CADOGANguides

take the kids Ireland

AMY CORZINE

Cadogan Guides
2nd Floor, 233 High Holborn
London, WC1V 7DN
info@cadoganguides.co.uk
www.cadoganguides.com

The Globe Pequot Press
PO Box 480, Guilford,
Connecticut 06437–0480

Maps © Cadogan Guides.
Maps of Northern Ireland based on Ordnance Survey of Northern Ireland mapping with the permission of The Controller of Her Majesty's Stationery Office, Permit No 50527 © Crown Copyright 2006
Maps of the Republic of Ireland based on Ordnance Survey Ireland, Permit No. 8149 © Ordnance Survey Ireland 2006 and Government of Ireland
All maps drawn by Maidenhead Cartographic Services Ltd

Original Photography: © Tim Mitchell
Cover Photographs: © Tim Mitchell, BL Images Ltd/ Alamy, Adrian Muttitt/Alamy, Dynamic Graphics Group/Creatas/Alamy, Vincent MacNamara/Alamy, Joe Fox/Alamy

Art director: Sarah Rianhard-Gardner
Managing Editor: Natalie Pomier
Editor: Rhonda Carrier
Editorial Assistant: Nicola Jessop
Proofreading: Daphne Trotter
Indexing: Isobel McLean

Printed and bound in Italy by Legoprint
A catalogue record for this book is available from the British Library
ISBN 10: 1-86011-315-X
ISBN 13: 978-1-86011-315-4

Please help us to keep this guide up to date. We have done our best to ensure that information is correct at the time of printing, but places and facilities are constantly changing, and standards and prices fluctuate. We will be delighted to receive your comments concerning existing entries or omissions. Authors of the best letters will receive a copy of the Cadogan Guide of their choice.

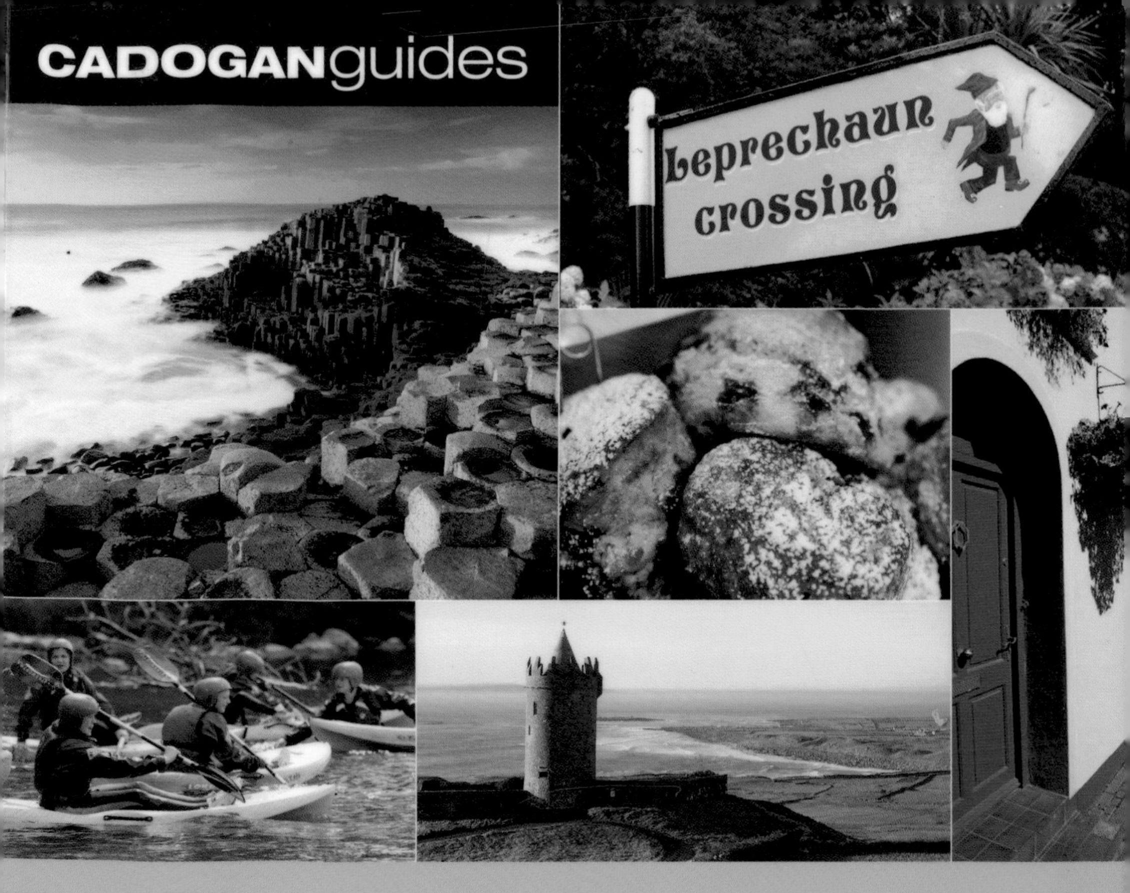

take the kids

IRELAND

Amy Corzine

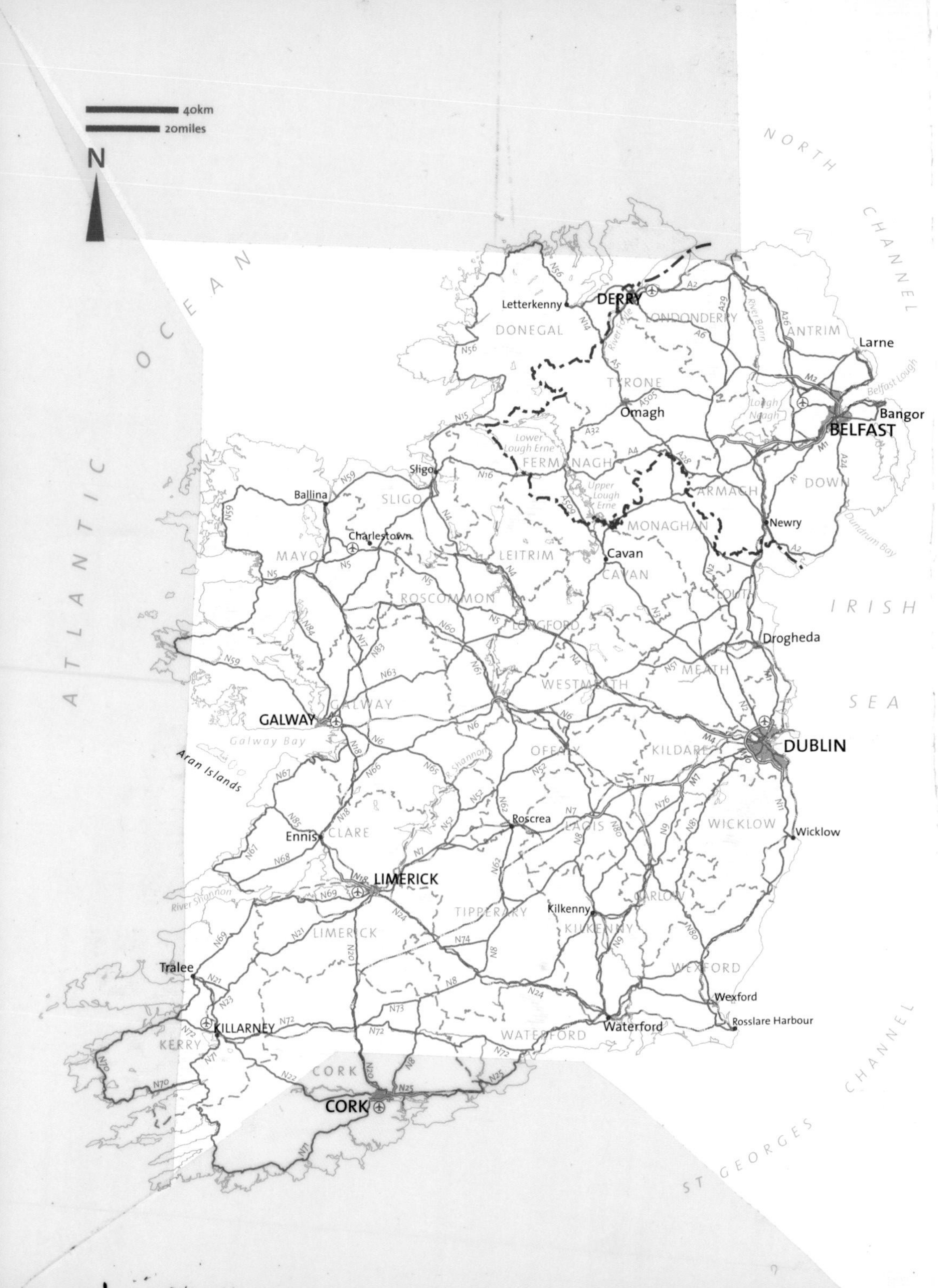

40km
20miles
N
ATLANTIC OCEAN
NORTH CHANNEL
IRISH SEA
ST GEORGES CHANNEL
Letterkenny
DERRY
DONEGAL
LONDONDERRY
ANTRIM
Larne
TYRONE
Omagh
Bangor
BELFAST
Lower Lough Erne
Lough Neagh
Belfast Lough
FERMANAGH
Upper Lough Erne
Sligo
SLIGO
Ballina
ARMAGH
DOWN
MONAGHAN
Newry
Dundrum Bay
Charlestown
MAYO
LEITRIM
Cavan
CAVAN
ROSCOMMON
LOUTH
LONGFORD
Drogheda
MEATH
WESTMEATH
GALWAY
Galway Bay
Aran Islands
DUBLIN
OFFALY
KILDARE
WICKLOW
Wicklow
Roscrea
LAOIS
Ennis
CLARE
LIMERICK
River Shannon
TIPPERARY
Kilkenny
KILKENNY
CARLOW
Tralee
WEXFORD
Wexford
Rosslare Harbour
KILLARNEY
KERRY
Waterford
WATERFORD
CORK

Snapshots of Ireland

Top towns

1
2
3
ULYS ES
JAM
DUB
LIN
ERS
4
LIBRARY
5
CIRQUE
AND
GRAND OPERA HOUSE
6
WOODEN HEART
WICE AS NICE

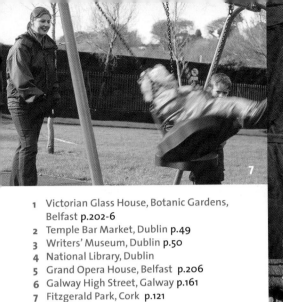

1 Victorian Glass House, Botanic Gardens, Belfast p.202-6
2 Temple Bar Market, Dublin p.49
3 Writers' Museum, Dublin p.50
4 National Library, Dublin
5 Grand Opera House, Belfast p.206
6 Galway High Street, Galway p.161
7 Fitzgerald Park, Cork p.121
8 Waterford Treasures Museum, Waterford p.148
9 Playground, Dublin Zoo p.58
10 Phoenix Park, Dublin p.61
11 Spanish Arch, Galway p.161
12 Toy shop, Cork p.121

Bricks and mortar

About the author

Amy Corzine

Amy Corzine is a writer and editor who lives in London. Fascinated by fairy tales as a child, she sought their source upon reaching adulthood. Discovering that many came from Ireland, she ventured there, only to become enchanted by its invisible, otherworldly denizens and very worldly inhabitants.

For my late mother, who helped me follow my dream, and my father, who helped me complete it

About the series

take the kids guides are written specifically for parents, grandparents and carers. In fact, they're the perfect companion for anyone who cares for or about children. Each guide not only draws on what is of particular interest to kids, but also takes into account the realities of childcare – from tired legs to low boredom thresholds – enabling both grown-ups and their charges to have a great day out or a fabulous holiday.

Series consultant

Helen Truszkowski is series consultant of Cadogan's *take the kids* series, and author of *take the kids Travelling* and *take the kids Paris & Disneyland® Resort Paris*. Helen is an established travel writer and photographer. Over the past decade her journeys have taken her around the globe, including six months working in South Africa. Helen's seven-year-old son, George, has accompanied her on her travels since he was a few weeks old.

Contents

Snapshots of Ireland 5

01
Introduction 21

02
History 27

03
Dublin 43
GETTING AROUND 46
THINGS TO SEE AND DO 50
AROUND AND ABOUT 58
WHERE TO EAT 62

04
Leinster 65
COUNTY DUBLIN 68
WICKLOW AND CARLOW 74
KILKENNY AND WEXFORD 82
KILDARE, LAOIS AND OFFALY 91
MEATH AND LOUTH 97
WESTMEATH AND LONGFORD 105
WHERE TO EAT 109

05
Munster 115
COUNTY CORK 120
Cork City 121
COUNTY KERRY 127
COUNTY LIMERICK 136
Limerick City 136
COUNTY CLARE 140
Ennis 141
TIPPERARY AND WATERFORD 146
WHERE TO EAT 151

06
Connacht 155
COUNTY GALWAY 159
Galway City 161
COUNTY MAYO 172
COUNTY SLIGO 181
Sligo Town 182
LEITRIM AND ROSCOMMON 186
WHERE TO EAT 191

07
Ulster 195
COUNTY ANTRIM 201
Belfast 202
COUNTY DOWN 211
Downpatrick 212
COUNTY ARMAGH 216
Armagh City 216
COUNTY LONDONDERRY 221
Londonderry/Derry City 222
COUNTY TYRONE 225
COUNTY FERMANAGH 229
Enniskillen 230
CAVAN AND MONAGHAN 233
COUNTY DONEGAL 235
Donegal Town 236
WHERE TO EAT 240

08
Sleep 245
WHERE TO STAY 246
Useful addresses and sources 248
RECOMMENDED ACCOMMODATION 249
Dublin 249
Leinster 251
Munster 257
Connacht 265
Ulster 271

09
Travel 279
GETTING THERE 280
By air 280
By bus 284
By sea 284
Border formalities 286
GETTING AROUND 286
By air 286
By bus 286
By car 287
By train 288

10
Practical A–Z 289

Index 301

Maps
Orientation map *inside front cover*
Chapter divisions 20
Area maps
Dublin 44
Leinster 67
Munster 116
Connacht 156
Ulster 196

7

8

9

10

1 Doonagore Castle, the Burren, Co. Clare **p.141**
2 Rock of Cashel, Co. Tipperary **p.147**
3 Staigue Fort, Co. Kerry **p.134**
4 The Lios, Lough Gur, Co. Limerick **p.138**
5 Charles Fort, Summercove, Co. Cork **p.124**
6 Cat Stone, Co. Westmeath **p.106**
7 Tintern Abbey, Co. Wexford **p.88**
8 Pádraic Pearse's Cottage, Co. Galway **p.169**
9 Dunguaire Castle, Co. Galway **p.166**
10 Clonmacnoise, Co. Offlay **p.93**

11
12
13
14

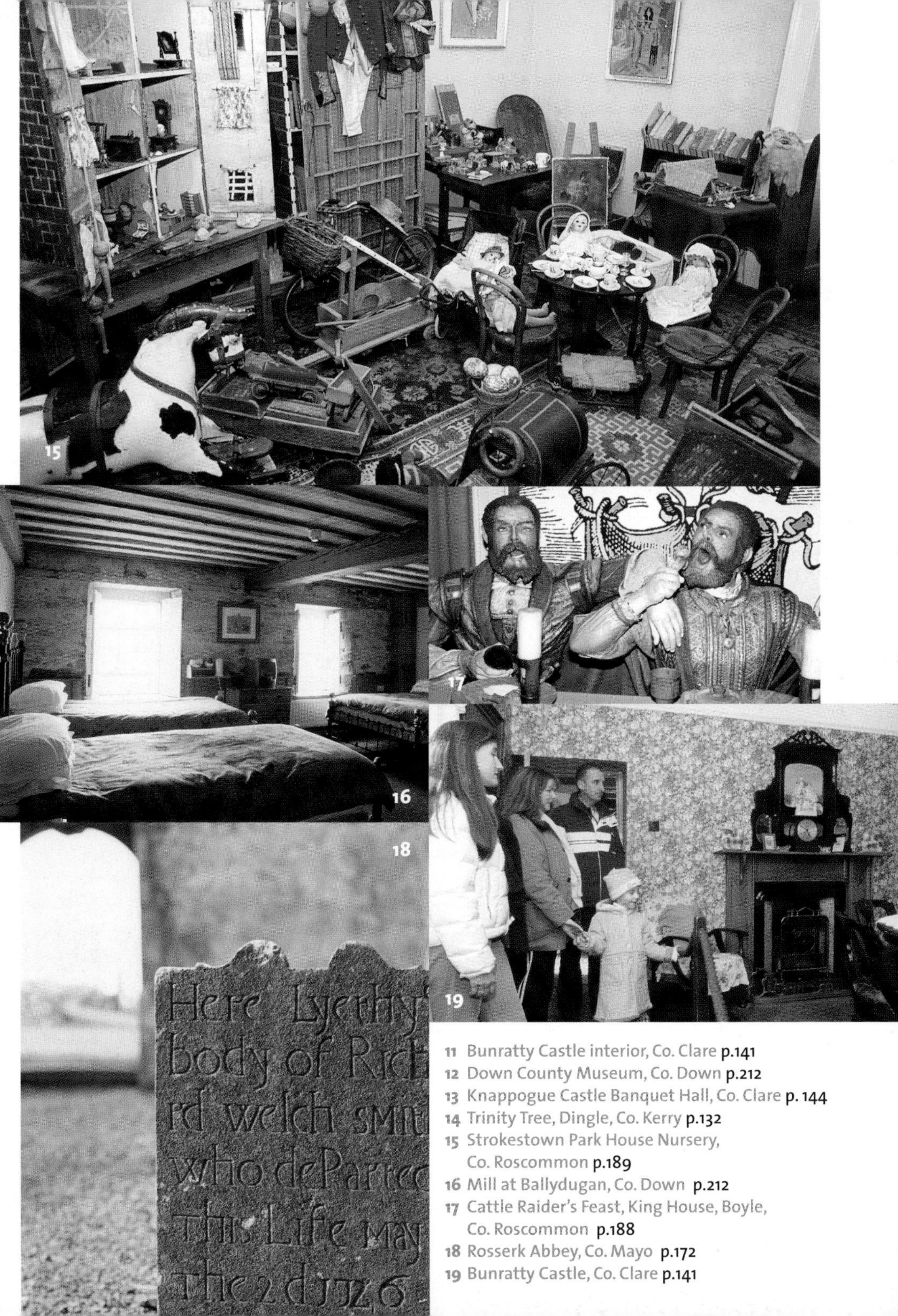

11 Bunratty Castle interior, Co. Clare p.141
12 Down County Museum, Co. Down p.212
13 Knappogue Castle Banquet Hall, Co. Clare p. 144
14 Trinity Tree, Dingle, Co. Kerry p.132
15 Strokestown Park House Nursery, Co. Roscommon p.189
16 Mill at Ballydugan, Co. Down p.212
17 Cattle Raider's Feast, King House, Boyle, Co. Roscommon p.188
18 Rosserk Abbey, Co. Mayo p.172
19 Bunratty Castle, Co. Clare p.141

Buckets and spades

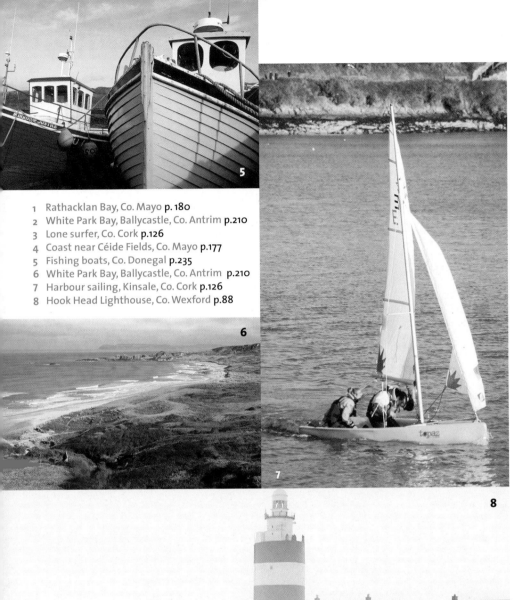

1 Rathacklan Bay, Co. Mayo p. 180
2 White Park Bay, Ballycastle, Co. Antrim p.210
3 Lone surfer, Co. Cork p.126
4 Coast near Céide Fields, Co. Mayo p.177
5 Fishing boats, Co. Donegal p.235
6 White Park Bay, Ballycastle, Co. Antrim p.210
7 Harbour sailing, Kinsale, Co. Cork p.126
8 Hook Head Lighthouse, Co. Wexford p.88

Animal magic

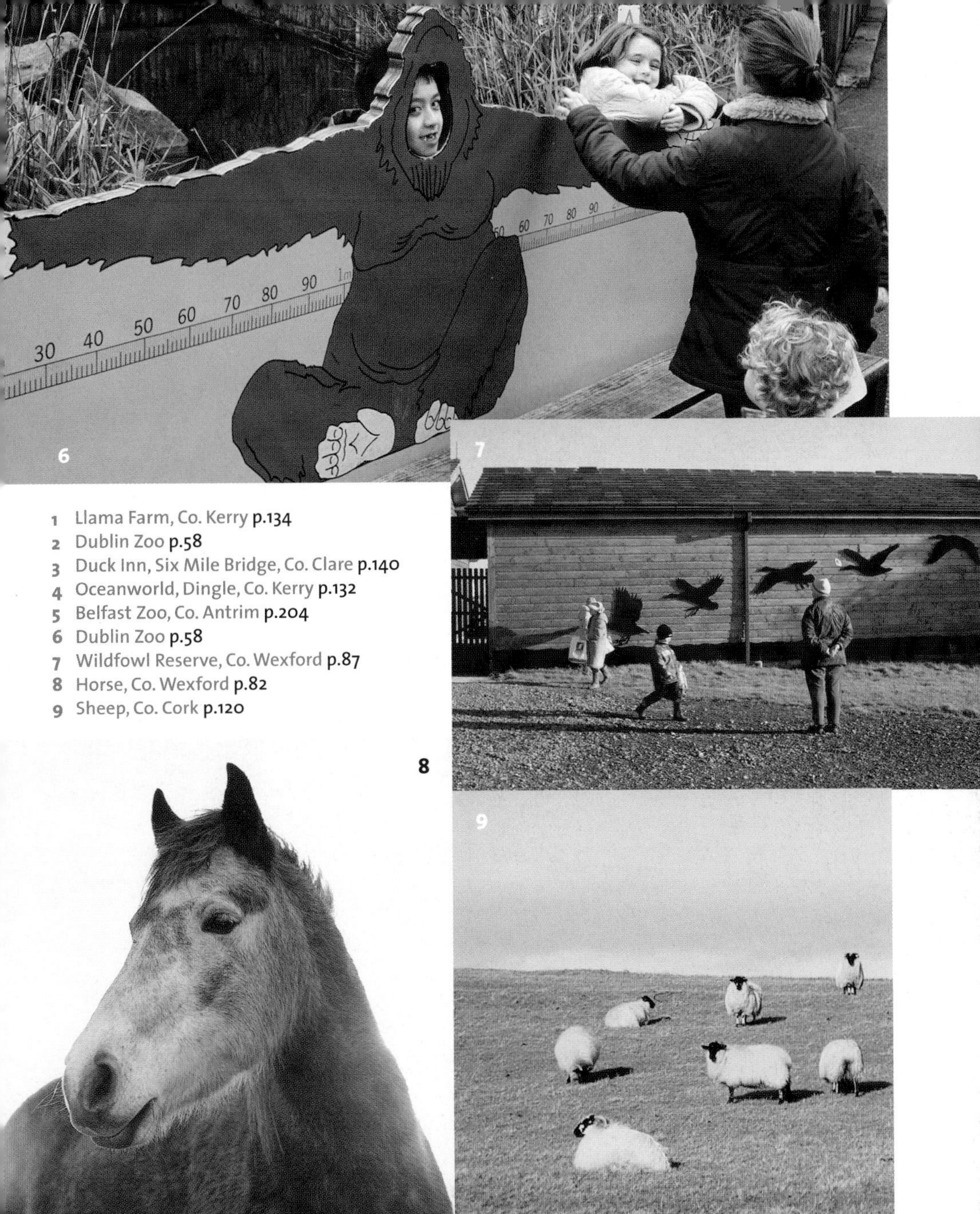

6

7

8

9

1 Llama Farm, Co. Kerry **p.134**
2 Dublin Zoo **p.58**
3 Duck Inn, Six Mile Bridge, Co. Clare **p.140**
4 Oceanworld, Dingle, Co. Kerry **p.132**
5 Belfast Zoo, Co. Antrim **p.204**
6 Dublin Zoo **p.58**
7 Wildfowl Reserve, Co. Wexford **p.87**
8 Horse, Co. Wexford **p.82**
9 Sheep, Co. Cork **p.120**

Nature lovers

Introduction

INTRODUCTION 22
PLANNING YOUR TRIP 23
TRAVELLING WITH KIDS 24
STORYTELLERS AND TOURS 26
TRADITIONAL MUSIC 26

INTRODUCTION

The *Tuatha Dé Danaan*, or faeries, first came to Ireland in a cloud. That's how I first arrived there too.

I recall looking down beyond the blues of sea and sky to an emerald-green land ringed by a line of white nimbus as far as the eye could see, as if cloud soldiers were standing sentinel around Ireland, guarding it and welcoming some foreign dignitary to their sacred treasure...as if Ireland itself were saying *Fáilte agus beannacht Dé* ('Welcome and the blessings of God be upon you'). I felt embraced by a warm kind of presence, a feeling that even now I think of with awe.

I didn't know then that Ireland is shaped a bit like the Cauldron of Plenty, or a giant bowl with mountains ridging a lower-level centre. Nor did I know that it is also encircled, and so kept temperate, by the Gulf Stream, the warm-water current that had flowed along with me all the way from my home near the Gulf of Mexico. And neither did I know that this island's ancient peoples once conceived the land itself as being a goddess with her own will – one that they named *Eiru*.

As I emerged from the plane, the air smelled sweet with the scent of burning turf and rainwashed fields – clean yet invigorating – with the softest mist I had ever felt upon my face. Lone trees sparkling with raindrops on small hills were pointed out to me as faery trees. The magical world of faery tales suddenly had substance here.

For children, this is a remarkable discovery – that an otherworldly dimension is taken seriously by adults who know more than they do, that there is history behind the stories they have heard. Despite the pall that adulthood casts on us, this small island enchants as no other can.

Geographically there are few boundaries but water in Ireland – whether lake, river or sea – but politically there are many, and not just between Northern and Southern Ireland, for people here have been warring for centuries. For all that, this seems a markedly peaceful country. Its people will sometimes take you by surprise by being unremittingly generous – for absolutely no other reason than that they just feel like being so. Such moments are like little solar flares that rise up from a sun that burns within them, reminding the fortunate recipient of the humanity we all hold within us. The Irish will tell you that there is nothing extraordinary about being kind – it is simply being human.

Statistically, the facts are that this 5,456-square-mile island with 5.7 million inhabitants is run by two different governments. Northern Ireland's six counties are governed from Stormont, which is overseen by the British government from London. The rest of Ireland is an independent republic run from Dublin. Since 1973 both have been part of the European Union, although only the Republic uses the European single currency, the euro.

The facts of history, however, may be altered slightly according to imaginings. For the Irish, history is a story. That is how they have told and retold what has happened to them over the centuries. And they love stories. One might say there are as many histories of Ireland as there are people in it, from the mythological past of the country's ancient oral tradition to the endlessly complicated political stories of more recent centuries, not to mention the influences from other cultures that the Irish have visited or been visited by. Added to this are the elaborations of the Christian monks, and of the all-important *shenachies* or storytelling tradition-bearers, who have been present in Ireland since the time of the druids, bards and Brehon Laws. Everyone, the Irish say, used to be a storyteller.

Have you heard the story in the Bible, someone might tell you, about the angel who goes from house to house asking for a little food and water? Well, some people gave, and some didn't. Those who didn't were visited later by another angel who was not so kind, one who made someone die in the house where people were not so generous. The Irish haven't forgotten the old stories completely. In the past, if there was some food in the press (Irish-English for larder), it was hard for a family not to offer it all to a stranger – as much as he'd have, until he said no thank you, I'm stuffed and replete with your generosity, your hospitality.

Ireland today

Foreigners often complain about how much Ireland has changed in recent years. In response, the Irish tend to say that visitors have always liked to imagine it as remaining the same, but the truth is that it is always changing, has always changed, and will continue to be changed by outside influences...which many Irish people welcome.

After all, its people have emigrated for the past couple of centuries to find work, and the notion of the homesick Irishman is famed in song and story.

Today there are more people with Irish ancestry outside Ireland than in it. You will find Irish theme pubs, with Irish beer and sometimes even Irish people in them, all over the world, from Australia to Russia. Half of North America seems to have some Irish blood. For the Irish, America was once the land of gold, of milk and honey, of opportunity, as millions emigrated there, while even those who stayed in Ireland learned to dream of one day going to the heaven-world of America. These days, however, the Irish no longer have to leave their own country to work, and have even become recipients of immigrants themselves from poorer countries. Nor do the modern Irish have to depend on foreigners to provide their industries and their businesses.

Nevertheless, for all the modernity that has exploded into Ireland with the birth of the now more kittenish 'Celtic Tiger' and the influx of settlers from countries that are as poor as Ireland used to be, the essential ingredients of an older, more leisurely way of life have not been entirely lost. Irish people retain a charm and vibrancy that is all their own. Laughter and the arts – including the most traditional Irish art of all, that of conversation – are important to them, not to mention the lifeblood of happy children and families. You and your children will find a creative imagination and a buoyant sense of fun still alive in the Irish people you meet, together with a certain respect for things unknown and otherworldly, especially among those who live close to nature. Vestiges of this island's ancient traditions, the roots of which are deeper than even the tree-centred beliefs of the druids, can be seen in the faery stories attached to many places. They hint of an earlier race who, sensibly, sought ways of protecting and regenerating their land, and whose deep respect for the unknown encouraged them to investigate what they could not see or experience ordinarily. The remnants of this attitude inspire the exhilarating kind of rebellious curiosity that is normal to Irish people beneath society's external veneers – controlled in the past by the druids, Brehon Laws, Christianity, later the British government, and nowadays by the modern 'religion' of technology.

The best of Ireland unites the old with the new, improving on the old by maintaining a high quality of architecture, food and natural surroundings inherited from the past while providing the comforts and variety of the modern world. When you find this, you may be forgiven for imagining you are in heaven, or in *Tír na n'Óg*, the Land of Eternal Youth so often mentioned in Irish mythology...the land of people who are young forever in their hearts.

Planning your trip

Long before you go to Ireland, think about the kind of holiday you want. Depending on what you and your family most want to do – explore Irish history or culture, try out new sports, fish, swim, hike or otherwise enjoy the countryside – you may prefer to base yourself in just one place, or to spend a few nights in each of a series of centres

Acknowledgements

A hundred thousand thank yous are in order for all the Irish people I have ever met, who have always given something of themselves to me, as a stranger and sometimes as a friend. It would be impossible to list them all, but noteworthy ones are: Jim and Anne Henry; Jimmy Gilvarry; Paddy Tuffy; Eugene and Geraldine Kielt; Eugene O'Kelly; Christopher Sweetnam (with American wife Colleen and daughters Ainé and Niamh); Bernard Waldron (who stoked the fire of my interest in Ireland for years); folklorist Dáithí Ó'hOgain of University College Dublin; Basil Nulty; John Kelly; Vicky Sutton; Michael McCaughan; the employees of Bord Fáilte/Tourism Ireland, especially Orla Carey, Ruth Moran, Damian O'Brien, Joe Lynam, Leanne Lyttle and Laura Duffy, and at the Northern Ireland Tourist Board, notably Maureen Durkan, Jan Nugent and Karen Houlahan; and the late Mrs Katherine Lambert Ball, Kevin Danaher, and Liza Mitchell.

To my non-Irish supporters, thanks to my father, brother Ed, Martyn Lucksford, inspiration Chime Radha, ex-Cadogan Editorial Director Vicki Ingle, Virginia Ivey Sullivan, Lyn Carr Harris, and the North London Steiner School children in my classes, 1989–93.

To Ireland, I apologize for my mistakes ('a man's mouth often broke his nose'). To the Otherworld beings, your stories are here because I hope others will respect you; I apologize for my impertinence, unconscious of it as I am, being nearly blind myself.

before travelling on to the next. The longer you stay in any of Ireland's counties, the more treasures you will discover there – whether they are difficult-to-find tourist attractions, archaeological sites or fascinating spots recommended to you by local people. You need to have time to savour and enjoy the full variety of Irish arts, crafts, sports, music and other cultural activities in the places you visit.

The destinations, attractions and places to stay featured in this guide include locations in cities, towns and the countryside across Ireland. When planning a visit, choose your base carefully so that you are near the sites you especially want to see. Ireland may appear small on the map, but the traffic in its big cities (especially Dublin and its environs) can be heavy enough to occupy plenty of your time, and in the countryside, once you've left the main highways, you can easily find yourself rolling along seemingly never-ending, winding roads looking for tourist attractions that remain inexplicably well hidden, particularly if a pooka or the faeries decide to play a trick on you. It's also not always simple navigating through Irish towns, where routes will not necessarily be clearly signposted. One thing that seems to work is to follow signs that indicate the direction of a highway to a main city such as Dublin or Galway, and not to worry that you're driving in the wrong direction as you go through the town; once you reach the main highway, you will usually find a roundabout with signposts showing a road towards the place you are looking for. Be wary, however, as occasionally you will see a sign turned in the wrong direction, or placed where you are certain never to see it, particularly at night. To complicate matters, soon all road signs in the Gaeltacht (Irish-speaking areas) will be only in Irish, so make sure that you have a map with translations in English.

To make the most of a family holiday in Ireland, don't start by driving a car as fast as you can. Speeding down roads at 60 to 80mph is not conducive to relaxation or to meeting any faery people. To get to know Ireland, you must slow yourself down and talk to human beings, meet the animals in the fields, and listen to the whispers in the breeze and the stream trickling by. Otherwise, you may go mad just trying to get out of Dublin via the new housing developments that surround it, and the newly built ring road that may not be on your map, or rushing from tourist site to tourist site without a word from an Irishman except 'Pardon' or 'Excuse me' as they sidestep you on the street as you practically run over them in your efforts to see everything in too short a time.

Remember the old Irish saying, 'When God made time, He made plenty of it', or you may not notice the leprechaun sitting on the pavement, or in the tree you're rushing past. A word to the wise: see everything in Ireland all at once and you'll see nothing. Especially with kids in tow, you won't have much fun if you run yourself ragged dashing from place to place. In Ireland, everything takes time, so take it easy and let the inevitable unexpected detours lead you where they will.

Travelling with kids

For children, these unexpected detours and discoveries can be exciting, so long as their adult companions don't convey tension to them by being too goal-oriented. Remember that the calmer and happier you are, the less anxious kids will be. Planning ahead helps take some of the anxiety out of a trip. Children will be better-tempered, also, if you pause for frequent breaks beside roadside ruins, and in the parks and green spaces you come across while touring around. Always take along the basics of a picnic (snacks, drinks), in case you want to stop and eat wherever you are rather than carry on to the next town. And in between, be sure to stop for plenty of special treats at ice cream parlours and souvenir shops.

When packing, it's best to keep it simple, especially if travelling with a baby or small child. There's no need to take along a whole nursery; just be sure you have enough nappies/diapers, wipes, etc., for the first 48 hours, then buy replacements locally. Take only a few carefully chosen toys – you'll almost certainly pick up more later in your trip. A favourite teddy bear or other soft toy will help younger kids settle at night; a personal stereo is popular with older ones, and is useful if you're sharing a room with them. Make sure to leave space for souvenirs.

Listed in this book are attractions and activities to amuse, engage and enchant children and their parents in their exploration of Ireland. However, all kids grow bored at least a few times while travelling, especially on long car journeys. To keep their mood swings at bay, instead of just relying on familiar

Fun and games: Some traditional Irish children's games

Here's a sampling of traditional games to learn from the Irish, and to try out as you travel around the country. As well as these, you might play 'I Spy' as you go along the country roads to find faery hills (usually identifiable with a solitary tree on top of them, or a ring of three or seven red rowanberry trees); faery raths (raised rings of earth that are the sites of ancient settlements); oddly shaped hills or islands (such as the pointed Croagh Patrick in County Mayo, and Dead Man island off the Dingle peninsula), or funny little sculptures of animals or faeries on the tops of walls made of stone or specially cut trees or bushes.

Dogs and Hares

Play this with a group. The children form two teams – of 'Hares' and 'Dogs' – then choose four 'safe corners'. The Dogs chase the Hares as they try to reach the safe corners. If the Hares get to the safe areas before the Dogs catch them, they stay there until the Dogs stand aside and chant 1-2-3, at which point the Hares get a chance to set off for another corner before the Dogs chase them again. If a Hare is caught, it must run with the Dogs. The last Hare to be caught wins the game.

Marbles

Marble games have long been very popular in Ireland, generally with boys. One simple common game of marbles goes as follows. Each player needs at least one glass marble. One throws his marble into an enclosed circle or space. When it stops rolling, another boy shoots, trying to hit the first marble with one of his own. If he hits it, it becomes his. If he doesn't hit it, the first player gets a chance to shoot at his opponent's marble. Whoever gets the most marbles wins the game.

Soldier's Tig

This is another game that was traditionally played by boys. One boy chases the others in a group and tries to strike one of them with his hand. The victim struck then has to hold one hand on the spot where he was touched, keeping it in that position while chasing the other boys and trying to hit them with his other hand, until all but the last boy are caught. For the next game, the last boy who evaded being struck becomes the one who chases the others.

Ring games

In Ireland, children used to hold hands and dance in a circle as they sang or recited different rhymes like these, especially under a new moon.

'I see the moon and the moon sees me,
God bless the moon and God bless me;
There's grace in the cottage and grace in the hall,
And the grace of God is over us all.'

A ring game popular in Co. Offaly involved singing the following rhyme:

'Sally go round the moon
Sally go round the stars
Sally go round in a gypsy van
Some day afternoon.'

After each verse, everyone falls down, and then rises from the ground and starts again.

Skipping games and verses

Skipping was thought of as a girl's game in Ireland; few boys learned to skip. In one popular Irish rope-skipping game, while two girls turned a rope for another who skipped, a group formed a circle around them and chanted:

'One, two, three, Mother caught a bee,
Bee died, Mother cried, out goes she...'

As the skipper recited 'out goes she', she would point to another person, who then became 'it'. Thus the skipper, and the game, would carry on.

A variation on this, without a rope, was: one girl would skip in the middle of a circle of girls while singing the verse. When the skipper pointed to someone in the circle, everyone would chase the 'it', who, if caught, had to skip in the centre and sing the verse, thus repeating the game.

Verses for this game from Co. Limerick are:

'Abben a babben a baby's knee
Holsum polsom, wait and see
Potato rows, single toes
And out she goes!'

'Hide and seek all the week,
Sheeps' heads for Sunday.
Half a crown for Mister Brown
To pay the rent on Monday.'

(One child would point at 'Mister Brown', who would be 'it'.)

'Mary Mac, dressed in black,
Three gold buttons behind her back.
Hi ho, tipsy toe,
Turn the ship and away we go.'

(This time the chosen 'Mary Mac' would be 'it'.)

games, toys and audiobooks from home, a range of Irish pastimes and games may be discovered in Ireland that are linked to all the new things your children will see on the trip and the people they will meet. Mythological story books or Irish songs and stories on CD or cassette will help introduce your children to Ireland's fascinating historical and fictional characters, some of whom are presented in the chapters of this guide. In the evenings, try telling an Irish story linked to a place you're going to visit the next day. After your visit, children (and you) could make something related to the places you've visited – like a *súgawn* (rope) or St Brigid's Cross braided from straw, or an animal or faery creature of putty, beeswax or plasticine – or learn some Irish songs (from traditional to U2), draw and colour your own postcards, or play a game, perhaps one of the Irish ones on p.25.

Storytellers and tours

Above all, Ireland offers one very special and unique means of entrancing children and adults – the telling of traditional stories, always best done by a storyteller or *shenachie*. Rooted in a love of story and language, storytellers use only the simplest resource – the human voice. True storytelling can fascinate even children apparently permanently addicted to electronic gadgetry, and bring alive the tales associated with historic sites in a way no ordinary tour guide can. Any opportunity to see and hear a real storyteller is not to be missed.

There are many more storytellers around Ireland than the ones noted below, but those listed are fairly well known. Real *shenachies* are increasingly rare these days, and so are harder to find; however, you'll recognize the difference when you meet a real one. The first on the list below, Eddie Lenihan, is one of a small breed of modern storytellers who are closest to the *shenachie* tradition.

Eddie Lenihan, Co. Clare, **t** (065) 27191
Windhorse Productions, Sounds True, PO Box 8010/ Dept. WH, Boulder, CO 80306-8010; or see **www.soundstrue.com** (**t** 1 800 333 9185 in the US).

This Irish folklorist, author and ex-teacher, based in Co. Clare, masterfully tells stories of myth, magic and mystery to children and adults. Highly recommended for car listening is his *The Good People*, available on cassette in the *Storytelling from Ireland* collection, issued by Sounds True in their *Secrets of the World* series. He has also produced several books; one of his most recent is *Meeting the Other Crowd, the Fairy Stories of Hidden Ireland*, co-authored and edited by Carolyn Eve Green (*see* **www**.carolynevegreen.com). Eddie Lenihan's story recordings are available from Windhorse/Sounds True in the USA, or via Amazon in the USA and UK.

Martin Byrne, Sacred Island Tours, Co. Sligo, t (079) 66241, www.gofree.indigo.ie

Byrne trained as a painter and printmaker in Galway, then set off to visit the ancient places of Ireland and learn about the old stories that had always fascinated him. He now documents the alignments and artwork of chambered cairns.

Richard Marsh, Legendary Tours, www.legendarytours.com

Transplanted American ex-journalist and Hibernophile Marsh conducts tours of countryside sites in Leinster, notably in counties Wicklow and Meath. Wellington (waterproof) boots are provided as needed. Some of the stories told are legends and sagas that may be too long for kids who don't have a big interest in folklore or history, and certainly will not be appropriate for under-10s. Walks may also go over rough terrain, and your children will need to be able to cope with being in the outdoors for 8 hours or so, but it's a very rewarding trek.

Michael Roberts, Co. Sligo, **t** (071) 916 8868

Mr Roberts, a student of mythology and folklore for more than 40 years, arranges tours of the sacred sites of Sligo. He can tell the stories and show the sights associated with the two battles of Moytura, Ben Bulben, Carrowmore, Knocknarea and Lough Gill for a day or a week, as there is a multitude of places to see and stories to hear around the county.

Pat Speight, Co. Cork, **t** (021) 455 1023, **www.patspeight.com**

Pat Speight also makes commercial tapes of his Irish stories, which you can obtain via his website.

Traditional music

For details of music sessions and festivals (*fleadhs*) around the country, contact:

Comhaltas Ceoltóirí Éireann, 32 Belgrave Sq., Monkstown, Co. Dublin, **t** (01) 280 0295, **www.comhaltas.com**

History

IRELAND'S HISTORY 28
Mythical Ireland and the Early Celts 28
Irish Mythology: Facts and Figures 30
The Isle of Saints and Scholars 31
Troubles 1: The Vikings 32
Troubles 2: The Normans and the English 33
A New Division 33
Britain's 17th-Century Wars Come to Ireland 34
The Protestant Ascendancy 35
The Great Famine and Exit 36
The 20th Century: War, Partition and Independence 37
The Troubles in the North 39
A Modern Place 41
Some Names in Irish History 42

IRELAND'S HISTORY

For more than one and a half million years, Ireland was covered in ice. A little irony of the universe is that Ireland was joined to both Britain and the rest of Europe at that time, during the Ice Age, about 20,000 years ago. Perhaps nature spirits, or even unicorns, lived there, but there were definitely no people around. One fascinating example of the strange landscapes that were left behind in Ireland by its giant ice-shield is the great stone plateau of the Burren, in Co. Clare (*see* p.141).

Ireland was then part of a peninsula that pointed north from Europe. Around 12,000 years ago, warm ocean currents began to melt the ice, causing flooding that broke the peninsula off from the continent. Eventually Ireland separated from Great Britain too, but not before giant animals had moved there. Great elk, woolly mammoths, brown bears and arctic foxes fed on soft carpets of grass that stretched across the island. As the weather warmed, birds flew to Ireland with the seeds of the great forests that began to fill the Irish hills. Hazel, birch and pine trees appeared first, then elms and the great oaks that centuries later were so important to the druids. The giant animals that had depended on the grasslands for food began to die as trees became giants themselves and covered the island – trees such as the huge ancient trunk at the prehistoric site of Céide Fields, Co. Mayo (*see* p.178).

Not until the Mesolithic era, or Middle Stone Age, (8000–4000 BC) did people finally move to Ireland, possibly from Scotland over the last land bridge. These hunter-gatherers roamed the forests hunting elk and bears, and moved along the coasts, where they fished and dug for clams and oysters. Many of their tools have been found near lakes, such as Lough Boora in Co. Offaly, and along the coasts of Waterford, Dublin, and Sligo. The first settlement we know about was at Mount Sandel in Co. Derry. Round huts were built there 6,000 years ago.

About 4000 BC, Neolithic or New Stone Age farmers moved to Ireland, bringing a new way of life based on stable settlements and growing crops instead of constant nomadic wandering. The remains of the largest Neolithic farming town in Europe are at Céide Fields, Co. Mayo, from around 3000 BC. Ireland's most dramatic prehistoric site is the round stone monument at Newgrange, Co. Meath, from about 3200 BC (*see* p.99).

By 2000 BC tribes had spread all over Ireland. Their chieftains often lived in the middle of lakes, on man-made islands or *crannógs*, in order that they could fight off attackers more easily. Examples can be seen at at Craggaunowen (*see* p.142). Some *crannógs* were still used as homes until the 17th century.

Traders from countries with more advanced metal-working and mining skills soon discovered Ireland's metals, as the European Bronze Age developed. Beautiful Bronze Age gold metalwork can be seen in the National Museum in Dublin (*see* p.54).

Mythical Ireland and the Early Celts

Ireland's mythology is another kind of gold. The *Tuatha Dé Danaan* or faery people and old gods of the Irish myths are thought by some to be connected with the Beaker people (so-named because of the special pottery they made) who arrived in Ireland during the Bronze Age.

The Greek and Roman writers who left us the first written descriptions of most parts of Europe made only passing comments on Ireland, and never visited it – perhaps due to outlandish notions such as those of Greek historian Strabo, who wrote: '[the Irish] think it decent to eat up their dead parents.' Many Irish place names refer to mythological figures such as Cúchulainn, Queen Maeve and Finn McCool, and stories attached to them are often the most concrete evidence we have of real events that may have occurred in them. Documents and records may be scarce, but these myths provide Ireland with a rare and richly elaborate 'parallel history'.

Did you know...?

The mythical battles between the Nemedians/Fir Bolg (see opposite) and the Fomorians could be rooted in a folk memory based on fact. Some scholars think that a roaming Mesolithic hunter-gatherer tribe (the Fomorians) were living on the fringes of Ireland at the time that a farmer tribe (the Nemedians) arrived to compete for land. Others think maybe a sea-going race such as the Phoenicians were the Fomorians, and that a farming tribe from Scotland called the Scythians were the Nemedians.

A story to tell: The Invasions of Ireland

Invasions occurred long before history was written down, and some are recalled in Irish myths. They carry the flavour of an earlier, forgotten history, and in them one senses something of Ireland's ancient people and a way of thinking that disappeared long ago.

Invasion 1 – Cessair

Ireland's first invasion is linked to the Bible story of Noah's Ark, when God was angry about the way people were behaving down on Earth, especially in Sodom and Gomorrah. People there only wanted to have fun, not caring what happened to anyone else. So God declared that He would get rid of all the living things He had created with a flood that would cover the entire world.

However, there was one good man that he refused to harm: Noah. God promised to save him and his family if he followed His instructions. Noah was to build a giant boat or ark, and fill it with a male and female of every animal he could find.

The Bible does not mention the Irish legend about three other ships that set sail with the ark, though, nor Noah's granddaughter Cessair. Forty days before the Flood, Cessair took with her 50 women and three men – her father Bith ('Cosmos' in Irish), her sailor brother Ladra and her husband Fiontánn – to seek a place with no human inhabitants in the hope of avoiding the Great Flood.

One day Cessair spotted land that glittered like an emerald, and landed somewhere in Munster, perhaps at Waterford Harbour, or on the Dingle Peninsula in Co. Kerry. There were no other human beings around, so they felt safe enough.

But Cessair's father and her brother died, leaving Fiontánn to take care of all the women. This was too much for Fiontánn, so he ran away, leaving Cessair and the other women broken-hearted. Then the Great Flood came and drowned them all, except Fiontánn, who survived by magically changing himself into a fish. This trick saved him for the next 5,500 years. He changed his shape as it suited him, from a salmon to an eagle to a hawk.

This sly one observed many a subsequent invasion of Ireland, and told humans about them long after they happened until, one day, his luck changed. The druid Finegas caught him on a hook in the form of the Salmon of Knowledge, the name by which Fiontánn was known (*see* p.234).

Invasion 2 – The Partholonians

Next to invade were the Partholonians – led, predictably, by Partholón. They came from central Europe (possibly Greece) to the plain of Elta Edar (now Howth, Co. Dublin), with Partholón's three sons. One enjoyed cooking and duelling, another spent his time making home-brew, while the last brought the art of hospitality to Ireland. Partholón created four lakes and cleared four plains with the four oxen he brought with him. Then he drove out of Ireland the demonic, giant Fomorians. A mere 550 years later, Partholón's people were wiped out by plague – except for one man named Tuán mac Cairill, who, like Fiontánn before him, shape-shifted into various animal guises through the centuries to observe the doings in Ireland.

Invasion 3 – The Nemedians

The third invasion was by the Nemedians, led by Nemedh, his wife Macha and their sons. Nemedh lit the first fire on Ireland's most central point, the Hill of Uisneach, and then on Ard Macha ('Macha's height') in Armagh. The Nemedians also cleared 12 plains and created four lakes, pushing the Fomorians – who had returned – out to the coasts and islands.

Tory Island off Donegal is where the Fomorians are said to live today, though you'd be hard pressed to actually catch one. They are described as badly formed in body and mind, and can be one-legged and one-eyed as well, but mainly it's the spirit inside that makes a Fomorian.

Their leader Balor had only one eye, which would destroy whomever it looked upon. In battle, when he was tired, other Fomorians would prop his eye open with planks of wood. Thus they conquered the Nemedians, and every Samhain (Halloween), they demanded a tribute from the Nemedians of corn, wine and sometimes children. If they did not pay, their noses were cut off.

The Nemedians finally attacked the Fomorians again, but their response was so vicious that the Nemedians ran away, in two groups. One fled to Greece and the other to unnamed northern lands. The Nemedians who went to Greece returned to Ireland later, by which time they were called the Fir Bolg. Their leaders were five brothers, who won a battle against the Fomorians and divided Ireland into five provinces. The fifth, called Mide (Meath), had the Hill of Uisneach at its centre. They declared that 'order, justice and the fruits of the island's prosperity should be granted to everyone'.

Irish Mythology: Facts and Figures

Aengus Óg Aengus the Young, the God of Love, son of the Daghda, whose palace was at Newgrange.
Balor Evil Fomorian leader with one eye that destroys everything upon which it gazes; his grandson Lugh killed him by casting a stone into his single eye in the Second Battle of Moytura (*see* p.183).
Banshee Faery woman who screams in the wind to foretell the deaths of descendants of Irish chieftain families; if you see her, you better not let her know you do or she may come after you too.
Beltaine 1 May or May Day: in pre-Christian times a day when the door between the realms of the dead and living was open.
Brigid Goddess of healing, poetry and fertility: her festival on 1 February (Imbolg) became linked with a Christian saint: St Brigid.
Conchobhar Mac Nessa King of Ulster and lord of the Red Branch warriors; betrothed to marry Déirdre, he killed her lover Naoise out of jealousy.
Cormac MacArt High King AD 254–77 and patron of the Fianna, whose daughter Gráinne eloped with Diarmuid after being betrothed to Finn McCool.
Cúchulainn 'The hound of Culann', a warrior-hero whose name was Sétanta until he killed the hound of Culann, a smith god from the Otherworld, to whom he pledged himself as the dog's replacement.
The Daghda Patron god of the druids and 'father' of all the gods of ancient Ireland.
Déirdre 'of the Sorrows' Conchobhar promised to marry her after being told by a druid that she would be the most beautiful woman in Ireland, but that she would cause Ulster's ruin.
Diarmuid Foster-son of Aengus Óg, and a Fianna warrior who had a 'love spot' no woman could see without falling in love with him. He eloped with Gráinne, pursued by Finn McCool.
The Fianna Warriors who guarded Ireland, whose greatest leader was Finn McCool.
Finn McCool or **Fiónn MacCumhail** 'The Fair One', a legendary warrior made head of the Fianna by Conn of the Hundred Battles, Cormac MacArt's grandfather. Finn had a son, Oísín, with the goddess Sadh, suffered for love of Gráinne (*see* p.184), and built the Giant's Causeway (*see* p.207).
Fionnbharr God of the Tuatha and King of the Faeries (his wife Oonagh is Queen).
Fir Bolg 'Bog Men' or 'Men of the Belgae', possibly descendants of the Nemedians (*see* p.29).
Fomorians Evil beings of Irish myth (*see* p.29).
Gráinne Daughter of Cormac MacArt, who eloped with Diarmuid upon being betrothed to Finn.
Imbolg 1 February, feast of St Brigid and the pre-Christian festival of spring and the end of winter.
Leprechaun Shoemaker for the Sidhe who loves music, singing, dancing and riddles, and is fond of home-brew (potcheen); also known for tricking mortals who try to take his pot of gold.
King Lir Ocean god of the Tuatha Dé Danaan, whose children were turned into swans (*see* p.177).
Lugh Half-Tuatha, half-Fomorian sun-god who slew his grandfather Balor and fathered Cúchulainn with a mortal woman.
Maeve or **Medh** or **Mebh** Mythical queen of Connacht, and adversary of Cúchulainn.
Milesians The sons of Míl or Milesius, the 'humans' who sailed perhaps from Spain or Turkey to Ireland and took the island from the Tuatha (*see* p.119).
Nemedians The third tribe to invade Ireland, possibly the ancestors of the Tuatha (*see* p.29).
Niall of the Nine Hostages High King of Ireland around AD 380–405: apparently a real figure, and the ancestor of the powerful O'Neill clan of Ulster.
Niamh of the Golden Hair Daughter of the sea god Manannan Mac Lir, who invited Oísín to live in Tír na n'Óg with her.
Oísín Champion warrior of the Fianna and the son of Finn and Sadh, who refused to help his father wreak vengeance on Diarmuid and Gráinne and went with Niamh to the Land of Youth.
Partholón Leader of the second invasion (*see* p.29).
Pooka or **Púca** Black dog or horse-like creature who brings bad luck to anyone rude to it and carries those who sit on its back on terrible rides.
Red Branch Warrior guardians of Ulster during the reign of Conchobhar Mac Nessa, whose headquarters was at Emain Macha, Co. Armagh.
Samhain Celtic festival marking the second time of the year when the door opens between the worlds of the living and the dead, now called Halloween.
Sídh, Sidhe Faeries who live in the hills, waters or Otherworld of Ireland, a form of the Tuatha.
Tír na n'Óg The Land of Youth or Promise, a heaven inhabited by immortals who stay young forever.
Tuatha Dé Danaan The Sídh, Sidhe, Gentry, Good People or faeries, descendants of the goddess Danu who defeated the Fir Bolg (*see* p.163). Often thought of as the old gods of Ireland, but perhaps representing an advanced pre-Celtic people, once revered as gods and then sent to the Otherworld.

Back in the realm of more ordinary history, accounts vary about when the Celts first arrived in Ireland, but there seems to have been a steady stream of them from Spain, France and Germany from about 400 BC onwards. After the Celts took control of Ireland around 350 BC, the eastern province of Leinster became a centre for Iron Age metal-work. At this time, swords and jewellery were decorated in what is known as the European Celtic or La Tène style, which makes spectacular use of whorls and spirals.

In the next few centuries, most of the other Celtic regions of Europe fell under the rule of the Roman Empire, but in isolated Ireland Celtic culture was able to continue unhindered for more than 1,000 years. It was during this time that Ireland was first described as divided into five provinces – Ulster, Connacht, Munster, Leinster and Mide (or Meath, later absorbed into Leinster). Irish legends tell of a society divided into many tribes (*túath*), each ruled by its *rí* (king), helped by druids (philosopher-judges), and *cúire* (priests). The king of each tribe paid a tax to a stronger chieftain of his encompassing province, for the king's protection. At times there was also an honorary 'High King' or *Ard Rí* over all five provinces, who had his base initially at the Hill of Uisneach in Westmeath, and later at Tara (*see* pp.102–3). However, no single king ever ruled over the whole of Ireland, as tribal leaders were always fighting among themselves.

This was the world in which Irish myths were first told and retold. Within Celtic society, there were poet-musicians called bards, who kept alive the histories and traditions of each clan by telling stories and singing songs they had memorized, since they were not written down. Some bards who showed special wisdom rose in society to become *vates* or seers, who also acted as advisors and teachers to the leaders of the tribe. At the top of the social ladder were the druids. A druid was a combination of wizard and wise man – one who had all the skills of the bards and *vates*, plus the authority to make laws and act as a judge.

The early Celts did not have writing as we know it, but used line markings known as *ogham* to mark directions or graves, or possibly to indicate 'magic' formulas. Carved on stones or tree bark, *ogham* had 20 characters, formed by drawing straight parallel marks on either side of, or across, a horizontal or vertical line. Each mark was named after a tree, so ogham is said to have a 'tree alphabet'.

Did you know...?

Leprechauns could be linked to a Viking god, but in Irish folklore they're also associated with Lugh, the sun-god of the Tuatha Dé Danaan.

The Isle of Saints and Scholars

Christianity came to Ireland in the 5th century AD, just as the Roman Empire was collapsing. Non-Christian Irish tribes had been raiding the west coast of Roman Britain for some time and creating colonies there. A boy named Succat was kidnapped in one of these raids and brought to Ireland, where he worked as a slave and began to have visions. After a few years, Succat was freed and went home to become a monk. However, he dreamt the Irish were calling him to come back to them, and in AD 432, now known as Patrick, he did return, and began converting the locals to the new religion and, as the legend goes, driving all the 'snakes' out of Ireland (*see* p.178). Although he was not the first Christian to grace its shores, St Patrick is often given credit for bringing Christianity to Ireland. He and his followers focused on converting tribal or clan leaders, believing, correctly, that the people they ruled would follow after them. Patrick first won the support of King Dichu in Co. Down, and later King Laoghaire (or Leary) of Co. Dublin.

Helped in part by Laoghaire, St Patrick rewrote Ireland's ancient Brehon Laws, to ensure they fitted in with Christianity. This book of laws was called *The Senchus Mór*. The Irish, though, mixed pagan ideas with their new religion to create what became Celtic Christianity. The pagan Irish worshipped at spring wells and went on pilgrimages to mountains such as the pointed Croagh Patrick (*see* p.178) and islands such as those in Lough Derg in County Fermanagh. These became Christian shrines and are still visited today. A strong tradition of hermits, solitary pilgrims and like-minded spiritual groups seems to have always existed in Ireland.

Part of the training that bards underwent included spells spent memorizing poems alone in dark caves, through which, it was said, one could enter the many-coloured mystical land of *Tír na n'Óg*. This tradition was carried on by the early Irish Christian monks, who often became hermits and

A story to tell:
Faery Origins

When Christians brought handwriting to Ireland, the old tradition-bearers, the poets and storytellers, became less important to society, since history could be written instead of told. People began to lose the habit of remembering long stories, and with them too the orally transmitted memories of the past.

Monks, for example, began telling everyone that the faeries were angels who had fallen from Heaven. Some of Heaven's angels, they said, led by the Archangel Lucifer, had gone against God. God grew mightily angry about this, and began sweeping his angels out of Heaven so that they fell to Hell. He was in such a fury that there was a great danger that soon there would be no angels at all left up there.

But luckily he stopped, and then all the angels froze on whatever level they had fallen to on their way down to Hell. Earth was midway between Heaven and Hell, and those angels who had fallen halfway to Earth became faeries, stuck in what the Irish called the Otherworld.

Humans could die and go to Heaven, but faeries, being immortal, could not, and so were jealous of humans. Because of this, the monks said they were to be feared as well as avoided. Their magic could be countered and mischief combatted only by praying to God, and with the help of monks and Christian teachers such as St Patrick.

The priests began to say this sort of thing at about the time that people started using up the earth for cities and stone towers to protect themselves from invaders such as the Vikings, and from bad weather and the dangers of nature. If Ireland's 'faery faith' does come from a pre-Christian nature religion, the monks' dislike of faeries makes sense.

chose the most uncomfortable and hostile places possible for their spiritual retreats – their disregard for cold and hunger was a sign of their faith. Remains of the lonely places where monks sought isolation can be found everywhere in Ireland, in places such as Glendalough (*see* p.77) and, most impressively of all, on the wind-blasted Skellig Rocks off the coast of Co. Kerry (*see* p.128 and p.133).

The centuries from 500 to 800 were Ireland's 'Golden Age'. While the rest of Europe suffered the many plagues and wars of the Dark Ages, the flame of learning was kept alight in Ireland. Monasteries grew up around many of its early hermitages, and grew rapidly in wealth and importance. Monasteries such as Clonmacnoise and Durrow were major centres of learning and art, like today's universities. It was during this time that Christian monks first wrote down Ireland's oral legends, such as the Ulster Cycle, including the great epic *Táin Bó Cúailgne*, and Irish monasteries produced magnificent illuminated manuscripts, the most famous of which is the *Book of Kells*, now in Trinity College Library, Dublin (*see* p.56).

Irish monks also travelled as missionaries to take Christian learning back to pagan, chaotic Europe. Irish scholars were respected advisors to many kings across the continent. Donegal produced its own home-grown saint in Columcille (521–597), better known in Britain as St Columba. In 561, he left Ireland to found a monastery on the inhospitable Scottish island of Iona, and returned to St Patrick's homeland what Patrick had brought to Ireland by converting much of Scotland and northern England to Christianity.

Troubles 1: The Vikings

Around 800, Vikings from Norway discovered Ireland's rich farming land and its monasteries, and began raiding and plundering all across the country. Used to fighting among themselves, the Irish had no united military force to fight them off, and the monks built tall round towers beside their monasteries to shelter from Viking attacks. The Uí Néill high kings of Ulster had a try at throwing out the Vikings in the 860s, destroying their settlements north of Dublin. Despite this, still more Vikings arrived and began to settle there, marrying the native Irish and establishing trading ports that eventually became Dublin, Waterford and Wexford (the Dublinia Museum has fine displays on Viking Dublin; *see* p.53). Battles between Irish tribes and Viking settlers lasted for 200 years.

During this struggle, the only native Gaelic King ever to take over the whole of Ireland emerged from Munster: Brian Boru (942–1014), whose name means 'Brian of the Tributes'. He was called this because the men of Leinster resented the heavy taxes he demanded after he became High King. They allied with the Vikings against him, but Brian defeated them both in the Battle of Clontarf.

After this victory, Brian became High King over all Ireland – for a few hours. Then a Viking stole into his tent and murdered him. Still, this battle ended major Viking wars in Ireland. Viking settlers kept control of Dublin, while various Irish families continued to fight each other for the high kingship.

Troubles 2: The Normans and the English

At about the time that the Norman William the Conqueror was vanquishing England in 1066, in Ireland Archbishop Malachy of Armagh was establishing four centres – at Armagh, Tuam, Cashel and Dublin – to control Ireland's churches. He had built Mellifont Abbey in 1140. St Malachy was famous for his prophecies and for bringing the Irish church into line with the rest of the European Christian church, then based in Rome.

Disunity and battles among the Irish, though, continued. In 1169, the High King of Leinster, Diarmait McMurrough, was defeated by the High King of Connacht. McMurrough, however, has been remembered forever after in Irish history because he went to King Henry II of England for help, offering him loyalty if he would assist him to regain his kingdom. In response, Henry II sent a band of Anglo-Norman warriors led by the Earl of Pembroke, known as Strongbow because he was so powerful in battle. The Normans were experienced in European warfare, and soon overcame the less organized Irish. Strongbow won the war for McMurrough in 1170, and in return demanded his daughter (Aiofe) in marriage and the throne upon his death. A year later, McMurrough died and Strongbow became King of Leinster.

After that, other Norman adventurers tried their luck. Henry II, though, got nervous about the growing power of some of his subjects and so in 1171 he set sail for Ireland with his own troops to impose his authority. With the support of the Pope he had himself declared 'Lord of Ireland', and made Dublin the capital of an English colony. This is how English rule began in Ireland.

Norman ways seemed quite strange to the Irish. The fact that a king became King simply because he was born to it – not chosen for his ability or physical qualities – seemed odd to Ireland's High Kings. However, the Anglo-Normans controlled only a few dozen square miles and, like the Vikings, many of the old Norman noble families – later known as the 'Old English' – had begun marrying Irish people, adopting local customs and speaking Irish, so they didn't seem much of a threat. The Normans also built fortifications on the east coast, such as Carrickfergus Castle, north of Belfast (*see* p.206), but for centuries the only part of Ireland directly ruled by English governors was a small area around Dublin called 'The Pale'. Outside of it, Irish life continued unchanged. This is where the expression 'beyond the Pale' comes from, meaning an 'area beyond control'.

A New Division

In 1533, King Henry VIII (1491–1547) of England divorced his Spanish first wife Catherine of Aragon because she could not give him a son and so that he could marry Anne Boleyn. The Catholic Church did not allow divorce, so the Pope denounced Henry, who then rejected the authority of Rome and gave England its own independent, Anglican, church. This soon joined the Protestant side in the Europe-wide split between Protestants and Catholics, the process known as the Reformation. In Ireland, however, the vast majority of people stayed loyal to the Roman Catholic Church.

From this came centuries of trouble for Ireland. Henry and later English governments worried that their Catholic enemies in Spain, France and England would use Ireland as a base for invading England. Determined to bring Irish leaders under his control, Henry VIII declared himself King of Ireland and took over the lands of Irish lords who wouldn't submit to him. Then he closed Ireland's monasteries, seizing their wealth for the Crown, and in 1534 crushed a revolt by the Catholic 'Old English' Fitzgeralds of Kildare. Henry's government also began the policy of trying to 'plant' communities of English Protestants in Ireland, to create a more loyal population. These actions were deeply resented by the Catholic Irish, for whom the terms Protestant and Catholic gained new importance; for them, Protestantism now meant English rule.

Elizabeth I, Queen from 1558 to 1603, continued her father's policies, only with still more determination to gain control over the whole of Ireland and not just the Dublin 'Pale'. She seized the lands of Catholic Irish lords who rebelled against her and gave them to English Protestants. She kept careful watch for invaders, especially those of her most powerful enemy, Spain, and by the time the survivors of the storm-wrecked Spanish Armada were washed up on Ireland's coasts in 1588, her henchmen and soldiers were able to ensure that they posed no threat to English power.

Ulster, however, was a big problem for Elizabeth. It was the part of Ireland where Gaelic culture and the Catholic lords lived most freely. The Earl of Tyrone, Hugh O'Neill – who claimed descent from the old Uí Néill high kings of Tara – and the Earl of Tyrconnell, Red Hugh O'Donnell, fought back bitterly against her governors in what became known as the Nine Years' War (1594–1603). At first, the Irish lords won a string of victories. In 1601, Spain sent an army to Kinsale, Co. Cork, to help. O'Neill marched south to join them, but, fighting in unfamiliar territory, they were badly defeated. The Spaniards withdrew, and O'Neill gave himself up to the English in 1603, not knowing that Elizabeth I would die the very next day. When the Earl heard the news, he wept with rage and grief.

O'Neill and O'Donnell were allowed to keep their lands, but the government in Dublin then harassed them and took away bits of their land on various excuses, and barred them from worshipping as Catholics. In 1607, O'Neill, O'Donnell and 90 other Ulster chieftains or 'earls' sailed away from Donegal, in the 'Flight of the Earls'. They hoped to get the help of one of Europe's Catholic kings and come back with a fresh army to fight on, but they never found enough support, and never returned. This left Gaelic Ulster without leaders, so that the door was wide open for Britain to take over completely, which it lost no time in doing.

Elizabeth I was succeeded on the throne by the Stuart King of Scotland, James, as James I of England and Ireland, which brought all three kingdoms under the same monarch for the first time. James I got rid of Ireland's Brehon Laws and began the 'Ulster Plantation', on a bigger scale than the earlier 'plantations' of Protestant settlers further south. All the land of the Ulster lords was given to English and Scottish Protestants, who were expected to be loyal to the Crown. The native Irish were pushed out to poorer quality land or wild regions such as Donegal, which was practically left alone. British domination of Ulster was complete.

The new 'Plantation' settlers formed much larger, more self-contained communities than earlier immigrants such as the Anglo-Normans, who had gradually blended in with the Gaelic Irish. The Ulster 'Planters' were a mix of Anglicans and other more radical Protestant groups, such as the Scottish Presbyterians. They tended to remain separate and inward-looking, and lived apart from the Catholic Irish communities around them. Co. Tyrone's Ulster History Park (closed at the time of writing) has a fascinating reconstruction of a Plantation-era house.

Britain's 17th-Century Wars Come to Ireland

In 1625, King James I was succeeded by his son Charles I (1600–49), whose angry conflict with England's increasingly powerful Parliament and the more extreme Protestants or Puritans led to the outbreak of the English Civil War in 1642. In Ireland many Catholics, both Gaelic and Anglo-Norman, thought they could benefit from this situation. A rebellion broke out across the country, and Catholics, many of whom had only recently lost their land to Plantation settlers, launched vicious attacks on Protestants throughout Ireland, killing an estimated 12,000 people. These massacres stayed in the memories of Ulster Protestants and Plantation settlers believed that even larger numbers had died. Reported figures of more than 100,000 dead were impossible, given that only 34,000 Protestants allegedly lived in Ulster, but these stories helped draw a still worse enemy of the Catholics to Ireland's shores: Oliver Cromwell (1599–1658).

By 1649 Cromwell, the leader of England's Puritans, had won the Civil War and beheaded King Charles I. He then set sail for Ireland with his battle-hardened Roundhead soldiers – one of the best fighting forces in Europe – to settle scores in Ulster and flatten the Catholic rebellion. In Drogheda and Wexford, especially, thousands of Catholics were killed by Cromwell's soldiers. He also took still more land from Catholic landowners who opposed him, which he gave to his soldiers and supporters. Enemies who were not killed were forced out of the country or sent to rocky, barren Connacht (hence the saying 'To hell or Connacht', attributed to Cromwell). To this day, Cromwell is referred to as 'the butcher' by Catholics in Ireland.

After Cromwell died in 1658, the monarchy was restored in 1660 under King Charles II, whose reign was a time of relative peace in Ireland. Ironically, problems arose again in 1685 with the succession of a king who was a Catholic, Charles II's brother James II (1633–1701). He wanted to permit Catholicism to be practised openly again and possibly to restore it as England's state religion. He appointed Catholics to powerful jobs in England and Ireland, arousing the suspicions and fears of Protestants, especially in Ulster. In 1688 England's Protestant ruling class rose against him and invited his son-in-law, the Dutch Protestant Prince William of Orange, to take over the throne as King William III. James II fled to Ireland, hoping to find supporters there and use it as a base to win back the British crown.

Irish Catholics flocked to support him, and James II soon took over the whole country except for the Protestant cities of Enniskillen and Londonderry, or Derry. When the citizens of Londonderry saw Catholic regiments marching towards them, 13 apprentice boys rushed to slam the city gates shut before the troops could enter, in an incident that has become an Ulster Protestant legend. For 105 days the city was besieged by James' followers, the Jacobites. A third of its population died, mainly from starvation. People ate rats, dogs, starch for laundering linen, and even candle wax. Eventually, though, British ships arrived with supplies, and James II's army was forced to withdraw.

The Jacobites retreated southwards, pursued by a Protestant army led by William III himself. They met at the Battle of the Boyne in Co. Meath on 12 July 1690, when William and his Protestant supporters decisively defeated James II and his Catholic followers. James lost heart and fled to France, leaving his army to fight on without him.

This is the most remembered of all of Ireland's wars. For the Protestant community in Northern Ireland, the Battle of the Boyne took on mythological significance (12 July is a holiday in Northern Ireland), and all over Ulster you'll see images of King William, or King Billy. The yearly marches held in memory of the Siege of Derry and the Boyne have led to violent clashes over the years because these battles led to William's – and therefore the Protestants' – definitive takeover of Ireland.

Afterwards, the Irish were defeated by William at Aughrim, Co. Galway, and then besieged in Limerick, resisting as long and heroically as the Protestants had in Londonderry. The siege and the war only ended with the Treaty of Limerick in October 1691, when the Catholics (Jacobites) made peace in return for religious tolerance. The treaty, though, was ignored by Ireland's Protestant parliament, and many of the Catholic 'Old English' nobility left Ireland to serve as soldiers for Catholic France and Spain. Their exit is known as the 'Flight of the Wild Geese'.

The Protestant Ascendancy

In the 18th century, with Protestantism triumphant, many of Ireland's aristocracy grew extremely wealthy, and built elegant European-style mansions for themselves within beautiful landscaped gardens, such as Powerscourt in Co. Wicklow (*see* p.79). Irish landowners had total control of vast estates, so their way of life was often even more resplendant than that of similar aristocrats in Britain or France (these mansions became symbols of Anglo-Irish control to Catholics, so many were burned down in the conflicts of the 1920s, often regardless of whether their owners were supporters of independence or not).

Literature and fine speech were very important among the ruling classes of the 'Ascendancy' (as the dominant regime after 1691 was known), and the arts, music and things of beauty were treasured. Dublin grew into an elegant Georgian city. The Ireland of this era produced many great writers, such as Jonathan Swift, author of *Gulliver's Travels* and many satires on British rule in Ireland, and the playwrights Congreve, Goldsmith and Sheridan. All were Anglo-Irish Protestants, since most Catholics were barred from education. Some Ascendancy Protestants were also interested in traditional Irish arts, and the early 18th century was also the time of the last and greatest of traditional Irish harpists, Turlough O'Carolan, from Co. Roscommon (*see* p.186 and p.189).

Most Catholics, though, were humbled and treated as inferior people. By 1750, while 75 per cent of Ireland's population were Catholic, they owned just five per cent of the land. Most were poor tenant farmers, many of them living in harsh conditions. Their landlords were often absentees – descendants of Cromwell's soldiers, or followers of Elizabeth I – who never even visited their estates. Catholics were kept in check by a series of harsh measures introduced after 1691 to prevent them ever gaining power, known as the Penal Laws.

In response, Catholics organized secret open-air Masses and 'hedge schools', where Catholic priests taught religion, Greek, Latin, the Irish language and history outdoors among bushes and hedges.

Not all Catholics opposed those in power, however, for many were in awe of their wealth and fine manners. Some became Protestants themselves to protect their careers. The Penal Laws also did not only discriminate against Catholics, but against

Some of Ireland's 18th-Century Penal Laws

1 Catholics were banned from joining the army or navy, or becoming Members of Parliament, and were forced to pay a tax to the Anglican (Protestant) church.
2 No Catholic could vote or buy land.
3 Catholic priests were expelled, and Catholic churches closed.
4 No Catholic schools were allowed.
5 A son of a Catholic who became a Protestant could take his parents' land for himself.
6 Speaking 'Irish' in public was banned.
7 Heavy taxes were placed on Irish products – such as cloth, glass, wool and cattle – so that Ireland could not compete with Britain economically.

many non-Anglican Protestants, such as the Presbyterian 'Dissenters'. Non-wealthy Protestants were also excluded from power by the aristocracy. Many Dissenters left Ulster for Puritan New England, where, known as 'Scots-Irish', they played a major role in founding the United States (Co. Tyrone's Ulster American Folk Park gives some fascinating insights on this; *see* p.226).

Secret societies formed in the countryside among Catholics, in rebellion against the laws that stopped them from getting jobs and owning land. Outbreaks of violence were frequent. Protestant gangs fought Catholic gangs, and in 1795 one clash led Ulster Protestants to found the 'Orange Order' to protect their interests (at 'The Diamond' in Co. Armagh; *see* p.219). Named in honour of Prince William of Orange, it would become one of the most powerful of such groups in Protestant Ireland. Ireland still had its own Parliament, which, even though it was only made up of rich Protestants, tried to win more powers from the British government, and managed to relax the worst of the Penal Laws by the 1780s. Even so, dissatisfaction continued among Catholics and many Protestants.

Inspired by the American and French Revolutions, some Protestants formed a radical society called the United Irishmen, in 1790. Its aim was Irish independence; its most famous member, lawyer Wolfe Tone, urged people 'to substitute the common name of Irishman in place of... Protestant, Catholic and Dissenter'. Promised help by France, then at war with Britain, they launched an armed rebellion along the Donegal, Mayo and Wexford coasts in 1798.

The revolt was strongest in Leinster and the Ulster counties of Antrim and Down, but spread to most of Ireland. However, the French troops sent to aid the rebels made little impact, and the rebellion was finally crushed in the Battle of Vinegar Hill, near Enniscorthy in Co. Wexford (*see* p.85), leaving nearly 30,000 people dead.

Following the 1798 Rebellion the British government shut down the Irish parliament, and in 1801 instituted the Act of Union, putting Ireland and Britain together into a single United Kingdom with one parliament at Westminster. However, this solved nothing, as the Irish still demanded reform.

The United Irishmen had planted the seed of a new idea, that of self-rule achieved by political means, but the bloody failure of their revolution caused a loss of heart among radical groups, who continued demanding reform. Then along came one of Ireland's most inspiring leaders, the Kerryman Daniel O'Connell (1775–1847). He believed that 'no political change is worth the shedding of a single drop of human blood', and stood for election in 1828. As a Catholic, he was banned from taking his seat in the Westminster parliament, yet he won by a landslide. Fearing another Irish revolt, the British government granted the Catholic Emancipation Act of 1829 so that 'the Liberator' – as O'Connell became known in Ireland – could sit in the House of Commons. Catholics were thus finally granted some basic political rights. However, Ireland was about to be plunged into a new disaster, as dramatic and devastating as any it had seen before.

The Great Famine and Exit

In the early 19th century, Ireland's population doubled to around 8 million between 1800 and 1840. The potato had become the staple food of the poor, and was often the only thing they could afford to grow and eat. Then potato blight, a plant disease, destroyed almost all of Ireland's potato crop in 1845 and again in 1846. Left with nothing to eat, destitute families wandered the land seeking food, eating grass and berries just to stay alive, building rough shelters on the roadside when they could and dropping dead when they couldn't. Many poor farmers were evicted from their homes as soon as they could no longer pay their rent, by landlords who refused to help them. Around 1.5 million people starved to death or died from disease, while more than 1 million others left

Ireland for other countries. The famine's effects were worst in the west, in Connacht and Munster, where poor farmers had been most dependent on potatoes for food.

Matters were made worse by the attitude of many British politicians, who felt the problems of the Famine were Ireland's responsibility. After all, there was still plenty of food in Ireland; the poor simply had no money with which to buy it. Cattle, sheep, oats and flour continued to be exported, and in Dublin life went on as normal. Ireland's unique situation, though, with so many absentee landlords, meant that many parts of the country were not well governed.

Some landowners were deeply disturbed by what was happening, and made themselves penniless trying to feed the wandering hordes of starving people. However, many absentee landlords, who lived in Britain or Dublin and sometimes never even visited their estates themselves, were unconcerned about Ireland's poverty, especially since their own and Britain's fortunes were growing. Others wanted to control more of their land themselves, for more profitable uses such as grazing sheep. The famine gave them a good excuse to clear their land of people, and so farmers and their families were evicted after they became too weak to work and too poor to pay rent. Sometimes landlords even paid their tenants to emigrate.

The famine years began the great flow of emigration out of Ireland. Thousands of people made their way to ports such as Cobh, hoping to find a boat to their great hope, America. Conditions on the ships were so terrible they became known as 'coffin ships', because so many people died while crossing, though there were still plenty more ready to sail on them. By the end of the 19th century, the population of Ireland halved, to just 4 million.

All over Ireland, you'll find the Famine mentioned, but one of the best places to take children to see its effects for themselves is Dan O'Hara's cottage in Connemara (*see* p.168). Here you can learn how the famine destroyed the lives of an ordinary family.

Thanks to emigration, a strong Irish community formed in the United States. Many Irish immigrants hated Britain for expelling them from their homeland. A new movement was founded among Irish-Americans, the Irish Republican Brotherhood (IRB). Its members called themselves Fenians, after the mythical Fianna warriors. Their aim was revolution to win complete Irish independence from Britain. Back in Ireland, though, they did not have much impact.

In 1879, another potato crop failed in Ireland, and evictions again became widespread. Land ownership was a burning issue. A new movement of poor farmers appeared called the Land League, led by an ex-Fenian named Michael Davitt (*see* p.176), who had been evicted from his Co. Mayo home as a child during the Great Famine, emigrated to England to work in a cotton mill, where he lost his arm at age 12, and eventually returned to Ireland to start political action. The League sought fair rents and improvements in tenants' rights, encouraging tenants to defy their landlords by refusing to pay rent. One of its most famous actions involved tenants who refused to work for a Mayo landlord named Captain Boycott (a campaign that gave us the word 'boycott').

Davitt and the League worked in cooperation with the politician Charles Stewart Parnell, whose Irish Party had become an important group in the British House of Commons. Parnell's arguments and unrest over land problems finally persuaded Britain's Liberal Prime Minister Gladstone that Ireland needed major reform. His government introduced laws that at last gave Irish Catholics complete religious freedom and the right to own land. The Irish, however, wanted more, and hoped that Gladstone would give them self-government, or 'Home Rule'. Their champion Parnell pushed the Home Rule issue to the top of the agenda in British politics. However, he was disastrously discredited by his affair with a married woman, Kitty O'Shea, in 1891, and Gladstone's Home Rule Bill collapsed in 1893, bringing this attempt at peaceful change to an end.

The 20th Century: War, Partition and Independence

Ireland's drive for independence intensified in the 20th century. Winds of change were blowing in other fields as well as politics. More and more people across the country – apart from eastern Ulster – felt a new pride in a strong, separate cultural identity distinct from that of Britain. The time from the 1890s to 1914 were the peak years of the 'Irish Cultural Renaissance'. Writers and artists re-examined and began to value Ireland's historic culture, literature and traditions. Many were from

Protestant, Anglo-Irish backgrounds and hoped that by strengthening awareness of Ireland's cultural heritage they would encourage eventual Irish independence. Lady Gregory, an Anglo-Irish aristocrat, brought back to people's attention Ireland's mythology, much of which had been virtually ignored for centuries. With her wealth, she also helped nearly every Irish writer of the time (regardless of their ethnic or religious background) and, with the poet WB Yeats, founded the Abbey Theatre, the hub of Ireland's new theatre movement.

Major initiatives to promote Irish culture were created by forward-thinkers. For example, the Gaelic Athletic Association popularized the Irish sports of hurling and Gaelic football and the Gaelic League was founded to support the Irish language by the man who would be the first president of the Irish Republic: Douglas Hyde. Even Dubliners began to study the Irish language, among them the writer-to-be James Joyce.

This growing Irish confidence was among the reasons why Britain's Liberal Party introduced a new Home Rule Bill for Ireland in 1912. It won enthusiastic support in most of Ireland, but alarmed the Protestant majority in eastern Ulster, who feared it would lead to Catholic supremacy – or 'Rome Rule' – and that a parliament in Dublin would favour the rural south against the industrialized north. This threat revived the Orange Order, and big demonstrations were held at which Protestant leaders such as Sir Edward Carson openly stated their willingness to defy the British government by force, by creating their own paramilitary army, the Ulster Volunteer Force or UVF. In response, former Fenians set up their own smaller paramilitary force, the Irish Volunteers, while a new group called Sinn Féin (Irish for 'Ourselves Alone') suggested that Irish MPs should withdraw from Westminster and set up their own parliament in Dublin. Trades unions had also been set up among the workers of Dublin's slums, many led by James Connolly, both a nationalist and a believer in socialist revolution. After a strike in 1913, he formed his own paramilitary force, the Irish Citizen Army.

Things had reached a stalemate when the outbreak of the First World War in August 1914 put everything on hold, at least so far as the British government was concerned. Having other things to do, Parliament suspended the Home Rule Bill. Ulster Protestants, including the UVF, volunteered in thousands to fight in the British Army. Many Catholics – although this is often forgotten – volunteered as well, hoping their loyalty would be rewarded by a grateful Britain with Home Rule after the war. Irish regiments were among the most prominent in the British Army's front line, and more than 5,000 Ulstermen alone were killed on the first day of the Battle of the Somme in July 1916.

Many Irish nationalists were intensely frustrated by the end of the Home Rule debate. Feeling that Britain's battles had nothing to do with them, they began to see the war as an opportunity. On Easter Monday 1916 the Irish Volunteers and Connolly's Irish Citizen Army launched the 'Easter Rising', seizing control of Dublin's General Post Office and other buildings around the city and proclaiming an independent Irish Republic. Fewer than 2,000 nationalists took part in the Rising, and 20,000 British Army soldiers had no trouble putting it down in a mere six days. At first the rebels were treated with scorn by the Dublin crowds, until the British committed the mistake of executing some of them. Fifteen rebel leaders, including popular figures such as Pádraic Pearse and James Connolly, were shot, and the only ones spared were Constance de Markievicz, because she was a woman, and Eamon de Valera, because he was an American citizen. Making them martyrs, their executions enraged the Irish public, turning it against British rule, and created great sympathy in America for the Irish revolutionaries.

By the time a new general election was held at the end of the World War in 1918, Irish politics had changed entirely. Sinn Féin won a majority of Irish seats, but refused to go to Westminster and instead formed their own parliament in Dublin, the *Dáil Éireann* ('doyle-air-an') or Assembly of Ireland, acting as representatives of an independent Ireland. Eamon de Valera was made *Taoiseach* ('tee-shock') or Prime Minister. Michael Collins was his deputy.

This amounted to a declaration of war – and a bitter, bloody guerrilla war ensued. Though Collins was officially Minister of Finance, he was also the foremost leader of a highly effective campaign of violence carried out against the British by the new Irish Republican Army (IRA). Against them were the Protestant Unionists, British soldiers, the police or Royal Irish Constabulary, and a newly formed paramilitary force: the notorious Black and Tans, whose undisciplined, uncontrolled violence later became a focus for anti-British feeling in Ireland.

Did you know...?

The Irish flag was designed in the 1840s. The green symbolizes Catholics and the orange Protestants, while the white stands for peace between them.

British power over Ireland became impossible to maintain. In 1921, this war came to an end with the signing of an Anglo-Irish Treaty. This divided Ireland. The six Protestant-majority counties of Ulster were given the chance to opt out of the Irish state, which they duly took. They remained part of what was now called the United Kingdom of Great Britain and Northern Ireland, but had their own regional government and parliament at Stormont. The remaining 26 counties, or most of Ireland, became a self-governing dominion within the British Commonwealth, and was called the Irish Free State. Michael Collins and Arthur Griffith, the Dáil Vice President, agreed this compromise with Britain's Prime Minister Lloyd George, believing it essential to bring the fighting to an end. All of them, though, believed that the new province of Northern Ireland would not take root and would eventually be absorbed into the Irish Free State.

The ink was scarcely dry when civil war broke out among Irish Nationalists (between 'Free Staters' and 'Republicans'). Hardline Republicans, led by De Valera, refused to take the oath of allegiance to the British Crown that members of the Dáil were expected to swear, as the Free State was still part of the Commonwealth. They also refused to accept partition and continued British rule in the North. They walked out of the Dáil when the majority ratified the treaty, and fighting began between former comrades. De Valera resigned as president and was imprisoned, while his supporters ambushed and murdered their former hero Michael Collins (*see* Argideen Valley, p.124). This civil war finally ended in 1923 when De Valera called for a ceasefire, leaving much bitterness and some IRA members who still believed in fighting on for the goal of a united Ireland.

In 1926, De Valera set up a new party, Fianna Fáil, which gained power in 1932 and has been the Irish Republic's foremost political party ever since. He cut political and economic ties with Britain with a new constitution in 1937, which got rid of the oath of allegiance to the British Crown, declared Ireland a sovereign state with its own president and established the use of the Irish word for Ireland, Eire, on government documents. Irish was made the national language, so that every teacher and child in state-funded schools was obliged to study it. Crucially, this Constitution claimed sovereignty over all of Ireland, including the six counties of the north. Eire remained neutral in the Second World War (1939–45), even though Churchill tried to bring it into the fray by promising immediate reunification. De Valera rejected the offer, and pulled Ireland out of the Commonwealth in 1949.

Emigration continued in the 1950s, and the Republic was a poor place. Few cars or telephones troubled it, and fewer than half its households had indoor toilets or running water. The Catholic Church played a central role in education and social policies, and kept a close eye on many other things: birth control and divorce were illegal, and many books published freely elsewhere were banned, including those by Irish authors Samuel Beckett, James Joyce and Edna O'Brien. Catholics and Protestants often regarded each other with suspicion. One of the best books about this time is Frank McCourt's *Angela's Ashes*, a vivid description of his experiences in Limerick as a poor Catholic.

In the North, meanwhile, after the partition of 1921, Unionists (Protestant supporters of the Union with Britain) moved fast to ensure that only property-owners were allowed to vote in local elections. This meant that most Catholics, who were usually poor and lived in rented houses, could not vote. In this way, Unionist councils could favour Protestants seeking employment and housing. For years, until the 1960s, this situation was ignored by Britain's governing parties, even though they held supreme authority over the six Northern Ireland counties.

The Troubles in the North

In 1967, encouraged by the success of the Civil Rights movement in America, John Hume, Bernadette Devlin and other Catholic politicians in Northern Ireland formed the Civil Rights Association (CRA). They organized non-violent street protests about housing, jobs, exclusion from voting, policing and the other more blatant ways in which Catholics were discriminated against in Northern Ireland. The Unionist Northern Irish government at Stormont had promised reform for years, but so far had done little, and was afraid to confront its own hardliners. These promises and the civil rights agitation, though, were enough to alarm large sections of the Protestant community, who were encouraged to believe that any concession to Catholic nationalists would threaten their way of life. Protestant organizations like the Orange Order revived and put pressure on the Stormont government to resist the civil rights campaign, and paramilitary groups such as the Ulster Volunteer Force were secretly re-formed. The British government did nothing, missing the chance, perhaps, to avoid decades of violence.

This violence flared up during civil rights marches in 1968 and 1969. Most Northern Catholics had long had little trust in the almost completely Protestant Royal Ulster Constabulary (RUC, or Northern Irish police), and their confidence shrank more each time the RUC obstructed marchers, or did nothing to protect them, especially when some joined in to attack them with Protestant mobs. This undermined confidence in the Ulster state. Wholescale violence erupted in August 1969 after the Protestant Apprentice Boys' parade to commemorate the Siege of Londonderry in 1689 (*see* p.35), when barricades went up around the Catholic Bogside area of the city to prevent the hated parade from going through the district. Rioting and street battles also spread to Belfast. The Northern Irish government was forced to admit it had lost control, and asked London to send in troops to restore order.

At first, the Catholic community welcomed British troops as their protectors against local Protestants and the police, but things changed as their presence and occasional heavy-handed tactics grew more obvious on their streets, and links between the British Army and the old Northern Irish state reasserted themselves. This led to the re-emergence of the IRA. It had been relatively inactive for many years and was at first split about how to respond to the civil rights campaign, but not long after the 1969 riots, a new faction gained the upper hand, the Provisional IRA or Provos, who believed that violence was the best way of achieving their goal of a united Ireland. So clashes with the army and other violence escalated, and more British troops were sent in, moving events in a downward spiral. In August 1971, the British government gave the IRA another recruiting card when it accepted Unionist demands to introduce internment, or imprisonment without trial. It was claimed that this would make it easier to stamp out terrorism on all sides, but nearly all of the 1,600 people arrested were Catholics, and civil rights lawyers accused the British government of mistreating and torturing internees.

On 30 January 1972, a march demanding the end of internment was held in the Bogside area of Londonderry. When the crowd reached army barricades, stones were thrown, to which soldiers responded with rubber bullets and water-cannon. Firing began, and 13 civilians were killed. This event, known as Bloody Sunday, boosted recruitment to the IRA and pushed the conflict to new depths. The British Army have said they were fired on first, but the marchers have denied this. A report from an official enquiry into the incident, led by Lord Saville, is expected some time in 2006.

After Bloody Sunday, the Northern Irish parliament was closed and Northern Ireland was placed under direct rule from Westminster, but violence continued. At around the same time, the IRA began a bombing campaign in Britain and Ulster. Hardline Protestants, meanwhile – who, despite being known as 'Loyalists', never trusted the British government to protect them – expanded their own paramilitary squads like the UVF (Ulster Volunteer Force) and UDA (Ulster Defence Association), occasionally launching violence against the IRA.

For years the conflict went on, with no visible end but occasional dramatic events, such as in 1981, when IRA prisoners in the Maze prison went on hunger strike to demand to be treated as political prisoners. The British government of Margaret Thatcher did not give way, and when the hunger strikers' leader, Bobby Sands, died, more than 50,000 people attended his funeral. Although Sands was unable to take his seat when elected to Parliament thereafter, it played a part in making Provisional IRA leaders think they could succeed politically rather than through violent action.

Despite the continued violence, politicians in Dublin, London and Northern Ireland carried on searching for a peaceful solution. In 1985, the governments of Britain and the Irish Republic signed the Anglo-Irish Agreement, which gave Dublin a consulting role in Northern Irish affairs. Northern Irish Protestants expressed outrage and there was an upsurge of violence and paramilitary activity on the Loyalist side, but tentative moves towards a real peace process had begun.

In the 1993 Downing Street Declaration, the British government stated that it had 'no selfish, strategic or economic interest in Northern Ireland', but assured Unionists that their consent would be required for any constitutional change. In August 1994, the IRA announced a ceasefire, and Loyalist groups announced their own shortly afterwards.

After May 1997, when a landslide election victory brought the Labour Party's Tony Blair to power in Britain, the British government began to push peace negotiations in Northern Ireland to the top of the agenda.

The talks that followed produced the Good Friday Agreement in 1998. A major breakthrough on the road to a peaceful settlement, it provided for no change in the status of the North except by majority consent; the devolution of a variety of powers to a Northern Ireland Assembly; a North–South Ministerial Council between Northern Ireland and the Republic; and a British–Irish Council that would include representatives from other parts of the British Isles. The Constitution of the Irish Republic would also be amended to renounce its territorial claim to Northern Ireland. A referendum in both parts of Ireland endorsed this agreement on 22 May 1998. Since then, Irish politics have been dominated by the difficulties of implementing the Good Friday Agreement.

Northern Ireland remains a divided society, but the year 2005 brought the final decommissioning of the IRA's weapons, establishing the organization's commitment to settling disagreements with politics instead of guns. Small protests about this from Loyalists are nothing, however, compared to the destruction that greedy corporations and businessmen are now wreaking upon the country.

A Modern Place

While the North was entangled in its problems, society in the rest of Ireland had begun to change. In the 1960s, TV, radio and cinema brought images of a wider world into Irish society, altering its long-held customs and habits, including its storytelling and music-making traditions. In 1972, the Irish Republic, like Britain, became a member of the European Community (later renamed the European Union). And in 1973, Eamon de Valera, a symbol of the old-fashioned Ireland, finally left office as president, and died two years later.

Ireland began to take on a new persona. While previously – despite its apparent independence – it had remained dependent on Britain, EU membership opened it up to an international economy. Grants of all kinds from the EU flooded in, joining the tax incentives being offered to foreign investors by the Irish government. The aim was to industrialize an economy still dominated by agriculture. And in the 1990s, Ireland exploded with the years of its so-called 'Celtic Tiger' economy. A media-based, international style of work and living, fuelled by new technology, from TV to computers and mobile phones, was energetically encouraged by business and government. Irish expatriates returned from countries like the United States with new ideas, 'blow-ins' arrived from other parts of the world to work in hotels and on farms, and Ireland even began to attract immigrants itself, often refugees from eastern Europe or Africa.

With all of these changes came a new openness in Irish society. In 1990 a woman, the lawyer and champion of liberal causes Mary Robinson was elected president. The political problems in the North had repercussions in the South, where people began to reassess their history, religion and society. Joint British and Irish membership of the European Union, prosperity and secularization did much to change sectarian attitudes, and smoothed the way in the south for the acceptance of the Good Friday Agreement. The Catholic Church was rocked by scandals, and its hold over society weakened. Although birth control and abortion are still hotly debated, divorce was legalized in 1995.

In 2002, the Republic adopted the euro, cementing its involvement with Europe and separation from Britain. With industrialization, a car-based transportation system and the intensification of influences from alien cultures have come new dangers that the Republic must address. It is now part of Europe, and looking outward at a more expansive universe. Although this new status exposes Ireland to many good things, it shouldn't be forgotten that the door is also open to the bad.

Modern enemies include a corporate landlord mentality that encourages blandness, soulless buildings and motorways, polluting chemical industries and a supermarket-based mono-agriculture, all of which sound the death knell for small farms and local businesses. This small country is more suited to having self-sustaining communities that use local resources and clean energy forms.

Ireland's complex history has given many of its inhabitants a unique perspective that could help it avoid others' mistakes. They should be heard before it's too late, for the sake of the future and the children of this special island.

Some Names in Irish History

Gerry Adams (b. 1948). Leader of Sinn Féin and a key figure in the Northern Ireland peace process.

Black Pig's Dyke A long, intermittent line of earthworks between natural obstacles that is thought to have been a series of massive defences guarding routes into Ulster. Folktales say an enchanted boar ploughed it up with his tusks.

Brian Boru (942–1014). The only High King of all Ireland, murdered by a Viking on the day he won the crown, after winning the Battle of Clontarf. His castle was at Kincora on the Clare–Tipperary border.

Sir Edward Carson (1854–1935). Unionist leader and Protestant lawyer from Dublin who led the Ulster opposition to Home Rule in 1912–14.

Michael Collins (1889–1922). Organized and led the IRA in a guerrilla war against the British, 1918–22, then signed the treaty that partitioned Ireland, which led to Ireland's Civil War, during which he was killed in an ambush in Co. Cork.

St Columcille, or **Colum Cille**, **Colmcille** or **Columba** (521–93). The 'Dove of the Church', a prince of the O'Neills of Donegal who became Ireland's greatest native saint, and founded the famous monastery on the Scottish island of Iona.

James Connolly (1868–1916). Key leader of the 1916 Easter Rising; born to Irish immigrants in Scotland, he returned to organize Ireland's trade unions.

Oliver Cromwell (1599–1658). English general and leader of the Parliamentarians who crushed the Irish rebellion in 1649 with notorious brutality.

Michael Davitt (1846–1906). Founder of the Land League, supporting the rights of tenant farmers.

Eamon de Valera (1882–1975). The dominant figure in Irish politics for 50 years, Prime Minister of the Republic 1932–48 and 1951–4, and President 1959–73.

Eóghan Mór (died late 2nd century). Semi-mythical High King of Munster's Eóghanachta dynasty.

Eoghanacht or **Eoghanachto** Kings of Munster who lost their seat at Cashel to Brian Boru.

William Ewart Gladstone (1809–98). British Liberal statesman and many-times Prime Minister who gave strong support to Home Rule for Ireland.

Lady Augusta Gregory (1852–1932). Benefactress of the Irish Literary Renaissance, who founded Dublin's Abbey Theatre in Dublin with WB Yeats and wrote many books on Irish myths and folklore.

James II (1633–1701). Deposed Catholic King of England who lost the Crown in Ireland to William of Orange; his followers were called Jacobites.

John Hume (b. 1937). Northern Irish Catholic leader from Derry who led the non-violent nationalist Social Democratic and Labour Party (SDLP).

Constance de Markievicz (1868–1927). Born into the Anglo-Irish Gore-Booth family, she married a Polish Count, and became an Irish Nationalist and socialist. She took part in the Easter Rising and was the first woman elected to the British Parliament, although she did not take her seat.

Daniel O'Connell (1775–1847). Lawyer from Co. Kerry known as 'the Liberator' after his successful campaign for voting and other rights for Catholics.

Hugh O'Neill (16–17th c.). Earl of Tyrone and the last of Ireland's powerful Gaelic lords, who led resistance to Elizabeth I in the 1590s, until he left for Europe in the 'Flight of the Earls' in 1607.

Pádraic Pearse (1879–1916). Poet, teacher and promoter of the Irish language who led the 1916 Easter Rising.

Rev. Ian Paisley (b. 1927). Presbyterian minister who has been an outspoken leader of hardline Unionism in Northern Ireland and founder and leader of the Democratic Unionist Party (DUP).

Charles Stewart Parnell (1846–91). Anglo-Irish Protestant landowner who led the 1880s campaign for Irish Home Rule.

St Patrick (5th c.). Patron saint of Ireland, credited with converting the Irish to Christianity.

Strongbow (12th c.). Earl of Pembroke, a Norman warrior who was the first Anglo-Norman to gain power in Ireland (1169–71).

Jonathan Swift (1667–1745). Dublin Protestant cleric and writer, and author of *Gulliver's Travels*.

David Trimble (b. 1944). Ex-leader of the Ulster Unionist Party and ex-head of Northern Ireland's regional government.

Wolfe Tone (1763–98). Protestant lawyer who sought support from Revolutionary France for Irish independence, and led the 1798 Rebellion.

Oscar Wilde (1854–1900). Notorious, extravagant Anglo-Irish dramatist, novelist, poet and wit.

William of Orange (1650–1702). Dutch Protestant prince who threw out Britain's Catholic King James II in 1688 and replaced him as King William III. He became a hero for Ulster Protestants after defeating James II at the Battle of the Boyne.

William Butler (WB) Yeats (1865–1939). Great Anglo-Irish poet and Nobel prizewinner who was a champion of Irish folklore and was most associated with counties Sligo and Galway.

Dublin

GETTING AROUND 46
Dublin Tours 48
Tourist Information 49
Shopping 49

THINGS TO SEE AND DO 50
North of the Liffey 50
South of the Liffey 52
Other Ideas 56

AROUND AND ABOUT 58
Animal magic 58
Bricks and mortar 58
Look at this! 59
Nature lovers 61

WHERE TO EAT 62

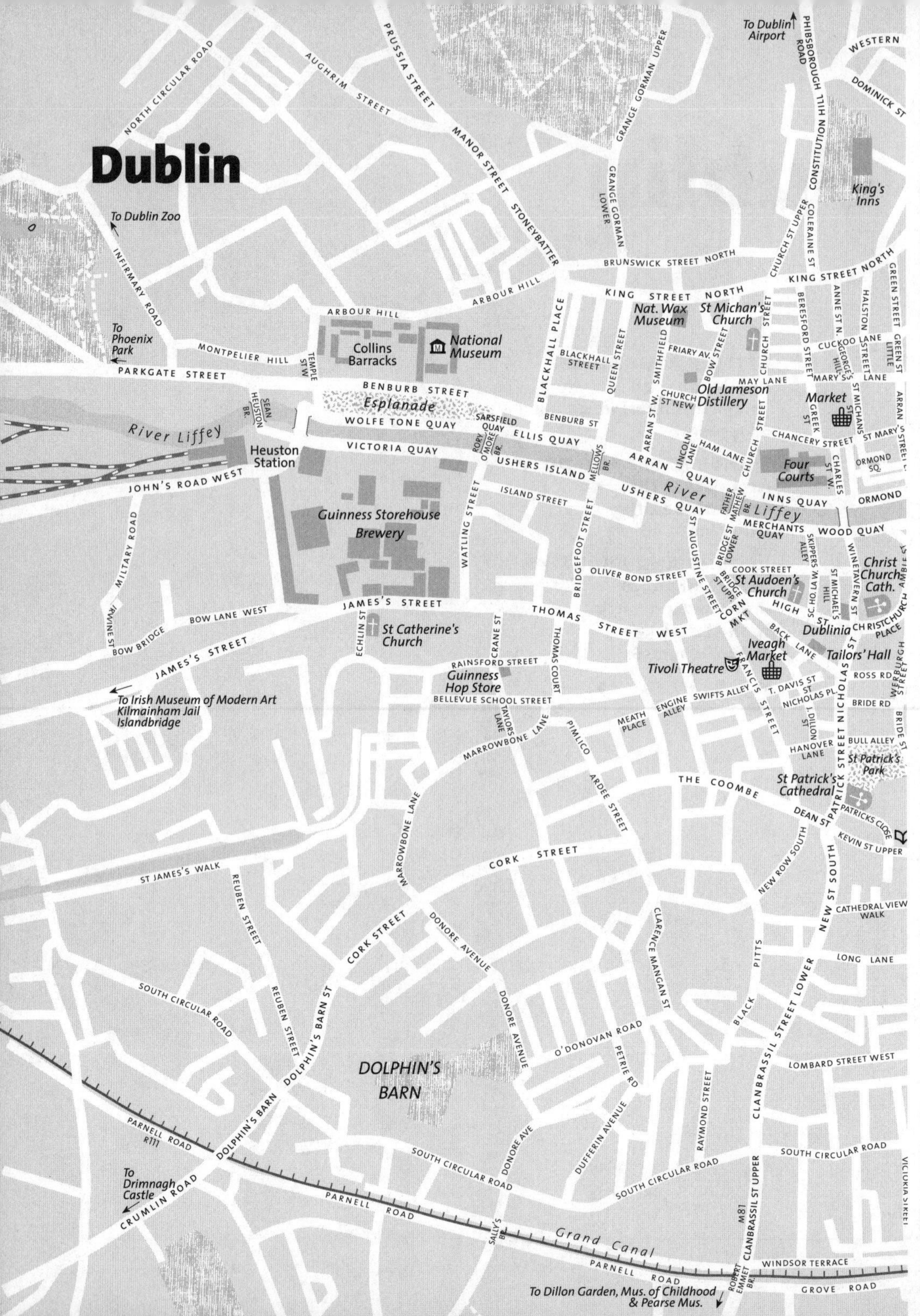
Dublin
To Dublin Zoo
To Phoenix Park
To Dublin Airport
Collins Barracks
National Museum
Esplanade
River Liffey
Heuston Station
Guinness Storehouse Brewery
St Catherine's Church
Guinness Hop Store
Nat. Wax Museum
St Michan's Church
Old Jameson Distillery
Market
King's Inns
Four Courts
Christ Church Cath.
St Audoen's Church
Dublinia
Tailors' Hall
Iveagh Market
Tivoli Theatre
St Patrick's Park
St Patrick's Cathedral
To Irish Museum of Modern Art Kilmainham Jail Islandbridge
DOLPHIN'S BARN
Grand Canal
To Drimnagh Castle
To Dillon Garden, Mus. of Childhood & Pearse Mus.

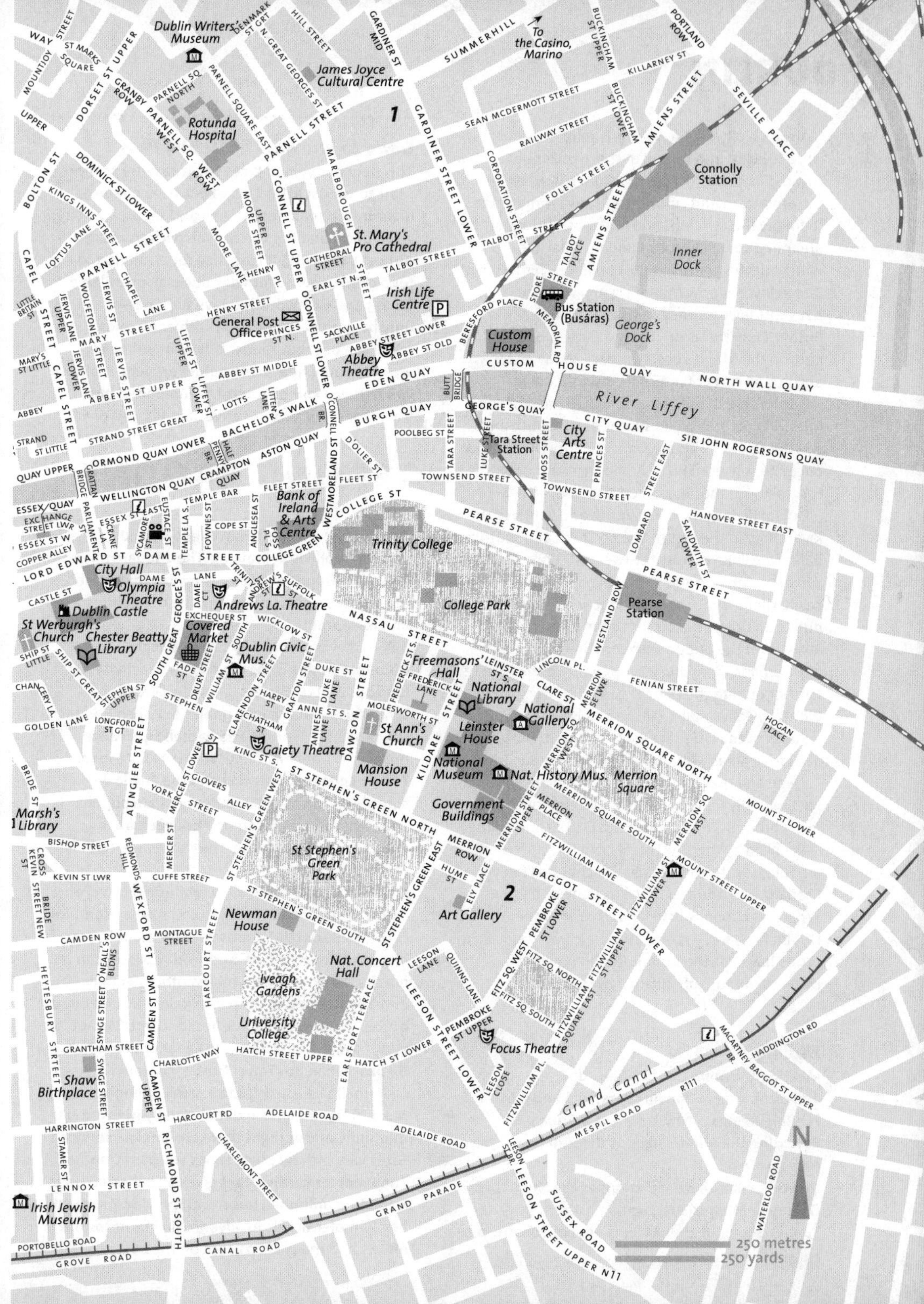

Dublin Writers' Museum
James Joyce Cultural Centre
To the Casino, Marino
Rotunda Hospital
1
2
St. Mary's Pro Cathedral
Connolly Station
Inner Dock
Bus Station (Busáras)
George's Dock
Custom House
Irish Life Centre
General Post Office
Abbey Theatre
River Liffey
Tara Street Station
City Arts Centre
Bank of Ireland & Arts Centre
Trinity College
College Park
Pearse Station
City Hall
Olympia Theatre
Dublin Castle
St Werburgh's Church
Chester Beatty Library
Covered Market
Andrews La. Theatre
Dublin Civic Mus.
Freemasons' Hall
National Library
National Gallery
Leinster House
St Ann's Church
Gaiety Theatre
Mansion House
National Museum
Nat. History Mus.
Merrion Square
Government Buildings
Marsh's Library
St Stephen's Green Park
Newman House
Art Gallery
Nat. Concert Hall
Iveagh Gardens
University College
Focus Theatre
Grand Canal
Shaw Birthplace
Irish Jewish Museum
N
250 metres
250 yards
Parnell Street
O'Connell St Upper
O'Connell St Lower
Gardiner Street Lower
Summerhill
Sean McDermott Street
Talbot Street
Amiens Street
Seville Place
Custom House Quay
North Wall Quay
Eden Quay
Burgh Quay
George's Quay
City Quay
Sir John Rogersons Quay
Bachelor's Walk
Ormond Quay Lower
Wellington Quay
Aston Quay
Pearse Street
Westmoreland St
College Green
Dame Street
Lord Edward St
Nassau Street
Grafton Street
Dawson Street
Kildare Street
Clare St
Merrion Square North
Merrion Square South
St Stephen's Green North
St Stephen's Green West
St Stephen's Green South
St Stephen's Green East
Baggot Street Lower
Leeson Street Lower
Harcourt Street
Aungier Street
Wexford St
Camden St Lwr
Richmond St South
Adelaide Road
Grand Parade
Canal Road
Portobello Road
Grove Road
Leeson Street Upper N11
Sussex Road
Haddington Rd
Mespil Road
Baggot St Upper
Mount Street Upper
Fitzwilliam St Lower
Waterloo Road

DUBLIN

Always a city for the young, Dublin is the largest city in Ireland and capital of the Irish Republic. Located in its busiest county, Dublin is where the ambitious and curious have always moved to to follow their dreams and find jobs. No longer the dreaming town of Molly Malone, today it bursts with youthful energy as never before. This home of James Joyce is now that of U2 and Westlife.

A short ferry journey across the Irish Sea from Britain, Dublin was originally a convenient trading port on the island's eastern coast. Today it still absorbs all sorts of international influences.

Dublin's suburbs have gobbled up most of the little villages and green spaces north, south and west of the city. This area, now County Dublin and once the sole domain of Anglo-Irish and British control in Ireland, was called 'the Pale'.

Dublin divides itself into north and south of the River Liffey. In the centre, the northern and southern halves are linked across the river by O'Connell Bridge. You can walk through the whole of central Dublin easily, though with children in tow it could be tiring due to all the traffic. North of the Liffey, running away from the bridge with the same name, is the city's broadest and busiest street, O'Connell Street. Further out are the old, congested areas of Marino, Clontarf, Dollymount, Sutton and Howth.

South of the Liffey are some of old Dublin's most attractive areas, with pub-filled Temple Bar, Trinity College and the lovely St Stephen's Green. Beyond, past wealthy Ballsbridge, the suburbs south of the river through Dun Laoghaire to Dalkey and Killiney – all linked by the DART local train (*see* opposite) – are full of writers like Maeve Binchy and Hugh Leonard, and pop stars such as Bono and Enya. Whatever happens to Ireland usually happens to Dublin first, and years of economic boom since the 1990s have left their mark. Children will find Dublin's mixture of old and new fascinating.

Highlights

Meeting the animals at Dublin Zoo and picnicking in Phoenix Park, p.58 and p.61
Playing Vikings on a Viking Splash Tour, p.48
Revisiting the Middle Ages at the Dublinia Museum, p.53
Drawing your own conclusions at the Hugh Lane Gallery of Modern Art, p.51
Puppet Shows at the Lambert Puppet Theatre, p.57

Good to know... The Dublin Pass

This new visitor card gives you free entry to more than 30 tourist attractions, bypassing queues; discounts in some restaurants and shops; a 76-page guidebook; and trips on the Aircoach from Dublin Airport (*see* p.283). It costs €29 for an adult and €17 for a child under 16 for 1 day but is also available for 2, 3 and 6 consecutive days. Kids' passes can only be used in conjunction with adult ones.

You can buy it at tourist offices or online at **www.thedublinpass.com** before arriving. It allows you to buy a Rambler ticket for unlimited bus travel for 1, 3 or 5 consecutive days (€5, €10 or €15).

GETTING AROUND

On foot The cheapest way to get around central Dublin is by walking. The 2 square miles (6 sq km) around the River Liffey contain most of the city's sights, museums, theatres, shops and restaurants.

The Liffey is spanned by several bridges; **O'Connell Bridge** is the main focus of activity (and bus routes). Streets lining the Liffey are called quays, and change names between bridges. **O'Connell St**, **Henry St** and **Parnell Square** are north of O'Connell Bridge; **St Stephen's Green**, **Trinity College**, **Grafton St** and the **Castle** lie south. Grafton Street and **Henry St** are popular pedestrian shopping areas. **Phoenix Park** is about 2 miles (3km) from the centre, westwards along the river.

Rambler tickets These allow unlimited travel on Dublin's public transport system. You can combine DART trains or LUAS trams with buses, or buy a bus pass alone. One-, 7- and 30-day passes can be purchased from Dublin tourist offices or railway and bus stations, or from Irish Rail or Dublin Bus offices. A combined LUAS/bus (or Combi) ticket for 1 day costs €6 for adults and €3 for under-16s.

By bus Dublin Bus Travel Centre, 59 Upper O'Connell St, **t** (01) 873 4222, **www.dublinbus.ie** Most of Dublin Bus's 150 routes daily run 7am–12 midnight, and at night there are Nitelink services. Fares vary by how many zones you pass through. The **Rambler family ticket** gives 2 adults and up to 4 children unlimited bus travel for 1 day. You must buy Rambler tickets in advance (in bus or tourist offices and many shops), not on the bus.

For **Airport** buses, *see* p.283.

By train DART, Iarnród Éireann, **t** 1 850 366 222 and **t** (01) 836 6222, **www**.irishrail.ie/dart

DART (Dublin Area Rapid Transit) local trains run around Dublin Bay through 25 stations from Greystones and Bray, just inside Co. Wicklow in the south, through the city and north to Howth, with 4 trains an hour in each direction, daily about 6am–11pm. One-day unlimited tickets are available: a DART-Suburban Rail family ticket (2 adults and up to 4 under-16s) for 1 day (for all DART and Suburban Rail services between Balbriggan, Kilcoole, Maynooth and Hazelhatch/Celbridge, including the Airlink/Aircoach service but excluding Nitelink, ferries and tours) is €12.50.

Dublin's mainline stations are **Heuston**, at the west end of the river quays, for trains to the west and south, and **Connolly**, northeast of the centre, for the east coast and Northern Ireland (*see* p.288).

By tram LUAS, **t** 1 800 300 604, **www**.luas.ie

Dublin's new tram sytem has overground trams along 2 lines: the Red Line from Connolly Station through Heuston Station to Tallaght, and the Green Line from St Stephen's Green to Sandyford. Trams run every 5–10 mins (5.30am– 12.30am Mon–Fri, 6.30am–12.30am Sat, 8am–11.30pm Sun). There are kids' fares (about half the price of adults') and student discounts. Seven-day 'specified zone' tickets cost €10 for adults, €6 for children, and Flexi Tickets for 1 and 7 days are available (1 day is €4.50/€2.50). You can also get Combi Tickets for LUAS trams and Dublin buses for 1, 7 and 30 days. Irish Rail (Iarnród Éireann; *see* above) sells LUAS tickets.

By taxi Ranks are found outside hotels and railway stations, in special taxi parks in central Dublin, and on St Stephen's Green and O'Connell St; they are often hard to flag down in the street. They charge extra per piece of luggage and at night.

Blue Cabs, **t** (01) 676 1111

Metro Cabs, **t** (01) 668 3333/478 1111/677 2222

By car Parking is difficult in the centre. Main car parks are in Frederick St and the St Stephen's Green Shopping Centre, and there is metered parking around St Stephen's Green and Merrion Square. North of the river there's parking in the Irish Life Shopping Centre (Lower Abbey St). Driving in Dublin is chaotic, so be on your guard. Using your horn is the worst insult, so keep it as a last resort. Car theft and burglaries are increasing, so check whether a hotel has secure parking when booking.

Car hire

AVIS, Dublin Airport, **t** (01) 605 7500

Budget Rent A Car, Dublin Airport **t** (01) 844 5150

Murrays Europcar, Baggot Street Bridge, **t** (01) 614 2800; Dublin Airport, **t** (01) 812 0410

Bike Hire (not advisable for central Dublin)

The Bike Store Ltd, 58 Gardiner St, D1, **t** (01) 872 5399

Irish Cycling Safaries, Belfield Bike Shop, University College, D4, **t** (01) 260 0749

Special Events and Festivals

February–March

Six Nations Rugby Lansdowne Road Stadium, Lansdowne Rd, Ballsbridge, D4, **t** (01) 647 3800, **www**.irishrugby.ie. Matches on several Saturdays.

March

St Patrick's Festival, **t** (01) 676 3205, **www**. stpatricksfestival.ie. Celebrations, music and parades starting on O'Connell St around the 17th.

May

Fleadh Nua, Monkstown, **t** (01) 456 9569, **www**. fleadhnua.com A lively traditional music festival.

June

Bloomsday Festival, Information: James Joyce Centre, **t** (01) 878 8547, **www**.jamesjoyce.ie

Dublin's peculiar holiday on 16 June, anniversary of the day (in 1904) when all the action in James Joyce's *Ulysses* takes place. Various events are held in places visited by the fictional Leopold Bloom.

AIB Music in Great Irish Houses, 1st Floor, Blackrock Post Office, Co. Dublin, **t** (01) 278 1528

A 10-day festival of chamber music in mansions.

August

RDS Dublin Horse Show, Ballsbridge, D4, **t** (01) 668 0866 An international annual equestrian event.

September

All-Ireland Hurling and Gaelic Football Finals, Croke Park, **t** (01) 836 3222, **www**.gaa.ie Local sports..

Dublin Fringe Theatre Festival, **t** (01) 679 2320.

A vibrant event for theatre fans.

Heritage Week, D2, **t** (01) 647 2466

A celebration of Irish heritage at historical sights.

October

Dublin Theatre Festival, **t** (01) 474 0154, **www**.dublintheatrefestival.com

A globally respected festival with a family series.

Samhain Halloween Festival, **t** (01) 855 7154

All kinds of events around 31 October.

On tour: Dublin tours

Bus tours

Dublin Bus 59 Upper O'Connell St, D1, **t** (01) 873 4222, **www.**dublinbus.ie
City tours depart Mon–Sat, every 10mins 9.30–5, every 30mins 5–7pm. **Tickets** Adult €12.50; under-14s €6; students, over-65s €11
The city bus company offers handy 'hop-on, hop-off' daily tours on green and cream buses, beginning at its O'Connell St office and going on a circular route around all Dublin's main sites. The full tour lasts 1hr 15mins, but each ticket is valid for 24hrs, so you can get on and get off the bus as many times as you like the same day. Ticket-holders also get discounts on admission to a range of attractions. Tickets can be bought on the bus or at Dublin Bus offices or Dublin Tourism, Suffolk St.

Dublin Bus also offers fun nightly **Ghost Bus Tours** around haunted houses and other places to do with the city's more ghoulish history (Mon–Fri 8pm, Sat and Sun 7.30, 9.30pm; €22), not suitable for under-14s.

Irish City Tours 33 Bachelor's Walk, D1, **t** (01) 872 9010, **www.**irishcitytours.com
Tours depart from 12 Upper O'Connell St, D1, daily every 15mins April–14 July and Oct 9.30–5; 15 July–Sept 9.30–5.30; Nov–Mar 9.30–4
Tickets Adult €14; under-12s €5; students, over-65s €12; family ticket (2+3) €35
Three 'hop-on hop-off', 24hr-ticket tours, with discounts for some attractions. The best, with a human guide, is aboard the yellow open-top bus marked 'Dublin Tour' and sporting a blue diamond logo. Though it goes to Kilmainham Jail but not Phoenix Park, you can use your ticket for the other 2 routes, which go to Phoenix Park but not the jail (both are red; one is marked 'City Sightseeing' and its driver does the commentary, the other has multilingual headsets and sports language flags).

The Viking Splash Tour 64–65 Patrick St, D8, **t** (01) 707 6000, **www.**vikingsplashtours.com
Tours run mid-Feb–Nov; call for current times.
Tickets Mar–June (Mon–Fri) and Sept–Nov daily, adult from €15.50, under-13s from €8.50, family (2+3) €47; Mar–June (Sat and Sun) and July and Aug daily adult €15.95, under-13s €8.95, family (2+3) €58
This tour starts from Bull Alley, by St Patrick's Cathedral, but tickets can be bought from tourist offices. Witty, costumed tour captains, aka 'Viking chieftains', settle you on board a reconditioned World War II amphibious vehicle ('Duck') to teach you about how Dublin natives behave. You are instructed in Viking customs (goats make a good tip for your Viking host) and behaviour (roaring at passers-by as loudly as you can, raising your fists in the air). Then your chieftain drives you through the streets, pointing out historical facts about the city. At the Grand Canal Basin docks, you don lifejackets before the 'Duck' drives into the water and proves its other function as a boat. (Children under 2 must leave the bus for this part of the tour, which takes 20mins). Advance booking is advisable in summer.

Guided walking tours

Signs around the city guide you to historical sites. Dublin Tourism in Suffolk St has details. Several guided walking tours are also on offer, such as:

Historical Walking Tour of Dublin 64 Mary St, D1, **t** (01) 878 0227, **www.**historicalinsights.ie
Tours Oct and Apr daily 11; May–Sept daily 11 and 3; Nov–Mar Fri–Sun 11. **Tickets** €10

Assemble at the front gate of Trinity College, where a knowledgeable guide will meet you.

Literary/Georgian Walk t (01) 496 0641 or **t** (01) 269 7021.
Tours June–Sept Mon, Wed, Fri and Sat 10.30am.

A 2hr literary walk.

Tours from Dublin City

Dublin Bus 59 Upper O'Connell St, D1, **t** (01) 873 4222, **www.**dublinbus.ie
Dublin Bus also offers 2 daily bus tours, of 3–5 hrs each, to nearby areas: the 'Coast and Castle' tour (north Co. Dublin, Malahide, Howth) and the 'South Coast' tour (Dun Laoghaire down the coast to Bray, and back through the Wicklow Mountains).

Irish City Tours 33 Bachelor's Walk, D1, **t** (01) 872 9010, **www.irishcitytours.com**
This firm also offers 1-day tours: Powerscourt, Malahide, Wicklow, Newgrange, Kilkenny.

Legendary Tours, www.legendarytours.com
American storyteller Richard Marsh leads tours of countryside sites in Leinster, leaving Dublin at 8–9am, and returning 4–5pm. Wellies are provided as needed. Not recommended for under-10s.

Over the Top Tours, www.overthetoptours.com
One-day small-group tours (max 14 people) leave the Dublin Tourism office in Suffolk St daily about 9am on 2 main routes: the 'Celtic Experience' (Boyne Valley, Tara) and the Wicklow Mountains. Longer trips to Connemara, Cork and Kerry are offered. Not suitable for small children.

Can you spot... The Halfpenny Bridge?
It's across the River Liffey, just west of O'Connell Bridge – the next (arched) bridge down the river. It was first built by an Englishman in 1816, when you had to pay a halfpenny to walk across it.

Tourist information

Dublin Tourism Centre, St Andrew's Church, Suffolk St, D2, **t** (01) 605 7700, information line **t** 1 850 230 330, **www.visitdublin.com**
Open Sept–June Mon–Sat 9–5.30, Sun (Sept only) 10.30–3; July and Aug Mon–Sat 9–7, Sun 10.30–3.
Dublin's excellent main tourist office in a restored former church near Trinity College includes information desks for both Dublin and Ireland as a whole, accommodation information and bookings (hotels, B&Bs, hostels), bus, LUAS and DART ticket sales, car hire, bus tour and theatre bookings, currency exchange, a café and a souvenir/gift shop.
Dublin has 5 more information offices:
Dublin Airport Arrivals Hall; **open** daily 8–10
Dun Laoghaire Ferry Terminal; **open** Mon–Sat 10–1, 2–6
14 Upper O'Connell St, D1; **open** Mon–Sat 9–5
Failte Ireland, Baggot Street Bridge (south of centre, by Grand Canal), D2; **open** Mon–Sat 9.30–12, 12.30–5
Temple Bar Information Centre, 12 East Essex St, D2; **open** times vary throughout the year.
Dublin Welcome Centre, 15–17 Eden Quay, D1, **t** (01) 878 3347; **open** Mon–Fri 8–8 and Sat 11–5.

Shopping

The old song 'In Dublin's Fair City', with the line 'cockles and mussels alive alive o', is about Molly Malone, who sold fish on Moore St in the 19th century. You'll still find street-sellers in this area, near Henry St and the landmark department store of Clery's on O'Connell St. This is Dublin's most traditional shopping area for basics, where things tend to be a bit cheaper. Modern Dublin's prettiest, most varied and most fashionable shopping zone, though, is south of the Liffey around Grafton St.

Fancy a souvenir?

For high-quality crafts, head for Nassau St, on the south side of Trinity College, where you will also find souvenir shops, or the area west of Grafton St. Among these winding streets is the **Powerscourt Townhouse Shopping Centre** (South William St, D2), in a beautiful Georgian building, with inviting cafés and **Fresh Vegetarian Restaurant** (*see* p.63).

On Grafton St itself there are branches of British chains such as Jigsaw and Monsoon, along with the Harrods of Ireland: Brown Thomas. At the bottom end of Grafton St is **St Stephen's Green Shopping Centre**, with a branch of Mothercare, if you need baby supplies of any kind.

Avoca Handweavers

11–13 Suffolk St, D2, t (01) 677 4215

Lovely handwoven woollens and tweeds., for kids and adults, made at Avoca in Co. Wicklow (*see* p.74), plus craft-made Irish cosmetics, foods and other things, and a great wholefood café (*see* p.62).

Celtic Note

14–15 Nassau St, D2, t (01) 670 4157

Traditional Irish music.

Claddagh Records

2 Cecilia St, D2, t (01) 677 0262, www.claddaghrecords.com

Traditional Irish and folk music.

Cleo

18 Kildare St, D2, t (01) 676 1421, www.cleo-ltd.com

Original handmade woollens, including kidswear.

Down to Earth

73 South Great Georges St, D2, t (01) 671 9702

A health food and vitamin store

Eason/Hanna's Bookshop

1 Dawson St, D2, t (01) 677 1255

A conveniently located shop on the tourist trail.

Eason's

40–42 Lower O'Connell St, D1, t (01) 858 3800, www.easons.ie

The flagship store of Ireland's largest bookshop chain, with all kinds of books for adults and children, and large magazine and stationery sections.

Hughes and Hughes

St Stephen's Green Shopping Centre, D2, t (01) 478 3060, www.hughesbooks.com

An attractive bookstore with a big kids' section.

Magill's

14 Clarendon St, D2, t (01) 671 3830

A wonderful old-fashioned food store.

THINGS TO SEE AND DO

Dublin songs to sing...
In Dublin's Fair City (Molly Malone), Raglan Road, The Little Beggar Man, The Rocky Road to Dublin, The Spanish Lady, Lanigan's Ball, The Town She Used to Call Home

North of the Liffey

Dublin Writers' Museum

18 Parnell Square North, D1, **t** (01) 872 2077
Getting there 5mins walk from the north end of O'Connell St and 15mins walk from Connolly DART Station, or on buses 10, 11, 13, 16 or 19
Open Mon–Sat 10–5, Sun and bank hols 11–5; late opening June–Aug Mon–Fri to 6
Adm Adult €6.50, child €4, family €18 (combined tickets available for James Joyce Museum and Shaw Birthplace)
Volumes Bookshop, ***t*** *(01) 872 2218; restaurant* ***t*** *(01) 873 2266, café, audio-guides*

There's a special room dedicated to children's literature here, among the books and personal items of just about all the Irish literary giants of the last 300 years. Housed in an 18th-century Georgian mansion with sumptuous plasterwork and stained glass, the exhibits highlight Ireland's literary tradition, one of the most illustrious in the world thanks to its early oral storytelling and bardic beginnings. Ireland has produced 4 Nobel Prize winners and many writers of international renown, including Beckett, Joyce, Shaw, Sheridan, Swift, Wilde and Yeats.

A story to tell:
The Death of Cúchulainn

The most dramatic monument in the General Post Office is Oliver Shepherd's sculpture: *The Death of Cúchulainn*. Although it commemorates the 1916 Rising, it portrays the legend that the great Irish mythical hero Cúchulainn, after he was mortally wounded in battle, insisted that his comrades tie him to a tree with his sword in his hand so that he would look as if he was still standing. None of his enemies dared approach him, for fear it was a trick and that Cúchulainn would kill them if they went near, until a raven landed upon his shoulder, so that everyone realized that he was dead. For more on who Cúchulainn was, *see* p.30 and p.219.

GAA Museum

St Joseph's Ave (off Clonliffe Rd), Croke Park, D3, **t** (01) 819 2323, **www.gaa.ie**
Getting there 15mins walk north from Connolly Station, or on buses 3, 11, 11A, 16, 16A, 51A
Open Mon–Sat 9.30–5 (last adm 4.30), late opening July and Aug to 6 (last adm 5.30), Sun and bank hols 12 noon–5; no stadium tours on match days; closed Good Fri and Christmas week
Adm Adult €5.50 (*€9.50), child €3.50 (*€6), student €4 (*€7), family €15 (*€24); * with stadium tour

For children who love sport and want to learn about Ireland's most traditional games – hurling and Gaelic football – this is the place to come. Croke Park (*see* p.57) is headquarters to the Gaelic Athletic Association (GAA), which runs and promotes Irish games throughout Ireland. It's also Ireland's best sports stadium, although only Gaelic games are played here (as well as the odd pop concert). Gaelic games are closely bound up with Irish nationalism, and the museum's film *National Awakening* tells of Irish sport's cultural and political history. There are also interactive exhibits in which kids can try the art of hurling, and the tour's closing film (*A Day in September*) leaves you with a sense of the thrill of All-Ireland Finals Day.

General Post Office

O'Connell St, D1, **t** (01) 705 7000
Open Mon–Sat 8–8 (some services close at 7), Sun and bank hols for stamps and bureau de change only 10–6.30

The main post office (or GPO) for Dublin and the Republic, this imposing neoclassical building was built in 1818 halfway down Dublin's O'Connell St. It is most famous for being the site of the 1916 rebellion by the Irish Volunteers and Irish Citizen Army, otherwise known as the Easter Rising (*see* p.38), the repercussions of which resulted in a majority of Irish people demanding independence from Britain. Pádraic Pearse read out his 'Proclamation of the Irish Republic' from the Post Office steps, but after defending the building in fierce fighting for nearly a week he and the other rebels gave themselves up to the British troops. Subsequently, 14 of the rebels were executed by the British in Kilmainham Gaol, which turned Dublin public opinion in favour of the rebels. Bulletholes from 1916 can still be seen in the steps and columns beside the main entrance, and inside there are several monuments to the Rising and the rebels.

Hugh Lane Gallery of Modern Art

Charlemont House, Parnell Sq North, D1,
t (01) 874 1903, **www.hughlane.ie**;
Bookshop and workshop bookings, **t** (01) 874 9294
Getting there Beside Dublin Writers' Museum (*see* opposite)
Open Tues–Thurs 9.30–6, Fri and Sat 9.30–5, Sun 11–5.
Adm Free

This was the first public gallery of modern art in these islands. Hugh Lane was the nephew of Lady Gregory, who helped Yeats and other Irish artists and fuelled the Irish Literary Renaissance of the early 20th century. Lane bought and sold paintings in London and decided to set up a gallery for Irish and international artists in Dublin, in 1908. Works by Monet, Renoir, Degas and Jack B Yeats are on show, and it now houses Francis Bacon's unbelievably messy studio as well (it may not be such a great idea to take children to see this as, forever after, they may claim you are stifling their creativity by making them clean up their rooms).

On weekends children can ask at the front desk for some paper and crayons (you have to return the latter as you leave). Monthly children's art workshops, usually on Saturday afternoons, are very popular; numbers are limited so booking is essential (via the bookshop).

National Museum of Ireland at Collins Barracks

Benburb St, D7, **t** (01) 677 7444, **www.museum.ie**
Getting there Buses 90 (Aston Quay), 25, 25A, 66, 67 (Middle Abbey St); DART Tara St, with connecting bus; LUAS Red Line 'Museum' stop.

An Irish proverb –
Do not mistake a goat's beard for a fine stallion's tail.

Good to know... Dublin's postcodes

Dublin is divided into several postcode zones, which are given with all the Dublin addresses in this guide (as D1, D2 and so on). Postcodes north of the Liffey have odd numbers; those south of the river are even. In the centre, the area north of the O'Connell Bridge is Dublin 1; south of the river down to St Stephen's Green is Dublin 2.

Open Tues–Sat 10–5, Sun 2–5; closed Christmas Day, Good Fri. **Adm** Free
Shop, café, supervised parking, wheelchair access

Housed in an impressive army barracks dating from the 1700s, this section of the National Museum is Ireland's new showcase for the decorative arts and the economic, social, political and military history of Ireland. The collections are enormously varied, and arranged to chronicle the development of a vast range of craft skills and arts, including silverware, glassware and ceramics. For younger kids, seek out the Dolls' House and the sections on folk life, costumes and period furniture. Older children may more be intrigued by the exhibits on weaponry and glassware. Many rooms have interactive screens that give comprehensive information on the displays.

National Wax Museum

Smithfield Square, Smithfield, D7, **t** (01) 872 6340
Open/adm Call for details after reopening in Autumn 2006

At the time of writing this museum was relocating, possibly to Smithfield Square. It's likely to contain much the same elements as its previous incarnation, which included a faerytale dimension for very young children, with models of fantasy characters from the Frog Prince (changing from prince to frog constantly) to more modern storybook and cinema creations; a video of a Disney film; horror characters, including a 'victim' on a stretcher in a dungeon; and a historical section with wax models of Ireland's past revolutionaries and presidents, Pope John Paul II with the Popemobile he used when he visited Ireland, various sports and entertainment personalities and Irish intellectual, political and literary figures, all in appropriately decorated rooms. The historical exhibits had recorded explanations, and sometimes even the voices, of the people they depicted. After that, models of Ireland's pop stars and their noisy outpourings sent you out into modern Dublin again.

A story to tell: The Black Pool

On the east coast of Leinster, there was a very rough river that flowed down to the sea. It was called Ruirtheach ('the impetuous one') because of its flash floods. Around the 6th century, someone built a raft over it, of interwoven wood, which was called an *áth cliath* (hurdle). At low tide, people could walk over it, and some set up their mud huts nearby, in a place they called Átha Cliath ('the ford or shallow place of hurdles'). Later this became Baile Átha Cliath ('the town of the ford'), which is the name Dublin is known by in Irish.

A pool of water lay by this ford. Nearby lived a sorceress named Dubh ('black'), with her chieftain husband Enna, who had another wife he preferred. Dubh grew so jealous of her that she whipped up some magic and whisked her rival into the Otherworld. King Enna found out and was so angry that he threw Dubh into that pool of water – where she stayed. Thereafter, it was called Dubhlinn (or Dubh's Pool, i.e., 'black pool'), which is where Dublin's other name comes from.

Another sad tale about this place comes from a medieval poem. A great warrior's wife died while having a baby beside the Ruirtheach. Her name was Liphe, which means life, so gossips began to call the river 'Liffey'. People felt unhappy about these terrible things, so they started to pray there, and built a monastery nearby. Some say, too, that the Liffey was named after Livia, the wife of the Roman emperor Augustus...but then, the Romans are said never to have lived in Ireland.

St Michan's Church

Church St, D7, **t** (01) 872 4154

Getting there By the Four Courts and the Inns Quay, on the west side of central Dublin; bus 79 from Aston Quay

Open Mar–Oct Mon–Fri 10–12.30, 2–4.30, Sat 10–12.45; Nov–Mar Mon–Fri 12.30–3.30, Sat 10–12.45; closed Christmas, bank hols and some of Holy Week

Adm By guided tour: adult €3.50, child €2.50

The current St Michan's was built in 1685–86 on the site of a much older church constructed by Christian Vikings in the 11th century. It was the only church north of the Liffey for some 500 years. The church is most famous, though, for the mummified bodies stored in its vaults. St Michan's has a peculiar ability to preserve bodies, some think due to the magnesian limestone in its walls or to its position, closer to the bed of the Liffey than any other Dublin church. Bodies tend to harden, while hair and skin remain rather than deteriorate.

Here you can find the death mask of Wolfe Tone and the corpses of many of the leaders of Ireland's 1798 rebellion. Some children, especially little ones, might find the dead bodies disturbing. You might prefer to take them into the church to look at the organ and the exquisite carvings of musical instruments above the choir, while their older siblings get their gruesome thrills.

South of the Liffey

Chester Beatty Library

Clock Tower Building, Dublin Castle, Dame St, D2, **t** (01) 407 0750, **www**.cbl.ie

Getting there In Dublin Castle gardens; *see* right

Open May–Sept Mon–Fri 10–5, Sat 11–5, Sun 1–5, Oct–Apr Tues–Fri 10–5; closed banks hols, Good Fri, 24–26 Dec and 1 Jan

Adm Free

Free guided tours Wed 1pm and Sun 3 and 4pm or by request, gift/bookshop, café and restaurant, baby-changing facilities, disabled access, roof garden

This collection of approximately 22,000 rare books, miniature paintings, artistic works and objects from Early Christian, Islamic and East Asian cultures was bequeathed to Ireland by the late Sir Alfred Chester Beatty on his death in 1968. Highlights include Chinese dragon robes, Japanese wood block prints and Buddhist paintings.

Christ Church Cathedral

Christchurch Place, D8, **t** (01) 677 8099, **www**.cccdub.ie

Getting there Buses 49, 50, 51B, 54A, 56A, 65, 77, 77A, 78A, 123

Open Mon–Fri 9.45–5, Sat and Sun 10–5

Adm Adult €5, child €2.50

Can you spot...

The 8ft-tall Crusader in St Michan's Church crypt? It is said to be good luck to touch his leathery hand upon leaving.

This is Dublin's oldest building and Ireland's oldest cathedral. Built on the site of a wooden Viking church (founded in 1030), the current Norman design dates from 1172, when Christ Church was commissioned by Strongbow, the Anglo-Norman conqueror of Dublin, and Archbishop Laurence O'Toole. There are family monuments and treasures in the fascinating crypt, where the 19th Earl of Kildare is buried. Like Dublin's other historic cathedral nearby, St Patrick's (*see* below), it is Church of Ireland (Anglican).

Dublin Castle

Dame St, D2, **t** (01) 677 7129
Getting there 5mins walk from Trinity College along Dame St; buses 49 (Eden Quay), 56A, 77, 77A, 123 (O'Connell St), stopping at Palace St Gate
Open Mon–Fri 10–4.45, Sat, Sun and bank hols 2–4.45; closed bank-hol Mon, Good Fri, 24–26 Dec and 1 Jan
Adm Adult €4.50, under-12s €2
Restaurant, heritage centre, craft shop

This is the heart of historic Dublin, at the junction of the River Liffey and its tributary the Poddle. A ring fort probably stood here first, and later a Viking fortress, the remains of which can be seen in the undercroft. The oldest surviving part of the medieval castle, though, is the 13th-century Record Tower; most of the current castle was rebuilt in the 18th century, after several disastrous fires. Visitors tour the elegant Georgian interiors, where excellent classical music concerts are also held (for information contact tourist office or the Music Network, **t** (01) 671 9429, **www**.musicnetwork.ie).

Dublin Civic Museum

58 South William St, D2, **t** (01) 679 4260
Getting there Buses 10, 11, 13 and others
Open Tues–Sat 10–6, Sun 11–2. **Adm** Free

A small collection of artefacts mainly from the 18th and 19th centuries in a fine building redolent of Georgian Dublin. Other material covers the city's history from the Vikings to the present, notably the head of a statue of Nelson blown off his column on O'Connell St by an IRA bomb in 1966.

Dublinia

Synod Hall, St Michael's Hill, Christchurch, D8, **t** (01) 679 4611, **www.dublinia.ie**
Getting there Buses 50 (Eden Quay), 78A (Aston Quay)
Open Apr–Sept daily 10–5, Oct–Mar Mon–Sat 11–4, Sun and bank hols 10–4.30, closed 24–26 Dec

> ***Tell me an Irish riddle...***
> ***Question – What's 'long and lanky, deaf and dumb, has no legs and still can run'?***
> ***Answer – A river.***

Adm Adult €6, child €3.50, family (2+3) €16
Guided (pre-book)/headset tours available, shop, tea room (June–Aug), disabled access

In the Middle Ages, the name given to Dublin by Latin-speakers and scholars was Dublinia. Today this is also the name of a notably child-friendly, interactive museum. It occupies the old Synod Hall of Christ Church Cathedral, and overlooks Wood Quay, where modern government buildings stand beside the Liffey. The story of how they came to be there is one topic of the exhibition: historians and archaeologists fought to keep Wood Quay un-developed so they could study it further, as it may be the most important Viking settlement in Europe. Magnificent artefacts found there are on display in the museum, which focuses on the years 1170–1540. At that time, Anglo-Normans lived within the city walls; the native Irish built their own cathedral (St Patrick's) outside.

The first thing you notice when you walk into Dublinia is the noise of some strange-tongued city, while your eyes make out the timeline on the wall. Eventually you discover that the languages you're hearing were those spoken in Dublinia around 1170; the Irish, English and Vikings had been intermarrying for years and developed a new language they spoke with each other. This became mixed with a form of French spoken by the most recent invaders, the Anglo-Normans led by Richard de Clare, better known as Strongbow. Meanwhile, Latin was spoken by the clergy, and Gaelic by the Irish people allowed to trade or work in the city.

As your eyes get used to the darkness, you'll see you're in a re-creation of a fair in 13th-century Dublin. People bought hot swan pies from vendors, or had their blood let using leeches, the most popular way of curing the sick at the time. You can try on clothes made by a tailor, and a knight's chain-mail and helmet. Look for a cure for what ails you at the apothecary's shop, where medicines were mixed from herbs, spices and insects. Copy a will, grant or pardon at the scribe's booth, and play with counters at the 'bank' and learn what 'debtors' sticks' were.

Later rooms tell you how the Black Death plague swept from England to Ireland, and how medieval dockyards worked. Look for the figure of Silken Thomas Fitzgerald, who led a rebellion against Henry VIII in 1534 and was hanged together with his 5 uncles. A scale model shows how Dublin looked in the 1500s: in the middle of the old town walls stands Christ Church Cathedral, and beside the southeastern wall is Dublin Castle. Particularly noticeable is how wide the Liffey was in comparison to today, and how much open space stretched between the city walls and the pasture land then held in common for the townspeople's animals (an area still known as St Stephen's Green).

At the end of the exhibit, you can walk to the top of St Michael's Tower to view modern Dublin and the tower's lovely stained glass, and cross a bridge into Christ Church Cathedral itself.

Marsh's Library

St Patrick's Close, D8, **t** (01) 454 3511, **www**.marshlibrary.ie
Getting there Buses 49, 50, 54A, 77, 77A, 150
Open Mon and Weds–Fri 10–1 and 2–5, Sat 10.30–1
Adm Adult €2.50, child free

If you want to inspire a love of learning in your children, bring them to Ireland's oldest public library, founded in 1701 and virtually unchanged. Set in its lovely Queen Anne house in a quiet lane beside St Patrick's Cathedral, it's almost like a time capsule: dark oak bookcases and elegant wired alcoves or 'cages' house rare leatherbound books kept exactly the same as they were 300 years ago.

National Gallery of Ireland

Merrion Sq West, D2, **t** (01) 661 5133, **www**.ngi.ie
Getting there Buses 5, 7, 7A (Burgh Quay), 8, 10 (O' Connell St), 44, 48A (Hawkins St) or Museumlink (172); DART to Pearse Station
Open Mon–Weds, Fri and Sat 9.30–5.30, Thurs 9.30–8.30, Sun 12–5.30. **Adm** Free, exc special exhibitions
Guided tours, restaurants, shop, disabled access

This spacious art museum is easy to visit with toddlers and pushchairs. Children who know the west of Ireland will like the mystical quality of the modern landscape paintings as much as the more famous artworks. Family activities offered by the Education Department (**t** (01) 661 5133) take the form of Sunday talks (12.30), Little Masters Drawing Classes in July, Children's Hours in mid-term breaks, and an annual Christmas Art Holiday.

National Museum of Ireland

Kildare St, D2, **t** (01) 677 7444, **www**.museum.ie
Getting there Buses 7, 7A, 8 (Burgh Quay), 10, 11, 13 (O'Connell St); DART to Pearse Station; beside National Library
Open Tues–Sat 10–5, Sun 2–5, closed Christmas Day and Good Fri. **Adm** Free
Guided tours, restaurant, shop, lecture theatre

A impressive 1890 building with exhibitions, such as Neolithic, Egyptian, Viking and Medieval, covering a timespan from 7000 BC to the 20th century. The world's finest collection of Celtic art and ornaments features the jewelled Ardagh Chalice, Tara Brooch, Derrynaflan Hoard and Europe's most important collection of prehistoric gold artefacts.

A story to tell: The Vikings are coming

The Viking invaders who sailed from Norway and Denmark to Dublin were mostly pirates and thieves. They weren't nice people. If you happened to own a good house, with a well-thatched roof, or live in a monastery with any kind of gold or money stored away, these red-haired fellows in their hats with the horns would break down your door and one way or another bump you off as soon as they got their hands on your gold. Around the year 800, some Vikings discovered the rich monastery at Dubhlinn and plundered it. They settled nearby for a few years, but then the Irish High Kings got together and drove them away. By the 900s, they were back again, destroying the best of the Uí Néill warriors. With their eye on settling down this time, the Norsemen gave up their marauding and built a town to the east of Átha Cliath, which they called Dyflinn. They began to be more sociable, marrying the locals, and some even became Christians. Putting their energies to good use, they built the town and the first bridge over the River Liffey (Dubhghall's Bridge).

By the 11th century, Dyflinn was an organized place, with wooden houses made of thatch, mud and dung (which doesn't stink when it dries, by the way), and with streets, paths and plots, all behind an earth and timber wall. Dyflinn grew together with Átha Cliath. They say that the area now called Wood Quay, near Christ Church Cathedral, covers the oldest part of Dublin.

Did you know... What a torc was?
It was a metal plate worn at the neck by the ancient Celts, usually made of gold. There are wonderful gold torcs on show in the National Museum on Kildare St.

National Museum of Natural History

Merrion St, D2, **t** (01) 677 7444
Getting there Buses 7, 7A, 8 (Burgh Quay); DART to Pearse Station
Open Tues–Sat 10–5, Sun 2–5; closed Christmas Day and Good Fri. **Adm** Free

This wonderful, unchanged Victorian museum is part of the National Museum of Ireland. Called Dublin's 'Dead Zoo' because it is full of stuffed animals and has a musty old atmosphere, it is famous for its Victorian cabinets and decorated panels depicting mythological characters. Its ground floor contains Irish insects, strange-looking earth and sea creatures in jars, and mammals, including skeletons of the extinct giant deer known as the Irish elk and the skeleton of a basking shark. In the upper-floor galleries are remains of creatures from around the world, the centrepiece being the skeleton of a 60ft (18m) whale suspended from the roof. Buffalo and deer trophies are also on show, as are the pygmy hippopotamus and giant panda, and the Blaschka Collection of reproductions of marine life.

Number Twenty Nine: Georgian Townhouse

29 Lower Fitzwilliam St, D2, **t** (01) 702 6165
Getting there Buses (from city centre) 7, 8, 10 or 45; by train, DART to Pearse Station
Open Tues–Sat 10–5, Sun 2–5; closed 2wks before Christmas; groups must book ahead
Adm Adult €4.50, students €2, under-16s free
Tea room, gift shop

This 18th-century house just off Merrion Square, in the heart of Georgian Dublin, belonged to a merchant and his wife. An explanatory video about middle-class Dublin life from 1790 to 1820 greets you, giving the historical background to goings-on inside the house, where you'll see life-sized mannequins of its original inhabitants. Then a tour guide leads you through the rooms on its 5 floors, tailoring his talk to suit visitors' ages.

The tour first takes you to the basement, with the kitchen. Baking was done here in the morning, meat being cooked last because the coal-fuelled oven would grow warmer as the day progressed. Ironing was done in the evenings, often by candlelight, by the head servant in her own bedroom, with irons heated in fires. Household servants were summoned from here by a set of bells. Each bell denoted a different room in the house, which the servants had to remember.

Food from the basement had to be carried to the dining room on the floor above for the family's meals. The times for these and going to bed varied according to the season, since people lived by candlelight, so that the evening meal might be served as early as 2.30pm during the winter.

Visitors were received on the first floor in the front drawing room. Behind it is the drawing room, where friends and family would read and play card games, or play music on clavichords, lyres and other instruments of the era.

On the second floor, beside the mistress of the house's bedroom, is her boudoir or private sitting room. This was where she would entertain close female friends, who might sew together as well as gossip. Alongside it is her toilet and bathroom, with its very advanced system of piped hot water.

The family's children and their governess occupied the whole of the third floor of the house. Here, the children slept together in one room, where they could play with its most impressive dolls' house, and received their lessons from the governess, whose bedroom was just next to them. She would create elaborate embroidery and samplers in order to prove her fitness as a wife to any suitable gentlemen who might appear. Educated women without dowries generally became governesses; if they grew old without marrying, their lives often ended in poverty, in the harsh conditions of the public workhouse.

Back downstairs, visitors can also enjoy some fine barm brack (*see* p.103) in the coffee shop.

Did you know...?
The Dublin-born writer Bram Stoker, who created Dracula in 1897, was inspired by his own insomnia to invent the vampire's fear of daylight.

Oscar Wilde House

1 Merrion Sq, **t** (01) 662 0281
Getting there Buses (from city centre) 6, 7, 8, 10 or 45; DART to Pearse Station
Open Mon, Weds and Thurs for tours (10.15, 11.15am)
Adm €2.50

The house where Oscar Wilde lived from 1855 to 1876, with ground and first floors restored by its owners, the American College Dublin.

St Patrick's Cathedral

St Patrick's Close, D8, **t** (01) 475 4817, **www.stpatrickscathedral.ie**
Getting there Buses 49, 50, 54A, 77, 77A, 150
Open Mar–Oct Mon–Fri 9–6, Sun 9–6; Nov–Feb Mon–Fri 9–5, Sun 9–3; closed 24–26 Dec and 1 Jan
Adm Donations requested: adult €4, child €2, family €9 (2+2)

Don't miss this famous cathedral – which is Church of Ireland (Anglican), like Christ Church – known for its association with writer and satirist Jonathan Swift, who was Dean here, and with Handel's *Messiah*, which was first performed here in 1742. The cathedral was begun in 1190, but it is said that St Patrick himself preached on this spot centuries earlier. An exhibition illustrates the role of St Patrick and the cathedral in Dublin's history.

Shaw Birthplace

33 Synge St, D8, **t** (01) 475 0854
Getting there 10mins walk south of St Stephen's Green; buses 16, 16A, 19, 19A, 122; DART to Grand Canal Walk, then 15min walk
Open May–Oct Mon–Tues and Thurs–Sat 10–1, 2–5, Sun and bank hols 2–5; Nov–Apr by appointment (call **t** (01) 872 2077)
Adm Adult €6.50, child €4, family €18

The fount of George Bernard Shaw's genius lies hidden somewhere in this neat terraced house, where he was born on 26 July 1856, feet first – a portent of his tendency to go against the ordinary way of things. A peaceful yet slightly oppressive atmosphere pervades this simple Victorian house. Its master bedroom, the drawing room where Shaw's mother held musical evenings, G.B.'s own box room and little walled garden outdoors are all restored to look as they did in the 19th century. It feels almost as if the Shaws have only just left.

After working in an estate office in Dublin, at age 20 Shaw followed his pianist mother to London. She had left her tippling husband four years earlier to follow her music teacher there, a man who had lived in the Shaw family home for years. Thereafter, Shaw earned around 50 pence a year for nine years, in which he wrote five unsuccessful novels. Then a friend helped him get a job as a book reviewer and music critic, while he wrote six unsuccessful plays. Then in 1896, his seventh play, *The Devil's Disciple*, struck gold in America. From 1898 on, he produced nearly a play per year. His plays' political and social themes did not always make him popular (he was an avowed socialist and anti-war vegetarian), but he lived amid great fame until his death in 1950.

Did you know...?
Which building houses the Republic of Ireland's Parliament?
... Leinster House, beside the National Museum of Ireland on Kildare St.

Trinity College Library

College St, D2, **t** (01) 608 2320, **www.tod.ie/library**
Getting there 2mins walk from O'Connell Bridge
Open Mon–Sat 9.30–5; Sun May–Sept 9.30–4.30 and Oct–May 12 noon–4.30
Adm Adult €7.50, child free, students and over-65s €6.50, family €15; Dublin Experience adult €4.20, under-18s, students and over-65s €3.50

The grand Georgian quadrangles of Dublin's esteemed seat of learning contain one of Ireland's greatest treasures, the astonishing illuminated manuscript the *Book of Kells*, made by monks around 800 AD. Almost as impressive is the *Book of Durrow*, from about 670. An interesting background exhibit helps bring the manuscripts alive, and there's also the Dublin Experience (late May–early Sept, 10–5), an optional audio-visual exhibit on the city's past. The College Library itself is magnificent, with a superb barrel-roofed Long Hall.

Other Ideas

ENFO, Environmental Info

17 St Andrew St, D2, **t** (01) 888 3910, **www.enfo.ie**
Getting there Near Dublin Tourism on Suffolk St

This centre has a children's corner for ecology information, plus environmental videos, an exhibition and a library.

Theatre and music

Abbey Theatre

Lower Abbey St, D1, **t** (01) 878 7222, **www**.abbeytheatre.ie
Getting there 2mins walk from O'Connell St
Box office open Mon–Sat 10.30–7

This theatre, imagined into being by poet WB Yeats and Lady Gregory, has occasional performances for children. Plans are afoot to move it to a new location.

The Ark

11A Eustace St, D2, **t** (01) 670 7788, **www**.ark.ie
Getting there Off Dame St, west of Trinity College
Open Mon–Sat, hrs vary

A cultural centre for ages 4–14, with a theatre, gallery and workshops. Call to find out about arts workshops, short sessions, one-off events, music and theatre festivals, and the regular drawing, printmaking and performance classes.

Gaiety Theatre

South King St, D2, **t** (01) 677 1717
Getting there Off St Stephen's Green

Popular traditional pantomimes at Christmas.

Lambert Puppet Theatre

5 Clifton Lane, Monkstown, **t** (01) 280 0964, **www**.lambertpuppettheatre.com
Getting there Buses 7, 7A, 8 or DART to Salthill.

A long-running theatre staging more than 30 productions a year, for both the very young and older children, this also has a puppet museum and puppetry workshops.

National Concert Hall

Earlsfort Terrace, nr St Stephen's Green, D2, **t** (01) 417 0000, **www**.nch.ie
Getting there Buses 6, 7, 8, 10 or 45
Box office open Mon–Sat 10–7

Occasional concerts and plays for children.

Storytellers Theatre Company

3rd Fl, Aston Quay, D2, **t** (01) 671 1161
Getting there On the River Liffey
Box office open daily, with answerphone out of hrs

An ensemble theatre with a storytellers' service.

Whelan's

25 Wexford St, D2, **t** (01) 478 0766
Getting there West of St Stephen's Green
Box office open daily 11–8

A live music venue hosting traditional, folk and pop for older teenagers and adults.

Parks and gardens

Iveagh Gardens

Clonmel St, D2, **t** (01) 475 7816. **Getting there** Buses 6, 7, 8, 10 or 45. **Open** Mon–Sat 8–6, Sun and bank hols 10–6; closes at dusk in winter. **Adm** Free

A hidden garden with a grotto, fountains, maze, archery grounds and woodlands in one of the busiest parts of south Dublin.

Merrion Square

D2. **Getting there** Buses (from city centre) 6, 7, 8, 10 or 45; by train, DART to Pearse Station

One of the best Georgian squares in Dublin, with gardens, space to picnic, a playground and a modern statue of Oscar Wilde across the street from the house where he grew up (*see* opposite).

St Patrick's Park

Patrick's St, D8
Getting there Beside St Patrick's Cathedral

St Patrick is said to have baptized the first Irish Christians here with water from the River Poddle, which now flows underground beneath the park.

St Stephen's Green

D2, **t** (01) 475 7816. **Getting there** Bottom of Grafton St, D2. **Open** Mon–Sat 7.30–dusk, Sun and bank hols 9.30–dusk. **Adm** Free

A lovely 19th-century park with a lake, fountains, playground, scented garden for the blind and statues of historical and literary figures. Now full of peaceful ducks, it's where people were once hanged.

Sports

Croke Park

Croke Park, D3, **t** (01) 836 3222, **www**.gaa.ie.
Getting there 15mins walk north from Connolly Station, or buses 3, 11, 11A, 16, 16A, 51A

The lavish venue for Gaelic games – hurling (mainly in summer) and Gaelic football (winter). You can also visit the GAA Museum (*see* p.50).

Lansdowne Road Stadium

Lansdowne Rd, D4, **t** (01) 668 4601

The main Rugby stadium, hosting the annual Six Nations tournament, plus international soccer games.

An Irish proverb –
There is no need like the lack of a friend...

AROUND AND ABOUT

Animal magic

Dublin Zoo

Phoenix Park, **t** (01) 474 8900/677 1425 or freephone **t** 1800 924 848, **www.dublinzoo.ie**
Getting there 2 miles (3km) from central Dublin in Phoenix Park. By bus: 10, 10A (from O'Connell St), 25, 25A, 26 (from Middle Abbey St), 66, 66A, 66B, 67, 67A, 68, 69; DART feeder bus 90 from Connolly and Tara St stations; walk from Heuston Station and LUAS stops
Open Mar–Sept Mon–Sat 9.30–6, Sun 10.30–6; Oct–Feb Mon–Sat 9.30–dusk, Sun 10.30–dusk; last entry 1hr before closing
Adm Adult €13, under-16s €8.50, under-3s free, family (2+2) €36, (2+3) €41, (2+4) €45
Gift shops, restaurant and snack kiosks, children's play areas, train, discovery centre, picnic area

You can easily spend a day at this award-winning zoo, so it's a good idea to bring a picnic (on-site facilities sell mainly fast food). The zoo has a policy of protecting endangered species and educating the public about them, such as its lemurs from Madagascar. At certain times, mainly in summer, zookeepers answer questions while feeding the animals (call **t** 01 474 8900 for times).

Large enclosed grassy spaces and water holes serve as homes for once-wild animals from all over the world. The World of Cats shows off big cats such as jaguars, tigers, lions and snow leopards. On an island isolated from visitors, you'll see Colobus and Celebes macaque monkeys, and the solitary 'old man of the forest', the orangutan, with his long beard and feet that look like hands. Baby monkey breeds are housed in warm sheds near wooden slides, climbing frames and a mirror, where children can see themselves making monkey faces and mimicking their acrobatics.

Pink flamingos congregate not far from the Fringes of the Arctic enclosure, where polar bears, arctic foxes, snowy owls and grey wolves live (the last wild wolves were seen in Ireland in the 18th century) . Nearby are water pools where seals and Humboldt penguins lounge about, as if on holiday.

Buggies must take the long path to the African Plains, where larger animals live in more spacious domains; those without can take the shorter stairway. A replica African village, this has children's play areas, toilets, a first aid and lost children hut, and the restaurant. Unless you take the African Plains Train, you may walk a while before you see the zebras, oryx antelopes, giraffes, elephants, rhinos and hippos. Lesser-known breeds include the Red River hog, Bongo, the miniature Reeve's Muntjac deer and the mongoose-like meerkats.

Near the zoo's exit are the hothouse homes of reptiles, including a few snakes (otherwise banished from Ireland by St Patrick; *see* p.178). In the specially heated buildings lurk Bell's hinged tortoises, mud turtles, Nile crocodiles and iguanas.

Did you know...?
The word 'reptile' comes from a Latin word meaning 'to crawl'. Reptiles never get beyond the crawling stage, and their body temperature goes up and down according to that of their surroundings, so they will literally freeze to death in very cold weather. They can't survive outdoors in Ireland, but you can see some at Dublin Zoo.

Bricks and mortar

Drimnagh Castle

Long Mile Rd, Drimnagh, D12, **t** (01) 450 2530
Getting there 3 miles (5km) southwest of central Dublin; buses 22, 22A, 50, 56A, 77, 77A
Open Apr–Sept Weds, Sat and Sun 12–5; Oct–Mar Weds 12 noon–5, Sun 2–5; last tour 4; other times by arrangement. **Adm** Adult €4, child €2

Inhabited until 1954, this is the only castle in Ireland that's still surrounded by a flooded moat. The tour includes its Great Hall, Norman keep with battlements, coachhouse, dairy and folly tower. Around it there's a pretty 17th-century garden.

Rathfarnham Castle

Rathfarnham bypass, near Rathfarnham Village, D14, **t** (01) 493 9462
Getting there 4 miles (6km) south of central Dublin; buses 16, 16A (city centre), 17 (Blackrock–Rialto), 75 (Dun Laoghaire–Tallaght)

Open May–Oct daily 9.30–5.30; call **t** (01) 647 2466 for Nov–Easter opening hours
Adm Adult €2, child €1, family €5.50
Car/coach park, restaurant/tea room (with disabled access)

Constructed around 1583 by Yorkshireman Adam Loftus, this semi-fortified castle has 18th-century interiors designed by Sir William Chambers and James Athenian Stuart. Layers of its earlier existence are now being uncovered by research at this ongoing conservation site, which will be of interest to budding archaeologists and conservationists.

Look at this!

Irish Jewish Museum

3–4 Walworth Rd (off Victoria St), South Circular Rd, D8, **t** (01) 490 1857/453 1797
Getting there 15mins walk south of St Stephen's Green; buses 16, 16A, 19, 19A, 22, 22A
Open May–Sept Tues, Thurs and Sun 11–3.30, Oct–Apr Sun 10.30–2.30, other times by appointment
Adm Free; donations welcome

This museum is in the restored Walworth Rd Synagogue (2 adjoining terraced houses) in the once-Jewish area of Portobello. Its exhibits include memorabilia from Ireland's Jewish communities, in Belfast, Cork, Derry, Dublin, Limerick and Waterford, over the last 150 years. The synagogue fell into disuse in the mid-1970s, when the area's Jewish population declined, and was made into a museum in 1984. Old photographs and paintings dominate the entrance area; on the ground floor there is a wide-ranging background display on the social and business life of Jews in Ireland. Upstairs are the rooms of the original synagogue. Jews have lived in Ireland since the 11th century, but never in great numbers. Their population peaked in the 1940s at around 5,500, but today there are only about 1,400 in the Republic and 400 in Northern Ireland.

James Joyce Museum

Martello Tower, Sandycove, **t** (01) 280 9265
Getting there 8 miles (13km) south of central Dublin along the coast; DART to Sandycove
Open Mar–Oct Mon–Sat 10–1 and 2–5, Sun and bank hols 2–6, Nov–Feb by appointment

Tell me an Irish riddle...
Question – Why is a dog like a tree?
Answer – They both have a bark.

Adm Adult €6.50, child €4, family €18 (combined tickets with Dublin Writers' Museum and Shaw's Birthplace available)
Guided tours by arrangement, parking

This is one of a series of 'Martello Towers' – battlemented brick watchtowers – that were built around Dublin in 1804 to guard against a possible invasion by Napoleon. The one in Sandycove is most famous, though, because James Joyce, the writer most closely associated with his native Dublin, lived here briefly in 1904 and used it for the opening scene of his classic *Ulysses*, one of the most influential novels of the 20th century. Since 1962 the tower has been open as a museum devoted to the life and works of Joyce. The tower itself, and the views over the sea beside it, will enchant children, while their parents read the literary displays.

Kilmainham Gaol

Inchicore Rd, D8, **t** (01) 453 5984
Getting there 2 miles (3.5km) southwest of central Dublin; buses 51B, 51C, 78A, 79 (Aston Quay) to Inchicore Rd
Open Apr–Sept daily 9.30–5 (last adm 4.45), Oct–Mar Mon–Sat 9.30–4, Sun 10–5; last tour 1hr before closing
Adm Adult €5, child €2, family €11
Guided tours only; toilets (also for disabled), café, access with special needs by prior arrangement

Some of Irish history's most famous events occurred in this, Europe's largest currently unoccupied jail, between 1795 and 1920. Charles Stewart Parnell, the 19th-century nationalist leader, was imprisoned here in 1881 for his part in the so-called Land War. Kilmainham's best-known prisoners, though, were the leaders of the 1916 Easter Rising, including a woman, Constance de Markievicz (*see* p.42). Pearse, Connolly and others were all executed here; Eamon de Valera (*see* p.42) only escaped the firing squad because he was a US citizen. The guided tours and displays don't pull any punches in describing 19th-century prisons and punishment, and younger children may find them all a bit gruesome.

Museum of Childhood

20 Palmerston Park, Rathmines, D6, **t** (01) 497 8696
Getting there Located 2 miles (3km) south of central Dublin; bus 13
Open Sun 2–5.30
Adm Adult €1, under-12s €0.75

A charming, privately owned collection of nursery memorabilia from all over the world. Most children will find the original Hornby train sets on show here interesting, as well as the toy soldiers, prams and dolls' houses of centuries ago, including the wonderful travelling dolls' house of Sissi, Empress of Austria. The oldest doll in Ireland is also here, as well as a strange three-faced doll.

National Print Museum

Garrison Chapel, Beggars Bush Barracks, Haddington Rd, D4, **t** (01) 660 3770
Getting there Bus 5, 7, 7A, 8, 45; DART to Lansdowne Rd
Open Mon–Fri 9–5, Sat, Sun and bank hols 2–5
Adm Adult €3.50, under-12s €2, family €7
Audio-visual show, café

A collection of machines and other artefacts (many in full working order) from every part of Ireland's printing industry, housed in a building that was created in the 1860s as a soldier's chapel. It was the first military barracks to be handed over by the British to the new Irish State in February 1922, and also the place where Irish revolutionary Erskine Childers was executed in 1922 during Ireland's Civil War. The exhibits on every aspect of printing have plenty of interest: children who are just learning to read may be intrigued to find out how books were first printed, while older children find the printing presses and processes amazingly archaic. An exhibit shows how the first printed book, the *Gutenberg Bible*, was produced in 1455, and how the invention of hot metal casting in the 19th century transformed the printing industry. Impressive ornate printing presses stand beside a Wharfedale press on which the 1916 Proclamation declaring Ireland's independence was printed. Next on show is a pen-ruling machine, used to make lines in the writing books that children used at school. Old newspaper headlines of world events are framed on the upstairs gallery wall, and children can be pleasantly surprised to discover that they enjoy the educational audio-visual show.

Pearse Museum

St Enda's Park, Grange Rd, Rathfarnham, D16, **t** (01) 493 4208
Getting there 2 miles (3km) south of central Dublin; bus 16 (from centre). Turn off Grange Rd into car park at bus terminus
Open daily Nov–Jan 10–1 and 2–4, Feb–Apr, Sept and Oct 10–1 and 2–5, May–Aug 10–1 and 2–5.30.
Adm Free
*Restaurant (**t** (01) 493 3053; open May–Sept daily, Feb–Apr and Oct Sat and Sun), guided tours on request, disabled access to ground floor and nature study room, nature trail, parking, concerts*

Set in one of Dublin's most charming and atmospheric parks, in the pleasant suburb of Rathfarnham, with riverside walks, a waterfall and walled garden, the Pearse Museum is a nature study centre that was once a school run by Pádraic Pearse, the Irish writer executed for his role as leader of the Easter Rising of 1916. His executioner said, 'There must be something terribly wrong in the world for a man of his calibre to be executed.' A strong proponent of the Irish language, Pearse briefly taught it to James Joyce before starting this school, which was bilingual in Irish and English and run on experimental, progressive principles. His mother and sister kept the school open until 1935. There's an audio-visual exhibit on Pearse and his life, but for many visitors the most attractive feature is the combination of the school building and its lovely, peaceful setting.

Waterways Visitor Centre

Grand Canal Quay, Ringsend, D4 (entrance off Ringsend end of Pearse St), **t** (01) 677 7510, **www.waterwaysireland.org**
Getting there Bus 3; by train, DART to Pearse Station
Open June–Sept daily 9.30–5.30, Oct–May Weds–Sun 12.30–5
Adm Adult €2.50, child €1.20, family €6.35

Called 'the box in the docks' by locals, this striking modern building houses an engaging exhibition about all the inland waterways (both canals and navigable rivers) of Dublin and Ireland. From inside the airy glass-walled building you get a real impression of being in 'a world of water'.

Good to know... The Organic Centre
For kids who like gardening, the Organic Centre, **t** (01) 985 4338, holds organic growing courses at Airfield Trust and Gardens, Upper Kilmacud Rd, D14.

Tell me an Irish riddle...
Question – 'The more you take out of it, the bigger it gets.' What is it?
Answer – A hole.

Nature lovers

Marlay Park and Demesne

Grange Rd, Rathfarnham, D14, **t** (01) 493 7372 and **t** (01) 204 7261
Getting there 2–3 miles (3–5km) south of central Dublin; bus 16 (from centre), turn off Grange Rd into car park at bus terminus. By car, an alternative route is to turn off the Southern Cross motorway at Kingston interchange
Open House: tours by arrangement; Gardens: Mon–Fri 10–5, Sat and Sun 11–6; closed Mon Oct–Mar
Adm Adult €3, child €2, family €6.50
Sports pitches, model railway, nature trails, lakeside walks, craft yard with retail units, coffee shop

About 200 acres of parkland, a 4.5-acre walled garden and an ornamental garden surround Marlay House, built in 1794 for the Governor of the Bank of Ireland, David La Touche. There's a miniature train ride here for children on Saturday afternoons, along with a playground, golf course, woodland walks and 2 lakes. Teenagers know it as a music venue for acts such as David Gray, Sting, Van Morrison, Westlife and Samantha Mumba.

National Botanic Gardens

Finglas Rd, Glasnevin, D9, **t** (01) 804 0300
Getting there 1 mile (1.6km) north of central Dublin, along Dorset St; buses 13, 19, 134
Open Summer Mon–Sat 9–6, Sun 10–6; winter daily 10–4.30; closed Christmas Day
Adm Free; guided tour €2; charge for parking
Toilets, gift shop, disabled access except Palm House, dogs on lead, parking outside gates on road

Ireland's premier botanical garden was established in 1795 on the 27-acre estate of minor poet Thomas Tickell, and acquired its magnificent Victorian glasshouses in the 1840s. The gardens contain more than 20,000 plant species, amid trees, shrubs and perennials. Botanically planned plots contain roses, poisonous plants, native plants, herbs and vegetables, along with a large rockery, bog garden, wild garden and curving herbaceous borders that bloom beautifully in summer. Must-see exhibits include the tropical treehouse, with orchids and flowering plants, and the gigantic Amazon water lily introduced in 1854 (the Victoria or Aquatic House was specially built to protect it). The cactus plant and fern glasshouses and the striking early Victorian chain tent draped with wisteria are equally special. Don't forget to look for the 'Last Rose of Summer' – an 'Old Blush' China rose raised from a cutting taken from a rose bush at Jenkinstown House in County Kilkenny, which inspired the poet Thomas Moore to write a famous sentimental Irish ballad with the same name.

Phoenix Park and Visitor Centre

Phoenix Park, D8, **t** (01) 677 0095
Getting there 2 1/2 miles (4km) from centre of Dublin; 20mins walk from the gate at Ashtown Cross or 30mins walk from the gate at North Circular Rd. Buses from central Dublin include 37 (Middle Abbey St to Ashtown Gate) and 10 (from O'Connell St)
Open Park: at all times;
Visitor Centre: Apr–Sept daily 10–6, Oct daily 10–5 Nov, Dec and Jan–mid-Mar Sat and Sun 10–5, mid–end-Mar daily 10–5.30
Adm Park free; Visitor Centre: adult €2.75, child €1.25, family €7
Toilets (also for disabled), restaurant, café, car park

Enlightened Victorians created this magnificent 1,760-acre green space for Dublin's city-dwellers. Inside the park are Dublin Zoo (*see* p.58) and some children's play areas and sports grounds. Located above water – which now flows underground – that was thought to have healing properties, the area was once called 'Clear Water', which is *fhionn uisce* in Irish, and this was later corrupted into 'Phoenix'. Around the park you will find several monuments, such as a giant column that was erected to commemorate the Duke of Wellington. From the No. 10 bus stop, you can walk for miles through Phoenix Park, so do go prepared for weather changes with decent walking shoes and rainwear.

The wildlife and history of Phoenix Park from 3500 BC to the present are displayed in the visitor centre. A restored medieval tower-house called Ashtown Castle, which was probably built in the 17th century, adjoins the centre and may be seen on Saturdays on a guided tour.

WHERE TO EAT

Dublin has become a city of restaurants, bars and cafés as well as ever-present pubs. Many are in the centre of the city, especially in tourist areas such as Temple Bar, but excellent ones can also be found in the suburbs. A 21st-century renaissance in food has arisen in Ireland, so there are many more good restaurants than can be listed here. Below is a selection of old- and new-style restaurants and cafés, chosen for comfort and value, as well as an accommodating attitude to children. Most offer a few vegetarian options.

It is a good idea to book Dublin restaurants ahead, particularly in the evenings and on weekends.

Avoca Café

Inside Avoca Handweavers, Suffolk St, D2, t (01) 672 6019 (*inexpensive*)

Open Mon–Sat 9.30–5.30

An excellent designer café decked out in wood, using organic produce where possible, and offering tempting baked desserts.

Aya Restaurant

49–52 Clarendon St, D2, t (01) 677 1544 (*moderate*)

Open Mon–Fri 8am–11pm, Sat 10am–11pm, Sun 11am–10pm

A Japanese restaurant with Dublin's first conveyor belt sushi bar, offering special prices at lunchtime and at weekends.

Bad Ass Café

9 Crown Alley, Temple Bar, D2, t (01) 671 2596 (*inexpensive–moderate*)

Open daily 11.30am–12 midnight

A diner-style spot for pizza, chops and burgers, famous because pop star Sinead O'Connor used to waitress here. You'll have to explain to your children that the restaurant's name refers to a donkey. A children's menu, a baby-changing area and highchairs are all available.

Beshoff

6 Upper O'Connell St, D1, t (01) 872 4400, and 14 Westmoreland St, D2, t (01) 677 8026 (*inexpensive*)

Open Mon–Sat 11–11 and Sun 12 noon–11

Good-quality fish and chips, eat in (self-service) and takeaway

Bewley's

78 Grafton St, D2, t (01) 635 5470 (*inexpensive–moderate*)

Open daily 7.30am–11pm

Bewley's was founded as a chain of coffeehouses in 1840, and the smell of its roast coffee and sticky buns is a nostalgic one for Dubliners and visitors alike. Most of its dark-panelled Art Deco and Art Nouveau architecture has been retained, and it is a central place to have a cup of tea and traditional barm brack, though its new restaurant, Mackerel, is drawing queues nowadays. The first floor, which once housed Bewley's chocolate factory, holds family portraits, old equipment, teapots made in the 1920s and an old penny lavatory lock, giving you some sense of Bewley's place in Dublin's social history.

Blazing Salads

42 Drury St, D2, t (01) 671 9552 (*inexpensive*)

Open Mon–Fri 10–6, Sat 10–5.30

A vegetarian takeaway deli selling its own wheat-free, dairy-free, organic baking.

Bretzel Bakery

1a Lennox St, South Circular Rd, D8, t (01) 475 2742 (*inexpensive*). Open Thurs 9–7, Fri and Sat 9–6

Mouthwatering caramel shortbread and other baked treats.

Captain America's Cookhouse

Grafton Court, 44 Grafton St, D2, t (01) 671 5266 (*inexpensive*)

Open daily 12 noon–12 midnight

This has been something of a rock'n'roll institution since it opened in 1971, as the first 'Hard Rock'-style restaurant in Ireland. Children love the noisy, casual restaurant, although it might be better to visit at midday rather than in the early evenings, as it'll be a bit less frenetic, although the music will still be loud. Activity sheets with crayons, a children's menu and highchairs are provided, and there's sometimes a clown on Sundays. As alternatives to burgers and all the classic American specialities, there are soups and salads on the menu too.

Chapter One

18–19 Parnell Sq, D1, t (01) 873 2266 (*moderate–expensive*). Open Tues–Fri 12.30–2.30, 6–11; Sat 6–11.

A gourmet restaurant reviewers are raving about. Lunch and pre-theatre meals (12.30–2.30 and 6–7) are the best times to bring well-behaved children.

Cornucopia

19 Wicklow St, D2, **t** (01) 677 7583 (*inexpensive*)
Open Mon–Weds, Fri and Sat 8.30–8, Thurs 8.30–9, Sun 12 noon–7.

Good-value, wholesome vegetarian and vegan food served in a casual place that was Dublin's first vegetarian restaurant. It's self-service at lunch, table service evenings.

Debenham's Restaurant

Jervis Shopping Centre, Mary St, D1, **t** (01) 878 1222 (*moderate*)
Open Mon–Sat 10–6

VIP baby service includes free jars of baby food (some organic) when you buy an adult meal here.

Dome Restaurant

St Stephen's Green Shopping Centre, D2, **t** (01) 478 1287 (*inexpensive–moderate*)
Open Mon–Sat 10–6.30

This large restaurant at the top of the shopping centre has views of St Stephen's Green and a varied menu, including children's portions if requested, plus highchairs and a baby-changing facility.

Frank's

Malting Tower, Grand Canal Quay, D2, **t** (01) 662 5870 (*inexpensive–moderate*)
Open Mon–Fri 11.30–11, Sat and Sun 12.30–11

Children who like restaurants will enjoy this one, which offers anything from a sandwich to a lamb tagine, plus good desserts, and has disabled access.

Fresh Vegetarian Restaurant

2nd Fl, Powerscourt Townhouse Centre, South William St, D2, **t** (01) 671 9669 (*inexpensive*)
Open Mon–Sat 9–6

This restaurant, a member of the Slow Food movement, has good vegetarian and vegan soups, hot dishes, salads, filled bagels, focaccia, tomato breads, smoothies, fresh juices, organic coffee and home-made cakes (organic where possible). Discounts are offered to students.

Gallagher's Boxty House

20–21 Temple Bar, D2, **t** (01) 677 2762 (*inexpensive–moderate*)
Open daily 12 noon–11.30

A 'traditional Irish' restaurant that has as its speciality *boxty* – potato pancakes. They come with a big choice of fillings and dishes on the side. Reservations are recommended for evenings.

Gotham Café

8 South Anne St, D2, **t** (01) 679 5266 (*inexpensive–moderate*)
Open daily 11am–12 midnight

Gourmet pizzas, speciality salads, pasta, vegetarian and noodle dishes are on offer at this popular American-style family café, with a children's menu, baby-changing room and highchairs.

Govinda's/Radha Govinda's

4 Aungier St, D2, **t** (01) 475 0309, and 83 Middle Abbey St, D1, **t** (01) 872 9861 (*inexpensive–moderate*)
Open Mon–Sat 11–10.30

This Asian duo consists of an Irish-Indian vegetarian café–restaurant (Govinda's) where you queue at the bar for tasty dishes, and its more upmarket sister restaurant (Radha Govinda's).

Hard Rock Café

12 Fleet St, Temple Bar, D2, **t** (01) 671 7777 (*inexpensive–moderate*)
Open daily 12 noon–late

Classic American food served in a tried-and-tested rock'n'roll atmosphere.

Harry Ramsden's

Naas Rd, D12, **t** (01) 460 0233 (*inexpensive*)
Open Mon–Sat 11am–11.30pm, Sun 12 noon–9

Weekends, this fish and chips institution has a face-painter and life-size version of Postman Pat, and colouring books and crayons are available.

Juice

73–83 South Great Georges St, D2, **t** (01) 475 7856 (*inexpensive*)
Open daily 8–2.30 and 6.30–10.30

Dublin's first juice bar, with all sorts of healthy and refreshing food: good vegan and vegetarian snacks, meals and veggie burgers, and tasty juices.

Kilkenny Restaurant

6 Nassau St, D2, **t** (01) 677 7066 (*inexpensive*)
Open Mon–Weds, Fri and Sat 9–5, Thurs 9–7, Sun 11–5

Traditional home cooking at an excellent self-service restaurant overlooking Trinity College.

Leo Burdock's

2 Werburgh St, D8, **t** (01) 454 0306 (*inexpensive*)
Open Mon–Sat 12 noon–12 midnight, Sun 4–12 midnight

Dublin's best and oldest fish and chip shop, offering takeaways next door to the Lord Edward pub and Christ Church Cathedral.

Luigi Malones

The Friary, 5–6 Cecilia St, Temple Bar, D2, **t** (01) 679 2723 (*inexpensive–moderate*)

Open daily 12 noon–11

A relaxed place serving modern Italian-influenced food, including pizza, and offering a children's menu. You'll find a second branch in Stillorgan, D4.

Mao Café and Bar

2–3 Chatham Row, D2, **t** (01) 670 4899 (*inexpensive–moderate*)

Open daily 10am–12 midnight

A hip spot for coffee, lunch and Sunday brunches, with Asian-based dishes, salads, juices and smoothies.

The Mermaid Cafe

69/70 Dame St, Temple Bar, D2, **t** (01) 670 8236 (*moderate*)

Open Mon–Sat 12.30–2.30 and 6–11, Sun 12.30–3.30 and 6–9

Wooden tables and good food have made this popular for weekend brunches.

Milano's

Dawson St, D2, **t** (01) 670 7744 (*inexpensive*)

Open daily 12 noon–12 midnight

Reliable pizzas and a supervised play area (Sundays until 5).

Nectar Juice Bar

53 Ranelagh Village, D6, **t** (01) 491 0934 (*inexpensive*)

Open daily 10am–11pm

A café-style restaurant serving nourishing juices, smoothies, wraps, salads and some hot dishes.

Nude

21 Suffolk St, D2, **t** (01) 672 5577 (*inexpensive*)

Open daily 11–11

Fresh juices, smoothies, panini and organic meals.

O'Connell's

Bewley's Aparthotel, Merrion Rd, Ballsbridge, D4, **t** (01) 647 3303, **www.oconnellsballsbridge.com** (*inexpensive–moderate*)

Open Mon–Sat 7.30–10.30, 12.30–2.30 and 6–10, Sun 8–11, 12.30–3 and 6–9.30.

Families have happy times in this lively basement venue with its child-pleasing meals and desserts.

101 Talbot's

101 Talbot St, D1, **t** (01) 874 5011 (*moderate*)

Open Tues–Sat 5–11pm

Older vegetarian children may find this place with its club-like atmosphere a treat for dinner.

O'Shea's

23 Anglesea St, D2, **t** (01) 671 9049 (*inexpensive*)

Open daily 12 noon–11pm

Traditional Irish family cooking.

Roly's Bistro

7 Ballsbridge Terrace, Ballsbridge, D4, **t** (01) 668 2611 (*moderate–expensive*)

Open Mon–Thurs 12 noon–3 and 6–6.45

A noisy, bright room where an excellent casual 'early bird' dinner of 3 courses may be enjoyed.

Thunder Road Café

Fleet St, Temple Bar, D2, **t** (01) 679 4057 (*inexpensive*)

Open daily 12 noon–12 midnight

Staff dress in 1950s gear and offer American-style food at this fun café with a children's menu, baby-changing room and highchairs.

Trentuno

Wicklow St, D2, **t** (01) 677 4190 (*inexpensive–moderate*)

Open Mon–Sat 11am–11.30pm, Sun 12 noon–9

A friendly place for Italian cuisine, with a children's menu and a baby-changing area.

Vermilion

Rathgar, Terenure, **t** (01) 499 1400 (*moderate–expensive*). **Open** daily 5.30pm–late

An Indian festival with dancers drew media types to this Terenure restaurant on Midsummer Eve. Its friendly chef will please the most critical vegetarian with his aromatic marinades, soft naan, perfectly cooked rice, vegetable dishes delicately balanced in a medley of textures and tastes, and rosewater and cardamom-flavoured desserts like shrikand and mango kulfi. Dine early with children as the winebar atmosphere attracts a lively crowd.

Wagamama

South King St, D2, **t** (01) 478 2152 (*inexpensive*)

Open Mon–Sat 12 noon–11pm, Sun 12 noon–10pm

A friendly, spacious branch of the well-known Oriental chain, with benches at long refectory-style tables and crayons and colouring paper for children.

Yamamori Noodles

71/72 South Great Georges St, D2, **t** (01) 475 5001 (*inexpensive*). **Open** Mon–Thurs 12.30–3 and 5.30–11, Fri and Sat 12.30–3 and 5.30–11.30, Sun 2–10pm

Authentic Japanese noodle and rice dishes. Child sizes, highchairs and a baby-changing area are available.

Leinster

COUNTY DUBLIN 68
Special Trips 69
Around and About 72

WICKLOW AND CARLOW 74
Touring Towns 76
Special Trips 77
Around and About 79

KILKENNY AND WEXFORD 82
Touring Towns 83
Special Trips 85
Around and About 87

KILDARE, LAOIS AND OFFALY 91
Special Trips 92
Around and About 92

MEATH AND LOUTH 97
Special Trips 98
Around and About 101

WESTMEATH AND LONGFORD 105
Special Trips 106
Around and About 107

WHERE TO EAT 109

04

LEINSTER

Around 300 BC, an Irish chieftain named Lavra the Mariner lost his kingdom to his thieving uncle, and hired mercenaries from France to help him regain it. The Gauls found his homeland so agreeable that they decided to stay on. They had triumphed in battle by using special broad-pointed spears, called *Laighen* in Irish, and so the people of the kingdom began to refer to it as 'The place of the broad-pointed spear' – that is, *Laighenster*, or Leinster.

The province's fertile farmland, lush forests, lakes and low mountains have always attracted outsiders, and each foreign invasion brought new building techniques and skills. All along Ireland's east and southeast coasts, down to the tip of Hook Head in County Wexford, Vikings, Norsemen, French Normans and Englishmen settled and lived together peacefully enough, after an initial period of strife. Evidence of Ireland's Christian 'golden age' – when Irish monasteries were among Europe's greatest seats of learning – may be found in abbeys, churches and monastic ruins throughout Leinster. This period (Ireland's 'enlightenment') occurred during Europe's so-called Dark Age.

Today Leinster is the most heavily populated province of Ireland. It includes two of Ireland's original provinces – *Mide* (now counties Longford, Meath and Westmeath) and the original, smaller Leinster (the other nine counties of present-day Leinster). Its busiest county by far is Dublin, and the influence of the Republic's capital reverberates out via the tentacles of its new, sprawling highways.

Ireland's laws have been made in Leinster for more than 2,000 years, first at the Hill of Uisneach and later at Tara (*see* p.100 and p.106). The first parts of Ireland brought under English control were Dublin and the small area around it known as 'the Pale'. At times, the border of the Pale changed, but at its largest it stretched from Dundalk to Waterford. 'Beyond the Pale', the Irish tribal leaders were a law unto themselves, at least until the time of Elizabeth I.

Not surprisingly, English settlers tended to congregate in the Pale. Leinster was also the favourite home of the Protestant Irish landed gentry, who gave the region many enormous stately homes. You can feel the influence of this community's writers, thinkers and men and women of action all around you.

Children can learn a lot from a visit to Leinster, as history seeps from every nook and cranny. Some facilities cater specifically for children, but they can be some distance from each other. The charm of this area lies in discovering things at your own pace and in your own way.

Regal houses or ruins from its long-inhabited past can be found around each corner or bend in the road, and you can wander through farmland, forests, mountainous hills and seascapes for days on end, letting the faeries take you in circles, maybe, around the place you are looking for. The coastal areas from Hook Head, in Wexford, to Louth are great for children who like to swim and cycle; Kilkenny, Westmeath and Wicklow are lush counties to visit for fresh air and country walks, some in mountains. Dublin, Meath, Westmeath and Kilkenny are especially noteworthy for ruins and castles. Horse-lovers will want to see Kildare, while the spiritually and ecologically minded enjoy Wicklow and Kilkenny. Southeast Leinster is the sunniest part of Ireland. Its marshes teem with wading birds – so pack binoculars and good pairs of boots. Low-lying pasture drops down to golden, sandy beaches, so in summer bring along a bucket and spade and swimsuits.

You might like to jump into the middle of Ireland first and visit its first-known ancient seat of power, the Hill of Uisneach in Westmeath. If you arrive via Dublin, you could first stay a couple of nights in Malahide. Not far from Uisneach is the Loughcrew cairn, near where a peaceful guesthouse, Mornington House (*see* p.256), sits on the edge of Lake Derravaragh. This lake is where the Children of Lir are said to have lived as enchanted swans for 100 years (*see* p.177).

Drive back east to the Hill of Tara (Co. Meath), where later high kings held counsel, and Newgrange, home of Aengus the Young, the Tuatha Dé Danaan god of love, in the Boyne Valley. Stop off at Newgrange Farm, then visit Dublin and

Highlights

All aboard for the Fry Model Railway Museum in Malahide, p.71
Walking in the Wicklow Mountains, p.81
Exploring the medieval delights of Kilkenny, p.83
Discovering Celtic ways at the Irish National Heritage Park, Wexford, p.85
Visiting Aengus Óg at Newgrange, p.99
Tracking the Vikings in Westmeath, p.106

Leinster
IRISH SEA
DUBLIN
Dundalk
Drogheda
Navan
Trim
Mullingar
Athlone
Tullamore
Longford
Cavan
Kells
Naas
Kildare
Newbridge
Portlaoise
Carlow
Kilkenny
Athy
Wicklow
Arklow
Bray
Enniscorthy
Wexford
New Ross
Waterford
Thurles
Roscrea
Birr
Rosslare Harbour
Howth
Holyhead
Liverpool
Douglas (Isle of Man)
Fishguard
Pembroke
Cherbourg
Roscoff
NORTHERN IRELAND
ULSTER
CONNACHT
REPUBLIC OF IRELAND
LEINSTER
MUNSTER
N
20km
10miles

drive south to Co. Wicklow to see St Kevin's monastery at Glendalough after climbing in the Wicklow Mountains. You could easily spend a few days wandering in the hills, or find out what life was like in a medieval town by visiting Kilkenny.

For big-city excitement, you'll have to stay in Dublin (*see* pp.43–64), but, instead of battling with its traffic, you may prefer to take a bus or tram to a museum or a tour to surrounding sites, like a working farm. That way, you'll be able to relax and look around, play with your children, and find out how easy it is to have a chat with the Irish, who have a habit of being welcoming, even in the age of the Celtic Tiger.

Tourist information for Leinster

Tourism Ireland, Freephones UK **t** 0800 039 7000, US and Canada **t** 1 800 223 6470,
Bord Fáilte, t (01) 602 4000 (Republic only), **www**.tourismireland.com (*see* p.300)
Dublin Tourism Centre, St Andrew's Church, Suffolk St, D2, **t** (01) 605 7700.
Open Sept–June Mon–Sat 9–5.30, Sun (Sept only) 10.30–3; July and Aug Mon–Sat 9–7, Sun 10.30–3. Dublin's central tourist office also provides all sorts of information and services (including accommodation advice) for the whole of Ireland as well as the city itself. *See also* p.49
The Office of Public Works (ex-Dúchas, the Heritage Service), 51 St Stephen's Green, D2, **t** (01) 647 6587/1890 321 421, **www**.heritageireland.ie The Irish government department responsible for running many monuments and historic sites throughout the country (*see also* p.300).

Getting there and around

By air Dublin Airport is the main flight arrival point for Leinster. *See* p.283.
By sea Leinster also contains Ireland's busiest ferry entry points: Dublin and nearly adjacent Dun Laoghaire, and Rosslare, near Wexford. Rosslare is a very useful entry harbour for anyone travelling to the south and southwest of the Republic, and wishing to skip the Dublin area. *See* pp.284–5.
By bus Bus Éireann coaches to every part of Leinster leave from Busáras bus station in Dublin.
By train In Dublin, trains along the east coast between Dundalk and Wexford/Rosslare and to northeast Leinster (Longford) leave from Connolly Station; trains to destinations further west and south (south Co. Kildare, Carlow, Kilkenny) leave from Heuston Station. *See* p.288

COUNTY DUBLIN

County Dublin is the area surrounding Dublin city centre, and includes the suburbs a little to the west and south of it, and the coastal area the north, up to Balbriggan on the border with County Louth. In ancient times, Howth, the point that closes off the north side of Dublin Bay, was named Elta Edar, and this is where Partholón (*see* p.29) is said to have arrived with the second wave of immigrants to settle in Ireland. On a grimmer note, it is also where a boat landed that brought the Black Death plague to Ireland in 1348.

Although you can still walk around Howth Head for a good view of Dublin Bay, the new plague upon the area is housing developments. It is to be hoped the movers and shakers will stop before they build over all of this county's beautiful surroundings, the forests, hills and clean waterways of which bring good health in mind and spirit to its children.

Everywhere in County Dublin is easy to get to from the city by public transport. The DART local rail line follows the coast around Dublin Bay all the way from Bray, County Wicklow (*see* p.76), to Howth. Mainline trains run further north, and there are plentiful buses. They are good alternatives to trying to drive and suffering the stress of getting lost due to maps that still don't have on them the roads to Dublin's new suburban realms.

Tourist information for Co. Dublin

Dublin Tourism Centre, St Andrew's Church, Suffolk St, D2, *see* p.49
Branch offices at: **Dublin Airport** Arrivals Hall
Dun Laoghaire Ferry Terminal
As well as Dublin Tourism's offices, there are local offices in:
Balbriggan George's Sq, **t** (01) 841 4884
Malahide Malahide Castle, **t** (01) 845 0490

Getting around

For anywhere along the shore of Dublin Bay the **DART** local train is the easiest way to get there (*see* p.47). In central Dublin you can get DART trains at Connolly, Tara St or Pearse St stations. For Malahide and the coast north of Howth, take **Northern Suburban** trains on the Dublin–Dundalk line, from the same stations. Many Dublin city **buses** run to the suburbs and surrounding towns, so coach services are not usually necessary.

SPECIAL TRIPS

Dalkey

Once an important port on Ireland's east coast, Dalkey is nowadays better known as Dublin's most fashionable suburb – inhabited by Ireland's top pop idols and film stars. It's easy to see why. It's the most charming of all the old villages around Dublin Bay, and still has a good deal of the look and feel of a fishing village, with good views over Dublin Bay, especially towards the neighbouring village of Killiney. Dalkey and Killiney also have good restaurants.

Dalkey Castle and Heritage Centre

Castle St, Dalkey, **t** (01) 285 8366
Getting there DART to Dalkey station or bus 8
Open Mon–Fri 9.30–5, Sat, Sun and public hols 11–5
Adm Adult €6, under-12s €5, family (2+4) €16

This is one of two tower castles left in Dalkey (there once were seven). It is known as the Medieval Goat Castle. You enter through the larger castle on Castle St, and from the top there is a fine view of Dalkey village. An adjoining 11th-century church is dedicated to a local saint called St Begnet, who also has a church dedicated to her on nearby Dalkey Island (*see* below). Children can scramble over the tiny graveyard, and may be interested in Dalkey Castle's Murder Hole, through which boiling oil (or worse) used to be thrown upon unwanted intruders. Teenagers may be interested in the exhibition scripted by local writer and playwright Hugh Leonard and in the theatre attached to the castle. The sea is about 10 minutes' walk from here.

Dalkey Island

Getting there Boats run regularly from Coliemore Harbour in Dalkey, roughly May–Sept, most frequently Sat, Sun and hols

Summer boat trips go to this tiny island just offshore of Dalkey, where there is a martello tower, bird sanctuary and medieval church (St Begnet).

Killiney Hill Park

Getting there DART to Dalkey or Killiney; from Killiney station, walk up Victoria Rd

A short, steep walk up the hill between Killiney and Dalkey will bring you here, for beautiful views of Killiney Strand, Dublin Bay and much of Dublin.

Tell me an Irish riddle –
Question – What has an eye but cannot see?
Answer – A needle

Howth

Round off a day in Howth with a trip to Ireland's Eye – which has another lonely martello tower – and the other tiny rocky islands just offshore; boats leave regularly daily from East Pier in Howth Harbour Apr–Sept, if there are enough people.

Howth Castle and Gardens

Off Howth Rd, Howth, D13, **t** (01) 840 0077
Getting there 5mins walk from Howth station; from Dublin centre, take DART to Howth station or buses 31, 31B, making sure you sit on the top deck to admire the view.
Open Daily 8am–sunset. **Adm** Free

This 15th-century castle, currently being renovated by its inhabitants, is surrounded by giant oak trees, and rhododendrons and azaleas that bloom in May and June. Co. Mayo's 16th-century pirate queen Grace O'Malley (*see* p.70) is credited as the reason the Castle's front gate is always left open and a table is set every evening with linen, crystal and candelabras to await a visitor. In the castle grounds are a portal tomb known as Aedeen's Grave and the National Transport Museum.

National Transport Museum

Howth Castle Demesne, Howth, D13, **t** (01) 832 0427, **t** (01) 848 0831, **www.nationaltransportmuseum.org**
Open Sept–May Sat, Sun and bank hols 2–5, 2 June–Aug Mon–Sat 10–5, 6 Dec–1 Jan daily 2–5
Adm Adult €3, child €1.50, family €8

Children fascinated by automobiles, models and moving things in general will love this very attractive and well-organized museum. On show are 60 of its 100 examples of historic means of transport, from military vehicles to trucks and cars. The buses, trams and fire engines of more than a century ago are here, going right back to horse-drawn carriages and even handcarts. It may be a surprise to discover that at the start of the 20th century, Dublin's public transport system was well ahead of most other cities', as it was one of the first places to bring electric trams to its streets.

A story to tell: The ransom of Grace O'Malley

Do you want to know why, every evening, even to this day, a table is laid for dinner, waiting for a stranger to call at Howth Castle?

In the 16th century, after the 'pirate queen' of Connacht, Granuaile, also known as Grace O'Malley, had gone to England to bargain with Queen Elizabeth I (*see* p.178), she landed on her return to Ireland at the port of Howth. She then walked up the slope to Howth Castle to ask for a place to spend the night – the logical thing to do, since she was of noble blood, and under Ireland's old Brehon Laws the local nobility were obliged to give her shelter.

When the door was opened by the Earl of Howth's butler, the pirate queen said, 'I am Granuaile, Lady of the Isles. Would you be so kind as to ask the Earl of Howth to grant me hospitality this evening?'

'I beg your pardon, my lady,' he replied, 'Who are you?'

'I rule the waves of the islands to the far west of the big island.'

'The big island?' he queried, 'I am sorry, but his lordship has already dined this evening, and is not expecting visitors.'

'Such ways you have, sir,' Granuaile's face turned red with anger. 'Have you no conscience about the rules of hospitality, especially to a lady of my birth?'

But already the door was slammed in her face.

According to the laws of her people, a stranger was always to be given food and lodging, even by the poorest in the realm. Granuaile spluttered with rage as she stomped down the hill to a tavern for her supper. Then, as fate would have it, she met the son of the Earl of Howth, who was friendlier to her than his butler had been. They ate and drank together for hours, until Granuaile had drunk him under the table. The next thing the Earl's son knew was when he woke up to hear the gulls circling Granuaile's ship, bound for a faraway place.

When the Earl of Howth was told about the kidnapping he sent word to Granuaile, promising whatever she wanted if she would only return his son. Her reply was this: 'That henceforth he honours the laws of hospitality. That the gates of Howth Castle are ne'er to be shut till after the dinner hour, and that an extra place always be set at his table just in case one shall come.'

By the standards of those times this was a mild demand, so the Earl immediately gave his promise, and his son was duly returned to him.

Malahide

One of the most pleasant seaside towns near Dublin, Malahide has some good restaurants and shops. The marina is lovely and there are good beaches, but look out for strong water currents. It's close to Dublin, yet far enough away for visitors to escape into the memory of the more tranquil way of life once enjoyed in the grounds of its castle.

Getting there Malahide is 8 miles (13km) northeast of Dublin City via Fairview and the Malahide road, and 4 miles (6km) from Dublin Airport

By bus Bus 42 from Beresford Place (near Busáras), or from Talbot St. Dublin Bus's 'Coast and Castle' tour also visits Malahide, *see* p.48

By car N1 Dublin–Belfast Rd, turn right at Swords bypass roundabout for Malahide

By train Some northbound Drogheda–Dundalk trains from Connolly Station, Dublin, stop here, or suburban trains from Connolly, Tara St or Pearse St stations

Getting around

Bike hire CGL, 9 Townyard Lane, Malahide, **t** (01) 845 4275.

Malahide Castle Demesne

Malahide, **t** (01) 846 2184/2516, **www**.visitdublin.com

Getting there The Demesne and sites within it are a 10–20min walk through the park from Malahide station. Everything is well signposted.

Open Apr–Oct Mon–Sat 10–5, Sun and bank hols 11–6; Nov–Mar Mon–Sat 10–5, Sat, Sun and bank hols 11–5; winter times may vary

Adm Free, see below for individual attractions

Toilets, tourist office, bookshop, restaurant, café, disabled access, audio-tours, playground, playing fields, cricket pitch, tennis courts, golf and pitch'n'putt course, parking

This 270 acres of rolling parkland just outside Malahide was once the home of the Talbot family, who occupied the castle for 800 years after Prince John granted it to them in 1185. The castle is the longest to have been continuously inhabited by the same family in all of Ireland. Oliver Cromwell displaced them briefly, but otherwise the Talbots lived here until 1975. The land around the castle does not seem to have changed much over the years, apart from the beautiful gardens created by the last Lord Talbot of Malahide. Here you can sense the peace the owners enjoyed when not defending their realm, eight centuries ago.

Contained within the grounds are the castle, the Fry Model Railway Museum, the Talbot Botanic Gardens, Tara's Palace Dolls' House, stableyards and many sports facilities. It is, in effect, nearly a town in itself. There are even ruins in the grounds, including an old chapel, so you gain a sense of what it was like to live alongside a castle in days of yore. Plus, there are all the wide, empty grassy spaces where children can play after poring over the exhibits in the museums. You can stop for lunch or a picnic in the grounds, and shop for locally made crafts in the former stableyard. If you've been stuck in Dublin traffic, it's a welcome relief to spend a day enjoying these grounds.

Malahide Castle

Malahide Castle Demesne, t (01) 846 2184
Open Mon–Sat 10–5, plus Apr–Sept Sun and bank hols 11–6, Oct–Mar Sun and bank hols 11–5
Getting there Bus 42 (Beresford Place near Busáras in Dublin); train and DART from Connolly Station to Malahide station, then 15min walk to castle
Adm Adult €6.50, under-12s €4, family (2+4) €8
Restaurant, disabled access, craft and souvenir shop, picnic areas, children's playground

A guide takes you into this well-preserved castle, its oldest part begun in 1185. It has an air of cloistered tranquility. The Great Hall – built in 1475, with additional parts added between the 15th and 19th centuries – is Ireland's only surviving original medieval great hall. Talbot family portraits hang on its walls. Fourteen Talbot cousins breakfasted here in 1690 before riding out to fight at the Battle of the Boyne; none returned (*see* p.35). The castle feels very much like a home, and gives children a good impression of what it was like to live here. They will probably be most curious about its nursery, library and bedrooms, but equally impressive are the oak room, Great Hall and drawing room, and the National Gallery of Ireland's national portrait collection, which adorns the walls.

Malahide Castle Craft Shop

Seaview, Yellow Walls Rd, Malahide, t (01) 846 2516

Interesting pottery, musical instruments and woven cloth.

Fry Model Railway Museum

Malahide Castle Demesne, t (01) 846 3779
Open Apr–Sept Mon–Thurs and Sat 10–1 and 2–5, Sun and public hols 2–6
Adm Adult €6.50, child €4, family €18
Model shop, bookshop

This purpose-built museum in the castle grounds, one of Ireland's most exciting places for model railway enthusiasts, has one of the largest working miniature railways in the world, covering 2,500 sq ft. Intricate handmade models of Irish trains, with replicas of stations in Dublin and Cork and other well-known landmarks, convey the history of railways in Ireland. Look for the giant model with stations, bridges, buses, trams and even barges on the Liffey, made to scale with incredible attention to detail. The collection was amassed in the 1920–30s by railway engineer and draughtsman Cyril Fry.

Sea Safari

Malahide Marina, t (01) 806 7626, www.seasafari.ie

Power boat trips along the coast.

Talbot Botanic Gardens

Malahide Castle, t (01) 816 9914
Open Daily May–Sept 2–5; guided tour of walled garden Weds 2pm; groups by appointment only
Adm Adult €3.50, under-12s free; guided tour €3
Toilets, teashop, disabled access

Refreshing botanic environs where children can play, with more than 5,000 varieties of trees and shrubs on display, a Victorian conservatory, 16 acres of shrubbery and 4 acres of walled gardens. The gardens as they are today were laid out by Milo, last Lord of Malahide Castle, between 1948 and 1973.

Tara's Palace Dolls' House

Malahide Castle Demesne, t (01) 846 4133
Open Apr–Sept Mon–Sat 10–1 and 2–5, Sun and bank hols 2–6
Adm Donations welcome: adult €2, child €1

Constructed over 10 years in the late 20th century, Tara's Palace combines the grandeur and elegance of three great 18th-century Irish mansions – Leinster House, Castletown House and Carlton House. It shows in miniature the best of Irish craftsmanship, worked into the interiors of a great Georgian house. Miniature porcelain and glassware, and paintings by Tom Ryan, RHA, adorn its rooms. Girls who enjoy dolls, and budding architects, find it fascinating. There's also a collection of 18th- and 19th-century dolls, silverware and furniture.

AROUND AND ABOUT

Animal magic

Animal Farm

Reynoldstown, Naul, **t** (01) 841 2615
Getting there 19 miles (30km) north of Dublin, 5 miles (8km) west of the N1

A working farm in an olde-worlde setting, where children can stroke and feed the animals.

Dublin Butterfly House

Harap Farm, Magillstown, Swords, **t** (01) 840 1285, **www.dublinbutterfly.com**
Getting there About 3 miles (5km) north of Dublin Airport; by car, take N1 north around Swords, then turn left onto the R125 (Ashbourne road)
Open May–Sept Tues–Sun and bank hols 10–6
Adm Adult €5, child €2.50, family (2+2) €12

The natural habitats of hundreds of the world's most beautiful butterflies are remarkably re-created on this family-run farm.

North Bull Island

Dollymount, D5
Getting there Bus 130 from Lower Abbey St, D1
Open Daily 7–4.30. **Adm** Free

A nature reserve and bird sanctuary near Dollymount Beach, on a 740-acre island created by the build-up of sand behind a sea wall built in Dublin Bay. There are sand dunes, mudflats and salt marsh, plus birds and many interesting plants.

Buckets and spades – Co. Dublin beaches

Dubliners have plenty of favourite beaches around them, not far from town.
Balscadden Beach, Howth – sandy but shallow.
Donabate – just north of Malahide and famous for its sand dunes, but watch out for dangerous tides.
Killiney – good for long walks taking in the view, but part of it is stony.
Malahide – a long, sandy beach, but beware of strong currents and undertows.
Portmarnock – a golden sand beach between Howth and Malahide, with summer donkey rides
Portrane – a beach with a bird sanctuary at the north end and, like Donabate next to it, lovely dunes.

Bricks and mortar

Ardgillan Castle and Victorian Gardens

Balbriggan, **t** (01) 849 2212
Getting there 19 miles (30km) north of Dublin. By car, N1; by bus, 33; by train, Northern Suburban from Connolly, Tara St or Pearse St stations
Open Castle: July and Aug daily 11–6; Apr–June and Sept Tues–Sun and bank hols 11–6; Oct–Mar Tues–Sun and bank hols 11–4.30, closed 23 Dec–1 Jan
Park: daily dawn–dusk
Rose garden: Mon–Fri 9.30–5, Sat and Sun and bank hols 11–5
Guided tours: June–Aug Thurs 3.30 or by arrangement
Adm Castle: adult €4, under-12s €3, family (2+3) €9; map exhibition and guided tours €3
Café, disabled access, parking

This was originally a Georgian country manor house, built in 1738 by the Reverend Robert Taylor, but over time it grew to become a castle. Children can explore its 198 acres of woodland and gardens, including a Victorian conservatory and a walled rose garden with a 20-alcove fruit wall. There is also an interesting permanent exhibition of 17th-century maps of Ireland.

Look at this!

Newbridge House, Demesne and Farm

Donabate Demesne: **t** (01) 843 6064,
House: **t** (01) 843 6534/5
Getting there 12 miles (19km) north of Dublin, off the N1. By car, turn east after Swords; by bus, 33B; by train, Northern Suburban to Donabate from Connolly, Tara St or Pearse St stations
Open House: Apr–Sept Tues–Sat 10–1 and 2–5, Sun and bank hols 2–6; Oct–Mar Sat, Sun and public hols 2–5
Grounds: all year.
Adm House: adult €6, ages 12–17 €5, 3–11 €3.50, family (2+2) €16.50.
Farm: adult €2.50, under-12s €1.50, family €6
Café, shop, children's playground, free parking

You could spend a full day looking around this 350-acre demesne, with a fine 18th-century manor house designed by George Semple. Built in

1737 for Charles Cobb, who became Archbishop of Dublin, the house was sold to Dublin County Council with much of its original contents. Works of art and antiques that belonged to the archbishop are on show on the ground floor, and don't miss the wing added in 1760 by his daughter-in-law Lady Elizabeth Beresford, whose red drawing room is one of the finest Georgian rooms in Ireland. Children enjoy the strange objects and souvenirs the Cobb family collected, though on a fine day they might prefer Newbridge's woodland and hilly pastures. There's also a playground and a farm with animals, managed by traditional methods. In the museum, in a cobbled courtyard, there's an old-time dairy, forge, carpentry shop, labourer's cottage with original furnishings, stableyard and the striking Lord Chancellor's Carriage.

Skerries Mills

Skerries, **t** (01) 849 5208
Getting there 19 miles (30km) north of Dublin. By car, off coast road (R126) or south from N1, signposted off N1/M1 roads, Fingal; by bus, 33 from Eden Quay; by train, Northern Suburban from Connolly, Tara St or Pearse St stations
Open daily Apr–Sept 10.30–5.30, Oct–Mar 10.30–4.30; closed 20 Dec–1 Jan and Good Fri
Adm Adult €5, child €4, family €10
Guided tours, tea room, craft shop, parking

In the seaside town of Skerries there are, next to each other, a watermill, 5-sail windmill and 4-sail thatched windmill, all in good working order. It's a fun place to see after visiting other sites nearby.

Nature lovers

Primrose Hill

Lucan, **t** (01) 628 0373
Getting there 8 miles (12km) west of Dublin in Lucan village; bus 25, 66, 67
Open daily Feb and Mar 2–5, June and July 2–6
Adm Adult €4, child €2.50
Guided tours, plants for sale

A Regency villa, attributed to architect James Gandon, amid 6 acres of grounds that include a garden with perennial plants, roses and lilies that provide continuous colour throughout summer, and a lovely spring garden and woods.

Sporty kids

Activity centres

Adventure Activities

t (01) 668 8047, www.adventure-activities-ireland.com

Canoe or kayak in Dublin Bay, rock-climb in Dalkey quarry, or walk in Wicklow: this agency organizes a raft of activities, all of them run by friendly, fully qualified instructors. Fees vary according to the activity; equipment is supplied, and transport is also available.

Fort Lucan Adventureland

Westmanstown, Lucan, **t** (01) 628 0166
Getting there 8 miles (12km) west of Dublin; bus 25, 66, 67
Open May–Aug daily 10–6, plus Sat and Sun until 31 Oct

An outdoor adventure playground complete with trampolines, swings, slides, maze, a waterslide and crazy golf.

Golf

Willie Fox's Golf

Glencullen, **t** (01) 295 9260
Getting there 12 miles (19km) south of Dublin

A mature golf range with scenic views, plus a pitch'n'putt course for youngsters.

Horse riding

Ashtown Riding Stables

Navan Road, Ashtown, D15, **t** (01) 838 3807
Getting there North of Phoenix Park, 10mins from central Dublin; bus 37, 38, 39, 70
Open Summer Mon–Sat 9–5. **Adm** Adult €25 for lesson, child aged 7+ €16 for a lesson or a ride

A likeable riding centre just north of Phoenix Park.

Water sports

Fingal Sailing School

Upper Strand Rd, Broadmeadow Estuary, Malahide, **t** (01) 845 1979
Getting there Malahide harbour, *see* p.70

Junior, youth and adult courses in sail training and windsailing.

Wind and Wave Watersports

16a The Crescent, Monkstown, **t** (01) 284 4177
Getting there DART to Salthill & Monkstown

Windsurfing tuition and gear.

WICKLOW AND CARLOW

Counties Wicklow and Carlow lie cheek by jowl just to the south of Co. Dublin. Wicklow is hilly, lush and has the most spectacular of the landscapes near Dublin, with sea views, low mountains, valleys, forests and lakes – so that the county has long been known as an ideal place to visit from the city. Carlow in contrast is open and flat, with tranquil rivers feeding its farmlands. In the quiet farming villages of Carlow (good cycling territory), you'll notice a subtle French influence, the result of the influx of Anglo-Normans around the 12th century. Meanwhile, Wicklow has remained 'rebel territory', full of people who can trace their ancestors back to folkloric warriors like Cúchulainn (*see* p.30). Some have managed to secrete themselves away in Wicklow's hills and glens without ever quite having given up their freedom to the waves of outsiders who have arrived over the years.

Many myth-laden ruins are hidden among Wicklow's trees, lakes and mountains. The monastery of St Kevin at Glendalough (*see* p.77) is only the most famous. One of the oldest roads in Leinster is *Bearna na Sciath* (Gap of the Shields), and western Wicklow contains the Glen of Imáil (or Imaal), seat of power of Leinster's kings in the Iron Age. Along one of many winding roads is Donard (*Dún Árd* or High Fort), a tiny village (with a very friendly pub) that is the site of one of three churches founded in Wicklow, circa AD 430, by Palladius, St Patrick's predecessor in bringing Christianity to Ireland. Other landmarks include the ruins of the 14th-century St Mary de Hogges nunnery, and, not far away in a wood on one side of Kilranelagh Hill is 'St Brigid's Headstone'. In Irish it's called *cloch na gceann* ('stone of the head'), as the son of 6th-century King Aed Ainmire lost his head here. According to local tales, Cromwell also put the stone to use for getting rid of the nuns from the nunnery. At any rate, Wicklow people believe that putting your head in the hole cures a headache. The respectful and the hopeful leave rosaries, coins, holy medals and pictures in and around it, in thanks to whatever invisible force may be there that can cure illnesses or answer prayers.

Tourist Information

Arklow, t (0402) 32484
Avoca, t (0402) 35022
Bray, t (01) 286 7128/286 6796
Carlow Town, t (059) 913 1554
Wicklow Town, t (0404) 69117

Getting there and around

By bus Bus Éireann coaches run to all the main towns in Co. Wicklow from Dublin, Rosslare and Waterford, and most towns in the north of the county are also served by Dublin Bus (*see* p.46)

St Kevin's Bus, t (01) 281 8119, has direct buses twice daily from Dublin to Glendalough, via Bray. Carlow Town has a few Bus Éireann connections each day with Dublin, Kilkenny and Waterford. Many villages have bus services provided by a local company, **Rapid Express, t** (059) 914 3081.

By train Dublin's **DART** trains run down to Bray and Greystones (*see* p.47). Towns further to the south along the coast (Wicklow Town, Arklow) are on the Dublin–Rosslare line, from Connolly or Pearse St stations in Dublin. Carlow is located on the Dublin–Waterford line, from Dublin's Heuston Station.

Bike hire

Bray Sports Centre, 8 Main St, Bray, **t** (01) 286 3046

Coleman Cycles, 19 Dublin St, Carlow, **t** (059) 913 1273

Celtic Cycling, Lorum Old Rectory, Bagenalstown, Co. Carlow, **t** (059) 977 5282

Tommy McGrath, Rathdrum, Co. Wicklow, **t** (0404) 46172.

Horsedrawn caravans

Clissmann Horsedrawn Caravans, Carrigmore Farm, Wicklow, **t** (0404) 48188
Travel the old-fashioned way through the Wicklow Mountains.

Shopping

Avoca Handweavers

Avoca Village, Co. Wicklow, **t** (0402) 35105, **www.avoca.ie**

The lovely and original handwoven woollens that are made in Avoca are rightly famous, and there is an attractive outlet for them in Dublin (*see* p.49). In Avoca village itself, as well as visiting the shop you can take a tour in the oldest weaving mill in Ireland (built in 1732), as well as watch the whole weaving process and examine the yarns being used.

Cloydagh Woodcraft

Milford, Co. Carlow, **t** (059) 913 2294

Fine carvings and other handmade woodwork; visits are by appointment.

Special Events – Wicklow and Carlow

May

Spring Wicklow Mountains Walking Festival, Wicklow Tourism: **t** (0404) 20070

Boots and warm clothing are recommended to those who take part; bring a packed lunch and some water too.

Wicklow Gardens Festival, t (0404) 20070

Alongside public gardens, more than 30 privately owned ones join this event, which lasts from May to July.

June

Bray Seaside Family Festival, Bray, **t** (01) 286 1702

A fun festival with races, a festival queen ball, GAA sports and soccer, live bands and fireworks, for a week at the end of June.

Carlow Eigse Arts Festival, Bridewell Lane, Carlow Town, **t** (059) 913 0065, **www.eigsecarlow.com**

Music, exhibitions, recitals and dances, from May into June.

Dunlavin Arts Festival, Dunlavin, Co. Wicklow, **t** (045) 401 459

A 3-day village festival complete with a parade, flower and agricultural shows, horse and dog shows, music, various forms of street entertainment and crafts.

July

Arklow Seabreeze Festival, Arklow, Co. Wicklow, **t** (0402) 33356

This 4-day street festival, during which you can enjoy plenty of music, includes a renowned pig race.

Greystones Arts Festival, 20 Hillside, Greystones, near Bray, **t** (086) 287 1470, **www.greystonesartsfestival.com**

Street theatre from Europe, workshops and music at the east coast's largest 4-day arts festival.

Wicklow Regatta Festival, Wicklow Town, **t** (086) 811 2809

Carnivals, treasure hunts and sports for 11 days.

August

Bray International Festival of Music and Dance, Bray, **t** (01) 286 0080, **www.brayjazz.com**

Varied, enjoyable programmes.

Rathdrum Festival and Fireworks, Rathdrum, Co. Wicklow, **t** (0404) 46262

A spectacular 1-day family event in Market Square, with a busking competition.

Tinahely Agricultural Show, Fairwood Park, Tinahely, Co. Wicklow, **t** (0402) 38953

Livestock, show-jumping, a craft village, a dog show, a food hall, dancing and music.

September

Music under the Mountains, Hollywood, Co. Wicklow, **t** (043) 867380

The east coast's premier traditional music event, which always presents some of Ireland's finest folk music artists.

October

Oscar Wilde Autumn School, Bray, **t** (01) 286 4943

Readings and talks by leading writers, for teenagers and up.

Autumn Wicklow Mountains Walking Festival, Wicklow Town, **t** (0404) 4042 0070

As in spring (*see* above), this event consists of a great range of organized and guided walks.

Honeysuckle Products

The Watermill, Hacketstown, Co. Carlow, t (059) 647 1375

A supplier of completely natural botanic goods, including essential oils, aromatic gifts, pot pourri and bath products.

Wicklow Vale Pottery

Arklow, Co. Wicklow, t (0402) 39442

Arklow was built around the pottery industry, and this pottery keeps the tradition alive. Visitors can watch pots being made and see all the many skills involved.

Wild Irish Crafts

Kilquigguin, Co. Wicklow, t (059) 915 6228

At the foot of the Wicklow Mountains in the very south of the county (6 miles/10km east of Tullow, Co. Carlow), this craft centre displays a wide range of products, all of them made in the same workshops, including decoupage, framed verses and Victorian jewellery, adorned with pressed flowers taken from the proprietors' own gardens. Around them they have also marked out well-maintained nature trails across 5 acres of the surrounding countryside (**adm**: adult €2, child free; accessible to wheelchairs) at the foot of the Wicklow Mountains. The main path is ideal for short walks, and leads up to a unique viewing point with panoramic views of the Wicklow and Carlow countryside. There's also a picnic area.

TOURING TOWNS

Bray

Now almost a residential suburb of Dublin, the Wicklow coastal town of Bray has also long been one of Dubliners' favourite seaside towns, with a long shingle beach, traditional resort attractions and bracing sea air.

Things to see and do

Killruddery House and Gardens

Bray, **t** (01) 286 3405, **www.killruddery.com**
Getting there 2 miles (3km) south of Bray off Greystones Rd
Open House: daily May, June and Sept 1–5
Gardens: Sat, Sun and daily Apr, May and Sept 1–5; other times by arrangement
Adm House and Gardens: adult €6.50, under-12s €2.50; Gardens only: adult €4.50, under-12s €1.50

This mansion has been the seat of the Earls of Meath since 1618 but was extensively remodelled in 1820. The gardens, Ireland's oldest formal ones, date from the 1680s. Special events are often held in summer, such as Irish Heritage Week in September; *My Left Foot*, *Angela's Ashes* and *Dancing at Lughnasa* are among the films that have used it as a location.

National Sealife Centre

Strand Rd (seafront), **t** (01) 286 6939, **www.sealife.co.uk**
Open Jan–Mar, Oct and Dec Mon–Fri 11–5, Sat and Sun 10–6; Apr–Sept Mon–Fri 10–6, Sat, Sun and bank hols 10–6.30
Adm Adult €9.75, child €6.50, student €7.50, family (2+2) €29, (2+4) €35

Twenty-four displays filled with Ireland's native fresh and saltwater marine animals from chub to stingrays, along with sea creatures from all over the world, including piranhas and seahorses (whose males give birth). It culminates in a 'theatre of the seas' presentation featuring sharks. Children may have a chance to hold some rockpool creatures.

Wicklow

Co. Wicklow is the home of many talented craftspeople, and their studios are often open to visitors, who can observe them at work. The county is known for pottery, weaving, jewellery, silverware, glasswork, sheepskin and traditional hand-knitting (*see* p.74, Shopping). Wicklow town is a pleasant little place that makes a good base for touring the area. Facing a shingle bay, it has pleasant beaches on both sides and the remains of a castle built by one of the first Norman lords in the 12th century.

Things to see and do

Wicklow's Historic Gaol

Kilmantin Hill, Wicklow, **t** (0404) 61599
Open Daily Mar–Oct 10–6; pre-book groups
Adm Adult €6.80, under-12s €3.95, under-5s free, family (2+3) €18.20
Café, shop

From 1702 to 1924 there was a jail here. The exhibition covers prisoners' stories from this time, including the 1798 rebellion, the famine and the 18th- and 19th-century transportation of prisoners to the penal colonies of Australia. The highlight is a reconstruction of a prison ship, which you climb aboard. A vivid insight into Ireland's social history.

Carlow

Carlow town lies where the Barrow and Burrin rivers meet. It is thought there was once a lake here, since the town's Irish name means 'quadruple lake' (*Ceathar Loch*). This unassuming place doesn't seem to mind that the world rushes past it, and appears happy to keep its treasures hidden among its musicians and artists, who quietly produce little gems. One part of the lively local music scene is the Carlow Traditional Singers Club, which brings together singers and storytellers in the Teach Dolmen pub in Tullow St every month.

Within the overlay of an ordinary old Irish town, little alleys lead to places such as the Cathedral of the Assumption, off College St, and the 18th-century seminary of St Patrick's College. Nearby is the Browneshill Dolmen, for budding archaeologists (*see* p.80). Having been a border town on the edge of the Pale, Carlow was once heavily fortified, but today only a small part of the castle remains.

Things to see and do

Carlow County Museum

Town Hall, Centaur St, **t** (059) 914 0730
Open Tues–Fri 9.30–1 and 2–5.30, Sat and Sun 2.30–5.30. **Adm** Adult €1.50, child €0.65

Displays on 19th- and early-20th-century folk life, local history and archaeology, plus some rare Celtic artefacts.

SPECIAL TRIPS

Clara Lara Fun Park

Vale of Clara, 11 Glenmalure Pines, Greenan, Rathdrum, Co. Wicklow, **t** (0404) 46161
Getting there 15 miles (24km) inland from Wicklow
Open Daily May–Aug 10–6
Adm Adult €13, under-12s €7, under-4s free

This former army assault course in mountains beside the Avonmore River was transformed into a 100-acre outdoor adventure park where children can play Tarzan on rope swings and climb about in treehouses, go rafting like Huckleberry Finn, play mini-golf or ride on an aqua shuttle, row a boat or go-cart. Bring a change of clothes and old shoes, as you'll get wet and muddy.

A story to tell:
Michael Dwyer the Rebel

Michael Dwyer is a legend around Wicklow. He was one of the United Irishmen, led by Wolfe Tone, who rose up against the British in 1798 (*see* p.36). Dwyer was at large in the Wicklow Mountains, and even after the main rebellion was over he continued the fight in a guerrilla campaign against the British troops. He was considered such an important adversary that the British built the 'Military Road' through the Glen of Imaal in an effort to capture him and his rebel followers, but he skilfully avoided them, since he knew the mountains and the Wicklow people so well.

Eventually they tracked him down to a small white stone cottage at Derrynamuck (*see* above). His colleague, a Presbyterian named McAllister, ran out of the cottage to draw the fire of the troops while Dwyer escaped. He finally decided to give himself up, but only on the understanding that he would be deported to America with his family. Once he was arrested, well-wishers lengthened his journey to Kilmainham Jail in Dublin by several hours, cheering him along the route. Once there, he was mistreated by a sadistic jailer and eventually sent to Australia. He died there 20 years later, aged 53, just a week after his by-then grown children had finally arrived to join him. McAllister's grave is still tended and in 1999, on the 200th anniversary of his arrest, local people placed fresh flowers upon it.

Dwyer McAllister Cottage

Derrynamuck, Co. Wicklow, **t** (0404) 45325
Getting there Off the Donard–Rathdangan road, southwest of Glendalough
Open Daily mid-June–mid-Sept 2–6
Adm Free

A traditional thatched cottage of local stone, whitewashed inside and out, nestling in the shade of Kaedeen Mountain at the top of a grassy lane. Restored in the 1940s after lying in ruin for 150 years following a fire, it stands as a monument to the famed Irish rebel Michael Dwyer (*see* left), who in 1799 fought encircling British soldiers here before escaping over snow-covered mountains.

Glendalough

Forever associated with the figure of St Kevin, Glendalough was one of the most important religious centres in Ireland during Europe's 'Dark Ages' (*see* p.31). Even after Kevin died, the monastery thrived as an educational and ecclesiastical centre. It contained some stone cells, workshops for cabinet-makers and metal-workers, a scribes' room, a refectory, a dairy, a bakery, a corn-drying kiln and a grain mill. The community around Glendalough continued to grow until by the 12th century it had become a major trading centre, and home to about 6,000 people. This was despite continuous Viking raids between 800 and 1000, in answer to which the monks built Glendalough's famous round tower as a refuge. It still stands there today. The monastery was finally destroyed in the 14th century, by a fire set by an English army.

Since then, the valley between Glendalough's 2 lakes (the Upper and the Lower) has generally remained the kind of quiet place that St Kevin would have approved of. It's a wonderful spot, set amid the kind of countryside that you probably imagined when you first thought of coming to Ireland. It gets very busy in summer, so visit early to catch the atmosphere, and make time for a stroll by the lake.

Glendalough Visitors' Centre

Glendalough, Co. Wicklow, **t** (0404) 45352
Getting there 30 miles (50km) from Dublin
Open Daily 9.30–5.15
Adm Adult €2.75, child/student €1.25, senior citizens and groups €2, family €7
Car and bicycle park, self-guided trails, picnic tables

A story to tell: St Kevin of Glendalough

Saint Kevin (or *Caoimhín*, 'fair begotten') lived alone in the Wicklow Mountains, in Glendalough, in the 6th century AD. Scholars say that Kevin studied with monks from the age of 12, and became an abbot before he went to Glendalough to be a hermit. One story about St Kevin claims he was born at a tiny spot on the map in Wicklow, but even that was too big for him, so he went off walking in the Wicklow Hills until he discovered the most peaceful place he had ever seen, a valley that lay between two lakes – the Glen of the Two Lakes, or Glendalough. He decided to settle there, in the stump of a great hollow tree at the end of the glen next to the larger of the lakes (the Upper Lake), with wild fruits and nuts for food and the skins of animals that had died nearby for clothing.

The legend goes that the woodland animals soon befriended him, watching as he sat or stood motionless for hours, in deep contemplation. He would wade into the lake and stand with his arms outstretched in prayer for the longest time. One day he stood so still that a blackbird put a twig into one of his hands, and then another and another until she had built a nest, and then laid her eggs in it. Not wanting to disturb the mother bird and her babies, he remained motionless until they hatched and flew away. This is why Kevin is often portrayed with a bird in his hand.

A cow is also said to have visited him while he was meditating. The cow would lick his feet and clothes and then wander back home to give the farmer who owned her as much milk as 50 other cows. One day the farmer followed his cow to find out what she was eating, and was surprised to discover the cow licking the immobile saint's feet. He was so amazed that he told everyone in the village, and they all brought their cows to lick Kevin's feet as well.

Thereafter, people sought him out from far and wide. Monks settled near him to live as hermits, creating a beehive of stone cells you can still find throughout Glendalough. The remains of at least seven churches can be seen in the area. The most famous one is called St Kevin's Kitchen, because the locals thought the spire looked like a chimney rising from a hearth.

The monks who followed Kevin elected him abbot, and soon he found himself in charge of a small city that grew up around the monastery. St Kevin was known to be happy with animals but not so much with humans, who disturbed the peace he sought. One day, during a drought, Kevin fed his monks with salmon brought to him by an otter that lived in one of the lakes. The otter overheard one of the monks say, ''T'would make a fine pair of gloves, that otter's pelt,' and so he left and never returned. Kevin was annoyed by this insult to one of his animal friends.

To get away from the crowds, St Kevin sometimes walked 12 miles (19km) west over the hills through the Wicklow Gap to a village now called Hollywood, where he stayed alone in a cave. Just above it today is a modern statue of St Kevin, erected in 1950. About 30 years ago a hermit lived in the cave and used to tell children that he was St Kevin, but the real Kevin died on 3 July 618. In the Irish calendar, however, he died on 3 June, and this is the day when people celebrate his life.

The centre provides history and background information about the monastic site started by St Kevin. Places to look out for around Glendalough include St Kevin's Cave, St Kevin's Chair, the 12th-century Norman tower of Geoffrey de Marisco, a replica road used in the film *Michael Collins*, the 4,000-year-old Athgreany Stone Circle and the 'Seat of Finn', a 5,000-year-old passage tomb associated with legendary hero Finn McCool.

Mount Usher Gardens

Ashford, Co. Wicklow, **t** (0404) 40205
Getting there 2 miles (3km) north of Wicklow town
Open Daily mid-Mar–end Oct 10.30–5.30
Adm Adult €6.50, child €5.50
Limited disabled access, craft shops, tea room

Woodland walkways and suspension bridges over babbling streams make these gardens, which are situated just off the Dublin road a little inland from Wicklow town, a tranquil, romantic place in which to wander. The gardens are particularly lush, containing 5,000 varieties of trees and shrubs, including rhododendrons, magnolias and maples. A clever mix of seasonal plants ensures the garden remains colourful throughout the year, and there's a particularly tempting tea room here: its cakes are excellent, and it has lovely views of the gardens.

Powerscourt Estate

Enniskerry, Co. Wicklow, **t** (01) 204 6000, **www.**powerscourt.ie
Getting there 12 miles (19km) south of Dublin off N11; bus 44 from Hawkins St, Dublin
Open Gardens and House daily 9.30–5.30, but times vary (i.e. winter 10.30–dusk, midsummer 9.30–7), so call to check; closed 25 and 26 Dec
Adm House and Gardens: Mar–Oct adult €8, under-16s €4.50; Nov–Feb adult €6.50, under-16s €3.80; reductions for garden- or house-only visits
Terrace restaurant, shops, garden centres

This is one of the most beautiful estates in Ireland and a fine example of the enormous stately homes built in the safe vicinity of Dublin in the 18th century by the Irish Protestant landed gentry. The main house, sadly, burnt down in the 1970s and has never been fully restored, but the estate is still a great place to take the kids to show them something of the splendour in which the aristocracy lived. The grounds contain Ireland's highest waterfall – Powerscourt Waterfall, 3 miles (5km) from the entrance across the 47-acre gardens. It's easy to spend a whole day here with children, exploring the tree trail, pet cemetery, Japanese and Italian gardens and Pepper Pot Tower.

AROUND AND ABOUT

Animal magic

Annamoe Leisure Park and Trout Farm

Annamoe, Co. Wicklow, **t** (0404) 45470
Getting there 2 1/2 miles (4km) north of Glendalough on the R755 (Dublin) road
Open 10.30–6.30 June–Aug daily, May and Sept Sat and Sun; junior bait pond 12 noon–6 June–Aug daily, Apr, May, Sept and Oct Sat and Sun
Adm Rod hire and bait: €5; fish caught must be bought at €3 each

A park in 9 acres of woodland, with a mile-deep lake with canoes and rafts, adventure play areas and a separate lake for fishing (rods and bait supplied). Be prepared for lots of mud and wet clothes.

Ballykeenan House Pet Farm and Aviary

Myshall, Co. Carlow, **t** (059) 915 7665
Getting there 10 miles (16km) east of Bagenalstown on R724 road
Open Mon–Fri 11–5, Sun 2–5. **Adm** Adult €3, child €2

The farm owners, the McCord family, give an enthralling guided tour on which kids can observe and pet a variety of animals and unusual birds.

Glenroe Open Farm

Kilcoole, Co. Wicklow, **t** (01) 287 2298, **www.**glenroefarm.com
Getting there 8 miles (12km) south of Bray
Open Apr–Aug Mon–Fri 10–5, Sat, Sun and bank hols 10–6, Mar, Sept and Oct Sat and Sun 10–6
Adm Adult €4.25, child €3.50, family €14
Indoor and outdoor picnic areas, gift shop

This family-run farm offers a pets' corner, aviary and a display of old Irish farm implements.

Greenan Farm Museums and Maze

Ballinanty, Greenan, Rathdrum, Co. Wicklow, **t** (0402) 36308, **www.**greenanmaze.com
Getting there 9 miles (14km) west of Rathdrum via a country lane through Ballinaclash
Open Easter weekend, May and June Tues–Sat and bank hols 10–6, July and Aug daily 10–6, Sept and Oct Sun 10–6, or by appointment
Adm Adult €7.50, under-16s €5.50, under-5s free, family (1+3) €20 or (2+2) €22, extra child €3.50; maze only: adult €4, child €3
Nature walk, craft shop, tea room

Spend a pleasant afternoon in the Glenmalure Valley, where a stream flows through a half-acre maze to a pond in the centre that is hard for adults to find, never mind children. Exhibits in the farmhouse (once a safe house used by Michael Dwyer, *see* p.77) show what life was like here in the 19th century. The large 2-storey barn exhibits traditional hill-farming methods from the days when ploughs were drawn by horsepower.

Lalor's Open Farm

Ballykealey, Ballon, Co. Carlow, **t** (059) 915 9130
Getting there 12 miles (19km) southwest of Carlow Town on the N80 Wexford road
Open call for tour times
Guided tour followed by traditional lunch

The Lalor family lead tours of their accolade-winning 100-acre dairy farm surrounding the 1830 Ballykealey House, where they show off their very high farming and environmental standards.

Bricks and mortar

Avondale House

Rathdrum, Co. Wicklow, **t** (0404) 46333, **www.coillte.ie**
Getting there 1 mile (1.6km) south of Rathdrum on R752 road towards Avoca and Arklow
Open Daily Mar–Oct 11–6
Adm Adult €5.50, child €3.50, family (2+2) €16
House tour, forest walk, children's play area, café and restaurant, picnic area, shop, disabled access to ground floor, coach and car park

Set in Avondale Forest Park – 500 acres of exotic forest beside the River Avoca – this restored Georgian building was the home of the celebrated politician Charles Stewart Parnell (1846–91), one of the most important figures in 19th-century Irish history (*see* p.37). His career came to a disastrous end when it emerged he was involved with a married woman. Exhibits give you an idea of how and why Parnell, son of a Protestant landowner, persuaded the British government to push through several laws called the Land Acts that greatly improved the lives of Irish tenant farmers, and of the later campaign for Irish Home Rule. When you've learnt enough, you can spend the rest of a very pleasant day here enjoying the lovely grounds and letting the kids run riot in the play area.

The Browneshill Dolmen

Rathvilly Road, Carlow
Getting there 2 miles (3km) east of Carlow Town on R726

Here since 3500–2900 BC, this stone dolmen (also called Brown's Hill) has the largest capstone in Europe, weighing an estimated 100 tons.

Old Leighlin Cathedral

Old Leighlin village, Co. Carlow, **t** (059) 972 1570
Getting there West of N9 Waterford road 9 miles (14km) south of Carlow Town
Open June–Aug Mon–Fri 10–5; rest of year groups only, by appointment
Adm Free; donations welcome

The village of Old Leighlin actually has a cathedral, the 13th-century church of Saint Lazerian, which replaced a 7th-century monastery that once had 1,500 monks. A church synod here in AD 630 decided on the formula that determined western Christianity's dates for Easter. The nearby holy well still attracts votive offerings.

Did you know?
Avoca, Co. Wicklow, is the tiny village used as the setting a few years ago for the TV series 'Ballykissangel'. It is also the home of the oldest mill in Ireland at Avoca Handweavers, which has additional sites at Kilmacanogue and Powerscourt.

Nature lovers

If you're hindered by buggies and so unable to take on too many walks in the hills, the drive along the 'Military Road', the road built by the British to track down rebels 200 years ago (otherwise now classified as the R755), will give you a glimpse of how beautiful Ireland is. Join the road at Enniskerry just south of Powerscourt (*see* p.79) and roll down to Glendalough to stroll by the lake. Make time to do this even if you are on a short break in Dublin.

Altamont Gardens

Tullow, Co. Carlow, **t** (059) 975 9510
Getting there Off the N80 Carlow/Bunclody road
Open Mon–Thurs 9–5, Fri 9–3.30, plus Easter–Oct Sat and Sun 10–6
Adm Adult €2.75, child €1.25, family (2+2) €7
Garden centre, toilets (with disabled access)

This beautiful garden has clipped yews sloping down to a lake, around which there are rare trees and a profusion of roses and plants. It was planted in the 19th century around Altamont House, parts of which are 16th-century. You can walk through its arboretum and bog garden to an Ice Age glen,where ancient oaks lead to the River Slaney. Birds, butterflies and squirrels are everywhere.

Kilmacurragh Gardens

Rathdrum, Co. Wicklow, **t** (01) 857 0909
Getting there 6 miles (9.5km) east of Rathdrum on local road towards Arklow
Open Mon–Sat 9–6, Sun 11–6 or dusk. **Adm** Free
Car park, limited disabled access

Budding botanists will find this 19th-century arboretum fascinating for its many species brought from around the world by David Moore and his son Sir Frederick, first curators of the National Botanic Gardens in Dublin (*see* p.61). Planted by Thomas Acton, it is especially famous for its conifers and calcifuges.

National Garden Exhibition Centre
Kilquade, near Bray, Co. Wicklow, **t** (01) 281 9890
Getting there 2 miles (3km) south of Bray.
Open Mon–Sat 10–6, Sun 1–6.
Adm Adult €4.50, under-16s free
Garden centre, tea house, guided tours

A centre with a 328ft (100m) Harlequin Walk with 8 rose arches with a rose garden in the middle.

Sporty kids

Activity centres

Blessington Lakes Leisure Pursuits Centre
Burgage, Blessington, Co. Wicklow, **t** (045) 865 092
Getting there 20 miles (32km) south of Dublin
Open Daily Mar–Dec 10–dusk (should reopen 2006)

Canoeing, boardsailing, tennis, sailing, orienteering and pony-trekking for ages 8 and up.

Tiglin National Mountain and White Water Centre
Ashford, Co. Wicklow, **t** (0404) 40169
Getting there 2 miles (3km) north of Wicklow town

Field courses in mountaineering, orienteering, canoeing, surfing and skiing.

Cycling

Celtic Cycling
Lorum Old Rectory, Bagenalstown, Co. Carlow, **t** (059) 977 5282 **Getting there** 11 miles (17km) sth of Carlow

A firm arranging cycling holidays in the region.

Glendalough Cycle Hire
Brockagh Ctr, Laragh, Co. Wicklow, **t** (086) 082 8355

McGrath's Cycle Hire
Main St, Rathdrum, Co. Wicklow, **t** (0404) 46172

Horse riding

Brennans Town Riding School
Hollybrook, Kilmacanogue, Bray, Co. Wicklow, **t** (01) 286 3778, **www.brennanstownrs.ie**
Getting there 1 1/2 miles (2km) inland from Bray

Rides in the hills behind Bray.

Carrigbeg Riding Stables
Bagenalstown, Co. Carlow, **t** (059) 972 1962
Getting there 11 miles (17km) south of Carlow

Indoor and outdoor arenas, cross-country rides and tuition.

Fishing

In Co. Wicklow, Brittas Bay, Ennereilly Strand and Arklow (South Beach) are good places to fish. The River Barrow in Co. Carlow is known for brown trout and coarse fishing. Several angling centres can be found in Bagenalstown and Tullow.

Dargle Anglers' Club
Bray Sports Centre, Main St, Bray, Co. Wicklow, **t** (01) 286 3046

Salmon and sea trout fishing on the Dargle.

Ray Dineen
Tara House, Redcross, Co. Wicklow, **t** (0404) 41645.

Gilly service on rivers on the eastern side of Wicklow. Fly fishing only.

Watersports

Adventure Canoeing
t (0509) 31307

Canoeing trips on the Barrow River in Co. Carlow.

Walking in Wicklow and Carlow

The Wicklow Mountains are wonderful to walk in, from easy walks through the woods to hikes over the hills. There are well-marked long-distance footpaths. The Wicklow Way begins in Co. Dublin near Marley Park, not far south of Dublin city, and climbs rapidly into the Wicklow Mountains, switching from glen to glen. The Dublin Tourism Centre and local tourist offices have maps and details of footpaths, walking tours and festivals in the hills.

In Co. Carlow, the South Leinster Way covering 64 miles (102km) through Carlow, Kilkenny and Tipperary has many attractive sections. Another lovely long-distance path is the Barrow Way (70 miles/113km), along the river through Carlow and Kildare. There is also a very pleasant forest walk by a canal at Bahana, in the southernmost point of Co. Carlow 3 miles (5km) to the south of Graiguenamanagh (on an unclassified road to St Mullins). Tourist offices, again, have details.

Some agencies that offer guided walks, long and short, in the Wicklow Mountains are:
Barry Dalby, 1555 Beachdale, Kilcoole, Co. Wicklow, **t** (01) 287 5990
Damien Cashin Outdoor Activities, Tomdarragh, Roundwood, Co. Wicklow, **t** (01) 281 8212
Footfalls Hiking Tours, Trooperstown, Roundwood, Co. Wicklow, **t** (0404) 45152

KILKENNY AND WEXFORD

County Kilkenny presents to any visitor an embracing, hilly lushness, making it one of the greenest and most idyllic pieces of the Irish countryside. Birdwatchers and fishermen love this area's rivers, such as the Slaney, which flows south through the county and down into Wexford Harbour. Centuries ago the Vikings made use of these same waterways in their plundering raids. Sophisticated country grace mixes with eccentric whimsy in these counties, in a unique, particularly Irish combination. The Normans founded the town of New Ross and County Wexford's breweries, farms and mills. From this rich, gently undulating countryside the people – more Celtic and Viking than Anglo-Norman – have exported fine produce and strong ales to the world.

County Wexford, Ireland's southeastern corner, is known for its birds, on the offshore Saltee Island and along the Wexford Slobs and Harbour. It also has many fine beaches and some lovely old fishing villages, especially along its south coast, and rare coastal rock formations, particularly near Hook Head.

Tourist information

Enniscorthy, The Castle, **t** (054) 34699
Gorey, Lower Main St, **t** (055) 21248
Kilkenny, Shee Alms House, Rose Inn St, **t** (056) 7751500
New Ross, t (051) 21857
Wexford Town, Crescent Quay, **t** (053) 23111

Getting there and around

By bus There are at least 6 Bus Éireann coaches each day between Dublin and Cork that stop in Kilkenny, and less frequent services from Waterford. Bus Éireann in Kilkenny, **t** (056) 776 4933. Many local bus routes are operated by **Kavanagh's, t** (056) 883 1106.

Bus Éireann coaches run every hour daily from Dublin to Wexford Town and Rosslare, and there are also many services running to Waterford and Cork.

By sea Rosslare Harbour is one of Ireland's busiest ferry ports, with sailings from Fishguard and Pembroke in Wales and the French ports of Roscoff and Cherbourg (*see* pp.285–6).

Special Events – Kilkenny and Wexford

March and April

Spring Music Festival, Wexford, **t** (053) 23923
A lively classical music festival.

Viking Festival, Wexford, **t** (053) 23401
A celebration of Wexford's Viking past, running from April into May.

May

The Cat Laughs, Kilkenny, **t** (056) 775 1254
There's fun for all at this annual comedy festival in Kilkenny town, from late May to early June.

June and July

Strawberry Fair, Enniscorthy, **t** (054) 33256
Ten days dedicated to the celebration of the strawberry harvest.

Kilmore Quay Seafood Festival, Kilmore Quay, Co. Wexford, **t** (053) 29922
A seafood celebration with horse races and music.

Wexford Hooves and Grooves Festival, **t** (053) 44634
Horse-racing and live music and street entertainment, in and around Wexford town.

Sandworld, Duncannon, Co. Wexford, **t** (051) 389 434
This international sand-sculpting event provides inspiration for castle-builders of all ages.

August

Blessing of the Fleet, Kilmore, Co. Wexford, **t** (053) 29922
An annual event to safeguard the fishing community when out at sea.

Kilmuckridge Mardi Gras Festival, Kilmuckridge, Co. Wexford, **t** (053) 30163
A fun non-traditional event.

Kilkenny Arts Festival, t (056) 775 2175, **www.kilkennyarts.ie**
One of Ireland's most important arts festivals, featuring opera performances, art exhibitions and music of all sorts, held during the last week of the month.

September

Blackstairs Blues Festival, Co. Wexford, **t** (054) 35364
An intimate blues music festival, best for teenagers and their parents.

October and November

Wexford Opera Festival, contact Wexford Festival Office, Theatre Royal, Wexford, **t** (053) 22400
A delightful event with an informal atmosphere, much loved by opera fans.

For up-to-date information on events, see www.southeastireland.com

Good to know...
Crossing Waterford Harbour
Waterford Harbour, between Co. Wexford and Co. Waterford in Munster (*see* pp.146–50), is a wide expanse of water. The quickest way to cross from Wexford to Waterford is via **Passage East Car Ferry** (**t** (051) 382 598, **www**.passageferry.com), not far from Arthurstown on the Wexford side.

There's not much in Rosslare Harbour, but you can catch trains and Bus Éireann coaches to other parts of Ireland from directly outside the ferry terminal, and also find taxis and buses that will take you to nearby Wexford.

By train Kilkenny Town is on the Waterford line from Dublin Heuston. Services are more frequent on the east coast line, from Rosslare and Wexford to Dublin, via Enniscorthy and other towns (*see* **www**.irishrail.ie).

Bike hire
The Bike Shop, 9 Selskar St, Wexford, **t** (053) 22514
Hayes Cycles, 108 South Main St, Wexford, **t** (053) 22462
JJ Wall, 86 Maudlin St, Kilkenny, **t** (056) 772 1236
Kenny's, Slaney St, Enniscorthy, **t** (054) 33255

Entertainment

The Sky and the Ground
South Main St, Wexford, **t** (053) 21273

This was once a shop and pub, and the present owners have left everything the way it was, including the groceries. Good traditional music is played here.

Shopping

Badger Hill Pottery
Enniscorthy, **t** (054) 35060

A place producing a range of attractive and original ceramics.

Cushendale Woollen Mills
High St, Old Rd, Graiguenamanagh, Co. Kilkenny, **t** (059) 972 4118

Handmade woollens, available from the mill's own shop.

Kilkenny Crystal
Rose Inn St, Kilkenny, **t** (056) 772 5132

Fine original glassware.

Kilkenny Design Centre
Castle Yard, Kilkenny, **t** (056) 772 2118

An excellent selection of crafts hailing from all over Ireland.

Kilkenny Irish Crystal
Canal Square, Kilkenny, **t** (056) 776 1377

The factory at Callan can be visited during the summer months.

Kiltrea Bridge Pottery Ltd
Kiltrea Bridge, Cairn, Enniscorthy, **t** (054) 35107

A place where you can watch clay earthenware being hand-thrown.

Nicholas Mosse Irish Country Shop
Bennettsbridge, Co. Kilkenny, **t** (056) 772 7505, **www**.nicholasmosse.com
Open Mon–Sat 9–6, Sun 1.30–5

This place produces what may be the loveliest pottery in Ireland: spongeware decorated with animals and flowers. Slight seconds are available, and there's an exhibition of pottery through the ages. Bennettsbridge is about 5 miles (8km) south of Kilkenny town.

Stoneware Jackson Pottery
Ballyreddin, Bennettsbridge, Co. Kilkenny, **t** (056) 772 7175

Attractive pottery recognizable by its swirly bright patterns.

TOURING TOWNS

Kilkenny

One of the most attractive medieval towns in Ireland, with a lovely old centre of cobbled streets and a lively atmosphere – if a bit too much traffic – Kilkenny makes a good place for a stop-over or base for exploring the region.

Things to see and do

Kilkenny Castle
The Parade, **t** (056) 772 1450
Open For tours daily Apr and May 10.30–5, June–Aug 9.30–7, Sept 10–6.30, Oct–Mar 10.30–12.45 and 2–5; pre-booking advised; closed Christmas and Good Fri

Adm Adult €5, child €2, family €11
Café in summer, children's play area, shop, art gallery, disabled access on ground floor

Children who like faery tales enjoy visiting this castle, built in the 12th century and remodelled in the Victorian era. From 1391 it was the main seat of the Butler family, who were earls, marquesses and dukes of Ormond, but the first castle here, still largely intact, was probably built about 1192. Acres of parkland surround it. Do have a look at the restored middle block of the castle.

Rothe House

Parliament St, **t** (056) 772 2893
Open Apr–Oct Mon–Sat 10.30–5 and Sun 3–5, Nov–Mar Mon–Sat 1–5
Adm Adult €3, child €1

A typical Tudor Kilkenny house built in 1594–1610 for merchant John Rothe, containing pictures and artefacts from Kilkenny's past, including fine oak furniture and paintings. A collection of period costumes and a large kitchen, bakery and brewhouse are also on view, and there's a good shop.

St Canice's Cathedral

The Close, Irishtown, **t** (056) 776 4971
Open Apr, May and Sept Mon–Sat 10–1 and 2–5, Sun 2–5; June–Aug Mon–Sat 9–6 and Sun 2–6; Oct and Mar Mon–Sat 10–1 and 2–4, Sun 2–4
Adm Cathedral: adult €3, 12–16s €2, under-12s free
Tower: adult €2, 12–16s €1.50, under-12s free
Shop, disabled access, guided tours by request

Kilkenny's atmospheric Norman-Gothic cathedral is the second-largest medieval church in Ireland. Completed in the 13th century, it still has some of its original carvings, and lovely, colourful stained-glass windows to look at. Next to the cathedral is a much older, 9th-century Irish round tower, which you can climb up in good weather, so long as you are steady on your feet and don't mind heights.

Did you know...?
Irish Protestants of the 18th century produced some very famous sons. The writer Jonathan Swift (1667–1745) went to school at Kilkenny College with fellow scholars William Congreve, the playwright, and the philosopher Bishop Berkeley, after whom Berkeley University, California, is named.

A story to tell...
The Kilkenny Cats

Some Kilkenny townspeople are said to have tied the tails of two cats together, and then watched them fight until only their tails were left behind. This – though some people say the story referred to warring Co. Kilkenny towns – is most often said to be the origin of the Irish saying, 'To fight like Kilkenny cats'. It's also why Kilkenny's hurling team, who have been many times All-Ireland champions, are known as 'The Cats'.

This limerick is about the cats –

There wanst was two cats of Kilkenny
Each cat thought there was one cat too many
So they fought and they fit
And they scratched and they bit
Til instead of two cats there weren't any.

Enniscorthy

Known for its river angling, craft studios, good restaurants and annual Strawberry Fair (*see* p.82), Enniscorthy is an excellent base from which to explore North Wexford. Its name has become synonymous with the craft of pottery, because one of Ireland's oldest potteries was established in the region more than 300 years ago. Several potteries in the area are open to visitors (*see* p.75).

Things to see and do

Friar Murphy Centre

Boolavogue, Ferns, Enniscorthy, **t** (054) 66898
Open May–Sept Mon–Sat 10–5, Sun 2–5
Adm Free
Picnic area, guided tours, craft shop, café

Next to an 18th-century farmyard is this restored thatched house with period furnishings and farm implements. Stories and pictures decorate the walls, and there are scenic views from the gardens.

National 1798 Centre

Millpark Rd, Enniscorthy, **t** (054) 37596, **www.1798centre.com**
Open Apr–Sept Mon–Fri 9.30–6, Sat and Sun 11–6 (last adm 5), Oct–Mar Mon–Fri 9.30–4, Sun 11–5
Adm Adult €6, child €3.50, family (2+2) €16
Gift shop, café, audio-visual show

Vinegar Hill, which lies outside Enniscorthy, was the site of the most important battle in Ireland's 1798 Rebellion (*see* p.36). This centre, near the battleground, tells the story of the rising and its aftermath via multimedia displays and interactive computers. The rebels' political strategy is conveyed via a chess game, in which 6ft (1.8m) chessmen represent political figures of the 18th century on a chequered floor – the 'king' on the Irish side is Wolfe Tone. A film relates how Wexford suffered 11 out of the 23 battles of 1798, and lost 20,000 people from a population of 120,000 over the course of 4 weeks. The enormity of this tragedy for the Irish people becomes all the more apparent when Ireland's losses are compared to the first 6 years of the French Revolution, which cost France's population of 30 million about 25,000 lives.

Wexford County Museum

Town centre, Enniscorthy, **t** (054) 35926
Open Feb–May, Oct and Nov daily 2–5; June–Sept Mon–Sat 10–5 and Sun 2–5
Adm Adult €4.50, child €1, family €11

Set in a magnificent Norman castle that was built in the 13th century by the Prendergast family, Co. Wexford's museum offers a fascinating insight into its agricultural, maritime, industrial, military and ecclesiastical history. Among the exhibits are commemorations of the uprisings of 1798 and 1916.

SPECIAL TRIPS

Irish National Heritage Park

Ferrycarrig, Co. Wexford, **t** (053) 20733, **www.inhap.com**
Getting there 2 1/2 miles (4km) north of Wexford off the Dublin road (N11)
Open Daily Mar–Oct 9.30–6.30 (last adm 5), Nov–Feb 9.30–5.30 (last adm 3)
Adm Adult €7.50, 13–18s €6, under-13s €3.75, under-4s free, student €6, family (2+3 under-18) €18; discounts in winter
Restaurant (with Celtic banquets on some evenings), picnic areas, shop, café, parking, walks, guided tours on request

Wexford's star attraction for children has won the European Year of the Environment award. Families can spend a whole day exploring 9,000 years of Ireland's history in this outdoor park, which shows how people lived in the Stone and Bronze ages and the Celtic, Early Christian and early-Norman periods. There are recreations of houses, communities and customs from 7000 BC to the arrival of the Normans in the 12th century, and of the ways in which the Celts, Vikings and Normans came together to create the unique Irish persona of today. Site attendants wear period costumes, and tell you all they can about how people lived. Children can explore all the replicas of historic homes freely, touching whatever they like.

A map shows you how to navigate the 35 acres of forest to each of 16 historical sites, designed by expert archaeologists. First you visit a site from the Mesolithic era, then move to an early farm where the crop-growing techniques of Neolithic times are displayed. Next is the Bronze Age, when more durable weapons and copper and bronze utensils were made. You can see pre-Celtic rituals and burials, and a re-created 'Stone Circle'. Then you walk into the Celtic era, and to the 4th century AD when Christianity came to Ireland, along with new foods, new cooking and water-milling methods, and writing. All this, plus the story of how Christian missionaries were sent here, is described inside a reconstruction of a 10th-century monastery. Nearby is a fascinating Viking home, with a shipyard and longboats for children to clamber over. Then there are round towers, which offered their owners some protection from Viking raiders, and then an early Norman castle and examples of the first Norman fortifications in Ireland.

At the end of your long walk, you may like to relax in the park's Fulacht Fiadh restaurant, which serves traditional Irish specialities – your children will enjoy a meal in the archaeologically themed surroundings, overlooking a *crannóg* (a round house on an island in a lake – an early Irish way of protecting oneself from intruders).

Kilkenny and Wexford songs to sing...
Bunclody, Kilkenny's the Best of Them All, Highland Paddy, Kelly from Killane, The Croppy Boy, Come to the Bower

Berkeley Costume and Toy Museum

Berkeley Forest House, New Ross, Co. Wexford, **t** (051) 421 361
Getting there In New Ross town
Open By appointment only **Adm** Adult €4, child €2

On display inside this house are 18th- and 19th-century costumes, beautiful embroidered textiles, dolls and toys, while outside are Victorian goat-carriages for children to ride in. The family of Bishop George Berkeley, after whom the California university town is named, own the property.

Dunbrody Abbey and Castle

Campile, New Ross, Co. Wexford, **t** (051) 388 603
Getting there 7 miles (11km) south of New Ross
Open Daily May–Sept 10–6
Adm Castle, maze, minigolf: adult €4, under-17s €2, family €10; Abbey: adult €2, under-17s €1, family €5
Maze, pitch'n'putt, picnic areas, tea room, craft shop, walks, free parking

Spend a quiet afternoon at this 13th-century Cistercian abbey while your children get lost in the yew-hedge maze and amuse themselves in the visitor centre and museum. A large dolls' house replicates Dunbrody Castle in miniature, and nearby is an excellent tea shop run by the Dunbrody Abbey Cookery Centre (**t** (051) 388 933), which offers day and evening cookery courses.

Dunbrody Heritage Ship

JFK Trust, South Quay, New Ross, Co. Wexford, **t** (051) 425 239, **www.dunbrody.com**
Open Daily Oct–Mar 10–5, Apr–Sept 9–6
Adm Adult €6.50, under-16s €4, family (2+3 under-16s) €18
Disabled access, guided tour, café and souvenir shop

Experience firsthand the conditions faced by Irish emigrants in the years after the Great Famine on this full-size replica of a 19th-century sailing ship moored at New Ross. You get your ticket for 18 March, 1849, and follow in the footsteps of emigrants bound for New York. Onboard, children find out what happened to those who went to America by ship in the 1840s. They may even meet the ship's captain, Mr Williams, or one of his crew or passengers, who will tell them in graphic detail what such a crossing was like. Cheer things up with a snack and hot drink in the more modern café, and check on the computer to see if any of your ancestors sailed to America.

Pirates Cove Adventure Golf and Fun Centre

Courtown Harbour, Co. Wexford, **t** (055) 25555
Getting there On the coast near Gorey, 31 miles (50km) north of Wexford by N11 (Dublin road)
Open Golf and Fun Cave: June–Aug daily 11–10; Sept–May bowling only Sun 2pm–late.
Adm Bowling: €21 for 1 hr, €11 for 1/2 hr
Golf: adult €5.50, child €4.20, family (2+2) €16.50, (2+3) €20
Fun Cave: €4.20 for 1hr
Picnic areas, coffee shop

The tropical gardens and waterfalls here create a magical atmosphere for children of all ages. Explore the Fun Cave (for 3–10-year-olds) or play golf in its adventure park (which includes a pirate ship).

Wexford Wildfowl Reserve

North Slob, Co. Wexford, **t** (053) 23129
Getting there 3 miles (8km) from Wexford via Curracloe or across Wexford Bridge and 8km northeast of Wexford town (signposted from Castlebridge Rd)
Open Daily mid-Apr–Sept 9–6, Oct–mid-Apr 10–5, closed Christmas Day (may be closed at other times for management operations). **Adm** Free
Guided tour on request, picnic area

The land spit known as the Wexford Slobs, on the north side of Wexford Harbour, is famous for the wild geese that winter there. Go birdwatching or explore the area on horseback; horses can be hired from Curracloe Equestrian Centre, *see* p.90.

Yola Farmstead Folk Park

Tagoat, Rosslare Harbour, Co. Wexford, **t** (053) 32611, **www.**geocities.com/wexgen
Getting there 2 miles (3km) south of Rosslare on N25
Open Mar, Apr and Nov Mon–Fri 10–4.30, May–Oct daily 10–5
Adm Adult €5, under-16s €2, family (2+4) €11
Crystal craft shop, children's playground, café

Step back to time when life was centred on the cycles of nature at this traditional Irish farmstead with thatched buildings, forge, church, schoolhouse, aviary and windmill. Kids can explore the enclosure for farm animals and rare breeds of poultry, and let off steam in the supervised play area. Take a stroll beside the flora and fauna of the past and find out about your own past at the genealogy centre.

AROUND AND ABOUT

Animal magic

Kia Ora Mini Farm

Courteencurragh, Gorey, Co. Wexford, **t** (055) 21166
Getting there 31 miles (50km) north of Wexford
Open Mid-Mar–Easter Sat and Sun 1–6, Easter–Sept hours variable, around 10–5.30, ring in advance
Adm €6 per person

Most animals are indoors here, so this is a good place to visit when the rain comes down. Tropical birds, fish, Jacob sheep, pheasants, deer, turkeys, mules and chipmunks are just some of those on show. Children can meet some in the play area, while you have coffee in the pleasant café. Santa Claus visits at Christmas time.

A story to tell…
The Witches of Wexford

It is whispered that there were, or are, witches in Kilkenny and Wexford. Some, of course, will have been of the good wise woman variety, but others may have been of the other sort. According to Irish tradition, there are still all kinds of good and bad beings out there, and you must be careful not to offend them. If you're untidy, dirty, discourteous, greedy or rude, you risk their ire. You need to have a few tricks up your sleeve to avoid spirits who mean you harm, or to counter their magic.

Christians had the Lord's Prayer and holy water as antidotes. Before that, the Irish used to carry a piece of iron or steel – a horseshoe or a fish hook – to protect them from supernatural powers. Salt and St John's Wort were said to counteract faery spells, and placing ash berries in a cradle would stop faeries from taking human babies and leaving one of their own (a 'changeling') in its place. Some Irish parents used to dress little boys as girls, as the faeries seemed to prefer stealing boys to girls.

One thing Irish country people knew better than to do, though, was to eat the faery food the Good People offered them, for if they ate even a morsel of it they would be trapped in Faeryland. If this happened, the horseshoe or bit of old iron could come in handy to wedge open the doorway of the faery fortress and make good an escape.

Nore Valley Park Open Farm

Bennettsbridge, Co. Kilkenny, **t** (056) 772 7229
Getting there 5 miles (8km) south of Kilkenny
Open Mar–Sept Mon–Sat 9–6
Adm €4 per person for a family with child over 2. Guided tour: adult €4.50, child €4.30
Café, shop, crazy golf, caravan and camping park

Children can help to feed lambs or kids and hold chicks and rabbits here, and a wooden American-style fort lets them watch the animals from up above. They can also enjoy a ride on a pony or donkey, have fun in a playground, sandpit and 'straw bounce', trundle off for a relaxed 2-mile (3km) walk by the river, picnic or have a home-baked scone in the café.

Bricks and mortar

Ballyhack Castle

Ballyhack village (off R733), Co. Wexford, **t** (051) 389 468
Getting there 12 miles (19km) north of New Ross
Open Daily mid-June–mid-Sept 10–6. **Adm** Free
Guided tours on request (pre-booking essential)

This tower-house stands on a steep slope overlooking Waterford Harbour. The Knights of St John built the castle in 1450. You'll also find the story of the marriage of Norman lord Strongbow to Aoife, daughter of the King of Leinster (*see* p.33).

Duiske Abbey and Abbey Centre

Graiguenamanagh, Co. Kilkenny, **t** (059) 972 4238
Getting there 12 miles (19km) north of New Ross
Open Mon–Fri 10–5, June–Aug also Sat and Sun 2–5
Adm Donations invited

A restored Cistercian abbey that was originally constructed in 1204. The abbey centre next door has a display of local historic artefacts, including some pieces of Christian art.

Jerpoint Abbey

Waterford Rd, Co. Kilkenny, **t** (056) 772 4623
Getting there Off N9, 2 miles (3.5km) from Thomastown and 11 miles (17km) from Kilkenny
Open Daily Mar–May 10–5, June–mid-Sept 9.30–6, Nov 10–4; rest of year groups only by appointment
Adm Adult €2.75, child €1.25, family €7
Shop, disabled access

This impressive 12th-century Cistercian abbey has a magnificent carved cloister arcade.

Tintern Abbey

Near Saltmills, Hook Peninsula, New Ross, Co. Wexford, **t** (051) 562 650
Getting there South of New Ross off R734 or off Wexford to Ballyhack road on R733, 20 miles (32km) west of Wexford
Open Daily mid-June–mid-Sept 10–6
Adm Adult €2, child €1, family €5.50

The tranquil grounds of this 13th-century abbey, with walled gardens, a battlemented bridge, ancient woods, a ruined church and a mill on a stream, are perfect for relaxation and peace.

Look at this!

Bród Tullaroan and Lory Meagher Heritage Centre

Tullaroan, Co. Kilkenny, **t** (056) 776 9202, **www.brodtullaroan.com**
Getting there 8 miles (12km) west of Kilkenny
Open Mar–Oct Mon–Fri and Sun 10–5, Nov–Feb Mon–Fri 10–4; Sat by appointment only
Adm Adult €4, family (2+4) €10
Children's play area, café, craft shop

Sports buffs might be interested to see the old home of a hurling hero of the 1920s, Lory Meagher. Bród Tullaroan is a thatched farmhouse built in the 17th century, and beside it is a museum on the history of Gaelic games in Kilkenny.

Duncannon Fort

Duncannon village, County Wexford, **t** (051) 389 454
Getting there 22 miles (35km) west of Wexford
Open Daily June–Sept 10–5.30
Adm Adult €4, child €2, family €10
Guided tours, café, shop, artists' studios, art centre

Older children will love exploring this intriguing 16th-century fortress built on a promontory at the mouth of Waterford Harbour. Built on top of a Celtic fort and Norman castle in 1588 in anticipation of the Spanish Armada, it is noted for its dry moat, exterior walls and shape. A lament is attached to Duncannon in which a 'croppy boy', who was betrayed, tried and hanged, is mourned by his mother.

Hook Lighthouse

Hook Head, Fethard, Co. Wexford, **t** (051) 397 055
Getting there R733 from New Ross or Wexford
Open Guided tours daily Mar–Oct 9.30–5
Adm Adult €4.75, student €3.50, 5–16s €2.75, under-5s free, family (2+2) €14
Restaurant, café, craft shop

The 13th-century circular Hook Lighthouse is the oldest lighthouse in the British Isles. It was first built when a Welsh monk named Dubhan was so appalled to see the bodies of shipwrecked sailors on the rocks that he began to shine a light here to help ships avoid disaster. An automated system now fills the almost intact stone lighthouse, perched on the tip of the Hook peninsula. You'll have to cover your ears if you find yourself below its foghorn when it sounds. The setting is magnificent, surrounded by roaring surf, and Hook Head is also a great place to spot seals and to hunt for fossils.

Irish Agricultural Museum

Old Farm Yard, Johnstown Castle, Co. Wexford, **t** (053) 42888
Getting there On N25 2 miles (3km) south of Wexford
Open June–Aug Mon–Fri 9–5, Sat and Sun 11–5, Apr, May and Sept–Nov Mon–Fri 9–12.30 and 1.30–5, Sun 2–5, Dec–Mar Mon–Fri 9–12.30 and 1.30–5
Adm Adult €5, child €3, family (2+4) €15
Grounds, craft shop, picnic area, café

Thousands of plant species are protected in the castle gardens here. Within the 50-acre grounds, the rustic farm buildings, dating from around 1810, house one of the best museums of rural life in Ireland, with old farm furniture, machinery and household implements. A permanent exhibit commemorates the Great Famine. Johnstown Castle was owned by the wealthy Grogan family, but its last owner left it to the state. The house is not open to the public.

Did you know...

During the 1798 Rebellion, which was inspired by the French Revolution, the United Irish rebels showed their allegiance to the cause by cropping, or cutting, their hair very short in the style of French revolutionaries. So people called them 'croppies', and a 'croppy boy' was a rebel for the cause of Irish independence.

Did you know...?

The saying 'by hook or by crook' relates to Hook Head peninsula and Crooke, across the bay near Waterford Town. It goes back to the 17th century, when Cromwell said that Waterford would be taken by assault at Hook in Wexford or at Crooke on the other side of the water.

Kennedy Homestead

Dunganstown, near New Ross, Co. Wexford, **t** (051) 388 264
Getting there 4 miles (6km) south of New Ross
Open Daily May and Sept 11.30–4.30, June–Aug 10–6, but check times before setting out
Adm Adult €2.50, child €1.50, family (2 + 3) €6
Visitor centre, museum, café, craft shop, picnic area, toilets, disabled access, parking

Dunganstown was the birthplace of Patrick Kennedy, great-grandfather of President John F. Kennedy, who left in 1848 for the United States. His house is long gone, but a plaque on the wall marks the spot. The road leading to it remains unchanged since Patrick senior walked down it to the famine ship. In the museum you learn how Patrick moved from being one of Ireland's poorest migrants to building a dynasty that became one of the most influential families in America. As it's told here, the tale ends with his most famous descendant taking office in the White House in January 1961 – only to be assassinated in Dallas in 1963. Admission also gives you reduced rates at the Kennedy Arboretum (*see* below) and Dunbrody Heritage Ship (*see* p.86).

Nature lovers

Dunmore Cave

Ballyfoyle, Co. Kilkenny, **t** (056) 776 7726
Getting there 7 miles (11km) north of Kilkenny
Open Daily Mar–mid-June 10–5, mid-June–mid-Sept 9.30–6.30, mid-Sept–Oct 10–5; Nov–Feb Fri–Sun and bank hols 10–5; last adm 1hr before closing
Adm Adult €2.75, 7–12s €1.25, under-7s free, family €7

A limestone cave with many strange rock formations. Visitors also learn all about a terrible Viking massacre that happened here in 928.

John F. Kennedy Arboretum

Near New Ross, Co. Wexford, **t** (051) 388 171
Getting there 7 miles (11km) south of New Ross
Open Daily May–Aug 10–8, Oct–Mar 10–5, Apr and Sept 10–6.30
Adm Free
Visitor centre, café, deck with picnic tables

Enjoy a peaceful morning or afternoon exploring these beautiful gardens, with 4,500 shrubs and forest plots covering 1,000 acres of Slieve Coillte.

Kilfane Glen and Waterfall

Kilfane, Thomastown, Co. Kilkenny, **t** (056) 772 4558
Getting there 11 miles (17km) south of Kilkenny off N9
Open July and Aug daily 11–6; other times groups by arrangement
Adm Adult €5.50, under-12s €4.50, family €15
Tea shop, guided tours, picnic area

This magical wild garden was created in 1790 and is perfect for letting children run free in lots of open space, although you'll need to watch younger and wilder kids on the clifftops. The cascading stream, hermit's grotto, waterfall and woodland trails combine to create a special atmosphere to feed the imagination and soothe the soul.

Kilmokea Country Manor and Gardens

Great Island, Campile, Co. Wexford, **t** (051) 388 109
Getting there 7 miles (11km) south of New Ross
Open Daily mid-Mar–4 Nov 10–5, and by appt
Adm Adult €5, 3–12s €2.50, under-3s free

Seven acres of delightful gardens behind a stone wall surround a restaurant and guesthouse (*see* p.111 and p.253). Children love these leafy grounds and little stone enclaves and bridges, but adults must accompany the very young, as space abounds for mischief and mishap near its stream. Freshly baked goods and lunch are available in a sunny conservatory, The Pink Teacup (open 12 noon–3pm), or dinner in the house's elegant dining room (open 7–10 pm), all made with produce from their organic gardens.

Woodstock Gardens and Arboretum

Inistioge, Co. Kilkenny, **t** (056) 854 9785
Open All year
Adm Free; car park €3.50 (season tickets available)

Walk among tall trees in the grounds surrounding the ruins of Woodstock House (1745). The gardens are currently being restored. Guided tours can be requested.

Sporty kids

Activity centres

Aqua Club

Kelly's Resort Hotel, Rosslare Strand, Co. Wexford, **t** (053) 32114

A club open to non-residents of the hotel, offering 2 swimming pools, a sauna, a Jacuzzi, a plunge pool, and more.

Shielbaggan Outdoor Education Centre

Ramsgrange, New Ross, Co. Wexford, **t** (051) 389 550

A centre offering sailing, kayaking, canoeing, archery, rock-climbing and more; residential and day courses are available.

Boat trips

Saltee Princess

Kilmore Quay, Co. Wexford, **t** (053) 29684, **t** (087) 252 9736.

Don't miss the chance from May to July to see Ireland's most famous bird sanctuary on the Saltee Islands, where puffins, gannets and many other birds and seals live.

Buckets and spades – Wexford's beaches

The Wexford coast has some of the best beaches in the whole of Ireland. To the north of Wexford town, the narrow R742 road winds behind the scenic east coast past many fine sandy beaches, especially around Courtown and Curracloe. The shallow waters of Curracloe and Ballinskar are where battle scenes for the film *Saving Private Ryan* were shot. On the other side of Wexford, meanwhile, Rosslare Strand, a long stretch of golden sand located to the west of Rosslare Harbour, is one of the most famous of all Irish beaches.

On the south coast, the working fishing village of Kilmore Quay is charming, with a number of thatched, white-washed cottages and a Blue Flag marina. Finding good food is no problem here if you like seafood. On the shores of Waterford Harbour, Arthurstown is a pleasant town by the water that also offers exceptional cuisine, and the clean beaches of Duncannon are popular with families.

Wexford Harbour Boat Club

Wexford, **t** (053) 22039

A boat club offering active families opportunities to water-ski and sail.

Fishing

Graiguenamanagh in Co. Kilkenny offers some of the best fishing to be had on the lower River Barrow.

The following shops can provide equipment and information:

Hook, Line & Sinker,
31 Rose Inn St, Kilkenny, **t** (056) 777 1699

Town and Country Sports Shop,
82 High St, Kilkenny, **t** (056) 772 1517

Horse-riding

Curracloe House Equestrian Centre

Curracloe, Co. Wexford, **t** (053) 37582 (call between 10 and 11.30am)

This equestrian centre provides excellent facilities for riders of all ages and levels of experience. Among the options are rides on Curracloe Beach or Wexford Slobs. Curracloe is 5 miles (8km) north of Wexford.

Glenmoor Riding School

Fethard-on-Sea, New Ross, Co. Wexford, **t** (051) 397 313

You can take riding lessons at this centre, or even own a pony for a week.

Walking

Guided walks of Kilkenny town are available through the tourist office. On summer evenings, walking tours of Wexford town are given by the local historical society; contact the tourist office for further details.

In the rest of the county, the Wexford Coastal Path stretches over 138 miles (221km), reaching all the way round the shoreline from Kilmichael Point to Ballyhack. Maps are available from the tourist offices.

Tynan Walking Tours

Depart from tourist office, Kilkenny, **t** (056) 776 3955

This firm runs walking tours of Kilkenny daily from mid-March to October, or on Saturdays only from November to mid-March. Note that winter times are subject to change, so be sure to check in advance. The tours cost €6 for adults, €5.50 for students.

KILDARE, LAOIS AND OFFALY

Kildare means 'church of the oak' in Irish, but when people think of County Kildare it is usually two things that come to mind – horses and St Brigid. Kildare town has Ireland's church most closely associated with Brigid and the order of nuns that followed her. As you enter the town on the busy main road from Dublin, though, you cannot see much of anything, so park your car and visit the Japanese Gardens and Tully Stud Farm before investigating the famous grassy heath known as the Curragh, Ireland's finest horse country and the site of its premier racecourse.

Neighbouring County Laois holds Stradbally, famed for its flower festival as well as what's known as the Stradbally Banshee (a white fairy lady). Every single Stradbally villager swore they heard a banshee one night about 70 years ago (her cry was likened to that of a hare being killed by a hound).

County Offaly is mostly bogland, but its western border is the River Shannon, so it's good for boat trips. Many Offaly people make a living via farming, turf-cutting or old trades like making clay pipes.

One interesting aspect of Kildare is that schools thrived here while most of Europe was stuck in the Dark Ages, and that long years later in the 19th century a similar pattern was repeated. In 1176 Strongbow, first Norman king of Leinster, gave a Norman called Fitzgerald the Maynooth area of Kildare, where his family later set up a Catholic college. This was closed with all of Ireland's Catholic monasteries by Henry VIII, so that later even the Fitzgeralds turned Protestant to survive. The only places where Irish priests could train at that time were the seminaries in the Catholic countries of Europe. Many of these were shut down in the French Revolution, but in 1793, while Britain was at war with France, the British government suddenly became concerned about appeasing Ireland's still-Catholic majority. So, when Irish Catholic bishops asked for permission to set up a seminary in Ireland, the government agreed, since they didn't want 'revolutionary' priests coming over from the continent. The son of Ireland's only duke, whom no one dared oppose, welcomed the seminary at Maynooth. This Duke of Leinster happened to be of the Fitzgerald family of Maynooth. Today the Fitzgeralds' ruined fortress still stands outside the main gates of Maynooth College.

Tourist information

Birr, Co. Offaly, **t** (0509) 20110
Clonmacnoise, Co. Laois, **t** (090) 967 4134
Kildare, Market House, Market Sq, **t** (045) 521 240
Naas, Co. Kildare, 38 South Main St, **t** (045) 898 888
Portlaoise, Co. Laois, **t** (0502) 21178
Tullamore, Co. Offaly, **t** (0506) 52617
www.shannonregiontourism.ie.

Special Events – Kildare, Laois, Offaly

January and February

Féile Bhríde, Kildare, **t** (045) 522 890
The festival of St Brigid, at St Brigid's Cathedral.

March

Kildare Drama Festival, Kildare, **t** (045) 521 907
A small but varied theatre festival.

May

Leixlip Salmon Festival, Co. Kildare, **t** (01) 624 3085
A festival including a mock battle with Vikings.

June

Derby Festival, Kildare, **t** (045) 521 858
A week of music, theatre and celebrations up to the big race at the Curragh (*see* p.96).

Music in Great Irish Houses, Co. Kildare, **t** (01) 278 1528
A festival held in various locations (*see* p.47).

July

Durrow Carnival Weekend, 10 Erkindale Drive, Durrow, Co. Laois, **t** (0502) 36327
Traditional music, dancing and street shows.

Maynooth Summer Festival, Maynooth, Co. Kildare
Music, drama, dance, football and a treasure hunt.

French Festival, Portarlington, Co. Laois, information from Portlaoise Tourist Office, **t** (0502) 21178
A celebration of the town's Huguenot ancestry.

August

Birr Vintage Week, Birr, Co. Offaly, **t** (0509) 20293
An 'Old Time Fayre', with art, antiques, parades, street entertainment, fireworks and singing.

Stradbally Steam Rally, Timahoe Rd, Stradbally, Co. Laois, **t** (0502) 25444
Bank-holiday steam engines, carousels and stalls.

October

Laois Arts Festival, Dunamaise Theatre and Centre for the Arts, Portlaoise, Co. Laois, **t** (0502) 63355
Traditional music, dancing and other events.

November

Slieve Bloom Storytelling Festival, Ardmore House, Kinnity, Co. Offaly, **t** (086) 278 9147.
Stories after sunset, in school halls and the like.

Getting there and around

By bus In Co. Kildare, Maynooth, Newbridge and Kildare town are stops on many routes into Dublin; services to Laois and Offaly are a bit less frequent.
By train Sligo trains from Dublin Connolly stop in Maynooth. Trains from Dublin Heuston on the Waterford, Cork, Limerick and Galway lines stop at Kildare town; Cork and Limerick trains go through Portlaoise, and Galway trains stop in Tullamore.
Bike Hire
M. Kavanagh, Railway St, Portlaoise, Co. Laois, **t** (0502) 21357

SPECIAL TRIPS

The Offaly town of Birr was one of many planned by Plantation landlords in the 17th century. An indelible graciousness has been left upon it by grand Georgian squares and streets. There's a fine walk by the river through the town, beside St Brendan's Church and the Convent of Mercy.

Birr Castle Demesne

Birr, Co. Offaly, **t** (0509) 20336, **www.birrcastle.com**
Open Mid-Mar–Oct 9–6 and Nov–mid-Mar 10–4
Adm Castle: adult €8, child €4.50, family €24
National Birds of Prey Centre: adult €5.50, child €3
Café, shop, picnics, guided tours, parking

The neo-Gothic castle is not open to the public, but 120 acres of 17th-century-style river gardens, parkland, a Historic Science Centre and a giant telescope are. Astronomical instruments and photographic and scientific equipment from the 1800s are exhibited along with information on the botanical work in the gardens, planted with Chinese and Himalayan trees.

Can you spot...?
Silken Thomas's tree? It's beside the path leading to Maynooth College. Garrett Óg Fitzgerald, son of the Earl of Kildare, refused to be ruled by Henry VIII, and instead wanted to rule all of Ireland himself. He was called Silken Thomas because he wore fine silk clothes, and he is said to have played his lute under this tree.

Larchill Arcadian Garden

Dunsaughlin Rd, Kilcock, Co. Kildare, **t** (01) 628 7354
Getting there N4, 19 miles (30km) west of Dublin
Open 12 noon–6 May bank hols, June–Aug Tues–Sun, Sept Sat and Sun; 6–23 Dec for Christmas grotto (3–7)
Adm Adult €7.50, 5–12s €5.50, under-5s free, family (2+4) €27.50

Your children may not appreciate that this is Ireland's last 18th-century *ferme ornée* or ornamental farm, but they will enjoy exploring the grounds to find the 10 follies that are set in its 63 acres of parkland. Among them are a circular Greek temple and fortress on an island in an 8-acre lake, and a tower lined with shells inside a walled garden. The follies lie on a circular walk through beech avenues, with wonderful views. Rare farm animal breeds graze among the follies, including Kerry Bog ponies, cattle, four-horned sheep, exotic wildfowl, puck goats and old breeds of pig. Larchill is said to have the largest number of rare breeds in Ireland.

A special grotto is created for children at Christmas time, with donkeys, farm animals, fairylights in the trees and hot chocolate and marshmallows after they meet Santa Claus.

AROUND AND ABOUT

Bricks and mortar

Castletown House

Celbridge, Co. Kildare, **t** (01) 628 8252
Getting there N4, 15 miles (24km) to the west of Dublin
Open Easter–Sept Mon–Fri 10–6, Sat and Sun 1–6, Oct Mon–Fri 10–5, Sun and bank hols 1–5
Adm Adult €3.50, child €1.25, senior citizen €2.50, family (2+3) €8.25
Guided tours, coffee shop, disabled access

Eighteenth-century paintings and furniture fill Ireland's finest Palladian country house, which was constructed in 1722 for the speaker of the Irish House of Commons.

A story to tell: St Brigid and Her Magic Cloak

There are actually two Brigids, although you'd think there were several, the name is spelled in so many different ways – Brigid, Brighid, Bridget, Bride, Brigit and more. All these names mean 'exalted one'. In Ireland Brigid is often called Mary of the Gael. In the days before Christianity, she was a goddess who looked after poets, scholars, metal-workers, blacksmiths and healers. People prayed to her for help with handicrafts, fertility, writing poems and when they wanted to learn something or heal someone. Some say she had two sisters with the same name, and the three became remembered as one goddess, named Brigantia and associated with nourishment and divination.

The first Brigid was a goddess of fire and illumination, linked with the festival of Imbolg on 1 February, celebrated by pre-Christian Celts to welcome the beginning of spring and say goodbye to winter. It was a time to encourage the new growing season; today it's St Brigid's Feast Day.

It is said that in County Kildare, in the house of the Daghda, leader of the Tuatha Dé Danaan, there was great rejoicing one morning, for at sunrise the Daghda's wife had given birth to Brigid. At that very moment a beautiful white cow appeared by the door in a puff of cloud, and her mooing made it clear she wanted to be milked. The cow nudged them to indicate that the new baby should have its milk to drink, and from then on that is what Brigid fed upon until she grew up into a lovely girl with cream-coloured skin, black curls and sky-blue eyes.

Every morning she lit the hearth fire. The house always seemed full of light whenever Brigid was about, for she sang songs and whispered little poems as she did her work, and always with a smile in her eye. The only trouble was, she had a habit of giving away whatever she saw in the house to any poor person who came asking, so that her mother had to keep an eye on her.

One day, the King of Leinster paused beside the family's well and asked Brigid for some water. She didn't know who he was, but she treated him kindly, as she did everyone, and the king was smitten by her beauty and gentleness of manner. Unable to forget her, he returned and begged for her hand in marriage. Brigid was shocked, as she had no desire to become the wife of a king; she had decided to dedicate her life to the needy. But the King would not take no for an answer, and so she was forced to agree to an engagement.

Then, she prayed to be made ugly so that the King would no longer want her. She fell ill and sallow-skinned, and her eyes lost their shine. When the King came to see her again, she told him she did not wish to marry him, so he freed her from the engagement and went away.

The next day her bloom and health returned, as did the bounce in her step. When the King saw her later, he was very downhearted he had lost her and asked if there was anything he could do for her.

'There is one thing,' she said. 'If you would give me a bit of land, just enough that my cloak will cover, then I will be happy indeed. Then I can start my church for the poor.' The King protested that her request was too little, but Brigid assured him it was enough. The King reluctantly agreed. Then Brigid spread out her cloak on the ground, and spread it, and spread it, for it kept growing, doubling in size, and then tripling, and quadrupling, until it covered the grasslands of the Curragh as far as the eye could see. The King couldn't help smiling, and gave her all the land beneath the cloak. Thereafter he often sought her advice, and they remained lifelong friends.

Brigid built a church of oak, a sacred tree to the druids, and 19 more women joined her to help minister to the poor. They dressed in simple white dresses so strangers would know them, and kept a fire going constantly at a shrine in a grotto in the grounds of what is now the Church of Kildare.

Clonmacnoise Monastic Site

Near Shannonbridge, Co. Offaly, **t** (090) 967 4114
Getting there 10 miles (16km) south of Athlone
Open Daily June–Aug 9–7, Sept–May 10–6
Adm Adult €5, under-12s €2, family (2+4) €11
Café, visitor centre, multi-lingual audio-visual show

Tour buses from Athlone depart daily for this peaceful monastic setting beside the Shannon. This beautiful Early Christian site was founded by St Ciaran in the 6th century, and includes the ruins of a cathedral, 8 churches (10th–13th-century) and 2 round towers. The original high crosses and grave slabs are on display in the Visitor Centre, where there is an audio-visual show as well as a number of exhibitions. The site gets very busy in the summer, so expect lengthy queues.

Durrow Monastery

Getting there Off the N52, 5 miles (8km) north of Tullamore, Co. Offaly

This ruined monastery is not open to the public, but you can stop to view the remains of the ancient buildings founded in the 6th century by St Columcille. It is famous for the 7th-century manuscript produced here, the *Book of Durrow*, which is now in Trinity College Dublin (*see* p.56).

A game for St Brigid's Day, 1 February

This game is based on a traditional ritual. Parents can take part, or children can take on the roles of the 'parents'. Younger children might just like to join in the active parts of the game.

One child plays Brigid, wearing a veil or scarf and carrying rushes or straw, and knocks three times on the closed door of a 'house' where the 'family' sits around a table on which food is spread. The house's boundaries can be marked however the players wish, so long as there is enough space for the participants to move around. Each time Brigid knocks, she calls, 'Kneel and let Blessed Brigid enter the house.' When she says this for the third time, those inside the house kneel and say, 'Oh come in, you are a hundred times welcome.'

The girl enters the 'house' and places her rushes under the table. The 'father' and 'mother' inside the house recite this verse: 'Bless us, O God, bless our food and drink, and deliver us from evil!'

Then everyone tries to run out of the house while Brigid tries to stop them. If she touches someone, they must sit down and stay where they are until someone who is free touches him or her so they are released. Brigid must chase and touch each person three times, before a player is 'out', at which point he/she must remain sitting until everyone else is caught. Once everyone is caught, they all say in unison '1-2-3', in order to give Brigid the chance to run away. Then each person must touch or tag her before they can return to the 'house'. Those freed first have to prepare Brigids seat and food at the table for her. Once Brigid is tagged by everyone, she can also return to the house.

Then the 'parent' gives a thanksgiving prayer and everyone eats the meal, after which they may plait the rushes or straw into a St Brigid's cross, sprinkle it with 'holy' water and hang it up where it will remain until the next St Brigid's Day.

Emo Court Demesne

Emo, Co. Laois, **t** (0502) 26573
Getting there 13 miles (20km) west of Kildare, just north of the N7 Portlaoise road
Open Grounds: daily until dusk; House: by guided tour 10.30–5 Mar–Oct Mon, mid-June–mid-Sept daily
Adm Adult €2.75, child €2

This lovely restored 18th-century house has an impressive domed rotunda room, but children may prefer the surrounding grassy spaces and walks near the large lough beyond it.

Leap Castle

Near Gloster, Co. Offaly, **t** (0509) 31115
Getting there 10 miles (16km) south of Birr
Open May–Sept daily 10–5, Oct–Apr by appointment
Adm Adult €6, child €2

This large, spooky tower was built by the Darby family around 1750. It was famous for its smelly ghost, one of many that inhabited it, until the castle was ruined in the Irish Civil War in 1922.

St Brigid's Church, Kildare

Kildare Town, Co. Kildare

This church is linked with St Brigid, since it was built on an ancient pagan site where Brigid and her nuns kept alight their eternal sacred fire.

Look at this!

Irish Pewter Mill and Moone High Cross Centre

Timolin, Moone, Co. Kildare, **t** (0507) 24164
Getting there 20 miles (32km) south of Naas
Open Showrooms/museum Mon–Fri 10–4.30, plus Sat and Sun 11–4 in summer; closed Good Fri, Easter Sun and Christmas. **Adm** Free

Watch pewter jewellery and tableware being made by hand at this 1,000-year-old mill.

Lullymore Heritage Park

Lullymore, Rathangan, Co. Kildare, **t** (045) 870 238
Getting there 17 miles (27km) north of Kildare
Open Easter–Oct Mon–Fri 9– 6, Sat and Sun 12 noon–6, Nov–Easter Mon–Fri 9–4
Adm €9 per person + €2 crazy golf, family (1+1) €14, (1+2) €18, (2+2) €22, €5 per extra child

This 13-acre community project has Early Christian, 1798 Rebellion and Famine exhibits, a train ride, a faery bower, a Celtic myth walk and a play area.

Rock of Dunamase

Getting there 3 miles (5km) east of Portlaoise, Co. Laois

Apparently a banshee and a hell hound (a big black mastiff with flaming breath) frequent this striking 13th-century ruin built on a Celtic ring fort. It has stood here since the Iron Age, and has been a ruin since Cromwell badly battered it in 1650.

Nature lovers

In the flood meadows on either side of the Little Brosna River in Co. Offaly, north of Tullamore, you can watch for golden plover, widgeon, whooper swans, curlews, lapwings and black-tailed godwits.

Bog of Allen Nature Centre

Lullymore, Rathangan, Co. Kildare, **t** (045) 860 133, **www.ipcc.ie**
Getting there 17 miles (27km) north of Kildare town
Open Mon–Fri 9.30–5, groups and tours Sat and Sun by appointment
Adm Donation €5
Restaurant, crafts and bookshop

Exhibits on the fauna and flora of the boglands and turf production since prehistoric times, together with an Irish farmhouse with a kitchen from the 1900s complete with turf fire.

Irish National Stud, Japanese Gardens and St Fiachra's Garden

Tully, Co.Kildare, **t** (045) 522 963/521 617, **www.irish-national-stud.ie**
Getting there Just south of Kildare town
Open Daily mid-Feb–mid-Nov 9.30–6
Adm Adult €9, student €7, over-12s €6.50, ages 5–12 €4.50, under-5s free, family (2+4) €20
Toilets with baby-changing room, restaurant, craft shop, Lego play area, disabled access, garden centre

Kildare is the hub of horse-lore in Ireland, and this museum on the stud farm's racehorses has a fine visitor centre. Also here is a real Japanese garden, which was created by landscape designer Tassa Eida, complete with Japanese plants, stone ornaments and a geisha house, which illustrates the symbolic journey of the soul through life on earth to eternity. St Fiachra's Garden is a new addition that uses rock and water to portray Ireland in its natural state.

> ***An Irish proverb –***
> ***A light heart lives long.***

Morell Open Farm

Turnings, Straffan, Co Kildare, **t** (01) 628 8636
Getting there 5 miles (8km) south of N4
Open Daily 10.30–5.30. **Adm** Adult €5, child €3
Picnic area, animal hospital, disabled access

Here your children can learn about many animal breeds and how they are looked after. They should wear wellies and old clothes so they can touch rare breeds of sheep, pigs, cows and exotic birds.

Sporty kids

Activity centres

Irish Canoe Union

t (01) 450 9838

Information on canoeing and courses.

Outdoor Education Centre

Birr, Co. Offaly, **t** (0509) 20029

A centre offering orienteering in the Slieve Bloom mountains.

Shannon Adventure Canoeing

The Marina, Banagher, Co. Offaly, **t** (0509) 51411

Canoeing trips on the Shannon.

Boat trips

Crean's Boat Hire

Vicarstown, Co. Laois, **t** (0502) 25189

Trips along the Grand Canal.

Lowtown Marine

Robertstown, Co. Kildare, **t** (045) 860 427

Rent a boat on the canal.

Fishing

For equipment and information on fishing spots in these counties, contact:

Mrs Travers, Curryhills House, Prosperous, Naas, Co. Kildare, **t** (045) 868 728
Ballaghmore Lake, Ballaghmore House, Borris-in-Ossory, Co. Laois, **t** (0505) 21366
J Hiney's Pub & Tackle, Main Street, Ferbane, Co. Offaly, **t** (0902) 54344.

Coarse fishing.

Did you know...?

William Hill-Walker, the founder of the National Stud at Tully, Kildare, in 1900, believed that astrology could influence the outcome of horse races, so he had skylights installed in his stables so that his horses could feel the influence of the stars.

Horse-racing

Look for upcoming events in the national newspapers, or in the racing calendar in the *Tourism Ireland Calendar of Events*, which is published every year.

The Curragh Racecourse

Co. Kildare, **t** (045) 441 205, **www.curragh.ie**

This is Ireland's foremost racecourse and the home of the Irish Derby, which is held every year in June.

Punchestown Racecourse

Co. Kildare, **t** (045) 897 704, **www.punchestown.com**

Horse-racing and events (occasionally family ones) take place here.

Horse-riding

Birr Equestrian Centre

Kingsborough House, Birr, Co. Offaly, **t** (0509) 21961

A centre offering riding and tuition in the Offaly countryside.

Fossey Mountain Springs Western Ranch

Timahoe, Co. Laois, **t** (0502) 36527

A Wild West-style trekking centre offering natural horsemanship courses.

Kill International Equestrian Centre

Kill, Co. Kildare, **t** (045) 877 208 or **t** (045) 879 9074

Getting there 5 miles (8km) east of Naas

A purpose-built centre, open all year, offering riding tuition for all ages and levels of experience, and very high-quality facilities.

Walking and cycling

The Slieve Bloom Way, a circular route extending 31 miles (50km), starts at Glenmonicknew Forest car park. Ask for information at any tourist office, or contact:

Slieve Bloom Walking Centre

Kinnitty Village, Co. Offaly, **t** (0509) 37299

Getting there 8 miles (13km) east of Birr

This centre offers a guided walking tours programme, maps and information.

Steam power!

Clonmacnoise and West Offaly Railway

Bord na Mona, Blackwater Works, Blackwater, near Shannonbridge, Co. Offaly, **t** (090) 967 4450

Getting there 18 miles (28km) north of Birr

Open Daily Apr–Oct 10–5, departures each hour

Tickets Adult €5.80, child €3.90, family €18

Guided train tours, picnic areas, café, craft shop, car park, disabled access

It's all aboard the Bog Train for a trip across Blackwater Bog to visit the turf bank and see a demonstration of turf cutting. This 6-mile (9km) circular journey through time takes about an hour, in the course of which your guide tells you everything you could want to know about the ecology of bogland. There is a daily bus tour to the site from Athlone.

Narrow Gauge Railway

Stradbally Hall, Stradbally, Co. Laois, **t** (0502) 25154

Getting there N7 from Dublin, near Portlaoise

Open Easter–Oct bank-hol Sun and Mon, plus special events; call for times

Adm Call for prices

Ireland's longest-established heritage railway.

Steam Museum

Lodge Park Heritage Centre, Straffan, Co. Kildare, **t** (01) 627 3155, **www.steam-museum.ie**

Getting there 5 miles (8km) south of N4 near Celbridge

Open June–Aug Weds–Fri, Sun and bank hols 2–6, May and Sept by arrangement

Adm Walled garden: adult €4, student €3, child €2, family €13

Disabled access, park, shop, tea room

Five big Victorian steam engines housed in this Gothic church actually work, as do the historic models of trains and plumbing systems. There is a hands-on area where kids can climb on everything, while outdoors you can visit an 18th-century walled garden and park.

MEATH AND LOUTH

Counties Louth and Meath are full of sites connected with Ireland's folklore and ancient history. The Boyne Valley and Hill of Tara in Meath are the most frequented tourist sites, but there are many others. Investigate the areas surrounding the Boyne Valley, Tara and Bective Abbey, or travel west to Oldcastle for ancient remains and delicious green spaces. Look around the peninsula beside the Irish Sea from Carlingford to Cooley Point, where there are many places to try watersports.

The Boyne Valley is the most important part of County Meath, historically and mythologically. It is filled with the homes of the Tuatha Dé Danaan, the Sidhe (pronounced 'shee') – or faeries, as they are better known. You will see the odd solitary 'faery tree' in the middle of a field, and 'faery raths' (grass-covered craters where ancient buildings stood) at nearly every turn in the road. The magnificent Hill of Tara has a great number of earthworks, including the ancient tomb or passage cairn of Niall and the Nine Hostages, and the Lia Fáil, the stone of destiny that is said to roar when the rightful king of Ireland sits upon it. Newgrange, ancient home of Aengus Óg, is also in the Boyne Valley.

This is also the place where one of the most important battles in Irish history was fought: the Battle of the Boyne, in July 1690, where Protestant William of Orange decisively defeated the Catholic James II (*see* p.35). On a lighter note, teenagers might like to know that Irish pop group The Corrs hail from Dundalk.

In County Louth, many sites are associated with the mythical hero-warrior Cúchulainn, and especially with the great Irish epic 'The Cattle Raid of Cooley', the *Táin Bó Cúailgne*. It is set in the Cooley Mountains in the northern part of the county, as is *Muirtheimhne*, where Cúchulainn is supposed to have been born. The county's name comes from the Tuatha Dé Danaan sun god Lugh of the Many Talents, who some stories claim was also the father of Cúchulainn. Louth village itself was a centre of a Lugh cult in St Patrick's time, and Louth also has a claim to be the county where St Brigid was born (at Faughart Hill), rivalling County Kildare for the honour.

Tourist information

For a full list of tourist information offices, *see* www.eastcoastmidlands.ie

Bru na Boinne, Donore, Newgrange, Co. Meath, **t** (041) 988 0305
Carlingford, Co. Louth, **t** (042) 937 3033
Drogheda, Co. Louth, **t** (041) 983 7070
Dundalk, Co. Louth, **t** (042) 933 5484
Kells, Kells Heritage Centre, **t** (046) 924 7840
Trim Visitor Centre, Co. Meath, **t** (046) 943 7227

Getting there and around

By bus Bus Éireann buses service both counties. An extensive timetable is available from Bus Éireann offices in Drogheda (**t** (041) 983 5023) and Dundalk (**t** (042) 933 4075). For more detailed information on bus services, *see* **www.buseireann.ie**.

By train The main Dublin–Belfast line runs through Drogheda and Dundalk. Trains run westward from Dublin to the midlands. For a full timetable, call **t** (01) 836 6222 or see **www.irishrail.ie**

Bike Hire

Bike hire is available from
Irish Cycle Hire, Ardee, Co. Louth, **t** (041) 685 3772
Newgrange Bike Hire, Co. Meath, **t** (086) 069 5771

Shopping

Bookwise Booksellers

Kennedy Rd, Navan, Co. Meath, **t** (046) 902 7722

A useful shop selling maps, guidebooks and books on Irish history.

Courtyard Craft Centre and Café

Cookstown House, Kells, Co. Meath, **t** (046) 924 0346

This is a good place to come to find locally hand-crafted ceramics, linen, textiles, woodwork, glass, jewellery, baskets and metal-work, and it has its own café.

Maguire's

Hill of Tara, Co. Meath, **t** (046) 902 6205

A shop selling Celtic theme and mythology books – including some aimed at children – plus Aran sweaters, crafts and jewellery. The café serves home-made scones.

Trim Visitor Centre

Mill St, Trim, Co. Meath, **t** (046) 37227, **www.meathtourism.ie**

Handmade silver jewellery, ceramics, textiles, leather goods, crystal glass and soaps.

Special Events – Meath and Louth

May–June

Dundalk International Maytime Festival, Dundalk, Co. Louth, **t** (042) 933 5253

Art, theatre, dancing, concerts, sport and events for children.

June

Moneley Oyster Pearl Regatta, Carlingford, Co. Louth; contact Dundalk and Carlingford Sailing Club, **t** (042) 937 3238

Races, held late in the month.

Blackrock Annual Raft Race, promenade/beach, Blackrock, Co. Louth, **t** (042) 932 1098

A local event with carnival and fancy dress.

Laytown Races, Laytown, Co. Meath, **t** (041) 984 2111

July

Kells Heritage Festival, The Courthouse, Headfort Place, Kells, Co. Meath, **t** (046) 924 7840

Crafts, art, walking tours and other attractions.

Le Chéile, Oldcastle, Co. Meath, **t** (049) 854 2197 **www.lecheile.com**

A mixed festival of arts and music.

Loughcrew Garden Opera, Loughcrew Historic Gardens, Oldcastle, Co. Meath, **t** (049) 854 1356, **www.loughcrew.com**

August

Carlingford Oyster Fest, Carlingford, Co. Louth, **t** (042) 937 3033

An oyster festival with arts, crafts and family fun.

Moynalty Steam Threshing Festival, Moynalty, near Kells, Co. Meath, **t** (046) 924 4390

A traditional farming festival with vintage machinery, together with ploughing, threshing and tilling demonstrations.

September

Carlingford Medieval Weekend, Carlingford, Co. Louth, **t** (042) 937 3033

Knights on horseback, battle reenactments, dancing and music. Local people dress up and the town is transformed into a medieval marketplace.

October

O'Carolan Harp Cultural and Heritage Festival, O'Carolan College, Nobber, Co. Meath, **t** (046) 905 2115

A celebration of Turlough O'Carolan, the blind harpist/composer/poet born in Nobber in 1670.

SPECIAL TRIPS

The Causey Experience

Lily or Angela Murtagh, Girley, Fordstown, Navan, Co. Meath, **t** (046) 943 4135, **www.causeyexperience.com**
Getting there About 8 miles (12km) west of Navan, south of Kells, on R164
Open Apr–Oct Sat 2–8, other times by arrangement
Adm Prices vary
Entry includes meals, tuition and Irish dancing; weekend camps available for teenagers.

This is a truly educational day out for children, as the family-owners of this farm, located just outside Kells in Co. Meath, recreate and offer a hands-on experience of Irish traditional country life. When you arrive, the matriarch of the Murtagh family, Lily, welcomes you with her homemade brown bread and scones. Ask her whatever you want to know about Ireland, whether it's the old mythologies or how people used to run a farm. If you have chosen to simply visit the farm rather than trek on the land, her husband, Tom, will take you with him on his tractor to cut turf. Upon returning to the stone cottage that has been especially converted for visitor activities, you don an apron and learn how to make the perfect brown bread. After that their son Matt will show you how Chip the sheepdog rounds up sheep, cattle or even Connemara ponies, and the Murtaghs' son-in-law Eoin Carton demonstrates how to hurl and shows how the hurley and ball, or *sliothar*, are made. Maybe you'll milk a cow or pair up to make *Sugán* rope out of straw. Lessons in goatskin drum (or *bodhrán*) making and dancing follow.

Your break for afternoon tea will take place somewhere in the midst of all this activity, and at the end of your day you will have a delicious 4-course evening meal with the family. By this time you will have picked up a few Irish words to include in your chatter with the Murtaghs and loosened up enough to enjoy the lively *ceilidh* that rounds off the day.

Bring a change of clothing and shoes, as you may get muddy and wet. For the geography trek, bring a packed lunch, raingear and old shoes or waterproof boots. The Murtaghs are flexible and friendly, so if you'd prefer a shorter visit than this one, simply let them know.

Loughcrew

Loughcrew Historic Gardens

Oldcastle, Co. Meath, **t** (049) 854 1060, **www**.loughcrew.com
Getting there 3 miles (5km) from Oldcastle off the Mullingar road
Open 17 Mar–Sept daily 12.30–5, Oct–16 Mar Sun and bank hols 1–4
Adm Garden and St Oliver Plunkett Church: adult €6, child €3, family €18
Book- and gift shop, parking, tea room, disabled access, garden guide for walks in area available

Beside Loughcrew Cairns, Charles and Emily Naper (who conduct residential courses in gilding) have restored these 17th–19th-century gardens to their former grandeur. They have also added touches that will appeal to children, such as the 'Celtic Legend' trail, watermill cascade, nature and history trails and fairy grotto. It is a wonderland for children, but adult supervision is needed at all times, for the grounds are extensive and there are many water features to fall into and plenty of meandering paths on which to get lost. Within the grounds you can picnic, play outdoor games or investigate the family church and tower-house of St Oliver Plunkett, among 350-year-old yews and many other varieties of trees. The modern entrance lodge with its comfortable, tasteful café is inviting and very much in keeping with its surroundings.

St Oliver Plunkett was a 17th-century Catholic archbishop who was hanged, drawn and quartered at Tyburn in London for going against the anti-Catholic laws of his time. His supporters managed to grab hold of his head, which after a long and complicated journey eventually ended up in St Peter's Church in Drogheda, where it is displayed as a relic. He was made a saint in 1975.

Loughcrew Cairns

Believed to be a Stone Age cemetery (3000 BC), this has around 30 passage tombs similar to the one at Newgrange, all on a hill called *Sliabh na Caillí* (the Hill of the Hag) in northwest Co. Meath. The best-preserved tomb is that of Ollamh Fodhla, believed to have been a poet-king at Tara around 1300 BC. The mound is known by local people as 'the witch's cave'; they say she will put a curse on those who enter it. Access to the cairns is steep, so it's not great for a hike with toddlers. Richard Marsh (*see* p.26) leads tours around the site.

Newgrange and Knowth

Brú na Bóinne (The Boyne Valley) Visitor Centre

Donore, Co. Meath, **t** (041) 988 0300
Getting there 2 miles (3km) off N51, 8 1/2 miles (13km) west of Drogheda
Open Daily Mar and Apr 9.30–5.30, May 9–6.30, June–mid-Sept 9–7, mid–end Sept 9–6.30, Oct 9.30–5.30, Nov–Feb 9.30–5; last admission 1hr before closing
Adm Centre only: adult €2.75, child €1.50, family €7; Centre and Newgrange: adult €5.50, child €2.75, family €13.75
Centre and Knowth: adult €4.25, child €1.50, family €10.50
Centre, Newgrange and Knowth: adult €9.75, child €4.25, family €24.25
Tourist office, café-restaurant, parking

Newgrange is Ireland's best-known prehistoric monument. Built between 3500 BC and 2700 BC, 500 years before the Egyptian pyramids and 1,500 years before Stonehenge, it fills almost a full acre of ground. Made of white quartz and granite, it is 36ft (11m) tall and has a 6-ton capstone, with other stones weighing up to 16 tons each. Inside it, tri-spiral and other designs such as chevrons and diamonds are carved into the stone. In Irish folk tales, this is the home of Aengus Óg, the Tuatha Dé Danaan god of love and birds.

All traffic for Newgrange is directed to the centre, eliminating direct access to it or to the similar nearby prehistoric sites of Knowth and inaccessible Dowth (which are currently being excavated). Visitors register at the centre for tours to Newgrange and/or Knowth, where they are taken by minibus. In summer the wait can be as long as 3 hours for a 1-hour tour (for a maximum of 25 minutes). Exhibits at the centre include a 7-minute introductory audio-visual show, and a walk-through replica of Newgrange with a simulation of the winter solstice.

Did you know...?
Aengus Óg, the ancient Irish god of love who lived at Newgrange, was always surrounded by birds, and he fell in love with a woman who was turned into a fly in one of her lives.

A story to tell: The Burning of the Hill of Tara

In the days when the Tuatha Dé Danaan (*see* p.163) roamed the earth freely, Aengus the Young (Aengus Óg), had his home at Newgrange, while other Tuatha Dé lived on high places such as the Hills of Tara and Uisneach. Then ordinary humans came along and took these over, with their High Kings. The Tuatha fought many battles, first against cruel magical beings that sought control of Ireland and later against humans, with whom they called a truce. The Tuatha agreed to let the humans take the upper surface of the world, while they themselves chose to move into the hills and the hidden realms of the Otherworld.

But there were some who disagreed with this truce, and did whatever they could to cause mischief for the upper-world dwellers. For a time, on every Samhain (Halloween) night an invisible enemy would burn down the palace at Tara. No one ever saw the enemy because every time it struck, they were fast asleep. All anyone could remember was hearing the most beautiful flute music and awakening in the morning to see the palace burned to a crisp. This was around the 2nd century AD, and in those days the best palaces were made of wood, so nothing could stop them from burning down. At the time Ireland's highest king was Conn of the Hundred Battles – so named because he had won that many battles without being injured, making him the greatest warrior of Ireland. So on Samhain, Conn assembled his best warriors at Tara to protect the palace. However, no one could ever stay awake long enough to even see who their attacker was, much less defeat him.

One year, Conn's most powerful warrior came from the west of Ireland to defend Tara. His name was Goll mac Morna (the 'One-eyed son of Morna'); he had been called Aed ('fire'), but was renamed Goll after he lost an eye in a battle between his men and the Fianna, when he slew the Fianna leader Cumall. Since then Goll had presided over the Fianna lands in eastern and southern Ireland. Their rightful leader, Cumhall's young son Finn, had been in hiding since his father's death because Goll's warriors, the Fir Bolg from Connacht, had sworn to kill him.

Now, this Samhain a great feast was being held at Tara, and again the assembled warriors awaited the attack. Just then there was a pounding on the gate of the palace, and in swept a tall, handsome young man with hair like spun gold.

'I am Finn, son of Cumhall,' he said. 'Since my father was leader of the Fianna, it is right that I should be leader, now that I am of age.'

Conn knew that if he didn't make Finn leader of the Fianna, Finn's faction would revolt, and there would be civil war. But if he took the leadership away from Goll, the Morna faction would revolt.

So Conn said, 'Not even the great Goll mac Morna can stop Tara from burning. Finn, you may be leader if you can prevent it.'

Soon the faery flute was heard and one by one each warrior fell snoring on the ground. Last to fall was Conn of the Hundred Battles – except for Finn, who had prepared himself with treasures from a crane-skin bag left to him by his father. It was actually made from the skin of Aoife, a warrior woman, who had been shape-changed into a crane by an enemy and then died. In the bag was a cap of silence and a poisonous spear.

Finn placed the cap on his head so as not to hear the music and watched as one of the Sidhe, named Aillén, opened his mouth and blew a flame at the palace. Quickly Finn caught the fire in a magic cloak and threw the fire back to Aillén, who fled in panic. Finn then hurled the magic spear at him, and it caught and slew him before he could return to the safety of the Otherworld. And that's how Finn became leader of the Fianna, so that now there are stories about Finn McCool and the Fianna all over Ireland.

The Battle of the Boyne Battlefield

t (041) 984 9873; access by guided tour only
Getting there Near Tullyallen, 2 1/2 miles (4km) west of Drogheda (signposted)

The children may wonder why you have brought them to see this green field when the country is covered in similar acres of verdant pasture, but this is no ordinary field. Here, in July 1690, William of Orange defeated the deposed Catholic King James II, and secured the Protestant succession to the British throne. The battle soon entered into Protestant mythology and William of Orange became an Ulster Loyalist hero. This turning point in Irish history is commemorated annually in Northern Ireland on 12 July (*see* p.203). At the site, there is a small monument.

Newgrange Farm

Near Slane, Co. Meath, **t** (041) 982 4119, **www**.newgrangefarm.com
Getting there 8 1/2 miles (13km) west of Drogheda on N51
Open Easter–Aug; call for days and times
Adm Adult €6, €5 per person in a family group
Café, disabled access, picnic areas, gift shop, pets' corner, rural life museum

This working farm offers tours around its 17th-century buildings and herb garden, and you can see vintage farm machinery and crops, and hold and feed poultry and farm animals. The café serves tasty home-made soups and desserts.

Stephenstown Pond and Agnes Burns Visitor Centre

Knockbridge, Co. Louth, **t** (042) 937 9019
Getting there 4 miles (6km) west of Dundalk
Open Daily Apr–Oct 9–8.30, Nov–Mar 9–4.30 (In winter hours may vary slightly)
Adm Free; parking €2
Children's playground with safety matting, picnic facilities, coffee and crafts shops, disabled access

Five acres of woodland, water walkways, decks for fishing and a pond with wildlife surround this 18th-century cottage where the sister of Scotland's national poet, Robert Burns, lived for nearly 20 years. Inside the period-furnished cottage are artefacts and information on animals, birds and local history, as well as on the poet's life and works. Home-cooking and cakes are available in the café.

AROUND AND ABOUT

Animal magic

Grove Gardens Tropical Bird Sanctuary and Mini Zoo

Fordstown, Kells, Co. Meath, **t** (046) 943 4276
Getting there About 5 miles (8km) south of Kells
Open Feb–Oct daily 10–6. Special activities at Easter and Christmas; call for details
Adm Adult €6, child €3.50, family €20
Tea room, barbecue and picnic areas, treehouse, summerhouse, shop, garden centre

Grove Gardens have four acres of gardens with one of Europe's biggest collections of clematis and climbing roses. Children will like the exotic and rare birds from around the world and the 10-acre enclosure full of friendly animals to meet, plus the soccer pitch where they can play.

Bricks and mortar

Dunsany Castle

Dunsany, Co. Meath, **t** (046) 902 5198
Getting there 10 miles (16km) south of Navan
Open Call for tour times and and open days
Adm Varies

Today this castle (hidden by a stone wall and parkland) is inhabited by the 20th lord of the estate, the artist Edward Plunkett, who inherited it after the death of the writer Lord Dunsany. It includes a 12th-century kitchen, a vaulted hall, a drawing room with fine plasterwork, family portraits, a distinguished library and the writing table where Lord Dunsany and writers like poet Frances Ledwidge worked.

Slane Castle

Slane, Co. Meath, **t** (041) 988 4400
Getting there 8 1/2 miles (13km) west of Drogheda
Open Mid-May–early Aug Mon–Thurs and Sun 12 noon–5 (call ahead to check times)
Adm Adult €7, child €4, family €20

This castle sits on top of the Hill of Slane, where a story claims St Patrick lit an Easter (Paschal) fire before Laoghaire, the High King, lit his Beltaine fire on the Hill of Tara. This gesture of defiance was a sign of the impending takeover of the High Kings' position by Christianity. In 1991, a fire gutted the interior of the 18th-century castle, including its fine ballroom ceiling, and it is not open to visitors. The grounds, however, contain a natural amphitheatre where the Rolling Stones, Robbie Williams, U2, REM and others have graced the stage, and occasional 'medieval festivals' occur; *see* **www**.mcd.ie

Trim Castle

Mill St, Trim, Co. Meath, **t** (046) 943 8619
Getting there 9 miles (14km) southwest of Navan
Open May–Oct daily 10–6
Adm Adult €1.50, child €0.75, family €4.25; with tour of keep: adult €3.50, child €1.25, family €8.25
Craft shop

Did you know...?
There were two great divisions of the year in the old Celtic calendar – Oíche Bheáltaine, the eve of 1 May (Beltaine), and Oíche Shamhna (Samhain or Halloween). On these two nights gateways between this world and the Otherworld are open. One gateway is the Hill of Tara.

Children need to be well supervised here, as there are all sorts of lumps and bumps in this part-restored ruined castle and grounds. Little ones might find the audio-visual show a bit grizzly. Trim Castle was on the farthest edge of the Pale, the area the Anglo-Normans ruled, and was the seat of a notorious 12th-century Norman warlord, Hugh de Lacy.

Old Mellifont Abbey

Near Drogheda, Co. Louth, **t** (041) 982 6459
Getting there 4 miles (6km) west of Drogheda
Open Daily May–mid-June and mid-Sept–Oct 10–5, mid-June–mid-Sept 9.30–6.30
Adm Adult €2, child €1, family €5.50

St Malachy of Armagh founded the first Cistercian monastery in Ireland here in 1142. Families can explore the site and visitor centre.

Look at this!

Drogheda Heritage Centre

Mary St, Drogheda, Co. Louth, **t** (041) 983 1153
Open Tues–Sat 10–5, Sat and Sun 2–6
Adm Adult €3.17, child €1.90, family (2+3) €7.62
Craft shops, café, disabled access, parking nearby

This wonderfully informative centre spans eight centuries of Drogheda life in a way both children and adults will appreciate. Families are invited to don period costumes and step back in time. Less pleasant aspects of history, such as the Battle of the Boyne and Cromwell's bloodthirsty activities (he killed 3,000 people in the town in 1649), are brought to life via a chilling audio-visual display.

Hill of Tara

t (046) 902 5903 or **t** (041) 988 0300
Getting there About 5 miles (8km) south of Navan off N3
Open All year; call for details of guided tours

Centuries ago this hill was the social and political centre of Ireland's nobility (*see* p.100). Today it's covered in grass, but you can see the sites of the circular dwellings of Cormac mac Airt and Gráinne, and the cairn, said to be the oldest of its kind in Ireland, where the sons of Uisneach are said to be buried and where there may be an opening into the Otherworld of the faeries. A Lia Fáil stone here was reputed to roar whenever the rightful heir to the High Kingship sat upon it, but whether it is the true Lia Fáil is another matter, as some say the original was stolen and became the 'Stone of Scone' on which Scottish kings were crowned, now in Edinburgh.

Kells Heritage Centre

Headfort Place, Kells, Co. Meath,
t (046) 924 7840
Getting there 10 miles (16km) to the northwest of Navan
Open May–Sept Mon–Sat 10–5, Sun and bank hols 1.30–6; Oct–Apr Tues–Sat 10–5
Adm Adult €4, child/student €3, family (2+2) €12
Gift shop

There's a fine Celtic High Cross in the grounds of this centre, while inside there are stone carvings, metal-work and a facsimile of the *Book of Kells*. Information on local sites is also available.

Ledwidge Cottage Museum

Janeville, Slane, Co. Meath, **t** (041) 982 4544
Getting there 8 1/2 miles (13km) west of Drogheda
Open Daily 10–1 and 2–5.30
Adm Adult €2.50, child €1, family €6.50

Frances Ledwidge (1887–1917) was a nature poet who lived in this stone cottage in the heart of the Boyne Valley, which is kept today as it was then. Ledwidge once got a job in Dublin, but he grew so homesick that one night he walked all the way back to Slane under the light of a full moon, neglecting to tell anyone he was going home. Ledwidge died as a soldier in World War I. Contact Betty Tallon on **t** (041) 982 4544 for details of the Ledwidge Day celebration in July.

Millmount Museum and Martello Tower

Drogheda, Co. Louth, **t** (041) 983 3097
Open Mon–Sat 10–5, Sun and bank hols 2–5
Adm Museum and Tower: adult €5.50, child €3, family €12; reduction for groups
Craft and genealogy centres, restaurant

This multi-purpose museum in an 18th-century military stronghold in Drogheda town houses a folk kitchen, medieval room, geological curiosities and exhibits on local history. There's also a good view over Drogheda and much of the Boyne Valley from its tower.

Monasterboice Round Tower

Near Drogheda, Co. Louth
Getting there 5 miles (8km) north of Drogheda

The ruins of this 5th-century monastery, amid fields just off the N1 road, contains a perfect Celtic high cross, known as Muireadach's Cross.

Proleek Dolmen

Cooley Peninsula, Co. Louth
Getting there About 4 miles (6km) north of Dundalk just east of N1, on R173

This is one of the most impressive of Ireland's late-Neolithic portal tombs (*c.*2500–2000 BC). Its capstone weighs 40 tons and is one of around 350 dolmens spread all over Ireland that are said to be 'Gráinne and Diarmuid's bed' (*see* p.184).

Nature lovers

Bective Abbey

Bective, Co. Meath, **t** (046) 943 7111
Getting there About 5 miles (8km) south of Navan on the Trim road

Stop for a picnic, a runaround or a peaceful walk around the ruins of Ireland's second Cistercian monastery, built in 1147. You can lunch overlooking the Boyne and then play hide and seek, but keep an eye on toddlers; most ruins have stone steps and precipices, and this one also has a river flowing by the hillock on which the abbey sits.

Cooley Hills

Cooley Peninsula, Co. Louth

It is within these hills that much of the action of the famous Irish epic poem 'The Cattle Raid of Cooley' – the *Táin Bó Cúailnge*, which is more often referred to as *The Táin* – took place. Visitors can follow a 'Táin Trail' and find many landmarks that are mentioned in the 12th-century book, with its battles between Conchobar, Cúchulainn and Queen Maeve. To get around the peninsula by car, you need to take the R173 road from Dundalk to Carlingford.

A traditional recipe – Irish barm brack

Every St Brigid's Eve (31 January), homemakers throughout Ireland would make a cake called barm brack. The same cake is also sometimes made for Halloween, but with a ring added into the mix too – so that whoever finds it gets to make a wish.

Ingredients

450g/1lb/3 1/2 cups of flour
pinch of salt
1 tsp mixed spice
15g/1/2oz/1 tbsp fresh yeast
1 tsp sugar
300 ml/1/2 pt/1 1/4 cups of warm water
85g/3oz/6 tbsp of butter
2 eggs
30g/1 oz/2 tbsp of candied peel
110g/4 oz/3/4 cup of raisins
110g/4 oz/3/4 cup of sultanas
110g/4 oz/3/4 cup of currants
110g/4 oz/1/2 cup of castor sugar
For glaze, 2 tbsp of castor sugar, and 1 tsp water

This makes 2 bracks, which take about 3 hours to make, although the mixing up does not take too long. Cream the yeast with a teaspoon of sugar. Add water. Sieve the flour with salt and mixed spice, and mix to a stiff dough with the yeast mixture. Knead until smooth and springy for about 5 minutes. Leave this in a bowl covered with a cloth in a warm place for 1 hour or until it has doubled in size.

Now add beaten eggs, fruit, sugar and melted butter. Beat it all together well. Half-fill 2 greased bread tins with the mixture and put to rise in a warm place, covered with a cloth. Leave for approximately another hour to rise to the top of the tins. Have ready a moderately hot oven, at 190°C, 375°F or Regulo 6. Bake for approximately 50mins or until it's fairly firm and brown.

To make the bracks gleaming brown, dissolve 2 tablespoons of sugar in 4 teaspoons of water over heat, boil for half a minute, and then brush this glaze over the bracks as they come out of the oven. Once they cool, they're ready to enjoy.

Thanks to Myrtle Allen for her permission to use the above recipe from The Ballymaloe Cookbook, *by Myrtle Allen, Gill and MacMillan Ltd.*

Faughart Hill

Faughart, Co. Louth

Getting there Just north of Dundalk off N1

St Brigid is supposed to have been born here, and to have founded a church on this hill. Beside the church you can see the grave of Edward Bruce, the brother of King Robert the Bruce of Scotland, who attempted to become king of Ireland and died here in 1318.

Knockabbey Castle and Gardens

Louth, Co. Louth, **t** (01) 677 8816, **www**.knockabbeycastle.com

Open May–Sept Tues–Sun and bank hols 10.30–5.30; groups by appointment

Adm Gardens: adult €6, child €4, family (2+2) €16 Tower-house and gardens: adult €10, child €6, family (2+2) €28

The approximately thirty acres of medieval and Victorian water gardens surrounding this privately occupied tower-house were begun in 1032. Inside is a display room that informs visitors about its history.

Sporty kids

Activity centres

Carlingford Adventure Centre

Thosel St, Carlingford, Co. Louth, **t** (042) 937 3100

Open All year

This centre offers professionally supervised windsurfing, sailing, tennis and canoeing lessons, as well as tours, hiking and a selection of other activities. Beginners' courses are available on a daily or half-day basis, and inexpensive dormitory accommodation is available.

Buckets and spades – Beaches in Meath and Louth

Meath's short stretch of coastline has wide Blue Flag beaches at **Mornington**, **Bettystown** and **Laytown**.

In Louth, there are a number of enjoyable beaches to be found, at **Termonfeckin** and **Clogherhead**, only a few miles to the north and east of Drogheda, and, on the Cooley Peninsula, at **Shelling Hill** and **Templeton** near Greenore, and at **Carlingford**.

Tell me an Irish riddle...

Question – *What has legs but cannot walk?*

Answer – *A table*

Boat Rides

Royal Canal Ventures

Hill of Down, Enfield, Co. Meath, **t** (046) 954 6731

This company offers you the chance to cruise to the Boyne aqueduct, go along the Royal Canal on a self-drive boat or try a pedal boat.

Cycling

Irish Cycle Hire

Ardee, Co. Louth, **t** (041) 685 3772, **www**.irishcyclehire.com

Cycling holidays and bike hire.

Fishing

For information on fishing locally, call David Byrne on **t** (046) 907 3375.

Horse-racing

See **www**.hri.ie and **www**.eastcoastmidlands.ie for details of horse races in the area.

Horse-riding

Bachelor's Lodge Equestrian Centre

Kells Road, Navan, Co. Meath, **t** (046) 902 1736

A centre offering riding lessons, farm treks and pony camps.

Rathe House

Kilmainhamwood, Co. Meath, **t** (046) 905 2376

Horse-riding, archery and other activities are available here.

Walking and cycling

The Táin Trail is a superb, well-signposted 18-mile (30km) circular walking and cycling path running through the Cooley Mountains in Co. Louth, from Carlingford almost round to Dundalk. A Tourism Ireland leaflet on the trail is available at all tourist offices. By car, take the R173 from Dundalk.

In Carlingford itself there is an enjoyable town walk – ask at the local tourist office for further information.

Keltic Walking and Adventures

White Gables, Headford Place, Kells, Co. Meath, **t** (046) 40322

Tailor-made walks for groups and individuals.

WESTMEATH AND LONGFORD

The quiet farming counties of Longford and Westmeath hold history and magic in equal measure. Until the arrival of Christianity in the 5th century, Westmeath was part of *Mide*, or Meath. In about the year AD 300 the palace of the High King of Ireland (the *Ard Rí*, *see* p.31) was at Uisneach, a small hill in the middle of the flat Westmeath countryside. Around 350, the seat of the *Ard Rí* moved to Tara (*see* p.102), but in the early 11th century it returned to Uisneach for a brief period. In a fairytale the children of King Lir were changed to swans on the shores of Westmeath's Lake Derravaragh, where they spent the first 300 years after their stepmother's curse (*see* p.177).

County Longford, which is also quite flat, is in the basin of the Shannon and known for its trees and rivers, and the pretty islands that dot its lakes. Many famous writers of different eras, including Oliver Goldsmith (1728–24), author of the play *She Stoops to Conquer*, and Padraic Colum (1881–1972), who wrote the children's story *The King of Ireland's Son*, were born here, and Anglo-Irish author Maria Edgeworth (whose *Castle Rackrent* denounced the hardships of Irish peasants in the 19th century) lived in Edgeworthstown, where her father had an estate.

Tourist information

Athlone, Co. Westmeath, **t** (090) 649 4630
Longford, Co. Longford, **t** (043) 46566
Mullingar, Co. Westmeath, **t** (044) 48650
East Coast and Midlands Tourism, Dublin Rd, Mullingar, **t** (044) 48761, **www.eastcoastmidlands.ie**

Getting there and around

By bus Bus Éireann buses from Dublin or Galway stop at Kinnegad, Mullingar, Moate and Athlone in Westmeath, and Longford and Granard in Longford. Many small-company local services to villages run from Athlone, Mullingar and Longford.

By rail The Galway line from Dublin Heuston stops in Athlone; the Sligo line from Dublin Connolly stops in Mullingar, Edgeworthstown (Mostrim) and Longford town.

Bike Hire

Buckley Cycles, Main St, Athlone, Co. Westmeath, **t** (090) 647 8989

Shopping

The Longford Bookshop

Ballymahon St, Longford, Co. Longford, **t** (043) 47698

A good general bookshop with plenty of material on attractions in the region, and a good children's section.

Tom McGuinness

Main Street, Longford, Co. Longford, **t** (043) 46305

Crafts and sweaters.

Glasson Arts and Craft Centre

Main St, Glasson, near Athlone, **t** (090) 643 9815
Open Summer Tues–Fri 10–6, Sat and Sun 12 noon–6; winter Wed–Fri 10–5, Sat and Sun 12 noon–5

See potters at work, and design and paint your own mug, bowl and so on.

Special Events – Westmeath and Longford

May

All Ireland Amateur Drama Festival, Deane Crowe Theatre, Athlone, Co. Westmeath, **t** (090) 647 4596

A busy arts festival, with many shows and stalls.

June

Annual Goldsmith Summer School, t (043) 71448

Lectures, adult and children's poetry competitions and art exhibitions celebrating the work of locally spawned writer Oliver Goldsmith.

July

Ballymahon Budweiser Festival, Main St, Ballymahon, Co. Longford, **t** (090) 643 2127

A town festival catering for all ages, with street tug-of-war, children's art and drama workshops, watersports and other street entertainment.

Viking Festival, Athlone, Co. Westmeath, **t** (086) 262 1136 or **t** (090) 647 3383

Relive the plundering of Clonmacnoise and capture of Viking king Olaf Scabbyhead with longboat races, reenactments, music and lectures.

August

Granard Harp Festival, Granard, Co. Longford, **t** (043) 86643

A renowned festival dating back to 1781. The main events are on the second Saturday of the month.

November

John McCormack, the Golden Voice of Athlone, Athlone, Co. Westmeath

An international classical singing competition named after celebrated local son John McCormack, a legend in Ireland and one of the greatest tenors in the world from the 1900s to the 1930s.

SPECIAL TRIPS

Adventure Viking Cruise

7 St Mary's Place, Athlone, Co. Westmeath, t (090) 647 3383, www.vikingtoursireland.com
Cruises daily June–Sept, by request Mar–May, Oct and Nov, to Lough Ree (90mins) and twice-weekly to Clonmacnoise (4 1/2hrs), departing from Strand Fishing Tackle Shop, **t** (090) 647 9277

Dress up in Viking costumes, swords, helmets and shields for your adventure cruise in a replica Viking ship on the Shannon, and follow the trail of the marauders who once plundered villages and monastic sites along the river, accompanied by historic tales told by your friendly Viking guide.

Athlone Castle

St Peter's Sq, Athlone, Co. Westmeath, t (090) 649 2912/4630 or t (090) 644 2100
Open Easter/May–Sept Mon–Sat 10–4.30
Adm Adult €5, child €3, family €11.50
Folk and military museums, tea room

Right on the Shannon, this 13th-century castle houses a museum of folk artefacts and a historical museum that focuses mainly on the Siege of Athlone in 1691, during the war between the forces of the deposed Catholic King James II and the Protestant William of Orange (*see* p.35). Soldiers' costumes and other exhibits complement an audio-visual display. More peacefully, there's information about the flora and fauna of the Shannon, and also on Ireland's most famous tenor and one of Athlone's most famous sons, John McCormack (1884–1945).

Fore Abbey

Fore, **t** (044) 61780
Getting there About 15 miles (24km) north of Mullingar and the N4 Dublin–Sligo road
Open Daily June–Sept and Sun all year; call for times
Adm Free
Guided tours by request

For a peaceful day out, take a picnic and drive to this sleepy village of ruins deep in the Westmeath countryside, near the valley where Norman landlords the De Lacys built a Benedictine priory in the 13th century. Once there, you can find out about the 'Seven Wonders of Fore':

* The water that flows uphill (it really does!)
* The monastery built in a bog
* The mill without a race
* The water that won't boil (don't try it, or you'll be cursed)
* The tree that won't burn (ditto)
* The hermit in a stone
* The stone raised by St Fechin's prayers (to sit above the entrance of the church)

A story to tell:
The Hill of Uisneach

It is said that the first High King to sit upon the Hill of Uisneach was King Midhe. As all kings do, he started making pronouncements, and he even had the audacity to light the Beltaine fire. The Druids didn't like this, for they were the ones who always lit the bonfire every year, the one that all the other tribal chiefs took as the signal to light their own fires on the highest hilltops on the eve of 1 May. It was a sight to see – Ireland lit up from coast to coast as if little golden eyes were opening all over it. This was an important time for the Druids; they were inviting the summer sun back into Ireland to make sure crops were good and cows healthy for the rest of the year. They'd throw a cow bone into the 'bone-fire' for the sake of their cattle, then drive them between two fires for good measure. Both of these rituals were said to keep disease and misfortune at bay.

Lugh, the hero-king of the Tuatha Dé Danaan, had ruled from Uisneach, with the Druids as his advisors. Ériu – who some called a sun goddess, and who was promised by the Milesians' chief poet Amergin that Ireland would be named after her in exchange for her giving Ireland to them (*see* p.119) – is also said to be buried beneath the Cat's Stone on the southwestern slope of Uisneach Hill. So it was no small thing when a king took it upon himself to start the Beltaine fire, and the Druids came together on Uisneach to discuss the matter.

King Midhe responded by cutting out all of their tongues and then setting himself above the spot where he buried them in the earth. His mother looked on fondly and said, 'It is *uisneach* [which means 'proudly' in Irish] you sit up there tonight!'

And that is how the great Hill of Uisneach got its name – and, of course, County Mide, or Meath, also took its name from the very same king.

St Fechin founded a monastery at Fore about 630, and a community of 300 monks gathered around him. Today you can visit the old church of St Fechin (you'll need to pick up the key in the Seven Wonders Pub) and, above it, a tiny chapel called the Anchorite's Church, where it is claimed that the last hermit in Ireland lived during the 17th century.

Did you know...?
According to Geoffrey of Monmouth, the wizard Merlin advised England's King Arthur to move Stonehenge (then called 'The Giants' Ring') from the Hill of Uisneach to Salisbury Plain, and so he did. The stones were believed to have healing properties, and each one had a unique purpose.

AROUND AND ABOUT

Bricks and mortar

Belvedere House, Gardens and Park

Tullamore Rd, Mullingar, Co. Westmeath,
t (044) 49060, **www**.belvedere-house.ie
Getting there 3 miles (5km) from Mullingar on N52, the Tullamore road to Kilbeggan
Open Gardens and Park: daily Mar, Apr, Sept and Oct 10.30–6, May–Aug 10.30–9, Nov–Feb 10.30–4.30
House: daily May–Aug 9.30–5.
Last adm 1hr before closing
Adm Adult €8, over-3s €4.50, family (2+2) €22
Restaurant, visitor centre, gift shop, play area, animal sanctuary, parking

A number of secluded woodland trails run from this 18th-century former home of the Earls of Belvedere and its lakeside and walled gardens. A multimedia presentation tells the story of how the cruel and jealous Lord Rochfort imprisoned his wife for 31 years here, behind Ireland's largest man-made folly, which is nicknamed the Jealous Wall. Younger children will enjoy the playground and the animal sanctuary, both of which are located close to the visitor centre. The new Lakeside Falconry Centre hosts two flying displays every day from Easter until the end of summer.

Tullynally Castle and Garden

Castlepollard, Co. Westmeath, **t** (044) 61159 or **t** (044) 62745
Getting there On the Granard road 1 1/2 miles (2.5km) outside Castlepollard
Open Garden: May Sat, Sun and bank hols, daily June–Aug 2–6;.Castle: call for times.
Pre-booked groups by arrangement
Adm Gardens: adult €5, child €2.50, family €14
Castle and Gardens: adult €8, child €4

The pleasure grounds here contain a Tibetan and a Chinese garden. The Gothic Revival castle itself is inhabited by the Earls of Longford, whose seat this is.

Look at this!

Mullingar Bronze and Pewter Visitor Centre

Greatdown, The Downs, Mullingar, Co. Westmeath, **t** (044) 48791
Open Mon–Sat 9.30–6, workshop tours Mon–Fri 9.30–4
Craft shop, showrooms, coffee shop, guided tours

At this co-operative studio, children can learn the secrets of making bronze- and pewterware, using methods that have remained unchanged for the past 800 years.

Dún na Sí Cultural Centre

Knockdomney, Moate, Co. Westmeath,
t (090) 648 1183
Getting there 10 miles (16km) east of Athlone
Open Mon–Thurs 10–4, Fri 10–3, or by appointment
Adm Folkpark: adult €3.50, child €1.50
Guided tours €5
Restaurant, ample parking, souvenir shop

An outdoor folk heritage park with farm machinery from days gone by. Inside there is a restored farmhouse with a cultural centre specializing in genealogical research, and featuring music, storytelling, song and dance evenings.

Nature lovers

Glendeer Pet Farm

Athlone, Co. Westmeath, **t** (090) 643 7147
Open Easter–Sept Mon–Sat 10–6 and Sun 12 noon–6, Dec Mon–Fri 5–8pm, Sat and Sun 3–8pm
Adm Adult €6, child €5

A child-friendly farm west of Athlone with a Christmas scene (28 Nov–23 Dec), café and play area.

Jonathan Swift Park/ Lilliput Adventure Centre

Lilliput, Lough Ennell, near Mullingar, Co. Westmeath, **t** (044) 26789/26545
Getting there 3 miles (5km) south of Mullingar
Café in summer, beach, children's playground

A lake with a rare inland Blue Flag beach and an activity centre running outdoor programmes, both day and residential.

Sporty kids

Activity centres

See above for Lilliput Adventure Centre.

Wineport Sailing Centre and Restaurant

Glasson, Athlone, Co. Westmeath, **t** (090) 647 4944
Open For sailing seasonally, restaurant all year
Sailing on Lough Ree, with instruction for beginners and experienced sailors (ages 10 and above).

Boat trips

Several companies offer trips and boat hire on the Shannon and Lough Ree.

Athlone Cruisers

The Jolly Mariner, Marina Athlone, Co. Westmeath, **t** (090) 647 2892

Cruiser and rowing boat hire on the Shannon.

Lilliput Boat Hire

Jonathan Swift Park (*see* above), **t** (086) 828 6849

Buckets and spades – beaches in Westmeath

This inland county has Blue Flag beaches on two of the region's beautiful lakes: the **Cut** on **Lough Leane**, 3 miles (5km) southeast of Castlepollard, and **Lilliput** on **Lough Ennell**, 3 miles (5km) to the south of Mullingar.

Did you know...?
Jonathan Swift used the name of Lilliput House on Lough Ennell, Co. Westmeath – now long demolished – for the country of the little people in his famous book entitled Gulliver's Travels.

Fishing

Brown trout fishing is good on Lough Sheelin, Co. Westmeath; for coarse fishing try loughs Owel, Ennell and Derravaragh. There is very good pike fishing all over Lough Ree, and Lough Gowna in northern Co. Longford is a coarse fishing centre.

For equipment and information contact:

Denniston Edward & Co, Centenary Sq, Longford, Co. Longford, **t** (043) 46345
Lough Derravaragh Boat Hire, Donore Shore, Multyfarnham, Co. Westmeath, **t** (044) 71500
Strand Fishing Tackle Shop, St Endas Place, The Strand, Athlone, Co. Westmeath, **t** (090) 647 9277.

Horse-riding

Ladestown House

Mullingar, Co. Westmeath, **t** (044) 48218

Raiding on trails along the lake.

Mullingar Equestrian Centre

Athlone Rd, Mullingar, Co. Westmeath, **t** (044) 48331

Year-round treks along Lough Derravaragh.

Walking

Boherquill Rambers Walking Club

Correally, via Rathowen, Co. Westmeath, **t** (043) 85116

Steam power!

An Dún Transport and Heritage Museum

Doon, Ballinahown, Athlone, Co. Westmeath, **t** (090) 643 0106
Getting there 7 miles (11km) south of Athlone
Open Daily Easter–Oct Mon–Sat 10.30–6, Sun 1–6
Video presentation, souvenir and coffee shop

On the *Slí Mór* or Chariot Way, one of the five ancient roads of Ireland, this private collection has forms of transport from trap cars to early cars, and old combine harvesters and other farm equipment. Its friendly owner, who has lovingly restored everything, will give an informative tour if you ask.

WHERE TO EAT

Co. Dublin

Dalkey

The Queens
12 Castle St, Dalkey, **t** (01) 285 4569 (*inexpensive*)

This pub serves good sandwiches and seafood chowder. It's pleasant for lunch on a sunny day, when you can sit outdoors with children.

Ragazzi
109 Coliemore Rd, Dalkey, **t** (01) 284 7280 (*inexpensive*)

An Italian restaurant that serves child-size portions, with attentive, welcoming staff.

Glencullen

Fox's Pub
Glencullen, **t** (01) 295 5647 (*inexpensive*)

A good seafood pub on the Wicklow border, very enjoyable for lunch.

Howth

Big Blue Restaurant
Howth, **t** (01) 832 0565 (*moderate*)

This restaurant has a children's menu, highchairs, colouring paper and pencils, plus a fish tank to help keep little ones amused.

Malahide

Giovanni's Restaurant
Malahide, **t** (01) 845 1733 (*inexpensive–moderate*)

An Italian restaurant with a relaxed, friendly atmosphere. Children can have reduced-size portions from the main menu and highchairs are available.

Malahide Castle
Malahide, **t** (01) 846 3027 (*inexpensive*)

Good soups, snacks and desserts for lunch and afternoon breaks.

Oscar Taylor's
Malahide, **t** (01) 845 0399 (*expensive*)

This place is known for its steaks, its seafood and its vegetarian dishes. The carvery inside the main bar is popular, bright and airy. There are no children's menu or reduced-price portions, but highchairs are available, and there's a baby-changing area.

Sandycove

Caviston's Seafood Restaurant
59 Glasthule Rd, Sandycove, **t** (01) 280 9245 (*moderate*)

An excellent deli on the south side of Dublin Bay, with a small restaurant attached, serving gourmet seafood. Note that it opens for lunch only.

Skerries

The Red Bank Restaurant
5–7 Church St, Skerries, **t** (01) 849 1005 (*expensive*)

This is a little upmarket and formal but still a great choice if you like fish. Families with small children who need highchairs usually have dinner in the adjoining Red Bank Guesthouse.

Wicklow and Carlow

Arklow

The Stone Oven
65 Lower Main St, Arklow, Co. Wicklow, **t** (0402) 39418 (*inexpensive*)

A great bakery and coffee shop.

Avoca

Avoca Mill Stores
Avoca Village, Co. Wicklow, **t** (0402) 35105 (*inexpensive*)

Home-made soups, bakes and cakes made from fresh produce, and much more are available at this child-friendly café in a knitwear centre.

Ballon

Ballykealey House
Ballon, near Carlow, Co. Carlow, **t** (059) 915 9288 (*inexpensive–moderate*)

This country-house-style restaurant serves home-made pizzas, ice cream and food that's as natural as possible. A children's menu is available in the bar, and in the dining room half-portions can be ordered from the main menu or there's a kids' menu and high tea.

Bray

Escape

1 Albert Ave, Bray, Co. Wicklow, **t** (01) 286 6755 (*inexpensive–moderate*)

Children are welcome at this friendly restaurant serving tasty vegetarian and vegan food opposite the Sea Life Centre.

Soprano's

51 Main St, Bray, Co. Wicklow, **t** (01) 286 0009 (*inexpensive–moderate*)

An Italian with a great children's menu.

The Tree of Idleness

Seafront, Bray, Co. Wicklow, **t** (01) 282 8183 (*expensive*)

A renowned Greek-Cypriot restaurant.

Carlow Town

The Beams Restaurant

59 Dublin St, Carlow, **t** (0503) 31824 (*expensive*)

A 300-year-old coaching inn with bistro-style modern Irish cuisine: fresh seafood, game and home-grown vegetables. Attached is an excellent wine and cheese shop.

Enniskerry

Poppies Restaurant

The Square, Enniskerry, Co. Wicklow, **t** (01) 282 8869 (*inexpensive*)

This is a good place for lunchtime salads, and gets lively at weekends.

Glendalough

Glendalough Hotel

t (0404) 45135 (*moderate–expensive*)

A child-friendly hotel where kids can choose between their own menu or small portions from the main menu.

Greystones

The Hungry Monk

Greystones, Co. Wicklow, **t** (01) 287 5759 (*expensive*)

This family-run fish restaurant has an impressive wine list and is a good spot for Sunday lunch.

Laragh

Lynham's Laragh Inn

Laragh, Co. Wicklow, **t** (0404) 45345 (*moderate*)

A family-oriented traditional restaurant.

Leighlinbridge

The Lord Bagenal Inn

Main Street, Leighlinbridge, Co. Carlow, **t** (0503) 21668 (*inexpensive*)

A very popular hotel pub-restaurant with a carvery, a varied menu and an excellent wine list. The children's play area is beside the bar.

Macreddin Village

The Brook Lodge Inn

Near Aughrim, Co. Wicklow, **t** (0402) 36444 (*expensive*)

Only free-range, organic and wild foods are served at this award-winning restaurant.

Rathdrum

Cartoon Inn

Rathdrum, Co. Wicklow, **t** (0404) 46774 (*inexpensive*)

Children enjoy examining the walls of this inn, which are covered with the work of many famous cartoonists. Take along some paper and crayons for them to doodle on.

Roundwood

Roundwood Inn

Roundwood, Co. Wicklow, **t** (01) 281 8107 (*expensive*)

A 17th-century inn with bar food – filling Irish stews – and a restaurant menu. Helpings are ample.

Tullow

Rathwood Home and Garden World

On R725, Rath, Tullow, Co. Carlow, t (059) 915 6285 (*inexpensive–moderate*)

Delicious home-baking in a garden centre with a heated outdoor garden patio.

Kilkenny and Wexford

There has long been a tradition of good cuisine in this part of Ireland, and around places such as Inistioge in Kilkenny you will find several independent cooks offering sophisticated modern food. Specialities of the area include oysters, potatoes and strawberries.

Arthurstown

Dunbrody Country House Hotel

Arthurstown, Co. Wexford, **t** (051) 389 600 (*expensive*)

A superior hotel with gourmet food, including a children's menu. Some of the local produce used is from the award-winning chef's organic garden.

Ballynabola

Horse and Hounds Inn

Ballynabola, Co. Wexford, **t** (051) 428 482 (*inexpensive*)

Gargantuan portions of simple food, including good stews. Accommodation is also available.

Campile

Kilmokea Country Manor

Great Island, Campile, near New Ross, Co. Wexford, **t** (051) 388 109 (*expensive*)

Cream teas and organic food are prepared especially creatively for kids in this health-oriented country hotel (*see* p.253) serving flower-strewn salads and delicious home-baking for dinner and at Sunday lunch in The Peacock Restaurant. High tea is served in the conservatory, The Pink Teacup.

The Shelburne Restaurant

Campile, Co. Wexford, **t** (051) 388 996 (*moderate–expensive*)

Seafood and French cooking by a gourmet traditionalist chef. Kids are welcome (book ahead).

Carne

Lobster Pot

Carne village, south of Rosslare, Co. Wexford, **t** (053) 31110 (*moderate*)

Great seafood and pub grub all day.

Duncannon

Squigl Restaurant

Quay Rd, Duncannon Fort Visitor Centre, The Hook, Co. Wexford, **t** (051) 389 700 (*moderate–expensive*)

A good fish restaurant. Dine early with children.

Graiguenamanagh

Waterside

The Quay, Graiguenamanagh, Co. Kilkenny, **t** (059) 972 4246 (*moderate–expensive*)

Refined cooking and especially good seafood for dinner, in an atmospheric riverside stone building.

Inistioge

Circle of Friends

The Bank House, High St, Inistioge, Co. Kilkenny, **t** (056) 775 8800 (*inexpensive–moderate*)

A café and evening restaurant set in a converted house on the village square, serving excellent cakes and snacks downstairs and fine meals upstairs.

The Motte

Main St, Inistioge, Co. KIlkenny, **t** (056) 775 8655 (*moderate–expensive*)

A charming little restaurant in this most picturesque of villages, with adventurous food and a cosy atmosphere.

Kilkenny Town

Edward Langton's

69 John St, Kilkenny, **t** (056) 776 5133 (*moderate–expensive*)

An award-winning hostelry where you can enjoy good pub lunches and dinners, including vegetarian dishes.

Kilkenny Castle

Kilkenny, **t** (056) 772 1450 (*inexpensive*)

This restaurant set within the old castle kitchen serves delicious lunches and teas, in the summer months only.

Kilkenny Design Centre

Castle Yard, Kilkenny, **t** (056) 772 2118 (*inexpensive*)

A place serving good soups, cooked meats and salads for lunch.

Lacken House

Dublin Rd, Kilkenny, **t** (056) 776 1085 (*expensive*)

A popular, family-run restaurant serving imaginative, perfectly cooked food.

Tynan's Bridge House Bar

St John's Bridge, Kilkenny, **t** (056) 772 1291 (*inexpensive*)

An unspoilt Victorian pub complete with its original fittings.

New Ross

Brandon House Hotel

New Ross, Co. Wexford, **t** (051) 421 703 (*moderate*)

An award-winning restaurant with a children's menu. The family-friendly hotel in which it is set has a health club and spa.

Cedar Lodge Restaurant and Hotel

Carrighbyrne, Newbawn, New Ross, Co. Wexford, **t** (051) 428 386 (*inexpensive*)

Quality food on the Wexford–New Ross road.

Thomastown

Thomastown Water Garden and Café

Thomastown, Co. Kilkenny, **t** (056) 772 4690 (*inexpensive*)

Teas and lunch served from Tuesday to Friday on the terrace of a lovely little water garden.

Wexford Town

Ferrycarrig

Reeds Hotel, Enniscorthy Rd, Wexford, **t** (053) 20999 (*expensive*)

An idyllic setting and good food, including breast of duck in a strawberry vinaigrette sauce and home-made ice cream and pastries. Kids get half portions at dinner or Sunday lunch. Book ahead.

Heavens Above

The Sky and the Ground, 112 South Main St, **t** (053) 21273 (*moderate*)

A delightful restaurant above a well-loved pub, serving excellent food from 5pm. The wine list is vast. It's a must if you're within striking distance.

Tim's Tavern

51 South Main St, Wexford, **t** (053) 23861 (*inexpensive–moderate*)

A lovely old-style, intimate restaurant noted for its traditional Irish cooking as well as French and vegetarian specials. Children are welcome.

Kildare, Laois and Offaly

Abbeyleix

Morrissey's Bar

Abbeyleix, Co. Laois, **t** (0502) 31281 (*inexpensive*)

Morrissey's is an award-winning pub and grocery shop with old cake tins and a stove, and good sandwiches.

Preston House

Abbeyleix, Co. Laois, **t** (0502) 31432 (*moderate*)

An ivy-covered stone B&B in a former school. Its restaurant serves wholesome traditional Irish food using organic produce where possible. Chips are never served to kids, who are always very welcome.

Athy

Tonlegee House

Athy, Co. Kildare, **t** (059) 863 1473 (*expensive*)

Imaginative and delicious cooking is on offer at this Georgian house restaurant situated in its own grounds. Extensive menus are available, together with children's meals.

Banagher

The Vine House

Banagher, Co. Offaly, **t** (0509) 51463 (*moderate*)

Good-value, simple cooking.

Birr

Spinners Town House & Bistro

Next to Birr Castle, Castle St, **t** (0509) 21673 (*moderate*)

Alongside this informal evening restaurant with highchairs and wheelchair access is a courtyard play area. Local fresh ingredients are prepared modern-Irish style, with many vegetarian dishes available. Rooms are offered too (children under 2 stay free).

Castledermot

De Lacy's

Kilkea Castle, Castledermot, Co. Laois, **t** (059) 914 5156 (*expensive*)

Local produce and fresh vegetables served in a dining room with a historic atmosphere, open all day Mon–Sat and for Sunday lunch. Book ahead.

Durrow

Woodview Restaurant

Bishopswood, Co. Laois, **t** (0502) 36433 (*moderate*)

This casual all-day establishment serving traditional, modern and vegetarian dishes has baby-changing facilities and wheelchair access.

Eustace

Ballymore Inn

Eustace, Co. Kildare, **t** (045) 864 585 (*inexpensive–moderate*)

This child-friendly local serves traditional Irish cuisine, pastas and pizzas.

Killenard

The Thatch Restaurant

Killenard, Co. Laois, **t** (0502) 23822 (*moderate*).

A quaint pub and restaurant in a charming village.

Moone

Moone High Cross Inn

Bolton Hill, Moone, Co. Laois, **t** (059) 862 4112 (*moderate*)

A friendly, old-fashioned pub serving above-average food, including home-cooked roasts, sandwiches and scrumptious apple pie.

Portlaoise

The Kingfisher Restaurant

Old AIB Bank, Main St, Portlaoise, **t** (0502) 62500 (*moderate*)

A very popular Indian restaurant open for both lunch and dinner

The Kitchen and Food Hall

Hynds Sq, off Main St, Portlaoise, **t** (0502) 62061 (*inexpensive–moderate*)

This casual eaterie can make up food hampers to take on picnics, with home-produced products. Both the deli and the restaurant are open from 9am to early evening.

Meath and Louth

Carlingford

Ghan House

Carlingford, Co. Louth, **t** (042) 937 3682 (*moderate–expensive*)

Book ahead if you want to experience the delicious gourmet evening meals made from organic produce served at this period guesthouse-hotel, which also runs cookery courses. Children are very welcome, and small or special meals are available for them.

Collon

Forge Gallery Restaurant

Church St, Collon, Co. Meath, **t** (041) 982 6272 (*expensive*)

A great place for vegetarians that serves organic food and is open in the evenings only. Children can get half-portions of everything.

Dundalk

No. 32 Restaurant

32 Chapel St, Dundalk, Co. Louth, **t** (042) 933 1113 (*inexpensive–moderate*)

Internationally inspired food at good prices, especially on the express menu (5.30–7pm).

Kells

Vanilla Pod

Headfort Place, Headfort Arms Hotel, Kells, Co. Meath, **t** (046) 924 0063 (*expensive–moderate*)

Global cuisine. Children are welcome.

Kilmessan

The Station House Hotel

Kilmessan, Co. Meath, **t** (046) 902 5239 (*moderate*)

Tasty food served in a former train station.

Navan

Dunderry Lodge Restaurant

Navan, Co. Meath, **t** (046) 943 671 (*expensive*)

A little restaurant with a tremendous reputation; Dubliners think nothing of driving out to sample its Mediterranean-influenced food and wine.

Hudson's Bistro

30 Railway St, Navan, Co. Meath, **t** (046) 29231 (*moderate*)

A casual place with an international menu.

Slane

Boyles Tea Rooms

Main St, Slane, Co. Meath, **t** (041) 982 4195 (*inexpensive*)

Very good home-made food for lunch.

Westmeath and Longford

Abbeyshrule

Rustic Inn

Abbeyshrule, Co. Longford, **t** (044) 57424 (*inexpensive*)

A good-value, family-run restaurant serving plain food and steaks.

Athlone

Conlon's Restaurant

5–9 Dublingate St, Athlone, Co. Westmeath, **t** (090) 647 4376 (*moderate*)

A good traditional Irish restaurant adjoining a pub; children are welcome during the day.

Kin Khao

Abbey Lane, **t** (090) 649 8805 (*moderate*)

Genuine Thai food served across the street from the Tibetan Buddhist Meditation Centre at lunch and dinner.

The Left Bank Bistro

Fry Place (behind Athlone Castle), Athlone, Co. Westmeath, **t** (090) 649 4446 (*moderate*)

This café by day, restaurant by night serves imaginative food with East/West flavours and excellent seafood, salads, dressings and vegetarian dishes. It has a heated walled garden, and children are welcome, with half-portions available.

Pavarotti's

Fry Place, Athlone, Co. Westmeath, **t** (090) 649 3066 (*moderate*)

A child-friendly Italian (without highchairs).

Restaurant Le Château

St Peters Port, The Docks, Athlone, Co. Westmeath, **t** (090) 649 4517 (*expensive*)

A friendly, informal and good-value place, welcoming children in the early evening.

Glasson

The Glasson Village Restaurant

Glasson, Co. Westmeath, **t** (090) 648 5001 (*moderate*)

This restaurant offers lovely plain Irish cooking, with lots of seafood options. Children are welcome for early dinners, and there is wheelchair access.

Wineport Lodge Restaurant

Glasson, Co. Westmeath, **t** (090) 643 9010 (*expensive*)

A very popular, casually elegant, friendly spot on the inner lakes of Lough Ree, north of Athlone. Families are welcome, and early-bird and special group menus are available for lunch and dinner.

Longford Town

The Longford Arms

Main St, Longford, **t** (043) 46296 (*moderate*)

Pub lunches and an à la carte menu.

Aubergine

17 Ballymahon St (above White House pub), Longford, **t** (043) 48633 (*inexpensive–moderate*)

A place recommended highly by locals for lunch and dinner, including vegetarian dishes.

Torc Café and Shop

Ballymahon St, Longford, **t** (043) 48777/47353 (*inexpensive*)

Good light lunches, cakes and chocolates.

Mullingar

Crookedwood House Restaurant

Mullingar, Co. Westmeath, **t** (044) 72165 (*moderate–expensive*)

This cellar restaurant, which has won awards for its excellent country cooking, welcomes children for early dinners of modern-Irish seafood, game and vegetarian dishes. Accommodation is available.

Tyrellspass

Tyrrellspass Castle Restaurant

Tyrellspass, Co. Westmeath, **t** (044) 23105 (*inexpensive–moderate*)

Medieval castle banquets and delicious home-cooked breakfasts, lunches, snacks, grills and Sunday lunches are offered at this historic building and museum site.

Munster

COUNTY CORK 120
Cork City 121
Special Trips 122
Around and About 123

COUNTY KERRY 127
Touring Towns 128
Special Trips 131
Around and About 134

COUNTY LIMERICK 136
Limerick City 136
Special Trips 137
Around and About 138

COUNTY CLARE 140
Ennis 141
Special Trips 141
Around and About 144

TIPPERARY AND WATERFORD 146
Touring Towns 147
Special Trips 148
Around and About 149

WHERE TO EAT 151

05

Munster
Kilronan
Aran Islands
South Sound
Ballyvaughan Bay
Burren
Fanore
Ballyvaughan
Burren Way
Aillwee Cave
The Burren
Poulnabrone Megalithic Tomb
Lisdoonvarna
N67
Carran
Doolin
Kilfenora
Cliffs of Moher
Liscannor
Inchiquin Lough
Lahinch
Corofin
Liscannor Bay
Dysert O'Dea
N85
Spanish Point
Miltown Malbay
The Hand Cross Roads
Atlantic
Ocean
CLARE
Doonbeg
N68
Kilkee
Deer Island
Kilrush
Killadysert
Killimer
Carrigaholt
Scattery Island
River Shannon
Foynes
Loop Head
Carrigafoyle Castle
Tarbert
N69
Glin
Mouth of the Shannon
Ballybunion
Cashen River
Listowel
Ardagh
Kerry Head
Newcastle West
Ballyheige
Magharee Islands
Banna Strand
Banna
N21
Abbeyfeale
Brandon Bay
Kilflynn
Brandon Head
Dingle Way
Tralee Bay
Broadford
Ballydavid Head
Brandon Mountain
Brandon
Fenit
Spa
Tralee
Mullaghareirk Mtns
Smerwick
Cloghane
Castlegregory
Ballydavid
Camp
Blennerville
Crag Cave
Gallarus Oratory
DINGLE PENINSULA
N86
Slieve Mish Mtns
N70
N23
Castleisland
Dunquin
Ventry
Dingle
Inch
Castlemaine
Blasket Islands
R. Maine
N22
Ballydesmond
Slea Head
Doonbeg Fort
Rossbeigh Creek
KERRY
Kanturk
Dingle Bay
Killorglin
Kells Bay
Rossbeigh
Glenbeigh
N72
Gap of Dunloe
KILLARNEY
River Blackwater
Ring of Kerry
Ross Castle
Lough Leane
Muckcross
Lough Coomasaharn
Macgillycuddy's Reeks
Muckcross Abbey
Millstreet
Valentia Island
Caherciveen
Killarney National Park
The Paps Mountains
Kerry Way
IVERAGH PENINSULA
Derrynasaggart Mountains
Portmagee
N71
R. Finnihy
St. Finan's Bay
Waterville
Staigue Stone Fort
Sneem
Kenmare
R. Roughty
Macroom
Skellig Islands
Ballinskelligs
Lough Currane
Kerry
Gougane Barra Forest Park
Carrigadrohid
Bolus Head
Inchiquin L.
Inishcarra Reservoir
Caherdaniel
Ring
Shehy Mountains
Derrynane House
Castlecove
Kenmare River
Scariff Island
Deenish Island
Ardgroom
BEARA PENINSULA
Glengarriff
Ballycrovane Harbour
Beara Way
Cod's Head
Castletownbere
Whiddy Island
Bandon River
Ballydonegan Bay
N
Bantry
Kilmichael
Dursey Head
Bantry Bay
Sheep's Head Way
Rossmore
R. Argideen
Bear Island
Durras
Clonakilty
Sheep's Head
Inchydoney Island
Dunmanus Bay
Ballydehob
Rosscarbery
Schull
Skibbereen
Drombeg Stone Circle
Three Castle Head
Goleen
Roaringwater Bay
Castletownshend
20km
10miles
Crookhaven
Heir I.
Baltimore
Lough Ine
Mizen Head
Clear Island
Sherkin Island
Fastnet Rock

GALWAY
Loughrea
N6
N65
N61
N66
R357
River Shannon
R355
R353
Portumna
Birr
Lough Cutra
Terryglass
N52
N62
Lough Graney
Lough Derg
R. Bow
Mountshannon
Holy Is.
Feakle
Dromineer
Nenagh R.
Cloghjordan
N7
Roscrea
Ennis
Cragganowen The Living Past
Portroe
Nenagh
Clarecastle
Quin
Doon Lough
Broadford
Knappogue Castle
Ballina
Killaloe
R. Suir
Newmarket on Fergus
Templemore
Bunratty Castle Folk Park
Birdhill
Silvermine Mtns
Shannon
Shannon Airport
Bunratty
N18
Castleconnell
Borrisoleigh
Moyne
LIMERICK
Kilcommon
Thurles
N69
Murroe
Slievefelim Mountains
Kilcooly Abbey
Kilcornan
Holycross Abbey
N21
Ballyneety
TIPPERARY
Franciscan Friary
Adare
GOLDEN VALE
N24
N8
Slieveardagh Hills
Croom
Dundrum
R660
LIMERICK
Lough Gur
R. Suir
Rock of Cashel
Ballingary
Limerick Junction
R689
N20
Cashel
Knockfierna Hill
Bruree
Tipperary
N74
Mullinahone
Kilmallock
R663
R692
Newtown
Bansha
Fethard
Galbally
Glen of Aherlow
Kilfinane
Cahir
Galtee Mountains
Swiss Cottage
Clonmel
Ballyhoura Mountains
Mitchelstown Cave
Carrick-on-Suir
Liscarroll
Mitchelstown
Clogheen
R671
Comeragh Mountains
Curraghmore House
R680
Buttevant
N73
Doneraile
Knockmealdown Mtns
Ballymacarberry
Nire R.
R676
Portlaw
R. Suir
Waterford
Mount Melleray Monastery
R668
R669
Ballynamult
N72
Kilworth
R666
Ballyduff
Mallow
Fermoy
Cappoquin
WATERFORD
N25
Knockeen Dolmen
Passage East
Lismore Castle Gardens
Lismore
Tramore
Bunmahon
R675
Aglish
Dungarvan
Doneraile Cliffs
Dunmore East
Waterford Harbour
Hook Head
R. Blackwater
R674
CORK
Blarney
Youghal
Ardmore
CORK
Barryscourt Castle
Carrigtwohill
N22
Ballincollig
Blackrock
Fota Is.
Midleton
Youghal Bay
Farnanes
Crookstown
Lough Mahon
Cobh
Cork Airport
Monkstown
Cluain Uamha Cathedral
Garryvoe
Shanagarry
Carrigaline
Bandon
Myrtleville
Kinsale
Summercove
Robert's Cove
Charles Fort
Swansea, Roscoff & Cherbourg
Timoleague
Kinsale Harbour
Garrettstown
Butlerstown
Courtmacsherry Bay
Old Head of Kinsale
Grand Canal
KILDARE
Kildare
R415
N9
Carlow
N78
CARLOW
Kilkenny
KILKENNY
R702
Stone Crosses
R697
R705
Drummin
New Ross
River Barrow
WEXFORD
R733
R734
Bannow Bay
NORTHERN IRELAND
ULSTER
CONNACHT
REPUBLIC OF IRELAND
LEINSTER
MUNSTER

MUNSTER

The first September morning I awoke on the west coast of Ireland's largest province – Munster (*Cuige Mumhan*) – in 1972, I recall looking out of my window with utter awe. It didn't seem possible that anything on earth could be more like paradise. Rainbow colours kaleidoscopically shifted across the Atlantic and the same unmoving island, altering its delicate beauty to a new beauty with each passing moment.

When I explored the seashore, I was delighted to discover that the water was so clean and clear that rocks, sand and seaweed on the ocean bottom appeared sharp and crystalline. This is not the case anymore in most parts of Ireland, but the Gulf Stream still flows around its coastline, making its climate temperate throughout the year.

Because of its beauty, Munster is popular with families, especially in summer – when, if you're lucky, it might not rain for two weeks or so. Come rain or shine, be prepared for weather changes. There is nothing more dramatic than an Atlantic storm here, although usually you will merely be treated to a fine mist, or perhaps a bit of ocean spray.

Be prepared for queues and traffic in the busier towns and attractions at the height of the summer season. For tourists, Kerry is the most popular county in Ireland, with Cork a close runner-up. Swimmers and hikers who enjoy lush greenery and environmental mysticism will love the Ring of Kerry's mountains, while those who seek the rocky drama of a more barren seascape will prefer County Cork's coastal walks around the Beara Peninsula.

Munster's other counties have fantastic attractions for children, not to mention ideal settings for relaxing holidays and Ireland's best unspoiled beaches and areas for watersports. Birdwatchers shouldn't miss County Clare, and horse-lovers will find many of their kind in County Tipperary. Young historians will be fascinated by the castle on a hill in the middle of Cashel, County Tipperary, seat of the Kings of Munster for more than 700 years, and the medieval castle that dominates the neighbouring town of Cahir. Days out at Bunratty Castle and at the history parks of Cragganowen, Lough Gur and Muckross will be enjoyed by the whole family. Those on the trail of the Vikings must visit Waterford, the first town they built in Ireland. County Waterford's history of seafaring intruders like Cromwell's soldiers will fascinate youngsters nearly as much as its fishing villages and bird life.

If you expect rain as well as sun, you'll thoroughly enjoy your time here, especially if you happen to see rainbows or leprechauns. And if you don't have 'the luck of the Irish', maybe it won't rain at all...

Did you know...?

Some believe the 'Milesians' described in Irish folk stories were actually the Celts. It's true that when the Celts first came to Ireland, they thought of the Tuatha as gods. But after the arrival of St Patrick and the spread of Christianity, the Tuatha gods became known as faeries, and their faery world was described as the realm of the spirits, or the dead. The monks, who wrote down most of the folk stories, were happy to retell the old tales with a Christian twist.

Highlights

Cork, Cobh and a bit of Blarney, pp.121–3
Island-hopping on the west coast, p.126
Killarney National Park, Muckross Farms and the Ring of Kerry, p.129 and p.133
Down Dingle way with Fungi the dolphin, p.132
Getting back to nature in the Burren, p.141
Discovering the Rock of Cashel and Tipperary's horses, p.147 and p.150

Tourist information for Munster

Cork/Kerry/South West Tourism (Cork, Kerry), Grand Parade, Cork, and Beech Rd, Killarney, **t** (021) 425 5100, **www**.corkkerry.ie

South East Tourism (Carlow, Kilkenny, Tipperary, Waterford, Wexford), 41 The Quay, Waterford, **t** (051) 875 823, **www**.southeastireland.com

Shannon Development (Clare, Limerick, Offaly, Shannon Airport, North Tipperary), **t** (061) 361 555, **www**.shannonregiontourism.ie

For information on selected sites, call **Shannon Heritage** on **t** (061) 360 788.

Getting there and around

By air It's easy to fly to Munster without going through Dublin: there are many flights from Britain to **Cork**, and many flights from the USA and Britain land at **Shannon**, north of Limerick. Smaller airports also with direct links to Britain and Europe are **Kerry** and **Waterford**. *See* pp.283–4.

By sea Swansea–Cork Ferries (in Cork, **t** (021) 427 1166) operate between Cork and Swansea in south Wales, and Brittany Ferries, **t** (021) 427 7801, has weekly ferries between Cork and Roscoff in France.

A story to tell: The coming of the Sons of Míl

The Tuatha Dé Danaan were good and decent rulers over Ireland. Theirs was a time when kindness reigned and noble thoughts filled the minds of the people. But ominous predictions and forebodings came from the Tuatha's Druids. Oracles implied that the Tuatha's rule over Ireland was nearing an end. Some Druids had seen visions of ships bringing men to their shores. The Tuatha leaders – the Daghda and his wife Ogma, Lugh and Aengus Óg among them – lived for a long while with the shadow of what was to come.

Then, one feast of Beltaine (May Day), the Druids' prophecies seemed to be coming true. Ships were seen on the horizon. There was a flurry at Uisneach, where the Druids and high chieftains held counsel. 'What did it mean? Was this the time?' they asked themselves again and again.

Every Druid in every part of Ireland began chanting in the hope that it would make the strangers return whence they came. The drumbeat of their chanting filled every nook and cranny until a mist formed that rose and thickened until heavy fog covered the island. Suddenly Ireland was no longer there; only a cloud was.

'What's this?' cried a captain on the leading ship. 'The island was there and now suddenly it is not. The Sons of Míl should not be deceived so in battle or in peace.'

'It is Druid magic, Captain Midhir,' murmured the dignitary sitting in the prow of the boat, Amergin.

'Druid magic!' the crew gasped, and a hush fell upon the ship, apart from the knock of ropes against the mast.

'Well then, Amergin,' said Midhir, 'do what you can do.'

So Amergin stood on the prow of the ship. Carefully arranging his robes and steadying himself, he began, in a tone soft and sonorous:

I am the wind on the sea
I am the wave of the sea
I am the bull of seven battles
I am the eagle on the rock
I am a flash from the sun
I am the most beautiful of plants
I am a strong wild boar
I am a salmon on the water
I am a lake in the plain
I am the world of knowledge
I am the head of the spear in battle
I am the god that puts fire in the head
Who spreads the light in the gathering
on the hills?
Who can tell the ages of the moon?
Who can tell the place where the sun rests?

The moment Amergin stopped chanting, a great wind rose and pushed the giant cloud away from Ireland in one big whoosh. The sun shone powerfully upon the three glistening ships of the Milesians. And then it was that the Tuatha Dé knew that the Druids had predicted 'true' about the arrival of Men. After the sons of Míl set foot upon Ireland, it quickly became obvious that no trick or magical device could repel their advances, and the Druids had to accept that the Milesians' poet Amergin had a magic stronger than their own. His was the greater gift. Amergin knew, as did the Druids, that the best words conjure the best spells.

Though they still had power over the land and its fertility, the Tuatha came to accept that their time for ruling the great island was at an end. And so they formed a truce with the Milesians, agreeing to take the hidden half of Ireland, the part that lay in the hills and Otherworld regions, while leaving the sons of Men (the Milesians) the rest. Ever since, the Tuatha Dé Danaan have kept to themselves, while Men have roamed Ireland's surface and treated the Tuatha with respect...until recently.

By bus There are frequent Bus Éireann services between Dublin, Wexford/Rosslare and Cork, Limerick and all the other main towns in Munster. Many regional services run out from Cork. Bus Éireann also runs a service between Cork city and Cork airport. For Bus Éireann details, *see* p.286.

By car From Dublin, take the N7 for Limerick, and turn south onto the N8 in Portlaoise for Cork or Kerry. Allow yourself plenty of time, because the roads are busy.

By train Irish Rail trains run from Dublin's Heuston station to Cork, Killarney, Tralee, Limerick, Ennis, Tipperary and Waterford, with many stops en route on slower trains. There are also many trains from Cork to other places in Munster.

For more information on Irish Rail/Iarnród Éireann, *see* p.288. They can be contacted in Ireland on **t** 1 850 366 222 or **t** (01) 703 4070, or check **www.**irishrail.ie.

COUNTY CORK

County Cork has some of Munster's finest countryside, and some of its most dramatically rugged, rocky coasts, laid along winding bays with many small islands to add extra fascination to the view. One of the greatest reasons for coming here is to meet this area's inhabitants, who are well known for their humour, love of parties and generous hospitality. Teenagers and young people will find lots to do in Cork City, with its vibrant street life. If you want a more languid holiday, though, base yourself outside the city, maybe in the seaside town of Cobh, in the gastronomic capital of Ireland: Kinsale, or in far West Cork.

Tourist information

Cork City, Grand Parade, Cork, **t** (021) 425 5100 or **t** 1 850 230 330, **www.**corkkerrytourism.ie
Bantry, t (027) 50229 (seasonal)
Blarney, t (021) 438 1624 (all year)
Clonakilty, Ashe St, **t** (023) 34051 (all year)
Glengarriff, t (027) 63084 (seasonal)
Kinsale, Pier Head, **t** (021) 477 2234 (all year)
Macroom, Castle Gates Lodge, **t** (026) 43280 (seasonal)
Midleton, t (021) 461 3702 (seasonal)
Skibbereen, North St, **t** (028) 21766 (all year)

Tours

Titanic Trail Guided Tours, Michael Martin, Mellieha, Carrignafoy, Cobh, **t** (021) 481 5211, **www.**titanic-trail.com

A guided tour around Cobh, visiting locations connected with the *Titanic* – including the White Star Line Office and embarkation pier – and learning about aspects of the port's history.

Getting there and around

By air Cork Airport is 3 miles (5km) south of Cork City on the Kinsale road (N27). There is a regular 20min shuttle bus service to and from the airport and the city. Airport information **t** 021 431 3131, **www.**cork-airport.com.

By bus The main bus station is Cork City Depot, Parnell Place, **t** (021) 450 8188. Most local buses pass St Patrick's St. During summer, open-top bus tours of Cork and Blarney are available.

Special Events – County Cork

May

Cork International Choral and Folk Dance Festival, Cork City, **t** (021) 484 7277

One of Ireland's foremost music festivals.

June

Cork Midsummer Festival, Shandon, Cork City, **t** (021) 450 7487

West Cork Chamber Music Festival, Bantry, **t** (027) 52788

July

Cahirmee Horse Fair, Buttevant, **t** (022) 23100

A community horse fair, more than 100 years old.

Schull Family Arts Festival, t (028) 28201

Workshops, art and drama.

West Cork Chamber Music and Literary Festival, 1 Bridge St, Bantry, **t** (027) 52788

Concerts, literary workshops and readings.

July–August

Garnish Family Festival, Lehanmore, Beara, **t** (086) 248 6500

Games and pet and talent shows.

Youghal Premier International Busking Festival, Upper Strand, Youghal, **t** (024) 92447

Four days of music, storytelling, mime, street and puppet theatre by artistes from the USA to China.

August

Ballydehob Gala Festival, Ballydehob Village and Community Hall, **t** (028) 37191

Dog, pony and baby shows; music, children's sports and art.

Regattas: Cobh, Glandore, Glengarriff, Schull and Baltimore

Events involving plenty of boats and salty tales for budding mariners of all ages, throughout the month of August.

Rosscarbery Family Festival, t (023) 48444

Irish music and games for all the family.

Timoleague Harvest Festival, Mill St, Timoleague, **t** (086) 169 7628

A family and music festival.

Youghal Ceolta Si, Youghal, **t** (087) 793 4504

A festival of Irish traditional music, storytelling and dance.

September

International Storytelling Festival, Cape Clear Island, **t** (028) 39116

This event is fun for the whole family, with its puppet theatre, boat trips around Fastnet Rock, and archaeological and ornithological explorations. A daily ferry service is available from Baltimore.

By train Trains run from Kent Station, including local lines to Cobh. Information: **t** (021) 450 6766.
By boat A car and passenger ferry crosses Cork Harbour at Ringaskiddy, 7 miles (11km) from Cork.

CORK CITY

Cork City is an important port and the second-largest city in the Republic. About AD 650, St Finbarr founded a monastery here. Cork grew slowly until the Georgian era in the 18th century, when fine, graceful buildings were constructed over the old town's narrow alleyways.

Until the last decades of the 20th century, Cork remained a beautiful port without much interference from the outside world. Today, it is undergoing unprecedented changes. It has grown in recent years, with many cars on new roads, and has become known for its vibrant arts community. It's an interesting place to shop and explore, and in the meanwhile you may happen upon its native inhabitants' way of talking in riddles, not to mention their great humour and generosity.

Things to see and do

Cork Butter Museum

O'Connell Sq, Shandon, **t** (021)430 0600
Open Daily May, June and Sept 10–1 and 2–5, July and Aug 9–6; Oct–Apr by arrangement
Adm Adult €3, child €2.50

Find out about Ireland's most successful food export and Cork's greatest trade.

Cork City Gaol Heritage Centre and Radio Museum

Convent Ave, Sunday's Well, **t** (021) 430 5022
Open Daily Mar–Oct 9.30–5, Nov–Feb daily 10–4 (last admission 1hr before closing)
Adm Adult €6, child €3.50, family(2+4) €15 for Gaol or Radio Museum; joint tickets for both available
Souvenir shop, tea shop, car and coach parking

Find out what 19th-century Cork was like inside this old prison, the majestic appearance of which belies the wretched conditions in which prisoners were kept. Sound effects bring to life wax figures in cells furnished as they once were, and a film conveys why people turned to crime at that time. The Radio Museum in the Governor's House, ex-residence of the prison governor, displays the collection of Ireland's national radio and TV network RTE. Dummies portray workers using old machines in the early days of Irish and world broadcasting, and exhibits convey the impact these new technologies had on the way we live.

Cork City Tour

Tourist Office, Grand Parade, **t** (021) 425 5100
Times daily 10–5
Adm Adult €12, student €10, under-14s €4, family (2+4) €28

A hop-on, hop-off bus tour of Cork's attractions.

Cork Public Museum and Fitzgerald Park

Off Western Rd, North Cork City, **t** (021) 427 0679
Open Mon–Fri 11–1 and 2.15–5 (until 6pm June–Aug), Sun 3–5; closed bank hols
Adm Free

This 18-acre park holds a museum covering 18th–20th-century political history and Cork's evolution and development. Set in a Georgian house, it contains many interesting items and information on some of Cork's most famous citizens.

Cork Vision Centre

St Peter's, North Main St, **t** (021) 427 9925
Open Tues–Sat 10–5 (Apr–Nov Thurs 12 noon–5)
Adm Free; donations welcome

Model and exhibitions of Cork City.

Crawford Art Gallery

Emmet Place, near Lavitt's Quay, **t** (021) 427 3377
Open Mon–Sat 10–6. **Adm** Free
Disabled access

The city's most important art gallery, in its original customs house, built in 1724. Named after the 19th-century art patron William Horatio Crawford, it became the Cork School of Art in 1884 and houses some of the best work by 19th- and 20th-century Irish artists. There are also 3 windows by Ireland's premier stained-glass artist Harry Clarke (1889–1931), and a small collection of international paintings. The gallery's restaurant, run by the Ballymaloe School of Cookery, serves some of the best modern-Irish gourmet cuisine at very decent prices.

St Ann's Shandon Church

Church St, Shandon, **t** (021) 450 5906
Open Mon–Sat 10–5; closed Christmas Day
Adm Adult €6, student/child €5, family €12

North of the River Lee is Shandon Steeple, built in 1720, which dominates the city. Here visitors may ring the famous 'bells of Shandon'.

An Irish Proverb –
The older the fiddle, the sweeter the tune.

St Finbarr's Cathedral

Bishop St, Cork City, t (021) 496 3387
Open Mon–Sat Apr–Sept 10–5, Oct–Mar 10–12.45 and 2–5; no adm during services
Adm Adult €3, under-18s €1.50

St Finbarr is said to have founded Cork City on this very spot in the 7th century, but the Church of Ireland cathedral – even though it may look medieval – was built in the middle of the 19th century, in extravagant Victorian Gothic style with giant spires that tower over the city.

Entertainment

Cork Opera House

Emmet Place, t (021) 427 0022

Despite the name, this grand building hosts theatre more often than opera – mostly new plays by Irish writers, often in its studio theatre, the Half Moon. Its season lasts for about 8 weeks every summer, and frequently has children's shows in the programme.

Everyman Palace Theatre

McCurtain St, t (021) 450 1673

Any play – tragedy or comedy – by any author, can be produced at this imaginative theatre, so long as it's good. Go prepared for anything and you won't be disappointed. In summer it produces shows with an Irish connection.

Triskel Arts Centre

Tobin St, off South Main St, t (021) 427 2022

This centre hosts a wide range of events – films, music, exhibitions, drama, poetry and more.

Shopping

The Coal Quay

Cornmarket St

An open-air Saturday market.

Easons

Patrick St, t (021) 427 0477

Cork's branch of Ireland's biggest bookshop chain, with a good children's section.

The English Market

Entrances on Grand Parade, Prince St and Patrick St

The site of a market since 1768, now held Mon–Sat 9–6. Look for The Organic Shop (**t** 021 427 9419).

SPECIAL TRIPS

Blarney Castle

Blarney, t (021) 438 5252, www.blarneycastle.ie
Getting there 5 miles (8km) west of Cork City
Open May and Sept Mon–Sat 9–6.30, Sun 9.30–5.30; June–Aug Mon–Sat 9–7, Sun 9.30–5.30; Oct–Apr Mon–Sat 9–dusk (or 6pm), Sun 9.30–dusk
Adm Adult €7, student €5, 8–14s (accompanied by an adult) €2.50, family (2+2) €16
Souvenir shops, toilets with disabled access and baby-changing facilities, park walks, parking

According to tradition you can get 'the gift of the blarney' by kissing the Blarney Stone here – but it could be dangerous for young children as they have to clamber to the top of the 1446 castle. 'Blarney' is the ability to talk your way out of any kind of difficult situation and give someone the runaround; the phrase was coined by Queen Elizabeth I when she told the castle's owner that he was speaking nothing but 'blarney' as he tried by devious means to avoid doing what she demanded. The surrounding 1,000 acres of woodland are magical to walk in – an excellent place for playing with the faeries.

The Queenstown Story

Cobh Railway Station, Cobh, t (021) 481 3591, www.cobhheritage.com
Getting there Great Island, Cork Harbour, 15 miles (24km) from Cork City; frequent trains run from Cork
Open Daily May–Oct 10–6, Nov–Apr 10–5; last admission 1hr before closing
Adm Adult €6, under-16s €3, family (2+4) €16.50
Multimedia exhibition, café, gift shop

Cobh was the *Titanic*'s last port of call before it set sail for its encounter with an iceberg in 1912, and this is where most of its victims embarked on their last voyage. This attractive, hilly seaside town, not far from Cork, has a fascinating museum that tells the story of how the fishing village of Cobh came to prominence during the French Revolution and Napoleonic Wars (1792–1815). It was an important ship-refuelling point, where you sometimes saw up to 300 ships at anchor. It was renamed Queenstown after Queen Victoria visited in 1849, and in the following years it serviced the tall ships that transported convicts to Australia and Irish emigrants to North America, and later transatlantic steamers and ocean liners. More than 2.5 million people emigrated through Cobh between 1848 and 1950, more than from any other port in Ireland. The multimedia exhibition inside Cobh's Victorian railway station brings its history to life, with real artefacts and a rolling ship's interior that will show you why people become seasick. Afterwards, relax in the railway café before returning to a more modern means of transportation.

Fota Wildlife Park

Carrigtwohill, near Cobh, **t** (021) 481 2678, **www.fotawildlife.ie**
Getting there 10 miles (16km) east of Cork City off N25, with access by rail: Fota station is by park entrance
Open Mid-Mar–Oct Mon–Sat 10–6, Sun 11–6; Nov–mid-Mar Mon–Sat 10–4.30, Sun 11–4.30; last admission 1hr before closing
Adm Adult €10.50, student and under-16s €6.50, under-2s free, family (2+4) €42
Playgrounds, wildlife train (adm extra), picnic areas, coffee shop, gift shop, restaurant, first aid, toilets with disabled access and baby-changing facilities, car park

This is one of Europe's best modern animal parks, with more than 90 species of wildlife wandering freely in 70 acres of open grass and woodland. There are no obvious restraints or cages (apart from the cheetah breeding area), yet everything is completely safe. You can easily spend a day exploring the grounds and meeting animals from five different continents. Bring good walking shoes, or else make sure the train is running so that you can look around without overtaxing little legs. Fota aims to conserve wildlife through education, the breeding of endangered species, and promoting and supporting international conservation programmes. After you've spent some time communing with the animals, visit the Fota Arboretum and Gardens nearby for a picnic.

County Cork Songs to Sing...
Blackwater Side, Bold Thady Quill, Skibbereen, The Wild Rover, Whiskey in the Jar, Goodbye Mursheen Durkin, O'Donnell Abu, The Holy Ground.

AROUND AND ABOUT

Animal magic

The Donkey Sanctuary

Knockardbane, Liscarroll, Mallow, **t** (022) 48398, **www.thedonkeysanctuary.org.uk**
Getting there About 10 miles (16km) northwest of Mallow, 30 miles (48km) north of Cork
Open Mon–Fri 9–4.30, Sat, Sun and bank hols 10–5
Visitor centre, shop, picnic area

Rescued donkeys are rehabilitated and protected at this sanctuary, which never turns away a donkey that needs a home or veterinary care. Some are placed in new homes, but welfare officers continue to check up on their wellbeing. They also offer educational programmes on donkey care.

Millstreet Country Park

Millstreet, **t** (029) 70810, **www.millstreetcountrypark.com**
Getting there 5 miles (8km) from Millstreet, 27 miles (42km) northwest of Cork
Open 17 Mar–Oct daily 10–5.30, or by appointment
Adm €15 per car/family
Restaurant, visitor centre, gardens, deer farm, picnic area, disabled access, gift shop, free parking

This 500-acre park in the Boggeragh Mountains has nature trails, ornamental grounds, waterfalls, rivers, wetlands, moorlands and reconstructions of archaeological sites that you can explore via park transporters or on foot, using the map you are given on arrival. Wild animals including birds and 700 red deer live in this park, which has a 4,000-year-old stone circle, and a *crannóg* at the base of Musheramore Mountain. Meals are available in the visitor centre, along with a gift shop, theatre and state-of-the-art interactive displays.

Bricks and mortar

Bantry House and Gardens

Bantry, **t** (027) 50047, **www.bantryhouse.com**
Getting there 55 miles (90km) west of Cork
Open Daily mid-Mar–Oct 10–6

Adm House, Gardens and Armada: adult €10, concessions €8; under-14s accompanied by an adult free. Gardens and Armada €5
B&B and tea room

In the gardens of this mid-18th-century house, with French and Flemish tapestries and works of art and furniture from 1800 to 1868, is the 1796 French Armada Exhibition Centre, a small exhibition about the failed French landing at Bantry Bay in 1796.

Barryscourt Castle

Carrigtwohill, **t** (021) 488 2218
Getting there 10 miles (16km) east of Cork City off N25
Open Guided tours June–Sept daily 10–6, Oct–May Fri–Wed 11–5; last admission 45mins before closing
Adm Adult €2, child €1, family €5.50
Restaurant, craft shop

This 15th-century tower-house with 16th-century additions has a bawn wall with three nearly intact corner towers. The remains of the keep house an exhibition telling the story of the Barry family who inhabited the castle until the 17th century. Sir Walter Raleigh lived here for a time.

Desmond Castle (French Prison)

Cork Street, Kinsale, **t** (021) 477 4855
Getting there 16 miles (26km) south of Cork City
Open Daily mid-Apr–mid-Oct 10–6; last admisson 45mins before closing
Adm Adult €2.75, child €1.25, family €7
Wine museum, guided tour on request

A custom house built by the Earl of Desmond c.1500, occupied by the Spanish in 1601 and used as a prison for American sailors captured during the American War of Independence, this became known locally as 'the French prison' after a fire in which mainly French prisoners died in 1747. In the Great Famine, it was used as a workhouse. An exhibition tells the story of Ireland's wine links with Europe.

Look at this!

Michael Collins Centre/ Argideen Valley Heritage Park

Near Timoleague, **t** (023) 46107
Getting there About 1 mile (1.6km) east of Clonakilty towards Timoleague; from Cork, 32 miles (51km) southwest on N71 towards Clonakilty
Open Mid-June–mid-Sept Mon–Sat 10.30–5 (last admission 3.45); other times by arrangement
Adm Adult €5, 12–18s €3, under-12s free
1 1/2hr Michael Collins presentation

On Crowley Way, a scenic tour and hill walk, park staff guide you round sites that are connected with Michael Collins (*see* pp.38–9). A 20min audio-visual is shown, then a 40min illustrated talk about Collins is given, and then for 15mins visitors are taken along an 'ambush trail', made to represent a road with a replica armoured car and other vehicles similar to those of Collins' time, which shows how he was killed.

Charles Fort

Summercove, Kinsale, **t** (021) 477 2263
Getting there 2 miles (3km) east of Kinsale
Open Daily mid-Mar–Oct 10–6, Nov–mid-Mar 10–5; last admission 45mins before closing
Adm Adult €3.50, child €1.25, family €8.25
Guided tours available on request, exhibition centre, restricted disabled access, parking

This huge star-shaped fort beside Kinsale Harbour was built in 1677 and used for coastal defence until British withdrawal in 1921. It's an impressive sight in this lovely coastal town.

Schull Planetarium

Schull, **t** (028) 28552
Getting there On Roaringwater Bay, 69 miles (111km) southwest of Cork near Skibbereen
Open Call for times of shows
Adm Adult €4.50, child €3.20, family (2+2) €12

Each summer, regular astronomy shows are offered to the public at the Community College in Schull.

Youghal Heritage Centre

Market House, by tourist office, Youghal, **t** (024) 20170
Getting there 29 miles (46km) east of Cork on N25
Open Daily 10–5.30. **Adm** Free

The exhibition here consists of reconstructions and an audio-visual display on the area's history since the 9th century. Sir Walter Raleigh stayed in Youghal for a while, where he brought the potato from South America; he is said to have been the first person to plant it in Irish soil. He also brought tobacco, and the first time he lit up to smoke in Ireland, his native Cork servant, seeing smoke rising from him, thought he had set himself on fire and threw a bucket of water over him.

West Cork Model Railway Village

Inchydoney Rd, Clonakilty, **t** (023) 33224
Getting there 32 miles (51km) southwest of Cork via N71
Open Daily Feb–Oct 11–5 (extended hrs in summer)
Adm Adult €6, students and 5–12s €3.50, under-5s €1.25, family €19
Train and entry: adult €10, student €8, 5–12s €5.50, under-5s €2.25, family €30
Café, gift shop in train carriages, disbled access, baby-changing facilities

This miniature copy of West Cork villages in the 1940s includes a 1:24-scale working model of the West Cork railway line. Conceived as a way to employ and train local craftspeople in the art of small-scale modelling and to regenerate reclaimed land, this has evolved into an excellent tool to help children develop a sense of where they are in place and time. Local children race around the miniature villages, exclaiming as they recognize familiar spots, then a small 'road train' bus carries them, with commentary, into the present real village of Clonakilty, thus perfectly orientating them in the here and now.

Prince August Toy Soldier Factory Visitor Centre

Kilnamartyra, Macroom, **t** (026) 40222
Getting there 23 miles (37km) west of Cork
Open June–Sept Mon–Fri 9–5, Sat 10–4; Oct–Apr Mon–Fri 9–5. **Adm** Free
Painting workshops by appointment

Watch a craftsman follow an artist's design for a toy soldier, then try casting a model and making a mould of it. Afterwards, look at hundreds of hand-painted figures, and perhaps buy a casting kit to take home or a 'Lord of the Rings' figurine.

Nature lovers

Cork Heritage Park

Bessboro, Blackrock, **t** (021) 435 8854
Getting there 2 miles (3km) from Cork City
Open May–Aug Thurs–Sun and bank hols 1–5
Adm Adult €5, student/child €3, family €10
Restaurant, play areas, baby-changing facilities

Six acres of grounds around the 19th-century Bessboro Estate, in which you can explore Cork's heritage. Displays feature local ecology, maritime history, the fire service, transport and archaeology.

Ilnacullin (Garinish Island)

Glengarriff, **t** (027) 63040
Getting there By boat from Glengarriff; from Bantry Rd just outside Glengarriff or 1 mile (1.6km) from Ellen's Rock on Castletownbere Rd
Open Mar and Oct Mon–Sat 10–4.30, Sun 1–5; Apr and June Mon–Sat 10–6.30, Sun 1–6.30; May and Sept Mon–Sat 10–6.30, Sun 12 noon–6.30; July and Aug Mon–Sat 9.30–6.30, Sun 11–6.30
Adm Adult €3.50, child €1.25, family €8.25 (plus short boat-ride fare)

A 15-hectare (37-acre) island garden of rare beauty.

Doneraile Wildlife Park

Turnpike Rd, Doneraile, **t** (022) 24244
Getting there North of Mallow, 27 miles (43km) north of Cork City
Open Mid-Apr–Oct Mon–Fri 8am–8.30pm, Sat 10–8.30, Sun and bank hols 11–7; Nov–mid-Apr Mon–Fri 8–4.30, Sat, Sun and bank hols 10–4.30
Adm Park only: adult €1.50, child €0.75, family €4.25

This elegant park was landscaped in the early 18th century in the Capability Brown style, which means it appears to have been created by nature. The 395-acre site is dotted with stone bridges and water features, mature groves of deciduous trees and herds of deer and other Irish wildlife.

A story to tell: 'Them'

Under their truce with each other, the Tuatha Dé Danaan and the sons of Mil agreed that neither would interfere in the affairs of the other, and that they would dwell alongside each other in peace so long as they treated each other with respect. In the centuries after the truce, certain places in Ireland were recognized by country people as 'theirs' – that is, the land of The Gentry, The Good People, Them or the Sidhe (pronounced *shee*). If you say the word 'faery' outdoors at twilight, which is the time when they come out, one of 'them' might overhear and play a trick on you, as it is said they do not like to be called faeries.

In the west of Ireland, people still exercise caution about Them. For instance, not long ago a farmer who merely swept clear the moat around a faery whitethorn bush was given a scare when, on his way home, driving his familiar lorry along a road he knew like the back of his hand, the lorry suddenly fell sideways into a ditch – leaving him unharmed (like the bush) but warned!

Good to know...
Getting to the islands of County Cork
Cruises are run to offshore islands from Kinsale by: **Shearwater Cruises**, Seaview Farm, Kilbrittain, **t** (023) 49610. The regular local ferries are these:
Bere Island: Off Castletownbere, Bantry Bay. Ferries are frequent in summer: contact Patrick Murphy, **t** (027) 75014
Cape Clear Island: May–Sept, 2 ferry services: from Schull, 1 ferry daily, **t** (028) 28138, and from Baltimore, 2 daily, **t** (028) 39159, **t** (028) 39119. West Cork Coastal Cruises, **t** (028) 39153, sails from Baltimore to Cape Clear and Fastnet Rock, and vice versa.
Sherkin Island: From Baltimore 7 times daily May–Sept, **t** (028) 20125 or **t** (087) 244 7828.
Whiddy Island: Off Bantry in Bantry Bay. Contact Tim O'Leary, **t** (027) 50310.

Sporty kids

Activity centre

Trabolgan Holiday Village

Midleton, **t** (021) 466 1551, **www**.trabolgan.com
Getting there South of Midleton (14 miles/22km east of Cork) on R630; turn south on to an unclassified road, the site is signposted
Open Daily mid-Mar–Oct
Adm Priced per activity, or day or half-day

This self-catering and caravan village offers day visitors aged 4 and over age-divided activities, including archery, swimming and adventure sports.

Boat trips

Carrig Water Ski Club

Carrigadrohid, Macroom, **t** (021) 487 3027
Open Daily May–Oct

Kinsale Harbour Cruises

t (021) 477 3188

Seafari Eco-Nature and Seal-watching Cruises

1 The Pier, **t** (064) 83171
Adm Adult €20, student €16, teenager €12, under-12s €10

Guided cruises introducing local marine life, plus fishing, kayaking and water-skiing. Booking needed.

Fishing

The Kinsale Angling Co-op

1 The Ramparts, Kinsale, **t** (021) 477 4946

Horse-riding

Bantry Horse Riding

Coonamore South, Bantry, **t** (027) 51412

Blarney Riding Centre

The Paddock, Killowen, **t** (021) 438 5854

Valley View Equestrian Centre

Gooseberry Hill, Newmarket, **t** (029) 68185

Walking

There are miles of great long-distance paths in Co. Cork, which you can follow a long way or for a short stroll: the **Beara Way**, a 122-mile (195km) circular route around the Beara peninsula from Glengarriff; the **Sheep's Head Way**, a 56-mile (90km) circular trail from Bantry; the **Ballyhoura Way**, 56 miles (90km) from Limerick Junction to John's Bridge near Kanturk; and the **Blackwater Way**, 104 miles (166km) along the Blackwater River from Clonmel to Muckross.

Good places for short walks include Charles Fort, Kinsale and Clear Island.

Water sports

Aquaventures

Lifeboat Rd, Baltimore, **t** (028) 20511

An impressive diving centre with abundant marine life and shipwrecks to explore.

The Baltimore Sailing School

The Pier, Baltimore, **t** (028) 20141

Courses on day boats.

International Sailing Centre

5 East Beach, Cobh, **t** (021) 481 1237, **www**.sailcork.com

Schull Watersports

Schull, **t** (028) 28554. Kayaking and sailing.

Buckets and spades – Beaches in Co. Cork

Around the Cork coastline there are many fine beach spots, many now with Blue Flag status.
Bantry Bay: one of Ireland's loveliest beach areas.
Clonakilty to Skibbereen: Inchydoney, Long Strand, Owenahincha (near Roscarbery) and Red Strand are some of the best Cork beaches for swimming, and there are more pleasant beaches at Tragumna, Tralispean, Sandycove and Sherkin Island.
Kinsale area: try the sandy beaches at Summercove and Castlepark; Harbour View and Coolmain (near Garretstown); or Garrylucas, on the Old Head of Kinsale.
Youghal: East Cork's best beaches are Front Strand and Claycastle, near Garryvoe.

COUNTY KERRY

The lush county of Kerry – known for its mountains, lakes and folklore – encourages story-making. This was one of the last large Irish-speaking parts of Ireland, and its *shenachie* or storytelling tradition continued well past the first half of the 20th century. Most of its people were fishermen and farmers who understood nature better than the machinations of Dublin society, before their children were caught up in pop music and all the blow-ins arrived from other countries.

Kerrymen don't have the attitude that one must entertain children all the time, but the genial kindness they offer them, alongside the beauty of these surroundings, will make city people relax. So many tourists visit in July and August, though, that you'll need to book accommodation in advance.

For many people, Kerry's coastal scenery is second to none. The famous 'Ring of Kerry' on the Iveragh Peninsula is hauntingly beautiful, with one of Ireland's earliest monastic settlements offshore on the Skellig Islands, but the Dingle Peninsula's Mount Brandon and Gap of Dunloe are more dramatic. Half of the Beara Peninsula, shared with County Cork, is also part of Kerry. Iron Age stone forts and beehive huts are scattered on private land, which you sometimes have to pay farmers to visit.

This is a place to ride bikes or hike in the hills and along the ocean shore. Play a musical instrument in a pub here and, so long as there's no football on TV, it will attract glances and the noise machines will be turned off. Before you know it, you'll have tourist-hardened Kerrymen asking you questions.

Despite all the foreign traffic, Kerry holds a sense of being cut off from the rest of the world, especially in winter, and Kerrymen often say the 'next stop', after the Atlantic, is America. The periodic wild storms that bash its shores intensify that feeling. And when rainbow colours dance upon sky and water, or heavy giant clouds fly fast across the mountains, it is easy to imagine that one is very close to the Otherworld of the faeries.

Tourist Information

Cork Kerry Tourism (South West Ireland), Beech Rd, Killarney, **t** (021) 425 5100, **www.corkkerrytourism.ie** (all year)

Caherciveen, t (066) 947 2589 (seasonal)

Dingle, The Quay, **t** (066) 915 1188 (all year)

Kenmare, next to Heritage Centre, **t** (064) 41233 (seasonal)

Listowel, St John's Church, **t** (068) 22590 (seasonal)

Tralee, Ashe Memorial Hall, **t** (066) 712 1288 (all year)

Waterville, t (066) 947 4646 (seasonal)

Special Events – County Kerry

April

Samhlaíocht – Kerry Arts Festival, t (066) 712 9934, **www.samhlaiocht.com**

A 10-day community arts festival in various venues, for established and emerging artists.

July

Féile Lunasa, Cloghane and Brandon, **t** (066) 713 8137/8282

A fine traditional festival. Dates vary each year.

August

Dan Paddy Andy Festival, Lyreacrompane, **t** (068) 48353

Music, dance and storytelling commemorating a great Irish matchmaker.

Puck Fair, Killorglin, **t** (066) 976 2366, **www.puckfair.ie**

One of Ireland's oldest – and wildest – annual festivals, dating back 400 years and including traditional cattle and horse fairs, the coronation and dethronement of a goat, and free family entertainment, including busking, parades, fireworks, street entertainment, concerts, traditional dancing and kids' competitions.

Rose of Tralee International Festival, Tralee, **t** (066) 712 1322, **www.roseoftralee.ie**

This 5-day international festival boasts carnivals, street parades, fireworks and free outdoor concerts alongside its fashion and beauty show and Rose Ball to choose the year's 'Rose of Tralee'.

Tours

Fios Feasa Holyground, Dingle, **t** (066) 915 2465

Archaeological tours.

Gap of Dunloe Tour, 7 High St, Killarney, **t** (064) 31068

Book ahead for day-trips in the Kerry countryside, combining hiking and/or cycling with boating, coach, pony or horse-drawn trap transportation.

Go Ireland, Killorglin, **t** (066) 976 2094, **www.govisitireland.com.**

Walking tours.

Getting there and around

By air Kerry Airport is at Farranfore, 9 miles (14km) north of Killarney on the road to Tralee (N22); there are shuttle buses to Killarney. Airport information: **t** 066 976 4644, **www.**kerryairport.ie (*see* p.283).

Flights to Kerry are operated by Aer Arann and Ryanair, *see* pp.280–2.

By bus Long-distance buses run to Killarney and Tralee. From Tralee, regular buses go to Dingle, from where there are infrequent services to other points on the peninsula. Bus Éireann runs daily coach tours (June–Sept) round the Ring of Kerry and Dingle between Killarney and Tralee, **t** (066) 712 3566.

By train Kerry is linked to Dublin Heuston by a rail line from Tralee via Killarney. Information, Tralee–Dublin–Cork line, **t** (064) 712 3522, Killarney **t** (064) 31067

By boat In North Kerry, you can avoid Limerick by taking the car ferry over the Shannon at Tarbert, to Killimer, Co. Clare. It sails hourly each way.

There is a ferry service around the Ring of Kerry from Dingle.

Bike Hire

Foxy John's Raleigh Rent-a-Bike, Main St, Dingle, **t** (066) 915 1316

A bar, hardware store and cycle hire centre.

Good to know...

Getting to the islands of Kerry

The situation with regard to insurance in boats for hire from local boat owners is complicated, so bear in mind that if you take such a trip you may do so at your own risk; check your insurance policy or ask about cover before you embark.

Blasket Islands: The **Blasket Island Boatmen** take day-trippers from Dunquin Harbour every half-hour in summer, **t** (066) 915 6422. Ask in Krugers Bar, Dunquin, **t** (066) 915 6127, about hiring a boat to the Great Blasket. **Mountain Man**, Main St, Dingle, **t** (066) 915 2400, offers bus and boat trips.

The Skelligs: Boats can be hired from Waterville, Caherdaniel, Derrynane Pier, Portmagee or Valentia Island – it's a matter of trying your luck with the local fishermen. Michael O'Sullivan of Waterville Boats does the trip from Waterville, fishing cruises and tours to the Skelligs; ask at The Oyster Bar, **t** (066) 947 4255. Sean Feehan arranges angling, boat hire and trips to the Skelligs, **t** (066) 947 9182.

Due to the popularity of the Great Skellig, and the fragile nature of its ruins and paths, a limit has been set on how many people can visit at once – book ahead in July and August. A waterbus tour is available from **The Skellig Experience**, **t** (066) 947 6306 (*see* p.133).

Killarney Rent-a-Bike, Killarney, **t** (064) 32578

This firm gives out a free map with rentals.

O'Neills, Plunkett St, Killarney, **t** (064) 31970

Standard and tandem bikes for rent, as well as fishing and camping gear.

Paddy's Bike Shop, Dykegate Lane, Dingle, **t** (066) 915 2311

Shopping

An Grianan

Green St, Dingle, **t** (066) 915 1910

A wholefoods supermarket.

Killarney Bookshop

32 Main St, Killarney, **t** (064) 34108, **www**.killarneybookshop.ie

A good selection of books for kids and adults.

Murphy's Ice Cream

Sráid naTrá, (An Daingean) Dingle, **t** (066) 915 2644

Heavenly ice cream and milk from organically farmed cows and sorbets from organic fruit. There's a second branch in Killarney.

The Pantry

Henry St, Kenmare, **t** (064) 42233

A wholefoods shop.

TOURING TOWNS

Killarney

Kerry's most popular tourist town, Killarney and its surroundings offer a multitude of sights. The town itself is rather small, but can get very busy in summer. It has an especially beautiful park, a range of accommodation and lots of restaurants to visit.

Things to see and do

Coolwood Wildlife Sanctuary

Coolcaslagh (off Cork Rd), **t** (064) 36288

Open Daily Apr–June, Sept and Oct 10–6, July and Aug 11–6

Adm Free exc children's zoo: adult €8, child €5, family (2+4) €22

Children's play and craft areas, pet shop, scenic walk, children's zoo, coffee shop, picnic area, parking

Bring your family here for a day of hiking in 40 acres of parkland, where you may see a wide range of wild birds, mink and red squirrels.

Killarney National Park

t (064) 31440
Getting there 4 miles (6km) from Killarney via N71
Open Park daily; visitor centre daily mid-Mar–June, Sept and Oct 9–6, July and Aug 9–7; last admission 1hr before closing. Closed Christmas.
Adm Free
Nature trails, lake swimming, restaurant, toilets with disabled access and baby-changing areas

This is Ireland's premier tourist attraction, so it attracts large crowds in high season. Still, your kids will enjoy the mystical, often misty, beauty of this giant park, encompassing the 3 Lakes of Killarney and set within thousands of acres of mountains and lush landscape. Muckross Abbey (a friary built in 1448 by Fransciscan monks), Dinis Cottage and the Torc Waterfall lie within yew and oak woodland inhabited by Ireland's only native herd of red deer. The park's fresh sweet air will exhilarate you even on the dampest of days.

Queen Victoria put the place on the map when she visited in 1861. Ladies View, a prime place to stop for a picnic, is so called because her ladies in waiting were delighted by the stunning view.

You can hire a traditional 'jaunting car' or a horse-drawn 'side-car', or cycle around the 26,000-acre grounds. There are snack places along the official 15-mile (24km) route, but it's a better idea to bring a picnic.

Muckross House, Gardens and Traditional Farms

t (064) 31440, **www.muckross-house.ie**
Getting there 4 miles (6.5km) from Killarney
Open House: daily 9–5.30 (to 6 in July and Aug); closed Christmas. Farms: call for times
Adm House: adult €5.50, child €2.25, family €13.75
Farms: adult €5.50, child €2.25, family €13.75
Joint ticket (House and Farms): adult €8.25, child €3.75, family €21. Gardens: free
Restaurant and craft shop (daily 9–5.30), vintage coach trip, information centre, restricted disabled access, toilets with disabled access, parking

Families visiting Killarney mustn't miss this exceptional estate. Muckross House is a splendid Victorian museum where in the summer months you can watch a blacksmith, bookbinder, potter and weaver working at their trades and see an informative film about the environment and geology of the park. You can also traverse the park by horse and cart to visit Muckross Friary or Muckross Traditional Farms.

Boats on the Lakes of Killarney

Killarney Waterbus, t (064) 32638

Beginning at Ross Castle, this trip offers a 1hr commentary about the Killarney Lower Lakes.

Lily of Killarney, Old Weir Lodge, Muckross Rd, Killarney, **t** (064) 31062, or Dero's Tours, **t** (064) 31251

Cruise around the lakes of Killarney from Ross Castle – 5 departures daily – with entertaining folklore and history of the area from your guide.

In the latter, a history park style is applied to a community in the countryside, where children can absorb the atmosphere of a way of life that has all but vanished in Ireland. No machine noise pollutes a wide expanse of land in this re-created early-20th-century rural community, where traditional organic farming methods are employed and dirt roads link farmhouses and farms. You smell the air and hear birds sing the way people did in Ireland until half a century ago, and suddenly find you have a spring in your step and a song on your lips just as people there used to. In each house you'll meet a lady who will tell you how people used to live. Talk to them about life and people's perspectives in Ireland then, while bread bakes over a turf fire.

Outdoors you'll probably find a farmer who looks after the land and animals in the traditional manner, without chemical pesticides. Maybe you'll meet an elderly Irish visitor who comes here just to remember the peace of living in this kind of dwelling without the noise of modern houses, TVs and computers. Survival in those days demanded that people be in tune with their surroundings. Today we can escape the hard work and damp houses of the past, but what price do we pay for it? How can we retrieve the good things of the past that we have lost and sometimes never even experienced? Visit this place and maybe you or your children will find some answers.

Museum of Irish Transport

Scotts Place, Killarney, **t** (064) 32638
Open Daily May–Sept 10–6, Apr–Oct 11–5
Adm Adult €5, child €2, family (2+2) €12

The entire history of bicycles is presented in this museum, from the Hobby Horse of 1825 to modern bikes. Also on show is a unique collection of Irish vintage, veteran and classic cars, fire engines and motorcycles. At the time of writing it was closed for rebuilding, with reopening scheduled for 2007.

A story to tell: Oísín and Tír na n'Óg

The son of Finn McCool was Oísín, meaning 'fawn'. He was so named because a sorceress jealous of his mother's beauty had transformed her into a deer.

For a long time, Oísín was watched over by an invisible faery presence, a warmth that cushioned him from the blows of training as a warrior of the Fianna (*see* p. 30). He did not know he was being admired by a faery princess called Niamh of the Golden Hair, who often rode far from her home of Tír na n'Óg, the Land of Eternal Youth. No sorrow or death disturb the Tuatha Dé Danaan's merrymaking there – a place where there is always feasting and never famine.

Still, the Tuatha have their work to do, regenerating and caring for the earth, which is how Niamh one day happened to see Oísín as his horse ran upon the white-sand shore, his cheeks as red as rowan berries. She began spying upon him then, invisibly. His manner was so gentle that love couldn't help rising in her heart. Oísín would wake in the night to see a bowl of stars glittering down upon him, or a curtain of moonbeams on his face from a silent sky, little knowing that faery magic was about.

One day Niamh decided to meet him. As Oísín rode along the shore, he saw the most beautiful shining woman, with hair like spun gold, floating above the ocean on a pearl white mare. He felt his heart lift as he looked into her smiling eyes.

'I am Niamh,' she said, 'of Tír na n'Óg. Perhaps you have heard of it?'

Oísín could barely speak. 'Until now I had thought it an old man's fantasy.'

'Well indeed it is not,' Niamh laughed. 'Would you like to see it?'

Her fingers touched his hand, and he was lost to ordinary mortals forever. Without a doubt in his heart, he answered, 'I would. Who would not?'

Then a pang of memory made him hesitate. Didn't he recall that people usually never returned from Tír na n'Óg? 'But,' he murmured, 'perhaps not at this very moment.'

Niamh smiled, 'Well, later then,' and dashed off on her faery steed before vanishing into thin air.

It was months before Oísín saw Niamh again, and still his love for her grew. The Fianna worried about him, whispering that he must be terribly lonely to be dreaming he had met a faery lady. They introduced him to the prettiest girls they could find, but they could not take away the spell that Niamh had cast upon Oísín's heart.

So when he saw Niamh again, his heart leapt into his eyes and she knew she had him. With barely a word, he joined her on her steed and off they flew to Tír na n'Óg.

There was much sorrow among the Fianna when they found Oísín's horse. They thought Oísín must have gone mad and cast himself into the sea. But Oísín had found the land of his heart's desire and was happier than he had ever been.

However after a time, he remembered his home and worried how his fellow Fianna were doing. He begged Niamh to let him return, just for a visit. She put off replying but couldn't refuse him, saying, 'My horse will take you.' Then, her eyes turning dark, she warned, 'But do not dismount or touch the earth of Ireland, or never more will you return to Tír na n'Óg.'

He promised her that he would return, and flew back across the waves to Ireland. But it was a changed land. Nothing looked familiar, and the people were so small. There were only weak little men struggling to lift what to him was a small rock he could move with one hand.

He looked at the ragged men, then asked them, 'Where might I find King Finn and the Fianna?'

One of the men sat down and wiped the sweat from his brow, unable to believe the giant he saw before him really existed. 'Where indeed?' he replied, 'just when you need them!' and waved his hand at his building work. A near-toothless man beside him piped up, 'Come here now, would ye ever be able to help us lift this boulder?'

'What? That stone?' Oísín started to dismount, then heard Niamh's voice in his ear, '...never more will you return to Tír na n'Óg,' so instead he leaned over from his saddle to pick it up, then, stretching too far, he lost his balance and fell to the earth.

In that moment, Niamh's horse fled and the young giant shrank to a white-haired old man nearly as small as the men he had formerly pitied. He lay in a heap on the ground silently weeping, knowing what he had lost.

'Whisht! Did you see that, man?',the men cried to each other. 'Are ye all right, sir?' one said to Oísín. And then the men heard the story of Oísín, and the tales of the Fianna – from the last there has been on earth of that proud race that is no more.

Ross Castle

Killarney, **t** (064) 35851/2
Getting there 1 1/2 miles (2.5km) outside Killarney off Kenmare Rd
Open Guided tours April 10–5, May and Sept 10–6, June–Aug 9–6.30; Oct Tues–Sun 10–5; last admission 45mins before closing
Adm Adult €5, child €2, family €11
Disabled access to ground floor by prior arrangement

This grand example of a medieval Irish stronghold was probably built in the 15th century by one of the O'Donogue Ross tribal chieftains, and was one of the last of its kind to fall to Cromwell's forces in the 17th century. It has 16th- and 17th-century furniture and is one of Kerry's finest castles, with a tower-house inside a bawn (fortified enclosure). Boats from here will take you to Innisfallen Isle in the middle of Lough Leane (book ahead in high season; *see* p.129). *The Annals of Innisfallen* were written there, in Innisfallen Abbey, founded around AD 600.

Tralee

Famous for its annual 'Rose of Tralee' festival, for which the whole town turns out – usually in August or September – Tralee boasts several attractions to interest children. It's a good place from which to travel around the whole of counties Kerry and Limerick, as it's slightly off the main tourist track of Killarney and the Ring of Kerry.

Things to see and do

Aqua Dome

Ballyard, **t** (066) 712 8899 (summer); information line for other seasons: **t** (066) 712 9150
Open Daily June–Aug 10–10; Sept–May call for times
Adm Adults €10, 4–16s €9, under-4s free; off-peak and family discounts available
Swimming pools, sauna, steam rooms, aqua and miniature golf, baby-changing facilities, restaurant

The biggest, and reputedly best, water-based complex in Ireland. The toddlers' pool has a bubble slide fountain and mushroom spray; older children can play in the medieval castle with water cannons, bubblers, gushers and geysers, whirlpools, rapids, a wave pool and the 296ft (90m) water chute. Adults can relax in the luxurious Sauna Dome. Aqua Golf, with an 18-hole miniature golf course, is next door.

Blennerville Windmill and Visitor Centre

Blennerville, near Tralee, **t** (066) 712 1064
Getting there 2 miles (3km) from Tralee on N86
Open Daily Apr–Oct 10–6
Adm Adult €5, student €4, child €3, family (2+3) €13
Craft shop, workshops, toilets with disabled access

An 18th-century windmill beside Tralee Bay. Displays explain all aspects of processing grain into flour. Also within the 5-storey building is an exhibit on emigration, with models of the 'coffin ships' on which Irish people travelled to escape the famine.

Kerry the Kingdom Museum

Ashe Memorial Hall, Denny St, **t** (066) 712 7777
Open Apr and May Tues–Sat 9.30–5.30; June–Aug daily 9.30–5.30; Sept–Dec Tues–Sat 9.30–5, bank-hol Sun and Mon 10–5; Jan–Mar Tues–Fri 10–4.30
Adm Adult €8, 5–15s €5, under-5s free, family (2+3) €22
Café, shop, free coach park, pay car park

Exceptional attractions detailing the last 8,000 years of Irish (particularly Kerry) history: a panoramic audio-visual tour of the county, where children can play with interactive devices; and the 'artefacts zone', with reconstructions from the Stone Age to today, including a street scene of medieval Tralee.

Siamsa Tíre – National Folk Theatre of Ireland

Godfrey Place, **t** (066) 712 3055
Shows 8.30 Apr and May Mon–Thurs and Sat, June, Sept and Oct Mon–Weds, July and Aug Mon–Weds and Fri; specials at other times
Adm Call for prices
Café, bar, shop, gallery, parking
Irish music, folklore and dance in plays for all the family.

SPECIAL TRIPS

The Dingle Peninsula

The most famous resident of Dingle Town, west of Tralee, is Fungi the dolphin, who has lived in Dingle Bay for some years and can be visited on boat trips. Out in the country and the smaller villages of the peninsula, the land is flat enough to ride bikes or go horse-riding along much of the coast. Explore caves, souterrains and beehive huts around Slea

Head, visit Dunbeg Fort west of Ventry, or take a boat out to wind-blasted islands like the now-uninhabited Great Blasket. Dingle is a walker's paradise too. Walk along the sea for glorious views, or swim off protected sandy beaches such as the one at Inch. The 1970 movie *Ryan's Daughter* was filmed here, although it isn't suitable for children.

Things to see and do

Dingle Maze

Tubberlispole, Dingle, Co. Kerry, t (0876) 109 563, www.mazemaker.com
Getting there **Walk towards hospital; field is beside new housing development**
Open **Daily mid-July–late Aug 11–6 (exact dates depend on weather, so call ahead)**
Adm **€5, under-5s free; ask about group rates for 10 or more people**

Children can explore six acres of a growing corn maze here, artfully planned and designed by Adrian Fisher, and incorporating everything from water to mirrors.

Dingle Oceanworld Aquarium

The Wood, Dingle, t (066) 915 2111, www.dingle-oceanworld.ie
Getting there **31 miles (49km) west of Tralee**
Open **Daily 10–5**
Adm **Adult €10, child €6, family (2+4 under-16s) €27**
Aquarium, gift shop, café overlooking harbour

Look at local sea life in the underwater tunnel here and learn about the creatures living off the west coast of Ireland. There is also a display about St Brendan the Navigator's voyages in the Atlantic.

Fungi the Dolphin

The Pier, Dingle; contact t (087) 285 8802; Dingle Boatmen's Association, t (066) 915 2626
Times **All operate in summer, daily 8–10am**
Cost **Around €11 per person**

For an experience that youngsters won't forget, take them to meet Fungi, the wild bottlenose dolphin who has chosen to live in Dingle Harbour since 1984. He normally comes to greet the boats that go out to see him. They say he really likes people, but be sensitive as he is not a pet.

Some people claim swimming with dolphins is therapeutic and that these unique sea creatures have a special empathy for humans in trouble or need. A meeting with Fungi is not a cure-all, but getting closer to animals and nature is likely to have a positive effect. To swim with Fungi, you need to hire a wetsuit from Flannery's (**t** (066) 915 1967), with whom you also can book an early-morning swim (about 2hrs long).

Gallarus Oratory

Kilmalkedar, Dingle Peninsula
Getting there **2 miles (3km) south of Kilmalkedar or west from Dingle on the road to Ballydavid**
Open **All year.** **Adm** **Free**
Craft shop, tea room

This impressive stone hut, built using the dry-stone corbelling technique of Neolithic tomb-makers, is still watertight after more than 1,000 years, and resembles an upturned boat. It is an Early Christian miniature church, built between the 6th and 9th centuries.

Ionad an Bhlascaoid Mhóir (The Blasket Centre)

Dunquin, t (066) 915 6444
Getting there **At the end of the peninsula 10 1/2 miles (17km) west of Dingle**
Open **Daily Easter–June, Sept and Oct 10–6, July and Aug 10–7; last admission 45mins before closing; available for bookings in winter**
Adm **Adult €3.50, child €1.25, family €8.25**
Guided tour on request, café with light lunches, bookshop, disabled access, car/coach park

Before a visit to the Blasket Islands, you can learn about them at this modern heritage centre, which sticks out like a sore thumb in front of the beautiful, and largest, Great Blasket island. The centre commemorates the Irish-speaking people of the seven islands that comprise the Blaskets. Their last inhabitants left for the mainland in 1953, but the islands are best known for their Irish-speaking storytellers, notably Tomás Ó' Crohan, Maurice O'Sullivan and Peig Sayers (a stone marks Peig's grave in the cemetery just outside Dunquin), who documented their people's last years on the Great Blasket. Today, their books are part of the Irish national curriculum. A video features islanders talking about their old way of life.

Thoughts from Peig Sayers –
Youth slips away as the water slips away from the sand of the shore... A person falls into old age unknown to himself. And a word is more lasting than the wealth of the world.

Lios na Croi

Ballynabuck, near Castlegregory, Co. Kerry, t (066) 713 9319
Open Mon 8–11pm. **Adm** €5
Refreshments provided (tea and biscuits)

The heart of County Kerry is its music, which is everywhere, but you should try to visit at least one music 'session', where musicians of all abilities come together to learn from each other while they are playing. This non-alcohol session for all ages and instruments, including voice, takes place within a traditional thatched cottage complete with a convivial hearth.

The Pottery Experience

Louis Mulcahy Workshop, Clogher, Ballyferriter, Dingle, Co. Kerry, t (066) 915 6229/6429, www.louismulcahy.com
Open Mon–Fri 10–5. **Adm** Free

A visitor centre that forms part of the Mulcahy pottery factory, where adults and children can watch potters at work or throw a pot themselves.

Scanlon's Pet Farm

Slea Head Drive, near Ballydavid, t (066) 915 5135
Getting there 5 miles (8km) west of Dingle
Open Apr–Sept Mon–Fri 10–6, Sun 2–6
Adm Adult €5, child €2.50, family (2+4) €15
Children's playground, picnic area, guided tours, refreshments, parking

This is a family-owned petting farm with a wide variety of animals and birds. You can explore it yourself, or take a guided tour round this gorgeous, windswept place.

The Ring of Kerry

The 'Ring' is one of the most famously beautiful roads in all Ireland, a 112-mile (180km) circuit all the way around the shores of the Iveragh Peninsula. The full round trip – clockwise or anti-clockwise – makes a natural excursion from Killarney.

Derrynane House

Derrynane National Historic Park, t (066) 947 5113
Getting there 1 miles (1.6km) from Caherdaniel, near the southwest corner of the Ring
Open Nov–Mar Sat and Sun 1–5, Apr and Oct Tues–Sun 1–5, May–Sept Mon–Sat 9–6, Sun 11–7; last admission 45mins before closing
Adm Adult €2.75, child €1.25, family €7
Disabled access to ground floor and toilets, guided tours available, café

> ***An Irish Proverb –***
> ***It's the quiet pigs that eat the meal.***

Explore the ancestral home of Daniel O'Connell, the 19th-century nationalist and campaigner for Catholic emancipation (*see* p.36), and its beautiful surroundings – 296 acres in a giant national park beside sand dunes and Derrynane Bay. Many relics of Ireland's 'Liberator' are on display, notably his desk, rosary and duelling pistols. A film tells you more about this eminent lawyer, politician and statesman. His old Gaelic family – hereditary constables of Ballycarberry Castle in the Middle Ages – got along with their Protestant neighbours despite fighting against Cromwell and William of Orange. They were even able to buy land during Penal times with the help of friendly Protestants.

The wild west of Ireland was far from the forces of law and order in the east, and before Daniel's birth the O'Connells made money from smuggling in France and Spain. He was born in Caherciveen, but was fostered out to some island people (an old Irish custom). He later stood for parliament to challenge the law that no Catholic could take a seat in the House of Commons, and won so decisively that the law was repealed in 1829.

After a tour, wander the grounds, walk along the rocky or sandy shore and in the national park, or swim on the nearby Blue Flag beach (*see* p.135).

The Skellig Experience

Valentia Island, t (066) 947 6306, or Killarney Tourist Office, t (064) 31633, www.skelligexperience.com
Getting there A boat trip is available for the Skelligs via Sea Quest, Seanie, Valentia Island, t (066) 947 6214. Boats depart from Valentia at 10am, Renard at 10.05 and Portmagee at 10.30
Open Daily June–Aug 10–6, Apr, May and Sept–Nov 10–5 (closing times may vary in Mar and Nov)
Adm Adult €5, under-12s €3, family (2+4 under-12) €14
Refreshment area, shop, toilets with disabled access and baby-changing facilities, audio-visual display

With sound effects, models and graphics, this exhibition tells how Early Christian monks lived on the Skelligs, 7 miles (11km) southwest of Valentia Island, and of the Skellig Michael lighthouses and the many species of sea birds and marine life that inhabit the area. Gannets and kittiwakes come here every February, while razorbills, guillemots and puffins arrive in April. Boat trips to the Skellig Islands – whose impressive rock-hewn dwellings were carved by monks seeking solitude – depart daily from the pier below this centre; you can circle the island rather than disembark if you like.

Staigue Fort

Near Castlecove, **t** (066) 947 5127
Getting there 27 miles (43km) west of Kenmare
Open Visitor Centre: daily Easter–end Sept 10–9; Fort: all year dawn–dusk
Adm Adult €3, child €2.50, family (2+3) €8
Animated audio-visual display, coffee shop

Thought to be 2,500 years old, this is probably the best stone fort in Ireland. The exhibition centre houses a complete model of the fort as well.

Valentia Island

Off Portmagee
Getting there You can cross to the island over a causeway at Portmagee, but in summer there is a ferry to the opposite end of Valentia from Renard Point near Caherciveen, **t** (066) 947 6141, or via Valentia Island Car Ferry, **t** (066) 947 6141
Open Daily Apr–Sept 10–7, Oct–mid-Nov 10–5.30

The Valentia Island Car Ferry operates a shuttle service to the island and its picturesque 1800s planned village of Knightstown. The island contains well-preserved pre-Christian remains, a famous grotto, a slate quarry and colourful flora and fauna.

AROUND AND ABOUT

Animal magic

Kissane Sheep Farm

Moll's Gap, Kenmare, Co. Kerry, **t** (064) 34791, **www**.adopt-a-sheep.ie
Getting there On Ring of Kerry (N71) surrounding Moll's Gap (between Kenmare and Killarney National Park)
Open Apr–Oct Tues–Sun 10–5; rest of year by appointment
Adm Adult €6, under-11s €3, family (2+3 under-11) €15

A working sheep farm with a unique eco-tourism idea: if you adopt one of the hundreds of lambs born in spring and summer for an annual fee, you can give it a name and visit the farm for free, and for sheep shearing (in season) and sheepdog demonstrations. Children can take an educational puzzle walk or follow a more adventurous treasure trail and help feed pet lambs with a bottle, and families can walk into the surrounding mountains.

Look at this!

Seanchaí

Kerry Literary and Cultural Centre, 24 The Square, Listowel, **t** (068) 22212
Getting there 15 miles (24km) north of Tralee
Open 9.30–5 daily June–Sept, Mon–Fri Oct–May
Adm Adult €5, student €4, under-12s €3, family €12
Café, gift shop, free car parking (at rear)

Ireland's storytelling tradition is celebrated in this museum in a 19th-century Georgian residence beside Listowel Castle. It's a must for young authors-to-be who want to learn how to tell stories, or who are perhaps already telling a few tall tales. There is an audio-visual display on north Kerry and its writers, and in July and August you can enjoy evenings of traditional Irish music, song and dance by top musicians.

Tarbert Bridewell Courthouse and Jail

Tarbert, Co. Kerry, **t** (068) 36500
Getting there 38 miles (58km) west of Limerick on the N69
Open Daily 10–6; closed Christmas
Adm Adult €5, student €3.50, 4–12s €2.50, under-4s free, family (2+4) €10.50
Coffee and gift shops, ample parking

This restored jail of 1831 gives an insight into the harsh penal system in Ireland in the 1830s and recreates the atmosphere of those tough times. Dummies in period dress with recorded voices and sounds of the time bring to life the experiences of the inhabitants of these tiny jail cells.

Nature lovers

Crag Cave

Castleisland, **t** (066) 714 1244, **www**.cragcave.com
Getting there 12 miles (19km) east of Tralee
Open Guided tours daily mid-Mar–1 Nov 10–6; last tour at 6 in July and Aug, 5.30 other months. Call for details of Santa's visits in Dec

Adm Adult €7.50, 5–16s €5, under-5s free, family (2+4) €20

Restaurant, gift shop, indoor play area (separate fee), toilets with disabled access

Learn about stalagmites and stalactites in this ancient limestone cave system that may well be more than 1 million years old. Coloured lighting effects and sounds add drama to the tour. The café sells home-baked specialities.

Glen Inchaquin Waterfall Park

Tuosist, Kenmare, **t** (064) 84235

Getting there Kenmare to Castletownbere; turn left after 8 miles (13km) at sign to Inchaquin Lake, then drive 5 miles (8km) to amenity area

Open Daily all year until sunset

Adm Adult €4, student €2, under-12s free

Picnic areas, car park

This is a good place for a day out when the weather is fine: there are pleasant walks around the waterfall, streams, lakes and woodlands, and you see all kinds of farm animals. The café has home-baked snacks.

Sporty kids

Activity centres

Activity Ireland and Skelligs Aquatics

Caherdaniel, **t** (066) 947 5277

This centre offers scuba-diving lessons and equipment, together with sea angling and guided hill-walking on the Kerry Way.

Horse-riding

Killarney Riding Stables

Ballydowney, near Killarney, **t** (064) 31686, **www.killarney-reeks-trail.com**

Treks in Killarney National Park.

Muckross Riding Stables

Mangerton Rd, Muckross, **t** (064) 32238

Hard hats, boots, ponies and horses for all ages.

Watersports

Dingle Sailing Club

The Wood, Dingle, **t** (066) 915 1984

Contact this club for week-long courses for children in the summer and Easter holidays. In the same area, you can hire wetsuits and bodyboards on Ventry beach.

Buckets and spades – Kerry's Beaches

Kerry has some of Ireland's finest beaches, of which the following is just a selection.

Dingle Peninsula You can swim on Ventry Beach (4 miles/6km west of Dingle), where lifeguards are on duty during summer, and you can dive in Ventry Bay. Other good places to swim are Beenbawn, near Dingle; Cappagh Strand, near Brandon; Wine Strand between the villages of Ballydavid and Ballyferriter; Smerwick Strand, near Ballyferriter; and Slea Head or Stradbally.

There's also a Blue Flag beach at Maherabeg, near Castlegregory in the north of the peninsula, and on the south side there's good surfing at Inch Strand (15 miles/24km east of Dingle) and Srudeen Strand, nearer Dingle (bring your own board).

Ring of Kerry Waterville is the main resort of the Ring of Kerry: its beach and St Finan's Bay are beautiful. Some other Blue Flag beaches are at Derrynane (west of Caherdaniel), with glorious sand dunes and a lovely 1-mile (1.6km) strand, Ballinskelligs (west of Waterville), Kells Bay (7 miles/11km northeast of Caherciveen), Rossbeigh (Glenbeigh) and White Strand near Castlecove.

North Kerry Try Banna (9 miles/14km northwest of Tralee), Ballyheigue (12 miles/19km northwest of Tralee) and Ballybunion (northwest of Listowel)

Waterworld

Castlegregory, **t** (066) 713 9292, **www.waterworld.ie**

Ireland's largest scuba-diving centre offers visits to the Blasket and Magharee islands. Dive holiday packages for all levels are available, as well as hill-walking and other energetic activities.

Steam power!

Tralee and Blennerville Steam Railway

Ballyard Station, Tralee, **t** (066) 712 1064

Operates Daily May–Sept

Adm Adult €5, student €4, child €3, family €15

The Tralee and Dingle Steam Railway, which ran from 1891 to 1953, was one of the world's most famous narrow-gauge lines. Now you can ride in one of its old carriages on the short (2-mile/3km) trip between Ballyard Station, near the Aqua Dome in Tralee, to the Blennerville Windmill.

COUNTY LIMERICK

A ghost in the town of Macroom
One night found a ghoul in his room
They argued all night,
As to which had the right,
To frighten the wits out of whom.

Scholars haven't yet proven that the Limerick five-line poem originated here, but it's certain that in the 18th century the taverns of Mungret, County Limerick, were renowned for their performing rhymers. This charming county of undulating farmland is known for picturesque villages such as Adare and old abbeys such as Kilmallock. You can take cruises on the Shannon and fish for salmon, or go on family walks in the history park at Lough Gur and explore a Neolithic settlement here since 3000 BC, not to mention the 4,000-year-old stone circle outside it. There's plenty of space here for children to play traditional Irish games (*see* p.25), and to pick blackberries along country lanes.

Tourist Information

Adare, Heritage Centre, Main St, **t** (061) 396 255
Limerick City, Arthur's Quay, **t** (061) 317 522
Shannon Airport, **t** (061) 471 664
www.shannonregiontourism.ie

Tours

***Angela's Ashes* Walking Tours of Limerick**, from Tourist Office, Mon–Fri 2.30, Sat by appointment.
Tickets €8

Getting there and around

By air Shannon Airport is just into Co. Clare, 16 miles (26km) along the N18 northwest of Limerick. There are shuttle buses to the city (40mins; *see* p.283). Information, **t** 1 890 742 6666 or **t** (061) 712 400

By bus Limerick's bus station for all services is on Parnell St. Bus Éireann, **t** (061) 474 311/313 333
By car Parking isn't easy in Limerick, and most of the city centre is a disc parking zone.
By train There are trains daily to Dublin, Cork, Waterford and Rosslare. Information, **t** (061) 315 555
Bike Hire
Emerald Cycles, 1 Patrick St, Limerick, **t** (061) 416 983

Special Events – County Limerick

May

Ballyhoura International Walking Festival, **t** (063) 91306, **www.ballyhoura.org**
Riverfest, Limerick, **t** (061) 400 225, **www.limerick.ie**
A family festival.

August

All-Breeds Championship Dog Show, Fitzgerald's Woodlands House Hotel, Adare, **t** (061) 304 433
More than 2,500 dogs are judged here.

October

Halloween Storyfest, Lough Gur Heritage Centre, information from HoneyFitz Theatre, **t** (061) 385 386
Storytelling, music and dancing.

Entertainment

Belltable Arts Centre

69 O'Connell St, Limerick, **t** (061) 319 866
Open Mon–Fri 9–7, Sat 10–9
Limerick's main live arts centre hosts very good plays and films, and has a gallery showing local work.

Irish Rambling House

Various locations in Limerick and Adare, **t** (068) 48353, **www.irishramblinghouse.com**
Open Summer
Adm €12 show only, €30 show and dinner
Traditional music, song, dance and storytelling.

Shopping

O'Mahony's Bookshop

120 O'Connell St, Limerick, **t** (061) 418 155
Open Mon–Weds, Fri and Sat 9–6, Thur 9–7
Ireland's oldest independent bookshop, a Limerick institution with lots for kids and on local interests. There are branches in Tralee and Ennis.

LIMERICK CITY

Limerick is cloaked in the colour grey, from the stones of its dwellings to its Custom House with the impressive Hunt Museum beside the blue Shannon. Founded in the 9th century by the Vikings, who named it *Laemrich*, 'rich soil or land', it is the Republic's third-largest city. Having gained notoriety as the home of Frank McCourt, who wrote *Angela's Ashes* about his poverty-stricken early days here, it still has the charm of the past lurking in its alleys and streets. Investigate its historic sites on a walking tour. For some, the town's rugby ardour makes it Ireland's sports capital. For others, it is an entertainment centre with its heritage precinct, where you can visit the 'Treaty Stone' on which was signed the treaty that ended the Jacobite–Williamite war in 1691 (*see* p.35), and visit King John's Castle.

Things to see and do

The Georgian House and Garden

2 Pery Square, **t** (061) 314 130
Getting there 5mins walk from Tourist Office
Open Mon–Fri 10–4, other times by appointment
Adm Adult €4.45, 5–16s €1.90, under-5s free, family €12.70

A faithfully restored house with Georgian furnishings, architectural details and decorations.

The Hunt Museum

Custom House, Rutland St, **t** (061) 312 833, **www.huntmuseum.ie**
Open Mon–Sat 10–5 (June 2–5)
Adm Adult €5.70, 6–16s €2.80, under-6s free, family (2+5) €14

Art and artefacts from the Stone Age to the 20th century, donated by noted art historians and Celtic archaeologists John and Gertrude Hunt. Teenagers interested in art find its early Celtic brooches and medieval crucifix figures fascinating, and there's also a bronze horse by Leonardo da Vinci and a cross belonging to Mary, Queen of Scots.

King John's Castle

Nicholas St, King's Island, **t** (061) 360 788
Open Daily Jan, Feb, Nov and Dec 10–4.30, Mar, Apr and Oct 9.30–5, May–Sept 9.30–5.30; last admission 1hr before closing. Times subject to change: call ahead
Adm Adult €7, 6–18s €4.20, under-6s free, family (2+6) €17.50
Souvenir shop, tea room, toilets with disabled access

There is a lot to see and explore in this authentic medieval castle, built between 1200 and 1210 and in the middle of Limerick's medieval heritage precinct. A state-of-the-art interpretative centre covers 800 years of local history from the 13th century onwards. The most family-friendly displays are reconstructions of medieval courtyards, crewed by actors demonstrating 16th-century trades. On other floors the castle's role in history is brought to life via audio-visual effects, 3D images, models and displays of early weapons, as well as excavated Norman fortifications and houses. Hear what King John says about himself, and find out how he made his own coins, on your way up to the battlement walkways on top of the castle's walls and towers. Learn what soldiers used in battle before gunpowder and cannons were available, and explore the southwest tower to discover what happened here in the 17th century. You can also see archaeological excavations below ground, which show that houses existed here before the castle was built.

A Limerick from Limerick, 1

A mouse in her room woke Miss Doud,
Who was frightened and screamed very loud,
Then a happy thought hit her,
To scare off the critter –
She sat up in bed and just meowed.

Can you spot?

Look for the shapes of imaginary animals such as the griffin and cockatrice on the 15th-century choir stalls in St Mary's Cathedral.

Limerick Museum

Castle Lane, off Nicholas St, **t** (061) 417 826
Open Tues–Sat 10–1 and 2.15–5. **Adm** Free

This award-winning museum houses Neolithic, Bronze and Iron Age artefacts and fragments of Limerick's civic and natural history, archaeology and traditional lace and silver crafts.

St Mary's Cathedral

Bridge St, **t** (061) 416 238
Adm Donation

Built in 1172 by the King of Munster, Donal Mor O'Brien, this is the oldest and the last ancient church left in Limerick City, and its most architecturally important building.

SPECIAL TRIPS

Celtic Park and Gardens

Cloonagulleen, Kilcornan, **t** (061) 394 243
Getting there Off the N69 10 miles (17km) west of Limerick and 5 miles (8km) northwest of Adare
Open Daily mid-Mar–Oct 9.30–6, other times by appointment
Adm Adult €5, free for up to 4 under-12s, family (2+4 under-12s) €10
Tea room, bookshop, free car and coach parking

Visit this landscaped garden and see whether you can tell the difference between the original and the reconstructed Celtic buildings. Sited on one of Cromwell's plantations, this is an excellent place to come to teach children something about Ireland's ancient buildings – with a lake dwelling (*crannóg*), a ring fort, a communal tomb and a stone church along with a dolmen, a stone circle, a mass rock, a cooking site, a lime kiln and a holy well, dotted within the beautiful gardens. End the day well by walking among the rockeries, lily ponds and roses in the ornamental garden and having tea amid beautiful views.

Lough Gur Heritage Centre

Killmallock Rd, Ballyneety, **t** (061) 360 788, **www.shannonheritage.com**
Getting there 7 miles (9km) southeast of Limerick City
Open Daily May–mid-Sept 9.30–5.30; by request at other times for groups
Adm Adult €4.75, child €2.50, family (2+4) €12.50, group rates €2.20
Guided tours, visitor centre, audio-visual display

This outdoor park on the shore of Lough Gur is possibly the most important Stone Age site in Ireland. It is easy to imagine that the Tuatha Dé Danaan still dwell here in some parallel universe, as Irish mythology indicates. Two small castles built by the Earls of Desmond stand at the ends of a horseshoe-shaped lake in which a *crannóg* (artificial island) stands. Around them lie the remnants of stone circles, including the 4,000-year-old Grange Stone Circle, which is made of 113 stones and may be the largest in Ireland. Reconstructions of the ritual, burial and dwelling places of this region's first farmers are present, along with standing stones, wedge-shaped cairns, a ring fort and a Neolithic house.

Thankfully, the site has been left alone without most of the disturbing elements and pollutants associated with modern tourism. Only a small visitor centre with an exhibition that tells the history of its last 5,000 years, plus a car park, impinge on it, and even these have been built in one place beside the lake and in keeping with the setting.

Wear good shoes and rainwear, as the pathways can be muddy. You will enjoy exploring this area most if you arrange to take a guided tour, as the grounds are quite extensive, but you must book a guide before you arrive.

AROUND AND ABOUT

Animal magic

Buttercup Farm

Ballygrennan, Croom, **t** (061) 397 556
Getting there 18 miles (29km) south of Limerick

Meet lambs, rabbits, pigs, peacocks and other farm animals at this old-fashioned farm. It offers a tree trail, nature quiz and picnic area.

Bricks and mortar

Croom Mills Visitor and Heritage Centre

Croom, **t** (061) 397 130, **www.croommills.com**
Getting there 18 miles (29km) south of Limerick
Open Exhibition: all year 9–5. Shop and bistro: daily 9–6. Restaurant: Thurs–Sat 5–9.30. **Adm** Free
Crafts and gift shop, restaurants, parking

An old grain mill – with a massive cast-iron waterwheel built in 1852 and a 1900s steam engine – has been restored and converted into this centre, where you can meet the descendants of local people who once worked it. First watch the film on the history of Croom Mills, then explore the mill itself, with its interactive exhibits that enable visitors to get involved in the corn-grinding process. Children can try turning a heavy stone quern and touching freshly milled grain as it is prepared via methods used more than a century ago. Afterwards, stroll along the Maigue River and return to the mill's restaurant for a home-baked meal. Sunday lunches are especially good.

De Valera Museum and Bruree Heritage Centre

Bruree, **www.bruree.net**
Getting there 30 miles (48km) south of Limerick off N20 Cork road
Open Mon–Fri 10–5, Sat and Sun 2–5. **Adm** Free

Older children may be interested in this museum in the National School attended by the late president of Ireland, Eamon de Valera (1882–1975). He was born in Manhattan, New York, to a Spanish father

A Limerick from Limerick, 2

A landlady mean in Ardee,
Served little of honey at tea.
A new lodger said,
As he shook a sad head,
"I'm glad, Ma'am, to see you've one bee."

and Irish mother. Following the death of his father when he was 2, he was sent to live in Ireland with his grandmother. As an adult, he became a maths teacher, then joined the Gaelic League and became a lifelong champion of the Irish language. Displays of his belongings and articles recording life in Bruree in the early 20th century are here, near the cottage where he spent his youth.

Look at this!

Flying Boat Museum

Foynes, **t** (069) 65416
Getting there On N69 23 miles (37km) west of Limerick
Open Daily Apr–Oct 10–6; last admission 5
Adm Adult €7.50, student €5, 6–14s €4, under-6s free, family (2+4) €18
Tea room, gift shop, free car and coach parking

A fascinating museum about the famous seaplane airliners of the 1930s, used to carry all kinds of passengers, from celebrities to refugees. This Atlantic port was a stopping-off and refuelling point for air traffic between the USA and Europe from the 1920s to the 1940s; 'Irish coffee', it is said, was created here to comfort cold passengers. Older children may be intrigued by the radio and weather room with original transmitters for Morse code, and the 1940s-style cinema with original footage.

Nature lovers

Ballyhoura Mountain Park

Kilfinane, Golden Vale
Getting there N20 south from Limerick to Killmallock, then southeast to Kilfinane (35 miles/56km)
Open All year
Interpretative panels, marked walking routes, fitness and orienteering routes, car parking

There is enjoyable birdwatching and walking in this natural woodland area covering about 25,000 acres. Within it there are mountains, peat bogs, wild berries and flowers, and it also has waymarked trails and nature walks.

Glin Castle, Pleasure Grounds and Walled Gardens

Glin, **t** (068) 34173, **www.glincastle.com**
Getting there 31 miles (50km) west of Limerick, on N69 to Tarbert (3 miles/5km east of Tarbert)
Open Strictly by appointment
Adm Castle and Gardens: €7 per person
Guided tours every half-hour

This Georgian Gothic castle is the ancestral home of the knights of Glin, part of the Fitzgerald family. A walled garden with fruit, herbs and vegetables slopes beyond the romantic house, where a few paying guests stay from March to November. The splendid Gothic-styled grounds feature a headless Ariadne statue in a rustic temple, a yew tree walk and hens roaming freely.

Sporty kids

Horse-riding

Clonshire Equestrian Centre

Adare, **t** (061) 396 770

A friendly and well-equipped riding centre.

Hillcrest Riding Centre

Galbally, **t** (062) 37915

Choose from cross-country, showjumping and trekking. You can see the Glen of Aherlow on horseback on the Ballyhoura/Glen of Aherlow Trail.

Walking

Knockfierna Hill

Getting there 6 miles (10km) southwest of Croom, 24 miles (39km) from Limerick

This hill is the home of the Tuatha Dé Danaan king of the Otherworld, Donn Forinne. A vast expanse of Ireland can be viewed from its summit, including the Shannon Estuary and the distant Blue Mountains. This is also the home of the National Famine Commemoration Park, and it contains 15 buildings associated with the famine; ask for directions in Ballingarry.

COUNTY CLARE

The Irish say that if you turn over a rock in County Clare (*Conndae an Chlair/An Clár*, 'a level surface or plain'), there's a story under it. It wouldn't be a surprise if music didn't sing out from under it as well. Near the Cliffs of Moher, Doolin has a fine tradition of Irish music and Ennis is home to the Fleadh Nua, an annual celebration of folk music.

Clare is a wonderful big-sky kind of place. Here, bird colonies may be observed off Loop Head in shale rock 'apartments', each inhabited every summer by the same bird until it dies. Dolphins leap in rough water (when they normally feed below the surface) for no reason at all but to show themselves to a dying child whose foremost wish is to see a real dolphin. A gentler kind of people inhabit this county, where protests about chopping down a faery tree in Ennis forced the council to reroute a new highway. Such occurrences are common in Clare, perhaps because its people's imaginations still dance with the natural world.

From the seaside towns of the west and castles of the south to the rugged Burren and Cliffs of Moher, there is remarkably good pasture in Clare. Numerous lakes and turloughs (lakes or ponds that disappear in dry periods) lie in land that's often fissured limestone, or a treeless terrain weathered to form peat bogs and rush-infested pastures.

Cromwell dismissed the Burren as 'a country where there is not water enough to drown a man, wood enough to hang one, or earth enough to bury him'. But there is a peace in Clare, especially in the Burren, that cannot be created by anything but nature, something the Cromwells (and faery tree choppers) of this world may not even notice.

Tourist Information

Bunratty, t (061) 360133
Cliffs of Moher, Liscannor, **t** (065) 708 1565
Ennis, Arthur's Row, off O'Connell St, **t** (065) 682 8366
Kilrush, Town Hall, **t** (065) 905 1577
Shannon Airport, t (061) 471 664
www.shannonregiontourism.ie

Getting there and around

By air Shannon Airport is located 13 miles (21km) from Ennis along the N18 road towards Limerick (*see* p.283). Information, **t** 1 890 742 6666 or **t** (061) 712 400

By bus Most buses leave from alongside Ennis train station, with regular connections to Shannon airport, Limerick, Galway and Dublin. There are a few buses daily to Lahinch and Doolin, Lisdoonvarna and the Cliffs of Moher.
Bus Information, Ennis, **t** (065) 682 4177 or Burren Coaches, **t** (065) 707 8009

By train Ennis is on the Galway–Limerick rail line and many trains continue on to Dublin.

By boat The Clare–Kerry ferry runs between Killimer and Tarbert: Shannon Ferries, **t** (065) 905 3124.

Bike Hire

Burren Cycling Holidays, t (065) 707 4300
David Monks, Monks Bar, Ballyvaughan, **t** (065) 707 7059
Gleeson's Cycles, Henry St, Kilrush, **t** (065) 905 1127
Tierney's, 17 Abbey St, Ennis, **t** (065) 682 9433
Williams Rent-a-Bike, Kilkee, **t** (065) 905 6041

Special Events – County Clare

May

Fleadh Nua, Ennis, **t** (086) 826 0300
www.fleadhnua.com

A festival of traditional music, dancing and singing that takes over the whole town for a week.

June

Shannon Dolphin Festival, Kilrush, **t** (065) 905 2522

Live street theatre for all the family.

July

Feile Brian Boru, Killaloe, **t** (061) 376 100

A weekend of music, parades and dancing to honour the reign of Brian Boru, High King 1002–14.

Glór Summer Festival, Ennis, **t** (065) 684 3103, **www.glor.ie**

A festival of traditional Irish music and dance, held all summer.

Willie Clancy Summer School, Milltown Mowbay, **t** (065) 708 4281/4148

Concerts and workshops in Irish traditional music and dance, held as a tribute to Ireland's greatest *uillean* piper, Willie Clancy (1921–73).

August–October

Matchmaking Festival of Ireland, Lisdoonvarna (late Aug–early Oct), **t** (065) 707 4005, **www.matchmakerireland.com**

Single women come all the way from America for the fun of this matchmaking festival; Mr Lisdoonvarna and the Queen of the Burren are the stars of the show.

ENNIS

Clare's county town straddles the River Fergus (*Inis* means an islet or river meadow). A market town dating back to the 11th century, it's famous today for traditional music. It's a friendly place with historic buildings and narrow streets, not to mention inhabitants, that give it great charm. In the centre is a memorial to Daniel O'Connell, and another to Eamon de Valera, who represented Clare in the Irish Parliament from 1918 to 1959.

Things to see and do

Ennis Friary

Abbey St, **t** (065) 682 9100
Open Daily mid-June–Sept 9.30–6.30

The O'Briens, kings of Thomond, founded this 13th-century Fransciscan friary, now in ruins.

The Riches of Clare

Clare Museum, Arthur's Row, off O'Connell Sq, t (065) 682 3382, www.clarelibrary.ie
Open June–Sept Mon–Sat 9.30–5.30, Sun 9.30–1; Oct–May Tues–Sat 9.30–1 and 2–5.30
Adm Free

Housed in a former convent built in 1861, this tells the story of Co. Clare from 6,000 years ago to the present day. There are impressive artefacts, special effects and works of art here, all organized along themes of Earth, Power, Faith and Water.

SPECIAL TRIPS

Beal Boru (Brian Boru's Fort)

Brian Boru Heritage Centre, Killaloe, t (061) 376 866 or t (061) 370 788
Open June–Sept Mon–Sat 9.30–5.30, Sun 9.30–1; Oct–May Tues–Sat 9.30–1 and 2–5.30
Adm Free

This display tells the story of the only High King of all of Ireland. Ask at the heritage centre for directions to the fort itself, just outside Killaloe.

Bunratty Castle and Folk Park

t (061) 360 788, www.shannonheritage.com
Getting there 8 miles (13km) from Limerick off N18 to Shannon and Ennis
Open Jan–Mar, Nov and Dec Castle 9.30–4, Park 9.30–5; May and Sept Castle 9–5.30, Park 9–4; closed Good Fri, 24–26 Dec
Adm May–Sept: adult €10, under-18s €5.60, family (2+ up to 6) €26.25
Oct–Apr: adult €8, under-18s €4.70, family €22
Tea room, shop, 'Irish Nights' Apr–Oct at 7pm, Medieval Castle banquets 2xnightly, 5.30 and 8.45pm year-round (subject to demand)

If you arrive in Ireland at Shannon, this is one of your first must-sees. It presents a microcosm of Irish history, with a replica 19th-century Irish village, complete with people dressed as country folk did 100 years ago. There are eight farmhouses, two watermills, a blacksmith's forge and a church, plus a pub, post office, school, doctor's house, hardware shop, printers, drapery store, pawn shop and hotel. Their informative attendants will tell you all about their work and times.

The exhibits are as authentic as possible. Roofs are thatched and stone walls are whitewashed. And you may see animals and fields being tended as they were before the days of machines, milk being churned or bread baked over an open fire.

Children can go even farther back into history by investigating the tower-house known as Bunratty Castle, which was built in 1425 by the MacNamara clan. It has been magnificently restored so that visitors can imagine what it was like to live in such a place, with its dungeon, great hall and cavernous kitchen. To really appreciate its past, you should indulge in the castle's medieval banquet, where you are treated to a sumptuous feast while being enchanted by the songs and stories of the Bunratty Entertainers. The early feast at 5.30 would most suit children.

The Burren

In the north of Clare is one of Ireland's most rare and magical landscapes – the Burren ('the stony district'), a giant limestone plateau. Apparently barren, the Burren is full of life amid its strangely shaped rocks, with ancient ruins, old villages, animals and an amazing range of scented plants.

Aillwee Cave

The Burren, Ballyvaughan, t (065) 707 7036, www.aillweecave.ie
Getting there 23 miles (37km) north of Ennis
Open Daily Jan–June 10–5.30, Sept–Nov 10–5.30, Dec 10–12

Adm Adults €10, 4–14s €4.50, under-4s free, family (2+2) €25, (2+4) €30
Guided tours, tea room, farm shop, parking

The Burren has the most important and extensive cave systems in Ireland, but only one is safe enough for the general public to explore (with a guide). Aillwee Cave was formed millions of years ago by an underground river that cut through the limestone left behind after the Ice Age. Older kids who have never been inside a cave will enjoy seeing the rock formations caused by dripping water, and the hibernation indentations caused by brown bears sleeping there through long winters.

It's important that your children are not afraid of the dark, as the tour is quite slow. Have a warm jumper or sweater to hand too. After exploring the cold grey hollows of the underworld, you can eat a baked potato in the café and shop for minerals or fossils. Outdoors you can picnic or climb over the Burren limestone pavements, or walk in coppice woods on a nature trail. After that, pay a visit to the dairy and watch cheese being made or honey extracted from combs, then try fudge or chutney made in the farm kitchen.

The Burren Centre

Kilfenora, **t** (065) 708 8030, **www.**theburrencentre.ie
Getting there 15 miles (24km) from Ennis on R476
Open Daily mid-Mar–May, Sept and Oct 10–5, June–Aug 9.30–6; last adm 30mins before closing
Adm Adult €5,95, under-16s €3.75, under-6s free, family (2+2) €17
Guided tours on request, shop, tea room, toilets with disabled and baby-changing facilities, garden

Here in the village that has more Celtic crosses than you can shake at a druid, you will find one of the most thoughtfully planned and impressive small museums in Ireland. Discover how 350 million years of life on Earth have shaped the limestone of the Burren. Fascinating exhibits explain its archaeology, flora, fauna, geography and geology and the effects of people on the landscape.

Most notable are the history sections, with life-size models showing prehistoric Irish people in their habitats, plus sound recordings of traditional music and local folk stories recounted by children. Don't miss this centre if you want to appreciate the Burren and its unique features.

Burren Perfumery and Floral Centre

Carran, **t** (065) 708 9102, **www.**burrenperfumery.com
Getting there 14 miles (22km) north of Ennis
Open Daily Oct–Apr 9–5, May–Sept 9–6, June–Aug 9–7; tea room Easter–Sept daily 9–5, Oct–Dec Sat and Sun 9–5
Adm Free
Organic tea room

This small centre now imports its floral essences due to recent laws on the local environment, but you can watch an audio-visual exhibit on the history of perfume-making in the Burren, then head outside to visit the essential oil distillery and the extensive organic garden.

Gregan's Wood

Getting there On N67 between Lisdoonvarna and Ballyvaughan

This is a veritable gold mine for amateur archaeologists, as you'll find cairns, ring forts, megalithic tombs and the like everywhere. A great place from which to look out over the Burren, the surrounding hills are good for fishing, swimming and walking.

Poulnabrone Portal Dolmen

Getting there 5 miles (8km) south of Ballyvaughan on R480

This 5,000-year-old portal tomb was excavated in 1986 and is one of Ireland's finest dolmens. It's a huge 3-legged tomb, standing alone on the rocky landscape.

The Salmon of Knowledge Experience

Burren Smokehouse, Lisdoonvarna, **t** (065) 707 4432, **www.**burrensmokehouse.ie
Getting there 20 miles (32km) from Ennis on R476
Open Daily Apr–Sept 9–6, Oct–Mar 9–5
Adm Free
Visitor centre, exhibition, audio-visual tour, crafts and gourmet food store and pub, parking

It is worth visiting this attraction to hear the story of the 'Salmon of Knowledge' (*see* p.234) and to learn about the ancient Irish custom of oak-smoking salmon.

Craggaunowen – The Living Past

Quin, **t** (061) 360 788 (Shannon Heritage), **www.**shannonheritage.com
Getting there 10 miles (16km) east of Ennis
Open Daily mid-Apr–Sept 10–6 (call ahead, as dates may vary), last admission 5
Adm Adult €7.50, student €5.60, child €4.50, family (2+2) €17.50, family (2+4) €18.50, family (2+6) €19.50
Guided tours, tea shop, craft shop, picnic area

The past is brought to life at this award-winning museum on all aspects of Celtic life. Guides in authentic period shoes and rough-hewn costumes demonstrate the daily work of the people who lived in Ireland 1,000 years ago. They know all sorts of fascinating details, such as how to spin wool or dry animal skins, or make Celtic crosses out of reeds. You may get the chance to do some of these things yourselves. Imagine what it was like to be a Celtic chieftain, peeking at intruders through the stick walls of a *crannóg* (lake dwelling). See a ring fort and Iron Age roadway, and learn how Finn McCool and the Fianna cooked whole deer in man-made pools filled with hot stones. Look around to spy on the Soay and Jacob sheep, the Kerry cattle and the tusked, wild Irish boars (cordoned off behind a fence).

Don't miss 'The Brendan' – a re-created leather curragh used in the 6th century by St Brendan the Navigator and other Irish mariners on the high seas. In the 1980s, the late Tim Severin sailed in it to North America to show that St Brendan could, indeed, have reached America first, long before the Vikings.

When you've finished walking through the ancient woods, visit the cottage tea shop, with its traditional decorated hearth, for afternoon tea. Be sure to telephone Craggaunowen before you go, to ask for their best guide for your children.

A story to tell: The Way to Sing a Song

One twilight, a hunchback who had been watching over sheep all day heard strange high-pitched singing in the wind, as if from far, far away. He followed the sound towards a faery hill, from which he saw an orange-gold light shining out, as if from the last rays of the evening sun.

As he ventured nearer, the words of the song became clearer. Many voices seemed to be singing, 'Monday, Tuesday, Wednesday', over and over again in Irish. Then he saw them – the Little People, the Sidhe – all merrily repeating the verse as they danced around together in swirls of colour.

After a time, he thought maybe the Sidhe didn't know the next day of the week and so, to help them, he took his courage into his voice and sang, 'Monday, Tuesday, Wednesday, Thursday', adding a new twist in the melody for good measure.

Suddenly all was silent. The hunchback broke into a cold sweat. What would they do to him, he wondered? Then the voices sang again, adding his melody and 'Thursday' to their song, immediately after which he found himself surrounded by them.

A tiny, elegant fellow with a golden crown strode up. 'Thank you, kind sir, for your addition to our song. We have been singing it for hundreds of years and couldn't find the next bit of it.'

Another little plump man piped up, 'Do you think you could add something more to it for us?'

'Certain so', replied the hunchback, singing, 'Monday, Tuesday, Wednesday, Thursday, Friday', adding yet another melody to the end, which was repeated by the faery people, who cheered and tossed the hunchback into the air.

The next thing he knew, it was pitch dark and he was alone and there were millions of diamond stars smiling down on him from the night sky. He rose quickly, thinking he must have fallen asleep and dreamt of the faeries, and worrying where his sheep were. But somehow he felt lighter, straighter – yes, for the first time in his life he was standing up straight! He rubbed his back where his familiar hump always was and – it was gone!

The hunchback's story spread, and another hunchback heard it. Determined to find these faeries and get them to take away his hump, he arrived at the faery hill one afternoon, muttering that the faeries were taking their sweet time arriving. Finally, at twilight, he heard them singing their song, along with the other hunchback's melody. This went on and on until he could stand it no longer and finally burst out, 'Would ye stop your infernal racket! It's Saturday and Sunday next!'

Again, there was silence. Only this time the song was not sung again and the hunchback was surrounded by hundreds of tiny angry faces. The fellow with the crown rushed up to him and said, 'How dare you disturb our songmaking!'

The plump one added, 'Would you mind adding a tune to that Saturday and Sunday of yours?'

'If you'll take off this hump of mine, I will,' sneered the hunchback.

At that point he was thrown high into the air, and the next thing he knew it was night and thick clouds were dripping rain upon him. He found he could barely stand at all, so heavy had his hump become. And, when he rubbed the usual spot where it ached, he found that he had two humps instead of one!

Scattery Island Dolphin Tours

Scattery Island Ferries/Gerald Griffin Boat Tours, The Marina, Kilrush, **t** (065) 905 1327, **www.**discoverdolphins.ie
Getting there 27 miles (43km) from Ennis by N68
Open Apr–Sept, with daily sailings June–Aug; call for sailing times and rest of year
Adm Dolphin watching: adult €18, under-16s €9
Scattery Island Ferry: adult €12, under-16s €6

Boat hire and cruises from here take you dolphin-watching or out to Scattery Island's monastic sites. Ferries run from Kilrush Creek Marina to the uninhabited island in the Lower Shannon, weather permitting. Booking is advisable.

There is something special about seeing dolphins frolicking in the waves around Scattery Island, with its ruined churches, round tower and lighthouse. The friendly crew tell you all about Ireland's only known resident group of bottlenose dolphins. This Shannon Estuary haven allows more than 100 to breed each year (May–Aug). Even getting through the elaborate locks from the bay into the Atlantic is exciting to those unused to such things, on a rough day with thick foam on the water. Once the dolphins see your boat, they may swim alongside it.

Scattery Island Centre

Merchants Quay, Kilrush
Open Daily June–mid-Sept 10–1 and 2–6. **Adm** Free

In the 6th century, St Senan defeated a horrible monster on an island called *Inis Cathaig*, and founded a monastery on the spot. It was destroyed in the time of Elizabeth I, when the island became known as Scattery Island, and a castle was built there. Today you can see the ruins of the monastery, seven churches and a round tower.

Did you know?
Lisdoonvarna has the only active spa, from iron and magnesium springs, in Ireland. Farmers came to relax here when they finished harvesting each year, and also looked for wives. The tradition by which women and men of marriageable age were 'matched' by a matchmaker was common in Ireland until quite recently, and still thrives at the matchmaking festival every September in Lisdoonvarna (see p.140).

AROUND AND ABOUT

Bricks and mortar

Dysert O'Dea Castle and Clare Archaeology Centre

Corofin, **t** (065) 683 7401
Getting there 5 miles (8km) north of Ennis
Open Daily May–Sept 10–6, other times by appointment
Adm Adult €4, child €2.50, family €10
History trail, 1–3hr guided walks, shop, tea room

Follow the archaeology trail here to find out more about the history of this 15th-century castle. Under the 12th-century Dysert O'Dea Church sits an Early Christian monastery that was founded by St Tola in the 8th century. With an illustrated guide from the shop, children can have fun tracking 25 historical and archaeological sites within 2 miles (3km) of the castle.

Knappogue Castle

Quin, **t** Bunratty Folk Park: (061) 360 788, **www.**shannonheritage.com
Getting there 7 miles (10km) southeast of Ennis
Open Daily May–mid-Sept 9.30–5, last adm 4.15
Adm Adult €4.20, child €2.40
Craft shop, picnic area, toilets with disabled access

An audio-visual display tells the story of this 15th-century castle. Medieval banquets take place twice nightly Apr–Oct at 6.30 and 8.30, subject to demand, similar to those at Bunratty (*see* p.141); reservations are required. Knappogue's speciality is a show with music, song and dance about famous women of Ireland through the ages.

Nature lovers

Cliffs of Moher (Ailltreacha Mothair)

Visitor Centre, **t** (065) 708 1565
Getting there 20 miles (32km) northwest of Ennis
Open Site all year; Visitor Centre daily Sept–May 9.30–5.30, June–29 Aug 9–8; O'Brien's Tower: daily Mar–Oct (weather permitting) 9.30–6

***Good to know...* Organic Gardening**
The Organic Centre, t (071) 985 4338, www.theorganiccentre.ie, holds lessons in organic gardening in Co. Clare, on Jim Cronin's farm near Bridgetown.

You can't visit Clare without seeing the Cliffs of Moher – but hold on to young children, especially when winds are high. These dramatic 600ft (185m) cliffs, confronting the might of the Atlantic Ocean, are horizontal layers of flagstones that extend for 5 miles (8km) from Hag's Head to beyond O'Brien's Tower. Hag's Head resembles a seated woman looking out to sea, and is linked with the story of an old witch named Mal of Malbay at Loop Head.

Aill na Searrach ('Cliff of the Colts') is the northernmost point of the Cliffs. It is linked with a story about some colts of faery origin who leapt over the cliffs to the sea. To view the cliffs, walkers should start at O'Brien's Tower. Watch for ravens and the puffins (with highly coloured beaks) that nest on Goat Island and near the tower.

Sporty kids

Boat trips

Dolphin Watching

The Pier, Carrigaholt, **t** (065) 905 8156
Operates Daily Apr–Oct, but always book ahead
Adm Adult €18, 2–16s €9

These 2hr cruises from the old fishing port of Carrigaholt, between Kilrush and Loop Head, are in a boat custom-built for watching the dolphins of the Shannon and eavesdropping on their conversations (via a hydrophone). An evening cruise goes around Loop Head to observe dolphins, sea birds and cliffs. Early-morning trips are available.

Buckets and spades – Clare's Beaches

Clare has both sea- and freshwater beaches. **Lahinch** (16 miles/26km to the northwest of Ennis) is a popular seaside resort with a fine Blue Flag beach, good surfing and a fun-packed leisure centre with a sealife centre and indoor full-size and children's pools.
Other Blue Flag beaches: **Kilkee**, **White Strand**, **Spanish Point** (Milltown Malbay), **Lough Graney**, **Fanore** and **Doonbeg**.
Freshwater swimming: **Lough Derg** is the largest of the River Shannon's lakes, and at Killaloe (*see* below) there are several points where you can swim (children should always be supervised).

Shannon Castle Line

Williamstown Harbour, Killaloe, **t** (061) 927 042, **www.shannoncruisers.com**

Trips from Killaloe on the Shannon and Lough Derg on a 48-seat river bus, daily in summer.

Horse-riding

Burren Riding Centre

Fanore, **t** (065) 707 6140

Clare Equestrian Centre

Deerpark, Doora, near Clarecastle, **t** (065) 684 0136

A well-organized centre with ponies for children.

Walking

The **Burren Way** stretches 20 miles (32km) west of Ballyvaughan over the Burren to the Cliffs of Moher, with superb ocean views. Other fine walks are at **Ballyalla Lake**, near Ennis, **Ballycuggaran**, north of Killaloe on the Shannon, and **Doon Lough**, between Ennis and Lough Derg.

Burren Hill Walks, Ballyvaughan, **t** (065) 707 7168

Able guides leading a varied range of walks.

Watersports

Killaloe (Shannonside) Activity Centre

Killaloe, **t** (061) 376 622

A centre custom-built for a wide selection of land- and water-based activities. Special weeks are organized in summer for different age groups.

Steam power!

West Clare Railway

Moyasta Junction, **t** (065) 905 1284
Getting there On N67 Killrush to Killkee road
Open Mar–Aug Mon–Sat 10–6, Sun 12 noon–6; Sept–Mar Sat 10–6 and Sun 12 noon–6
Tickets Adult €7, child €3.50; free in Sept

A narrow-gauge steam locomotive, the No.5 Slieve Callan, runs for 3 miles (5km) through an area rich in birdlife. You need to pay at the adjoining Taylor's Pub before entering the site.

TIPPERARY AND WATERFORD

County Tipperary is known for horses and lakes. It's perfect for a quiet family holiday – just far enough from cities to avoid traffic yet close enough to popular tourist sites in nearby counties. A riding tour with overnight stays planned in advance is a leisurely way to holiday here, but if you prefer to see the sights, the rambling country roads are ideal for touring unhurriedly by car and Bus Éireann offers tours.

Lough Derg is a pleasant spot for a boating trip. With an abundance of trout, roach, bream, perch, pike and eels, it's also an angler's paradise. Other fine places to visit are Cashel, with the Rock of Cashel as its centrepiece; the village of Bansha for horse lovers; the Glen of Aherlow, if you prefer forest views; or Cahir, a market town with a castle.

Just to the south, the rather flat southeastern county of Waterford is known for its scenic coast and fishing villages. Within it is one of the most famous and most curious Irish-speaking areas of Ireland – far away from other such areas on the west coast – An Rinn (Ring), south of Dungarvan on Helvick Head. Noteworthy for being the first part of Ireland to have a city established by the Vikings, County Waterford has a history beset with invasions, thanks to the easy access its geography gives to seafarers. Interestingly, once people settled here, they became very peaceful – a quality you will find today throughout Waterford.

Tourist Information

Ardmore, Co. Waterford, **t** (024) 94444
Cahir, Co. Tipperary, Castle St, **t** (052) 41453
Cashel, Co. Tipperary, Main St, **t** (062) 62500
Clonmel, Co. Tipperary, **t** (052) 22960
Dungarvan, Co. Waterford, **t** (058) 41741
Lismore, Co. Waterford, **t** (058) 54975
Tramore, Co. Waterford, Railway Sq, **t** (051) 381 572, **www**.tramore.ie
Waterford, 41 The Quay, **t** (051) 875 823
www.southeastireland.ie
www.shannonregiontourism.ie

Tours

Day Tours by Rail, **t** (051) 873 711, **www**.railtoursireland.com
Trips from Dublin to Waterford
Easy Wheelin' Scenic Guided Cycle Tours, **t** (051) 390 706
Walking Tour of Historic Waterford, Waterford Tourist Services, Jenkins Lane, **t** (051) 873 711 or **t** (051) 851 043
Cost Adult €5, under-12s free with adult
Guided tours daily Mar–Oct at 11.45 and 1.45

Local historian and storyteller Jack Burtchaell takes you through the history of his home town and Ireland's oldest city. The 1hr tour brings to life the town's 'gallery of rogues and rascals' and departs from the Waterford Treasures Museum.

Getting there and around

By air Waterford has an airport, 8 miles (13km) south of the town on the road to Clohernagh (*see* p.280 and p.284). Information, **t** 051 875 589, **www**.flywaterford.com
By bus There are frequent Bus Éireann buses (**www**.buseireann.ie) from Dublin and Cork to Tipperary, Cashel, Waterford and other towns. From Cashel, Kavanagh's, **t** (062) 51563, runs other local services.

In Waterford, most buses leave from the Quay opposite the tourist office; as well as Bus Éireann services, Suirway, **t** (051) 382 422, **www**.suirway.com, runs buses to places all along the River Suir. Bus Éireann in Waterford, **t** (051) 879 000.
By train The Dublin–Cork line passes through Tipperary, and Waterford has frequent trains on the Dublin–Kilkenny and Rosslare/Wexford–Cork lines. Tor Tipperary town, trains stop at Limerick junction, a few miles north. Local information, Tipperary, **t** (062) 51206, Waterford, **t** (051) 873 401; **www**.irishrail.ie

A co-ordinated train and bus service operates with Northern Ireland; see **www**.translink.co.uk
By ferry Passage East Car Ferry offers a shortcut between Waterford and Wexford; **http**://homepage.eircom.net/~passferry/
Bike Hire
McInerneys, Cashel, Co. Tipperary, **t** (062) 61225
Murphy's Toys and Cycles, Main St, Dungarvan, Co. Waterford, **t** (058) 41376

Entertainment

Brú Ború Heritage Centre

Beside Rock of Cashel, Cashel, Co. Tipperary, **t** (062) 61122, **www**.comhaltas.com
Open Mid-June–mid-Sept Tues–Sat 9am–11.30pm, Sun and Mon 10–5; mid-Sept–mid-June Mon–Fri 9–5; evening performance 9, pre-show dinner 7.30
Adm Free. Exhibition: adult €5, child €3; Show: adult €16, child €9; Dinner and show: adult €42, child €20

A centre for the study of Irish traditions and also the venue for an Irish music and dance show run by Comhaltas Ceoltóirí Éireann each summer. Subterranean chambers run beneath here at the base of the Rock of Cashel.

Special Events – Tipperary and Waterford

February

Merriman Winter School, Dungarvan, Co. Waterford, **t** (098) 27758, **www.merriman.ie**

A celebration of all aspects of Irish culture.

April

Sean Dunne Literary Festival, Waterford, **t** (051) 309 983

Readings, workshops and music.

June

Clonmel Show, Clonmel, Co. Tipperary, **t** (052) 22611

A lively horse show, with showjumping.

July

Kilcommon Festival, Kilcommon, Co. Tipperary, **t** (062) 78103

An 8-day affair in the rural highlands, with traditional music and dance, games, sheepdog trials and street entertainment.

July–August

Spr Ogi Pre-Spraoi Festival, Garter Lane Arts Centre, 22A O'Connell St, Waterford, **t** (051) 877 153

Entertainment for children aged 5–8.

August

Aonach Paddy O'Brien, Newtown, Co. Tipperary, **t** (067) 42900

A traditional music and arts festival, named after a local composer and accordionist.

Spraoi Street Festival, Waterford, **t** (051) 841 808

'Ireland's biggest street festival', held in Waterford town over the whole of the August bank holiday weekend.

September–October

Waterford International Festival of Light Opera, Theatre Royal, Waterford **t** (051) 311 270, **www.operafestival.com**

A charming festival of high-quality music.

Waterford Show

City Hall, The Mall, Waterford, **t** (051) 381 020
Performances 4 May–Sept Tues, Thurs and Sat 8.45pm, plus Weds July and Aug. **Adm** €12

A comic tale with Irish music and folklore.

TOURING TOWNS

Cashel

Once the home of the High Kings of Munster, Cashel is just small enough for those who want to explore an Irish town in a day. Several attractions are within easy reach and it's a good place to take a break if you're driving from Dublin to Cork. Don't forget to try some Cashel Blue cheese too.

Things to see and do

Cashel Folk Village

Dominic St, **t** (062) 62525
Open Daily Mar–Apr 10–6, May–Oct 9.30–7
Adm Adult €3.50, student/child €2.50
Guided tour available, audio-visual presentation of the Irish Wars 1916–23, disabled access

Behind a wall near the Rock of Cashel lie informal reconstructions of traditional thatched shops, a forge and other businesses, complete with old signs and historical displays. Wish yourself back in time at Dominic's Well. Visit Widow Breen's House. Learn how tools were used in the Trades Hall and enter a Tinker's Caravan, then learn about the famine before meditating in the movable chapel that was hidden from official view in Penal times.

Cashel Heritage Centre

Town Hall, **t** (062) 62511
Open Daily Mar–June 9.30–5.30, July and Aug 9.30–8, Sept–Feb Mon–Fri 9.30–5.30, Sat and Sun on request; tram operates June–Sept
Adm Adult €1.27, child €0.63, family €3.81
Disabled access

A large-scale model of Cashel dominates this centre about the history of this ancient site. The royal relics of the MacCarthy Mur kings are on display, alongside changing exhibitions on the area.

Rock of Cashel

Cashel, **t** (062) 61437
Open Daily mid-Mar–mid-June 9–5.30, mid-June–mid-Sept 9–7, mid-Sept–mid-Mar 9.30–4.30; last admission 45mins before closing
Adm Adult €5, child €2, family €11
Guided tour available

This medieval castle sits spectacularly above the Golden Vale and town of Cashel on a great mound: the Rock of Cashel itself. Cashel rock was the seat of the Eóghanachta clan from the 4th century. From here they conquered much of Munster to become its High Kings. For 400 years, Cashel rivalled Tara as

Ireland's centre of power. In the 10th century, the clan lost it to the O'Briens, led by Brian Boru, and in 1101 King Muircheartach O'Brien gave Cashel to the Church. It was a great ecclesiastical centre until Cromwell's army killed 3,000 Catholic devotees here in 1647. Visitors may watch a film entitled 'Strongholds of the Faith'. Inside the castle walls, keep an eye on young children, as there are lots of rocky surfaces to negotiate.

Waterford Town

Ireland's oldest town was created by the Vikings before they settled in Dublin. An old-fashioned quiet hovers above its grey streets, reminiscent of Irish towns in the 1970s. Folk music and fun walking tours are available in summer (*see* p.146).

Things to see and do

Christ Church Cathedral

Cathedral Sq, **t** (051) 858 058
Open Easter–Oct Mon–Sat 10–5, Sun 11.30–5 (Apr, May and Oct closed for lunch 1–2)
Adm Adult €3, child €1.50, family €6
Guided tours on request for individuals

Waterford's main architect, John Roberts, designed this in the 18th century. Under its stucco plasterwork ceiling sit an 1815 Elliot organ and the tombs of a 16th-century knight and 14th-century town mayor.

Reginald's Tower Museum

The Quay, **t** (051) 304 220
Open Easter–May, Oct and Nov daily 10–5, June–Sept daily 10–6, Oct–Easter Wed–Sun 10–5
Adm Adult €2, child €1, family €5.50
Shop, guided tour

A round tower has stood here for more than 1,000 years, but the current round, fat building has been here since the 12th century. Around that time, in this place, the Norman warrior Strongbow first met Aoife, the daughter of the King of Leinster (*see* p.33). Viking-era and medieval artefacts are on show.

Waterford Treasures at the Granary

The Granary, Merchants Quay, **t** (051) 304 500, **www.waterfordtreasures.com**
Open Daily Apr, May and Sept 10–5, June–Aug 9.30–9
Adm Adults €6, students €4.50, under-16s €3.20; ask about family rates
Shop, restaurant, tourist office

This excellent museum has many interactive and audio-visual presentations to appeal to school-age children, and some fun activities for younger ones. As you enter, you can watch a short film about how Viking settlers first came to Waterford – on benches that roll as if you're on a ship, to give you a sense of Viking life at sea. You move on to a reconstruction of the wedding between Strongbow and the King of Leinster's daughter Aoife, and later Georgian Ireland and its artefacts, including Waterford crystal. Also here are computers and child-friendly music, song, dance and storytelling, **The Waterford Viking Show** (**t** 051 303 500, shows June–mid-Sept Mon, Wed, Fri 8pm).

Waterford Crystal Factory

Kilbarry, Cork Rd (N25), t (051) 332 500, www.waterfordvisitorcentre.com
Open Daily Mar–Oct 8.30–6, Nov–Feb 9–5; factory tours daily Mar–Oct 8.30–3.15, Nov–Feb 9–3.15 (closed 17 Mar)
Adm Adult €8, students €4, under-12s free
Guided tours, toilets with baby-changing facilities and disabled access, café, tourist office

Learn how this world-famous crystal is made via a film and a tour of the glass-making factory, with modern technology used alongside traditional skills. The informative staff welcome children.

SPECIAL TRIPS

Cahir Castle

Castle St, Cahir, Co. Tipperary, **t** (052) 41011
Getting there 11 miles (18km) from Cashel by N8
Open Daily mid-Mar–mid-June 9.30–5.30, mid-June–mid-Sept 9–7, mid-Sept–mid-Oct 9.30–5.30, mid-Oct–mid-Mar 9.30–4.30; last admission 45mins before closing. Closed 24–30 Dec
Adm Adult €2.75, under-18s €1.25, family €7
Audio-visual presentation

Sitting on a rocky island on the River Suir, this impressive castle is one of Ireland's largest and best preserved. Founded by Conor O'Brien in 1142 and passed on to the Butler family in 1375, it imbues the town that has grown up around it with medieval grandeur. It has survived nearly intact through the centuries, largely because it surrendered to Cromwell in 1650 without a fight.

AROUND AND ABOUT

Animal magic

Holycross Rare Breeds Farm

Holycross, Thurles, Co. Tipperary, **t** (0504) 43173
Getting there 9 miles (15km) north of Cashel
Open Daily May–Sept 10–7; Apr and Oct Sat, Sun and bank hols or by appointment
Adm Adult €3.50, child €2.50
Pets' corner, picnic areas, toilets with disabled access

You can learn about 70-plus breeds of birds and animals at the interpretative centre here, then meet Kerry Bog ponies, once used to pull turf from the bogs, tiny brown Soay and blue Herdwick sheep (which were rescued from extinction by Beatrix Potter), and more.

Parson's Green Pet Farm

Clogheen, Co. Tipperary, **t** (052) 65290
Getting there 8 miles (13km) south of Cahir
Open Daily mid-Mar–June 10–6, July and Aug 10–8
Adm Adult €5, child €2.50, family (2+3) €12
Pet farm, picnic area, café, caravan park

Spend a day here with kids playing in the garden or on the beach, or taking trap, boat and pony rides.

Bricks and mortar

Ormond Castle

Castle Park (off Castle St), Carrick-on-Suir, Co. Tipperary, **t** (051) 640 787
Getting there 16 miles (25km) from Waterford
Open Daily mid-June–Sept 10–5.15
Adm Adult €2.75, child €1.25, family €7
Guided tours only, shop

Ireland's best Elizabethan manor house, begun by the Earls of Ormond in the 14th century.

Look at this!

Carrick-on-Suir Heritage Centre

Main St, Carrick-on-Suir, **t** (051) 640 200
Open Mon–Fri 10–1 and 2–4
Adm Adult €3, student/child €2, family €6.50

Photographs of the town's famous inhabitants, such as the Clancy Brothers musicians, and other artefacts displayed in a pre-Reformation church.

Lismore Heritage Centre

The Courthouse, Lismore, **t** (058) 54975
Open Daily Mon–Sat 10–5.30, Sun 12 noon–5
Adm Adult €4, child/student €3.50, family (2+4) €12
Audio-visual show

The town of Lismore's Celtic beginnings in AD 636 through its monastic period and involvement with Sir Walter Raleigh and the building of its cathedral, castle and church may be learned about here.

Swiss Cottage

Kilcommon, Cahir, **t** (052) 41144
Getting there 1 mile (1.5 km) south of Cahir off R670 to Ardinnan; enter via Cahir Wood
Open Mid-Mar–mid-Apr Tues–Sun and bank hols 10–1 and 2–6, mid-Apr–mid-Oct daily 10–6, mid-Oct–mid-Nov Tues–Sun and bank hols 10–1 and 2–4.30; last admission 45mins before closing
Adm Adult €2.75, student/child €1.25, family €7
By guided tour only (book in advance)

Access to this 'cottage orné' is by stone steps, so it's only suitable for older children. Built in the early 1800s to a design by Regency architect John Nash, it has a thatched roof and internal spiral staircase.

Nature lovers

Lismore Castle Gardens

Lismore, Co. Waterford, **t** (058) 54424
Getting there 15 miles (24km) from Dungarvan
Open End Mar–Sept daily 1.45–4.45pm (11am opening in high season)
Adm Grounds only: adult €6, under-16s €3

This castle, presented to Sir Walter Raleigh in 1589, can only be viewed from outside but its magical gardens are open to visitors.

Mitchelstown Cave

Burncourt, Cahir, Co. Tipperary, **t** (052) 67246
Getting there 10 miles (16km) west of Cahir on N8
Open Daily May–Sept 10–6, Oct–Apr 10–5
Adm Adult €9.50, child €2, family (2+2) €12.50
Guided tours available (minimum 2 adults)

This limestone cave, which was discovered in 1833, extends over an area of 10 miles (16 km) between Mitchelstown and Cahir, and has some impressive stalagmites and stalactites.

Sporty kids

Boat trips

Shannon Sailing Centre
New Harbour, Dromineer, Nenagh, **t** (067) 24499

Lunch/dinner cruises on Lough Derg, plus boat hire, water-skiing, sailing, windsurfing and canoeing.

Ireland Line Cruisers
Ballina, Co. Tipperary, **t** (061) 375 011, **www.irelandlinecruisers.com**

Cruises on Lough Derg and the River Shannon.

Horse-riding

Colligan Equestrian Centre
On R672, Crough, Colligan, Dungarvan, Co. Waterford, **t** (058) 68261

Kilcooley Equestrian Centre
Gortnahoe, Co. Tipperary, **t** (056) 883 4222

Lake Tour Stables
Tramore, Waterford, **t** (051) 381 996

Nire Valley Equestrian Trail Riding and Trekking
Ballymacabry, via Clonmel, Co. Tipperary, **t** (052) 523 6147

Walking

The **Ballyhoura Way** stretches 56 miles (90km) from John's Bridge in west Limerick to Limerick Junction in Co. Tipperary. The **Cahir Way** is another signposted path from Cahir to Ballydavid through the Galtee Mountains. There are also fine paths between Carrick-on-Suir, Clonmel and Clogheen in the Knockmealdown Mountains. In Co. Waterford, walk through the Comeragh Mountains south of Clonmel on the **Munster Way**, or **St Declan's Walk**, a popular pilgrimage route from Lismore to Ardmore.

Buckets and spades – Tipperary and Waterford

In Co. Tipperary there is enjoyable lake swimming on Lough Derg at **Ballina**, opposite Killaloe in Co. Clare, and around **Portroe**.

In Co. Waterford there are excellent beaches for swimming at **Dunmore East**, **Ardmore** and around Dungarvan – especially **Clonea Bay**, 5 miles (8km) to the east. The seaside resort of **Tramore** is typically touristy but is a popular spot for surfing.

Watersports

Ardmore Scuba Diving
Gorteen, Dungarvan, **t** (058) 46577

Inshore diving training in an enclosed bay.

Dunmore East Adventure Centre
The Harbour, Stoney Cove, Dunmore East, Co. Waterford, **t** (051) 383 783, **www.dunmoreadventure.com**

Sailing, windsurfing and canoeing, for everyone from beginners to experts.

Oceanic Manoeuvres Surf School
The Red Cottage, Tramore, **t** (051) 390 944

Surfing lessons for adults and children, summer camps and guided beach walks.

Seapaddling.com
Unit 112, Dunhill Enterprise Park, Dunhill, Tramore, **t** (051) 358 995

Kayaking explorations, even for beginners.

Splashworld
Tramore, Co. Waterford, **t** (051) 390 176
Open Summer daily 10am–10pm
Disabled access, baby-changing facilities, café, under-10s must be accompanied by adult

An aqua-adventure playground with bubble pools, a river ride, a wave machine and waterslides.

T–Bay Surf Centre
Tramore beach, Co. Waterford, **t** (051) 391 297, **www.surftbay.com**
Environmental and wildlife visitor centre

Surf hire, beach facilities and activity camps.

Steam power!

Waterford and Suir Valley Railway
Kilmeadan, Co. Waterford, **t** (051) 311 137
Getting there From Waterford–Cork Rd (N25), take R680 towards Portlaw/Carrick-on-Suir for just under 1 mile (1.3km); Kilmeadan train station is opposite Old Kilmeadan Rd junction
Open Feb–Sept; call for operating times
Fares Adult €7, child/student €5.50, family (2+2) €18, (2+4) €22

This heritage narrow-gauge rail line runs along 4 miles (6km) of an abandoned Waterford–Dungarvan route past Mount Congreve Gardens and a recently discovered Viking site.

WHERE TO EAT

County Cork

Baltimore

Customs House Restaurant
t (028) 20200 (*inexpensive–moderate*)
Imaginative fresh dishes in a seaside setting.

Glebe House
t (028) 20232 (*inexpensive*)
Organic gardens here produce the ingredients for great salads and baking for this daytime café.

Bandon

Otto's Creative Cooking
Dunworley, Butlerstown, **t** (023) 40461 (*moderate–expensive*)
This restaurant's owners rear their own animals and grow their own produce.

Bantry

The Snug
The Quay, **t** (027) 50057 (*inexpensive*)
An eccentric bar by the harbour, with simple home-cooked dishes.

Clonakilty

Richy's Bar and Bistro
4 Wolfe Tone St, **t** (023) 21852 (*inexpensive–moderate*)
Open for both lunch and dinner, this dark, cool spot offers children crayons and colouring books as well as a kids' menu or half-portions of its wholesome gourmet cooking.

Cork City

Café Paradiso
16 Lancaster Quay, Western Rd, **t** (021) 427 7939 (*inexpensive–moderate*)
Great vegetarian food made solely from organic ingredients. Many consider this the best vegetarian restaurant in Ireland.

Crawford's Art Gallery Café
Emmet Place, **t** (021) 427 4415 (*inexpensive*)
Run by one of the Allen family of Ballymaloe (*see* p.258), this has light, original food for lunch or supper, excellent fresh orange juice and gooey cakes.

Gino's
Winthrop St, **t** (021) 427 4485 (*inexpensive*)
Fabulous pizzas for large and small appetites. This is a famous diner amongst Corkonians.

Kelly's
64 Oliver Plunkett St, **t** (021) 427 3375 (*inexpensive*)
Friendly, charming and simple surroundings for home-style Irish lunches. Children are welcome.

Tony's Bistro
69 North Main St, **t** (021) 427 0848 (*inexpensive*)
A place popular with all ages for breakfast, lunch and dinner, including great fry-ups.

Durrus

Good Things Café
t (027) 61426 (*inexpensive–moderate*)
Good, adventurous food. Dinner is only served on summer weekends.

Kilbrittain

Casino House
t (023) 49944 (*moderate*)
Good food produced from local produce. Children are welcome.

Kinsale

The Blue Haven
3 Pearse St, **t** (021) 477 2209 (*expensive*)
This very good restaurant is in a cosy hotel. Seafood is a speciality but the steaks are good too.

Fishy Fishy Café
Market Place **t** (021) 477 4453 (*inexpensive–moderate*)
Kinsale's best and busiest restaurant, with an outside terrace in good weather.

Toddies
Sleaveen House, Eastern Rd, **t** (021) 477 7769 (*moderate*)
A place recommended for its very good cooking.

Midleton

The Farm Gate
Coolbawn, **t** (021) 463 2771 (*inexpensive–moderate*)
Traditional dishes made from local ingredients.

Rosscarbery

O'Callaghan-Walshe Restaurant
The Square, **t** (023) 48125 (*moderate–expensive*)
A very popular fish restaurant for dinner.

Schull

Adele's

Main St, **t** (028) 28459 (*inexpensive*)

A bakery and restaurant offering excellent lunches, salads and desserts.

Youghal

Aherne's Pub and Seafood Restaurant

North Main St, **t** (024) 92424/92533 (*moderate*)

A good atmosphere and delicious seafood dishes. This is perhaps the best pub-restaurant in the south.

Browne's County Restaurant

Killeagh, **t** (024) 91373 (*moderate*)

This family-run restaurant offers breakfast, brunch, lunch, tea and Sunday lunch in a snug ambience beside Browne's Equestrian Centre.

County Kerry

County Kerry is known for its good local produce. Fenit and Castlegregory are renowned for vegetables, Cromane for mussels, Tralee Bay for oysters, Dingle for seafood and North Kerry for beef.

Ballinskelligs

Skelligs Chocolate Company

The Glen, **t** (066) 947 9119

Drive along the Ring of Kerry to this factory, where you can watch chocolates being made and take home an artistically packaged box of them.

Brandon

O'Shea's Bar & Restaurant

Near Castlegregory, **t** (066) 713 8154 (*inexpensive*)

Food is served all day at this pub with its beer garden and children's play area.

Caherdaniel

The Blind Piper

t (066) 9475126 (*inexpensive*)

A pub with a good, lively atmosphere in a pretty village. It has a play area and a garden.

Dingle

An Café Liteartha

t (066) 915 2204 (*inexpensive*)

A combined bookshop and café serving delicious open sandwiches.

Doyle's Seafood Bar and Restaurant

John St, **t** (066) 915 1174 (*expensive*)

Fine seafood served in a room like an old Irish kitchen, with stone floor and simple furniture. The hosts are very welcoming.

The Forge

Holy Ground, **t** (066) 915 2590 (*moderate*)

A popular family-owned pub in the centre of Dingle, with a children's menu and decent steaks and seafood.

Murphy's Ice Cream

Strand St, **t** (066) 915 2644 (*inexpensive*)

Organic ice cream, sorbets and chocolate cakes for that perfect summer children's treat may be had at this award-winning ice-cream parlour run by two American-Irish brothers who have plans to expand into the hot dessert arena.

Kenmare

An Leath Phingin

35 Main Street, **t** (064) 41559 (*moderate*)

Fresh pasta, scrumptious sauces and stone-baked pizzas made by an Italian chef.

The Lime Tree

Shelburne St, **t** (064) 41225 (*moderate–expensive*)

A popular evening restaurant offering Asian and vegetarian dishes and herbal teas made from loose leaves, prepared by a Café Paradiso (Cork) graduate.

Mulcahey's

Henry St, **t** (064) 42383 (*moderate–expensive*)

Very highly reputed food.

The Purple Heather

Henry St, **t** (064) 21016 (*inexpensive*)

Great bar food during the day and early evening.

The Wander Inn

2 Henry Street, **t** (064) 42700 (*inexpensive*)

A perfect spot for the classic combination of a plate of Irish stew, a pint of Guinness and traditional music.

Killarney

Foley's Seafood and Steak Restaurant

23 High St, **t** (064) 31217 (*moderate*)

A place serving delicious seafood, lamb and vegetarian dishes.

Gaby's Restaurant
27 High St, **t** (064) 32519 (*moderate*)

A Med-style café with tasty seafood. It's very popular, and no bookings are taken, so arrive early.

Murphy's Ice Cream
37 Main St, **t** (064) 265 544 (*inexpensive*)

A second swish ice cream shop set up by the Murphy brothers (*see* opposite).

Killorglin

Nick's Restaurant and Pub
Lower Bridge St, **t** (066) 976 1219 (*expensive*)

A friendly, fun place serving large portions of seafood and steaks, and often packed with local people singing around the piano.

County Limerick

Adare

The Blue Door Restaurant
t (061) 396 481 (*inexpensive–moderate*)

Afternoon snacks, light lunches and evening meals of Irish food in an old-fashioned cottage atmosphere.

The Inn Between Restaurant
t (061) 396 633 (*inexpensive–moderate*)

One of the famous Adare thatched cottages, open for lunch and dinner.

The Maigue Restaurant (Dunraven Arms)
t (061) 396 633 (*moderate–expensive*)

A gourmet site that has won many awards, open for lunch and dinner.

The Wild Geese
t (061) 396 451 (*expensive*)

A mix of classic French and modern-Irish cooking. It's open evenings only; booking is advisable.

Limerick City

Copper and Spice
2 Cornmarket Row, **t** (061) 313 620 (*moderate*)

A superior, popular Asian restaurant that serves Indian and Thai dishes.

Greene's Café Bistro
63 William St, **t** (061) 314 022 (*inexpensive*)

Beautiful stained-glass features and wholesome dishes make this a very pleasant spot for lunch.

County Clare

Ballyvaughan

Gregan's Castle Hotel
t (065) 707 7005 (*moderate*)

Delicious food served all day in the family-friendly Corkscrew Bar, where a fire crackles beneath a low-beamed ceiling – very welcoming after a long hike.

Bunratty

Gallagher's of Bunratty
t (061) 363 363 (*moderate*)

A charming thatched cottage with local seafood.

The Burren

The Burren
Carran, **t** (065) 708 9109 (*inexpensive*)

Burgers, steaks, baked potatoes and sandwiches are sold here. It's a great spot in the middle of the Burren, with beauty nearby (and a play area).

Cassidy's of Carran
t (065) 708 9109 (*inexpensive*)

A remote pub in the wildest part of the Burren, with excellent lunches using local produce.

Linnane's Lobster Bar
New Quay, **t** (065) 707 8120 (*moderate*)

This pub specializes in lobster and oysters.

Doolin

Aran View House Hotel and Restaurant
Coast Rd, **t** (065) 7078 4061 (*inexpensive–moderate*)

This family-friendly hotel restaurant specializes in fresh seafood and the best local produce, and also has good vegetarian dishes. The views are superb.

Ennis

Brogan's Bar and Restaurant
24 O'Connell St, **t** (065) 682 9480 (*moderate*)

Family meals of steak, lamb and so on, served from 10am until late.

Kilfenora

Vaughan's Pub
Kilfenora, Co. Clare, **t** (065) 708 8004 (*inexpensive–moderate*)

Music and good food are important to the family who run this pub, so you will have both.

Lahinch

Bartrá Seafood Restaurant

t (065) 708 1280 (*expensive*)

A simple but good restaurant with fine bay views.

O'Looney's

Promenade, **t** (065) 708 1414 (*moderate*)

A pub popular with surfers and families, offering good seafood, bar food, sandwiches, music and an outdoor eating area.

Liscannor

The Mermaid

t (065) 708 1076 (*inexpensive–moderate*)

A restaurant with an open fire on the outskirts of the village. Mainly fish is served, but also very good inventive veggie dishes made from local ingredients.

Lisdoonvarna

Roadside Tavern

Kincora Rd, **t** (065) 707 4494 (*inexpensive*)

This charming wood-panelled pub-cum-smoking house specializes in delicious smoked fish.

Spanish Point

The Cape Restaurant

Armada Hotel, **t** (065) 708 4110 (*moderate*)

Hearty, traditional Sunday roasts or informal bar food, and uninterrupted views over the Atlantic.

Tipperary and Waterford

Ardmore

White Horses

Main St, Ardmore, Co. Waterford, **t** (024) 94040 (*inexpensive–moderate*)

Sandwiches, light lunches and good-sized dinners, with interesting sauces and scrumptious desserts, and special little treats for children.

Cashel

The Bakehouse

7 Main St, Cashel, Co. Tipperary, **t** (062) 61680 (*inexpensive*)

Irresistible breakfastes, lunches and snacks, with gourmet coffee and goods baked daily on site.

Cashel Palace Hotel

Cashel, Co. Tipperary, **t** (062) 61411 (*moderate–expensive*)

Two restaurants in a house built in the Queen Anne style in 1730. The formal Three Sisters is more adult, the Bishop's Buttery is welcoming for kids.

Clonmel

Angela's Coffee Emporium and Restaurant

14 Abbey St, Clonmel, Co. Tipperary, **t** (052) 26899 (*inexpensive*)

A relaxed place for good light lunches.

Clifford's

29 Thomas St, Clonmel, Co. Tipperary, **t** (052) 70677 (*inexpensive–moderate*)

The chef here has an excellent reputation, and the restaurant, open for lunch and dinner, is bright and pretty. Children are welcome.

Dunmore East

The Ship Restaurant and Bar

Dunmore East, Co. Waterford, **t** (051) 383 141 (*moderate*)

A casual, fun atmosphere, fine for kids during the day and early evening. Good seafood is served.

Waterford Town

Haricots Wholefood Restaurant

11 O'Connell St, **t** (051) 841 299 (*inexpensive*)

Comfortable and relaxing surroundings for vegetarians, vegans and omnivores alike, with wholefood dishes created daily. The home-made soups and freshly squeezed juice are very good. It's open through the day up to 8pm.

Waterford Castle

The Island, Ballinakill, **t** (051) 878 203 (*moderate–expensive*)

Having to take a ferry to get here, plus the high standard of the classical cuisine offered, makes dining in this castle especially charming.

The Wine Vault

High St, **t** (051) 853 444 (*inexpensive–moderate*)

Open for lunch and dinner, this small, smart restaurant offers dishes such as chicken Kiev and pumpkin quiche within what is actually a vault full of wines from which you can choose.

Connacht

COUNTY GALWAY 159
Galway City 161
Special Trips 164
Around and About 167

COUNTY MAYO 172
Special Trips 174
Around and About 176

COUNTY SLIGO 181
Sligo Town 182
Special Trips 183
Around and About 184

LEITRIM AND ROSCOMMON 186
Special Trips 187
Around and About 189

WHERE TO EAT 191

06

Connacht

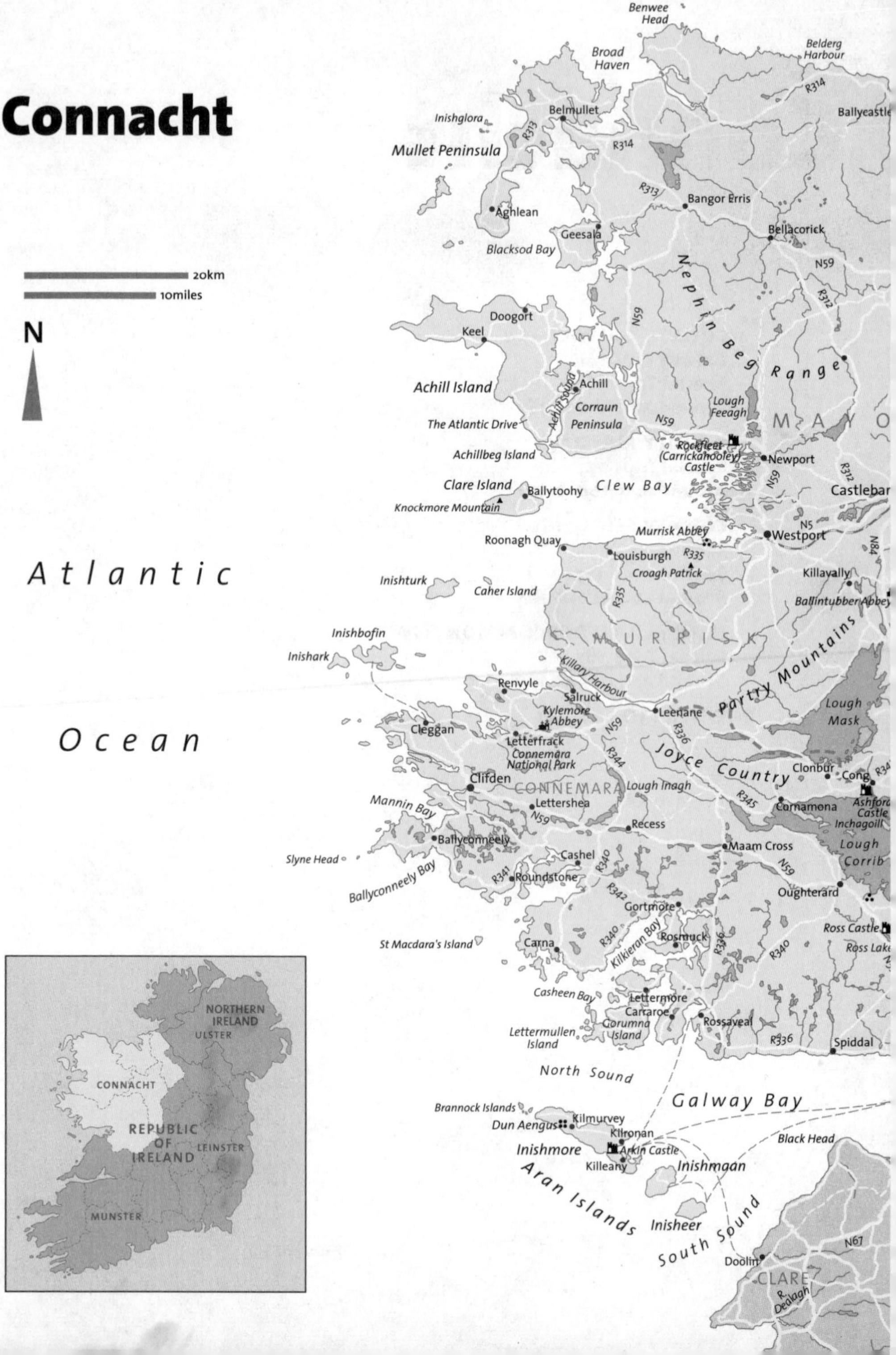

20km
10miles
N

Atlantic Ocean

Benwee Head
Broad Haven
Belderg Harbour
Inishglora
Belmullet
R313
R314
Ballycastle
Mullet Peninsula
Bangor Erris
Aghlean
Geesala
Bellacorick
Blacksod Bay
Nephin Beg Range
N59
R312
Doogort
Keel
Achill Island
Achill Sound
Achill
Corraun Peninsula
Lough Feeagh
MAYO
The Atlantic Drive
Rockfleet (Carrickahooley) Castle
Achillbeg Island
Newport
Clare Island
Ballytoohy
Clew Bay
Castlebar
Knockmore Mountain
Murrisk Abbey
N5
Roonagh Quay
Westport
N84
Louisburgh
R335
Croagh Patrick
Inishturk
Caher Island
Killavally
Ballintubber Abbey
MURRISK
Inishbofin
Inishark
Partry Mountains
Killary Harbour
Renvyle
Salruck
Lough Mask
Leenane
Kylemore Abbey
Cleggan
R336
Letterfrack
Connemara National Park
R344
Joyce Country
Clonbur
Cong
Clifden
CONNEMARA
Lough Inagh
Ashford Castle
Mannin Bay
Lettershea
R345
Cornamona
Inchagoill
Recess
Ballyconneely
Maam Cross
Lough Corrib
Slyne Head
Cashel
R340
Ballyconneely Bay
R341
Roundstone
Oughterard
R342
Gortmore
Ross Castle
St Macdara's Island
Carna
Kilkieran Bay
Rosmuck
Ross Lake
Casheen Bay
Lettermore
Carraroe
Gorumna Island
Rossaveal
Lettermullen Island
Spiddal
North Sound
Galway Bay
Brannock Islands
Kilmurvey
Dun Aengus
Kilronan
Black Head
Inishmore
Arkin Castle
Killeany
Inishmaan
Aran Islands
Inisheer
South Sound
N67
Doolin
CLARE
R. Dealagh

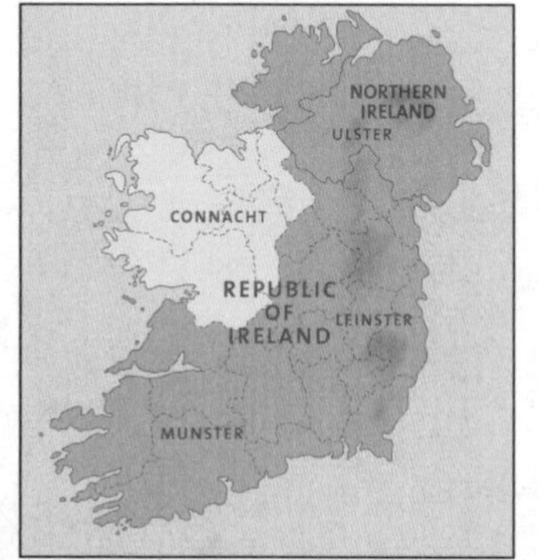

Mullaghmore
Bundoran
N15
Inishmurray
River Erne
A46
Lower Lough Erne
A35
Kinlough
Lough Melvin
N15
Downpatrick Head
Lissadell House
Benbulben Mountain
B81
Rossinver
Ulster Way
A32
FERMANAG
Sligo Bay
Drumcliff
R280
N16
Manorhamilton
R283
Enniskillen
Easky
Killala Bay
R. Easky
R297
R281
Strandhill
N15
Sligo
R286
N16
Ballysodare Bay
Carrowmore
Killala
Dromore West
Inniscrone
N59
Lough Gill
R291
River Bonet
Dromahair
R287
N59
Slieve Gamph/The Ox Mountains
R289
Collooney
R280
R314
A509
Ballina
SLIGO
R284
R200
R294
Riverstown
Lough Allen
Arigna Mountains
Lough Talt
N4
CAVAN
Ballymote
Lough Conn
Tubbercurry
Castlebaldwin
Lough Arrow
LEITRIM
Waterway
N26
Lough Meelagh
Ballinamore
Ballinafad
Drumshanbo
Pontoon
Lough Cullin
Foxford
R294
Curlew Hills
Gorteen
Lough Key
R284
R202
Corrawaleen
N26
Leitrim
Boyle
Straide
N5
Swinford
Charlestown
Lough Gara
Lough Key Forest Park
Carrick-on-Shannon
N4
Knock Airport
Mohill
Cloone Grange
Kiltimagh
Ballaghaderreen
Ballinameen
N5
Frenchpark
Clougher
Elphin
R202
Dromod
Knock
Clonalis House
Castlerea
Claremorris
N60
N60
R367
Tulsk
Strokestown
N4
Lough Forbes
Killoe
Lough Carra
ROSCOMMON
N5
R. Camlin
Longford
R194
Ballintober
N84
Cloonfad
Ballymore
Four Mile House
N4
Ballinrobe
LONGFORD
R334
Royal Canal
Roscommon Castle
Roscommon
R332
Glennamaddy
N84
N83
Castlestrange Stone
R366
Athleague
Knockcroghery
Lisacormack Fort
Tuam
R333
River Clare
Saint's Island
R332
Lough Ree
Mount Bellew
N61
Inchmore
Curraghboy
WESTMEA
N59
Moycullen
N84
Claregalway Abbey
Claregalway
Athlone
GALWAY
N17
N6
Galway (Carnmore)
N6
N6
R348
River Shannon
Salthill
Athenry
Moyode Castle
Aughrim
Ballinasloe
GALWAY
Oranmore
N6
N18
N6
R. Suck
Grand Canal
N52
Clarinbridge
R355
Clonfert Cathedral
Clonfert
Tullam
Loughrea
N6
R357
N52
Doorus House
N67
Lough Rea
N65
OFFALY
Dunguaire
Kinvara
Banagher
N66
Slieve Aught Mountains
R355
River Shannon
R. Barrow
Thoor Ballylee
Coole Park
R353
Gort
Portumna
Priory
Lough Cutra
Portumna Forest Park
Glendine Gap
R460
N52
N62
CLARE
TIPPERARY
LAOIS

CONNACHT

Arthur Colaham's old song *If You Ever Go Across the Sea to Ireland* speaks of a time in Galway when children would run barefoot from May to September to save their shoes for the winter, and women would work in the fields digging potatoes and harvesting hay. It is a world that no longer exists but still echoes in modern Connacht.

The province's recent history includes great poverty. Connacht was deeply harmed by the Great Famine in the middle of the 19th century. Already the majority of its people were struggling to survive, often under landlords of a different culture and faith. Many of the ancestors of Connacht's inhabitants had been dumped there by Cromwell in the 17th century. Life was hard, so you made the best of it with music and stories. The stony vastness of Connemara symbolizes its people's struggle, and the tiny colourful wild-flowers that grow every year in the gaps between the rocks their spirit.

Known for the barren sweep of its rocky land and thin topsoil, this was a part of Ireland where few chose to live, and those who did tended to be fishermen, farmers or turf-cutters. In the 19th century, life was not made any easier for Connachtmen by the developing industrialization of Europe. The arrival of the mass market in Ireland was made manifest in its wool and textile industries, where the money to be made rarely trickled down to the hand-knitters of Connemara and the Arans, whose human-speed artistry was not (and still is not) a particularly lucrative trade. Foreign landlords with no loyalty to the land were deeply resented by those whose lives depended upon it for survival. This and the arrival of the Famine triggered mass migration to America. After that, young and old grew ever more determined to find gold on the streets of the New World, so that for generations of displaced Connachtmen, Ireland became a distant, nagging memory.

Today Connacht is a much more cosmopolitan province, even though it is much less so than the towns around Dublin. As more natives return home after years of working abroad, a mixture of European, British and American influences are coming with them, affecting the buildings and appearance of the countryside and transforming once-peaceful towns such as Galway into cities with all their attendant problems.

But still the old habits linger in the countryside, where traditional music and culture are nearer ordinary life. Rarely are they ever done merely 'for the tourists' there. In Connacht you will find a more careful approach to strangers than in other provinces, but perhaps a less contrived one too, with the old Irish laws of hospitality still working as they have for centuries.

Highlights

Finding out how Galway crystal and traditional *bodhrán* drums are produced, p.162 and p.169
Wandering in wild Connemara, p.170
Sailing to the magical Aran Islands of Galway or Clare Island, Co. Mayo, p.164 or p.179
A whole day of fun at Westport House, Co. Mayo, p.176
Visiting Sligo's faeries at Knocknashee and Gillighan's World, p.183

Tourist information for Connacht

Ireland West Tourism (Galway, Mayo, Roscommon), Aras Fáilte, Forster St, Galway, **t** (091) 537 700, **www**.irelandwest.ie
Self-catering information, t (091) 537 777
North West Tourism (Sligo, Leitrim, Cavan, Monaghan and Donegal), Aras Redden, Temple St, Sligo, **t** (071) 916 1201, **www**.ireland-northwest.ie

Getting there and around

By air Connacht has 2 airports with direct links with Britain, **Galway** (used by Aer Arann) and **Knock** (British Airways, MyTravel, Ryanair). Galway is also the airport for Aer Arann flights to the Aran Islands. For travellers from North America the best airport to use is **Shannon**. *See* pp.280–4.
By bus Frequent Bus Éireann coaches run between Dublin and Galway, Westport, Sligo and other towns. Many local services operate from Galway. For Bus Éireann details, *see* p.286.
By car From Dublin, for north Connacht follow the N4 via Longford; for Galway, take the N4 as far as Kinnegad, then the N6 via Athlone.
By rail Trains to Galway run from Dublin Heuston, and there are also west coast lines to Ballina or Westport, via a change in Athlone or Athenry. Trains to Sligo run from Dublin Connolly, via Longford. For more on Irish Rail/Iarnród Éireann, *see* p.288. They can be contacted in Ireland on **t** 1 850 366 222 or check **www**.irishrail.ie.

COUNTY GALWAY

County Galway will be most enjoyed by families who love active holidays – fishing, cycling, horse-riding or walking along spectacular Atlantic beaches and through unique landscapes. Junior archaeologists and geologists will especially enjoy exploring the wind-blown Connemara peninsula, its landscape bereft of most things but rock dotted with strikingly blue eyelet lakes. This is the land that Cromwell was thinking of when he banished Catholic landowners from the rest of Ireland 'to Hell or Connacht' in the 17th century. Apart from these cosy fishing holes, anglers can visit Connemara's largest lake, Lough Corrib, and the numerous bays leading to the Atlantic Ocean, which holds the special world of the Aran Islands.

Connemara is loosely defined as the area between Lough Corrib and the Atlantic Ocean, with a northern boundary at Killary Harbour and its southern coastline beside Galway Bay. Hours may be spent traversing it, looking for forgotten cairns.. This is the largest area of Ireland that is still a *Gaeltacht*, a place where Irish is spoken as a first language. In the far west of Connemara, road signs and directions are often only in Irish. This is perhaps something of a political statement stretching back to the 17th century, when Irish people are said to have been hanged for speaking in their native tongue.

Traditional culture was a lively part of life on the Arans and in western Connacht until near the end of the 20th century. Vestiges of the old habits can still be found here, and there is a quiet renaissance going on that is regenerating communities, with folklorists as the new holders of tradition and ecologists bringing new vigour and support for organic farming. Faerylore is still present here also, although it might take some uncovering, which you can only do through getting to know the often-cautious country people.

County Galway's greener eastern region is a place of farms and romantic woodland, among which Ireland's greatest 20th-century poet WB Yeats chose to live. His magical home, Thoor Ballylee, sits beside a rushing stream in the middle of a countryside that, reassuringly, doesn't seem to have changed for a very long time. Not far from there are the extensive grounds of Coole Park, once the home of the folklorist Lady Gregory, co-founder with Yeats of Dublin's Abbey Theatre and the wealthy benefactress behind the early 20th century's Irish Literary Renaissance.

Good to know...

Try to find a real storyteller to tell you all about what might happen if you mix with the Gentry (faeries), or listen to stories recorded by Irish storytellers (*see* p.26).

Tourist information

Aran Islands, Comharchumann Forbartha Arann, **t** (099) 61354, **www.visitaranislands.com**.

Also:

Kilronan, Inishmore, **t** (099) 61263
Ballinasloe, **t** (0905) 42131
Clifden, Galway Rd, **t** (095) 21163
Galway, Aras Fáilte, Forster St, **t** (091) 537 700
Oughterard, **t** (091) 552 808
Salthill, Promenade, **t** (091) 520 500
Thoor Ballylee, **t** (091) 631 436
Tuam, **t** (093) 25486/24463

Tours

Bus Éireann (*see* below) also offers bus tours of Connemara in summer, from Galway.

Lally Tours, **t** (091) 562 905, **www.lallytours.com**

Connemara and Burren day tours by bus with a guide, departing from Galway and Salthill on a daily basis.

O'Neachtain's, Burren, **t** (091) 553 188

Full- and half-day tours.

Getting there and around

By air Galway Airport is 4 miles (6km) to the east of the city in Carnmore. Buses are infrequent, but Aer Arann often provides its own shuttle buses, or there are taxis (*see* p.283) between the airport and the city.

Galway Airport, Carnmore, **t** (091) 755 569, **www.galwayairport.com**

By bus In Galway City buses depart from the train station, in the centre off Eyre Square. Galway is one of Bus Éireann's main hubs, and you can get to almost every town in Connacht and the surrounding counties quite easily. Other private operators provide services to Co. Galway towns, especially in summer. Galway City bus Information, **t** (091) 562 000; Nestor Bus, **t** (091) 797 144; Bus Éireann, **t** (091) 562 000, **www**.buseireann.ie

By train Galway has a few trains daily from Dublin via Athlone. Information, **t** (091) 564 222

Bike Hire

Celtic Rent-a-Bike, Queen St, Galway, **t** (091) 566 606

Europa Bicycles, Earls Island, Galway, **t** (091) 563 355
Flaherty Cycles, Upper Dominic St, Galway, **t** (091) 589 230
Irish Cycle Hire, Victoria Place, Galway, **t** (091) 561 498
John Mannion, Bridge St, Clifden, **t** (095) 21160
Kearney's Bicycle Hire, Headford Rd, Galway, **t** (091) 563 356
Renvyle Stores, Tullymore, **t** (095) 43485
Rothar Arainn TEO, Frenchman's Beach, Kilronan, Inishmore, Aran Islands, **t** (091) 61132/61203

Special Events – County Galway

Easter

Easter Egg Hunt, Turoe Pet Farm, Bullaun, Loughrea (*see* p.167), **t** (091) 841 580

Seasonal fun for youngsters.

May

Fleadh nag Cuach ('Cuckoo Festival'), Kinvara, **www.kinvara.com**

A traditional festival, with fun for all the family.

Walks the Ancient Celtic Way, Inishmore, Aran Islands, **t** (099) 61424 or **t** 0041 1252 0918 (Jan–June)

The shorter walks are good for youngsters.

May

Ragus, Halla Ronain, Kilronan, Inishmore, Aran Islands, **t** (099) 61515

A 1hr show of traditional Irish music, song and dance, presented through the summer (May–Sept).

June

Corrandulla Show, Corrandulla, **t** (091) 791 714

Showjumping, horse and pony showing classes, a dog and a sheep show, sideshows for families, arts, crafts and baking competitions.

Roundstone Arts Week, Roundstone, **t** (095) 35709, **www.roundstoneartsweek.com**

Seven days of children's events, music, theatre and other cultural goings-on.

Summer Fun at National Children's Museum, Ballybrit Industrial Estate Upper, Galway, **t** (091) 766 829, **www.childrensdiscoverymuseum.ie**

Children's workshops and activities (June–Aug).

July

Spiorad, Inisheer, Aran Islands, **t** (099) 75067, **www.araninisheer.com**

Inis Oirr International School of Celtic Spirituality offers a week of lectures, sacred rituals and Irish culture on Inisheer island.

August

Connemara Pony Show, Clifden, **t** (095) 21863

The annual show of the world-famous Connemara ponies, by Connemara Pony Breeders Society. A lovely event for horse-struck kids.

Crinniu na mBad ('Gathering of the Boats'), Kinvara, **t** (091) 637 579, **www.kinvara.com**

A traditional boat festival, with *curragh*-racing, arts, sports, children's events and traditional music.

September

Clarinbridge Oyster Festival, t (086) 226 1537

Oyster-opening competitions, traditional music, dance and fun during the day for families.

Clifden Community Arts Festival, t (095) 21644

Top-quality arts events – poetry, recitals, exhibitions – with some family-friendly activities.

Lady Gregory of Coole: An Autumn Gathering, t (091) 524 329

A weekend of lectures, discussions and drama, highlighting the ideas of Lady Gregory.

October

Baboró International Arts Festival for Children, t (091) 509 705

Irish and international theatre, dance and music, with workshops for 3–12-year-olds, in Galway and around the county.

Ballinasloe International Horse Fair and Festival t (090) 964 3453

This traditional festival, dating back to 1772, includes a children's workshop along with puppet shows and other street entertainments.

Cooley-Collins Traditional Music Festival, Gort, **t** (091) 632 370

Traditional music, *ceili* and stories for children.

Maam Cross October Fair, t (091) 552 306

The sale of sheep, cattle and Connemara ponies via stalls, trailers and cars parked for miles on each of the 4 roads leading to Maam Cross village.

December

Christmas Winter Wonderland, Turoe Pet Farm, Bullaun, Loughrea, **t** (091) 841 580

Visits by Santa Claus on this pet farm (*see* p.167) from Thursday to Sunday evenings

Woodford Mummers' Feile, Woodford, **t** (090) 974 9028

Traditional folk activities for all the family on 26 and 27 December.

GALWAY CITY

Galway is a provincial college town whose enterprising citizenry have long traded wine with Spain and encouraged tourism. Built on the Corrib River, which runs from Lough Corrib north of the city, it is the gateway to the Connemara Gaeltacht. Also the home of University College Galway, it has long been a favourite of students and foreign visitors. The arts are very much alive here, with fine traditional music and the internationally renowned Druid Theatre Company.

Busy with traffic that is reminiscent of Dublin's at times, central Galway's Eyre Square is no longer a peaceful empty expanse you can just walk across to the shops, where someone may speak to you curiously because they know you're a stranger. It is now even difficult to park a car there (car parks can be found beside the new centrally located hotels). Galway's main tourist office stands on an offshoot of the square, but if you get lost, orientate yourself via Galway Bay. At the west end of the town (right, looking bay-wards) you will find the seaside resort area of Salthill, with a tourist office open in summer near Atlantaquaria and Leisureland.

If you want to hear some Irish music in one of Galway's lively pubs, you'll need a babysitter. Sessions don't start until about 9 or 10pm.

Things to see and do

Atlantaquaria

National Aquarium of Ireland, Toft Park, The Promenade, Salthill, t (091) 585 100
Open Daily Mar–Oct 10–6
Adm Adult €7, child €4, under-3s free, family (2+2) €21
Guided tours available, gift shop, café

A small shock awaits you just after you enter Atlantaquaria on the ground floor, but don't worry – you won't get wet! Suddenly you will feel as though you have been submerged in a ship deep in the ocean, where sea creatures dwell in tanks behind glass and in open-surfaced saltwater pools. This is the place to meet Galway's underwater inhabitants – from starfish to conger eels, sea anemones to mussels. The conditions that sea creatures normally inhabit are re-created in some tanks, while other containers protect the young of certain species. Baby plaice come to the surface of their pool periodically and cling to its sides, while starfish lie on the sandy gravel bottom beneath them. Accompanying text panels provide information about feeding patterns, tides, and the size, habitat and habits of the many species that are exhibited in each tank.

Young children will enjoy the small submarine-like Deep Submergence Vehicle. They can crawl into it for a 'fish-eye' view of what life is like under the water for fish, starfish and crabs (the crabs eat

A story to tell: The Claddagh Ring

Once upon a time there was a king who so loved a woman he could not be with that it drove him mad. Since she was a peasant and therefore of lower status than him, society would not allow him to marry her. He instructed his servants to cut off his hands after he died and place them around his heart as a symbol of his undying love for her. This macabre little tale may not be true, but it conveys the emotions people can have in this part of the world and describes the origins of the famous Claddagh ring.

Another story claims the symbol was worn and also painted on ships and sails by fishermen from Claddagh, a poor fishing village that stood on the outskirts of Galway town in the Middle Ages. They are said to have killed fishermen they found in their waters who were not wearing it.

Whatever the truth of the symbol's beginnings, to the fishing kings of Claddagh it meant 'in love and friendship let us reign'. Two hands (signifying friendship) hold a heart (indicating love) on which sits a crown (symbolizing loyalty).

In the 17th century a goldsmith named Richard Joyce – who had earlier learnt his craft when he had been captured by North African pirates and sold as a slave to a Moroccan goldsmith – returned to Galway and opened a shop in the Claddagh. He began to make Claddagh rings, and they became popular as wedding rings, worn with the heart pointed towards the wearer's fingers when betrothed, and towards the body after marriage. According to tradition, love and friendship will reign supreme in the life of its wearer.

The ring's fame spread with the vast exodus from the west of Ireland after the Great Famine. Kept as heirlooms, Claddagh rings were passed from mother to daughter all over the world. Today they are still worn all over Ireland.

Special Events – Galway City

April

Cuirt Literary Festival, t (091) 565 886, **www.**galwayartscentre.ie

Readings and performances held in venues across the county.

May

Galway Early Music Festival, t (087) 930 5506, **www.**galwayearlymusic.com

A traditional music and song festival incorporating art and drama.

June

Bloomsday, Nora Barnacle House, Bowling Green, **t** (091) 564 743

Open-air readings from the works of James Joyce, on 16 June

Salthill Air Show, Salthill seafront, **t** (091) 526 158/ 771 111

A fun, free air show on Galway Bay.

Siamsa, Galway Folk Theatre, Eyre Sq, **t** (091) 755 479, **www.**siamsaireland.com

Irish music, singing, dancing and folk plays, including plenty for young audiences, with performances a few times a week June–August.

July

Galway Races, Ballybrit Racecourse, **t** (091) 753 870, **www.**galwayraces.com

The most exciting meetings here are at the end of July, and feature the Galway Plate and the Galway Hurdle – a mixture of high society and smooth-talking bookies. Races go on through August.

Galway Arts Festival, t (091) 509 700, **www.**galwayartsfestival.ie

Ireland's biggest arts festival, lasting 15 days and including a children's festival with clowns, puppets and events especially for them.

Galway Film Fleadh, Town Hall Theatre, **t** (091) 751 655

Previews of high-quality films.

September

Galway Oyster Festival, Galway City, **t** (091) 522 066

These oyster-opening championships attract international participants. Kids are a bit peripheral as the affair snowballs into dances, shows and speeches, and you may spot a celebrity or two.

November

The Junior Film Fleadh, t (091) 751 726

Films and seminars for youngsters.

anything, including fish excrement, and so are generally put in tanks to clean them up). Skeletons of a fin whale and a porpoise are on view, as are models of canal gates, a *curragh* and lighthouse, and some deepwater corals.

Staff here can tell you all about Ireland's marine ecosystem and the efforts that are now being made to protect and support it. After exploring the displays, you can have a snack or buy a souvenir in the shop, then go outside to walk along Galway Bay or swim at Leisure World next door.

Galway Irish Crystal Heritage Centre

Merlin Park, **t** (091) 757 311, **www.**galwaycrystal.ie

Open Daily 9–5.30

Adm Adult €4, child €3, family €10

Guided tours only

Visit this glass-making factory and find out what etching and acid polishing are and how lead crystal glassware is made. You can watch glass-blowers at work, and see a complete range of Galway Irish Crystal displayed in the showroom.

Nearby at the Hall of the Tribes museum, you can learn about the merchants and artists who were the original leading families of Galway known as the '14 tribes'. There you'll also find out history about the Claddagh ring and Claddagh Village. Don't miss the boatbuilders' workshop and exhibit on Galway's fishing vessels known as the 'Hooker'.

Galway Leisure World/Leisureland

Headford Rd, Salthill, **t** (091) 562 820/521 455

Open Daily 10am–midnight

Adm According to activity

Adventure rides, bowling, laser games, disabled access, baby-changing facilities and buggy storage, café, shop, outdoor funfair in summer

A great place to come after visiting Atlantaquaria next door. Different sections cater for different age groups; under-7s must be accompanied by an adult in the water, and a learner area for toddlers has an adjustable floor for controlling water depth. For older children, the Treasure Cove has pirate ships on a beach-style pool with a water cannon, bubble pool and 213ft (65m) waterslide.

In summertime there's an outdoor funfair here with miniature train rides, a ghost train, a giant wheel, virtual reality games, a fun house, crazy golf, carnival rides, adventure playgrounds and bumper cars.

Royal Tara China Visitor Centre

Tara Hall, Mervue, **t** (091) 705 602, **www.royal-tara.com**
Open Mon–Sat 9–6, Sun 10–6
Adm Free
Café, free guided tours, showrooms

Take a guided tour of this china and pottery factory: it's best to visit on a weekday before 4.30 if you want to see craftspeople in action.

Entertainment

Druid Theatre

Chapel Lane, **t** (091) 568 617, **www.druidtheatre.com**

Producing very exciting performances, Druid has built up a good international reputation.

Taibhdhearc na Gaillimhe

Middle St, **t** (091) 562 024/530 291/755 479

An intriguing Irish-language theatre that also hosts traditional music and bilingual folk presentations. It's home to the acclaimed Siamsa festival (*see* opposite).

Shopping

Charlie Byrne's Bookshop

Manguard St, **t** (091) 534 494

A bookshop full of character.

Claddagh Jewellers

Eyre Sq, **t** (091) 563 282

A good place to buy souvenir claddagh rings.

A story to tell: The Tuatha Dé Danaan, or People of the Goddess Dana

Long ago the People of the Goddess Dana – or Danu, or Anu – flew within clouds from far northern lands to Ireland. They called themselves the Tuatha Dé Danaan.

A fine white mist spread below them over County Leitrim as they landed on the mountain of Sliabh an Iarainn, and around Mayo and Lough Corrib, near what may have been their blood-kin, the Fir Bolg. Some say they were all of the race of the Nemedians, who had escaped centuries earlier from the Fomorian monsters (*see* p.29).

The Tuatha asked the Fir Bolg if they could share Ireland. The Fir Bolg leader Eochaí said no quite boldly as he cowered below the tall, shining Tuatha. Little did he know how much magic they had. He soon found out, during what became known as the First Battle of Moytura (*see* p. 175).

The Tuatha were a handsome race – tall, fair, with blue or grey eyes and round heads. Well versed in the mystic sciences and medicine, they were skilled horsemen and excellent inventors. They were fond of music and brought to Ireland new musical and poetic arts, metal-working skills and a kind of magic for healing the earth and living things, as well as for winning battles.

Head of the Tuatha was the Daghda ('the great father'), who brought along Oghma, his wife, to Ireland, and four talismans:

The Stone of Destiny or *Lia Fál*, which roared when the rightful candidate sat upon it as he was made king on the Hill of Tara, where some claim it is still. Others say it became the 'Stone of Scone' over which Scottish kings were crowned – which was under the coronation throne in London's Westminster Abbey for several centuries and was recently returned to Scotland.

The Spear of Lugh, whose bearer never failed in battle.

The Sword of Nuadhu, from which no attacker ever escaped.

The Cauldron of Plenty, which satisfied all hunger.

Later the Tuatha had to fight the Fomorians again, in the Second Battle of Moytura (*see* p.183), and later still to resist the humans when they arrived (*see* p.119). The Tuatha called for a truce, as they knew it was their fate to lose any battle with the humans (or Milesians). They agreed that the Milesians could have the surface world of Ireland so long as they, the Tuatha, were left in peace to inhabit the interior of its hills. Some say the Tuatha moved to the Otherworld, where dreams and magic are entwined.

Irish country people maintained this truce as best they could for centuries afterwards, by offering the Tuatha respect and leaving 'them' alone as much as possible. But today many people aren't keeping the Tuatha's secret places sacred... which perhaps isn't such a good idea.

Just because you don't see something doesn't mean it isn't there. A hill may be just mud and rock to you, but, for the Tuatha, it could be home. What fool can say that those who live in a world unseen (that is, the one that you yourself cannot see) are not affected by your actions and whatever else goes on in the dimension you occupy?

Easons

Shop St, **t** (091) 562 284

A branch of the large bookshop chain, with a stock that covers all areas, including an extensive children's range.

Galway Woollen Market

21 High St, **t** (091) 562 491

A good place to come if you want to buy tweeds and knitwear.

Hughes & Hughes

Galway Shopping Centre, Headford Rd, **t** (091) 563 903

An excellent modern bookshop boasting a comprehensive stock for children, and also hosting special events.

Kenny's Bookshop

Tuam Rd, **t** (091) 773 311, **www.kennys.ie**

This is a famous bookshop, stocking Irish literature and children's books and more. It also has an art gallery.

Smyths Toy Shop

Galway Shopping Centre, Headford Rd, **t** (091) 561 520

The largest toy shop in Galway.

SPECIAL TRIPS

The Aran Islands

The Arans are made up of three main islands – Inishmore, Inishmaan and Inisheer – and a few smaller ones. For most native Aran islanders, English is their second language; others don't speak it at all.

Riding a bike is probably the best way of travelling independently on the Aran Islands, although the weather can be unpredictable. The best thing to carry with you for this purpose is a lightweight plastic poncho that covers your head and leaves your arms free. You will need strong legs and lungs for cycling here, although the air is invigorating for those who are out of shape. Otherwise, you'll have a choice of a bus tour or a horse and cart. The latter is a fantastic experience on a sunny day, even if you don't cover as much ground as you would on the bus.

Inishmore

Inishmore, or *Inis Mór*, the 'Big Island', is the largest of the Arans. The islanders' traditional way of life is still maintained here, and Irish is still the language of the majority – although the Islanders speak English as well. Inishmore has a regular public bus service, but you may want to take one of the minibuses that meet the boats arriving in Kilronan, its main town. Minibus tours of the whole island cost about €10 – good value if you want to find your way to all of its archaeological sites, ruined churches and bays where seals live.

Inishmore has a wealth of historic ruins dating back to the Iron Age. Dún Aonghasa is the largest, but others are Dún Eóghanachta, a circular stone fort northwest of Kilronan; Dún Eochla, between Kilronan and Dún Aonghasa; Dún Duchathair, south of Kilronan; and Teampall Bheanain and Chiarain. The tourist office stocks an excellent guide to the archaeological jewels of Inishmore called *Legends in the Landscape, a Pocket Guide to Árainn*, by Dara O'Maoildhia. The book's author has started organic farm training courses here, so that the islanders can grow vegetables unique to Inishmore without using pesticides.

Should you choose to visit Kilronan first, see the Aran Heritage Centre (*see* opposite), then have a look at the locally made and imported Aran knitwear. There are also restaurants on the island, but take a picnic and drinks if you don't want to stay in town but prefer to roam about the island.

Dun Aonghasa Visitor Centre

Kilmurvey, Inishmore, **t** (099) 61008
Open Daily Mar–Oct 10–6, Nov–Feb 10–4
Adm Adult €2, child €1, family €4
Limited parking for bicycles only, toilets with disabled access, nearby coffee shops

This Iron Age fort is the most famous and spectacular of Inishmore's national monuments: the ancient stone ruin is so old that no one knows when it was built. Situated right on the edge of the cliff, part of it appears to have fallen into the sea, although some scholars have suggested that fort-dwellers there built it this way on purpose in order to evade intruders. You will need to hang on to younger children, as there are no barriers to stop them from going over the edge. You may want to take advantage of the wonderful guided tours on offer at the visitor centre, as they employ excellent

Good to know...
Getting to and around the Aran Islands

Tourist information Comharchumann Forbartha Arann, **t** (099) 61354, **www**.visitaranislands.com. The main tourist office is in Kilronan, **t** (099) 61263.
By air Aer Arann (*see* p.280) flies to all 3 islands, with several flights daily all year from Galway and from Connemara Airport in Inverin (19m/30km west of Galway, with buses to the city). Flights take about 10mins; fares are around twice the cost of the ferry – but look out for special packages, which include a night's stay on the islands. Galway Airport, **t** (091) 755 569; Inverin, **t** (091) 593 034; Inishmore, **t** (099) 61109; Aer Arann, Galway, **t** (091) 593 034, **www**.aerarann.ie.
By boat From 3 mainland harbours: Galway, Rossaveal, 23 miles (36km) west of Galway City, and Doolin, Co. Clare. The main island port is Kilronan on Inishmore. Crossings from Rossaveal take 40mins–1hr; return tickets on all lines are about €20. Tourist offices have current timetables.
Aran Island Ferries, **t** (091) 568 903, **www**.aranislandferries.com. Two boats: the *Galway Bay* runs between Galway and Inishmore, late May–Oct daily, and the *Aran Flyer* between Rossaveal and Inishmore, Apr–Sept daily.
Doolin Ferries, **t** (065) 74455. Ferries run from Doolin to Inisheer and Inishmore, Easter–Sept. You can arrange through tickets to make the islands a stepping-stone from Clare to Galway.
Island Ferries, **t** (091) 561 767. Ferries between Rossaveal and all 3 islands year round; in summer there may be 6 boats a day to Inishmore. Day-trips are also available.
O'Brien Shipping, **t** (091) 567 283. Services to all 3 islands from Galway, June–Sept daily.
Queen of Aran II, **t** (091) 566 535, **www**.queenofaran2.com. Nov–Mar, Rossaveal to Inishmore.
By bus There is a regular bus service on Inishmore, from Kilronan around the island. Many islanders also offer inexpensive minibus tours.
Bike Hire Bicycles can be hired at several places in Kilronan: **Aran Bicyle Hire**, **t** (099) 61132.

folklorists. Before you go, tell your children about the Fir Bolg (*see* p.29), who allegedly built this fort after losing Ireland to the Tuatha Dé Danaan.

At the bottom of the hill where Dún Aonghasa is located, you can have tea and shop at the crafts stores congregated there for woollen goods, or visit the site's tourist office, where you can sometimes find noted Aran folklorist Padraigín (pronounced pora-geen) Clancy, who often guides tours there – in Irish as well as English (her book *Celtic Threads*, Veritas Publications, Dublin, 1999, is a collection of essays on Ireland's Celtic spiritual heritage by Irish scholars and celebrities).

Afterwards, look for the seals that sometimes lounge off the coast of Inishmore, and contemplate what life must have been like – and the way it still is – for islanders here. You may even catch a glimpse of the enchanted island of *Hy Brasil* ('island of the blessed'), which some say appears every seven years west of Inishmore. Others claim it appears elsewhere or is the modern name for *Tir na n'Óg*, the land of eternal youth, or merely an optical illusion created by weather conditions. Still, it has been on maps since the 16th century. The 6th-century sailor-monk St Brendan the Navigator is said to have discovered America long before Columbus while seeking this illusive isle.

Ionad Arann/Aran Heritage Centre

Kilronan, Inishmore, **t** (099) 61355
Open Daily Apr, May, Sept and Oct 11–5, June–Aug 10–7; other times by appointment
Adm Adult €3.50, under-16s €2
Book/craft shop, restaurant, toilets

This small exhibition centre constantly runs Robert Flaherty's classic film *Man of Aran*, and exhibits old artefacts found on the largest of the Arans. Older children enjoy seeing the vintage boats once used for fishing and transport.

Celtic Spirit

Inis Mór, Árainn, **t** (099) 61424 (July–Dec), **t** 0041 44 252 0918 (Jan–June), **www**.celticexperience.net

Irish culture weeks on Inishmore Island.

Inishmann and Inisheer

The middle of the three islands that make up the Arans is Inishmann, and the smallest, most southern one is Inisheer. These are less popular with tourists, and people who do go there generally hire bicycles or hire spots on horses and carts. The largest, best-preserved of the Arans' stone forts is on Inishmann, while the best beach is on lonely little Inisheer.

Before you leave the Arans, or the Gaeltacht, you may like to surprise the shopkeepers by speaking in Irish: *go rev muh hah gut* (thank you) and *shlan* (good health to you/goodbye).

Dunguaire Castle

Kinvara, t (061) 360 788
Getting there 17 miles (28km) south of Galway City: N6 and N18 to Kilcolgan, then N67 to Kinvara
Open Daily mid-Apr–Sept 9.30–5 (last adm 4.30); times subject to change so call ahead
Adm Castle: adults €4.20, 5–12s €2.40, under-5s free, family (2+4) €10.50; Banquet: adults €44, 9–12s €33, 6–8s €22, under-6s free
Guided tours, banquets 2xnightly Apr–Oct 5.30 and 8.45 (booking required)

In an ocean-side corner of Co. Galway, you'll notice this fascinating 400-year-old tower-house on the outskirts of Kinvara on Galway Bay. After exploring the restored castle – which was built by the Hynes clan in 1520 – take your children to an early-evening medieval banquet, to be transported back to a time of candlelight and kings, cold grey stone walls and acoustic music, and greetings by ladies in medieval attire. A harpist opens the evening with a serenade, then your regal host welcomes you and takes you back to the time of King Guaire, renowned for his banquets in the 7th century. Your first course follows, and then there are intervals of serving and performing, as your servers illustrate the castle's history through a series of playlets incorporating faerytales, poems and music. Other works cited include those of past owners of the castle such as writer Oliver St John Gogarty and his visiting friends: WB Yeats, Lady Gregory, George Bernard Shaw and JM Synge, all of whom came here in the early 20th century.

The ambience makes it easy to chat with neighbours on the wooden benches at long oak tables. Food is the one thing that could be improved here – maybe with more authentic dishes from the Middle Ages – as the feast is a bit too 21st century. However, sweet mead and wine are served to adults to ensure that the evening is merry, while children receive something less potent.

Thoor Ballylee

Near Ballaba, outside Gort, t (091) 537 700 (Oct–May), t (091) 631 436 (June–Sept)
Getting there From Galway, N6 then N18 to Gort (23 miles/38km). From Gort, take N66 north.
Open June–Sept Mon–Sat 10–6
Adm Adult €4.45, child €1.27, student €3.81
Audio presentations, book/craft shop, gardens, picnic area, tea room, toilets

It is obvious why Ireland's best-loved lyric poet WB Yeats chose this fairytale tower-house (pronounced 'toor bahh-lilee') as a place in which to live and write. Its pastoral surroundings remain much as they were when he lived here with his family in the early 20th century. Yeats never allowed his son or daughter to enter his writing alcove at the top of the tower, nor to make noise while he was writing. He generally left his wife 'George' to settle squabbles. Only once did he come down from his study to discipline his children, his daughter claimed, by reciting a poem about little dogs that bark and bite, which so shocked them they fell silent for the rest of the day.

The tower has been kept true to its original, rather bare condition, so that one can understand Yeats's complaints about floods and draughts. Press a button to learn how each room was used in his time; the best people to talk to about this, though, are the locals, whose relations knew him. Take note of the inscription on the tower, which goes:

I, the poet William Yeats
With old millboards and sea-green slates
And smithy work from the Gort forge
Restored this tower for my wife George;
And may these characters remain
When all is ruin once again.

A story to tell: A Galway folk tale

Galway is known for its folk tales, and stories about giants and faeries from the Otherworld are common around the Ballylee and Gort area.

One story filed at the Kiltartan Gregory Museum near Gort is about a poor old woman with only a piece of bread left in her press (larder or cupboard). On the day of her worst poverty, a poor stranger appeared at her door begging for bread. The kind old lady had only a small bit left but gave it gladly to 'the poor craithur' (creature), who was hobbling on two sticks and seemed so much worse off than herself. At twilight she fell asleep with the pangs of the hunger upon her and had a dream in which she was wandering in a wood looking for berries to eat. There she met a faery lady who told her to go home, where she would find her fortune in the press. The next morning, remembering the dream, she opened her press, where she found bread, faery cakes and foods of all kinds, which never emptied until she died many years later. In the evening, a purse filled with gold was left at her door that, no matter how much she took out of it, always remained full.

AROUND AND ABOUT

Animal magic

Dartfield Horse World

Kilreekil, Loughrea, **t** (091) 843 968
Getting there on N6 Galway–Dublin road
Open daily 9.30–6
Adm Adult €6.50, child/student €4, family (2+2) €16
Indoor displays, exhibits, videos, café, shop, play area

Explore 350 acres of parkland on horseback, in a horse-drawn carriage or on foot, and pet and feed horses or ride ponies.

Ocean and Country Visitor Centre

Derryinver, Letterfrack, Renvyle Peninsula, Connemara, **t** (095) 43473
Getting there 22 miles (35km) north of Clifden
Open Daily mid-Feb–Oct 10–6
Adm Centre: adult €5, student €4, child €2.50, under-6s free, family €20
Children's play and picnic areas, telescope, toilets

Connemara's marine life and heritage are the focal point of this small, independent centre, which includes an aquarium and maritime museum. Scenic and wildlife cruises and short sea-angling trips are available, and the centre hosts traditional Irish music on summer evenings.

Turoe Pet Farm and Leisure Park

Turoe House, Bullaun, **t** (091) 841 580
Getting there 25 miles (40km) east of Galway; N6 to Loughrea, then north 4 miles (6km) to Bullaun
Open Easter–Sept daily 10–7, Oct–Easter Sat, Sun and bank hols 2–6; 1–22 Dec Thurs and Fri 6–8, Sat and Sun 2–8 for Christmas Village; other times by appointment
Adm Adult €5, child €10, up to age 2 1/2 €7
Farm tour, shop, café, BBQs and entertainment, picnic areas, pets' corner, playground, indoor play area, football pitch, nature walk, guided tours, disabled access, toilets, baby-changing room

Meet an Irish farming family and feed and cuddle farm animals or enjoy special events such as the Easter Egg Hunt, Halloween Party and Christmas Village. Bring the right footwear to walk the nature trail that winds around this tranquil farm and the famous Turoe Stone, a beautifully carved standing stone made around 300 BC. Children like making a wish at the wishing well, feeding ducks, playing on the swings and slides or petting the animals. Look at the old farm machinery before stopping at the tea shop for home-baked goodies, or book to have Irish music, song and dance with lunch or dinner.

Bricks and mortar

Athenry Castle

Athenry, **t** (091) 844 797
Getting there 15 miles (23km) north of Clifden
Open Apr, May and mid-Sept–Oct Tues–Sun 10–5, June–mid-Sept daily 10–6
Adm Adult €2.75, child €1.25, family €7

This medieval walled town was made famous by the popular song *The Fields of Athenry*, and its 13th-century Norman castle ruin is worth a look.

Aughnanure Castle

Oughterard, **t** (091) 552 214
Getting there 17 miles (27km) north of Galway
Open Daily May–Oct 9.30–6
Adm Adult €2.50, child €1.20, family €6.30

A 15th-century tower built by the Norman De Burgo clan but captured by the rival O'Flahertys, as their stronghold beside Lough Corrib.

Clonfert Cathedral

Clonfert Village
Getting there 55 miles (88km) east of Galway by the River Shannon
Open Daily; hours vary

This atmospheric ruined church – known as a 'cathedral' despite being small – is thought to have been built in the 12th century over a monastery founded in 563 by St Brendan the Navigator, who some claim discovered America before Columbus.

Kylemore Abbey and Garden

Kylemore, Connemara, **t** (095) 41146, **www.kylemoreabbey.ie**
Getting there 11 miles (18km) north of Clifden on N59 between Letterfrack and Recess
Open Abbey: daily Nov–Mar 10–4, Easter–Oct 9.30–6, except Christmas week and Good Fri Garden: daily Easter–Oct 10.30–4.30
Adm Abbey and Garden: adult €11, student €7, under-12s free
Visitors' centre, abbey, tea room (Easter–Oct), craft shop and pottery (Mar–Oct), toilets

One of few human-built monuments in this wild part of Connemara, the abbey is also a place to pause for some home-cooking and excellent desserts. This is Ireland's only convent of Benedictine nuns, who also run an international girls' boarding school here. The nuns fled here from their parent convent in Belgium in World War I. Today they open the grounds and part of the house to the public, along with the neo-Gothic chapel. Kylemore Abbey was built in 1868, and its chapel is a beautiful miniature cathedral. After seeing the exhibition and rooms open to visitors, stroll along the Lake Walk and take a bus to the Victorian walled garden. Once one of the most impressive in Ireland, with flower and kitchen gardens separated by a mountain stream and woodland, its restoration was begun by a single nun. Distinctive pottery is made in the abbey's studio.

Look at this!

Aughrim Heritage Centre

Near Ballinasloe, **t** (090) 967 3939
Getting there 36 miles (58km) east of Galway
Open Daily June–end Sept 10–1 and 2–6. **Adm** €4
Book/craft shop, restaurant, toilets

Older children fascinated by history may enjoy reliving one of Ireland's most important – and bloodiest – wars. The 1691 Battle of Aughrim, reconstructed very well here, took place after the Battle of the Boyne and Siege of Athlone during the war between Catholic James II and his Jacobite followers and the Protestant William of Orange (*see* p.35). Just as the Jacobites were about to win, a cannonball killed their French general St Ruth, and panic ensued. The Williamites got the upper hand and killed 6,000 Jacobites that day, while only 2,000 of their own men died. This decisive Protestant victory was Ireland's last great land battle. The centre has a Children's Day on the second Sunday in June (telephone for times).

Galway songs to sing...
Connemara Cradle Song, Galway Is Where I Want to Be, Sweet Marie, The Galway Races, The Hills of Connemara, The Waxies Dargle, Dan O'Hara, The Galway Shawl, The Fields of Athenry.

Athenry Arts and Heritage Activity Centre

St Mary's Church, The Square, Athenry,
t (091) 844 661, **www**.athenryheritagetown.com
Getting there 15 miles (23km) north of Clifden, off Galway–Dublin road (N6)
Open Apr–Oct daily 10–6, Nov–Mar Tues–Sun 10–5
Adm €3.50, family (2+2) from €12
Archery lessons, guided tours of Athenry, toilets

This display on Athenry's medieval past will provide you with all the details you need for exploring the 13th-century walled town. Activities include arts, crafts, archery, and puppetry workshops, and you can dress up in reproductions of medieval costumes and hold replica weaponry.

Dan O'Hara's Homestead Farm

Lettershea, **t** (095) 21246
Getting there 5 miles (8km) inland from Clifden, Connemara, on N59 from Galway
Open Daily Apr–Oct 10–6; rest of year by request
Adm Adult €7, child €3.50, student €6, family (2+4) €17
Audio-visual display, guided tours, turf-cutting and other demonstrations on request, craft shop, tea room, restaurant (opening 2006), accommodation , toilets

This eight-acre organic farm is run exactly as it would have been in the 19th century. Teach your children *The Ballad of Dan O'Hara* in honour of your visit here, where they can learn the tale of a tenant farmer whose eviction after the famine ruined his life. Reconstructions of a *crannóg* (island house), ring fort and *clochaun* (stone hut) and the exhibition on how farming began here 6,000 years ago, with a bit of history of Connemara thrown in, give them a context in which to consider Dan O'Hara's thatched stone cottage and deepen their insight into the life of a non-English-speaking 19th-century tenant farmer. They will find out how turf was cut in the nearby bogs and used to fuel the hearth, around which O'Hara's family and friends gathered to tell stories and dance *céilis* (group dances).

People of O'Hara's time lived quite well on a diet of potatoes and buttermilk, supplemented with fish, seaweed, eggs and a little meat from animals they raised. Self-sufficient, O'Hara rented the house in which they lived and the land they worked. One day he enlarged his windows, not realizing he would have to pay a higher rent for them. This and the arrival of the potato blight and the Famine in the 1840s made it impossible for him to pay his landlord, and eventually he and his family were evicted. They got a ship to New York – one of the terrible coffin ships (so called because so many people died in them). On the voyage, his wife and three of his seven children died. Arriving in America broken and destitute, O'Hara had to put the rest of his children into an orphanage and ended up selling matches on the streets of New York, far from home.

Kiltartan Gregory Museum

Kiltartan Cross, north of Gort, **t** (091) 632 346
Getting there 23 miles (38km) from Galway on N18
Open June–Aug daily 10–6, Sept–May Sun 1–5
Adm free
Souvenir shop

A little museum in a former schoolhouse, where a dedicated (plain-clothes) nun tells lots of stories about the mementoes of Lady Gregory, the Great Famine and the Celtic Revival on display. It offers a history of Lady Gregory's life and times, covering everything from records of the Famine on the vast lands her family owned to her correspondence with many renowned Irish artists. Of special note is a letter from James Joyce to Lady Gregory just before he left Ireland for Paris. Children will perhaps be most interested by the replica of an early-20th-century Irish classroom, with its mannequin teacher in period costume, old maps of Ireland and the world, textbooks and other accoutrements.

Leenane Sheep and Wool Centre

Leenane, **t** (095) 42323
Getting there 40 miles (65km) northwest of Galway via Oughterard
Open Apr–Oct daily 9–6 (times may vary)
Adm Adult €5, child €3, family €12
Craft shop, audio-visual display, restaurant, toilets

This centre overlooks Killary Harbour and on a good day is a wonderful place to come to show children something about sheep and the wool industry in Ireland. They can see how wool gets from sheep to humans, and all the related processes.

Roundstone Music and Crafts

IDA Park, Roundstone, Connemara, **t** (095) 35808, **www.bodhran.com**
Getting there 13 miles (21km) south of Clifden on N59
Open Mar–Oct daily 9–7, Nov–Feb Mon–Sat 9–7
Craft shop, workshop, coffee shop, toilets

The famous *bodhrán* (pronounced bow-rawn), a drum made of goatskin stretched across a round Irish beech tree rim, is one of Ireland's oldest known instruments. You'll often hear it played in traditional Irish music, and Irish traditional musicians around the world use bodhráns that were made here. You can book a time to watch Malachy Kearns make one for you, which can be decorated with a Celtic design, family crest or even your child's initial or name while you wait, free of charge. Malachy also specializes in smaller custom-made instruments (wooden flutes, harps, tin whistles). Another of their shops may be found on Main St, Clifden, but it is open only in summer.

Afterwards, you might be inspired to climb Mt Errisbeg, a 300m (984ft) mountain overlooking the Atlantic, to which you can walk from Roundstone village, or take a walk along the beach at Dog's Bay.

A story to tell: Knockma: The Great Hill

The very first people to live in Ireland, allegedly, were a granddaughter of Noah named Cessair and her companions, who came here to avoid the Great Flood (*see* p.29). Cessair, it is said, was buried under a cairn on top of Knockma (*Cnoc Meadha*, 'the great hill'), near Belclare, west of Tuam, in Co. Galway. Later, Knockma became known as the home of Fionnábar (or Finnveara), the King of the Faeries. Rumour has it that it's a good idea not to disturb this place or you may attract the ill will of the immortal King who lives there, and it's a certainty that if you throw something into a hole on the top of Knockma, it will be thrown right back out at you with as much force as it dropped.

Now, why is the King of the Faeries living inside a hill? The answer goes back to long, long ago before the days of Men (the Sons of Míl, *see* p.119), deep in the mists of time when magic was taken as a real and common thing in the world. The best magicians of all were the Tuatha Dé Danaan, later known as the faeries among country people. Fionnábar is one of the Tuatha, and therefore dwells in the shadowy nether regions of the earth.

Teach an Phiarsaigh (Pádraic Pearse's Cottage)

Near Ros Muc (Rosmuck), **t** (091) 574 292
Getting there On Kilkieran Bay, 21 miles (34km) southwest of Oughterard
Open 30 Mar–Easter Sat and Sun 10–5, mid-June–mid-Sept daily 10–6, mid–end-Sept Sat and Sun 10–6
Adm Adult €3, child €1.50, family €7
Guided tours on request, toilets

This cottage, a bit difficult to find on Connemara's winding roads, doesn't contain a lot of information, apart from some memorabilia belonging to its owner, but it's notable as the modest thatched house where poet-teacher Pádraic Pearse (1879–1916), leader of the 1916 Easter Rising, spent several summers. Pearse was an ardent supporter of the Irish language, and improved his knowledge of it by talking to local people in the lonely village of Rosmuck.

Nature lovers

Connemara National Park

Visitor Centre, Letterfrack, **t** (095) 41054/41006
Getting there 10 miles (16km) north of Clifden
Open Visitor Centre: daily Mar–May, Sept and Oct 10–5.30
Adm Adult €2.75, student €2, child €1.25, family €7
Guided walks (June Mon–Wed, July and Aug Mon–Fri; boots and rainwear needed for boggy terrain), disabled access, indoor picnic area with kitchen, coffee shop, toilets with disabled access and baby-changing room, free parking, summer events

This is one of Ireland's six national parks, covering 2,000 hectares of Connemara's mountains. Extra activities in July and August include 2–3hr guided walks, nature mornings (for children aged 5+) and evening talks. There are also self-guided trails, including two short ones. In the visitor centre, children can watch an audio-visual show, see 3D models and plans of the park, and get to grips with interactive exhibits. Summer Tuesdays and Thursdays are activity days – involving games, the arts, animals and nature – for ages 4 and up.

Coole Park

Gort, **t** (091) 631 804
Getting there 23 miles (38km) south of Galway
Open Park: all year; Visitor Centre: Easter–May Tues–Sun 10–5, June–Aug daily 10–6, Sept daily 10–5
Adm Adult €2.50, child €1.20, family (2+2) €6.30
Visitor centre, disabled access, tea room, toilets

Just northeast of Gort lie the vast grounds that once held the home of folklorist Lady Gregory, who offered it as a haven to Yeats, Synge and many other writers. The house was demolished in the early 1940s, and now only fragments of it remain, but the park is a nature reserve with majestic yews. The Coole Visitor Centre provides historical background and maps of the area. You can spend a whole day here exploring Coole's nature trails and lakeside walks among graceful trees. Enjoy the excellent café, and watch the video about the days when Lady Gregory and her friends planned a better future for Ireland in this very setting. In the walled garden, you can still find the famous copper chestnut tree known as the 'autograph tree' on whose trunk many of Coole Park's illustrious visitors carved their names.

Portumna Forest Park

Portumna, Lough Derg

This large area, beside Lough Derg on the Shannon in eastern Co. Galway has lakeside and forest walks, a nature trail, an observation point and a tower that children can climb to look down upon the beautiful lough and surrounding forest.

Sporty kids

Activity centres

Delphi Adventure Sports Centre

Delphi, Leenane, **t** (095) 42208/42307
Adm Price according to activity
Indoor sports hall with climbing wall, tennis court, shop, café, sauna, instruction, equipment included

Buckets and spades – Beaches in County Galway

There are fine beaches all along the twisting Galway coast, scattered around its hundreds of inlets and coves. In particular, **Ballyconneely** in western Connemara is surrounded by beaches: **Aillebrack** is good for swimming, and **False Bay** is better for surfing.

Omey Strand is a huge, magnificent sandy beach near **Cleggan** in Connemara. At low tide you can also drive over to the beautiful Omey Island, where there's a freshwater lake near the beach on the western edge. The island is a paradise for walkers – but watch the tides, or you'll get cut off.

Other beaches that stand out in the county are at **Salthill** just west of Galway, **Traught Beach**, further south at **Kinvara**, **Tra na mBan** beach at **Spiddal**, and **Tra na Doilin** beach on the inlet at **Carraroe**. More unusual options are **Cill Muirbhthe** beach on **Inishmore** in the Aran Islands and, for freshwater swimming, **Loughrea Lake** beach.

Tell me an Irish riddle...
Question – How many 'o's can you put in potatoes?
Answer – Put eight o's

A centre offering adventure holidays for children aged 8–17. Day or half-day activities include sailing, raft-building, canoeing, rock-climbing, surfing, hill-walking and snorkelling, and there are also evening events such as *céilis*.

Killary Adventure Centre

Renvyle, Salruck, near Leenane, t (095) 43411/42276

Half-day, day, weekend, or week-long sea- or land-based activities, including archery, canoeing, sailing and rock-climbing.

Boat trips

Several companies offer cruises on Lough Corrib, in the heart of Connemara. Most of them last about 90 mins.

Aran Watersports

Kilronan, Inishmore, The Arans, t (087) 904 2777
Open May–Sept

Fishing trips or boats for hire, including a traditional *curragh*.

Corrib Cruises

Oughterard, t (092) 46029/46292
Guided commentary, open-top deck, bar

Cruises twice-daily in summer (May–Sept) on the Irish Republic's largest lake, the surface of which shines like polished glass. The Corrib is also one of Ireland's cleanest and most scenic loughs, with 365 islands, one for each day of the year.

Corrib Princess River Cruises

Furbo Hill, Furbo and Woodquay, Galway, t (091) 592 447, www.corribprincess.ie

Twice-daily cruise tours in the summer season around Lough Corrib from the Woodquay on the north side of Galway city, with a bar on board, and an optional buffet and dinners.

Island Discovery

Cleggan, Connemara, t (095) 44642/21520

Several sailings daily to Inishbofin Island, leaving from Cleggan, just north of Clifden.

Killary Cruises

Leeane, t 1 800 415 151

Cruises on Ireland's only fjord.

Fishing

For brown trout, sea trout and salmon fishing on Lough Corrib, contact the tourist office in Galway City for details and regulations.

Blue Water Fishing

John Brittain, Sharamore House, Streamsdown, Clifden, t (095) 21073

Deep-sea angling.

Galway Fishery

Nun's Island, t (091) 562 388

Horse-riding

Cleggan Beach Riding Centre

Cleggan, Connemara, t (095) 44746

Trek on sandy beaches or, if you prefer, for 2hrs on one of the offshore islands.

Clonboo Riding School

Corandulla, t (091) 791 362

A small family-owned riding school with day and week-long courses, or half-hour sessions for very small children.

Rockmount Riding Centre

Claregalway, t (091) 798 147

A few miles north of Galway, this centre with an indoor arena offers instruction and trekking.

Rusheen Riding Centre

Salthill, t (087) 681 1837 or t (095) 521 285

Beach riding and trekking, AIRE-approved lessons for beginners, and horses and ponies for all ages and standards.

Walking

There are many wonderful walks in Connemara and the rest of Co. Galway, but the beautiful wildness of the terrain makes it more important than in other parts of Ireland to have a good map with you, or, preferably, to join a guided walk.

Guided Nature Walks with Seán

Coismeigmór, Na Forbacha, t (091) 503 936, www.seansafari.com

Morning walks (Mon–Sat), with a minibus available. Ensure you have suitable footwear.

Michael Gibbons' Walking Ireland

Connemara Walking Centre, Dun Gibbons Inn, Clifden, t (095) 21379, www.walkingireland.com

A choice of archaeological and heritage walks, with accommodation arranged en route.

COUNTY MAYO

Mayo (*Mag nEo na Sacsan*) in Irish means 'The Plain of the Yew Trees of the Saxons', which indicates how long ago it got its name. The secrets County Mayo holds are found in quiet places where the past is still relatively unbothered by tourism. Archaeological treasures and ancient monuments in the form of standing stones, *fulachta fiadh* (outdoor water-cooking troughs), ring forts and intriguingly shaped hills such as the pointed Croagh Patrick will draw your attention.

There are welcoming amateur historians everywhere in Mayo who want to talk about the old stories of this part of the world, but you may not meet them if you don't adjust to the gentler pace of its people, who prefer slower ways to the glitz of the city. You will be able to relax in this part of Ireland, walking in its gardens, riding horses, climbing mountains, exploring prehistoric settlement sites and just making conversation. Taking the time to talk will lead to unexpected adventures. Often these will have something to do with the Mayo landscape, where you'll find lakeland scenery, the highest sea cliffs in Europe, safe beaches and islands such as Inishglora, where four small graves are alleged to be those of the Children of Lir, or Clare Island, the home of the 16th-century pirate queen Grace O'Malley. Families can fish for salmon on the River Moy in the middle of Ballina or make a pilgrimage to Croagh Patrick on Reek Sunday in July for a sense of what pagans and Christians have long experienced there. Try to understand how Irishmen felt after the Great Famine when so many saw the Knock apparition, while the practical joined Michael Davitt's Land League. Then discover the proud Gaelic heritage that people in Mayo have never quite forgotten, and the sense that women are not on Earth to be meek or mocked, as their High Queen Grace O'Malley demonstrated (*see* p.178).

Beneath Mayo natives' generosity and easygoing hospitality burns a special independence of spirit and love for freedom. They are not slow to tell you about the terrible Famine, which they periodically remember with a long-distance 'famine walk'. Nor are they embarrassed when they speak of their nature-based remedies that heal people when modern medicine does not. There is great respect here for the traditions and lessons of the past, allied with a staunch determination not to dwell on what has been but to make the most of what is.

Ballina, Castlebar and Westport are Mayo's main towns. Ballina is a lively grey town through which heavy lorries pass; the more anglicized Castlebar is bigger, with modern buildings. The ancestors of Diana, Princess of Wales, the Spencers, were land-owning gentry here – given land in Castlebar during a British loyalist plantation after Cromwell's takeover. Westport retains the charm of its Georgian past, as its leaders have heroically combatted 'development', which outsiders claim is necessary if Ireland is to keep up with the rest of the world. Westport's strength is that its people know better. That is why it is still a beautiful, inviting town, while its counterparts elsewhere have fallen to the drill. It is an ideal base, with pleasant shops, restaurants and hotels.

Did you know...?

Over each joint and sinew of the buried corpse of the Tuatha healer Miach grew 365 herbs, each one growing above the spot in the body that it could cure. His sister collected them, carefully noting the position of each one on her cloak, but when her father the healer Dían Cécht discovered this he was so jealous of his dead son's greater powers that he mixed them up – and so today we do not have the cures known by the Tuatha healers – all because of one man's selfish heart.

Tourist information

Achill Tourism, Achill Island, **t** (098) 47353, **www.achilltourism.com**

Ballina, t (096) 70848

Castlebar, t (094) 902 1207

Cong, t (092) 46542

Knock, t (094) 938 8193

Knock Airport, t (094) 936 7247

Westport, James St, **t** (098) 25711

www.visitmayo.com, www.irelandwest.ie

Tours

Clew Bay Heritage Centre, The Quay, Westport, **t** (098) 26852

Guided tours of Westport, plus an exhibition.

Mayo Horsedrawn Caravan Holidays

See p.180.

Mayo Island Tours, t (098) 26015

Guided tours of the islands off the Mayo coast.

Michael Maye, e michaelmaye@eircom.net

A historian-guide to Ashford Castle and the Cong region of Co. Mayo.

Special Events – County Mayo

June

Achill Archaeological Field School, t (098) 43564

Explore the deserted village of Slievemore on Achill Island. Best for teenagers and young adults.

Westport Horse and Pony Show, t (098) 26206

Children who love horses will enjoy this, but don't be surprised if they want you to buy one.

Westport International Sea Angling Festival, t (098) 27297

This festival in late June is only of interest to really keen youthful fishermen.

July

Ballina Street and Arts Festival, t (096) 79814

Fun for the whole family.

Castlebar International Walking Festival, t (094) 24102

Walkers need to be fit for this, so be ready to carry small children on walks.

Clare Island Regatta, t (098) 25087

One day of *curragh* and yawl racing and children's sports.

Croagh Patrick Pilgrimage, Westport, **t** (098) 28871

A harsh climb for the super-fit, and serious pilgrims, on the last Sunday in July.

Feile Iorras, Belmullet and Erris region of the Mullet Peninsula, **t** (097) 81952, **www.feileiorras.org**

A local traditional festival for families.

Mulranny Mediterranean Heather Festival, t (098) 36287

Sheepdog trials, community sports, angling and children's events.

Siamsa Sraide (Street Festival), Swinford, **t** (094) 925 1179

Céilis, busking competitions and the like.

August

Westport Horse Fair, t (098) 25616/26206

A real fair for those seeking horses to buy.

September

Westport Arts Festival, t (098) 25711

A fun festival, especially for teenagers.

October

Roola Boola Children's Arts Festival, Linenhall Arts Centre, Castlebar, **t** (094) 902 3733

A children's festival with shows, workshops, a parade and other events.

SONAS, Louisburgh Children's Arts Festival, Louisburgh, **t** (098) 66218

A local community festival of children's arts.

Getting there and around

By air Mayo has an international airport at Knock, in the countryside near Charlestown by the N17 Galway–Sligo road, 24 miles (38km) east of Castlebar (*see* p.283). It has flights from airports in Britain with bmibaby, easyJet, Aer Arann and Ryanair (*see* pp.280–2). The only transport from the airport is taxi or airline bus. Knock Airport, **t** 1 850 67 22 22, **www.knockairport.com**

By bus Bus Éireann coaches from Dublin and other cities run to Ballina, Castlebar, Westport and several other towns. You can get around by bus almost anywhere within Mayo, or points beyond. There are a number of obscure local lines; tourist offices are the best sources for bus information. Bus Éireann, Ballina, **t** (096) 71800, **www**.buseireann.ie

By car Dublin to Castlebar takes 4–5hrs (by the N4, then the N5 from Longford). A car is the best way to get around Mayo with children, but journey times are long and roads are narrow and bumpy. Don't expect to get anywhere fast!

By train Rail services are infrequent: Westport, Castlebar and Ballina each have about 3 trains daily to and from Dublin Heuston, and there are also trains from Dublin to the west coast, to Galway and Limerick. Stations: Westport, **t** (098) 25253; Castlebar, **t** (094) 902 1222; Ballina, **t** (096) 71820.

Bike Hire

Achill Sound Hotel, Achill Island, **t** (098) 45245

P. Breheny and Sons, Castlebar St, Westport, **t** (098) 25020

Mayo Leisure Cycling, Newantrim St, Castlebar, **t** (094) 902 5220

Self-guided cycling tours, with accommodation.

O'Connor's, Main St, Cong, **t** (092) 46008

O'Malleys Island Sports, Dooagh, Achill Island, **t** (098) 43125

Sean Sammons, The Fuel Yard, James St, Westport, **t** (098) 25471

Boat Tour

Corrib Cruises, Cong, **t** (087) 679 6470 or **t** (094) 954 6029, **www.corribcruises.com**

Live ballad sessions and guided tours to Lough Corrib's Inchagoill Island's 5th–12th-century ruins from Ashford Castle by a scholar of this lake, from April to October.

Good to know...
Getting to Mayo's offshore islands
Clare Island: O'Malley Ferries, t (098) 25045, make 5 runs a day from Roonagh Quay; tickets can also be bought from Westport Tourist Office.
Chris O'Grady also operates boats out to Clare Island, and can organize sea-fishing and boating via **Clare Island Ferry and Clew Bay Cruises**, Westport, **t** (098) 28288 (or via Westport Tourist Office). They have 2 boats, the *Pirate Queen* and the Clare Island mail boat, and also operate from Roonagh Quay. Both boat operators run all year round, but with much less frequency from October to April.
Inishturk and Caher: Boats also run from Roonagh. Service is somewhat informal; negotiate with local fishermen, or Chris O'Grady (*see* above). The *Caher Star* and *Lady Marilyn* make trips in summer from Roonagh via Inishturk, **t** (098) 45541.
Inishglora and Inishkea: There is no regular service to these islands, and you'll have to find someone with a boat to take you over, such as **Matthew Geraghty** in Belmullet, **t** (097) 85741.

SPECIAL TRIPS

Hennigan's Heritage Centre

Killasser, near Swinford, **t** (094) 925 2505
Getting there North of Swinford about 19 miles (30km) east of Castlebar by N17
Open Daily Mar–Sept 10–6; tours from 12 noon
Adm Adult €7, child €2
With (recommended) guided tours: adult €9, child €4, family (2+2) €22 + €4 per extra child
Guided tours, boat hire, fishing, tea room, toilets

Proprietor Jim Hennigan offers what is most likely the best folklore tour in Mayo. He tells the story of the way life used to be here for him and his family, who lived in a thatched cottage on this 10-acre farm for 200 years. Human-sized models hold farm tools, exhibiting in 3D the working, as well as bad, habits of the past. A mannequin waits for illegal alcohol, *potcheen*, to distill in a real *potcheen* still. To avoid dying from this lethal, normally potato-based brew, it was important to distill it at least three times before you drank it. The finer points of similar matters Hennigan can explain, such as why boys were made to wear dresses and why their hair wasn't cut until they were old enough to look after themselves (to make the faeries think they were girls so they wouldn't steal them).

Here you can see the real way of life of Mayo people, and how they lived in frugal, self-sufficient communities and used a 'barter and meitheal' system without money in order to survive the terrible conditions they lived under from Penal times until the 19th century. A large collection of agricultural implements and a schoolhouse carry detailed explanations. Outdoors spuds grow in fields as they used to do, with fowl and animals in an unchanged farmyard.

A tour around the lake, with more from Mr Hennigan about local history, rounds off your personalized tour, along with home-baked scones and fresh coffee in the tea room. Tours are available at 12 noon, 2, 4 and 5.30pm (later on request).

Knock

Knock, Ireland's National Marian Shrine

Knock, **t** (094) 938 8100, **www.knock-shrine.ie**
Getting there By N17 7 miles (11km) north of Claremorris
Open Daily. **Adm** Free

In 1879, a total of 15 people of different ages – some of them children – saw an apparition of the Virgin Mary in the Mayo village of Knock, in the pouring rain. It lasted for more than two hours. On her left was the spirit of St John the Evangelist holding an open book in his left hand, his right hand raised as if he were preaching, and a lamb on an altar farther left with a large cross behind it. To Mary's right was St Joseph. Around the altar were hovering angels, and the vision was enveloped in a bright light that could be seen from miles away. No message was given and no word spoken. Today a modern complex of buildings stands on the site, with holy water available from lines of outdoor water fountains. If you want to learn about the apparition and Knock, do visit the on-site Knock Folk Museum, which will also interest children.

Knock Folk Museum

Knock, **t** (094) 938 8100
Open Daily May– Oct 10–6; other times by appointment. **Adm** Adult €5, child €4
Guided tours on request, shop, disabled access

This small, excellent museum tells the story of the Knock Apparition of 1879 and places it in the context of life in Ireland at that time. It occurred not long after the Great Famine, when poverty was rife and much social unrest manifested in the formation of the Land League (*see* p.37). It was against this background that people in Knock saw a vision of the Virgin Mary. The museum's exhibits include reconstructions of rooms, with information on crafts, education, clothing and transport of that period, alongside religious life and traditions.

Museum of Country Life

Turlough Park, Castlebar, **t** (094) 903 1755, **www.museum.ie**
Getting there 4 miles (7km) east of Castlebar on N5
Open Tues–Sat 10–5 and Sun 2–5; closed bank hols
Adm Free
*Guided tours on request (**t** (094) 903 1751; call 10–2), full disabled access, shop, café, gardens, workshops, craft demonstrations and activity sheets for children (book in advance)*

This modern museum looks out of place in its beautiful 19th-century setting beside a lake in the grounds of Turlough Park, next to the restored 18th-century Turlough Park House. But once inside, you can immerse yourself in an unmissable exhibition on Irish rural life from 1850 to 1950. You can find out how furniture, utensils and even thatched roofs were made. Films of real people making things like *curraghs* and straw ropes fascinate anyone, and free teaching sessions in Irish craft skills are offered. Modern city kids are impressed by the skill, patience and strength required to make traditional products, and it's an education for them to realize the importance of knowing how to look after oneself in the wild, and how helpless modern civilization makes many of us. The demands of living with the elements are emphasized in displays on hunting, fishing and farming. Equally interesting are exhibits on religion and education, where you listen to lessons as they were taught in Irish schools, and learn how clothes and shoes were made. Children may find out about the games Irish children played; what they did on holidays such as St Bridget's Day, May Day, Samhain and Christmas; and how people mourned at wakes. Highlighted are the political history of the time and Ireland's geography. Home to the National Folklife Collection, this is the first branch of the National Museum of Ireland outside Dublin.

A story to tell: The First Battle of Moytura

When they first arrived in Ireland, the Tuatha Dé Danaan challenged the Fir Bolg for control of the island (*see* p.163). These 'Bag Men' were busy digging turf and husbanding the bogland at the time, and were overwhelmed by these god-like, glittering magicians with their golden torcs and jewellery, and their fine cloaks embroidered in yet more gold. But the Fir Bolg and their king, Eochaí, still fought the Tuatha proudly on the Plain of Moytura in Mayo, around Cong and along the shore of Lough Corrib.

They managed to cut off the arm of the Tuatha King, Nuadhu, but then three Tuatha warriors caught King Eochaí bathing at a well near a little hill (now called *Tulach an trír*, 'The Hill of the Three'). A small monument called *Carn an éinfhir* ('Cairn of the One Man') stands where they killed him. Of course the Tuatha won after this, especially with their superior magic, herbal medicines and special healing baths used for the wounded.

After losing the First Battle of Moytura, the Fir Bolg retreated to find freedom in the faraway places of Ireland, such as Rathlin Island in Co. Antrim and the Aran Islands of County Galway. On Inishmore, their leader Aonghus built a fort you can still see, at Dún Aonghasa ('Fort of Aonghus', *see* p.164).

According to Tuatha laws, no king was allowed to have a bodily imperfection, so now that Nuadhu had only one arm, he gave the kingship to the half-Tuatha warrior Bres the Beautiful, whose father was a Fomorian. However, Bres was unkind to the Daghda, and proved stingy and inhospitable to visitors to his fort. His Fomorian genes must have got the better of him, because he showed none of the kingly virtues valued by the Tuatha, and grew very unpopular.

Meanwhile, Nuadhu was given a silver arm by the Tuatha's great healer, Dían Cécht, whose son Miach was a still better healer and restored Nuadhu's natural arm. Dían Cécht grew so jealous of his son for this that he had him killed.

Now whole again, Nuadhu told Bres that he wanted to take back his kingship, especially since Bres had been wreaking havoc among the Tuatha with his mean-spirited behaviour. But Bres refused to comply, and turned to his evil relatives the Fomorians for help, and so began the Second Battle of Moytura (*see* p. 183).

Westport House and Country Park

Westport House Estate, Westport, **t** (098) 27766, **www**.westporthouse.ie
Getting there 2 miles (3km) north of Westport
Open Hours vary for different attractions; most are open 6 Apr–May Sat and Sun 2–5, June daily 1.30–5.30, July–24 Aug daily 11.30–5.30, 25 Aug–21 Sept daily 1–5.30, but call to check what's operating on the day of your visit
Adm All attractions: adult €24, child €15, family (2+4) €75; House and Gardens only: adult €15, child €10, family (2+4) €49
Exhibition, shop, tea room, restaurant, baby-changing facilities, toilets, disabled access

Combining a historic house with a fun park makes for a perfect family day-trip. Westport House, built in 1685 and set within delightful grounds, is owned by the 13th great-grandson of Grace O'Malley (*see* p.178), who apparently retorted, when offered the title of Countess by Queen Elizabeth, that the latter had no right to offer her that for they were equals. Little children enjoy the animal farm, ball pond, playground, boating area, miniature railway, swan pedal boats, pitch'n'putt and flume ride. You could spend all day here and even fish on the lake or river. The grand interior of Westport House should be seen also, with its statue of Grace O'Malley nursing a baby, its old children's nursery and its playful dungeon.

AROUND AND ABOUT

Animal magic

Partry House

Partry, **t** (094) 954 3004
Getting there 12 miles (19km) south of Castlebar
Open Limited times; call for details
Adm €5

A pleasant outing may be had at this ecologically friendly organic farm and garden with abundant wildlife in its peaceful grounds.

Bricks and mortar

Ballintubber Abbey

Ballintubber, near Claremorris, **t** (094) 903 0934
Getting there 8 1/2 miles (14km) south of Castlebar, on N84
Open Daily June–Aug 9am–12 midnight; guided tours May–Sept 10–4.30, other times by appointment
Adm By donation
Video, interpretative centre, shop, guided tours available with advance notice

This historic abbey, founded in 1216 by Cathal O'Connor, King of Connacht, is overseen by the charismatic Father Fahey, renowned in the area for his knowledge of history and local folklore. Looking like a white-haired John Lennon in Lennon's opposite universe, he leads pilgrims on cross-country walks to ancient shrines and local places, such as Croagh Patrick (*see* p.178). A panel display describes how Ballintubber became known as 'the abbey that wouldn't die'. Despite robberies and the abbey being roofless for 250 years, local people continued to attend Mass in rain, wind and snow. Guides here are as entertaining as professional actors, telling you all sorts of stories about Ballintubber, which, with its cemetery, retains a sense of bygone times.

Father Fahey oversees the nearby Celtic Furrow museum when he is not busy with retreats and his duties for local parishioners, not to mention weddings, as for the actor Pierce Brosnan.

Celtic Furrow

Visitor Centre, Ballintubber Abbey, **t** (094) 903 0934
Getting there 8 1/2 miles (14km) south of Castlebar
Open June–Aug daily 10.30–5 (but call in advance)
Adm Adult €4, child/student €2.50, family €9; tour of Celtic Furrow and Ballintubber €4
Exhibition, toilets, tea shop

This small museum covers the past 5,000 years in Ireland, showing Neolithic farming methods (*c*.3000 BC) and paintings of Celtic celebrations (*c*.600 BC). An outdoor maze traces the Early Christian period with displays on Irish folklore and Celtic festivals.

Michael Davitt Memorial Museum

Straide, **t** (094) 903 1022, **www**.museumsofmayo.com/davitt
Getting there 12 miles (19km) north of Castlebar
Open Daily 10–6
Adm Adult €3.50, child €1.50, family €8

A story to tell:
The Children of Lir

King Lir, the Tuatha Dé Danaan father of sea god Manannan mac Lir, married the eldest daughter Aebh (or Eve) of King Bodh Dearg. Their union brought a daughter and a son, and then twin sons, at which point Aebh died in childbirth.

Lir would have died himself of grief but for his children, whose beauty and singing soothed his heart, and made their grandfather Bodh Dearg and all their peoples love them. Lir was so miserable that when Aebh's younger sister Aoife attracted him with her magic arts, he married her. But Lir loved his children and their singing more than Aoife, and she grew very jealous.

One day, she told Lir, 'I'm taking the children to see their grandfather.' But on the way she paused at Lough Derravaragh (the 'lake of the oaks' in Co. Westmeath, *see* p.105), and cursed the beautiful children with a druid rod, saying, 'As swans with feathered companions will you live through the length of your lives.'

The children wept as a white cloud rose from the lake and moved to envelop them within its mist. Lir's eldest child, his daughter Fionnuala, begged Aoife to limit their time on the lake.

Aoife declared, 'It is bad for you that you have asked me, but, since you ask, you will remain here at Lough Derravaragh for 300 years, and on the Sea of Moyle [between Antrim and Scotland] for 300 years, and then 300 more on the island of Inishglora [off the coast of Mayo].'

The children, now swans, mourned, and their pitiful sounds made Aoife's heart soften a little, so that she declared, 'You may keep your own speech and continue singing the sweet music of the Sidhe. There will be no music in the world equal to yours until your swan shapes leave you when you hear the first bells of a new religion in Ireland. But go away out of my sight now, children of Lir, with your white-feather faces and stammering Irish.'

Aoife went on to Bodh Dearg and lied, 'I'm sorry, my father, but Lir would not let your grandchildren come to visit you.'

King Bodh Dearg did not believe her and sent word to Lir, who, fearing something terrible, set out to follow them. But on the way, he heard the singing of his children over Lough Derravaragh. The swans flew to him and he slumped in sorrow as he heard what Aoife had done.

After Bodh Dearg heard the story, he went to Aoife, not telling her what he knew, and asked her, 'What shape do you fear most?'

'A witch of the air in the cold north wind.'

To which Bodh Dearg replied, 'It is that you will be until the end of time, Aoife, for your cruel deed to Lir's children,' and Aoife immediately flew away as a witch of the air, in which you can still hear her screaming when a north wind blows.

After 900 years, the swans followed the ringing of church bells on Inishglora, where they returned to their human forms as withered ancient people before dying. Graves for them were tended on Inishglora well into the 20th century.

The hardships of Irish nationalist hero Michael Davitt (1846–1906) and how he overcame them may be an inspiration to children. Born in Straide at the height of the Famine, he was thrown out of his home with his parents for being unable to pay rent, which marked him for life. They went to England and aged 11 he began working in a cotton mill, where he lost his right arm to a machine. He later joined the Irish Republican Brotherhood and was sentenced to 15 years in prison for arms running. Returning home, he decided peaceful political action was the best way to help Ireland and founded the Land League (*see* p.37). He later travelled the world, collecting and spreading humanitarian ideas and campaigning for the rights of all oppressed peoples.

Opposite the museum you can see a ruined Franssciscan abbey.

Look at this!

Achill Folklife Centre

Dooagh, Achill Island, **t** (098) 43564
Getting there 25 miles (40km) south of Castlebar
Open Mon–Sat 9.30–5.30
Adm Varies according to exhibition

Occasional exhibitions on local folklife.

Ballymagibbon Cairn

Cross village, near Cong
Getting there 25 miles (40km) south of Castlebar

Cross (An Crois), on the Plain of Moytura, marks the site of the battle between the Tuatha and the Fir Bolg (*see* p.175). Oscar Wilde roamed this area as a youngster, while holidaying nearby.

Céide Fields

Ballycastle, **t** (096) 43325, **www**.heritageireland.ie
Getting there 5 miles (8km) west of Ballycastle
Open Daily mid-Mar–May 10–5, June–Sept 10–6, Oct and Nov 10–5
Adm Adult €3.50, under-18s/student €1.25, family €8.25
Guided tours, tea room, toilets, disabled access

There is a modern pyramid-shaped interpretative centre with a viewing area over this Stone Age site, where people farmed long before the bog formed. Dating from 5,000 years ago, it's the most extensive settlement of megalithic tombs and field systems discovered anywhere in the world. Try out the archaeologists' technique for finding old fence poles by pushing a rod of wood into the bog (guides show you how). In the visitor centre, warm up with a hot drink before examining the huge trunk in the middle of the hall, the discovery of which proved that this barren area was once a forest of giant trees. Friendly, well-informed guides tell you all you could want to know about the site and more – just ask.

Croagh Patrick (the Reek)

Information Centre, Murrisk, near Westport, **t** (098) 64114, **www**.croagh-patrick.com
Getting there 5 1/2 miles (9km) west of Westport
Open Mar–Nov. **Adm** Free
Craft shop, café, guided tour (book ahead), toilets

The pointed summit of this mountain, 2,510ft (765m) high, dominates the north Mayo coast. It gained its holy status after St Patrick fasted here for 40 days in AD 441, when it was called the Reek. From the summit, he prayed to God that he might intercede for all Irish people. Blackbirds tormented him, perhaps seeking the food they were used to getting from druids during their rituals (in some folk tales, blackbirds are druids who have 'shape-shifted'). They surrounded him and turned into demons and serpents who attacked him. He threw his holy bell at them, and banished them to a hollow on the north side of the mountain. The story grew to include all the snakes of Ireland, and St Patrick's banishment is said to be why no poisonous snake or reptile can live wild in Ireland today.

A story to tell: Connacht's Pirate Queen

Ireland's pirate queen was called *Granuaile* in Irish, or Grace O'Malley in English. The English termed her a pirate, which the Irish found galling, as she was one of Ireland's last tribal chieftains, controlling the waters off the coast of Connacht from Mayo to Clare. She was well matched against England's queen, only not so rich or powerful.

For 200 years Granuaile's family the O'Malleys had been Lords of the Isles, seafarers who ruled the land around Clew Bay and the islands of Clare, Inishturk, Inishbofin and Caher. In Granuaile's time, English feudalism was replacing Ireland's system of clan chiefs, and English law displacing Ireland's ancient Brehon Laws. Irish lords had very little power. So Granuaille resorted to unusual methods to get her taxes, which the foreigners never seemed to want to pay.

From her Clare Island stronghold, Granuaile told her lads to row out to the merchants in their ships on their way to sell wines and such in Galway.

'Fáilte,' one of Granuaile's men would cry out from their boat, 'I thought I should warn you, Sir, that your ship is in dangerous waters.'

'But the sea appears quite calm here,' the captain would reply.

'Ach, sure your honour, but there's trouble down below,' the boatman would say. 'Many's the captain whose goods have been washed up ashore because he broke his craft upon our rocky secrets.'

'Hmph, that's very hard to believe,' came the retort.

'Well, suit yourself,' Granuaile's seaman would smile, 'but if I was you I'd pick meself as your captain to guide you inwards.'

A long silence began as the sailor rowed away and the captain weighed his options, then shouted, 'Err, look here, how much will you take us in for?'

'A mere pittance,' Granuaile's man grinned.

'Right then,' said the captain, 'up aboard.'

And that is how many a ship ended up wrecked on the shores of Connacht, which, oddly enough, did not prevent their goods from turning up at Galway market.

Granuaile felt that her seafaring warriors were merely demanding the taxes due from the ships trading in her domain. In 1593, aged 63, she went all the way to the Queen of England to tell her so. Amazingly, Elizabeth I let her out of her sight without taking off her head, and even agreed to allow Granuaile to police the waters off Ireland's western shore without interference from British soldiers. On her way home, she had a famous encounter at Howth Castle (*see* p.70).

The Reek was named Croagh Patrick, after Ireland's most famous saint, and became one of the foremost shrines of Irish Catholicism. But megalithic peoples held an annual festival here for the god Lugh at least 3,000 years before Christ was born (about 5,000 years ago), so it is possible that the tradition of every pilgrim carrying a rock to its summit and leaving it there started that long ago. The present Christian Pilgrimage to Croagh Patrick begins in Murrisk on the last Sunday of July, Reek Sunday.

Foxford Woollen Mills

Visitor Centre, Foxford, **t** (094) 925 6756
Getting there 15 miles (24km) north of Castlebar, via N26
Open Mon–Sat 10–6, Sun 2–6
Adm Adult €6, child/student €5, family €18
Tours, mill/craft shop, restaurant, baby-changing facilities, tourist information, toilets

The fascinating story of how Mother Agnes Morrogh Bernard began this woollen mill in an impoverished post-famine village in 1892 is told via an ingenious self-guided exhibition, part of the tour of the factory where you see woollens being made. Afterwards, have a snack in the restaurant or perhaps buy something made in the mills.

Granuaile Centre

Louisburg, **t** (098) 66341
Getting there 14 miles (22km) west of Westport
Open July and Aug Mon–Sat 10–5 (call ahead to check) or by appointment
Adm Adult €4, child €2, family (2+4) €8
Bookshop, crafts centre, video, café

On your way to Roonagh to take the boat to Clare Island (*see* p.174), find out about the 'Pirate Queen of Clew Bay' Grace O'Malley (1530–1600). Born to a clan with land from Achill Island to Inishbofin, she married a neighbouring clan member. When he was murdered by the rival Joyce family, she set up a base on Clare Island, from which her men attacked foreign ships. When the English viceroy in Ireland, Sir Richard Bingham, tried to halt the activities of local chieftains, Granuaile appealed to Queen Elizabeth I for protection (*see* opposite).

Murrisk Abbey

Murrisk, near Westport
Getting there 5 1/2 miles (9km) west of Westport

In the shadow of Croagh Patrick, this ruined abbey was built in the 1450s by the Augustinians, and destroyed in the 17th century by Cromwell's soldiers.

The Quiet Man Heritage Cottage

Cong, **t** (094) 954 6089, **www.quietman-cong.com**
Getting there 25 miles (40km) south of Castlebar
Open 17 Mar–Oct daily 10–5
Adm Adult €3.75, student €2.25, child €1.50, family €6.50

This is an exact replica of a typical Irish cottage of the 1920s, exactly like the set (filmed in Hollywood) for the 1952 movie *The Quiet Man*. Cong, chosen for much of the location shooting, remembers the film fondly, hosting an annual 'Quiet Man' festival.

Nature lovers

Clare Island

Getting there *See* p.174

Synonymous with Grace O'Malley, this 6-square-mile (1,500 hectare) island at the mouth of Clew Bay has quartzite hills that rise to the 1,510ft (460m) peak of Knockmore. The island's archaeological remains include a court-tomb at Lecarrow, ancient cooking sites, standing stones, forts and many other sites from later times. One of the most interesting places to visit is the remains of a 15th-century Cistercian friary, founded by monks from Abbeyknockmoy, Co. Galway. Substantial patches of frescoes remain in a faded condition in the chancel vault. Local legends say that after O'Malley's death in 1600, her body was buried in the decorated O'Malley wall tomb in the friary.

Overlooking the harbour, note the O'Malley castle, which in 1831 became a coastguard station. Pack a picnic if you're making a day-trip, and head for the lovely sandy beaches, where you may spot otters, seals and dolphins offshore.

Sporty kids

Activity centres

Glenans Sailing Centres

Collanmore Island, Westport, **t** (098) 26046

Residential courses in sailing.

Mayo Leisure Point

Moneen, Castlebar, **t** (094) 902 5473

An indoor swimming pool, Jacuzzi, sauna, steam-room, gym, cinema, bowling, go-karts and more.

Buckets and spades – Mayo's Beaches

Achill Island: Keel Beach, in Keel village; Keem Strand, near the western tip of Achill; Dugort Beach, in Doogort village; Golden Strand; and Dooega Beach in Dooega village.
Clare Island: many fine beaches around the island, *see* p.179
Clew Bay: Bertra Beach, near Westport; Old Head Beach and Carrowmore Beach near Louisburgh
Mullet Peninsula: Belmullet, at Elly Bay Beach and Mullaghroe Beach.
North Coast: Ross Strand, Killala to the northwest of Ballina.

Tír na n'Óg Venture Fun Park

Enterprise House, Aiden St, Kiltimagh, **t** (094) 938 1494

The supervised play areas here are for children aged 1–13 and are environmentally friendly. Fees are charged for the indoor adventure maze and toddler area (€3/30mins, €5/hr), but outside there's a free play area and good picnic spots.

Westport Leisure Park

James St, Westport, **t** (098) 29160

An indoor children's fun pool, swimming pool, gym, sauna, plunge pool, and other facilities. Under-8s must be accompanied when using the pools.

Horse-drawn caravans

Mayo Horsedrawn Caravan Holidays

Belcarra, Castlebar, **t** (094) 903 2054, **www.horsedrawn.mayonet.com**

These caravans come with full self-catering facilities and instruction in managing your horse. Stops are planned to give you 3hrs' travelling time per day.

Horse-riding

The centres listed below offer 1hr to full-day rides with experienced guides for all ages in the Mayo countryside. Headgear and other essentials are supplied.

Carrowholly Stables

Carrowholly, Westport, **t** (098) 27057, **www.carrowholly-stables.com**

Claremorris Equitation Centre

Galway Rd, Claremorris, **t** (094) 936 2292

Drummindoo Stud and Equitation Centre

Castlebar Rd, Knockranny, Westport, **t** (098) 25616

Westport Woods Riding Centre

Westport Woods Hotel, Quay Rd, Westport, **t** (098) 25811.

Rides along the seashore or in the hills.

Walking

Local tourist offices (*see* p.172) have excellent guidebooks for all Mayo's walks. Especially enjoyable are **Westport town walks** and the **Foxford Way**, 52 miles (84km) long, which links Western Way in the Ox Mountains to loughs Conn and Cullin via many sites of archaeological interest. Others are the **Bangor Trail** (29 miles/48km) from Newport through Nephin Beg to Bangor, and the **Western Way**, from Killary Harbour and the Ox Mountains across Croagh Patrick to Westport.

The **North Mayo Sculpture Trail** has 15 outdoor sculptures by living artists, created to highlight the beauty of the coastline. The trail stretches from the Moy Estuary through Erris to the southern tip of the Mullet peninsula.

Cong Wood

Just north of the border with Co. Galway is Cong, the location for the 1952 film *The Quiet Man* (*see* p.179). Long before, Cong Abbey was the home of the last High King of Connacht, Rory O'Connor. The surrounding woods, from Cong to Ashford, are a maze of roads, forest walks and high stone walls where you will even find an old tower. In Cong Park, note the romantic spot where the Monk's Fishing Cottage sits, and picnic in the park in the nearby village. Enter it via Cong Abbey so you don't have to pay

Walking tours

Clew Bay Heritage Centre, The Quay, Westport, **t** (098) 26852

Historical walking tours in summer.

Croagh Patrick Walking Tours, Westport, **t** (098) 26090

Guided hill-walking tours for adults, with selected walks for older, accompanied children.

Doon Peninsula Nature Archaeological Walk, Burriscarra, **t** (094) 936 0287

Tochar Phadraig, **t** (094) 903 0934

An ancient pilgrim cross-country path from Ballintubber Abbey to Croagh Patrick.

Watersports

Glenans Irish Sailing School

Collanmore Island, Kilmeena, Westport, **t** (098) 26046

Sailing and other watersports facilities.

COUNTY SLIGO

Perhaps the Tuatha Dé Danaan still wander in the clouds in County Sligo, or the ghost of the poet Yeats haunts visitors in this place he loved so well. Whatever the reason, Sligo hangs heavy with mystical enchantment. Here you can almost hear the ancient lovers Diarmuid and Gráinne whispering to each other as they hide from jealous Finn McCool, or Diarmuid rasping for water somewhere on the high mist-hidden plateau of Benbulben.

You will see traffic-stopping trains of cars following funerals in slow solemn procession here, pall-bearers walking before them, and giddy bridesmaids dressed to the nines giggling with their wedding flowers next to young bucks in their tuxedos, and somehow it seems that the past is no different from today in this dreamy place. Only the rush of cars, the new bungalows built outside towns and the cold, modern bridge inside Sligo town remind you of the inexorable march of time.

Sligo has beaches to swim beside, woods to walk in, waterfalls to discover, ancient stone megaliths to stumble over and the occasional hill to climb, including Knocknarea, where the grave of Queen Maeve is covered by a cairn, to which every pilgrim should add their own stone. Near enough to Donegal to make its wilds and the woodlands of Fermanagh accessible, yet close to Mayo and the Gaeltacht, County Sligo is a peaceful place in which to base yourself if you wish to listen for the slow heartbeat of a lore and an old, old spirit now much besieged by the 21st century.

Tourist information

Sligo Town: Temple St, **t** (071) 916 1201; Douglas Hyde Bridge, Yeats Building, **t** (071) 913 8772

Tours

Sacred Island Tours, Carrowkeel, Castlebaldwin, **t** (079) 966 6241

Martin Byrne offers guided tours of ancient and mythical sites, conveyed with the eye of an artist, by car or coach. Some walks are unsuitable for small children.

Getting there and around

By air Sligo has an airport, 5 miles (8km) west of town at Strandhill, **t** (071) 916 8280/916 8318. It only has domestic flights from Dublin.

Special Events – County Sligo

June–July

Ballymote Heritage Weekend, **t** (071) 918 3112

A good event for families.

Sligo County Fleadh, Ballintogher, **t** (071) 916 7560

A classic country festival of traditional music.

Sligo Vintage Festival, Riverstown, **t** (071) 916 5001

Vintage displays, crafts, music, dance, drama, poetry and traditional foods.

Seisiún, Sligo Town, **t** (071) 916 4250

A traditional festival of music, storytelling and dance that children enjoy.

South Sligo Summer School of Traditional Music and Dancing, Tubbercurry, **t** (071) 918 2151

A festival where dance-loving, musically minded children may want to get up and take part in the proceedings.

August

Gurteen Agricultural and Horse Show, Gurteen, **t** (071) 916 5082

End-of-month fun for animal-lovers.

Michael Coleman Traditional Festival, Gurteen, **t** (071) 918 2250/918 2599

A family music event.

Queen Maeve International Summer School of Irish Music and Song, Institute of Technology, Ballinode, Sligo Town, **t** (071) 916 2008

Sean Nós singing, flute, fiddle, *bodhrán*, and so on, classes, and concert and music sessions.

Tubbercurry Old Fair Day Festival, Tubbercurry, **t** (087) 681 5956

An old-fashioned fair day, held in memory of the monthly fair.

Warriors Festival, Strandhill, **t** (071) 9168633

This comprises the Culleenamore Horse and Pony Races and the Warriors' Run to Queen Maeve's legendary grave on Knocknarea Mountain.

October

Ballintogher Feis, Ballintogher, **t** (071) 916 4250

A community family festival.

November

Sean Nós Singing, Coleman Heritage Centre, Gorteen, **t** (071) 918 2599

This music-school-based event is interesting for young singers keen to learn about Ireland's unusual unaccompanied traditional singing.

Sligo International Choral Festival, Sligo Town, **t** (086) 259 2290

This includes choral events for children.

By bus Sligo bus station is on Lord Edward St. Bus Éireann has daily buses between Sligo and Dublin, Ballina, Derry and Galway. Local buses link the county's villages.

Bus information, **t** (071) 916 0066

By car N4 from Dublin via Longford

By train There are several trains daily between Sligo and Connolly station in Dublin via Longford. Sligo information, **t** (071) 916 9888.

Bike Hire

North West Tourism, **t** (071) 914 3149, produces a very good local *Hiking and Biking Guide*, available from tourist offices.

For bike hire, try:

West Coast Cycles, Quigabara, Inniscrone, **t** (096) 36593

SLIGO TOWN

The face of County Sligo's main town has been altered in recent years by modern shopping centres and cars, and, while the sleepy romanticism of the quiet town that entranced Yeats and Yeatsian scholars until the late 20th century still exists, it is no longer quite the charmer that it once was. But get out of your car and you will find people who are very friendly and happy to get to know you, and who enjoy conversation and the new perspectives strangers bring into what is essentially still a small town. Here you will sniff a bit of the 'old romantic Ireland' that is not quite dead and gone, which can be missed altogether in a big city such as Dublin. Yet enough outsiders pass through Sligo all the time to make it a little bit cosmopolitan, especially thanks to its place on the literary map.

Things to see and do

Model Arts and Niland Gallery

The Mall, **t** (071) 914 1405

Open Tues–Sat 10–5.30, Sun 11–4

Adm Free exhibitions but charges for events

Atrium café, toilets

This large modern building hosts international artists and a daring mixture of local, national and international works – from Sligo youth theatre groups to Baroque and contemporary music festivals. It also has a permanent exhibition of paintings by Jack B Yeats, who was the brother of the poet WB Yeats, and one of the world's largest collections of Irish artwork, the Niland Collection of Contemporary Irish Art.

Sligo Abbey

Abbey St, **t** (071) 914 6406, **www.heritageireland.ie**

Open 17 Mar–Oct daily 10–6, Nov and Dec Sat and Sun 10–6 (but call ahead to check times)

Adm Adult €2, under-18s €1, family €5

Guided tour on request, visitor centre, toilets (also for disabled), coach/car park nearby

Find out what the love knot is at this Dominican friary, built in the mid 13th century. It holds Gothic and Renaissance carved tombs, cloisters and the only 15th-century sculptured high altar left in any Irish monastic church.

Sligo Art Gallery

Yeats Society, Yeats Memorial Building, Douglas Hyde Bridge, **t** (071) 914 2693/7264, **www.yeats-sligo.com**

Open Mon–Fri 10–5

Adm Free

A small fine art gallery.

Sligo County Museum and Branch Library

Stephen St, **t** (071) 914 2212

Open Tues–Fri 10–12.45 and 2–4.45

Adm Free

This small museum in the branch library building displays artefacts related to the prehistory of Co. Sligo along with a special section on Yeats and his family's connections with Sligo.

Entertainment

The Factory

Sligo, **t** (071) 917 0431

A venue hosting productions by the Blue Raincoat Theatre Company.

The Hawk's Well Theatre

Temple St, **t** (071) 916 1526, **www.hawkswell.com**

Revivals and contemporary Irish theatre.

Did you know... what a geis is?

In Irish tradition, it was a binding spell or obligation put upon someone from birth to death that was much stronger than honour or faith.

SPECIAL TRIPS

Carrowmore Megalithic Cemetery

Sligo, **t** (071) 916 1534
Getting there About 2 miles (3km) south of Sligo Town; ask at tourist office for directions
Open Daily May–Oct 10–6
Adm Adult €2, child €1.50, family €5.50
Guided tours on request, exhibition (restricted access for those with disabilities), toilets, car park

This once-lofty, windy ancient site is said to be where the warriors of the Second Battle of Moytura (*see* right) are buried, and where some of the battle itself was fought. It once contained the largest collection of megalithic monuments (or tombs) in Ireland. They are also among the country's oldest prehistoric relics, predating Newgrange by some 700 years. Sadly, only 30 of the original 100 or so monuments remain; much of it was apparently quarried, presumably for the gravel that bedevils most Irish tourist sites these days.

Older children will be engaged if you provide some historical background, as well as stories about the area; younger ones may be entranced by the faerylore associated with the megaliths. There is little shelter here, so long treks can be tiring and you need to bring along water and a snack. Be sure to wear clothing and shoes suitable for changeable and wet weather, and for uneven, rocky terrain too.

Gillighan's World

Knocknashee, Lavagh, near Tubbercurry, **t** (071) 913 0286, **www**.gillighansworld.com
Getting there Near Lavagh village, 17 miles (26km) south of Sligo Town
Open May and Sept Fri–Sun 12 noon–6 and by appointment; June–Aug Tues–Sun and bank hols 11–7 (last adm 6). Phone ahead to check times and activities, inc 'Santa in Fairyland' in Dec
Adm Adult €7, child/student €6
Shop, picnic areas, baby-changing facilities, tea room

From Sligo town, drive out to the impressive hill of Knocknashee ('hill of the faeries'), at the base of which is this adventure centre for young children. Older kids will be interested to hear the stories associated with the hill, smaller ones will feel big as they come upon tiny houses and toy creatures among the trees, rocks and streams, and everyone will enjoy petting the small animals and meeting the tame pig. There are model faery villages, competitions and quizzes for children, and magical events at Christmas and Easter.

A story to tell: The Second Battle of Moytura

After refusing to let Nuadhu take back the kingship of the Tuatha Dé Danaan (*see* p.175), King Bres sought the help of his evil relatives the Fomorians, who asked for taxes from the Tuatha. They of course refused to pay the Fomorians anything at all, and war ensued.

While the Tuatha were waiting to fight Bres and the Fomorians, a young, handsome warrior with all the virtues of the most noble of beings called Lugh (known as 'the shining one') arrived to help them. Lugh had survived the attempt of his grandfather, the one-eyed Balor, leader of the Fomorians, to kill him. Balor had been told by Fomorian prophets that he would die at the hands of his own grandson, and so had ordered all his grandchildren to be drowned. But Lugh was rescued and raised by the sea god Manannan mac Lir ('son of the ocean'). Lugh was better than anyone at every skill, which he proved when he won every test the Tuatha gave him. Nuadhu made him King of the Tuatha Dé Danaan, so that he could lead the Tuatha in battle against the Fomorians. This was the Second Battle of Moytura.

The Fomorians' most deadly weapon was the eye of Balor, whose lid it took several men to lift. Any man it looked upon disintegrated into nothing.

Lugh cast a stone straight into Balor's eye and killed him. So the prophecy was fulfilled, and Balor fell at the hands of his own grandson. This is how the Tuatha Dé Danaan won the battle and the Fomorians were expelled from Ireland. For years afterwards, Ireland prospered, with Lugh or the Daghda taking turns to be king.

Sligo Folk Park

Millview House, Riverstown, **t** (071) 916 5001, **www**.sligofolkpark.com
Getting there 10 miles (16km) south of Sligo
Open May–Oct Mon–Sat 10–4.30, Sun 12.30–5 (last adm); Nov–Apr by appointment or for special events
Adm Adult €5, child €3, family (2+3) €15; ask about special group rates
Disabled access, free parking, craft shop, exhibition, café

This folk park was created by a consortium of locals to salvage what was left of their vanished way of life and to educate others about it. They are slowly building a museum to hold the discarded antiques that have been donated. Thus far, they have a working forge, restored 19th-century house, thatched cottage that was once moved to the USA for an exhibition, farm implements and a museum with displays on rural history. Its star exhibit is a replicated village street with the kinds of shops that existed in every Irish town. The park holds events such as a Vintage Day in June, Santa Town in December (call **t** (071) 916 7013), plays and live music. The café offers lunch and dinner, and home-baking in the afternoon, even when the park is closed.

AROUND AND ABOUT

Bricks and mortar

Lissadell House

Drumcliffe, **t** (071) 916 3150, **www.lissadellhouse.com**
Getting there 11 miles (18km) north of Sligo
Open Daily Easter and May–Sept 11–6; gardens and groups by appointment. **Adm** Adult €6, child €3

Don't visit Sligo without seeing this house, where WB Yeats and other early-20th-century luminaries exchanged ideas with suffragette Eva Gore-Booth and her sister Constance de Markievicz (*see* p.42).

A story to tell: Diarmuid and Gráinne

King Finn McCool was due to marry a young woman half his age – Gráinne (pronounced 'grawn-yuh'). When she was born, druids had predicted her beauty would cause great trouble in the land, so Finn decreed he would marry her to keep his kingdom safe. But when Gráinne saw her future husband just before their wedding, her heart sank, as he was old, very old. She drifted off to her chambers, wondering how she might avoid what seemed a fate worse than death.

Finn's famous warriors, the Fianna, had come to the castle to join in the wedding festivities and were playing games in the courtyard beneath Gráinne's window. Among them was Diarmuid, an honourable character, without fault or blemish. Apart from being very handsome, he had a 'love spot' on his forehead, which made any woman who saw it fall instantly in love with him. Knowing the trouble it caused, Diarmuid always wore a cap to hide it. But as Gráinne gazed wistfully at the young men her own age, leaping about with the blush of health upon them, Diarmuid's cap fell off, and the inevitable happened.

That evening in the king's banqueting hall, Gráinne waited until the old men were dozing over their mead and made her way to Diarmuid. Before he knew it, she was asking him to take her away from Finn and marry her himself. He cried, 'Oh no, that is not possible. I am loyal to King Finn. A man of the Fianna never breaks faith with his own kin.'

'Then I put *geis* upon you,' wept Gráinne, 'you must take me away from here this very night. Steal out of the castle now and I will follow you.'

Now Diarmuid was ruined. Gráinne had put *geis* upon him – a binding demand that a faithful member of the Fianna could not refuse (*see* p.182). So Diarmuid and Gráinne ran away from King Finn, sleeping in a different place every night for many moons to avoid his warriors, leaving behind their 'beds' (flat smooth stones on top of earthworks) all over Ireland, before finally settling beside Mt Benbulben in County Sligo.

At last King Finn found out where they were and sent word he wanted to see them. Suspicious, Gráinne sent a servant to spread the rumour she had lost her looks, from years of hard living. But Finn sent a spy to find out the truth, and he reported back that she was even more beautiful, and that the pair were as happy as two swans on a lake. This enraged the king, but he kept it secret.

Gráinne encouraged Diarmuid to make peace with Finn, and eventually, after many entreaties, Diarmuid agreed to hunt with him on Benbulben, as in old times. However, Finn conjured up a magical boar, which chased Diarmuid and gored him. The king found his former warrior gasping for breath upon the ground, and his heart softened as Diarmuid begged for water from his hands, for Finn had the gift of healing in them. He rushed to a well to carry water back to Diarmuid. Three times he tried, but each time anger rose in his heart about his former warrior's deceit and the water fell through his fingers. And then Diarmuid died.

At first Gráinne was inconsolable – but, after a while, Finn won her affection. And do you know, the terrible truth of it all is that in the end, she married King Finn...

The latter was an ardent Irish nationalist who married a Polish count and took part in the 1916 Easter Rising. Spared execution because she was a woman, in 1918 she became the first woman ever elected to the British House of Commons, although she did not take her seat.

The Gore-Booths lived near Drumcliffe from the time of Elizabeth I until 2004. Sir Robert Gore-Booth built this house in the 1830s in a Greek Revival style, which its new owners are keeping. The idealistic Gore-Booths gave away much of their fortune to the poor in the Great Famine. Walk in the well-loved parkland around the house and you may experience a bit of old Ireland's quiet nobility.

Look at this!

Ceoláras Coleman

Gurteen, **t** (071) 918 2599
Getting there 25 miles (40km) south of Sligo
Open Mon–Sat 10–5
Adm Adult €4, child/student €3, family €10; shows €10
Audio-visual show, shop, lessons

This venue was set up in honour of traditional Sligo fiddler Michael Coleman to educate people about Irish music.

Yeats' Grave

Drumcliffe Church, Drumcliffe, **t** (071) 914 4956
Getting there 6 miles (10km) north of Sligo
Open Mon–Fri 8.30–6, Sun 1–6. **Adm** Free

Beneath Benbulben, outside the little white Protestant church at Drumcliffe, a plain gravestone is inscribed: *Cast a cold eye on life, on death; Horseman, pass by*

This is the simple message that WB Yeats left to posterity (although the Sligo tourist industry has certainly not passed it by). Yeats died in France in 1939, and his body was brought here in accordance with his wishes by Sean Macbride, son of Maude Gonne, Yeats' English muse and love.

Nature lovers

Benbulben

Getting there 10–15 miles (16–24km) north of Sligo

This flat-topped mountain marks the view just north of Sligo town, rising up like some great upturned ship that was left behind by giants long ago. It is where Diarmuid is said to have died after a false reconciliation with Finn McCool (*see* left).

Buckets and spades – Sligo Beaches

Inniscrone: Almost in Mayo on Killala Bay, about 30 miles (48km) west of Sligo, this big beach has a well-developed seaside look, with good facilities and play areas for small children, and a fairground in summer. **Easky**, further north, is quieter and a bit of a surfing centre.

Mullaghmore: Near the Leitrim borde, this broad beach is safe for smaller children.

Strandhill: Sligo's 'town' beach, 5 miles (8km) to the west, has little shops and beach cafés, and is also good for surfing. For information and equipment, try **Malibu Surf Shop, t** (071) 916 8302.

Sporty kids

Boat trips

Boat tours are available on Lough Gill, or trips can be made to Inishmurray Island (Apr–Oct; contact Rodney Lomax, Mullaghmore, **t** (071) 916 6124, or Tommy McAllion, Rosses Point, **t** (071) 914 2391).

Lough Arrow Boats, t (071) 916 5491

Boat rental on one of Sligo's inland loughs.

Wild Rose Waterbus (The Rose of Innisfree), Lough Gill, Kilmore, Fivemilebourne (R286), **t** (071) 916 4266, **www.roseofinnisfree.com**

Tours of Lough Gill with readings of Yeats' poetry.

Horse-riding

Ard Chuain Equestrian Centre

Corbally (near Ballina), **t** (096) 45084

Children's riding holidays for all abilities.

Markree Castle Riding Stables

Collooney, **t** (071) 913 0727

Rides on the Markree estate and forest trails.

Sligo Riding Centre

Carrowmore, **t** (071) 916 1353

One of Ireland's major equestrian complexes.

Walking

Some of the best walks in Co. Sligo are around Lough Gill. On the north side of the lake there are forest paths at **Carns**, **Deerpark** and **Hazelwood**; on the south side at **Slish Wood**, on the R287, there is a kids' paddling pool in a small river by the car park.

LEITRIM AND ROSCOMMON

The unassuming strip of Ireland known as Leitrim, the place where in legend the Tuatha Dé Danaan are said to have first settled when they came to Ireland, and its next-door inland county of Roscommon, once coal- and iron-mining centres, are today known for fishing and farming. Visitors come to them to cruise on their rivers and lakes, or to cycle along picturesque roads observing these rolling hills, pastures and boglands. Leitrim lies between County Sligo and the province of Ulster, with just 2 1/2 miles (4km) of Atlantic coastline. Roscommon has fewer hills and level plains, and blends into Leinster's midlands.

Quiet farmers fill this area, with German settlers doing a good job of regenerating the land, so the locals claim. Notably, near Rossinver, County Leitrim, lies what may be Ireland's only official organic farm. Health is not a new concern in this vicinity. People with aches and pains have long gone to Lough Allen for sweathouse therapy. This once consisted of sitting on a pile of straw inside a stone hut, in which a fire burned steadily for hours, and then taking a dip in a stream.

Perhaps past smallpox sufferers – such as Jonathan Swift and his friend, Meath-born musician Turlough O'Carolan, who set up home for his wife and children in Mohill, Co. Leitrim, while he travelled around the country as a blind harpist – also found better health here. In fact we have smallpox to thank for O'Carolan's music. He caught the disease while a teenager, but survived, after which his Roscommon benefactor, a Mrs MacDermott, felt sorry for him and financed his musical education. She then set him on a horse with a guide to ply his trade as a blind harpist roaming 18th-century Ireland. The first place O'Carolan is known to have performed was the house of a certain Seóirse Ua Raghnall (George Reynolds) on the banks of Lough Scur in Leitrim. Apparently he wasn't such a great harp player and, after hearing him, Reynolds suggested perhaps he might be more successful if he wrote music well, as opposed to playing it badly. That night O'Carolan composed his first tune, naming it after a local story of warring faeries: *Sí Beag Sí Mór* – still one of his most famous compositions and a favourite of Irish traditional musicians.

Special Events – Leitrim and Roscommon

March

Cavan and Leitrim Easter Bunny Trains, Dromod, Co. Leitrim, **t** (071) 963 8599

Special Easter trains for children.

May–June

An Tostal, Drumshanbo, Co. Leitrim, **t** (071) 964 1069, **www**.antostalfestival.ie

A traditional festival of Irish music, song and dance, complete with children's entertainment, street parades, dog show, car treasure hunt, fishing competition and a cast of national and international artists.

John McKenna Traditional Music Festival, Drumkeeran, Co. Leitrim, **t** (071) 964 8049

A 3-day festival of concerts, workshops and flute and tin whistle competitions held in memory of locally born flute-player John Mckenna (1880–1947).

Josie McDermott Memorial Festival, Ballyfarnon, Boyle, Co. Roscommon, **t** (071) 964 7024

Traditional music.

Lough Allen Festival, Ballinaglera and Dowra, Co. Leitrim, **t** (071) 964 3117

Watersports and windsurfing tasters, cruises and competitions, and family entertainment.

July–August

Douglas Hyde Summer School of Traditional Irish Music and Dance, Ballaghaderreen, Co. Roscommon, **t** (086) 827 2300, **www**. ballaghaderreen.com

Joe Mooney School of Traditional Music, Song and Dance, Drumshanbo, Co. Leitrim, **t** (071) 964 1213

A music festival with daily workshops and *ceilis*.

Boyle Arts Festival, Greatmeadow, Boyle, Co. Roscommon, **t** (071) 966 3085, **www.boylearts.com**

O'Carolan Harp and Traditional Irish Music Festival, Keadue, Boyle, Co. Roscommon, **t** (071) 964 7204, **www.ocarolanharpfestival.ie**

A harp competition and Irish music summer school.

September

Green Festival, Manorhamilton, Co. Leitrim and beyond, **t** (071) 985 4338, **www.thegreenfestival.com**

Conservation, organic food, ecology, nature walks.

Sliabh an Iarainn, Co. Leitrim, **t** (071) 964 1569

A hill-walking festival.

October

Feile Frank McGann, Strokestown, **t** (086) 815 1119, **www.feilefrankmcgann.com**

Traditional music and dance commemorating the *bodhrán* player Frank McGann.

Halloween Magic, King House, Boyle, Co. Roscommon, **t** (071) 966 3242

A story to tell:
Cruachan and the Brown Bull of Cooley

The legendary Cruachan was once a royal palace, the inauguration site and burial place of the kings of Connacht. At one time, Cruachan was also the home of Maeve, or Mebh – 'she who intoxicates' – the famed warrior queen (some say earth goddess) whose burial mound is on top of Knocknarea near Strandhill in Co. Sligo. Fierce and proud, Maeve was responsible for launching the famed cattle raid of Cooley, as recounted in one of the greatest works of early Irish literature, the *Táin Bó Cúailnge* or 'Brown Bull of Cooley'. Born queen of the southern part of Ireland, she married Ailill, who was king of the northern part. Their alliance made them the most powerful people in the country.

But that was not enough for Maeve. One morning she had an argument with her husband over which of them held the greatest power in Ireland. Agreeing that their wealth should be the deciding factor, they separated their fortunes and counted everything against the other. They found that they were equal in every respect but one. Ailill had one thing more than she had – the finest bull of their combined stocks. However, in Ireland there was one bull finer even than Ailill's, and that was owned by a farmer in Louth – the 'Brown Bull of Cooley'. Secretly, Maeve asked the farmer to let her borrow it. Intending merely to make her husband think she had more than he, she planned to return the bull to the farmer immediately afterwards. But he grew suspicious of her motives, and didn't let her have it. For no money would he part with it, even temporarily. So Maeve turned her army upon the farmer to steal the bull from him. This started a terrible war, which ended in her husband Ailill's white bull and the brown bull of Cooley fighting to the death, and tearing each other to bits.

Tourist information

Athleague, Co. Roscommon, **t** (090) 666 3602
Boyle, Co. Roscommon, **t** (071) 966 2145
Carrick-on-Shannon, Co. Leitrim (Apr–Sept): The Market Yard Centre, **t** (071) 962 0170, **www**.leitrimtourism.com
Roscommon Town, **t** (090) 662 6342, **www**.roscommon.ie, **www**.visitroscommon.com

Getting there and around

By bus Bus Éireann's Sligo–Dublin and other routes stop in Carrick-on-Shannon, Roscommon, Boyle, Strokestown and other towns. There's also a good local network. For Bus Éireann information phone Sligo, **t** (071) 916 0066, or Athlone, **t** (090) 647 3322.

By train Carrick-on-Shannon and Boyle are on the Sligo line from Dublin Connolly; the Dublin Heuston–Ballina line passes through Roscommon town and Castlerea. Boyle, **t** (071) 962 0036; Roscommon town, **t** (090) 662 6201.

Bike Hire

For cycle routes in Roscommon, contact Athleague tourist office or check the Suck Valley Tourism website, **www**.suckvalley.firebird.net

Brendan Sheerin, Main St, Boyle, Co. Roscommon, **t** (071) 966 2010
Buckley's Cycles, Astor Buildings, Roscommon town, **t** (090) 662 7318
Riverside Cycles, Bridge St, Boyle, Co. Roscommon, **t** (071) 966 3777

SPECIAL TRIPS

Cruachan Ai Visitor Centre

Tulsk, Co. Roscommon, **t** (071) 963 9268, **www**.cruachanai.com
Getting there 22 miles (35km) west of Longford
Open Jan–Mar, Nov and Dec Mon–Sat 9–5 (closed bank hols); Apr–Oct daily 9–6
Adm Adult €5, under-18s €2.75, family (2+4) €11
Café, exhibition, toilets

In this legendary home and inauguration place of the kings of Connacht, there is said to be an opening that leads straight into the Otherworld. Deep in the crevice of Crúachain lies the Owenygat (or Cat Cave) of the faeries, which is protected by a giant King of the Cats, whose minions travel through it between this world and that of the faeries.

Myths aside, school-age children with any curiosity about archaeology will think this little exhibition centre a real find. Ask at the desk for information on the sites in this area. It holds a good exhibition about how a Galway University project has determined – through ground-probing radar and other modern techniques – that the area around Tulsk, Rathcroghan and Carnfree holds some 60 Iron and Bronze Age earthworks.

The visitor centre also has exhibits about later buildings, such as Tulsk Castle and a 15th-century Dominican abbey on the River Ogulla. At Ogulla there is a well that is said to be where St Patrick converted to Christianity the daughters of the High King of Ireland, who immediately died and went to heaven. It is still a place of pilgrimage.

Children won't want to spend long indoors here, though, while their parents read all the displays, as they will be eager to explore the surrounding sites. You have to tour these independently, on foot, by car, or with a guide. Major sites include:

Rathcroghan Mound, a large circular mound thought to have been used in pre-Christian ceremonies, possibly also containing a passage tomb.

Rathmore (opposite Rathcroghan School), an impressive raised ring fort.

Rathnadarve (*Ráth na dTarbh*), the site in the Táin where the brown bull of Cooley and the white horned bull of Connacht did battle (*see* p.187).

Relignaree (*Relig na Rí*), the burial ground of the kings, a large enclosure in Glenballythomas.

Dathí's Stone, where the last pagan king of Ireland is reputedly buried.

Educational visits for groups of children can be arranged in advance.

Who was... Douglas Hyde?

Douglas Hyde (*see* p.190), a Protestant Anglo-Irishman, planted the seed for the revival of the Irish language with a lecture he gave in 1892 on de-Anglicizing Ireland. He said, 'In Anglicizing ourselves wholesale, we have thrown away with a light heart the best claim which we have upon the world's recognition of us as a separate nationality.'

In 1893, with the poet Yeats, he co-founded an organization in Dublin called Conradh na Gaeilge, the 'Gaelic League', to promote a revival of the Irish language. Though not a political group, it was very influential in creating an Irish national consciousness. Hyde later became disillusioned when other members such as Pádraic Pearse took up a more political stance. An opponent of the 1916 Easter Rising, Hyde believed in building identity through education about Irish history, arts and traditions.

Still, he took political office himself, becoming a member of the Irish Parliament. This enigmatic figure was so popular that De Valera asked him to become the first President of Ireland in 1938, an office he kept until 1945, aged 85. During his presidency he lived in Dublin's Phoenix Park, but he returned to his native Frenchpark in Roscommon afterwards, ending his days there in 1949.

Derryglad Folk Museum

Curraghboy, Co. Roscommon, t (090) 648 8192
Getting there 7 miles (11km) north of Athlone on the Roscommon road
Open May–Sept Mon–Sat 10–6, Sun 2–6
Adm Adult €3.50, child €2.50, family €11
Full disabled access

Talk to the friendly proprietor of this award-winning rural artefacts museum – he grew up and worked on a traditional Irish farm, and has a passion for conveying to people what he feels was a superior way of life to that lived in modern Ireland. He brings the implements that Irish farmers once used to life, and is accustomed to teaching school groups all about how people used to make butter, iron and wash clothes, cook food and harvest crops. He also plays old records on a wind-up gramophone to bring voices of the past to life for children weaned on computers. His knowledge and enthusiasm make this a gem.

King House

Main St, Boyle, Co. Roscommon, t (071) 966 3242
Getting there 24 miles (38km) south of Sligo
Open Daily Apr–Sept 10–6, last adm 5; other times by request
Adm Adult €4, child €2.50, family (2+2) €10
Guided tours by request, restaurant, shop, full disabled access, adjacent adventure playground and park, special events all year

The life-size models and dynamic effects used in this 18th-century mansion combine to help you explore the world of landlords, monks, soldiers and craftsmen in the Ireland of 1600–1800. The story of the house, its inhabitants and locality is told in an informative, entertaining manner, focusing on dramatic episodes, such as the King family's lives, Gaelic Ireland, the construction and restoration of the house and its military history. The King family were the Earls of Kingston in England and arrived in 1603 to control nearby Rockingham Estate, now Lough Key Forest Park. Sir Henry King built the present Georgian mansion about 1730, and its grand scale was created to impress outsiders with the wealth of its owners. Visitors are led through stunning tableaux and interactive exhibits that let you, for instance, build part of a brick vault like craftsmen of the time. Children enjoy banging the regimental drum of the Connaught Rangers, based here when it became a barracks in 1788.

Strokestown Park House

Strokestown, Co. Roscommon, **t** (071) 963 3013, **www**.strokestownpark.ie
Getting there 14 miles (23km) west of Longford
Open Daily mid-Mar–Oct 10.30–5.30; all year for pre-booked groups
Adm Gardens and Museum €12; 2 of the 3 sites €8.50; 1 site €5
Shop, guided tours, tea room, disabled access

Strokestown Park House was the family home of the Pakenham Mahon family from the 1600s to 1979. The 18th-century mansion has been restored with virtually all of its original furnishings intact. Its cavernous kitchen will impress children who only know modern kitchens. They will also enjoy seeing the clothing and toys used by 18th-century children in the nursery. Built in the Palladian style, this mansion also houses the Irish National Famine Museum. Outside the house is an impressive 6-acre walled garden, faithfully restored to its 1740s layout. You can buy some of its organic produce in the shop by the entrance.

The village of Strokestown ('Ford of the Blows') is a curiosity itself. Peculiarly grand for a country village, it probably has the widest street in the whole of Ireland, the ends of which are marked by an octagonal church and Strokestown House. The street was created by a local landowner called Lord Hartland, who was inspired by and copied the Ringstrasse in Vienna, Austria.

AROUND AND ABOUT

Bricks and mortar

Boyle Abbey

Boyle, Co. Roscommon, **t** (071) 966 2604
Getting there 24 miles (38km) south of Sligo
Open Apr–Oct daily 10–6; guided tours hourly 10–5
Adm Adult €1.20, child €0.50, family €4
Visitor centre in restored gatehouse, toilets

Founded in 1161 by the MacDermott family, Boyle Abbey is a fairly well-preserved ruin, considering its history: it was built as a companion house to the first Irish Cistercian monastery at Mellifont and consecrated in 1220, after which it was attacked many times by the MacDermott and O'Conor clans.

A story to tell... O'Carolan's last tune

The musician O'Carolan returned one day to the home of his first patron, Mrs MacDermott of Ballyfarnon. She was the lady who had first taught him the harp, and the one who had suggested he tour professionally, giving him a horse to travel with. After telling her that he had come to her house to meet his maker, he asked her for whiskey and composed his heartbreaking *Farewell to Music* before retiring to bed. A week later, he died.

O'Carolan is buried in Kilronan Church, a few miles from his own home in Mohill over the border in Leitrim, in the MacDermott family vault.

Clonalis House

Castlerea, Co. Roscommon, **t** (094) 962 0014
Getting there 6miles (9km) west of Castlerea
Open June–Aug Mon–Sat 11–4
Adm Adult €7, child €5, enquire about family rates

The descendants of the last high kings of Ireland lived here, in the ancestral home of the O'Connors, kings of Connacht. The harp of O'Carolan, who often played here, is also on display, along with the O'Connor inauguration stone. The house itself was built in 1880 but stands on ground which has been in the O'Connor family for 1,500 years. Owen O'Connor was dispossessed for short periods in the 17th century, but their remarkable tenure survived even wars and penal laws. A fascinating archive of over 100,000 documents is maintained at Clonalis. Other exhibits include uniforms belonging to the O'Connor family, and Louis XV-style furniture.

Look at this!

Cavan and Leitrim Railway

Dromod, Co. Leitrim, **t** (071) 963 8599, **www**.irish-railway.com
Getting there 11 miles (17km) south of Carrick-on-Shannon
Open Mon–Sat 11–5.30, Sun 1–5.30
Adm Adult €7, student/child €5, family(2+4) €16

A small exhibition with pictures of the old railway in a period ticket office and waiting room and a transport museum of military and other vehicles, where you can catch an old-fashioned train that ran on a narrow-gauge line to the Leitrim towns of Drumshanbo, Mohill and Ballinamore.

The Claypipe Visitor Centre

Knockcroghery, Co. Roscommon, **t** (090) 666 1923
Getting there On N61 in the village
Open Mon–Fri 10–6 summer, 10–5 winter. **Adm** Free

This centre has reinvigorated Knockcroghery's traditional method of making clay pipes. You can learn how, for 250 years, villagers produced them.

Douglas Hyde Interpretative Centre

Frenchpark, Co. Roscommon, **t** (090) 967 0016
Getting there 9 miles (14km) south of Boyle
Open Daily May–Sept; call for times
Adm Free; donations welcome

Dr Douglas Hyde was the first President of the Republic of Ireland and a co-founder of the Gaelic League (*see* p.188). This centre, dedicated to him, is located in the church where his father was rector, and contains an informative exhibition on his life and times.

Elphin Windmill

Ballyroddy, Elphin, Co. Roscommon,
t (071) 963 5695
Getting there 6 miles (9km) north of Tulsk
Open Daily 10–6
Adm Adult €4, child €2, family €10
Guided tours all year by arrangement

This early 18th-century windmill is in full working condition and is the only one of its kind in the west of Ireland. Restored as a local community project, the tower was built to grind oats and wheat.

Hell's Kitchen Bar and Railway Museum

Main St, Castlerea, Co. Roscommon,
t (094) 962 0181, **www.hellskitchenmuseum.com**
Getting there 40 miles (64km) west of Longford
Open Pub hours, or by request
Adm Adult €5, child €3, family €10

This Aladdin's cave of a place in a small country town has a very friendly proprietor, Sean Browne, who thoroughly enjoys showing people his collection of memorabilia in the rooms behind his pub. Old-fashioned knick knacks fill the pub and attached room that holds an impressive diesel locomotive. Children find it fascinating, especially given the unstoppable enthusiasm of its owner.

Nature lovers

Lough Key Forest Park

Boyle, Co Roscommon, **t** (071) 966 2363,
www.loughkeyboats.com
Getting there 24 miles (38km) south of Sligo
Open Dawn–dusk daily. **Adm** €5 per car

With woods, a lake and several islands, this is one of Ireland's most attractive forest parks. It has lots of facilities and great walks and, on the lake, which connects with the Shannon, boats for hire.

The Organic Centre

Near Rossinver, Co. Leitrim, **t** (071) 985 4338,
www.theorganiccentre.ie
Getting there 24 miles (38km) northeast of Sligo
Open May–Sept Sat–Thurs 11–4 (but call ahead)
Adm Adult €5, child free
Café

This farm offers educational visits and courses on organic gardening, here and nationally.

Sporty kids

Boat trips

The most popular waterways are the Shannon, from Carrick-on-Shannon, Lough Garadice, from Ballinamore, and Lough Key (*see* above) from Boyle.

Carrick Craft, The Marina, Carrick-on-Shannon, Co. Leitrim, **t** (071) 962 0236

Horse-riding

Moorlands Equestrian Centre, Drumshanbo, Co. Leitrim, **t** (071) 964 1500

Unaccompanied children are catered for here.

Una Bhan Rural Tourism Cooperative, King House, Boyle, Co. Roscommon, **t** (071) 966 3033

A company that organizes fishing and bike tours in addition to riding.

Walking

Suck Valley Visitor Centre, Athleague, **t** (090) 666 3602, **www.suckvalley.com**

On the banks of the River Suck, this centre has full information on local attractions and walks: the **Suck Valley Way** is a 60-mile (100km) path through woods, bogs and wetlands, and there's also a 135-mile (217km) **Green Heartlands Cycle Route**, in a paradise of unspoiled countryside.

WHERE TO EAT

County Galway

The Arans

An Dun
Inishmaan, **t** (099) 73047 (*inexpensive–moderate*)
Simple meals, B&B accommodation and a small spa where aromatherapy massage is available.

Aran Fisherman's Restaurant
Kilronan, Inishmore, **t** (099) 61363 (*inexpensive*)
A children's menu is available during the day here, with dishes made from organic vegetables.

Fisherman's Cottage
Inisheer island, near the pier, **t** (099) 75073 (*inexpensive*)
A reasonably priced seafood restaurant.

Mainistir House Hostel
Kilronan, Inishmore, **t** (099) 61322 (*inexpensive*)
Good vegetarian buffets are offered in this somewhat ragged hostel, but be sure to book and turn up for 8pm, for food disappears fast.

Man of Aran Cottage
Kilmurvey, Inishmore, **t** (099) 61301 (*inexpensive–moderate*)
A small restaurant situated in the double thatched-roof cottage that featured in the classic film of the same name, serving produce and speciality drinks from its organic garden during the tourist season. Book in advance for lunch, afternoon tea or dinner.

The Mermaid's Garden
Castle Village, Inisheer, **t** (099) 75062 (*inexpensive*)
Lunches or dinners of home-grown produce, made by an excellent, imaginative cook.

Teach Osta
Inishmaan, **t** (099) 73003 (*inexpensive*)
This is the only pub on Inishmaan and offers good bar food and conviviality.

Tig Conghaile
Moore Village, Inishmaan, **t** (099) 73085 (*inexpensive–moderate*)
An all-day place using organic and local ingredients, offering seafood and home-baking.

Ballinasloe

Haydens
Dunlo St, **t** (090) 964 2347 (*moderate*)
Good pub snacks and an excellent dining room.

Clarinbridge

Moran's on the Weir
Kilcolgan, near Clarinbridge, **t** (091) 796 113 (*inexpensive*)
This seafood bar, open for lunch and dinner, is tucked away in an old cottage overlooking its own oyster beds in Galway Bay.

Old Schoolhouse
Clarinbridge, **t** (091) 796 898 (*inexpensive–moderate*)
An establishment run by genial hosts, with a special €10 children's menu (available 12.30–2 Sun and 6.30–10 Tues–Sun).

Clifden

Derryclare Restaurant
Main Square, **t** (095) 21440 (*moderate*)
A reliable place to come to for pasta dishes, steak and seafood.

Quay House
Beach Rd, **t** (095) 21369 (*expensive*)
A very high standard of cooking and a friendly, relaxed atmosphere in Clifden's oldest building.

Galway City

Antonio's
Salthill Rd, **t** (091) 581 100 (*inexpensive*)
A place with New-York-style pizzas, a children's menu and highchairs. It's closed on Sundays.

Busker Browne's
Cross St, **t** (091) 563 377 (*inexpensive*)
An all-day, bright and breezy seafood bar.

Delight
29 Upper Abbeygate St, **t** (091) 567 823 (*inexpensive*)
A café serving light lunches, snacks and takeaways.

Eddie Rocket's
Eglinton St, **t** (091) 566 026 (*inexpensive*)
A 1950s-style American diner with good service; very child friendly.

The Galleon
Salthill, **t** (091) 522 963 (*inexpensive–moderate*)

Plain yet substantial food served up by efficient and family-friendly staff. Highchairs, children's menus, baby-changing facilities and colouring pads are all provided.

Goya's Fine Confectionery and Pastry Shop
2/3 Kirwans Lane, **t** (091) 567 010 (*inexpensive–moderate*)
Delicious cakes and coffee, and excellent light meals for children.

McDonagh's Seafood House
22 Quay St, **t** (091) 565 001 (*inexpensive*)
Excellent eat-in or takeaway fish and chip meals. McDonagh's has a reputation as one of Ireland's best fresh fish restaurants.

Milano's
Middle St, **t** (091) 568 488 (*inexpensive*)
Helpful staff, highchairs and baby-changing facilities make for a winning combination at this contemporary child-friendly pizza restaurant.

Nimmo's
Spanish Arch, Galway, **t** (091) 561 114 zzz (*inexpensive–moderate*)
A popular restaurant encouraging bonhomie in a Galwegian way.

Inishbofin Island

Day's Hotel Bar
Inishbofin, **t** (095) 45809 (*inexpensive*)
Good seafood and soups.

Kylemore

Kylemore Abbey Restaurant and Teahouse
t (095) 41146 (*inexpensive*)
Lunch and snacks with hot and cold dishes and home-baking. Children are welcome.

Letterfrack

Pangur Ban
t (095) 41243 (*moderate–expensive*)
A thatched-roof stone cottage serving exceptional food (though not in children's portions).

Moycullen

The White Gables
t (091) 555 744 (*expensive*)
A restored cottage offering seafood for Sunday lunch and for dinner, except Mondays in winter.

Recess

Ballynahinch Castle
Ballinafad, **t** (095) 31006 (*luxury*)
A very popular dinner venue.

Roundstone

Beola Restaurant
t (095) 35871 (*moderate*)
Seafood is a speciality here.

Spiddal

Boluisce Seafood Restaurant
t (091) 553 286 (*inexpensive*)
A good place to come to try fish chowder with home-made bread.

Tuam

Cre-na-Cille Public House
High St, **t** (093) 28232 (*inexpensive–moderate*)
An intimate, relaxing, family-run restaurant that specializes in seafood, game and local produce.

County Mayo

Achill Island

The Beehive Craft and Coffee Shop
Keel, **t** (098) 43134 (*inexpensive*)
Snacks and light lunches served daily.

The Chalet
Keel, **t** (098) 43157 (*inexpensive*)
Fish and chips.

Ballycastle

Mary's Bakery
Main St, **t** (096) 43361 (*inexpensive*)
Home-cooking in a comfortable, casual setting.

Castlebar

Café Rua
New Antrim St, **t** (094) 26159 (*moderate*)
Light lunches made using fresh locally grown food.

Charlestown

Riverside Restaurant
Church St, **t** (094) 54200 (*inexpensive–moderate*)

Children's menus and even baby dinners are available in this quaint, family-friendly restaurant specializing in seafood, steak and Irish cuisine.

Cong

Ashford Castle

t (094) 954 6003 (*luxury*)

Gourmet Irish food in a sumptuous setting. Families might prefer afternoon tea in the thatched cottage nearby. Of most interest to youngsters will probably be the evenings in the Dungeon Bar, where a storyteller sometimes tells stories and myths from Irish folklore.

The Hungry Monk Café

t (094) 954 6866 (*inexpensive*)

Light lunches, desserts and Internet access.

The Quiet Man Café

t (094) 954 6034 (*inexpensive*)

Excellent cakes and scones, made daily.

Foxford

The Sun House

Swinford Rd, **t** (094) 56506 (*inexpensive*)

A casual café where you can get good coffee and light snacks.

Newport

Newport House

t (098) 41222 (*expensive*)

It is a treat just to see inside this house, with its elegant furniture, but the food is good too. This is a good place for a treat with teens, but younger kids may be a bit fidgety around the fine china.

Westport

The Helm

The Quay, **t** (098) 26194 (*moderate–expensive*)

Breakfasts, lunches and dinners here are recommended by locals.

The Olde Railway Hotel Bistro and Bar

North Mall, **t** (098) 25166 (*inexpensive–moderate*)

A range of excellent dinners and desserts is available in the comfortable 18th-century surroundings of Thackeray's Brasserie.

Quay Cottage

The Harbour, **t** (098) 26412 (*moderate*)

A folksy seafood restaurant open for dinner, with good bread and a vegetarian menu.

County Sligo

Castlebaldwin

Cromleach Lodge

Lough Arrow, **t** (071) 916 5155 (*expensive*)

Traditional, hearty Irish cooking in the hills above Lough Arrow, close to Boyle in Roscommon.

Castlegarron

Ben View Restaurant and Mullarkey's Bar

t (071) 916 3149 (*inexpensive–moderate*)

Simple, straightforward meals, good for families.

Collooney

Glebe House Restaurant

Coolaney Rd, **t** (071) 916 7787 (*moderate–expensive*)

This award-winning country house restaurant offers homely French-based cooking with lots of herbs and vegetables from the garden. Children are welcome, and there's a children's menu.

Drumcliffe

Yeats Tavern

t (071) 916 3117 (*inexpensive–moderate*)

Casual dining daily, with good home-cooking and salads, and good facilities for children.

Mullaghmore

Eithna's Seafood Restaurant

The Harbour, **t** (071) 66407 (*moderate–expensive*)

Organic coastal ingredients used with fresh fish and shellfish, and vegetarian dishes.

Sligo Town

Bistro Bianconi

44 O'Connell St, **t** (071) 914 1744 (*moderate*)

An informal pizza joint with a pleasant modern interior, offering pasta and pizza, eat in or take away.

Fiddler's Creek

Rockwood Parade, **t** (071) 914 1866 (*inexpensive–moderate*)

A family-friendly place recommended by locals.

Hargadon's

O'Connell St, **t** (071) 917 0933 (*inexpensive*)

An atmospheric pub with cosy snugs and mirrors decorated with gold Guinness slogans. The lunchtime pub fare goes down well with kids.

Hy-Brasil Espresso Bar

Bridge St, **t** (071) 916 1180 (*inexpensive*)

Good coffee, juices, snacks and lunches.

McGrath's

Tobergal Lane, **t** (071) 914 5030 (*inexpensive–moderate*)

Serving unpretentious food for both lunch and dinner, this place is especially well geared to families.

Leitrim and Roscommon

Ballinamore

Glenview

Ballinamore, Co. Leitrim, **t** (071) 964 4157 (*moderate*)

This restaurant, part of a B&B, is in a lovely setting beside the river at Woodford. Advance booking is required.

Boyle

Donnellan's

Clarendon House, Knockvicar, Boyle, Co. Roscommon, **t** (071) 966 7016 (*moderate*)

A place with a good children's menu.

The Royal Hotel

Bridge St, Boyle, Co. Roscommon, **t** (071) 966 2016 (*moderate*)

This hotel coffee shop serves salads and snacks.

Dromahair

Stanfords Village Inn

Main St, Dromahair, Co. Leitrim, **t** (071) 916 4140 (*inexpensive–moderate*)

A cosy pub boasting a simple restaurant and its own garden.

Drumshanbo

Maguire's Cottage

Drumshanbo, Co. Leitrim, **t** (078) 41033 (*moderate*)

A friendly restaurant with an open fire and traditional furnishings, serving good steaks, seafood and salads.

Frenchpark

Sheepwalk Bar and Restaurant

Frenchpark, Co. Roscommon, **t** (090) 987 0391 (*moderate*)

Children are welcome in this restaurant south of Boyle, with highchairs and a children's menu. It's just down the road from the Douglas Hyde Interpretative Centre.

Kinlough

Courthouse Restaurant

Kinlough, Co. Leitrim, **t** (071) 984 2391 (*moderate–expensive*)

A mixture of Italian and Irish dishes made from organic produce.

Roscommon Town

Abbey Hotel

Abbeytown, Galway Rd, **t** (090) 326 250 (*expensive*)

A comfortable, bright 18th-century house offering fine French-style cuisine, Irish dishes and a children's menu in a 60-seat restaurant. It's a good place for a treat.

Gleeson's Restaurant

Market Square, **t** (090) 662 6954 (*moderate*)

Try breakfast in the 'Manse' restaurant, or eat in the café for lunch, afternoon tea or dinner.

Ulster

COUNTY ANTRIM 201
Belfast 202
Special Trips 206
Around and About 208

COUNTY DOWN 211
Downpatrick 212
Special Trips 212
Around and About 214

COUNTY ARMAGH 216
Armagh City 216
Around and About 219

COUNTY LONDONDERRY 221
Londonderry/Derry City 222
Special Trips 223
Around and About 224

COUNTY TYRONE 225
Special Trips 226
Around and About 227

COUNTY FERMANAGH 229
Enniskillen 230
Special Trips 230
Around and About 231

CAVAN AND MONAGHAN 233
Around and About 233

COUNTY DONEGAL 235
Donegal Town 236
Special Trips 236
Around and About 237

WHERE TO EAT 240

07

20km
10miles
N
Malin Head
Ballyhilfin
Lag Sand Dunes
Tory Island
Fanad Head
Doagh Isle
Culdaff
Tory Sound
Horn Head
Sheep Haven
Ballyliffin
Inishbofin
Dunfanaghy
Downings
Portsalon
Carndonagh
Marblehill
Dunree Head
Carrigart
Lough Swilly
INISHOWEN
Gweedore
Gortahork
Crana River
Redcastle
Buncrana
White Castle
Bunbeg
Rathmullan
Millford
Lough Foyle
Donegal Airport
Derryveagh Mountains
Glenveagh Nat. Park
Inch Island
Inch
Burnfoot
Aranmore Island
The Rosses
Kilmacrenan
Burt
Derry City Airport
Burtonport
Newtown-cunningham
Grianan Aileach
DERRY
Dungloe
Letterkenny
River Swilly
Gweebarra
Ardmore
Ness Wood
Gweebarra Bay
Lough Finn
Dunmore Head
Naran
Portnoo
Maas
DONEGAL
Convoy
River Foyle
Loughros Beg Bay
Glenties
River Deele
Ballyneaner
Maghera
Lifford
Strabane
Ardara
Blue Stack Mountains
Ulster Way
Ballybofey
Dergalt
Sperrin
Glencolmcille Folk Village
Glencolmcille
River Finn
Glengesh Pass
Lough Mourne
Malin Bay
Plumbridge
Glenelly Valley
Lough Eske
Mourne River
Castlederg
Newtownstewart
Gortin
Kilcar
Killybegs
Bruckless
Donegal
Ulster History Park
Strule
Gortin Glen Forest Park
Greencastle
Ulster American Folk Park
Mountfield
Doorin Point
Lough Derg
St John's Point
TYRONE
Carn
Omagh
Donegal Bay
Rossnowlagh
Camowen
Pettigo
Ballyshannon
Boa Island
Kesh
Bundoran
Lower Lough Erne
White Island
Dromore
Belleek
Tully Castle
Castle Archdale
Irvinestown
Ballygawley
Blaney
Augher
Devenish Island
FERMANAGH
Fivemiletown
Blackwater
Sligo
Upper Lough Macnean
Enniskillen
Castle Coole
Ulster Way
River Easky
Lough Gill
Lower Lough Macnean
Brookeborough
Blacklion
Marble Arch Caves
Bellanaleck
Knockatallon
Gubaveeny
Florence Court Forest Park
Florence Court
Lisnaskea
Upper Lough Erne
Monaghan
Rossmore Forest Park
SLIGO
Dowra
Crom Estate
Drumswords Church
Arigna Mountains
Lough Allen
MONAGHAN
Ballyconnell
Annagh-makerrigh House
Belturbet
Rockcorry
LEITRIM
Blackwater River
Milltown
Cootehill
NORTHERN IRELAND
ULSTER
CONNACHT
REPUBLIC OF IRELAND
LEINSTER
MUNSTER
Leitrim
Killykeen Forest Park
Killashandra
CAVAN
Carrick-on-Shannon
Cavan
MAYO
River Erne
Baileborough
Lough Gowna
Lough Gowna
Ballymachugh
Virginia
LONGFORD
Lough Sheelin
Lough Ramor
N15
N56
N13
N14
R245
R247
R238
A2
A40
A6
B74
A5
B48
B84
A505
A35
A46
B81
A32
A4
B83
N16
R281
R286
R280
R283
N59
R292
R287
R289
R284
A509
A34
R200
R189
R202
N4
R198
N3
R178
N5
N60

Ulster

Rathlin Island
Rathlin Sound
Campbeltown
Inishowen Head
Greencastle
Giant's Causeway
Dunluce Castle
Portrush
Portstewart
Downhill
Magilligan
Castlerock
Coleraine
Bushmills
Ballycastle
Fair Head
Ballyvoy
Torr Head
Ballypatrick Forest
Runabay Head
Benvarden
Dervock
Limavady
Ulster Way
Ringsend
Balleymoney
ANTRIM MOUNTAINS
Glens of Antrim
Layde Church
Cushendall & Hill of Tivereagh
Garron Point
Glenariff Forest Park
River Main
Carnlough
NORTH CHANNEL
NDONDERRY
Dungiven
Glenarm
River Bann
Glenshane Pass
Carntogher
Broughshane
Slemish Mountain
Carnagee
Cairnryan
Mountains
Maghera
Ballymena
Ballygalley
ANTRIM
Larne
Portmuck
Draperstown
Castledawson
Magee Island
Magherafelt
Balleyclare
Stranraer
Whitehead
Antrim
Beaghmore Stone Circles
Moneymore
Springhill
Carrickfergus
Liverpool
Belfast International Airport
Douglas (Isle of Man)
Belfast Lough
Cookstown
Newtownabbey
Helen's Bay
Copeland Islands
Drum Manor Forest Park
Ardboe High Cross
Crumlin
Holywood
Cultra
Bangor
Lough Neagh
Belfast City Airport
Donaghadee
Glenavy
BELFAST
Coalisland
Mountjoy
Newtownards
Dungannon
Coney Island
Upper Ballinderry
Giant's Ring
Mount Stewart
Temple of the Winds
Maghery
Lisburn
Comber
Ballywalter
Grey Abbey
Ards Peninsula
Moira
Moy
Ardress House
Strangford Lough
Lurgan
River Lagan
Hillsborough
Kircubbin
Benburb
R. Blackwater
Portadown
Craigavon
Loughgall
Dromore
Rowallane Gardens
Navan Fort
Armagh
Killylea
Gilford
Ballynahinch
Tandragee
Banbridge
DOWN
Portaferry
Glaslough
ARMAGH
Castle Ward
Strangford
Cusher River
Saul
Milltown
Markethill
Downpatrick
Ballyquinton Point
Seaforde
Ballynaskeagh
Newry Canal
Castlewellan Forest Park
Keady
Castlewellan
Dundrum
Tyrella
Ardglass
Tullymore Forest Park
Newcastle
Newtownhamilton
Newry
Ulster Way
Dundrum Bay
Ballybay
Slieve Gullion Forest Park
Castleblaney
Mourne Mountains
Silent Valley
Narrow Water Castle
Dunmore
Mullaghbane
Warrenpoint
Rostrevor
Crossmaglen
Annalong
Carlingford Lough
Mannan Castle
Kilkeel
Greencastle
Fane River
Cranfield Point
Inishkeen
Dundalk
Carrickmacross
Dún a Ró Forest Park
Kingscourt
LOUTH
MEATH

ULSTER

Ever since the time of Macha (*see* opposite, *The curse of Ulster*), Ulster has had its share of political ups and downs. Its high kings held out longest against outside invaders, until the 17th century when English and Scots 'planters' set up shop there. Their descendants, the tough 'Scots-Irish', were later welcomed with open arms by the United States to settle its frontier.

For nearly a century, Ulster has been divided, with the consequences that are well known. You might not think of Ulster as a good holiday destination for children, but if you want to stimulate an interest in politics and history in them, this is the place to come. Some of the finest museums on the whole island can be found here.

And, intriguingly, some of the loveliest and most peaceful countryside and landscapes in the whole of Ireland can be found here too – in Antrim, Down and Fermanagh in Northern Ireland, or in Cavan and Donegal in the Republic. And, with the peace process now in place – despite its glitches – there has never been a better time to come and enjoy them. Northern Ireland is experiencing a social renaissance, with gourmet restaurants and cultural ventures springing up in main towns. People are helping one another to rebuild communities and businesses. Some of the world's most forward-thinking humanitarian efforts have begun here too, such as Antrim's Corrymeela Community near Ballycastle, which brings together Catholic and Protestant kids for holidays. You also may find things – especially accommodation – less expensive in Northern Ireland than in the Republic.

Although many Northern Irish towns have been redeveloped in recent years, you might prefer to stay in the countryside or villages with children in tow, and make day-trips to museums and tourist sites, which are often outside its major cities. Perhaps the most peaceful, pleasing landscapes are in Antrim, Down, Derry and Fermanagh, but well worth discovering are lesser-known areas such as the Sperrins forest area in County Tyrone.

Highlights

Talking to the animals at Belfast Zoo, p.204
Exploring Finn McCool's bridge: the Giant's Causeway, p.207
Visiting the faeries in the Glens of Antrim, p.208
Discovering St Patrick in Downpatrick and Armagh, p.212 and p.218
Island-hopping on Lough Erne and walking in the forests of Fermanagh, pp.229–32
Playing on remote beaches and riding horses in Donegal, pp.235–9

Did you know...?

Six of the 9 counties of historic Ulster make up Northern Ireland, while 3 (Cavan, Monaghan and Donegal) are in the Republic. A few border towns are still dominated by fortress-like police stations, and remnants of guard posts can sometimes be seen, but otherwise movement between the Republic and Northern Ireland is unrestricted.

Older children will find a visit to Northern Ireland fascinating, particularly if they've grown up in Britain, but seeing an ordinary street transformed by political murals, or the (now much rarer) army patrols, will get anyone asking questions. Most likely they'll never have seen anything like the Red Hand flags and multicoloured pavement curbs that show you're in a Catholic or Protestant area.

In the mainly loyalist counties of Antrim and Down, you can have a great time wandering through the pristine Nine Glens of Antrim, north of Belfast, and the Giant's Causeway along the glorious shores of the northern coast, not to mention Rathlin Island, where you may glimpse puffins. Blatant child-pleasers such as County Antrim's high-tech Dunluce Centre and the 5Ws (who-what-where-when-why) science museum in Belfast are well worth visits, as are Downpatrick's St Patrick's Centre, Cultra's Ulster Folk Museum and Portaferry's Exploris aquarium.

Moving west into Co. Armagh, you'll find the Hill of Navan, where King Conchobar and his Red Branch Knights lived, near Armagh City. In Armagh City itself youngsters will be delighted with the Gulliver's Travels show at St Patrick's Trian Museum and meeting living history characters at the Palace Stables, before moving on to Armagh Planetarium. Nearby on Lough Neagh, Ireland's largest lake, is Oxford Island's Lough Neagh Discovery Centre, for outdoor sports. In Fermanagh, you will find restorative woodland walks, rich Irish folklore and the intensely peaceful Lough Derg. Storytelling and traditional music festivals abound in the southern part of County Armagh and places like Magherafelt, Co. Derry.

In the countryside of Co. Derry (or Londonderry), you will find beautiful nature spots on the coast such as those near Mussenden Temple and the impressive Mountsandel Estate. Londonderry/Derry City itself is fascinating, with its virtually intact ancient walls and award-winning Tower Museum.

For a real interactive experience, visit the fantastic Ulster American Folk Park in County Tyrone. Nearby are Gortin Forest Park and the Sperrin Mountains, where you can pan for gold (but watch out for leprechauns, especially if you try to take away their hidden pots of it!).

Over the border in the Republic, Co. Donegal's people are much closer psychologically to Ireland's ancient high kings than anywhere else in Ireland. At the mouth of the Inishowen Peninsula, just north of Londonderry, you'll find the prehistoric seat of Ulster's high kings. Said to have been built by the Daghda, leader of the Tuatha Dé Danaan, before them, the Grianán Aileach is an awe-inspiring stone ring fort. Its nearby museum at Burt should not be missed by young children who like their faery tales mixed with a bit of history. Donegal has some of the most magical mountain- and seascapes in Ireland, and after travelling for miles to the county's coastal towns, at the end of long, winding roads, you will be rewarded with magnificent views, open skies and plenty of time for storytelling. In South Donegal, Ardara embraces those who want to know about folklore and woven crafts, while nearby Bruckless offers young riders country and seaside treks. South of Northern Ireland lies the 'buffer zone' of counties Cavan and Monaghan, where there is nothing to attract wild holidaymakers – only tranquility. Once an important flax and linen area, now fishermen and equestrians tend to keep it as their secret holiday hideaway.

A story to tell: The curse of Ulster

One morning an Ulster farmer rose with the sun, as he did every day, but such a shining light lay upon the land that he decided to stroll through the woods to find some wild berries for his breakfast. Named Crunnchu, he was a practical, hard-working man, especially now that his wife had died, but today, the truth was, some strange magic had drawn him out of his dreams and into this wood.

Suddenly the early-morning chatter of the birds stopped, and Crunnchu saw something flash past the trees beyond the clearing where he was picking berries. It was fast as lightning. It couldn't be a horse, he thought – the trees were too close together for an animal that size to run between them, and the golden-red flash he'd seen was too light on its feet. It must be some strange animal, he concluded, and went back to his berry-picking.

Little did he know that he had attracted the interest and attention of the goddess Macha, who had stopped and was peeking at him from behind the trees. Eventually Crunnchu glanced up, and saw a beautiful red-haired woman gazing at him.

Well, one thing led to another, and Macha went to live with him and eventually fell pregnant. They were very happy together, but he did notice that his wife had one small quirk: at times she would dash out of the house without a word and run faster than any horse he had ever seen.

One day Crunnchu was invited to a feast of Ulster's powerful King Conchobar Mac Nessa, whose hospitality was well known. His greatest warrior, Cúchulainn, would be there too, so Crunnchu was very excited. Knowing her husband well, Macha warned him not to boast, especially since she couldn't be there to keep an eye on him because she was about to have their baby.

The banqueters grew merry with drink, and Crunnchu was no exception. Then King Conchobar began to boast about the speed of his horses, until Crunnchu burst out with, 'My Macha runs faster than any horse I have ever seen, including your own, King Conchobar.'

Blood rushed to the king's face as he demanded, 'Then so. Your wife must race my horses.'

Crunnchu, unable to refuse the King, brought a raging, pregnant Macha to the palace.

'Please, your majesty,' said she, 'may I not participate in this race, as I am weighty with child.'

But none of Conchobar's men would listen to her, and they made her race. So Macha ran, and ran – faster than all King Conchobar's horses put together. And while the cheers flew about her, she fell to the earth, went into labour and bore twins.

Then she said, 'Men of Ulster, hear me! From this day forward, in times of great danger, you will become as weak as a woman in labour. Her pains will be yours in every battle.'

And then she died upon the dusty ground.

Tourist information for Ulster

Tourism Ireland, freephones UK **t** 0800 039 7000; USA and Canada **t** 1 800 223 6470; **www**.tourismireland.com

Travel information for the whole of Ireland.

Northern Ireland Tourist Board (NITB), 59 North St, Belfast BT1 1NB, **t** (028) 9023 9026, **www**.discovernorthernireland.com

Affiliated to Tourism Ireland.

Belfast Welcome Centre, 47 Donegall Place, BT1 5AD, **t** (028) 9024 6609, **www**.discovernorthernireland.com, **www**.gotobelfast.com, **www**.belfastconventionbureau.com, **www**.belfastvisitor.com

Causeway Coast and Glens Ltd, 11 Lodge Rd, Coleraine, BT52 1LU, **t** (028) 7032 7720, **www**.causewaycoastandglens.com

Derry Visitor Centre, 44 Foyle St, Derry, BT48 6AT, **t** (028) 7137 7284, **www**.derryvisitor.com

Fermanagh Lakeland Tourism, Wellington Rd, Enniskillen BT74 7EF, **t** (028) 6634 6736, **www**.soeasygoing.com

Kingdoms of Down, 40 West St, Newtownards, BT23 4EN, **t** (028) 9182 2881, **www**.kingdomsofdown.com

North West Tourism (Cavan, Monaghan, Donegal), Aras Redden, Temple St, Sligo, **t** (071) 916 1201, **www**.irelandnorthwest.ie

Tours

Minicoach From Belfast Welcome Centre (*see* above), or Belfast International Youth Hostel, 22 Donegall Rd, Belfast, **t** (028) 9032 4733, **www**.minicoachni.co.uk

These 1-day tours by minibus cover the whole of Northern Ireland from Belfast: the Giant's Causeway, Belfast City, St Patrick's Tour in Co. Down, Carrickfergus Castle, the Antrim coast and more.

Good to know... Phoning Northern Ireland

The whole of Northern Ireland has the UK area code **028**. You do not need to use this code with the individual number within Northern Ireland. To call a Northern Ireland number from the Irish Republic, you have to change the code to **048**. Phoning the Republic from the North counts as an international call, but at low rates: dial **00**, then **353**, then the number, **omitting** the first 0 from the area code.

Good to know... Pounds and euros

While the euro (€) is the currency used in the Irish Republic, in the six counties of Northern Ireland it is the British pound sterling (£). However, many businesses across the North will accept and/or exchange both currencies – especially in border towns such as Derry or Newry. *See also* pp.294–5.

Getting there and around

By air There are a great many flights between Britain and Belfast, with several airlines, and some have direct flights to Northern Ireland's 'other' airport, **Derry**. Note that Belfast has 2 airports, **Belfast International** and **Belfast City**; you need to be clear which one your airline is using. Derry is also the best airport for Donegal and the northeast Republic. At present there are no scheduled flights between North America and Northern Ireland, so the best way to get there is via a change in Britain or Dublin or Shannon in the Republic. For all airline and airport details, *see* pp.280–4.

By bus Most public transport in Northern Ireland is run by **Translink**, which has several sub-divisions: **Ulsterbus** operates most buses across the 6 counties, with a comprehensive network. In Belfast, buses heading west and south (Armagh, Tyrone, Derry, Fermanagh and West Down, the Republic) leave from the **Europa Centre**; buses to Antrim and North Down leave from the **Laganside Bus Centre** (*see* p.202). Both Ulsterbus and Bus Éireann also have plenty of long-distance coaches between the North and many towns in the Republic. For more on buses and ticket information, *see* p.286.

By rail Another part of Translink is **Northern Ireland Railways** (NIR), which has suburban lines around Belfast and trains to Coleraine, Portrush and Derry. **Enterprise** trains, run by NIR with Irish Rail, provide a very well-priced service between Belfast and Dublin, with several trains each day. For more on trains and fares, *see* pp.287–8.

Translink, for bus and rail information, **t** (028) 9066 6630, **www**.translink.co.uk

By sea There's a wide choice of ferry routes and companies from Britain: from Cairnryan and Troon in Scotland and Fleetwood, near Blackpool, to Larne; from Troon, Stranraer and Liverpool to Belfast; and from spring to autumn there's also a ferry between Campbeltown in Argyll, Scotland, and Ballycastle, Co. Antrim. For companies and further details, *see* pp.284–5.

COUNTY ANTRIM

This is one of the most visited parts of Northern Ireland, not least because it contains the capital, Belfast. Places that children enjoy are dotted all over Antrim, and include Northern Ireland's most famous tourist site, the Giant's Causeway, which was originally named *Clochan na bhFómharach* ('the stones of the Fomorians'). In legend it was once inhabited by a giant seafaring race, the Fomorians, known for preying on others and depicted as monsters in many of Ireland's mythological tales. Antrim has castles, gardens and museums, together with many opportunities for walking, riding and watersports. For faerylore enthusiasts, the 'capital' of Ireland's faeries is said to be near Cushendall, as is the grave of Oisín (*see* p.130).

Tourist information

Antrim, 16 High St, **t** (028) 9442 8331
Ballycastle, 7 Mary St, **t** (028) 2076 2024
Ballymena, 76 Church St, **t** (028) 2563 8494
Ballymoney, **t** (028) 2766 2280
Belfast Welcome Centre,
47 Donegall Place, **t** (028) 9024 6609,
www.discovernorthernireland.com
Tourism Ireland/NITB Information Centre,
59 North St, Belfast, **t** (028) 9023 1221,
www.discovernorthernireland.com
Carrickfergus, Knight Ride, Antrim St,
t (028) 9336 6455, **www**.carrickfergus.org
Cushendall, 25 Mill St, **t** (028) 2177 1180
Giant's Causeway, Visitor Centre,
44 Causeway Rd, Bushmills, **t** (028) 2073 1855
Larne, Narrow Gauge Rd, **t** (028) 2826 0088
Portrush, Dunluce Centre, Sandhill Drive,
t (028) 7082 3333

Getting there and around

By air For information on Belfast's 2 airports (Belfast International and Belfast City) and transport into town, *see* p.284.

By bus Ulsterbus, **t** (028) 9066 6630, in addition to its regular services, operates the Antrim Coaster, which runs in summer between Belfast and Portstewart, stopping at most towns around the Antrim coast. Ulsterbus and the Bushmills Distillery operate an open-topped bus, 27 June–28 Aug, from Coleraine along the Giant's Causeway, via Portstewart, Portrush, Portballintrae, Bushmills, and back. For bus stations in Belfast, *see* p.202.

By train From Belfast (Central Station or Great Victoria St) there are trains along the north side of Belfast Lough via Carrickfergus to Larne Ferry Port, and on a line through Antrim town and Ballymena to Coleraine. Larne trains connect with ferry arrivals and departures. NIR information, **t** (028) 9066 6630.

By car Roads are often in much better condition in Northern Ireland than in the Republic. The M2 motorway provides a fast route out of Belfast towards the north; turn off at Antrim onto the A26 for the Glens and the Giant's Causeway. Note that if you arrive and hire a car at Belfast International Airport, you do not need to go into Belfast at all.

Car hire

The best places to hire a car are at the airports and in Belfast. Rates often work out lower than those in the Republic, especially in Dublin.

AVIS, 69–71 Great Victoria St, Belfast, **t** (028) 9024 0404; Ferry Terminal, Larne Harbour, **t** (028) 2827 0381; Belfast City Airport, **t** (028) 9045 2017, Belfast International Airport, **t** (028) 9442 2333
Budget, 96–102 Great Victoria St, Belfast, **t** (028) 9023 0700; Belfast City Airport, **t** (028) 9045 1111; Belfast International Airport, **t** (028) 9442 3332
Dan Dooley, 175B Airport Rd, Aldergrove (near Belfast International), **t** (028) 9445 2522
Europcar, City Airport, **t** (028) 9045 0904; International Airport, **t** (028) 9442 3444
Hertz, International Airport, **t** (028) 9442 2533
McCausland Car Hire, 21–31 Grosvenor Rd, Belfast, **t** (028) 9033 3777

Bike Hire

Many bike hire shops in Northern Ireland are part of the linked Raleigh Rent-a-Bike network.

Ardclinis Outdoor Adventure Centre,
11 High St, Cushendall, **t** (028) 2177 1340
RF Linton and Sons, 31 Springwell St, Ballymena,
t (028) 2565 2516
The Skerries Pantry, 6 Bath St, Portrush,
t (028) 7082 4334

Check too with Portrush tourist office (*see* left) for other cycle shops in the summer season.

Cushendall Activity Centre, **t** (028) 2117 1340
This is well placed for the Glens of Antrim.

A Belfast Skipping Game...
Cinderella dressed in yella,
went upstairs to kiss a fella.
How many kisses did she get?
1... 2... 3... 4... (Count until misstep)
From Michael McCaughan (1968)

BELFAST

Belfast, from *Beal Feirste*, 'mouth of the sandy ford', can seem more peaceful than Dublin these days – apart from the odd boom around Halloween, when youngsters like to frighten everyone with fireworks. If you've never been to Northern Ireland, you'll be surprised what a friendly place it is and how normal life is here. If you have been before but not for some years, you'll be amazed how much the city has been redeveloped around beautifully preserved examples of Georgian, Victorian and Edwardian architecture.

The unique constellation of qualities that Belfast possesses seems to produce inventive creators in literature and music. Of particular interest to families is the verbal cleverness of its childrens rhymes and street games. Among the many luminaries of this fascinating city are singer Van Morrison and writer CS Lewis, who both grew up here. Read Lewis' *The Lion, the Witch and the Wardrobe* and other tales of Narnia to your children before you go to Belfast. If they've seen the movie *The Chronicles of Narnia*, they may want to learn more about him, in which case you can take a CS Lewis Homeland tour with Harper Taxi Tours, Belfast, **t** (028) 9074 2711, **www**.harpertaxi tours.co.nr. Regarding more technological pursuits like engineering, Belfast's shipping industry built the Titanic and many British battleships. This industry is only a memory now, but the money being poured into the city in recent years shows in its many new buildings. The big British superstores are here and near the West Belfast neighbourhoods with political wall murals, you'll find busy shopping streets. Signs of a more peaceful political situation are everywhere and, while there are still occasional disputes, tourists are unlikely to encounter any problems.

Much of the city centre is pedestrianized, and young people will find its nightlife pretty lively. Queen's University attracts an international student population, which fills the 'Golden Mile' – from Donegall Square down Great Victoria Street to Dublin Road and University Road – of clubs, pubs and restaurants on weekend evenings.

Children will have fun visiting the zoo, the W5 centre, Aunt Sandra's Candy Factory and the special events put on for youngsters in Dixon's Park. After a visit to the Ulster Museum, you can walk in the gentle Victorian grounds of the Botanic Gardens just outside.

Belfast and Antrim songs to sing...

Belfast Town, I'll Tell Me Ma, The Belle of Belfast City, The Great Shipyard Protest Parade, Carrickfergus

Getting around

On foot Much of the city centre is pedestrianized, and the main shopping streets and many city attractions are within easy walking distance of each other. To get to some places such as Stormont or the zoo, it's best to use buses or cabs.

By bus For all **Translink** services, including Metrobus, Ulsterbus and NIR, call **t** (028) 9066 6630 or see **www**.translink.co.uk

A branch of Translink, **Metro**, runs all buses in Belfast, with more than 60 routes around the city. Most routes operate around 7am–12 midnight daily, and on Sat nights Nightlink late-night buses run. If you travel more than a few journeys it's worth buying a Smartlink card, either the MultiJourney (MJ) card, valid for 5–50 journeys, or a weekly Travelcard. They can be bought from Metro offices and many shops, like the **Metro** Ticket and Information Kiosk, Donegall Sq West.

For **Ulsterbus** coach services, the main stations are the **Europa Bus Centre**, Great Victoria St (for the west and south) and **Laganside Bus Centre**, Donegall Quay (for Down and Antrim).

By car Parking is heavily restricted in central Belfast, but there are plenty of parking meters there. Car parks and pay-and-display areas ring the centre of the city; the tourist office has a list and map.

By train Central Station, East Bridge St, near the Albert Bridge over the Lagan, is the hub of NIR rail services, but most trains also pass through Great Victoria St Station, on the west side of the city centre. Information, **t** (028) 9066 6630, **www**.translink.co.uk

By taxi Ranks can be found at City Hall in Donegall Sq, Upper Queen St, Wellington Place and Castle St.

Black Taxi, **t** (028) 906 2264

Freephones are available round the city for:

FonaCab, **t** (028) 9033 3333

Value Cabs, **t** (028) 9080 9080

Activities & Tours

Belfast Welcome Centre, 47 Donegall Place, **t** (028) 9024 6609
Open June–Sept Mon–Sat 9–7, Sun 12 noon–5, Oct–May Mon–Sat 9–5.30

Ask for copies of *Whatabout?* magazine, *NI4 Kids* newspaper and *Walk This Way* (walking tours leaflet), and, if you're a fan of CS Lewis, the booklet *Northern Ireland and CS Lewis*.

Mini Coach Tours, t (028) 9031 5333

KM Tour Guiding Services, t (028) 3884 0054, **www.kmtgs.co.uk**

Tours of Belfast by car with a fascinating commentary by actor-playwright Ken McElroy.

Things to see and do

Aunt Sandra's Candy Factory

60 Castlereagh Rd, Belfast, **t** (028) 9073 2868
Getting there Metro 5A, 5mins from centre
Open Mon–Fri 9.30–4.30, Sat 9.30–5
Adm Free (but advance booking essential)

A fascinating confectionery factory, where honeycomb, chocolate macaroon cake and traditional fudge are made from 100-year-old recipes. A viewing window lets children watch the sweets being made in a building kitted out with the original fittings, brick walls, wooden ceilings and slate floors of a small candy shop of 1953.

Special Events – County Antrim

May

Ballyclare May Fair, t (028) 9034 0000

Horse trading, a community fair and other equestrian events.

Country Lifestyle Festival, Shanes Castle, Lough Neagh, Randalstown, **t** (028) 9048 3873

The largest family event in Northern Ireland, with a big medieval show, children's learning area, equestrian display, water-based activities and more.

Feis nGleann, t (028) 2076 2024

A feast of Gaelic music, crafts and sports held through May and June in the Glens of Antrim.

Larne Irish Dancing Festival, t (028) 2826 0088

A week of Irish dance competitions, for all ages.

July

Lughnasa Medieval Fair and Craft Market, Carrickfergus Castle, **t** (028) 9335 1273

An event for young damsels and brave knights.

August

Heart of the Glens Festival, Cushendall, **t** (028) 2177 1378

Traditional music.

Ould Lammas Fair, Ballycastle, **t** (028) 2076 2024

Northern Ireland's oldest traditional market fair, held on the last weekend in August.

Events and Festivals – Belfast

May

Belfast City Summer Festival, t (028) 9032 0202

Family fun, including the Lord Mayor's Show, through May and June.

Cathedral Quarter Arts Festival, t (028) 9023 2403

An impressive arts programme.

Ulster Drama Festival, The Lyric Theatre, **t** (028) 9038 1081, **www.lyrictheatre.co.uk**

A treat for young thespians.

July

12 July The Boyne Anniversary

Parades are held and bonfires lit in Protestant areas of Belfast and throughout Northern Ireland to commemorate William of Orange's victory at the Boyne in 1690 (*see* p.35).

Note that watching the Orange March along Belfast's Lisburn Rd is quite safe, but it's best to avoid marches on controversial routes. If you don't know if a place is safe, ask someone; people are very friendly and will almost certainly give you the right advice.

August

Ardoyne Fleadh, Ardoyne, **t** (028) 9075 1056

Local and international performers and traditional *ceili* (dance).

Feile an Phobail, t (028) 9031 3440

An annual festival of Irish music, drama and Irish-language events, with a carnival and a parade.

October/November

Belfast Festival, Queens University, information **t** (028) 9097 2600, bookings **t** (028) 9097 2626, **www.belfastfestival.com**

Three weeks of music, films, plays, poetry and art exhibitions, fringe shows from Edinburgh and international stars. Events take place mainly around the university area.

Cinemagic Festival, t (028) 9023 0606

This children's film festival offers free film workshops, acting, production and screen-writing sessions in addition to a film programme.

Belfast City Hall

Donegall Sq, **t** (028) 9027 0456
Getting there Via Centrelink bus, most Metro buses and City Airlink 600
Open Mon–Sat; call for times
Adm Free
Guided tours by appointment (book in advance)

Belfast City Council sits in this 1906 Edwardian building, where the parliament of Northern Ireland held its first meeting in 1921. It was built with Portland stone in Renaissance style after Queen Victoria gave Belfast city status in 1888, in recognition of its growth from a mere village in the 17th century. Today this rectangular monolith dominates central Belfast, covering some 1.5 acres within gardens open to the public.

Belfast Castle and Cave Hill Country Park

t (028) 9077 6925, **t** (028) 9037 1013 (bookings), **www**.belfastcastle.co.uk
Getting there 3 1/2 miles (6km) north of Belfast city centre, off Antrim Rd; entrances at Belfast Castle and near zoo, via Metro 1/A6
Open Visitor centre (2nd floor of castle): Mon–Sat 9am–10pm, Sun 9–6
Castle: Mon–Sat 9am–10.30pm, Sun 9–6
Playground: Apr and May Mon–Fri 2–5, Sat and Sun 10–6; June Mon–Fri 2–8, Sat and Sun 10–8; July and Aug daily 10–8; Sept Mon–Fri 2–7.30, Sat and Sun 10–7.30; Oct Sat and Sun 11–4.30; Nov and Dec Sat and Sun 11–3.30; Jan Sat and Sun 11–4; Feb and Mar Sat and Sun 11–4.30
Adm Castle and Park: free; Playground: £1.70
Waymarked trails, visitor centre, restaurant

Spend a sunny day at this 740-acre park. Two nature reserves surround the castle (*c*.1870) on the slopes of Cave Hill, overlooking Belfast Lough. Five caves on its east side contain evidence of prehistoric occupation, as does its highest point, McArt's Fort. There's an elaborate adventure playground for 3–14-year-olds only, with supervisory staff (though children must be accompanied by an adult). Its junior area has cradle swings, slides, spring rockers, a sand pit, a bicycle roundabout and play ships. Older children can climb a space net, whizz down an aerial runway or explore tunnels and tube slides.

Belfast Zoo

Antrim Rd, **t** (028) 9077 6277, **www**.belfastzoo.co.uk
Getting there 5 miles (8km) north of the city on A6, in the park below the slopes of Cave Hill; via Metro 1/A6 from City Hall
Open Daily Apr–Sept 10–5, Oct–Mar 10–2.30; closed Christmas Day
Adm Apr–Sept adult £7, 4–18s £3.60, family (2+2) £19.20
Oct–Mar adult £6, 4–18s £3, family £16
Restaurant, shop, tea house, children's playground, facilities for the disabled, free parking

A 50-acre world-class zoo on the side of Cave Hill just outside Belfast, with panoramic views over the city and Belfast Lough. Highly regarded for its conservation and education programmes, it looks after more than 160 rare or endangered species. Enclosures replicate natural environments. Chimps and spider monkeys can be seen on their island, alongside slower-moving gorillas. Watch penguins and sea-lions swim underwater from the viewing enclosure. Two very rare white tigers, Jack and Jill, live here alongside lemurs, tamarins and pelicans.

Botanic Gardens Palm House

Between Stranmillis Rd and Botanic Ave, next to Ulster Museum, **t** (028) 9032 4902
Getting there Metro BA-C
Open Apr–Sept Mon–Fri 10–12 noon and 1–5, Sat and Sun 2–5; Oct–Mar Mon–Fri 10–12 noon and 1–4, Sat and Sun 1–4 **Adm** Free

Delightful for a stroll, these formal gardens (*c*.1827) hold a 'tropical ravine' with a fish pond full of giant water-lilies and a jungle glen, the centrepiece of which is the restored Palm House with its exotic trees and flowering plants.

Lagan Lookout Visitor Centre

Donegall Quay, **t** (028) 9031 5444
Open Apr–Sept Mon–Fri 11–5, Sat 12 noon–5, Sun 2–5; Oct–Mar Tues–Fri 11.30–3.30, Sat 1–4.30, Sun 2–4.30
Adm Adult £1.50, student £1, child £0.75, family (2+2 or more of school age) £4; boat trip £6
Disabled access

Take a boat trip to see Belfast old and new along the River Lagan from this exhibition about the city's industrial and folk history.

Queen's University Visitor Centre

University Rd, **t** (028) 9097 5252
Open May–Sept Mon–Sat 10–4; Oct–Apr Mon–Fri 10–4. **Adm** Free

Northern Ireland's most prestigious university, built in 1845–49, was designed by Charles Lanyon. It was founded by Queen Victoria as part of a trinity of 'Queen's Colleges', the other two being Cork and Galway. Today it's one of the most respected universities in the British Isles. Nobel Prize-winning poet Seamus Heaney is just one of its distinguished ex-students.

Sir Thomas and Lady Dixon Park

Upper Malone Rd, **t** (028) 9032 0202
Getting there Metro 8A/B
Open Daily dawn–dusk.
Adm Free

A park with a playground, Japanese gardens and rose garden. In summer it hosts a Teddy Bears Picnic.

Stormont

Upper Newtownards Rd
Getting there Just east of Belfast on A55 (between A2 and A20); Metro 4A (19/19A, 20/20A)

Older kids may be interested to see the home of the Northern Ireland Assembly at Stormont. It's an impressive neoclassical building at the end of an imposing avenue, and the huge park around it is a good place to let children run off some excess energy. The statue at the front of the entrance is of Lord Carson, who led the Protestant opposition to Home Rule 100 years ago.

Ulster Museum

12 Malone Rd/Stranmillis Rd, **t** (028) 9038 3000, **www.ulstermuseum.org.uk**
Getting there Metro 8A
Open Mon–Fri 10–5, Sat 1–5, Sun 2–5
Adm Free exc special exhibitions
Art gallery, shop, café

Spend at least half a day exploring this great museum with its large collections of archaeology, art, history and the natural sciences. Children may not entirely appreciate the variety and quality of its collection, but they might be taken by the steam engines from old mills and factories, the treasures of the Spanish Armada, the relics from prehistoric to medieval Ireland, the ethnography exhibits on subjects such as Native Americans, and the natural history displays. Its gallery has a collection of Irish paintings, and there are always family activities to complement the changing programme of exhibitions, lectures, films and workshops. The good café overlooks an ancient graveyard.

West Belfast Wall Murals

Getting there The Falls and Shankill Rd are 5mins from the centre by car. To see them with children you'll need a car or to take a black taxi or bus tour. It's a long walk with children, and it's hard to find your way without a guide.

West Belfast by black taxi cab or tour:
Black Taxi Tour, t (028) 9064 2264, **www.belfasttours.com**
Cost Tours from £25 per person or group of 3, then £8 per extra person up to a maximum of 7, for a 90min tour taking in the murals on the Shankill and Falls roads and other places around the city
KM Tour Guiding, *see* p.203

It would be a pity to visit Belfast and not take a look at the city's most famous area. Over the last 30 years, the Catholic Falls Road and Protestant Shankill Road have become household names as the battlefronts of the Troubles. These days they're safe enough during the day, and over-8s will find them fascinating, above all for the giant murals all over this part of town. On the Falls Road they commemorate events such as the 1981 Hunger Strike (*see* p.40) and the Famine (*see* p.36), while on the Shankill Rd they commemorate the Battle of the Boyne, Cromwell, and other Protestant heroes (see p.35).

Black cabs, called 'people's taxis', were used during the Troubles as a substitute bus service, since normal buses didn't run in this part of town. You'll still see them today, and there are many to choose from if you feel like taking a tour. They now have something of a cult status and songs have even been written about Falls Road taxi drivers.

Whowhatwherewhenwhy – W5

2 Queen's Quay, at The Odyssey Centre, **t** (028) 9046 7700, **www.w5online.co.uk**
Getting there City Airlink 600
Open Mon–Sat 10–6, Sun 12 noon–6; last adm 5
Adm Adult £6, child £4, family £15.27

This science and discovery centre contains more than 100 interactive exhibits and has something for the whole family. It's divided into five areas, including the 'Wow, Start' exhibition for children up to age 8, and 'Go, See and Do' for older children, where they can see a laser harp and watch a fire tornado rise to the ceiling. You also can try creating cloud rings, build a house, try a lie detector, design a robot or a bridge, play with a flying machine or make music by walking on a floor piano.

The museum is inside The Odyssey Centre, a multifunctional venue with an indoor arena seating up to 10,000, a 12-screen multiplex cinema, an IMAX® cinema and a wide choice of bars, restaurants and other leisure facilities.

Entertainment

Belfast Waterfront Hall

2 Lanyon Place, t (028) 9033 4455/9033 4400
www.waterfront.co.uk

A concert hall where up to 2,200 people watch performances by stars of classical and pop music.

Grand Opera House

2–4 Great Victoria St, t (028) 9024 1919/9024 0411,
www.goh.co.uk

Matinées and early performances (11am on) of musical and theatrical entertainment in architect Frank Matcham's Victorian 'pleasure dome'.

The Ulster Hall

Bedford St, t (028) 9032 3900

Lunchtime recitals, concerts and comedy shows.

SPECIAL TRIPS

Carrickfergus

Carrickfergus Castle

Marine Highway, t (028) 9335 1273
Getting there Train from Belfast (Larne line)
Open Daily Apr, May, Sept and Oct Mon–Sat 10–6, Sun 2–6; June–Aug Mon–Sat 10–6, Sun 12 noon–6; Nov–Mar Mon–Sat 10–4, Sun 2–4 (closed 25 Dec)
Adm Adult £3, child £1.50, family (2+2) £8
Visitor centre, gift shop, guided tours, disabled access, café, activity room, baby-changing facilities

On the coast just north of Belfast, you'll find this impressive four-storey rectangular castle built in 1180 by the Anglo-Norman John de Courcy to guard the entrance to Belfast Lough. He led an invasion of Ulster in 1177, and he and his kinsmen conquered much of Down and Antrim. Ireland's best-preserved Norman castle, it is enclosed in a way that makes it easy to keep track of wandering children. The castle was besieged by King John in 1210 and Edward Bruce in 1315, and briefly captured by the French in 1760. You can watch a very good historical documentary about the castle's history here, made in a manner that young people will absorb. Outdoors on the ramparts, models of soldiers stand poised with real cannons. Present also are medieval games for children to play and armour they may have an opportunity to don. Periodic pageants or military tattoos are held here, especially in summer.

Mountsandel Fort

t (028) 2955 6000 (Forest Office),
www.forestserviceni.gov.uk
Getting there Outside Coleraine
Open daily dawn–dusk

This large oval mound dominates the Bann River beside the remains of the oldest houses in Ireland (dating from 6000 BC), on the outskirts of Coleraine. This is an intriguing, beautiful place to explore. There is a riverside walk and an area perfect for picnicking.

Dunluce

Dunluce Centre

10 Sandhill Drive, Portrush, t (028) 7082 4444
Getting there On A2 east of Portrush
Open Easter (2wks) daily 10.30–6.30, June Mon–Fri 12 noon–5, Sat and Sun 12 noon–6, July and Aug daily 10.30–6.30, Sept–May Sat and Sun 12 noon–5
Adm All-inclusive ticket (all 3 areas): £8.50, family (2+2) £27 plus £7.50 per person for extra members to maximum of 3
Finn McCool's Playground: 0–3s £2.75, 4–14s £4.50; Treasure Fortress or Turbo Tours: 0-14s £3.50
Shop, restaurant, viewing tower, tourist office

Children could spend the whole of a rainy day quite happily at the Dunluce Centre with its three themed game areas (aimed at ages 6–13). The Finn McCool Adventure Playground has three floors of games that a spectrum of ages can play alone or in a group, including ones called Shadow Cave, Echo Well, Ball Swamp and Make Your Own Weather. Treasure Fortress is a high-tech treasure hunt that is set in a real castle, where players must find quiz clues hidden in secret portals, in order to collect enough 'magic' to free the spellbound princess and acquire her dowry of Spanish treasure.

Once they have burned off some energy and are ready to sit down for a bit, they can take the Turbo Tour ride, which synchronizes moving seats with sound and imagery from top action films. Then, after they have had a look in the shop for a souvenir or two, and after the excitement of the day has been discussed over a good meal in the restaurant, maybe they will go to bed early.

Dunluce Castle

Portrush, t (028) 2073 1938
Open Apr–Sept Mon–Sat 10–6, Apr–May and Sept Sun 2–6, June–Aug Sun 12 noon–6,

Oct–Mar Tues–Sat 10–4, Oct and Mar Sun 2–4, also Mons and bank hols
Adm Adult £2, child £1
Shop, guided tours, limited disabled access

These dramatic ruins on a rocky chalk headland west of Portballintrae date back to the 14th century.

Giant's Causeway

Giant's Causeway Centre and Causeway School Museum (Visitor Centre), 44 Causeway Rd, Bushmills, **t** (028) 2073 1855/1582, **www.nationaltrust.org.uk**
Getting there 2 miles (3km) N of Bushmills on B146
Open Causeway: daily. Shop and tea room: daily June–Sept 10–6, Oct–May 10–5; closed 25 Dec and 1 Jan. School: daily July and Aug 11–5
Adm Visitor centre: adult £1, child £0.50
Guided tours of stones (June–Aug) £2
Shuttle bus: £1 (National Trust members free). Car £3
Visitor centre with disabled access, shop, restaurant, toilets with baby-changing facilities, picnic tables

Northern Ireland's number one tourist attraction is a World Heritage site. You could spend a long afternoon or more exploring these polygonal columns of layered basalt rocks and caves, formed by a volcanic eruption 60 million years ago. Various legends describe the chunks of basalt as 'stepping stones' to Scotland, usually associated with a giant named Fiónn MacCumhail (Finn McCool; *see* below). Similar rock formations can be found on the Scottish island of Staffa, which features in some of the stories. Watch the fun film that tells one of these Finn stories before hiking out to the stones. Be prepared for lots of walking, or take the shuttle bus to the place where the Causeway's famous

A story to tell: Finn McCool and the Giant's Causeway

Like many warriors, Finn was the size of a giant, and one day he decided to build a bridge of stones between the coast of Antrim all the way to Scotland across the narrow Sea of Moyle, in case he ever wanted to walk over in a hurry to buy the good whisky that he had heard was there. But a Scottish giant named Benandonner got wind of his plan and thought, 'Hmph, he's going to bring his Fianna warriors over this bridge and try to conquer my lands,' so he went stomping through the waters from Scotland with the idea of stopping Finn from building his bridge.

With his special long-distance sight, Finn saw big Ben approaching and realized he was much larger than himself, so he fled homeward and asked his wife Oonagh for advice. Fearing for her husband's life, she told him, 'Quickly now, build a baby's cradle large enough to hold a man your size.' And then she sewed some giant baby clothes and a bonnet and put her husband in them.

When Finn's wife saw Benandonner bounding through the waves, her heart sank at his size. 'He is much bigger than you, Finn McCool,' she whispered to her husband.

'Don't I know it,' Finn replied as big Ben's shadow darkened their shore like a great grey storm cloud.

'Whist, husband, keep your mouth shut and close your eyes here in this cradle. No matter what the giant says to me, no matter what he does, behave as if you are asleep. Mind yourself now...'

As the Scottish giant came to shore, Oonagh was humming to herself and gently rocking the cradle with her husband in it.

'Pleased to meet you,' Ben boomed on reaching the place where Finn's bridge began.

'Shhh,' whispered Finn's wife, placing her forefinger to her lips. 'You'll wake the baby.'

The giant peered at the supposed baby, marvelling at its size. 'And whose child might this be?' he whispered to Finn's wife.

'Finn McCool, the great leader of the Fianna,' she replied with pride.

Finn couldn't help but manufacture a little extra baby snore to further emphasize his high status.

Mightily nervous, the Scottish giant began to shake as he considered how big Finn McCool must be to have such a large baby, but only the merest tremble was in his voice as he said, 'And where might this Finn McCool be at the moment?'

'Oh not far. He's hunting but should be back this noon. Will you come in for tea?'

'Well,' said the Scot, 'I must be off to my own dinner myself. It'll take some walking to get there from here.'

Oonagh laughed heartily as she watched the Scottish giant splashing away as fast as he could back towards Scotland.

As soon as he was out of sight, Finn kissed his wife for her cleverness and then tore up the parts of the bridge nearest to Scotland, to make sure that no Scottish giants would ever venture Ireland's way again.

octagonal geological formations start and have a gentle stroll. Do bring along a raincoat and wear good walking shoes that won't slip easily on wet or rocky surfaces. Next door to the Visitor Centre, the Causeway School Museum (**Open** July and Aug daily 11–5; **Adm** Adult £0.75, child £0.50, family £2) re-creates a 1920s Irish classroom.

Giant's Causeway and Bushmills Railway

Runkerry Rd, Bushmills, **t** (028) 2073 2844, **www**.giantscausewayrailway.org
Open Summer; call for running times
Adm Call for prices

An old steam train along the coast between the Giant's Causeway and Old Bushmills station.

The Glens of Antrim

Glenballyeamon, Glenaan and Glencorp are especially beautiful glens near Cushendall, north of Belfast. Maps for 14 walks in the Glens are available, and you can also ride, visit beaches, cycle (if you don't mind steep roads) and enjoy many sports events and festivals, not to mention search for the hideouts of the Good People, whose main haunts are said to be Lurigethan Mountain and Tiveragh Hill. On the slopes of Tieve Bulliagh, about 2 miles (3km) west of Cushendall in Glenaan, you'll find **Oisín's Grave**, the supposed burial site of Finn McCool's son.

Glenariff Forest Park

Waterfoot, Glenariff, **t** (028) 2955 6000, **www**.forestserviceni.gov.uk
Open Daily 10–dusk
Adm Car: £4; Pedestrians: adult £1.50, child £0.50
Visitor centre, shop, restaurant, picnic areas

For families tired of the city, a day spent exploring this 2,927-acre park at the heart of the 'Nine Glens of Antrim' won't go amiss. Some people call it 'the Queen of the Glens', the most beautiful of the nine. There are mountain views along the waymarked trails and its waterfall walk offers spectacular views along the Glenariff River.

Hezlett House

Hezlett Farm, 107 Sea Rd, Castlerock, **t** (028) 7084 8728, **www**.nationaltrust.org.uk
Getting there On A2 5 miles (8km) from Coleraine
Open June Sat and Sun 1–5, July and Aug 1–5 Weds–Mon
Adm Adult £3.70, child £2.20, family £9.60

A thatched cottage dated 1690, making it one of Northern Ireland's oldest buildings.

AROUND AND ABOUT

Animal magic

Brookhall Historical Farm

2 Horse Park, Ballinderry Rd, Magheragall, near Lisburn, **t** (028) 9262 1712
Getting there 5 miles (8km) southwest of Belfast off A3
Open Easter–Oct Weds–Sat 11–5, Sun 2–6
Adm Adult £3, child £1.50, under-2s free
Museum, cottage garden, gift shop, nature walks, tea house, guided tours for groups, no dogs allowed

Artefacts used on Irish farms in the past are displayed on this historical farm with gardens and a wildlife pond. Children may see and pet farm animals, including some rare breeds, then follow nature walks and visit the enclosed garden – an ancient burial ground – a fishing lake, a 12th-century church and a holy well that never runs dry, with waters reputed to have healing powers. Before you leave, stop for refreshments in the tea house.

Leslie Hill Open Farm

Macfin Rd, Leslie Hill, Ballymoney, **t** (028) 2766 3109
Getting there 7 miles (11km) southeast of Coleraine
Open Easter–May and Sept Sun and bank hols 2–6, June Sat and Sun 11–6, July and Aug Mon–Sat 11–6, Sun 2–6. House: only open to pre-booked groups
Adm Call for prices
Playground, walled garden, forge, gift and tea shops, horsetrap and pony rides

Visit 18th-century farm buildings, including the Bellbarn (a threshing barn), a dovecote, a typical cattle byre and old stables that sometimes house piglets. The estate has been lived in by the Leslie family for 350 years, and the Big House is a classic Georgian stone-cut building dating from 1760.

Did you know?
The Hill of Tiveragh, near Cushendall, is alleged to be the capital of the faeries, who live inside the hill – a rounded volcanic plug. From here there are good views of the coast.

Watertop Farm

188 Cushendall Rd, Ballyvoy, Ballycastle, **t** (028) 2076 2576
Getting there 2 miles (3km) east of Ballycastle
Open July and Aug daily 11–5.30 (caravan and campsite all year)
Adm Adult £2, child £1
Caravan and campsite, tea room (July and Aug), electric hook-ups, showers, museum

A family activity centre in a scenic area beside a lake. You can ride ponies or take a boat out, walk along the historical trail and take a farm tour, then pet and feed the small animals. Your children may have the chance to watch a shearing demonstration or take part in an assault course. Afterwards, refresh yourselves in the tea room beside the lake. If you want to stay longer, you can camp here if you have a tent or caravan.

Look at this!

The Giant's Ring

Getting there Off B23, 1 mile (1.6km) south of Shaw's Bridge, near the Lagan Valley, Belfast

This impressive prehistoric hill fort, a giant earth mound almost within the city of Belfast, is more than 600ft (180m) wide.

Irish Linen Centre and Lisburn Museum

Market Sq, Lisburn, **t** (028) 9266 3377, **www.lisburn.gov.uk**
Getting there 9 miles (14km) south of Belfast
Open Mon–Sat 9.30–5
Adm Free
Exhibition, guided tour, linen and craft shop, café

This is a must if your children are interested in crafts. They can talk to weavers in the damask handloom workshop and watch as they spin and weave, then try it themselves. The old-fashioned factory and 'Flax to Fabric' exhibition show Northern Ireland's world-renowned linen industry from the past to the present, and include Egyptian linen from the tomb of Tutankhamun as well as Irish damask napkins made for European royal courts. After the factory, be sure to visit the spinner's cottage and hear the tape of Victorian mill girls gossiping before you learn how modern linen fashions are created via a combination of traditional skills and high technology.

Patterson's Spade Mill

Antrim Rd, near Templepatrick, **t** (028) 9443 3619
Getting there 11 miles (17km) north of Belfast
Open Mid- to end Mar Sun 2–6, Apr, May and Sept Sat and Sun 2–6, June–Aug Weds–Mon 2–6
Adm Adult £3.80, child £2.20, family £9.80
Guided tour

This is the only water-driven spade mill left in Ireland. Its forge produces nine kinds of spades, although in its heyday it made around 300 types. A fascinating tour takes you to a busy, glowing workshop full of bangs and clangs, where people make things the way they used to. You can take away your own sturdy spade to show your neighbours.

Nature lovers

Benvarden Garden

36 Benvarden Rd (off B67), Dervock, Ballymoney, **t** (028) 2074 1331
Getting there 7 miles (11km) north of Ballymoney
Open May–Aug Tues–Sun 12 noon–5.30, exc bank hols
Adm £2.50

One of the few fully maintained walled gardens in Ireland, Benvarden has an attractive 18th-century rose garden and pleasure grounds. Its river is spanned by a Victorian iron bridge, near a woodland pond surrounded by gardens. The owners will show around pre-booked tour groups.

Carnfunnock Country Park

Drains Bay, Coast Rd, Larne, **t** (028) 2827 0541,
Getting there 3 miles (5km) north of Larne
Open Daily spring/summer 9–dusk, July and Aug 9–9, autumn/winter 9–4.30, closed Christmas Day and New Year's Day
Attractions: daily Easter–Oct (times vary, call ahead)
Adm Park: free, but charges for each activity
Wildlife garden, partial disabled access, wheelchair hire, toilets (also for disabled), walks, café, shop

On a fine day, lots of activities for all ages may be found in the 470-plus acres of woodland, gardens, ponds, walking trails, beaches and coastline here. Original features include an icehouse and lime kilns, outdoor man-made attractions like a maze shaped like Northern Ireland and a walled garden with sundials from different eras. Those who can't read clocks may see where their shadows fall on the Human Sundial.

Ecos Millennium Environmental Centre
Kernohans Lane, Broughshane Rd, Ballymena, **t** (028) 2566 4400, **www**.ecoscentre.com
Getting there Off Junction 11 of M2
Open Mon–Fri 9–5, Sat 10.30–5, Sun 12 noon–5; closed 24 Dec–1 Jan
Adm Adult £4, child £3, under-4s free, family (2+4) £12.50
Café and gift shop, nature trails, play areas, caravan park, baby-changing and disabled facilities

The ecos Centre promotes natural energy sources such as wind and sun. Its interactive exhibits on environmental issues are geared to older children.

Rathlin Island
Getting there Daily boat crossings from Ballycastle, June–Sept. Boats leave Ballycastle at about 10.30am and return in the afternoon. Call **t** (028) 2076 2024 or Rathlin Island Ferry, **t** (028) 2076 9299

The island is 6 miles (9km) off Ballycastle and 16 miles (26km) from the Mull of Kintyre in Scotland. It is 8 miles (13km) long and less than a mile (1.6km) wide. You may see some of the endangered species of puffins nesting on the cliff.

Sporty kids

Activity centres

Dundonald International Ice Bowl
111 Dundonald Rd, Belfast, **t** (028) 9048 2611

This entertainment complex has an Olympic-size ice rink, bowling centre, Indiana Land jungle-themed play paradise for children, and more.

Lagan Valley LeisurePlex
12 Lisburn Leisure Park, Lisburn, **t** (028) 9267 2121, **www**.lisburn.gov.uk

An impressive complex with a swimming pool with various thrills, diving pool, fitness suite, four squash courts, main hall and restaurant.

Did you know...?
Throughout the Middle Ages, Ireland and Scotland disputed the ownership of Rathlin Island. The argument was finally settled in Ireland's favour in 1617 on the grounds that on Rathlin, as in Ireland, there weren't any snakes.

Buckets and spades – Beaches in Co. Antrim

From Larne northward, there are golden stretches of sand all along the Antrim coast road. **Cushendall** has a particularly lovely beach, and **Ballycastle** is definitely worth a visit – pretty and quiet, with cliffs and caves to explore. You can camp, park a caravan or dock a boat, as well as swim on a Blue Flag beach and take a boat to Rathlin Island; *see* below. More Blue Flag beaches are at **Portrush** and **Magilligan**.

Horse-riding

Castlehill Equestrian Centre
86a Fenaghy Rd, Cullybackey, Ballymena, **t** (028) 2588 1222

Drumaheglis Riding School
89 Glenstall Rd, Ballymoney, **t** (028) 2766 5500

Maddybenny Riding Centre
20 Maddybenny Park, Coleraine, **t** (028) 7082 3394

Fishing

The Bann, Main, Braid and Glenwhirry rivers and Lough Neagh are renowned for trout and salmon. Sea-fishing is also good all along the Antrim coast. For a list of centres contact Tourism Ireland.

Sailing

Ulster Cruising School
Carrickfergus Marina, **t** (028) 9336 8818

Sailing training for families, May–Sept; adults must accompany children.

Walking

As well as the Glens of Antrim or Giant's Causeway, there are many great walks here. One is the **Slemish Mountain**, 4 miles (6km) east of Ballymena. The **Ballypatrick Forest Drive**, between the Glens and Ballycastle, combines a scenic drive with stops for leisurely walks. Tourist offices have full guides.

Steam Power!

Railway Preservation Society of Ireland
Whitehead Station, York St, Whitehead, **t** (028) 2826 0803. **Times** June–Aug Sun pm. **Fares** Call for info

Two-hour runs between Whitehead and Portrush on the charming vintage Portrush Flyer.

COUNTY DOWN

One of Ireland's most famous and poignant emigrant songs comes from County Down. *The Mountains of Mourne* compares the life that's lived 'digging for gold in the streets' in a foreign city (there are different versions, where the migrant is in London or New York) with the satisfactions of being in a place where mountains 'sweep down to the sea'. In other words, in a foreign land you have to dig for the beauty you already have in your own country, and most of the 'gold' you find there is no more than faery dust.

A little ironically, in terms of the song, Down was one of the two most densely 'planted' counties of Northern Ireland in the 17th century, giving it and Antrim Ulster's heaviest Protestant population. Before that, even St Patrick hailed from England; he landed in Saul in AD 432. A local chieftain called Dichu, Patrick's first convert, gave him a barn where he preached. St Patrick founded a church in Armagh, and his remains are buried on top of a hill outside Down Cathedral in Downpatrick, where he shares a grave with Sts Brigid and Columcille.

As well as the Mourne Mountains, Down is known for lush woods and quiet coastal towns, and the wetlands around Strangford Lough. Families wanting a leisurely holiday will find many attractions, from the Ulster Folk and Transport Museum in Cultra to the Exploris aquarium and Castle Espie wildfowl centre. For a more active time, try watersports off the east coast or riding in the Mournes.

Tourist information

Ards, Newtownards, **t** (028) 9182 6846
Banbridge Newry Rd, **t** (028) 4062 3322
Bangor, **t** (028) 9127 0069
Downpatrick, **t** (028) 4461 2233
Groomsport, **t** (028) 9145 8882
Kilkeel 6 Newcastle St, **t** (028) 4176 2525
Newcastle, **t** (028) 4372 2222
Newry, **t** (028) 3026 8877
Newtownards Kingdoms of Down, 40 West St, **t** (028) 9182 2881, **www.kingdomsofdown.com**
Warrenpoint, **t** (028) 4175 2256

Tours

Mourne Cycle Tours, **t** (028) 4372 4348
Mourne Heritage Trust, 87 Central Promenade, Newcastle, **t** (028) 4372 4059

Guided walks in the Mourne Mountains.

Getting there and around

By bus Ulsterbus has excellent services to all parts of Co. Down, from Laganside Bus Centre, Belfast.
By rail NIR has a suburban line from Belfast along the south side of Belfast Lough through Holywood to Bangor, and the Belfast–Dublin line runs down the west of the county via Newry. Bus and train information, **t** (028) 9066 6630, **www.translink.co.uk**

Bike Hire

Ross Cycles, Newcastle **t** (028) 4372 5525
Mike the Bike, Newtownards, **t** (028) 9181 1311

Special Events – County Down

March–April

St Patrick's Day, information **t** (028) 4461 0800

The county's biggest celebrations on 17 March are in Downpatrick, Newry and Cultra.

Ulster Folk and Transport Museum Events, **t** (028) 9042 8428

Irish culture, storytelling, crafts and seasonal events for all the family, throughout the year.

June

Castle Ward Opera, **t** (028) 4461 5283

An opera festival in the lovely setting of Castle Ward and its gardens (*see* p.214).

Fleadh Amhran agus Rince, Comhaltas Ceoltóirí Éireann, Newcastle, **t** (028) 4377 8989

Traditional music, dancing, competitions and so on.

Green Living Fair, Castle Espie, **t** (028) 9187 4146

Ireland's biggest environmental weekend event, in the Castle Espie wetlands centre (*see* p.212). Months in which it occurs vary from year to year.

July

As in all Protestant areas of Northern Ireland, there are big celebrations on 12 July (*see* p.35).

All Ireland Pipe Band Championships, Donard Park, **t** (028) 4372 2222

Pipers piping.

Kingdom of Mourne Festival, Kilkeel, Cranfield and Annalong, **t** (028) 4176 2166, **www.kilkeel.org.uk**

A community festival for families.

August

Fiddlers Green Festival, Rostrevor, **t** (028) 3026 8877 or **t** (028) 473 9819

A 5-day arts and music festival.

September

Boley Fair, Hilltown, **t** (028) 4063 8200

Demonstrations of vanishing skills such as weaving, stone-carving and shoeing horses, with traditional music, dancing, storytelling, street stalls and a sheep fair. The fair, held early–mid-July, is appropriate for the whole family.

DOWNPATRICK

The county's main market town, Downpatrick, bears the weight of its many associations with St Patrick. After landing in Ireland close to Strangford Lough, the saint spent a lot of time around here, converting the warrior-heathen to a gentle form of Christianity and casting demons into oblivion. Locally, Patrick is also strongly associated with Saul, just east of the town near Slieve Patrick.

Things to see and do

Down County Museum

The Mall, English St, t (028) 4461 5218
Open Mon–Fri 10–5, Sat and Sun 1–5
Adm Free

A brief history of the area is displayed and carved stones from Saul are displayed here, inside what used to be a jail. Model inmates wear 17th-century costume in the cells. Children can also try on the costumes of various religions, learn about an ancient chess game that was played by the Vikings and make simple brass rubbings.

Down Cathedral

t (028) 4461 4922
Open Mon–Sat 9.30–5, Sun 2–5
Adm Guided tour £1

The grave of St Patrick, some claim, is outside this Church of Ireland cathedral.

Downpatrick Railway Museum

The Railway Station, Market St, t (028) 4461 5779
Open For train rides July and Aug Sat and Sun 2–5, and first 2 weekends Sept; special trains for St Patrick's Day, Easter Sun and Mon; May Day; Halloween and Dec weekends with Santa Claus; guided tours of carriages and workshops June–Sept Mon–Sat 11–2
Open Prices vary; call for details

Model-train-mad children love this restored station with its museum of old railway carriages and its steam train that runs to a place called King Magnus's Halt, near the grave of a Viking king called Magnus Barefoot. Work is underway to extend the track south towards a restored cornmill at Ballydugan and on to Quoile River and Inch Abbey.

The Saint Patrick Centre

53A Market St, t (028) 4461 9000, www.saintpatrickcentre.com
Open June–Aug Mon–Sat 9.30–6, Sun 1–6; Apr, May and Sept 9.30–5.30, Sun 10–5.30; Oct–Mar Mon–Sat 10-5; St Patrick's Day 9.30–7
Adm Adult £4.90, child £2.50, family (2+5) £11.70; free entry to restaurant, shops and art shows
Internet café, crafts and gift shop, restaurant

Were there two Patricks? What kind of world did he live in? Was he crazy or a visionary? These and other questions will be answered as you explore this state-of-the-art museum. Its modern audio techniques combine with innovative visuals and interactive technology to absorb you in a world where a man's dreams led him to sainthood.

When you enter the museum, you are greeted by a hallucinatory film covering an entire wall, its kaleidoscopic narrative taking you over a 'bridge of time' into the past and turning your mind to St Patrick's Ireland of 1,500 years ago, when heathen warriors and Christian men of peace lived side by side in occasional harmony. Children may not have the patience to wait for it to end, before moving on to the more interactive part of the museum.

If we are to believe the stories about him, St Patrick overcame all doubters with great miracles and banished many a pagan demon to the deep. He bettered the druids in every respect, and overcame the magical beings that inhabited Ireland with even stronger magic – a magic that came not from him, he said, but from God.

Although folklore portrays Patrick as a being of mythic proportions, he was not a mythological character. We have proof, because he left two pieces he wrote himself: the *Letter to Coroticus*, in which he upbraided a chieftain who had murdered newly baptized Christians; and his *Confession*, a detailed account of his life's work and thoughts.

SPECIAL TRIPS

Castle Espie

Wildfowl and Wetlands Trust, Castle Espie, Ballydrain Rd, Comber, t (028) 9187 4146
Getting there On Strangford Lough 3 miles (5km) south of Comber and 13 miles (21km) southeast of Belfast, signposted from A22

A story to tell:
How St Patrick came to Ireland

It's a great irony that Ireland's greatest saint allegedly came from England. It appears he was kidnapped as a boy by Niall of the Nine Hostages, and brought to these shores to tend the sheep of an Irishman. He was not a particularly holy lad at first, but after his Irish adventure and return to his homeland, he began to have visions. This led him towards the Church, and so he took a monk's vows.

Then, one night in a dream, he heard all the voices of Ireland as if they were one voice. 'Come and walk among us again,' they called out. And so when the Church asked Patrick to take the place of Palladius, the ageing missionary sent to Ireland before him, he did not hesitate to return.

He arrived at the mouth of the River Slaney on Strangford Lough, and landed at Slán (which means 'health' in Irish) – now the Struell Wells area, whose waters have an ancient reputation for healing. St Patrick's first church in Ireland was in a large barn in the village of Saul, which the local Gaelic chieftain Dichu, his first convert, gave him.

Open July and Aug Mon–Sat 10.30–5.30, Sun 11–5.30; rest of year Mon–Sat 11.30–4, Sun 11.30–5; closed 24 and 25 Dec
Adm Adult £4.60, student £3.70, child £2.75, under-4s and helpers of disabled people free, family (2+3) £11.95
Coffee shop, gift shop, walks, organic garden, guided walks by arrangement, picnic area, free parking

Children come into close contact with birds and wetlands here. The landscaped gardens, kilns, quarries and more than 30 acres of woodland are home to Ireland's largest collection of ducks, geese and swans, as well as otters, badgers and foxes, amid rare flowers and grasses, moths and butterflies. From May to August, you can see hundreds of fluffy ducklings and goslings. Probably the best nature park in Northern Ireland, it takes 1hr to walk around fast, but you could spend hours here. The views of Strangford Lough are wonderful.

Exploris

The Ropewalk, Castle St, Portaferry, **t** (028) 4272 8062, **www.**exploris.org.uk
Getting there 28 miles (46km) south of Belfast by A20 around Strangford Lough
Open Mar–Aug Mon–Fri 10–6, Sat 11–6, Sun 1–6; Sept–Feb Mon–Fri 10–5, Sat 11–5, Sun 1–5
Adm Adult £6.20, child £3.70, under-4s free, family (2+4) £17.50
Shop, café, picnic area, playground, toilets with baby-changing facilities, disabled access

Perhaps Ireland's best aquarium, Exploris has a huge open sea tank housing rays and sharks. A virtual journey takes you out into Strangford Lough and the Irish Sea to encounter underwater creatures, then you can see real ones for yourself as you enter the walk-through tanks. Around 2,000 species are here. There are feeding shows and touch tank sessions at 10.30, noon, 1.30, 3 and 4.30.

Exploris also rehabilitates orphaned, injured and sick seals – which can sometimes be seen – and is in a park and wildfowl reserve with a caravan park, tennis courts, mini-golf area and bowling green.

Seaforde Tropical Butterfly House, Maze and Garden

Seaforde Nursery, Seaforde, **t** (028) 4481 1225
Getting there Off A24 between Ballynahinch and Newcastle, just outside Seaforde
Open Butterfly House: Easter–end Sept Mon–Sat 10-5, Sun 1–6; Gardens: all year
Adm Butterfly House or Garden: adult £3, under-16s £2; Butterfly House and Gardens: adult £5.50, under-16s £3, family (2+2) £15
Maze, children's playground, nursery, gift shop

Hundreds of free-flying exotic butterflies fill the Tropical Butterfly House here, and you can see their lifecycle firsthand. Insects and reptiles from every continent are displayed, behind glass. Young kids enjoy following the maze to its central 'treasure'.

The Ulster Folk and Transport Museum

Cultra, Holywood, **t** (028) 9042 8428, **www.**uftm.org.uk
Getting there 8 miles (13km) north of Belfast by A2, near Holywood
Open Mar–June Mon–Fri 10–5, Sat 10–6, Sun 11–6; July–Sept Mon–Fri 10–6, Sat 10–6, Sun 11–6; Oct–Feb Mon–Fri 10–4, Sat 10–5, Sun 11–5
Adm Folk or Transport Museum: adult £5, 5–16s £3, under-5s free, family (2+1) £10, (2+3) £12
Joint ticket: adult £6.50, 5–17s £3.50, under-5s free, family (1+3) £12, (2+3) £18

Craft and gift shops, tea rooms, Sunday carvery, toilets with baby-changing facilities, disabled access

This double museum hosts family-orientated events all year. Across the road from the indoor 'transport' part of the museum is an outdoor 'folk' part. A whole village – shops, school, church, houses – has been set in more than 60 acres to look like an Ulster town in the early 1900s. It even has a sweet shop where kids can buy old-fashioned sugar candies.

The transport exhibition shows everything from horsecarts, unicycles and Belfast trams of the 19th century to the DeLorean car, old Ulster buses and railway carriages. There are life-sized models of people on the buses and trams, cleverly depicted as if they're taking part in little everyday dramas. Look out for the very funny tableau of the last bus home in 1950s Belfast. Kids will love sitting in an early aeroplane to watch a film of man's earliest attempts at flight. Also here is a very moving exhibition about the *Titanic*.

AROUND AND ABOUT

Animal magic

Ark Open Farm

296 Bangor Rd, Newtownards, t (028) 9182 0445
Getting there 11 miles (17km) east of Belfast
Open Mon–Sat 10–6, Sun 2–6
Adm Adult £3.10, child £2.50
Coffee shop, disabled access

Rare breeds including Irish Moiled cattle, live in 40 acres here. Petting farms such as this tend to rotate the animals on show so that they stay as healthy as possible, but you're likely to see pigs, a midget pony kitted out with a saddle ready to take a toddler for a ride and some very intelligent-looking llamas.

Did you know...?
Ireland's famous shamrock emblem came from St Patrick. After a contest of magical power against the druids, which he won, St Patrick plucked a shamrock to illustrate the Trinity, the 'three in one' idea he was trying to convey as a means of understanding God.

Bricks and mortar

Castle Ward Castle and Gardens

Strangford, t (028) 4488 1204, www.nationaltrust.org.uk
Getting there 30 miles (48km) south of Belfast
Open Castle: Mar–June, Sept and Oct Sat and Sun 1–6; May–Aug Fri–Weds 1–6
Grounds: daily 10–8
Adm House and Wildlife Centre: adult £5.50, child £2.50, family £13.50
Grounds only: adult £3.80, child £1.80, family £9.40
Restaurant, shop, toilets, disabled access, baby-changing and -feeding facilities, children's play area

Crafts fairs, cultural and music events and historical re-enactments are held on this 700-acre estate of beautiful formal and landscaped gardens, woods, lakes and seashore. The 'castle' is an 18th-century house with classical and Gothic façades, a theatre in the stableyard, a fortified tower house, a sawmill and a Victorian laundry. An interpretative centre offers historical background too.

There are woodland and lough-side paths to explore, plus horse trails, the gardens and the Strangford Lough Wildlife Centre, where children can learn all about the seals, otters and many species of birds who live on the lough.

Grey Abbey and Nendrum Monastic Site

Ards Peninsula, Newtownards, t (028) 9054 3037
Getting there 18 miles (29km) south of Belfast by A20 around Strangford Lough
Open Apr–Sept Tues–Sat 10–7, Sun 2–7; Oct–Mar Sat 10–4, Sun 2–4
Adm Free (under-16s must be accompanied)
Guided tours, picnic area, toilets with disabled access

The beautiful 12th-century Grey Abbey – ruined, but with many intact rooms – has an exhibition on what life was like for monks here and demonstrating the skills of building and stone-carving. Nearby is another monastic ruin at Nendrum. The visitor centre has displays about St Mochaoi, and a film on Nendrum and Grey Abbey.

Look at this!

North Down Heritage Centre

Town Hall, The Castle, Bangor, **t** (028) 9127 1200, **www**.northdown.gov.uk/heritage
Getting there 14 miles (22km) northeast of Belfast
Open Tues–Sat and bank-hol Mon 10.30–4.30, Sun 2–4.30 (July and Aug to 5.30). **Adm** Free
Disabled access, courtyard restaurant (July and Aug)

Set at the back of Bangor town hall in the former outbuildings of the castle (1852), amid wooded grounds, this centre offers children a discovery quiz sheet to accompany the displays and audio-visual presentations. It has an observation beehive and also summer 'fun days'. As well as archaeological artefacts, you can see intriguing large-scale models of Bronze Age and Early Christian settlements.

Nature lovers

Castlewellan Forest Park

Main St, Castlewellan, **t** (028) 4377 8664
Getting there 4 miles (6km) north of Newcastle
Open Daily 10–sunset. **Adm** Per car: £4
Caravan and campsites, picnic and barbecue areas, café, walks, riding trails, fishing, guided tours

A 19th-century Scottish baronial-style castle sits among trees here, in grounds that are delightful for family walks. You can explore the walled garden, established in 1740, with hothouses, rhododendron beds and woodlands, around a lovely pond in the foothills of the Mountains of Mourne.

Delamont Country Park

Mullagh, Killyleagh, near Downpatrick, **t** (028) 4482 8333
Getting there 6 miles (10km) north of Downpatrick
Open Daily 9–dusk
Adm Per car: £3.50
Shop, picnic areas, tea room, licensed restaurant, playground, miniature railway

Summer events such as magic shows, concerts and puppet plays are held in this wooded park.

Mount Stewart House and Gardens

Portaferry Rd, **t** (028) 4278 8387, **www**.nationaltrust.org.uk
Getting there 5 miles (8km) SE of Newtownards

Buckets and spades – Down's Beaches

Going from north to south, there are 2 lovely, and popular, beaches at **Helen's Bay**, just west of Bangor, and there's an attractive Blue Flag beach at **Millisle**, just south of Donaghadee.

South of Downpatrick, one of Northern Ireland's best is **Tyrella Beach** on Dundrum Bay, long, sandy and backed by dunes. Also good for swimming is **Dundrum** itself.

Cranfield Bay, Co. Down's southernmost point near Kilkeel, has long been a favourite summer swimming and holiday spot, with Haulbowline Lighthouse not far away.

Open House: 12 Mar–Apr Sat and Sun 12 noon–6; May and June Mon and Weds–Fri 1–6, Sat and Sun 12 noon–6; July and Aug daily 12 noon–6; Oct Sat and Sun 12 noon–6
Gardens: 10–sunset; Temple of the Winds: Apr–Oct Sun and bank hols 2–5
Adm House, garden, Temple of Winds: adult £5.45, child £2.70, family (2+3) £13.60;
Garden only: adult £4.40, child £2.30, family £11.10
Shop, tea room, toilets with baby-changing facilities, disabled access, seasonal exhibitions and events

The gardens of this 18th-century house contain sculpted shrubs – such as a magnificent Irish harp above a blanket of red-leaf plants in the shape of a Red Hand, created to symbolize reconciliation between Catholic/Gaelic and Protestant Ireland. Stone images of all kinds of animals, including memorials to late family pets, decorate the grounds. Families could have fun by challenging children to spot the different stone sculptures and make up stories about them, such as why there's a monkey sitting on top of a Green Man, or why the Stewart family put sculptures of rabbits, boars, cats and even a stone ship in the garden. The comfortable tea room has good home-made cakes.

Rowallane Gardens

Saintfield, Ballynahinch, **t** (028) 9751 0131, **www**.nationaltrust.org.uk
Getting there 15 miles (24km) south of Belfast
Open Daily mid-Apr–mid-Sept 10–8, rest of year 10–4; closed 24–26 Dec
Adm Adult £3.70, child £1.70, family £9.10
Shop, tea room, disabled access

This beautiful, flower-filled garden is great for easy walks. Special events, concerts and fun days are occasionally arranged for families.

Tollymore Forest Park

Bryansford Rd, Newcastle, **t** (028) 4372 2428
Getting there 2 miles (3km) west of Newcastle
Open Daily dawn–dusk
Adm Adult £1.50, child £0.50, per car £4
*Visitor centre, guided tours (summer, **t** (028) 4377 8664), gift/craft shop, picnic areas, restaurant, caravan and camping park, disabled access*

This lush park of woodlands and mountains is huge, with lovely paths; pick up a map from the visitor centre. Look for the White Fort rath (perhaps built *c.* AD 500), bridges, grotto and arboretum.

Sporty kids

Activity centres

Mourne Activity Breaks

28 Bridge St, Kilkeel, **t** (028) 4176 9965

Falconry, riding and other outdoor activities.

Pickie Family Fun Park

Marine Gardens, The Promenade, Bangor, **t** (028) 9185 7030

Swan boats on a lake, pools, sandpits, a miniature train ride, fairground arcades and shore walks.

Boat trips

Weather permitting, boats leave Bangor and Donaghadee in summer at 10.30, 2.30 and 7.30 for short coastal cruises. Information is posted on the piers. Boats from Bangor also go out to uninhabited Copeland Island; Bangor Tourist Office has details.

Horse-riding

Drumgooland Equestrian Centre

29 Dunnanew Rd, Seaforde, Downpatrick, **t** (028) 4481 1956

Mount Pleasant Equestrian Centre

15 Banannstown Rd, Castlewellan, **t** (028) 4377 8651

Walking

The **Ulster Way** footpath goes along the shores of Strangford Lough, around the coast and into the Mourne Mountains. Tourist offices have guides.

Watersports

Bangor and Strangford Sailing School

13 Gray's Hill, Bangor, **t** (028) 9754 1883

Tropicana Swimming Pool

Central Promenade, Newcastle, **t** (028) 4372 5034

COUNTY ARMAGH

The name Armagh comes from *Ard Macha*, 'Macha's Height', which refers to the fortress built on top of a hill by a legendary queen called Macha around the first millennium BC. For 700 years, the high kings of Ulster held court at what is now Armagh City, and their capital was at Navan Fort, very near the town. These kings were always at war with Connacht, at least until the 5th century AD, when Christianity arrived in Ireland and St Patrick himself, supposedly, chose Armagh as his seat.

Armagh is known as the Orchard of Ireland, because its rich and beautiful landscape is renowned for its apples.

Tourist information

Armagh: St Patrick's Trian Centre, 40 English St, **t** (028) 3752 1800, **www.armagh-visit.com**
Craigavon: Civic Centre, Lakeview Rd, **t** (028) 3831 2400

Tours

Armagh Guided Tours, **t** (028) 3755 1119, **www.armaghguidedtours.com**, or via Armagh Information Centre, **t** (028) 3752 1800

Barbara Ferguson can tell you all about Armagh, from folklore to history, and take you all around its most fascinating corners.

Getting there and around

By bus Ulsterbus Express buses run from Belfast to Armagh, Mon–Sat every hr 6.30am–6.30pm; on Sun there is only 1.
Translink: **t** (028) 3752 2266
By rail The **Enterprise** trains between Dublin and Belfast stop at Portadown and Newry, and there also slower trains with more stops.
Bus and train information, **t** (028) 9066 6630, **www.translink.co.uk**

ARMAGH CITY

The City of Armagh is central to Ireland's ecclesiastical history. Little is known about it before the middle of the 7th century, when it was the centre of the cult of St Patrick and was fast becoming the religious capital of Ireland, but we do know that King Conor and his Red Branch warriors occupied Navan Fort, just outside the town.

The famous *Book of Armagh* was written here in 807 by a scribe named Ferdomnach. It contains the New Testament plus St Patrick's *Confession* and some of the earliest documents about the saint, including the *Book of the Angel* (c.640), a unique glimpse of 7th-century Armagh.

The heart of Armagh is called 'the Rath', and it is surrounded by 'the Trians', part of the monastic settlement that grew up around the centre of the city. Armagh's most famous home-grown saint was the 12th-century St Malachy, portrayed holding Armagh apples in sculptures and on the stained-glass inside St Patrick's Catholic Cathedral.

Today a strong military police presence occupies the city fairly benignly, a vestige of the Troubles. Mostly, it's a quiet town: shops close early and restaurants do slow trade off-season.

Just to the west of Armagh city stands Navan Fort, the ancient Emain Macha of Irish history and legend and the earliest capital of Ulster. It is the setting for the tales of Macha, Cúchulainn and the heroes of the Red Branch. On the hill of Emain Macha, where traces of a giant Celtic temple (128ft/39m in diameter) have been found, you are enveloped by the mysteries of Celtic rituals and prehistoric people's beliefs in the 'Otherworld'. Navan Fort, the cultural, political and spiritual capital of the Kings of Ulster from 600 BC, serves as the backdrop for a number of legends first written in the 7th century. Even today as you walk up the low hill, small in comparison to the weight of its mythology, you can sense an atmosphere of gravity and importance. King Conchobor Mac Nessa ruled from here, with his Red Branch Knights assisted by County Louth's demigod Cúchulainn; the stories surrounding them are similar to those of Britain's King Arthur and his Knights of the Round Table, with Cúchulainn a rougher version of Lancelot. A few years ago an attractive visitor centre was installed next to the hill but was subsquently closed; check with local tourist offices whether it is now open and ask what tours or other activities may be available at Navan when you visit.

A story to tell: Queen Macha

Macha was sovereign of an area west of Armagh City, marked by a hill called *Emain Macha* – which most agree means 'the Twins of Macha'. Like many a mythical goddess in Ireland, this queen seems to have had three sides to her character, and three main stories have been handed down about her. In one she was the wife of Nemedh, who built a fort in South Armagh called *Ard Macha* or 'Macha's Height' (*see* p.29). When she foresaw the sorrows of the future of Ireland, she died of heartbreak. In another, Macha was the only child of a king of Ulster. When he died, she challenged her father's two brothers, who refused to let her succeed to the throne because she was a woman. She challenged them to a fight, which she won, and so became Queen. For the third story, *see* p.199.

Special Events – County Armagh

March

St Patrick's Day, 17 March

A huge parade in Armagh City and a concert in St Patrick's Hall.

May

Apple Blossom Festival, Armagh City, **t** (028) 3752 1800

Street concerts, games and a 'jail break'.

June

Armagh Festival of Traditional and Folk Song, t (028) 3026 7517

A traditional music festival.

Things to see and do

Armagh County Museum

The Mall East, **t** (028) 3752 3070
Open Mon–Fri 10–5, Sat 10–1 and 2–5
Adm Free

Costumes, natural history and maps of the city and county are displayed in this building that includes a library and art gallery. The Newry tram that carried coal, flax and linen sits amid memorabilia of the Clogher Valley Railway and the lines that linked Armagh city to Belfast and the rest of Ireland.

Armagh Planetarium and Observatory

College Hill, **t** (028) 3752 3689,
www.armaghplanet.com
Open Reopening 2006; call for times
Adm Call for prices
Shop, café, disabled access

Mature grounds surround this attraction's 18th-century Astropark, an observatory with a model solar system, and the Eartharium, an earth science centre where children can find out all about volcanoes, earthquake activity and ozone layer depletion. Beyond the gardens you can visit the 20th-century planetarium, with a star show under a silver dome and interactive exhibits that allow you to look back through time to the Big

Bang that scientists believe created our universe millions of years ago. The space ice cream is highly recommended.

Palace Stables Heritage Centre
The Palace Demesne, Friary Rd, **t** (028) 3752 9629
Open Call for details after 2006 reopening
Adm Call for details
Restaurant, shop

Meander through the exhibit with its life-size models and audio commentary explaining a day in the life of a lady visiting this grand house in the 18th century, then get a guide to lead you through the stables, house, chapel and grounds. Converse with one of the 'living history' interpreters who act, speak and dress in the Georgian style of 1786. Look for the ice house, and make sure your guide explains how it was once used. During the winter, snow would be shovelled into it from a window near the top, so that the thick-walled round 'house', partially underground, would remain cold throughout the rest of the year.

The adventure playground, 'sensory garden' and perhaps a horse-drawn carriage ride will round off your visit. Once a month, the Armagh Pipers Club meets here to play music (**t** (028) 3751 1248).

St Patrick's Cathedral (Church of Ireland)
Cathedral Close, **t** (028) 3752 3142
Open Daily Apr–Oct 9.30–5, Nov–Mar 9.30–4
Adm Free
Small car park, bookshop, toilets

St Patrick founded his bishopric and chief church on the high Hill of Armagh, once a prehistoric settlement, in AD 444. The city spreads out below it. There is little left of a 13th-century cathedral built over the remains of St Patrick's original church, as it was 'renovated' by English architect LN Cottingham in the 1830s. Note the 11th-century Market Cross (one carved stone cross mounted on top of another). A nearby plaque claims the body of Brian Boru, High King of Ireland, lies in the vicinity.

Did you know...?
Archaeologists think that Navan hill fort may have been more of a ceremonial than a defensive site. Its importance must have lasted into the Middle Ages, as Brian Boru camped there in 1005. Navan Fort was abandoned after St Patrick's Church was built in Armagh City.

Did you know...?
Trians (pronounced 'tree-anns') means 'three sections' and is an ancient name for the way central Armagh was divided; Christian monks and their followers later settled in these three sections.

St Patrick's Cathedral (Catholic)
Cathedral Rd, **t** (028) 3752 2802
Open Daily 10.30–dusk. **Adm** Free

Like most Catholic churches in Ireland, Armagh's Catholic cathedral could only be built after the laws against Catholics were relaxed in the 1820s (*see* p.36). It was begun in 1840, but work was suspended during the Great Famine of the 1840s. Work began again in 1854, but it wasn't completed until the 20th century. It boasts some very impressive interior decorations.

St Patrick's Trian Visitor Complex
40 English St, **t** (028) 3752 1801, **www.saintpatrickstrian.com**
Open Mon–Sat 10–5, Sun 2–5
Adm Adult £4.50, child £2.75, family (2+3) £11
Tourist office, shop, periodic craft workshops, restaurant, disabled access, enclosed car parking

Two exhibitions here trace the development of Armagh from prehistoric times to its present incarnation as a world centre of Christianity. A film on this with displays on St Patrick and his effect on the city is followed by an interactive exhibit about the Book of Armagh.

A third exhibition will most interest young children: 'The Land of Lilliput', an extravaganza based on Jonathan Swift's *Gulliver's Travels*. Children are invited into a bright wooden fairytale castle where they put on costumes and enter the land of Lilliput, to encounter the sleeping giant, tied down by the tiny natives who wait to feed him hundreds of miniature loaves of bread. Gulliver's adventures are told in the next room, via hi-tech 3D effects, as you take part in his trial and Gulliver talks to you. This is a great way to interest children in a literary classic, and a must on a trip to Armagh.

Entertainment

Market Place Theatre and Arts Centre
t (028) 3752 1821

An arts centre, with drama, music and dance, two theatres, a gallery, restaurants and bars.

Shopping

A craft fair is usually held the last Sunday of the month at the Palace Stables Centre (*see* opposite).

Shambles Market

Cathedral Rd, **t** (028) 3752 8192
Open Tues and Fri 9–5
A large food, clothing and general market.

AROUND AND ABOUT

Animal magic

Ardress House

64 Ardress Rd, Portadown, **t** (028) 8778 4753, **www.nationaltrust.org.uk**
Open 2–6 mid-Mar–Sept Sat, Sun and bank hols, June–Aug Weds–Mon
Adm Adult £3.30, child £1.70, family £8.30
Guided tours, shop, disabled access

This 17th-century manorhouse and its outbuildings contain rare farm animals, farm implements and a blacksmith's shop. Kids can enjoy an adventure playground, family events and riverside walks.

Tannaghmore Gardens and Animal Farm

Silverwood, Craigavon, **t** (028) 3834 3244
Open Gardens: daily dawn–1hr before dusk
Farm: daily 10am–2hrs before dusk
Adm Free; small charge for bouncy castle
Picnic area, organized treasure hunts

A Victorian rose garden, rare animal breeds and nature walks alongside an adventure playground.

Bricks and mortar

The Argory

Derrycaw Rd, Moy, Dungannon,
t (028) 8778 4753/9598, **www.nationaltrust.org.uk**
Open Grounds: daily May–Sept 10–7, Oct–Apr 10–4
House: mid-Mar–May and Sept Sat, Sun and bank hols 1–6; June and Aug Mon–Fri 1–6; July daily 2–6
Adm Adult £4.50, child £2.40, family £11.40; £2 car park
Guided tours, shop, tea room, toilets with baby-changing facilities, disabled access

Everything in this 1820s mansion is the same as it was at the start of the 20th century. There is no electricity, and family possessions from 4 generations are on show. The house stands in 315 acres of woodland overlooking the River Blackwater, and also has a children's playground.

Dan Winter's House

9 Derryloughan Rd, 1 The Diamond, Loughgall, **t** (028) 3885 2777
Open Mon–Sat 10.30–5.30, Sun 2–5.30 (to 8.30 in summer); other times by request
Adm Free

This monument of Protestant Ulster is at the crossroads where the 'Battle of the Diamond' took place in 1795 – and so the birthplace of the Orange Order. It all began when the 'Orange Boys', a Protestant club, heard that the Catholic 'Defenders' planned to burn all Protestant homes in Richhill, Kilmore and Loughgall, and set out to catch them first. A short fight ensued next to Dan Winter's pub, between the 'Defenders' and many Protestant groups. The 'Defenders' were defeated in this 'Battle of the Diamond', and right afterwards, the leaders of the Protestant groups in the battle – notably pub-owners James Wilson, Dan Winter and James Sloan – formed an umbrella organization, supposedly to protect their faith, called the Orange Order, which still exists.

A story to tell: Cúchulainn

Chulainn was a man who held a feast for the Red Branch and King Conchobar. Setanta, the son of the god Lugh, who was half-god and not from Ulster at all but from Louth, arrived late at the banquet. The gates of Chulainn's palace were shut, and so Setanta simply scaled the walls and climbed over them – unfortunately straight into the vicinity of Chulainn's deadly guard dog, whose jaws were wide enough to swallow a man. Setanta wasn't too bothered by this, though, and simply threw a stone into the hound's mouth, which lodged in its throat and killed it instantly.

Hearing all the commotion, Chulainn came out of the palace and was most upset that his best protector had been killed. The honourable Setanta then promised to take the guard dog's place and be Chulainn's personal protector, so thereafter he came to be called 'the hound of Chulainn', or, in Irish, 'Cúchulainn'. Later he became the greatest hero of the Red Branch warriors, and of Ireland.

Did you know...?
Two Celtic warlords agreed to a contest for ownership of Ulster. The first to place his hand on the land would own it, after a race across the Irish Sea from Britain. One, named O'Neill, was behind in the race and, desperate to claim Ulster for himself, he cut off his hand and threw it ashore before his opponent could land. That is the origin of the Red Hand symbol you see in Ulster today.

The timbers of the cottage, said to have been Dan Winter's pub (although some say it was his neighbour James Sloan's pub, and that Winter's was burned to the ground), still bear scorch marks from being set alight in the battle. Thought to be the longest thatched cottage in Ireland, this 94ft (29m) home contains 18th-century furnishings in an area for selling alcohol, and a working loom.

Look at this!

Tayto Castle and Crisp Factory

Tandragee, **t** (028) 3884 0249, **www.tayto.com**
Getting there 11 miles (17km) east of Armagh
Open Mon–Fri 10–5, Sat 10–1 and 2–5
Adm Free (not suitable for under-5s);
Book guided tours in advance

This 300-year-old castle and factory makes one million packets of crisps and snacks daily. Kids can sample many, including products being developed.

Nature lovers

Gosford Forest Park

7 Gosford Demesne, Markethill, **t** (028) 3755 1277
Open Daily 10–dusk
Adm Adult £1.50, child £0.50, car £4
Guided tours and orienteering (book in advance), walled garden, deer paddock, caravan and campsite, horse-riding routes, disabled toilets

The vast forest around this fine neo-Norman 18th-century castle (closed to visitors) is ideal for a walk, with trees, lakes, ducks and a haunted round tower.

Loughgall Country Park

11–14 Main St, Loughgall, **t** (028) 3889 2906
Open Daily 9–dusk
Adm Park: £2; Fishing: adult £3 per day, under-18s £1.50 (must have coarse fishing licence)
Light refreshments, children's playground (free)

This 464-acre estate of open farmland and orchards has a play area, bridle path, 18-hole golf course, 37-acre coarse fishery, country walks, formal gardens and the Lake of Loughgall.

Lough Neagh Discovery Centre

Oxford Island, Lurgan, Craigavon, **t** (028) 3832 2205, **www.oxfordisland.com**
Open Centre: Weds–Sun Oct–Mar 10–5, Apr–Sept 10–7
Adm Centre: adult £4, child £2; Park: free
Shop, café

Scenic boat and birdwatching trips are available on Lough Neagh. The award-winning exhibition in the centre was closed at the time of writing; call for reopening details. Cycling is also available.

Sporty kids

Activity centres

Waves Leisure Complex

Robert St, Lurgan, **t** (028) 3832 2906

Wave- and child's fun-pools and a restaurant.

Boat trips

Lough Neagh

Paddy Prunty, Harbour Master, Kinnego Marina, Oxford Island, **t** (028) 3832 7573

Boats depart from Kinnego Bay, Lough Neagh; Mr Prunty can also arrange sailing courses.

Walking

The **Ulster Way**, a well-signposted trail, also goes through Armagh. There is an especially scenic stretch along the Newry Canal between Newry and Portadown. Carnagh and Slieve Gullion Forest Park also have fine paths. Details are available from tourist offices.

Watersports

Craigavon Water Sports Centre

Lakeview Rd, Craigavon, **t** (028) 3834 2669

Watersports of all types can be enjoyed at this centre.

COUNTY LONDONDERRY

The name of this county and its city may confuse outsiders. It originally came from the Druids' sacred wood of Derry, from which the city grew. Then, in the 17th century, after the 'Plantation' of Protestant settlers here, King James I renamed it Londonderry (*see* p.35). County Londonderry is a lively place of great beauty steeped in history and folklore. Mythology, Christian legends and dramatic landscapes entwine and wrap around the imagination.

Visit Derry City's Tower Museum for an introduction to its secrets, then stroll along the city walls before going further afield to see plantation settlements at Springhill House and Mussenden Temple. Investigate folklore at the storytelling festival at Magherafelt, and show your children how Christianity affected Ireland by following some of the legends about St Columcille and St Patrick, which permeate the countryside.

Tourist information

Coleraine: Railway Rd, **t** (028) 7034 4723; Causeway Coast and Glens, 11 Lodge Rd, **t** (028) 7032 7720, **www**.causewaycoastandglens.com

Derry/Londonderry: Derry Visitor and Convention Bureau, 44 Foyle St, **t** (028) 7126 7284, **www**.derryvisitor.com

Limavady: 7 Connell St, **t** (028) 7776 0307

Tours

City Sightseeing Derry, **t** (028) 9062 6888, **www**.derrycitysightseeing.com

City Tours, 11 Carlisle Rd, **t** (028) 7127 1996

Foyle Cruises, Harbour Museum, Harbour Sq, **t** (028) 7136 2857

Open Top Tour, **t** (0845) 226 0292, **www**.opentoptour.com

Getting there and around

By air City of Derry Airport is 7 miles (11km) northeast of the city on the Coleraine road (A2). It has flights from Britain with British Airways and Ryanair (*see* pp.281–2, p.284). From the airport taxis and lots of buses run to Derry, Coleraine and many places in Donegal. Airport information, **t** (028) 7181 0784, **www**.cityofderryairport.com

By bus Ulsterbus has regular buses between Derry and every part of Northern Ireland (in Derry, **t** (028) 7126 2261). There are also many Bus Éireann coach services from Derry to Dublin and other destinations in the Republic. The **Londonderry and Lough Swilly Bus Company**, **t** (028) 7126 2017, runs local buses from Derry to most of the loughs and small towns across the border in Donegal.

By train Derry is the terminus of the main NIR line from Belfast via Antrim town and Coleraine, with several trains daily in each direction.

Translink's Ulsterbus and NIR train information: **t** (028) 9066 6630, **www**.translink.co.uk

Bike Hire

Call Derry Visitor Centre, **t** (028) 7126 7284, for information about bike hire.

Special Events – County Londonderry

March

St Patrick's Day, 17 March, **t** (028) 7137 6645
Parades and events around the county.

City of Derry Drama Festival, **t** (028) 7126 4455
A dynamic theatre festival.

Guth an Earraigh, Derry City, **t** (028) 7126 4132
An Irish-language festival.

March–April

Feis Doire Cholmcille (Annual Derry Feis), **t** (028) 7126 4455
The northwest's largest Irish music festival.

July

Children's Art Festival, The Playhouse, Derry City, **t** (028) 7126 8027
Workshops and classes for those aged 7–11.

Walled City Cultural Festival, Derry City, **t** (028) 7126 7284
An outdoor carnival for the family.

July–August

Foyle Cup, Derry City, **t** (028) 7126 7432
A youth soccer tournament.

Gasyard Wall Féile, Derry City, **t** (028) 7126 2812
Events around the city, including music, workshops and exhibitions for the whole community.

Maiden City Festival, Derry City, **t** (028) 7134 9250

Sperrins Summer Storytelling Festival, Magherafelt, **t** (028) 7963 1510; Draperstown, **t** (028) 7962 9100
A very enjoyable showcase for Irish storytelling.

October

Banks of the Foyle Halloween Carnival, **t** (028) 7137 6545
Old-Gaelic Samhain revelry by the lough, with dressing up and fireworks, followed by loud music.

November

Foyle Film Festival, Derry City, **t** (028) 7126 7432

Craft Fair, Derry City, **t** (028) 7136 5151

LONDONDERRY/ DERRY CITY

This town's first name was *Doire*, meaning 'oak grove'. It is thought to have grown up around a sacred wood of the druids, for whom oak trees were especially significant. After AD 546, when St Columcille established a religious settlement here, it was known as Derry-Columcille. It became 'Londonderry' in 1613, when King James I enlisted support for the Ulster Plantation (*see* p.34) by giving London livery companies privileges in the town in return for sending young workmen (many of whom probably had little choice in the matter) to populate the country with loyal Protestants. During Northern Ireland's Troubles, you instantly gave away your political stance by the name you called it: Protestants termed it Londonderry and Catholics Derry. In local papers, they began to call the town Londonderry/Derry (or vice versa) to avoid offending anybody. A local radio presenter once suggested just renaming it 'Stroke City' instead.

Whatever its name, this is an important city for two reasons. The first is that it lies between Ireland's cosmopolitan east and rural, romantic west, and the second is that it had a prominent role in the events leading up to the outbreak of 'the Troubles'. The city's Bogside, where riots began in 1969, was a famous Republican/Catholic enclave known for its 'Free Derry' monument and murals. Today many leaders of social reconciliation efforts are from the Bogside and Catholics are in the majority in Derry. Slowly, Catholics and Protestants are beginning to integrate.

It is now a popular holiday destination and an excellent base from which to explore some of Northern Ireland's most beautiful places. Donegal, Mountsandel and the Giant's Causeway are all nearby. The Field Day Theatre Company began here, and you must see the award-winning Tower Museum set in the rejuvenated tourist area of the city.

Things to see and do

Cathedral of St Columb

London St, t (028) 7134 2303, www.stcolumbscathedral.org

A Derry song to sing...

Like everything else here, the song most closely associated with Derry has 2 names – The Londonderry Air, and Danny Boy. It's probably the most famous of all Irish songs.

Open **Mon–Sat summer 9–5, winter 9–1 and 2–4**
Adm **£1**

Audio-visual displays on local history; disabled access but shallow steps at entrance to chapterhouse

The most historic site in Derry is this Protestant 'Plantation Gothic' cathedral, built in the name of St Columba/Columcille by the Corporation of London in 1633. Stained-glass windows depict the life of the saint. You can also see the Catholic-fired cannonball that fell inside the cathedral during the Siege of Derry (1688–9), along with stained-glass scenes of the battle. The keys of the gates that were closed against the Jacobites are displayed in the chapterhouse; also on display are flags and artefacts from the various brigades that protected the Protestant camps in Ireland.

In 546, Aimire, a prince of Columcille's clan the O'Neills, granted an oak-clad hill in another part of Derry to St Columcille, the early missionary whose name is associated with ancient Christian sites all over Ireland and on the Scottish island of Iona.

City Walls

Derry tourist office, t (028) 7126 7284
Open **Daily dawn–dusk**
Adm **Free; guided tours £4**

Derry is the only remaining completely walled city in Ireland, and also one of the finest examples of its kind in Europe. These famous walls were constructed during the Plantation period in the early 17th century, when Derry was one of the British Crown's new settlements of English and Scots Protestants. Fine views can be had from the tops of the walls encircling the old city, a circuit of a mile (1.6km), over the River Foyle and to the hills of Donegal. If you head for the area near the Apprentice Boys' Lodge, you can look down on the Bogside.

Harbour Museum

Harbour Sq, t (028) 7137 7331
Open **Mon–Fri 10–1 and 2–4.30**
Adm **Free**

This museum has exhibits on maritime history and interesting Victorian artefacts. Highlights are old ship models, and a replica of a 30ft (9m) *curragh* in which St Columcille sailed to Iona in 563.

Tower Museum

O'Doherty Tower, Union Hall Place, **t** (028) 7137 2411
Open 10–4.30 Sept–May Mon–Fri, June–Aug daily
Adm £3 per person
Exhibition, shop, film, guided tour, disabled access

The loss of this museum for a while has been quite a blow for Derry. In 2005, the 17th-century grey stone tower that housed the city's best museum was closed for the installation of a new five-floor exhibition about the Spanish Armada. This section opened towards the end of the year and displays many artefacts recovered from *La Trinidad Valencera*, one of the largest ships in the Armada fleet, which foundered in 1588 on Donegal's northern coast during a violent storm.

The complex history of Derry – from its geological origins through the Celts and St Columcille's arrival to why the city walls were built and the origins of the Troubles – will be traced alongside the Armada exhibition in a new and improved form, they say, from May 2006. The square outside the museum has been 'improved' as well.

Workhouse Museum

23 Glendermott Rd, **t** (028) 7131 8328
Open Jan–June and Sept–Dec Mon–Thurs and Sat 10–4.30; July and Aug Mon–Sat 10–4.30
Adm Free

Teach your children about what happened to people who fell on hard times in the past by showing them this museum's famine and workhouse displays. Upstairs is the original workhouse dormitory, much as it was for the poor souls who were sent there. In another room is the Atlantic Memorial Exhibition, which shows the importance of Derry and the River Foyle during World War II.

Entertainment

Comhaltas Ceoltóiri Éireann

15 Crawford Sq, **t** (028) 7128 6359

Irish music, dance and storytelling evenings.

The Playhouse

5–7 Artillery St, **t** (028) 7126 8027, **www.derryplayhouse.co.uk**

A theatre, dance and visual arts centre.

The Verbal Arts Centre

Stable Lane and Mall Wall, **t** (028) 7126 6946, **www.verbalartscentre.co.uk**

A venue about storytelling and Ireland's oral arts that encourages visitor involvement.

SPECIAL TRIPS

The Forge

Castledawson, **t** (028) 7946 8310
Getting there 2 miles (3km) north of Magherafelt
Open Visitors welcome at any time; call in advance
Adm Free but gifts appreciated

Seamus Heaney's poem 'The Forge' was about this blacksmith's cottage, which its owner Barney Devlin can tell you all about, since he's related to Heaney's wife. Barney will tell you how people preferred to wash in cold water because they thought hot water would destroy the skin, or how putting your hand in the blacksmith's water (used for cooling hot metals) cures warts. If he likes you, he might give you some of his ironwork.

Springhill House

20 Springhill Rd, Moneymore, **t** (028) 8674 8210, **www.nationaltrust.org.uk**
Getting there 1 mile (1.6km) east of Moneymore
Open 12 noon–6 mid-Mar–June Sat, Sun and bank hols, July and Aug daily, Sept Sat and Sun; last adm 5
Adm Adult £4.10, child £2.20, family £10.40
Guided tours, tea room, caravan park

This charming 17th-century house was built for the Lennox-Conynghams, a Plantation family.

*What was...*The Siege of Derry

Derry's walls have weathered a few sieges, but the best known is the Siege of Derry of 1688–9, which lasted 105 days. After Catholic King James II had lost the throne of England to the Protestant William of Orange in 1688 (*see* p.35), he fled to Ireland and raised an army among his Catholic supporters, known as Jacobites. In Londonderry, when James's soldiers were about to enter and conquer the city, a group of apprentice boys – lowly trainee workers sent mostly from London to join the Protestant Plantation – famously locked a gate in the city walls just in time to keep them out.

Around it are some Dutch-style outbuildings, walled gardens and lovely grounds. Its well-trained guides tell of tragedies, triumphs and the resident ghost. Also here are a display of historic clothing and a chamomile lawn that made dirty feet smell better. Events with 'living history' actors also take place.

AROUND AND ABOUT

Look at this!

Amelia Earhart Centre

Ballyarnet Country Park, **t** (028) 7135 4040
Getting there Just outside Derry City
Open By advance booking
Adm Free

This exhibition commemorates Amelia Earhart's historic flight across the Atlantic and her unexpected landing in Derry on 21 May 1932. Earhart was the first woman to fly across the Atlantic solo. Mistaking Derry for Paris, she began speaking French on arrival, which amused the locals no end.

Nature lovers

Palace of Downhill and Mussenden Temple

Castlerock, **t** (028) 7084 8728, **www.nationaltrust.org.uk**
Getting there 5 miles (8km) west of Coleraine, 1 mile (1.6km) west of Castlerock
Open Palace and Temple: mid-Mar–May Sat, Sun and bank hols 11–6, June and Sept daily 1–6, July and Aug daily 11–7.30, Oct Sat and Sun 11–5
Glen and grounds: all year
Adm Car park at Lion's Gate: £3.70

The 18th-century estate of Downhill is set on a stunning wild headland with fabulous views over the Inishowen Hills and the Antrim and Derry coasts. Superb for walks is the area around the ruined 'palace' (called Downhill Castle), built with a temple and mausoleum in the 18th century by the famous Earl of Bristol and Bishop of Derry, Frederick Augustus Hervey (1730–1803).

Buckets and spades – Derry's beaches

A multiple recipient of European Blue Flag awards, **Benone Beach** on Lough Foyle near Limavady offers 7 miles (11km) of golden sand with a dramatic scenery of mountains, cliffs and views of Co. Donegal, and many leisure and sports facilities.

Between Portstewart and the mouth of the River Bann lies the 2-mile (3km) **Portstewart Strand**, which is now a sand dune reserve as well as a tourist beach. On the west side of Portstewart is **Downhill Strand**, which is popular for surf fishing, and there's a fine beach and sandhills at **Castlerock**.

Sporty kids

Horse-riding

Hill Farm

Castlerock, **t** (028) 7084 8629

Rides for children aged 4 and up.

Fishing

You'll find good coarse fishing on the Bann. Fishing for brown trout and salmon is available on the Agivey, Clady, Roe, Bann and Faughan rivers.

Loughs Agency, 8 Victoria Rd, Derry City, **t** (028) 7134 2100

A firm providing game-rod licences.

Walking

The **Sperrins Sky Way**, a 20-mile (32km) route, starts at Barony Bridge near Draperstown and runs along the Sperrin Ridge, finishing at Eden, to the east of Plumbridge, in Co. Tyrone. To the north, the **Ulster Way** runs towards the **Banagher Glen**, with fine walks and panoramic views.

Not far to the south of Derry City is the **Ness Wood Country Park**, which is the site of Ulster's highest waterfall, and near Limavady is the **Roe Valley Country Park**, where you will find a lovely riverside walk through sites that are associated with St Columcille.

COUNTY TYRONE

Dominated in much of the north of the county by the lofty, little-populated Sperrin Mountains, Tyrone is the heart of Ulster. It's one of Ireland's lesser-known counties, but it holds one of Northern Ireland's most impressive attractions: the Ulster American Folk Park, which is worth the trip on its own.

A kind of folk memory exists in Tyrone that encourages annual traditional walks, such as the one held on Cairn Sunday, the last Sunday in July, at Mullaghcarn (or *Mullach an Chairn*, 'the summit of the heap of stones') near Gortin Glen north of Omagh. It probably dates back to pagan times and the worship of the god Lugh, when people walked to the tops of hills on *Lúghnasa* for religious rituals, sports, bilberry picking, picnics, singing and dancing. On Mullaghcarn, this practice was phased out by disapproving Victorians and discontinued during the Great Famine, but today the custom is being revived as a way of restoring the Cairn. Walkers leave a stone when they reach the summit, as they have done intermittently for 1,000 years.

Omagh is Tyrone's capital, but it might be more enjoyable for families to base themselves in Strabane, where the novelist Brian O'Nolan (alias Flann O'Brien, author of *At Swim-Two-Birds*) was born, or in the hills and forests outside the town. Astride the River Strule, it is best known as a centre for exploring the Sperrin Mountains, which lie to the north and northeast. Omagh is ringed by beautiful, dense woodlands: Seskinore Forest, close to Fintona, Dromore Forest, further west, and Gortin Glen.

The Omagh bombing in August 1998, which killed 28 people and injured a further 200, was the worst single atrocity of the Troubles. It so shocked the community in Northern Ireland – and around the world – that it is said by many to have brought the effective end of large-scale terrorist activity here.

Tourist information

Cookstown: Durn Rd, **t** (028) 8676 6727
Cranagh: Sperrin Heritage Centre, 274 Glenelly Rd, Plumbridge, **t** (028) 8164 8142
Dungannon: Killymaddy Tourist Information Centre, 190 Ballygawley Rd, **t** (028) 8776 7259
Omagh: 1 Market St, **t** (028) 8224 7831
Sperrins: The Manor House, 30 High St, Moneymore, **t** (028) 8674 7700, **www.sperrinstourism.com**
Strabane: Abercorn Sq, **t** (028) 7188 3735

Getting there and around

There is no rail line in Tyrone, so buses are the only means of public transport.

By bus Ulsterbus has good services to all parts of the county, and Bus Éireann coaches link Co. Tyrone to many destinations in the Republic. Ulsterbus information, **t** (028) 9066 6630, **www.translink.co.uk**; Omagh bus station, **t** (028) 8224 2711; Strabane bus station, **t** (028) 7138 2393

Special Events – County Tyrone

March

St Patrick's Day, 17 March
Parades and celebrations are held around the county.

Mid-Ulster Drama Festival, Omagh, **t** (028) 8224 0537
Locally produced plays.

Strabane Drama Festival, **t** (028) 7138 3111
Another local theatre festival.

June

Fair Day Carnival, Strabane, **t** (028) 7138 2204
Street entertainment in vintage Strabane, for the whole community.

The Strawberry Fair, Sion Mills, Strabane, **t** (028) 8165 8350
A traditional village fête with music, dancing and lots of entertainments for children.

June

Ulster American Folk Park Festival, Ulster American Folk Park, **t** (028) 8225 6330 (*see* p.226)
Historical reenactments in costume, music and informal storytelling usually occur.

August–September

Glenelly Sheep and Dog Trials, Plumbridge, Strabane, **t** (028) 8164 8744
A fun event for dog-loving kids.

Johnny Crampsie Weekend, Strabane, **t** (028) 7188 2041, **www.johnnycrampsie.com**
Traditional Irish music and workshops, with musicians of all ages.

Storytelling Festival, Rural College, Draperstown, **t** (028) 7962 9100
An event that is always of interest to children who like stories.

SPECIAL TRIPS

Gray's Printing Press

49 Main St, Strabane, t (028) 7188 0055, www.strabanedc.com
Open Apr, May and Sept Sat 2–5, June Tues–Sat 2–5, July and Aug Tues–Sat 11–5; closed public hols; last admission 45mins before closing
Adm Free. Tour of press: adult £2.70, child £1.60, family £7
Disabled access

This National Trust Georgian property, used as a printing press in the 18th century, contains an audio-visual exhibition telling of how this 'publishing capital' on the borders of counties Donegal, Londonderry and Tyrone influenced the world. John Dunlop, the printer of the United States' Declaration of Independence and first daily newspaper, worked here as an apprentice. By the time he died in 1812, he owned 98,000 acres in Virginia, several pieces of land in Kentucky and a large part of central Philadelphia, Pennsylvania. You can also see several 19th-century hand-printing presses. It's best to time your visit to coincide with a costumed interpretation to learn how the press functioned (call for a schedule).

The adjoining Strabane council museum has displays on the local railway and canal.

The Ulster American Folk Park

2 Mellon Rd, Castletown, near Omagh, t (028) 8224 3292, www.folkpark.com
Getting there Off A5 4 1/2 miles (6km) N of Omagh
Open Easter–Sept Mon–Sat 10.30–4.30 (last adm), Sun and bank hols 11–5 (last adm); Oct–Mar Mon–Fri 10.30–5 (last adm), closed bank hols
Adm Adult £4.50, 5–16s £2.50, under-5s free, family (2+4) £11
Restaurant, special events, picnic areas, craft and gift shops, disabled access, parking

Did you know...?
The parents of American frontiersman Davy Crockett were from the area of Castlederg, Co. Tyrone. See opposite.

This wonderful museum depicts the life that 18th- and 19th-century emigrants left behind in Ulster, and the New World they found in America. Period-costumed guides encourage children to take part in what once were ordinary activities: spinning, open-hearth cooking, traditional corn craftwork and feeding the ducks at Mellon House.

Visit the indoor museum first for an introduction. It describes emigrants' reasons for leaving home for a new land and what they encountered there. In the 18th century, many Ulster Protestants left for America, where they became known as the 'Scots Irish'. It tells how some rose to fame and fortune, while others sank into penury. Children find the life-sized dioramas fascinating, as well as the Conestoga covered wagon, black bear, wooden dancing dolls, hobby horses and traditional games.

Afterwards explore the 18th-century Ulster farming village, where you can see, smell, touch and taste the past – the smell of soda bread cooking over a turf fire (the 'living history' guide may even hand out warm bread with home-churned butter), the sound of a hammer on metal or the whirr of the spinning wheel in a weaver's cottage. On a special-event day, children may hear someone playing music in a cottage. There might also be storytelling beside a cottage fire or by a teacher in the Castletown National School, where the kinds of slates and slate pencils that were used in 1845 may be seen, along with old maps and traditional games like skittles and hoop-a-stick.

Leaving rural Ulster, turn left towards Shipbouy Street and wander through the shops with their original signs and interiors. Then go to the dockside gallery and board the emigrant ship *Brig Union*, bound for the New World. The sounds of the creaking timbers provide a small insight into the conditions experienced by thousands of emigrants on an ocean crossing that took up to 12 weeks.

After 'arriving' (on the other side of the ship) at an American port resembling that of Boston or Baltimore, you can wander through a 19th-century American street. Notice the heady scents of cinnamon and coffee in the air. Imagine the sense of unreality that these people experienced after surviving their horrific sea journey.

As you leave the 'city', with its flea- and rat-infested flophouses where the poorest of the poor spent cold winter nights, you move 'west' and encounter a log cabin and other dwellings typical of those built by emigrants on the American frontier.

After a long walk through so much history (wear comfortable shoes and take raincoats), you may well want a snack in the museum restaurant.

An easy two-day lesson about Ireland's entire social history once could have been enjoyed by combining visits to this and the **Ulster History Park**, which is currently closed. Its accurate reconstructions of the kinds of dwellings built in Ireland from 8000 BC to the start of the 18th century still sit in vast grounds near Gortin Park, and have been bought by new owners, so perhaps the attraction will reopen in the not-too-distant future.

AROUND AND ABOUT

Animal magic

Barrontop Funfarm

35 Barron Rd, Dunnamanagh/Donemana, Strabane, **t** (028) 7139 8649
Getting there 8 miles (13km) N of Strabane on B49
Open Apr–June Mon–Fri 9.30–2, Sun 2–5; Easter hols, July and Aug Mon–Sat 9.30–5, Sun 2–5; 23 Nov–23 Dec Mon–Thurs 10–2.30, Fri and Sat 10–8, Sun 2–6. **Adm** £3
Bouncy castle, adventure playground, gift shop, tea room, disabled facilities

Young children will have fun here, bottle-feeding a lamb or cuddling calves, chicks, rabbits and puppies. Exotic breeds such as emus, pot-bellied pigs and ostriches may be seen alongside deer as children are taken around on a horse-drawn cart. Afterwards they can explore a playground and try an indoor bouncy castle. In December it has a nativity scene and Santa Claus visits the farm.

Bricks and mortar

Beaghmore Stone Circles

North of Dunnamore, near Cookstown
Getting there 10 miles (16km) west of Cookstown, signposted off A505

Seven impressive Bronze Age stone circles and cairns have been excavated from the bogland at this site.

Castlederg Visitor Centre

26 Lower Strabane Rd, Castlederg, **t** (028) 8167 0795 or **t** (028) 7138 2204, **www.strabaneedc.com**
Getting there 9 miles (14.5km) south of Strabane
Open Easter–Oct Tues–Fri 11–4, Sat 11.30–4, Sun 2–5
Adm Journey in Time exhibition: adult £1.50, concessions £1, family £4

Find out more about locals Joe Sheridan, creator of Irish coffee, and frontiersman Davy Crockett at this centre near Castlederg Castle on the River Derg, site of fierce battles between the native Irish and Plantation settlers, as well as the O'Neill and O'Donnell high kings before that. Crockett, famous for dying at Texas' battle with the Spanish general Santa Anna at the Alamo Spanish mission (of which there's a model here), was born in the townland of Ballyeglish in Cookstown District.

Grant Ancestral Home

Dergina, Ballygawley, **t** (028) 8555 7133
Getting there 13 miles (20km) west of Dungannon
Open Tour and video by appointment only
Adm Adult £1.50, child £0.75

Here you can see a video and exhibition on the American Civil War and Ulysses S Grant, the Union General and later the 18th president of the USA. His great-grandfather, John Simpson, was born here in 1738. Also here are agricultural implements, a butterfly garden and a wildlife pond.

Wilson Ancestral Homestead

Plumbridge Rd, Dergalt, **t** (028) 7138 2204
Getting there 2 miles (3km) southeast of Strabane on B536
Open July and Aug Tues–Sun 2–5. **Adm** Free

US president Woodrow Wilson was another distinguished American of 'Scots Irish' stock. His grandfather was reared in this humble abode before setting off to become a newspaper editor in the USA.

Look at this!

Wellbrook Beetling Mill

20 Wellbrook Rd, Corkhill, Cookstown, **t** (028) 8674 8210, **www.nationaltrust.org.uk**
Getting there Minor road through Dunnamore
Open mid-Mar–June Sat, Sun and bank hols 1–6; July and Aug daily 1–6; Sept and early Oct Sat, Sun and bank hols 1–5

Adm Adult £3, child £1.70, family £7.70
Shop, walk, guided tour

This water-powered 18th-century hammer mill was an important centre for beetling, the final process used in manufacturing linen. Try scutching, hackling, weaving and beetling by hand and on the old machines, then walk in the lovely surrounding glen.

Nature lovers

An Creagán Visitor Centre

Creggan, Omagh, **t** (028) 8076 1112, **www.an-creagan.com**
Getting there 12 miles (19km) east of Omagh off A505
Open Daily Apr–Sept 11–6.30, Oct–Mar 11–4.30
Adm Free

An introduction to the history of the Sperrins area, with bog trails and a small exhibition.

Drum Manor Forest Park

By the A505, near Cookstown, **t** (028) 8676 2774
Getting there 3 miles (5km) west of Cookstown
Open Daily 8am–dusk
Adm Car: £3. Pedestrians: adult £1, child £0.50

This contains a walled butterfly garden, arboretum, forest trail for the disabled and heronry.

Gortin Glen Forest Park

t (028) 8167 0666
Getting there 7 miles (11km) north of Omagh, on B48
Open Daily 10–dusk
Adm Car £2.50. Pedestrians: adult £1, child £0.50

Nature trails pass through 5 miles (8km) of conifer woods here, as does the Ulster Way.

The Sperrins Heritage Centre

274 Glenelly Rd, Plumbridge, **t** (028) 8164 8142
Getting there 24 miles (38km) north of Omagh off B47
Open Apr–Oct Mon–Sat 11.30–6, Sun 2–7
Adm Adult £2.50, child £1.25, family £7.85; Pan hire: adult £0.65, child £0.35
Craft shop, Glenelly Kitchen café

> **Did you know...?**
> ***When left in neutral gear in a certain area near Gortin Glen, along what is called the Magnetic Mile, your car will roll uphill.***

> **Did you know...?**
> ***Poets in ancient Ireland were forbidden from taking part in physical combat, so they composed poetic curses to recite at enemies before battle.***

This centre tells of how gold was discovered in the Sperrins, and describes the making of the illicit spirit *potcheen*. Pan for gold in the iron pyrite stream after finding out about Sperrin wildlife in the exhibition. Outside, walk in the glens.

Sporty kids

Horse-riding

Crocknagrally Forest Stables

100 Cooneen Rd, Fivemiletown, **t** (028) 8952 1991

Walking

Forest parks with good walks include **Favour Royal**, just south of Caledon, **Gollagh Woods**, and **Fardross Forest** near Clogher, with red squirrels. The **Ulster Way** also goes through the Sperrins, and lovely riverside walks are by Wellbrook Mill (*see* p.227). Contact Omagh and Strabane tourist offices or The Sperrins Heritage Centre (*see* left) about walking in the Sperrins. One of the best walks that's easy to get to is the **Gortin Loop** path.

Steam power!

Peatlands Park

The Birches, Dungannon, **t** (028) 3885 1102
Getting there 7 miles (11km) east of Dungannon
Open Park: daily Easter–Sept 9–9, Oct–Easter 9–5
Visitor centre: Easter–May and Sept Sat, Sun and bank hols 1–6, June–Aug daily 9–5
Railway: times vary; call ahead
Adm Railway: adult £1, child £1.50, under-3s free

A circular railway with open-top carriages pulled by a modern diesel engine moves through woods and peat bog on a narrow-gauge track near Lough Neagh, once used to carry turf from the bog. In the middle of the bog, you can wander along an unusual boardwalk with a hide that allows you to peer at its flora without endangering it.

COUNTY FERMANAGH

Fermanagh (*Firmanach*) means 'men of Manach'. It is thought a man named Manach, or Monach, a member of the family of a High King, settled beside Lough Erne around the 3rd century AD. Later the Maguire clan took control of the area and fought off potential usurpers for centuries, until losing Fermanagh in the 17th century to the British.

A wonderland of woods and lakes, Fermanagh holds a serenity and intense peace at its heart, which the visitor occasionally senses in ancient settlements around and on the two Lough Ernes. One-third of the county is underwater, and is divided by the Lough Erne Waterway, which is linked by canals and locks to the Shannon, forming Europe's largest navigable inland waterway network: the Shannon–Erne Waterway.

Ancient carvings and stone heads can be seen on Devenish and White islands on Lough Erne. Children who enjoy boat trips and maybe fishing will find Fermanagh magical, as will those who like folk tales, long walks in woods and making things. Craftspeople will be drawn to this county's old pottery and crystal-making traditions. Other sights not to be missed are Castle Coole, Florence Court Park and Marble Arch Caves, where you can float beneath stalactites on a boat.

Tourist information

Enniskillen: Fermanagh Tourist Information Centre, Wellington Rd, **t** (028) 6632 3110, **www.fermanaghlakelands.com**

Tours

Erne Heritage Tours, Commons, Belleek, **t** (028) 6865 8327, **www.erneheritagetours.com**

Qualified guides offering general and specific tours, town tours and site visits in Fermanagh, Donegal, Cavan, Monaghan and Tyrone.

Heritage Tours of Fermanagh, t (028) 6862 1430

Blue Badge Guide and broadcaster Breege McCusker leads fine tours through county history.

Getting there and around

By air Enniskillen has a small airport, at Trory, 4 miles (6km) north of town. At present the airport does not have scheduled international flights, but facilities for visiting pilots and their aircraft are excellent. Enniskillen Airport, t (028) 6632 9000.

By bus There are at least 6 Ulsterbus expresses a day between Belfast and Enniskillen, and good services around the county. Bus Eireann runs to Sligo and several other towns in the Republic. Enniskillen Bus Station, Wellington Rd, t (028) 6632 2633.

Special Events – County Fermanagh

There are lots of tiny festivals and sporting events thoughout the summer. Ask at the tourist office.

March

Enniskillen Drama Festival, t (028) 6634 3233

Community fare for theatre-mad youngsters.

May

Florence Court Country Fair, t (028) 6634 8249

A family fun day with pet and rare breed shows, crafts and more.

June

Fiddlestone Festival, Belleek, **t** (028) 6865 8201

A traditional festival with great music.

Lisnaskea Feis, t (028) 6772 1610

A fun, friendly town festival.

Summer Drama Season, Ardhowen Theatre, Enniskillen, **t** (028) 6632 3233

Imaginative fare for theatre-lovers.

July

Lady of the Lake Festival, Irvinestown, **t** (028) 6862 1656, **www.ladyofthelakefestival.com**

A varied and lively arts programme in honour of a mystical figure sometimes seen making her way among the islands of Lower Lough Erne, carrying wildflowers and clad in a gown filled with light.

August

Enniskillen Agricultural Show, t (028) 6632 2509

An event for outdoor types and animal-lovers.

Kesh Carnival, t (028) 6863 2158

A community festival.

By Bike

A waymarked trail stretches 230 miles (368km) through Fermanagh, Leitrim, Cavan, Donegal and Monaghan. Enniskillen Tourist Office has details: ask for the *Hiking and Biking Guide to the Waters and the Wild* or see www.cycletoursireland.com.

Kingfisher Cycle Trail Tour, t (07198) 56898, **www.cycletoursireland.com**

A 30–40-mile (48–64km) ride from Belleek, over Boa Island to Kesh, down through Irvinestown to Enniskillen and over to Florence Court.

Did you know...?

Fermanagh people believe that if you see the Lady of the Lake floating in the air above Lower Lough Erne in May, good times are ahead.

ENNISKILLEN

Enniskillen (*Inis Ceaithleann*) means 'the island of Kathleen'. It is said to be named after the legendary wife of Balor, who fled here from battle. Enniskillen Castle was the medieval seat of the Maguires, high kings of Fermanagh, who policed the lough with a private navy of 1,500 boats.

Chosen as the area's main town during the 17th-century Ulster Plantation (*see* p.34), it played a major role in wars and rebellions in 1641 and 1689. Later on, it was where Samuel Beckett and Oscar Wilde went to school (at Portora Royal School). Today about 14,000 people live here. Its Buttermarket is an attractive craft centre, and you may want to visit Mrs O'Malley's for hand-made chocolates and traditional sweets or try some Morelli's ice cream before leaving to explore the countryside.

Things to see and do

Enniskillen Castle and Museums

Castle Barracks, **t** (028) 6632 5000, **www.enniskillencastle.co.uk**
Open May–Sept Mon 2–5, Tues–Fri 10–5, Sat 2–5, July and Aug Mon 2–5, Tues–Fri 10–5, Sun 2–5, Oct–Apr Mon 2–5, Tues–Fri 10–5; all bank hols 10–5
Adm Adult £2.50, child £1.50, under-5s free, family (2+3) £6.50
Gift- and bookshop, children's activity corner, full disabled access in heritage centre, partial in castle

Enniskillen Castle houses exhibitions in its keep and also Fermanagh County Museum. Together they offer a good overview of the county's history from prehistoric times to the world wars and into the 1950s. Be sure to see the audio-visual display on the Maguires, the Gaelic clan that built the castle on the River Erne in the 15th century and ruled Fermanagh until the 1600s. Soldiers' uniforms, medals and memorabilia span the history of the famous Inniskilling regiments in the British army since their formation in 1689.

Enniskillen Craft and Design Centre (The Buttermarket)

Down St, **t** (028) 6632 4499, **www.thebuttermarket.com**
Open Mon–Sat 9.30–5.30

Watch traditional crafts being made by local craftspeople, designers and artists here, and pick up lace, knitwear and Belleek china as souvenirs.

SPECIAL TRIPS

Belleek Pottery Factory

Belleek, **t** (028) 6865 9300, **www.belleek.ie**
Getting there 25 miles (40km) north of Enniskillen
Open Mon–Fri 9–5.30 (times vary Apr–Oct); tours Mon–Thurs 9.10–4.15, Fri 9.10–3.15
Adm Adult £4, students £2, under-12s free
Guided tours (book ahead), showroom/shop, café

Potters here use the techniques Belleek has been known for since it opened in 1857. A film tells you all about this. Then tour the factory to watch potters make and delicately paint pottery baskets and flowers. The showroom has many discounted items.

Lough Erne

What Fermanagh people refer to as Lough Erne is two lakes connected by the River Erne in the middle (where Enniskillen sits). More than 150 islands fill Upper and Lower Lough Erne. Some are inhabited, such as Belle Isle, credited as the place where the *Annals of Ulster* were compiled in the 15th century. These waterways are home to a wide variety of birds.

Boa Island

Along the north side of Lower Lough Erne, this 'island' is accessible by road, between Kesh and Belleek, 16 miles (26km) north of Enniskillen. Here is the famous Janus Stone, in Caldragh Cemetery (signposted beside the island's road), about which Seamus Heaney wrote a poem. These stone figures are thought to be Celtic in origin, but their shape and style seem closer to the prehistoric inhabitants of Ireland than its modern ones, with two different faces and a hole in the top of the head that collects water. Close at hand is the 'Lusty Man', a smaller figure brought here from nearby Lustymore Island.

Can you spot...

The white limestone outline of a horse that shows through the scree at the foot of the eastern cliff of the steep mountain of Benaughlin ('peak of the horse') above Florence Court?

Benaughlin is said to be the dwelling place of a Tuatha faery called Donn Binn, who had a talking horse. At some point the horse was engraved on the side of the hill.

Devenish Island

Open Museum: Apr–Sept Tues–Sat 10–6, Sun 2–6
Adm Museum and ferry: adult £2.25, child £1.20

This island in the Lower Lough has extensive ruins, including a 12th-century round tower, abbey and St Molaise's House. The island was one of Ireland's most important monasteries.

White Island

Open Apr–June Sat and Sun 10–1 and 2–6, July and Aug daily 10–6
Adm Adult £3, child £2

On White Island, 3 miles (5km) to the south of Kesh, there are the ruins of a 12th-century church, with some impressive stone figures dating from the 6th century.

Marble Arch Caves European Geopark

Blacklion Rd, Marlbank, **t** (028) 6634 8855
Getting there On the 'Marlbank Scenic Loop', 8 miles (13km) north of Florence Court
Open Mar–Sept daily 10–5 (but advance booking essential)
Adm Adult £7, child £4, family £18
Disabled access, shop, restaurant, parking area

Here you can take an exciting 75min boat journey through an underground wonderland of cave formations and lofty chambers with rivers and waterfalls. Wear a sweater and good shoes. There are 120 steps at one point, so it isn't suitable for toddlers. The caves may be closed in heavy rain.

AROUND AND ABOUT

Bricks and mortar

Castle Coole

t (028) 6632 2690, **www.ntni.org.uk**
Getting there 1/2 mile (0.8km) south of Enniskillen
Open House: Mar–May and Sept Sat, Sun and bank hols 12 noon–6; June Mon–Weds and Fri 1–6, Sat and Sun 12 noon–6; July and Aug daily 12 noon–6
Estate: daily May–Sept 10–8, Oct–Apr 10–4
Adm Adult £4.20, child £2.10, family £10.50

Getting around Lough Erne

Devenish Island

The main ferry, **t** (028) 6862 1588, embarks at Trory Point (Easter–Sept daily at 10, 1, 3 and 5)

White Island

Ferries run from Castle Archdale, June–Sept, **t** (028) 6862 1333

Cruiser Hire

To explore these islands via one of the least congested waterways in Europe, rent a cruiser by the day or week. Prices range from around £400 a week for a 4-berth cruiser in low season to £1,600 for an 8-berth in high season. Free lessons on how to handle boats are provided for novices.

Carrick Craft, Castle Island, Enniskillen, **t** (028) 3834 4993. One-way boat rental between the Erne and the Shannon.

Lakeland Canoe Centre, Blaney, Enniskillen, **t** (028) 6632 4250. Canoeing, rowing, sailing and mountain biking, plus a campsite.

Tour Boats

MV Kestrel, Round 'O' Quay, Enniskillen, **t** (028) 6632 2882. This 56-seat waterbus departs from Enniskillen Easter–Sept on 90min to 3- or 4-hr tours of Lough Erne, with a stop at Devenish Island's monastic site. Sat dinner cruises to/from the Killyhevlin Hotel are available (May–Aug).

Lady of the Lake Tours, Inishclare Restaurant, Killadeas, **t** (028) 6832 2200. A 60-seat luxury tour boat hosting 2hr cruises on Lower Lough Erne, with full bar and catering facilities.

The Inish Cruiser, Share Centre, Lisnaskea, **t** (028) 6772 2122. A 57-seat luxury boat cruising around Upper Lough Erne Easter–Sept, with a fully licensed bar.

Canoe Trail

Northern Ireland's first canoe trail stretches for 31 miles (50km) between Lower and Upper Lough Erne within beautiful unspoilt scenery. Call **t** (028) 9030 3930 or see **www.niccanoeing.com**

Water sports

Drumrush Watersports Centre, Drumrush Lodge, Boa Island Rd, Kesh, **t** (028) 6863 1578
Water-skiing, jet-skiing, paddle boating, canoeing, sailing and other activities on the lake. The centre also has a 10-bed guesthouse, a restaurant, a tennis court, and a caravan and campsite.

Guided tours, disabled access to ground floor and visitor centre, gift shop, tea room, car/coach park

This very grand and beautiful neoclassical house, built in 1790–97, retains its 18th-century furniture and magnificent woodwork, fireplaces and library. There are family days in the school holidays, and baby-slings are available.

Florence Court

Near Enniskillen, **t** (028) 6634 8249, **www.**ntni.org.uk
Getting there 8 miles (13km) south of Enniskillen
Open House: Mar–May and Sept Sat and Sun 12 noon–6, June Mon and Weds–Fri 1–6, Sat and Sun 12 noon–6; July and Aug daily 12 noon–6
Grounds: daily Apr–Sept 10–8, Oct–Mar 10–4; last tour 1hr before closing
Adm Adult £4, child £2, family £10
Restaurant, tea room, gift shop, children's play area

This impressive 18th-century house belonging to the earls of Enniskillen, built for Lord Mountflorence, has fine rococo plasterwork and is set in woodland with views of the Cuilcagh Mountains. Free guided tours of the Forest Park are available (book ahead).

Tully Castle

Blaney, **t** (028) 9023 5000
Getting there 9 miles (14km) north of Enniskillen
Open Apr–Sept Tues–Sat 10–6, Sun 2–6
Adm Adult £1, child £0.50
Formal garden, visitor centre

Although it was the site of a bloody massacre by the Maguires in the 1640s, the ruins of this fortified house and bawn, built in 1613, are nearly intact.

Look at this!

Belle Isle School of Cookery

Lisbellaw, **t** (028) 6638 6123, **www.irishcookeryschool.com**

Over 8s can take 1- or 2-day cookery courses with an accompanying adult in this new building. Accommodation on-site is available.

Drumskinney Stone Circle

Getting there 4 1/2 miles (7km) north of Kesh

One of the best stone circles in Northern Ireland.

The Sheelin Antique Irish Lace Museum

Bellanaleck, **t** (028) 6634 8052, **www.irishlacemuseum.com**
Open Mar–May and Sept Sat and Sun 12 noon–6, June Mon–Weds and Fri 1–6, Sat and Sun 12 noon–6, July and Aug daily 12–6. **Adm** Adult £2.50, child £1.50

An award-winning museum of antique lace.

Nature lovers

Castle Archdale Country Park

Irvinestown, **t** (028) 6638 6938
Getting there 3 miles (5km) south of Kesh
Open Park: daily 9am–dusk; Museum and Visitor Centre: Easter–May bank hol Sun 12 noon–4, May bank hol–June Sun 11–6, July and Aug Tues–Sun 11–6. **Adm** Free
Tea room, pony trekking, ferry to White Island

Beautiful woodlands with a butterfly garden and more. Camp, fish or sail to Lough Erne's islands.

Crom Estate

Newtownbutler, **t** (028) 6773 8118, **www.ntni.org.uk**
Getting there 17 miles (27km) south of Enniskillen
Open Mar and Apr Sat, Sun and bank hols 10–6, May–Sept daily 10–6, Oct Sat and Sun 12 noon–6
Visitor centre: mid-Mar–mid-Apr Sat, Sun and bank hols 10–6, May–Sept daily 10–6
Adm Grounds and visitor centre: car or boat £4.70

A thousand acres of wood-, park- and wetland.

Macnean Organic Garden

Garrison Rd, Belcoo, **t** (028) 6634 1308
Open Easter–Sept Weds–Sun 10–2
Adm Adult £2.50, child £1

See how organic flowers, fruit and veg are grown.

Sporty kids

Activity centres

Corralea Activity Centre

Belcoo, **t** (028) 6638 6123

Canoeing, caving, windsurfing and more.

Share Holiday Village

Lisnaskea, **t** (028) 6772 2122, **www.sharevillage.org**

Banana skiing, dinghy sailing and more.

Horse-riding

The Forest Stables

100 Cooneen Rd, Fivemiletown, **t** (028) 8952 1991

CAVAN AND MONAGHAN

These low-key counties are the southernmost ones of Ulster, but since most of their people were Catholic rather than Ulster Protestants, they chose to remain part of the Republic when Ireland was partitioned in 1921. Little visited, they nonetheless have great charm. If you enjoy riding or want to learn about Carrickmacross lace, Monaghan may be your preferred stop. But if you want to fish in pristine lakes amid clean air and lush woodlands with manicured villages, or to learn Irish stone-building or mohair teddy bear making crafts, you will love unpolluted Cavan, which is perfect for families who prefer outdoor activities to sightseeing.

Pleasant undulating landscape surrounds Cavan town, and it is convenient for Ireland's lake district, although Belturbet is better placed if you want to spend a lot of time across the border on Lough Erne. Monaghan town is handier if you want to pop across to Belfast and the core of Northern Ireland.

Tourist information

Cavan: Farnham St, Cavan, **t** (049) 433 1942, **www.cavantourism.com**
Monaghan: Castle Meadow Court, Monaghan, **t** (047) 81122, **www.monaghantourism.com**

Getting there and around

By bus Bus Éireann runs to Cavan and Monaghan from Dublin, Belfast and other towns.

Local services include: Cavan Bus Depot, **t** (049) 433 1353; Monaghan Bus Station, **t** (047) 82377.

Bike Hire
Fitzpatrick Cycles, Castle Hill, Belturbet, Co. Cavan, **t** (049) 952 2866
McQuaid Cycle Hire, Glaslough, Co. Monaghan, **t** (047) 88108
On Yer Bike Tours, Abbeyset Buildings, Farnham St, Cavan, **t** (049) 31932

AROUND AND ABOUT

Look at this!

Ballyhugh Art and Culture Centre

Ballyconnell, Co. Cavan, t (049) 952 6044
Music evenings, *ceilis* and crafts courses.

Belturbet Railway Station

Belturbet, Co. Cavan, **t** (049) 952 2074
Getting there 10 miles (16km) north of Cavan
Open Visitor centre: daily 9.30–5
Adm Adult €2.50, student €1.90, under-12s €1.27
A restored station with a display on rural lines.

Special Events – Cavan and Monaghan

May

County Cavan Fleadh Ceoil, Ballinagh, Co. Cavan.
A traditional music festival held county-wide.

June

Carrickmacross Festival, Co. Monaghan, **t** (042) 966 1236, **www.carrickmacross.ie/festival**
Music, dancing, kids' shows, an arts and crafts fair, a carnival, a vintage parade and tug-of-war.

Cassandra Hand Summer School of Clones Lace, Clones, Co. Monaghan, **t** (047) 51729
Make lace in the traditional Clones manner.

Cathal Bui Weekend, Blacklion, Co. Cavan and Belcoo, Co. Fermanagh, **www.cathalbui.com**
A family festival.

Festival of the Lakes, Killeshandra, Co. Cavan, **t** (049) 433 4990
Music, dance, drama, kids' entertainment, racing.

Virginia Street Fair and Vintage Display, Virginia, Co. Cavan, **t** (049) 854 8299
Vintage cars, machinery and music in a lovely spot.

July

Belturbet Festival of the Erne, Belturbet, Co. Cavan, **t** (049) 952 2178/2239
A large family-oriented festival with watersports, music and heritage, held late July–early Aug.

Heritage Among the Drumlins, Maudabawn, Cootehill, Co. Cavan, **t** (049) 555 9504
A 1wk course on local heritage, natural and human.

Muckno Mania, Castleblayney, Co. Monaghan, **t** (042) 974 6087
An arts and music festival.

Raglan Road Festival, Iniskeen, Co. Monaghan, **t** (042) 937 8560
A 3-day music, poetry, theatre and song festival commemorating Monaghan's 20th-century poet–novelist Patrick Kavanagh in his hometown.

October

Cootehill Arts Festival, Cootehill, Co. Cavan, **t** (049) 555 2241
Music, arts and crafts, drama performances and literary events for crafts/arts-oriented families.

Carraig Craft Visitor Centre and Basketry Museum

Outside Mountnugent, Co. Cavan, **t** (049) 854 0179
Open Apr–Oct Mon–Fri 10–6, Sun 2–6; Nov–Mar by request
Adm Adult €3.50, children 7 and up/student €2.50, under-7s free
Demonstrations arranged, audio-visual, shop, café
Learn to make baskets in the traditional Irish way.

Cavan County Museum

Virginia Rd, Ballyjamesduff, Co. Cavan, **t** (049) 31799
Open Mon–Fri 10–5, Sat and Sun 2–5
Adm Adult €3, student/child €1.50, family €8
Shop, tea room
Displays on the story of Cavan since the Stone Age.

Cavan Crystal

Dublin Rd (N3), Cavan, **t** (049) 433 1800, **www**.cavancrystaldesign.com
Getting there Just south of Cavan town
Open Mon–Fri 9.30–6, Sat 10–5, Sun 12 noon–5 (but book ahead). **Adm** Free
Factory tours
Centuries-old glass craftsmanship and other crafts.

Maudabawn Cultural Centre

Cootehill, Co. Cavan, **t** (049) 555 9504
Getting there 15 miles (24km) north of Cavan
Guided tours of Co. Cavan and Co. Monaghan, music, storytelling, and pony-and-trap rides.

Monaghan County Museum

1–2 Hill St, Monaghan, **t** (047) 82928
Open June–Sept Tues–Sat 11–1 and 2–5. **Adm** Free
A place to find out about the history of Monaghan.

Patrick Kavanagh Rural and Literary Resource Centre

Iniskeen, Co. Monaghan, **t** (042) 78560
Open Mon–Fri 11–5, Sat, Sun and bank hols 2–7
Audio-visual display, library, guided performance tour
An exhibition all about the poet–novelist.

A story to tell: Finn McCool and the Salmon of Knowledge

The druid Finegas had long prepared himself for gaining the clairvoyant powers of the Salmon of Knowledge (*see* p.29), and one day he finally caught the fish. He asked his assistant Finn McCool, then a boy, to guard it while it cooked in the pan but to be certain not to let anyone taste it – neglecting to mention that the first person to do so would acquire its powers. After faithfully watching the salmon for a while, Finn noticed it was beginning to burn, and turned it with his thumb, and before he knew it, his thumb was in his mouth.

Soon after, Finegas returned, and immediately noticed that a great change had come over Finn. He saw the whole salmon still frying in the pan and said, 'Finn, lad, have you tasted the salmon?'

'Well, sir, I turned it with my thumb because it was burning and I burned my thumb and – '

...at which point Finegas went white with rage and shouted, 'You tasted MY salmon!'

Finn immediately braced himself for blows, not knowing what he had done but well knowing the temper of his master. Finegas, however, calmed down enough to explain that Finn was now in grave danger, since he was untrained and in possession of powers he could not control.

Thereafter Finegas looked after Finn's education in the druid ways. The boy learned quickly, and so when Finn visited King Conn at the Hill of Tara (*see* p. 100), he was well prepared to take his place as leader of Ireland's best warriors, the Fianna.

Sporty kids

Activity centres

Lough Muckno Leisure Park

Castleblaney, Co. Monaghan, **t** (042) 974 6356
Activities in a 900-acre lake and forest park.

Fishing

Fisheries Boards:
Cavan, **t** (049) 854 7722
Monaghan, **t** (046) 73375

Horse-riding

Cavan Equestrian Centre, Shalom Stables, Latt, Co. Cavan, **t** (049) 433 2017
Greystones Equestrian Centre, Castle Leslie, Glaslough, Co. Monaghan, **t** (047) 88100

Walking

The **Cavan Way**, a 15-mile (24km) path from Blacklion to Dowra, goes close to the source of the Shannon. Easier walks are in **Killykeen Forest Park**, **Lough Gowna** and **Castle Lake**. The **Ulster Way** runs into Co. Monaghan near Clones.

COUNTY DONEGAL

Also part of the Republic of Ireland, Donegal (*Dún na nGall*, 'the fort of the foreigners') has a kind of lonely magic that you feel you can almost touch when you see double and even triple rainbows forming arcs across its barren mountains. You can sail from the port of Killybegs, ride horses just about everywhere, splash around on superb beaches, learn how to make tapestries and explore Ardara's woollen shops. Donegal also contains one of the last of the Gaeltacht areas of Ireland, so if you want to hear Irish spoken and you like traditional music and folklore, it's a great place to go. Nothing moves fast, apart from the summer tourist traffic.

Donegal town is the 'capital', but the main market town of northern Donegal is Letterkenny. It's a good place to stock up before seeing nearby sights.

Tourist information

Buncrana, t (074) 936 2600 (May–Sept)
Bundoran, t (071) 984 1350 (Apr–Oct)
Donegal Town, t (074) 972 1148 (all year)
Dungloe , t (074) 952 1297 (June–Sept)
Letterkenny, Blaney Rd, **t** (074) 912 1160 (all year)

Getting there and around

By air Derry Airport (*see* p.200, p.284) is the most convenient airport for most of Donegal, with good bus connections across the border. Donegal has its own airport on the coast near Crolly, but so far it only has Irish domestic flights and some charters. Donegal Airport, Carrickfinn, **t** (074) 954 8284, **www.donegalairport.ie.**

By bus Bus Eireann coaches run from Dublin and other towns to Letterkenny and Donegal Town. To get around the villages of Donegal, you need a car, or to use one of several local bus companies.

Feda O'Donnell, t (074) 954 8114 or **t** (087) 246 8226. Glasgow–Donegal and Crolly–Galway buses.

John McGinley, t (074) 913 5201. Buses between Inishowen, Letterkenny, Donegal and Dublin.

Londonderry and Lough Swilly Bus Company, Derry, **t** (028/048 from Republic) 7126 2017. Links Derry with various towns, such as Ballyshannon, Burdoran, Donegal, Killybegs and Letterkenny.

McGeehan's, t (074) 954 6150. Regular services from Donegal town to Glencolmcille, Dungloe, Ardara, Killybegs, Kilcar and Carrick.

North West Busways, t (074) 938 2619. This links Buncrana and Letterkenny.

Bike Hire

The Bike Shop, Waterloo Place, Donegal Town, **t** (074) 912 2515
Church Street Cycles, Letterkenny, **t** (074) 912 6204
Donegal Tourist Office, t (074) 972 1148 (for info)

Shopping and Crafts

Glencolmcille Woollen Mill

Malin More, **t** (074) 973 0070

You can watch traditional and contemporary knitwear being made in this shop.

Simple Simon

Anderson's Yard, The Diamond, Donegal Town, **t** (074) 972 2687

Wholefoods, organic produce and cheeses.

Special Events – Donegal

Donegal is the location for some of the most renowned events in Ireland in the world of traditional music – especially those held in Buncrana, Letterkenny and Glencolmcille.

Easter

Oideas Gael, Glencolmcille, **t** (074) 973 0248

A traditional festival of hill-walking, music, cultural holidays and so on, lasting to the end of summer.

April

Ardara Walking Festival, Ardara, **t** (074) 954 7830

Walk in this lovely part of Donegal. Book ahead.

May

The Flough, Muff, **t** (074) 938 4024

A tea room with activities such as corn fiddle, spinning, rope-twisting, crafts, singing, poetry and baking scones over an open fire.

June

Buncrana Folk Festival, Inishowen, **t** (074) 937 4933

A classic, very friendly Irish folk festival.

July

Ballyshannon Folk and Traditional Music Festival, t (071) 985 1088, **www.donegalbay.ie**

Fun for visitors and locals in South Donegal.

Buncrana Music Festival, t (087) 246 8226

Mary from Dungloe Festival, Dungloe, **t** (074) 912 1254

Puppet shows, art workshops, sports, music and dancing.

August

Féile Ghleanncholmcille, Glencolmcille, **t** (074) 973 0111

A family-oriented traditional festival with a garden fête, *ceili*, toss-the-sheaf, pet show, music and so on.

Good to know...
Getting to the islands of Donegal
Arranmore Island: There is a regular ferry from Burtonport that takes approximately 25mins; there are about 6 sailings per day, year-round, **t** (074) 952 0532.
Tory Island: A passenger ferry operates daily from Bunbeg, Meenlaragh and Portnablagh (Weds only). Contact **Donegal Coastal Cruises**, **t** (074) 953 1991 or **t** (074) 913 5061, for times of sailings, which are subject to the weather and tide.

DONEGAL TOWN

South Donegal's capital is a pleasant small town – a lively place to refuel and relax before travelling on to more remote coastal areas.

Things to see and do

Donegal Bay Waterbus Tour

Harbour Office, Donegal Pier, **t** (074) 972 3666, **www.donegalbaywaterbus.com**
Open Sailing times depend on tide
Adm Adult €12, child €6, under-5s free, family tickets on request

On this 90-min boat trip around Donegal Bay, a friendly guide is happy to talk to children about the history and tales of the area. Hear stories about Red Hugh O'Donnell as you visit his burial place, and find out about *The Annals of the Four Masters*, compiled near the Old Abbey in 1632–36. Then learn about the Famine years as you visit the embarkation point where emigrants left for North America. Look out for wildlife, seals and Magherabeg Abbey, among many other magical things.

Donegal Castle

Tyrconnell St, **t** (074) 972 2405
Open Daily May–Oct 10–5.45 (last tour 5.15)
Adm Adult €3.50, child €1.25, family €8.25

Built in 1505, this was the stronghold of the princes of Tyrconnell, the O'Donnells. The last of them was Red Hugh O'Donnell, who tried to stop the English taking over Ireland in the 1590s. Finding their rule insufferable, he fled to Europe with Co. Tyrone's Hugh O'Neill in the so-called 'Flight of the Earls' (*see* p.34). A 'planted' colonist, Sir Basil Brooke, took over the castle in 1601, adding a Jacobean house to the stone tower and turrets. It now contains historical displays and beautiful antique furniture.

SPECIAL TRIPS

An Cláchán Folk Village Museum

Glencolmcille, **t** (074) 973 0017
Open Easter–Sept Mon–Sat 10–6, Sun 12 noon–6
Adm Adult €2.75, child €2, family €9.50
Café

The late Father McDyer almost singlehandedly regenerated this community by setting up this crafts venture that gave locals a percentage of its profits. These replica 18th–20th-century houses have been attracting tourists since the 1950s.

Glebe House and Gallery

Church Hill, near Letterkenny, **t** (074) 913 7071
Open Easter, July and Aug daily 11–6.30, mid-May–June and Sept Sat–Thurs 11–6.30 (last tour 1hr before closing)
Adm Adult €2.75, child €1.25, family €7

Teenagers may find this 1828 Regency house interesting, but its beautiful wooded grounds are delightful for any age. Budding painters and designers will be intrigued by the house with its Morris textiles and art from around the world, including work by leading 20th-century artists. They were amassed by former owner Derek Hill, a bohemian British theatre designer who bought and renovated this place, then invited famous friends to visit.

Glenveagh (Glenveigh) Castle

Glenveagh Park, Church Hill, **t** (074) 913 7088
Getting there 15 miles (24km) NW of Letterkenny
Open Easter–last Mon in Oct daily 10.30–6.30 (June–Aug Sun to 7.30)
Adm Adult €2.75, child €1.25, family €7
Tea room, visitor centre with parking

Morning and afternoon teas are served in a tea room in this castle (built 1870–3), a four-storey keep with ramparts, turrets and a round tower, and, inside, the furniture of its last owner. Surrounding it by a lake are gardens, and a lovely section called the Pleasure Ground.

Grianán Ailigh (or Aileach)

Near Burt, Inishowen Peninsula
Getting there 5 miles (8km) north of Derry City

From this stone ring fort, just across the border from Derry, you look out over seven of Ireland's counties. Its name means 'Stone Temple of the Sun', so it may have been a temple where prehistoric peoples worshipped the sun goddess Gráinne (or Ainé or Anu). In Penal times, Catholics came here for secret masses. On the top of Grianán Hill, 800ft (245m) above sea level, this magnificent circular rampart of rock is thought to have been built *c.* 1700 BC. In legend it was created by the king of the Tuatha Dé Danaan, the Daghda. It was originally a central 74ft (23m) 'cashel' or circular fortification, with a series of outer earthen ramparts 17ft (5m) high and 12ft (3.5m) thick. Two inner terraces, reached by a stone staircase, are set into the circular wall.

A story to tell:
The Fomorians and the arrival of Lugh

Possibly the first people in Ireland, the Fomorians (*see* p.29) treated others very cruelly, demanding crops and even children from those who lived on the land they considered their own. They were misshapen, and some say they often had only one leg or arm. They fought wars against the Nemedians, then the Fir Bolg and finally the Tuatha Dé Danaan. Their leader in these wars was Balor of the Evil Eye, whose one eye instantly killed every living thing it looked upon. In battle, when he grew tired, the Fomorians kept his eye propped open with planks of wood.

A druid predicted that Balor's daughter Eithne would bear a son who would kill him, so Balor put her in a tower where men were forbidden to enter. But one day Cian, a son of the Tuatha's great healer Dian Cécht, disguised himself as a woman and entered the tower, then secretly married her.

Shortly afterwards Balor found out that Eithne was pregnant and slew Cian on a white stone. Eithne bore triplets, and Balor cast them into the sea to drown. But the Tuatha sea god Manannan mac Lir rescued one of them and raised him in secret. His name was Lugh (the father of Cúchulainn, *see* p.219).

When Lugh reached manhood, the Tuatha were suffering greatly at the hands of the Fomorians, so he went to the court of the Tuatha to offer his help, later killing Balor in the Second Battle of Moytura, and fulfilling the prophecy (*see* p.183).

Thus, the Tuatha Dé Danaan remained rulers of Ireland, and they banished the Fomorians to Ireland's most northerly outpost, Tory Island off Donegal. Afterwards, the Fomorians were reduced to raiding coastal areas, often drowning seafarers and fishermen off Ireland's northwestern coasts.

There's a saying that any secret whispered inside the Grianán will not remain secret. And indeed, years ago an archaeologist noticed that, despite the sounds of gusting wind, conversations within its walls could be heard outside them quite easily.

AROUND AND ABOUT

Animal magic

Deane's Open Farm and Equestrian Centre

Darney, Bruckless, **t** (074) 973 7160
Getting there 12 miles (19km) west of Donegal
Open Farm: daily Easter–Aug (call for hours)
Horse-riding: daily 10–5
Adm Farm: about €5 per person

A welcoming, relaxing place to visit with children near Donegal town and the Atlantic. You can feed and walk farm animals, take a farm tour, stroll around the forest, or pony trek along country roads.

Millbridge Farm

Gobnascale, Convoy, **t** (074) 914 7125
Getting there 14 miles (22km) south of Letterkenny, signposted off N13
Open July and Aug Tues–Sat 11–5, Sun 1.30–5, bank hols except Good Fri
Adm Adult €5, child €3
Pets' corner, playground, picnic area, tea room

A 200-acre dairy farm by the River Deele, where children can pet pigs, goats, sheep and horses. The museum has curiosities of old farm life.

Look at this!

Cairn Visitor Centre

Greencastle, **t** (074) 938 1104
Open Summer daily 11–6; music and comedy drama: July–mid-Sept Weds 7.30pm (booking essential)
Adm Adult €7, concessions €5
History tour, craft shop, tea room

The story of Ireland and the changes in its countryside from the Celts through the Vikings and the Great Famine to the recent past are told here via stories, playlets and special-effects lighting.

Colmcille Heritage Centre

Gartan, Church Hill, **t** (074) 913 7306
Getting there 10 miles (16km) north of Letterkenny
Open Mon–Fri 10.30–6.30, Sun 1–6.30
Adm Adult €2, student €1.50, child €1

Illustrated panels tell the story of St Columcille (or Columba), patriarch of Irish monasticism and the Scottish Church. Artefacts and models in period clothing of Colmcille's time are on display.

The Courthouse Visitors Centre

The Old Courthouse, Lifford, **t** (074) 914 1733
Getting there 1 mile (1.6km) west of Strabane
Open Mon–Fri 10–5, Sun 12.30–5
Adm Adult €4.50, student €3.50, child €2.50, family (2+3) €12.50

An excellent introduction to Donegal, this exhibition – in a historic courthouse – describes what happened to Ulster in the 18th century when English and Scottish people were 'planted' here. As you enter, you see a film narrated by Manus, Red Hugh O'Donnell's grandfather. He tells the story of those who held power in Lifford from the time of St Columcille to 1938, when the last court was held in this courthouse. The O'Donnells themselves built a castle at Lifford in 1527. On the building's second level, the story is carried on until the Siege of Derry, and an audio-visual drama in the courtroom shows the severe sentences meted out to criminals in the 18th century. After this, you go down to the dungeons, to be charged and fingerprinted by prison warders/tour guides before you hear the stories of past prisoners there. Your bed of straw will only be changed monthly. Maybe the rats won't bite you much with your other inmates around, including the epileptic branded a 'maniac' who's given 'spinning' treatments. Whether you're 'sent for transportation' for seven or 14 years to Australia, for anything from burglary to telling bad Irish jokes, before you know it you're released into the café.

Doagh Famine Museum

Doagh Island, Inishowen, **t** (074) 937 8078
Open Famine Museum: Easter–Oct daily 10–5.30
Santa's Island: 19 Nov–24 Dec (shows at 5 and 7pm)
Adm €6 per person

You'll have to drive a long way to this attraction on a beautiful coastal plain on the northern edge of Inishowen, with an exhibition set up in traditional cottages to represent a village during Ireland's famine. A guide can tell you all about the traditions and history of the period, from wakes to entertainment, how people lived and ate, and whatever else you want to know. Small animals and a pond make up the outdoor part of the museum; children can play with them in summer. For Christmas, the buildings are transformed into a 'North Pole' where Santa gives a gift to each child.

Flight of the Earls Heritage Centre

Rathmullan, Lough Swilly, **t** (074) 915 8178
Getting there 10 miles (22km) north of Letterkenny
Open Easter–May Sat 10–6, Sun 12 noon–6; June–Sept Mon–Sat 10–6, Sun 12 noon–6
Adm Adult €5, child €2; ask about group rates

This small museum is near the spot where the last two High Kings of Ireland left their homeland in 1607 (*see* p.34). It is inside a fort built in 1810 by the British as a defence against a French invasion.

Fort Dunree Military Museum

Buncrana, Inishowen, **t** (074) 936 1817
Open June–Sept Mon–Sat 10.30–6, Sun 1–6, Oct–May Mon–Fri 10.30–4.30, Sat and Sun 1–6
Adm Call for prices
Cafe, audio-visual show

Near where Wolfe Tone was caught in 1798, this small 19th-century fort was built to ward off a possible French invasion.

Inishowen Maritime Museum and Planetarium

Old Coast Guard Station, Greencastle, Inishowen, **t** (074) 938 1363
Open Summer Mon–Sat 10–6, Sun 12 noon–6
Adm Call for prices
Cafe, shop

Boats up to 50ft (15.2m) long are displayed here, and a planetarium offers multimedia presentations and a laser light show at night, with accompanying pop music.

Newmills Corn and Flax Mills

Milltown, **t** (074) 912 5115
Getting there 5km west of Letterkenny
Open Tours: June–Sept daily 10–5.45
Adm Adult €2.75, child/student €1.25, family €7

Interactive exhibits tell you about millers, scutchers and this 400-year-old industry.

Tell me an Irish riddle...
Question – *What has teeth but cannot eat?*
Answer – *A comb*

Ramelton Heritage Centre and Donegal Ancestry

The Quay, Ramelton, **t** (074) 915 1266, **www.**donegalancestry.com
Open Easter–Oct Mon–Sat 10–6, Sun 2–6, Oct–Easter Mon–Fri 10–4.30; last adm 30mins before closing
Donegal Ancestry research service: Mon–Thurs 9.30–4.30, Fri 9.30–3.30
Adm Adult €2.50, child €1

Displays and an audio-visual show here tell you how Ramelton was the seat of the ancient High King O'Donnell and his clan before it was rebuilt as a Plantation town. King George IV's favourite nurse, whom he nicknamed 'Blackie', was also from here. If one of your relatives was too, you can check it out through a computerized genealogical databank.

Nature lovers

Donegal Organic Farm

Glenties, **t** (074) 955 1286, **www.esatclear.ie**
Getting there 19 miles (30km) north of Donegal Town, 2 miles (3km) outside Glenties village
Open Call for times. **Adm** Free, donations welcome

A biodynamic organic farm with dairy, meat and vegetables for sale, plus a nature trail.

Glenveagh National Park

Church Hill, near Letterkenny, **t** (074) 913 7090
Open Mid-Feb–end Nov daily 10–6.30 (last adm 5)
Adm Adult €3, child €1.50, family €7

This 40,873-acre park contains lakes, oak- and birch-clothed glens and woodlands, red deer, lots of bird life on the upper slopes of its mountains and Glenveagh Castle. Landscapes are magnificent, and Ireland's highest peaks, Mount Errigal and Slieve Snaght, are here. A visitor centre introduces you to the wildlife and flora of the area.

Sporty kids

Activity centres

Donegal Adventure Centre

Bundoran, **t** (071) 984 2844, **www.donegal-holidays.com**

Accommodation and guided or self-guided walking and cycling tours, plus surfing, canoeing, golfing, mountain biking and other activities.

Waterworld

Bundoran, **t** (071) 984 1172

An award-winning aqua-adventure playground, with swimming pools, a wave pool and a slide pool.

Horse-riding

Tourist offices have information on all the many riding centres in Donegal, which include:

Dunfanaghy Riding Stables, Arnold's Hotel, Dunfanaghy, **t** (074) 913 6208

Walking

There are many great walks in Donegal, often through wild and remote landscapes, but bear in mind that there are many areas that newcomers shouldn't explore without a guide and proper preparation. The organizations below offer guided walks. Glenveagh is one of the best places for more accessible walking (*see* p.236).

Ballytour, t (071) 982 2888

Visit characters from Ireland's past on a walk in Ballyshannon in July and August.

North West Walking Guides, Clunarra, Letterbarrow, **t** (087) 266 2248, **www.northwestwalkingguides.com**

The Blue Stack Centre, Drimarone, Donegal Town, **t** (074) 973 5564, **www.thebluestackway.com**

Súil Siar, Kilcar, **t** (074) 973 8211

Archaeological and themed guided walks.

Buckets and spades – Beaches in Donegal

Considered by many one of the most beautiful beaches in the world, the Blue Flag beach at **Portsalon** near Millford, north of Letterkenny, has a backdrop of heather-covered mountains that plunge into the blue seas of Ballymastocker Bay. Visitors are asked not to walk on its sand dunes so they can recover from overuse.

Rossnowlagh Beach, 10 miles (16km) south of Donegal town, is regarded by many as the most scenic beach in northwest Ireland, with miles of golden sand. Popular for watersports such as surfing and windsurfing, it's excellent for safe swimming.

Other Blue Flag beaches can be found at **Bundoran, Rathmullan, Naran, Portnoo, Marble Hill** and **Dunfanaghy**. Best for swimming are Silver Strand at **Malin Bay** and **Glencolmcille.**

WHERE TO EAT

Belfast

Alden's

229 Upper Newtownards Rd, **t** (028) 9065 0079 (*moderate–expensive*)

Comfort, service, ambience and good food. Children are made very welcome.

Café Renoir

95 Botanic Ave, **t** (028) 9031 1300 (*moderate*)

An all-day restaurant with a wood-burning pizzeria and a café. Ingredients are organic and highchairs are available.

Cargoes

613 Lisburn Rd, **t** (028) 9066 5451 (*inexpensive*)

An enjoyable modern café with good Mediterranean salads and other light meals.

Cayenne

7 Ascot House, Shaftesbury Sq, **t** (028) 9033 1532 (*moderate–expensive*)

A very child-friendly, casual restaurant, open for lunch and dinner, owned by Northern Ireland's celebrity chef Paul Rankin, with imaginative food, including many vegetarian dishes and good-value set lunches, plus highchairs and wheelchair access.

Equinox

32 Howard St, **t** (028) 9023 0089 (*inexpensive*)

A daytime café with sophisticated interior design, serving excellent salads, coffee and milkshakes.

Ginger Café

68–72 Great Victoria St, **t** (028) 9029 9496 (*inexpensive*)

Chef Simon McCance carries on his reputation for excellent, inventive cooking and artisan baking in his new restaurant, open in the daytime.

Maggie May's

50 Botanic Ave, **t** (028) 9032 2662 (*inexpensive*)

Big servings, good value veggie meals and all-day breakfasts in the university area.

Nick's Warehouse

35 Hill St, Cathedral quarter, **t** (028) 9043 9690 (*moderate–expensive*)

This popular, informal restaurant owned by renowned chefs Nick and Kathy Price comes highly recommended. Open all day until 9.30pm, it offers smaller portions and will change dishes according to a child's wishes. It also has highchairs.

Rain City

33–35 Malone Rd, **t** (028) 9068 2929 (*moderate*)

Paul Rankin's American-style restaurant attracts long queues, but the good-quality food and children's menus make the wait worthwhile.

Sun Kee

Donegall Pass, **t** (028) 9031 2016 (*inexpensive–moderate*)

One of Belfast's best Chinese restaurants.

Tong Dynasty

82 Botanic Ave, **t** (028) 9043 9590 (*moderate*)

Excellent Chinese food and fast, genial service.

Around Co. Antrim

Ballyclare

Ballylagan Organic Farm

10 Ballylagan Rd, **t** (028) 9332 2867 (*inexpensive*)

A place to buy fresh organic local produce, dried goods and imported organic fruit.

Bushmills

Bushmills Inn

25 Main St, **t** (028) 2073 2339 (*inexpensive–moderate*)

A Victorian-style coaching inn near the Bushmills Distillery, with enjoyable bar food and restaurant meals. Children get their own menu or half-portions.

Carnlough

The Londonderry Arms Hotel

20–28 Harbour Rd, **t** (028) 2888 5255 (*expensive*)

A child-friendly restaurant with good fish and a wide choice of dishes. Children are offered things to do so adults can finish their meals in peace and enjoy the views of the sea and glens.

Cushendall

Harry's Restaurant

10–12 Mill St, **t** (028) 2177 2022 (*inexpensive–moderate*)

A family-friendly restaurant at the foot of the Antrim Glens, with reasonably priced specialities: monkfish, grills, lamb, steaks, scampi, veggie dishes.

Portrush

The Wine Bar, The Harbour Bistro, Coast
The Harbour, **t** (028) 7082 4313 (*inexpensive–moderate*)

Children are welcome in the upstairs Wine Bar overlooking Portrush Harbour until about 9pm. Downstairs, the less expensive Coast has pizzas and pasta, and more gourmet meals are found in The Harbour Bistro. All are open for lunch and dinner.

County Down

Bangor

Shanks Restaurant
Blackwood Golf Club, 150 Crawfordsburn Rd, **t** (028) 9185 3313 (*moderate–expensive*)

A rich and varied menu for lunch and dinner, plus highchairs, special menus and wheelchair access.

Comber

Anna's House
Tullynagee, 150 35 LIsbarnett Rd, **t** (028) 9754 1566 (*moderate–expensive*)

Organic food and baking from lovely gardens.

Castle Espie Coffee Room
Wildfowl and Wetlands Trust, Ballydrain Rd, **t** (028) 9187 4146 (*inexpensive*)

Good food in the middle of a nature reserve.

Donaghadee

Grace Neill's Bar and Restaurant
33 High St, **t** (028) 9188 4595 (*moderate*)

Adventurous food in what is said to be Ireland's oldest pub (founded in 1611), where Russian tsar Peter the Great stopped for a pint in 1694. Children must leave by 7pm. It has a no-smoking area.

Dundrum

The Buck's Head Inn
77 Main St, **t** (028) 4375 1868 (*moderate*)

This restaurant in an 18th-century building is renowned for its warm atmosphere, with a cosy panelled bar, open fire and imaginative menus. Children go for its fantastic fishcakes, home-made burgers and fish and chips, and it has a walled garden. It's open for lunch, tea and dinner.

Hillsborough

The Pheasant
410 Upper Ballynahinch Rd, Annahilt, **t** (028) 9263 8056 (*inexpensive–moderate*)

A non-smoking restaurant offering early-bird and Kids' Club global, game and seafood cuisine.

Holywood

The Baytree Coffee House
118 High St, **t** (028) 9042 1419 (*inexpensive*)

Fabulous desserts and home-made food put together with fresh ingredients and a gourmet touch, including fantastic breakfasts, delicious mashed spuds and cakes. Children are very welcome. It's open until 4.30pm and for dinner on Fridays.

Camphill Organic Farm Shop and Bakery
Shore Rd, **t** (028) 9042 3203 (*inexpensive*)

Daytime organic meals and fresh home-baking.

Fontana
6A High St, **t** (028) 9080 9980 (*inexpensive–moderate*)

Mediterranean-based gourmet lunches and early dinners for children.

Portaferry

Portaferry Hotel
10 The Strand, **t** (028) 4272 8231 (*moderate*)

Seafood straight from the boats of Portavogie.

Strangford

The Cuan Bar and Restaurant
6 The Square, **t** (028) 4488 1222 (*moderate*)

A place open from noon to 9pm for venison, quail and a hot and cold buffet. Colouring books, a baby-changing room and highchairs are available.

County Armagh

Armagh City

Pilgrim's Table Conservatory Restaurant
St Patrick's Trian visitor complex, 38–40 English St, **t** (028) 3752 1814 (*inexpensive*)

The best lunches in town, offered self-service in pleasant Georgian surroundings, plus morning coffee and afternoon tea.

Killeavy

Annahaia

Slieve Gullion Courtyard, Killeavy, t (028) 3084 8084 (*moderate*)

Children are welcome here for early dinners of gourmet cooking.

Loughgall

The Famous Grouse

6 Ballyhagan Rd, t (028) 3889 1778 (*inexpensive–moderate*)

A reasonably priced, relaxed and cosy restaurant welcoming families. Try the pub grub at lunchtime (Thurs–Sun) or the main menu in the evening.

Markethill

The Court Rooms Restaurant

7 Main St, t (028) 3755 2553 (*inexpensive*)

Children will love the excellent selection of delicious home-baked desserts on offer here for lunch or afternoon tea.

Portadown

Yellow Door

Portadown Rugby Club, Bridge St, t (028) 3839 4860 (*inexpensive–moderate*)

A children's menu is available here during the week, featuring baby pizzas, soups, burgers and fish; half-portions of the adult menu can be ordered on Sundays. It's so relaxed in this rugby club restaurant that kids play quietly on the wooden floor.

Co. Londonderry

Coleraine

Strawberry Fayre

1 Blagh Rd, t (028) 7032 0437 (*inexpensive*)

Excellent lunches and teas made from fresh produce and natural ingredients.

Derry City

Danano

2–4 Clarendon St, t (028) 7126 6646 (*moderate*)

A lively Italian spot with pizzas galore.

Linenhall Bar

3 Market St, t (028) 7137 1665 (*moderate–expensive*)

A lively place popular with locals for relaxed lunches, with or without Guinness. Children are made to feel comfortable here.

Mange 2

Clarendon St, t (028) 7136 1222 (*expensive*)

Children are welcome to dine early in this dimly lit gourmet restaurant where vegetarians can get a good-quality entrée for £10.

Magherafelt

Ditty's Bakery and Café Slice

33 Rainey St, t (028) 7963 3944/3980 (*inexpensive–moderate*)

A bakery–café (daily 9–5) and restaurant/wine bar (Thurs–Sun 9am–9.30pm), with nouveau-Irish cooking, including excellent starters. A well-priced children's menu is available. Staff go out of their way to please.

Gardiner's Restaurant

7 Garden St, t (028) 7930 0333 (*inexpensive–moderate*)

Children are welcome for early dinners here, where friendly, media-popular, inventive chef Sean Owens offers tasty Ulster versions of a variety dishes, from Thai to vegetarian.

Portstewart

Morelli's

53–58 The Promenade, t (028) 7083 2150 (*inexpensive*)

With the Italian name, what else could be served here but good ice cream and pasta? Children are welcome, and are offered a children's menu.

County Tyrone

Castletown

Mellon's Country Hotel, Bar and Restaurant

Castletown, on road past Ulster American Folk Park, t (028) 8166 1224 (*inexpensive–moderate*)

Generous portions prepared with fresh ingredients and desserts such as soft pavlova with fruit compôte are offered in this genial family restaurant where vegetarians will be happy.

Cookstown

The Courtyard

56A William St, **t** (028) 8676 5070 (*inexpensive*)

There's a good set lunch in this farm-themed coffee shop with home-made pies and puddings, closed Sundays. Children are very welcome.

The Otter Lodge

26 Dungannon Rd, **t** (028) 8676 5427 (*inexpensive*)

Pleasant pub grub and home cooking.

Dungannon

Viscount's Restaurant

Northland Rd, **t** (028) 8775 3800 (*moderate*)

This popular medieval-style restaurant in a renovated church, complete with suits of armour, offers extensive main and children's menus for lunch (except Mondays) and grills until 9.30pm.

County Fermanagh

Enniskillen

Franco's Pizzeria

Queen Elizabeth Rd, **t** (028) 6632 4424 (*moderate*)

A popular family-friendly restaurant offering pizzas, seafood, salad, steak and chicken.

Leslie's Bakery

10 Church St, (028) 6632 4902 (*inexpensive*)

An artisan bakery with excellent regional breads.

Oscar's

Belmore St, **t** (028) 6632 7037 (*moderate*)

Salmon and local trout are served in this small, popular restaurant. Children are welcome.

Scoff's

17 Belmore St, **t** (028) 6634 2622 (*inexpensive–moderate*)

Considerate service, low lights, wooden tables, big salads, artisan breads and scrumptious desserts. In the downstairs section, the menu is inexpensive and the surroundings more casual.

Florence Court

Florence Court House

t (028) 6634 8249 (*inexpensive*)

Light lunches served all day in an old barn.

Cavan and Monaghan

Ballyconnell

Polo D Restaurant

Main St, Ballyconnell, Co. Cavan, **t** (049) 952 6228 (*inexpensive–moderate*)

Light country-style meals served all day and an imaginative dinner menu beckon families to this place.

Blacklion

MacNean Bistro

Blacklion, Co. Cavan, **t** (071) 985 3022 (*moderate–expensive*)

Children are welcome in this very popular, top-class restaurant (linked with MacNean House B&B; *see* p.277), which creates imaginative dishes, mainly with locally grown organic produce, and highly lauded desserts.

Cavan

Casey's Steak Bar

Main St, Ballinagh, **t** (049) 433 7105 (*inexpensive–moderate*)

This place offers a children's menu, highchairs and – according to some – the best steaks in Ireland.

Cloverhill

Olde Post Inn

Cloverhill, Butler's Bridge, **t** (047) 55555 (*moderate*)

The chef here is causing a stir with his good cooking for dinner and Sunday lunch.

Monaghan

Andy's Bar and Restaurant

12 Market St, **t** (047) 82277 (*inexpensive–moderate*)

A place offering a children's menu alongside a dinner menu featuring specialities of Monaghan mushrooms, steak in whiskey and beer sauce and good desserts.

Virginia

The Park Hotel

t (049) 854 6100 (*moderate*)

Children can have half-portions or fast food here, and highchairs are available. Imaginative, ambitious Irish and European cooking makes up the menu.

County Donegal

Ardara

Nesbitt Arms Hotel

Main St, **t** (074) 954 1103 (*inexpensive–moderate*)

Filling Irish food and a children's fast-food menu, plus highchairs.

Burtonport

Lobster Pot

t (075) 42012 (*inexpensive*)

Families are welcome in this casual seafood restaurant in a tiny harbour village opposite Arranmore Island. Highchairs and a children's menu are available.

Crolly

Leo's Tavern (Tabhairne Leo)

Meenaleck, Crolly, **t** (074) 954 8143 (*inexpensive*)

Music is intimately linked with this pub, which gave a start to the careers of Clannad and Enya. Bar food is available 1–8.30 daily, and Sunday lunch 1–3.30.

Donegal Town

Millcourt Coffee Shop

Behind the Simple Simon healthfood store, **t** (074) 972 3016 (*inexpensive*)

Good cakes and light meals in a wooden-tabled upstairs room.

Thai Food Restaurant

Central Hotel, The Diamond, **t** (074) 972 1027 (*inexpensive–moderate*)

A very family-friendly and locally popular dinner venue (closed Tuesday).

Dunfanaghy

Dunfanaghy Workhouse

t (074) 913 6540 (*inexpensive*)

A seasonal coffee shop that becomes a wine bar with traditional music in the evening.

Dungloe (An Clóchan Liath)

The Riverside Bistro

Main St, **t** (074) 952 1062 (*inexpensive*)

A bistro with a children's menu.

Glencolmcille

An Chistin

Ulster Cultural Foundation, **t** (074) 973 0213 (*inexpensive*)

Seafood, salads, soups.

Letterkenny

Yellow Pepper

Main St, **t** (074) 912 4133 (*inexpensive*)

A restaurant with an early-bird menu until 5.30, a children's menu of chips with everything, plus wraps and basic vegetarian dishes such as pasta and vegetable stir fries. Highchairs are available.

Lifford

Acquolina Restaurant

The Diamond (behind The Old Courthouse), **t** (074) 914 1733 (*moderate*)

Pasta and pizzas that have locals raving, open for dinner daily and Sunday lunch.

Portnoo

The Dolmen Centre

Kilcooney, **t** (074) 954 5010 (*inexpensive*)

Home-baking/sandwiches in an eco-centre café.

Ramelton

The Bridge Bar Seafood Restaurant

t (074) 915 1855 (*moderate*)

Children are welcome at this small upstairs restaurant whose chef ensures that vegetarians are well catered for with artisan breads, good salads and well-flavoured fresh vegetables. The frequently changing desserts are substantial.

Rathmullan

Rathmullan House Hotel

t (074) 915 8188 (*expensive*)

Delicious gourmet cooking using produce from the hotel's walled garden, including good-value Sunday lunches. Every mouthwatering course is a delight.

Tory Island

Ostan Thoraigh

t (074) 913 5920, **www.toryhotel.com** (*inexpensive–moderate*)

Awarded Ireland's 'Dining Pub of the Year' award, this hotel offers fresh seafood dishes in a wonderful location. Children are welcome.

Sleep

WHERE TO STAY 246
Price Ranges 247
Useful Addressses and Sources 248

ACCOMMODATION 249

DUBLIN 249

LEINSTER 251
County Dublin 251
Wicklow and Carlow 251
Kilkenny and Wexford 252
Kildare, Laois and Offaly 254
Meath and Louth 255
Westmeath and Longford 256

MUNSTER 257
County Cork 257
Cork City 257
County Kerry 259
County Limerick 261
County Clare 262
Tipperary and Waterford 263

CONNACHT 265
County Galway 265
County Mayo 267
County Sligo 269
Leitrim and Roscommon 270

ULSTER 271
Northern Ireland:
County Antrim 271
Belfast 271
County Down 273
County Armagh 274
County Londonderry 274
County Tyrone 275
County Fermanagh 276
Republic of Ireland:
Cavan and Monaghan 276
County Donegal 277

08

WHERE TO STAY

Irish attitudes regarding what visitors expect in accommodation have changed enormously in the past decade. But so has the cost to the traveller. You will find more superior hotels that only the super-wealthy can afford than ever before, and more rooms with en suite bathrooms, even in hostels. At the same time, you can also find more of the lowliest form of budget accommodation.

Hotels and guesthouses in Ireland usually cater pretty well for children's needs, but you may prefer to rent a cottage or house with its own kitchen and facilities (*see* right). Self-catering accommodation certainly offers more privacy and independence, although on the downside it can also make you feel a bit isolated, especially if you are driving your family around Ireland in a car.

Hotels

Fáilte Ireland, under the auspices of Tourism Ireland (which now unites the tourist offices of northern and southern Ireland), grades all types of accommodation with a system of stars and commendations. Lists of all categories can be found in pamphlets available at local tourist offices, which will also make bookings for you. But though Ireland's tourist boards do a fantastic job of grading and listing the wealth of accommodation available, a range of other information sources – e.g. specialist accommodation guides, websites, independent hotel associations – provide more. They vary a great deal, but independent groups such as the Blue Book and Hidden Ireland pay close attention to standards for their clubs of privately owned properties. For suggestions, *see* p.248.

In cities, some hotels cater mainly for business and/or older independent travellers, so get clear whether children are welcome (and what's provided for them) when booking. Hotels oriented to the young adult market, in trendy areas such as Dublin's Temple Bar, can be a problem for families. Check also whether hotels offer discounts for children and longer stays; sometimes small children stay free, especially off season. High season usually means Easter, July to mid-September, and Christmas. At these times, it's best to book well in advance.

Only the larger Irish hotels usually have a lot of leisure facilities, particularly indoor pools. You may have to balance the range of facilities offered against a loss of local character due to staying in a new, international-style hotel.

Prices in the Republic of Ireland are listed in euros, those in Northern Ireland are listed in British pounds.

Bed and breakfasts and guesthouses

B&Bs can be a good choice if you are on a budget, but they often charge per head rather than per room, which can make prices rise to a level that makes a family hotel room more economical. Note that, while most hotels will have a restaurant and offer breakfast and evening meals, traditionally B&Bs offer breakfast only. Many country guesthouses will also provide evening meals (and packed lunches) if you ask in advance, especially in more remote places where there are not many alternatives.

Many farmhouses accommodate families, but Ireland now has quite a few upmarket guesthouses and country-house hotels that are geared more to business travellers and couples, and so are not family friendly. Again, check this when booking.

Self-catering

Renting a self-catered cottage can often be the most amenable and economic option for a family. Self-catering allows you to come and go as you please without being restricted to set mealtimes, and gives kids room to spread out. However, it does tie you to one place, so make sure it's somewhere you want to spend the entire holiday. Choose accommodation in an area you want to visit, and consider places you want to explore and things you want to do and whether they are nearby.

Be a little cautious, also, if you don't want to spend your holiday in a new, purpose-built bungalow community. Many have sprung up all over Ireland, and you can find whole towns made up of holiday homes that are empty for most of the year. These new housing developments are fairly functional in look and atmosphere, although they have all the modern conveniences.

If a house is described as 'modern' or 'purpose-built', this generally means it's not an old-fashioned kind of country place with any period details. Rental homes such as this fit the bill if you want the assurance of certain conveniences but aren't too concerned about atmosphere, and may sometimes be cheaper than old houses with more character.

Horse-drawn Caravans around Ireland

Combine travelling with a place to stay by touring Ireland in a horse-drawn caravan. You get a trustworthy and solid horse and a barrel-shaped caravan that sleeps 4, and you can travel at a relaxing pace – usually about 9 miles (15km) a day. The cost per week is from around €260 in the low season to €700 in July and August.

For more information contact Tourism Ireland, or one of the following:

Clissmann Horse Drawn Caravans, Carrigmore Farm, Wicklow, Co. Wicklow, **t** (0404) 48288, **www.**clissman.com

Into the West Horse Drawn Caravans, Ballinakill, Kylebrack, Loughrea, Co. Galway, **t** (090) 974 5211

Kilvahan Horse Drawn Caravans, Kilvahan, Cullenagh, Portlaoise, Co. Laois, **t** (0502) 27048, **www.**horsedrawncaravans.com

Mayo Horsedrawn Caravan Holidays, Belcarra, Castlebar, Co. Mayo, **t** (094) 903 2054, **www.**horsedrawn.mayonet.com

Private homes

Owners of 'period houses' in Ireland who take paying guests are usually committed to a high standard of hospitality – of a kind that is traditional and natural to the Irish. However, under such circumstances you need to be especially conscious that you are visiting people's homes, no matter how professionally they are run. If you're planning to visit with children, do ask about their policy towards kids and check details such as furnishings and whether they have outdoor play areas. If you have a baby, you need to ensure that hoteliers and guesthouse owners know in advance; sometimes they can accommodate you in special wings or cottages outside their main houses where you and your children can enjoy more freedom.

'Home-baking' usually means the owners take care over their food and bake their own cakes and breads, but standards differ. The best places offer inventive gourmet spreads for breakfast.

'Special diets' implies that your hosts will do what they can to provide particular foods for you, if you give them advance notice. Owners of private homes will often provide or arrange babysitting, and advise on activities you and your children can enjoy in their area, or even organize them for you.

Activity centres

Centres with leisure activities or facilities often cater for families as well as school and youth groups. Accommodation can be anything from dorms to fully equipped apartments, but normally a laundry and a communal kitchen are provided.

Hostels

Several independent hostelling associations have sprung up in Ireland in recent years, in addition to the traditional An Oige and YHANI (*see* p.248). Standards vary enormously. It's best to investigate before committing yourself to more than a night in one. People of all ages and types stay in hostels, but those who most enjoy them are budget travellers on walking and outdoor holidays. Visitors usually have to leave the hostel during the day, and be in by a certain time at night. Self-catering is possible in some hostels with kitchen facilities, and breakfast and even dinner may be offered. Washing machines, drying rooms and Internet access may be found too. But anyone travelling with children should ensure that a hostel offers family rooms and not just dormitory-style accommodation.

Camping and caravanning

The amenities provided in Irish caravan and camping sites vary a lot. Electrical link-ups, toilets, showers and laundry areas are usually the bare minimum offered, while the best-equipped parks have kitchens, restaurants and games rooms.

Price ranges

All the accommodation listed in this chapter is categorized according to one of the price bands below, based on prices for B&B per person, per night. Bear in mind, though, that price alone is no guide to the quality offered in any category.

In low seasons most hotels, and often guesthouses and B&Bs, offer 'discounts' for families or family rooms. Check how spacious the latter actually are, as sizes and standards vary significantly.

High season = Easter, July and August, Christmas and New Year; Mid-season = April–June, September; Low season = the rest of the year.

Luxury	More than €200 (UK£135)
Expensive	More than €130 (UK£90)
Moderate	More than €60 (UK£40)
Inexpensive	Less than €60 (UK£40)

Useful addresses and sources

General Information

Tourism Ireland

Freephones UK **t** 0800 039 7000; US and Canada **t** 1 800 223 6470; **www**.tourismireland.com

The joint travel information service for the whole of Ireland. Affiliated to it are Bord Fáilte/ the Irish Tourist Board (ITB; **www**.travel.ireland.ie) and the Northern Ireland Tourist Board (NITB; **www**.discovernorthernireland.com) and it has links to all the regional and local tourist bodies.

Guides, brochures and websites

Bed & Breakfast Ireland
Ireland Accommodation Guide
Ireland Self-Catering Guide

Available from Tourism Ireland or the ITB.

Accommodation for Visitors on a Limited Budget
A Complete Guide to Self-catering Holiday Homes in Northern Ireland
Bed & Breakfast Guide, Northern Ireland
Northern Ireland Hotels and Guesthouses

From Tourism Ireland or the NITB.

Be Our Guest Hotels and Guesthouses Guide, from the Irish Hotels Federation, **www**.irelandhotels.com

Camping and Caravan Ireland, from **www**.camping-ireland.ie

Friendly Homes of Ireland, Tourism Resources Ltd, **www**.tourismresources.ie

Hostels Ireland, by Paul Karr, from An Oige, **www**.irelandyha.org

Independent Holiday Hostels of Ireland, 57 Lower Gardiner St, Dublin 1, **t** (1) 836 4700, **www**.hostels-ireland.com

Lóistín Gaeltachta (Accommodation in the Gaeltacht), Freephones, **t** IR 1 800 621 600, **t** (353) 6691 52423, **t** UK 0800 783 5708, **www**.gaelsaoire.ie

Hotel and tour organizations

Country House Tours, 71 Waterloo Rd, Dublin 4, **t** (01) 660 7975; US **t** 1 800 688 0363, **www**.tourismresources.ie

Tours of grand houses and castles.

Ireland's Blue Book, 8 Mount St Crescent, Dublin 2, **t** (01) 676 9914, **www**.irelands-blue-book.ie

Individual, opulent country houses and restaurants.

Irish Hotels Federation, 13 Northbrook Rd, Dublin 6, **t** (010) 497 6459 **www**.irelandhotels.com

Access to more than 1,000 hotels and guesthouses online, plus advice on specialist short breaks.

Holiday rentals and self-catering

Dream Ireland Holiday Rentals, Lodge Wood, Kenmare, Co. Kerry, **t** (064) 41170, **www**.dreamireland.com

Friendly Homes of Ireland, Adams & Butler, Dublin 4, **t** (01) 660 7975, **www**.tourismresources.ie

This site features plenty of affordable, family-run accommodation.

The Hidden Ireland, **t** (01) 662 7166; US **t** 1800 688 0299, **www**.hidden-ireland.com

Self-catering rentals, often in country houses of character, some so grand they'd be hard put to stay hidden.

Irish Country Holidays, Old Church, Mill St, Borrisokane, Co. Tipperary, **t** (062) 79330, **www**.country-holidays.ie

An association of rural homes all over Ireland offering a range of self-catering homes for visitors.

Irish Farmhouse Holidays Association, 2 Michael St, Limerick, **t** (061) 400 700, **www**.irishfarmholidays.com

Kerry Cottages, 3 Royal Terrace West, Dun Laoghaire, Co. Dublin, **t** (01) 284 4000, **www**.kerrycottages.com

Killarney Lakeland Cottages, Muckross, Co. Kerry, **t** (064) 31538, **www**.killarneycottages.com

Rent-an-Irish Cottage, 51 O'Connell St, Limerick, **t** (061) 411 109, **www**.rentacottage.ie

Rural Cottage Holidays Ltd, St Anne's Court, 59 North St, Belfast BT1 1NB, **t** (028) 9024 1535, **www**.cottagesinireland.com

Shamrock Cottages, 13 Clifford Terrace, Wellington, Somerset TA21 8QP, UK, **t** (01823) 660 126, **www**.shamrockcottages.co.uk

An excellent company that can advise on country and beachside rentals suitable for young families.

Hostels

An Oige (Irish Youth Hostel Association), 61 Mountjoy St, Dublin 7, **t** (01) 830 4555, **www**.irelandyha.org

The Republic's main hostel association.

Independent Holiday Hostels of Ireland, 57 Lower Gardiner St, Dublin 1, **t** (01) 836 4700, **www**.hostels-ireland.com

This offers a 'bed search' service. Some of their hostels are very rudimentary.

Youth Hostel Association Northern Ireland (YHANI), 22 Donegall Rd, Belfast, BT12 5JN, **t** (028) 9032 4733, **www**.hani.org.uk

Fine hostels on the Ulster Way footpath.

ACCOMMODATION

DUBLIN

Dublin's entrance into the club of the world's most popular tourist cities has brought a real explosion in new hotels and guesthouses. Below is simply a sample of what you will find. Dublin is a very popular city, so it's best to book well ahead.

Hotels

Buswells Hotel

Molesworth St, D2, t (01) 614 6500, www.quinn-hotels.com *(expensive–luxury)*

This old-fashioned family hotel is very central and offers price reductions for families, children's meals and babysitting.

Camden Court Hotel

Lower Camden St, D2, t (01) 475 9666, www.camdencourthotel.com *(expensive)*

Not far from St Stephen's Green, this modern 246-room hotel has family rooms specially fitted with all amenities, and offers highchairs, babysitting, children's menus and an indoor swimming pool – a rarity in Dublin hotels.

The Clarence

6–8 Wellington Quay, D2, t (01) 407 0800, www.theclarence.ie *(luxury)*

Pop music fans might be interested in the fact that this boutique hotel is owned by Bono and The Edge of U2. The children of the rich are catered to with 'VIP gifts' for under-16s and the like.

Georgian Hotel

18–22 Baggot St Lower, D2, t (01) 634 5000, www.georgianhotel.ie *(luxury)*

Children under 17 are charged less in this central Georgian house next to St Stephen's Green, with its snug, pastel-coloured rooms. Babysitting, children's meals and a car park are available.

The Gresham

Upper O'Connell St, D1, t (01) 874 6881, www.thegresham.com *(expensive)*

Built in the days when a first-class hotel had big bedrooms and enormous baths, this classic hotel retains a 1930s atmosphere. There are family discounts and children's meals in the restaurant.

Harcourt Hotel

60 Harcourt St, D2, t (01) 478 3677, www.harcourthotel.ie *(moderate)*

A 5min walk from St Stephen's Green and Grafton St, this former home of playwright George Bernard Shaw offers babysitting, evening entertainment and local car parking for a fee.

Jurys Ballsbridge Hotel

Pembroke Rd, Ballsbridge, D4, t (01) 660 5000, www.jurysdoyle.com *(expensive)*

This 5-star option has interconnecting rooms, babysitting, children's meals and family rates. There's a leisure centre on site, swimming pools and entertainment. It's part of the reliable Jurys chain, which has another first-rate, family-friendly hotel, The Westbury, on Clarendon St.

Longfield's Hotel

10 Fitzwilliam St, Lower Ballsbridge, D2, t (01) 676 1367, www.longfields.ie *(expensive)*

This pristine Georgian hotel with its highly rated restaurant is best suited to those with older, well-behaved children, as it's popular with business types.

Mount Herbert Hotel

Herbert Rd, Ballsbridge, D4, t (01) 668 4321, www.mountherberthotel.ie *(expensive)*

A smart Victorian residence in upmarket Ballsbridge , with an outdoor play area with climbing frames, swings, seasaws and treehouses, children's meals and half-portions in the restaurant, babysitting and access to a health club.

Sachs Hotel

19 Morehampton Rd, Donnybrook, D4, t (01) 668 0995 *(expensive–luxury)*

This small, traditional hotel in a Georgian terrace, renovated in 2005, offers ample parking, family rates, children's meals and babysitting.

School House Hotel

2–8 Northumberland Rd, D4, t (01) 667 5014, www.schoolhousehotel.com *(moderate–expensive)*

A hotel offering children's meals and babysitting. A child aged 2–12 can share a parent's room, using a rollaway bed for €27.

B&Bs and guesthouses

Aberdeen Lodge

53 Park Ave, Ballsbridge, D4, t (01) 283 8155, www.halpinsprivatehotels.com *(expensive)*

Two family rooms are available in this small, sedate hotel in a quiet, leafy neighbourhood of embassies and Regency houses – a pleasant home away from home yet not far from central Dublin. Everything is delivered promptly and with a smile, from room service to advice about what to do in Dublin. High teas and breakfasts are good too.

Albany House

84 Harcourt St, Ballsbridge, D2, t (01) 475 1092, (*moderate–expensive*)

In the heart of Ballsbridge with a LUAS tram line outside the front door, this hotel is surprising quiet – probably due to its thick walls (it's listed with Dublin's Georgian Society). Slightly worn antique wardrobes and dressing tables fill the curlicue-plastered, high-ceilinged rooms, and fresh flowers, mirrors and paintings add to the impression of being in a more langourous past. Breakfast is casual, and staff are informative about local history. Children are made to feel comfortable – appropriately, given that the buildings next door were given away 150 years ago by Lord Clonmel to establish the first children's hospital in Europe. Quote this guidebook when booking for a 10% discount on room rates.

Kilronan House

70 Adelaide Rd, Ballsbridge, D2, t (01) 475 5266 (*moderate*)

This white Georgian house has provided Grade A accommodation for more than 30 years. Not far from St Stephen's Green, it's a good-value, supremely welcoming find. You'll get lots of light from windows and skylights in the new part of the building, but en suite rooms in the older part feel like safe hideaways from the city bustle and retain some of the charm of the 19th century alongside pristine bathrooms and modern amenities. Many rooms have windows facing the Grand Canal. At breakfast in a cheerful Victorian-styled room with large bay windows, families are spoiled with a choice of full Irish breakfast or fresh strawberries, yogurt compôte whips, home-made breads and sweet breads, and more. Its considerate hosts, Terry and Katie Masterson, will give you invaluable advice on what to do in the city.

McMenamins Townhouse

74 Marlborough Rd, Donnybrook, D4, t (01) 497 4405, www.irishwelcome.com (*moderate*)

A warm welcome awaits you here from helpful, hospitable host Padraig McMenamin, who knows all about Donnybrook's history and sports activities. His wife Kay provides excellent home-baking and special breakfasts for vegetarians. A family room with a double and a single bed can be booked in conjunction with an adjoining small room with another single bed. You'll sleep peacefully in this residential street, not far from University College Dublin.

Waterloo House

8–10 Waterloo Rd, Ballsbridge, D4, t (01) 660 1888, e waterloohouse@eircom.net (*expensive*)

Two fine Georgian townhouses contain a 4-star guesthouse on a residential street within walking distance of the city centre. Friendly, efficient Mayo-born host Evelyn Corcoran welcomes children of any age. A wicker-furnished conservatory and a plush dining room face the back garden, a luxurious oasis of peace. This is perfection for those who want privacy and well-presented accommodation in the easygoing gentility of old Dublin.

Self-catering

Baggotrath

Off Landsdowne Rd (nr DART station), Sandymount, D4, t (01) 668 6463 or t (01) 679 2222 (*moderate*)

This purpose-built apartment complex offers private parking between the sea and city centre, and requires a minimum stay of two nights.

Hostels

Hostel facilities can be very rudimentary and both clientele and staff changes can affect the service significantly. Those listed here are only two of the many hostels in Dublin.

Avalon House

55 Aungier Str, D2, t 475 0001, www.avalon-house.ie (*inexpensive*)

Dublin's most central hostel is more suited to families than some of the backpacker hostels. This old building has been converted into a modern hostel with no-smoking twin, family and dormitory rooms and no curfew.

Dublin International An Oige Youth Hostel

Mountjoy St, D7, t (01) 830 1766, www.anoige.ie (*inexpensive*)

The headquarters-hostel of Ireland's oldest youth hostel association has a café, self-catering kitchen. laundry, and family and en suite rooms.

LEINSTER

County Dublin

Hotels

Gresham Royal Marine Hotel

Marine Rd, Dun Laoghaire, t (01) 280 1911 or t 1850 298298, www.gresham-hotels.com (*expensive–luxury*)

This 3-star Victorian hotel is comfortable and friendly, with an expanse of grass before it and, beyond new development, Dublin Bay. The suites facing Dun Laoghaire Pier have four-poster beds, sitting rooms, wide windows and high ceilings. Old-fashioned Dublin hotel-style breakfasts, babysitting, kid's meals and family rates are available.

B&Bs and guesthouses

Chestnut Lodge

2 Vesey Place, Dun Laoghaire, t (01) 280 7860 (*moderate*)

Gracious Georgian house near the ferry with lovely rooms, good breakfasts and a friendly atmosphere.

Druid Lodge

Killiney Hill Rd, Killiney, t (01) 285 1632, www.druidlodge.com (*moderate*)

An ivy-clad house high above Killiney Bay, with lush gardens. Inside, you are surrounded by paintings, artefacts and sculptures from the McClenaghans' world travels. On a sunny morning, the view is more like north Italy than a suburb of Dublin. A gourmet Irish breakfast prepares families for a morning's trek to Killiney Hill for an even better ocean view. Cynthia will advise on local restaurants or show you the way down to nearby Dalkey, and where to take a boat trip out to Dalkey Island in summer.

Sandycove Guesthouse

Sandycove seafront, Dun Laoghaire, t (01) 284 1600 (*inexpensive*)

A tidy B&B close to the DART station, beaches and Dun Laoghaire ferry port.

Self-catering

Harap Farm

Magillstown, Swords, t (01) 840 1285, www.dublinbutterfly.com (*moderate*)

Family-owned self-catering homes, with gardens and a tennis court. Sports facilities and restaurants are nearby, but you need to have a car to get there.

Wicklow and Carlow

Hotels

The Brooklodge Inn

Macreddin Village, near Aughrim, Co. Wicklow, t (0402) 36444, www.brooklodge.com (*moderate–expensive*)

This holiday village style hotel offers B&B in individual houses and organic food. Good rates for families, children's meals, a garden and a games room are available. A smokehouse, organic bakery, wine shop and outdoor-wear shop are onsite. A babysitter will even take your children to their country pub for meals while you dine at the Strawberry Tree Restaurant. It's only 15mins from Glendalough, with riding and fishing nearby.

The Lord Bagenal Inn

Main St, Leighlinbridge, Co. Carlow, t (059) 972 1668, www.lordbagenal.com (*moderate*)

A small hotel decorated with the owner's collection of paintings, with helpful staff and generous breakfasts. Enjoy fine wines in the restaurant and snacks and carvery meals in the bar. Amenable to families, with a children's menu, family rates and an enclosed playroom (until 8pm), it also offers a private river marina, fishing boat hire, and riding and walking in the Blackstairs Mountains.

Powerscourt Arms Hotel

Enniskerry, Co. Wicklow, t (01) 282 8903 (*moderate*)

An attractive town hotel at the foot of the Wicklow Mountains, with good Guinness, children's meals and price reductions for families.

Country houses

Ballyknocken House

Glenealy, near Ashford, Co. Wicklow, t (0404) 44627, www.ballyknocken.com (*inexpensive–moderate*)

A pretty, romantic farmhouse with iron beds and clawfoot baths, built in 1850. Advice is given on walks and pony rides are available on the farm. Children are welcome (ask about price reductions) and it has a garden and fishing facilities.

Lorum Old Rectory

Kilgreaney, Bagenalstown, Co. Carlow, **t** (059) 917 5282, **www.lorum.com** (*expensive*)

An ideal place for those travelling with children; Mrs Smith's farm has plenty to do on it, plus outdoor toys, dogs, pet sheep and croquet in the garden. Meals are tasty and the bedrooms are pretty and old fashioned.

Sherwood Park House

Kilbride, Tullow, Ballon, Co. Carlow, **t** (059) 915 9117, (*moderate*)

Children are welcome in this elegant Georgian farmhouse in rolling parkland. An accessible country retreat, it offers cosy log fires, candlelit dinners, quaint bedrooms with brass beds, excellent food, fishing, riding and a pet farm for children. Golf facilities are also available nearby.

B&Bs and guesthouses

Avonbrae Guesthouse

Rathdrum, Co. Wicklow, **t** (0404) 46198 (*inexpensive*)

This family-run village guesthouse will help to arrange hill-walking and other activities.

Bel Air Hotel and Equestrian Club and Holiday Village

Ashford, Co. Wicklow, **t** (0404) 40109, **e** belairhotel@eircom.net (*expensive*)

An equestrian village with a hotel and 4-star self-catering for those taking horse-riding courses.

Old Rectory

Wicklow Town, Co. Wicklow, **t** (0404) 67048 (*inexpensive*)

A place offering cosy rooms and delicious food for breakfast and dinner.

The Watermill

Rathvilly, Co. Carlow, **t** (059) 9161392 (*inexpensive*)

This delightful restored 16th-century mill on the River Slaney offers home-cooking and vegetables from the garden, plus free fishing.

Self-catering

Devil's Glen Holiday and Equestrian Village

Devil's Glen, Ashford, Co. Wicklow, **t** (0404) 40638, **www.devilsglen.ie** (*moderate*)

Apartments, bungalows and 4-star cottages available at an equestrian centre where guests can ride from morning to night.

Hostels

Glendalough An Oige

Glendalough, Co. Wicklow, **t** (0404) 45342 (*inexpensive*)

A straightforward, traditional youth hostel.

Camping and caravanning

Avonmore Riverside Caravan and Camping Park

Rathdrum, Co. Wicklow, **t** (0404) 46080, **www.avonmoreriverside.com** (*moderate*)

This site on the banks of the Avonmore, open Easter–Sept, also offers self-catering timber chalets.

Kilkenny and Wexford

Rosslare Harbour and the road that leads into Wexford have a number of hotels and B&Bs. Even so, in summer it's best to book ahead.

Hotels

Dunbrody Country House Hotel

Arthurstown, New Ross, Co. Wexford, **t** (051) 389 600/1 800 323 5463, **www.dunbrodyhouse.com** (*expensive–luxury*)

This antique-filled hotel in parkland not far from the sea on the Hook Peninsula offers gracious service, a new spa and delicious cuisine by the ex-chef of Dublin's famous Shelbourne Hotel, Kevin Dundon, who also runs courses at Dunbrody Cookery School. Babysitting, family rates and a children's menu are available, plus riding and fishing nearby

Kelly's Resort Hotel

Rosslare Strand, Co. Wexford, **t** (053) 32114, **www.kellys.ie** (*expensive–luxury*)

A 4-star, 100-bedroom hotel on 5 miles (8km) of safe, sandy beach near several golf courses. Children are catered for all day, with activities available for all ages: there's an indoor playroom, an outdoor playground and a special kids' dinner at 5.30pm. There's also entertainment, a leisure centre, a swimming pool, a tennis court and crazy golf. You can book full board or self-cater (book well in advance). Staff will arrange a minibus to collect you from Rosslare Strand Station if you wish.

Kilkenny River Court Hotel

The Bridge, John St, Kilkenny, t (056) 772 3388, www.kilrivercourt.com (*luxury*)

A 4-star on the river, with family rooms and a leisure centre with a swimming pool.

Langton House Hotel

69 John St, Kilkenny, t (056) 776 5133, www.lanton.ie (*expensive–luxury*)

A 3-star Art Deco-style hotel with family rooms.

Whites Hotel

George St, Wexford Town, Co. Wexford, t (053) 22311 (*moderate*)

Central and comfortable, this was the smartest hotel in town for years. It is now largely modern but still incorporates part of an old coaching inn. Facilities include a health and fitness club, price reductions for children, kids' meals and babysitting.

Country houses

Ballinkeele House

Ballymurn, Enniscorthy, Co. Wexford, t (053) 533 8105, www.ballinkeele.com (*luxury*)

Children are welcome to enjoy the peaceful atmosphere at this old family home in 350 acres of farm and woodland, with ponds, mature trees and rhododendrons.

Ballyduff House

Thomastown, Co. Kilkenny, t (056) 775 8488 (*moderate*)

This 18th-century manor house is set in wooded parkland overlooking the River Nore. A family suite is available, and all bedrooms are furnished with antiques and white linen. Your hostess Breda Thomas runs a pony club for youngsters, and can arrange activities for visitors young and old.

Belmore

Jerpoint Church, Thomastown, Co. Kilkenny, t (056) 772 4228 (*moderate*)

A fine old family home with gardens and a working farm on the site of a 1790 hunting lodge. Children are welcome, but you may not want to tell them that Santa Claus is reputedly buried nearby.

Cullintra House

The Rower, Inistioge, Co. Kilkenny, t (051) 423 614 (10am–2am), www.indigo.ie/~cullhse/ (*moderate*)

A magical place (especially for cat lovers), set in beautiful, flower-filled grounds, with antiques and bohemian furnishings. Lively proprietress Patricia Cantlon paints as well as runs her ancestral home and 230-acre estate at the foot of Mount Brandon. A separate building is available for those who prefer more private quarters, as well as a plant-filled art-studio conservatory for conference and guest use. Art lessons and guided walks may also be available. Superb dinners may last late into the night, and breakfast can be served until midday.

Garranavabby House

The Rower, Inistioge, Co. Kilkenny, t (051) 423 613 (*inexpensive*)

One family room is available in this farmhouse, parts of which were built in the late 17th century. It's in a scenic rural setting near charming Inistioge, on the outskirts of Rower village.

Horetown House

Foulksmills, Co. Wexford, t (051) 565 771 (*moderate*)

An old-fashioned 17th-century manor house in a beautiful parkland setting. Mrs Young offers good plain food in The Cellar Restaurant, and facilities include an equestrian centre in the courtyard.

Kilmokea Country Manor House

Great Island, Campile, Co. Wexford, t (051) 388 109 (*moderate–expensive*)

A perfect spot for families who enjoy a more genteel holiday, this Victorian house and its grounds have been carefully planned to create a sense of tranquil repose. Apart from the new Jacuzzi, sauna and heated pool in an unobtrusive, sweet-smelling, cedar-panelled building, Kilmokea's restaurant (*see* p.89 and p.111) and tea room, The Pink Teacup, offer gourmet meals comprising ingredients from its own organic plot. Seven acres of delightful walled gardens surround the house. Parents appreciate the quality and quiet of the place, while children love roaming from one walled garden to another to climb trees, play hide and seek or dream on leaf-cosseted secret seats. One garden has a stream and small bridges, so an adult should accompany children under 12. Tastefully decorated apartments or rooms, some en suite, with twin or double beds, are available.

B&Bs and guesthouses

Ballaghtobin

Callan, Co. Kilkenny, t (056) 772 5227, www.ballaghtobin.com (*moderate*)

Children are welcome in this Georgian home set in lovely grounds, with tastefully decorated and luxurious rooms.

Butler House
16 Patrick St, Kilkenny Town, **t** (056) 22828/65707 (*moderate–expensive*)

A smart, central, comfortable Georgian guesthouse.

Danville House
New Ross Rd, Kilkenny Town, **t** (056) 772 1512 (*moderate*)

A Georgian farmhouse with family rooms.

Self-catering

Blanchville House
Dunbell, Maddoxtown, Co. Kilkenny, **t** (056) 27197 (*moderate*)

Self-catering apartments in an old coachhouse.

Killowen House
Dunganstown, New Ross, Co. Wexford, **t** (027) 51184 (*moderate*)

An attractive cottage and apartment with a tennis court and gardens.

Somers' Fort Cottages
Coolroe, Ballycullane, Co. Wexford, **t** (051) 562 335, **www.somersfort.com** (*moderate*)

Three 19th-century tenant farmers' cottages.

Hostels

Arthurstown An Oige Youth Hostel
Coastguard Station, Arthurstown, Co. Wexford, **t** (051) 389 411 (*inexpensive*)

Small family rooms available in summer (from 1 June) in a good cycling and walking area.

Rosslare Harbour An Oige
Goulding St, Rosslare, Co. Wexford, **t** (053) 33399 (*inexpensive*)

An 85-room hostel open all year, with a courtyard where toddlers can play. You can swim, ride horses or play golf nearby, and eat at a nearby hotel.

Kildare, Laois and Offaly

Hotels

Castle Durrow
Durrow, Co. Laois, **t** (0502) 36555, **www.castledurrow.com** (*luxury*)

Children are welcome at this country-house hotel with a 30-acre orchard on its estate, offering family rooms and organic meals.

Kilkea Castle
Castledermot, Co. Kildare, **t** (059) 914 5156, **www.kilkeacastle.ie** (*luxury*)

The oldest inhabited castle in Ireland, with views over tranquil gardens. As well as accommodation, it offers good health and sporting facilities.

Kinnitty Castle
Kinnitty, Co. Offaly, **t** (0509) 37318, **www.kinnittycastle.com** (*luxury*)

Atmospheric rooms in a 17th-century neo-Gothic mansion that hosts medieval banquets. A large luxury cottage is also available for rent. Dinner is served in the Georgian restaurant; other facilities include children's meals, babysitting, gardens, tennis courts and a gym. Falconry, riding, fishing and golf are available nearby.

Country houses

Griesemount
Ballitore, Co. Kildare, **t** (059) 8648 1205 (*expensive*)

A small, genteel B&B in a Georgian house.

Ivyleigh House
Bank Place, Portlaoise, Co. Laois, **t** (0502) 22081, **www.ivyleigh.com** (*moderate*)

Children are welcome at this antique-furnished Georgian townhouse, although no family rooms or cots are available. Breakfasts are magnificent.

The Manor House
Ballaghmore Castle, Borris-in-Ossory, Co. Laois, **t** (0505) 21453, **www.castleballaghmore.com** (*expensive*)

One of the oldest houses in Ireland. Families are welcome, and unbeatable breakfasts are served.

Roundwood House
Mountrath, Co. Laois, **t** (0502) 32120, **www.hidden-ireland.com/roundwood/** (*moderate*)

This Palladian mansion built in the 1740s near the Slieve Bloom Mountains is run by a delightful couple who instantly make you feel welcome. The atmosphere is relaxed, and antiques, books and paintings fill the house to absorb you on cold, wet afternoons. For good weather, riding and golf are on hand. There's lots for kids to do – animals to feed, woods to explore and games to play in the nursery. A self-catering apartment is available.

B&Bs and guesthouses

Kilkea Lodge Farm

Castledermot, Co. Kildare, t (059) 914 5112 (*moderate*)

A charming 18th-century farmhouse where riding holidays can be arranged.

Preston House

Abbeyleix, Co. Laois, t (0502) 31432 (*moderate*)

Children are welcome in this ivy-covered Georgian B&B, just as they were when it was a school. Its award-winning restaurant serves Sunday lunches, where vegetarians and the health-conscious can find nutritious options.

Spinners Townhouse and Bistro

Castle St, Birr, Co. Offaly, t (0509) 21673, www.spinners-town-house.com (*moderate*)

Set in a garden courtyard, this modern, stylish B&B has a backdrop of Birr Castle. The bistro offers tasty dishes made from local ingredients.

Self-catering

Coolanowle Country House

Ballickmoyler, Co. Laois, t (059) 862 5776, www.coolanowle.com (*moderate*)

This organic farm offers a self-catering cottage and B&B, with home-baking, a fully equipped gym and steam room on site.

Kilrush Holiday Homes

Narraghmore, Athy, Co. Kildare, t (059) 862 6631 (*moderate*)

One and two-bedroom apartments are available in this 18th-century house on a 120-acre estate.

Meath and Louth

Hotels

Ballymascanlon House Hotel

Dundalk, Co. Louth, t (042) 935 8200, www.ballymascanlon.com (*moderate–expensive*)

A Victorian country house set in an 18-hole parkland golf course. In the grounds is a fine example of a portal dolmen, as well as a pool, gym and tennis courts. Families are welcome, and encouraged by price reductions, children's meals, babysitting, and riding and fishing nearby.

Smarmore Castle

Smarmore, Ardee, Co. Louth, t (041) 685 7167 (*luxury*)

A refurbished 14th-century building with a fitness and leisure complex including a 72ft (22m) indoor heated swimming pool, toddler's pool, gym, sauna, steam room and Jacuzzi.

The Station House Hotel

Killmessan, Co. Meath, t (046) 902 5239, www.thestationhousehotel.com (*moderate*)

A converted 1850s railway station that's now a very pleasant hotel with price reductions for kids, children's meals and gardens, plus fishing nearby.

Country houses

Ghan House

Carlingford, Co. Louth, t (042) 937 3682, www.ghanhouse.com (*luxury*)

You'll find luxury and comfort at this 18th-century Georgian manor in this medieval town, with views over Carlingford Lough near the Mountains of Mourne. Owners Paul and Joyce Carroll go out of their way to make you welcome. It's the variety and quality of the cooking that really makes this place special, though. The proprietors also run a cookery school and hold gourmet nights in their renowned restaurant. Everything is perfectly judged, and children are offered their own choice of simple gourmet-style dishes. More independent and quieter en suite family accommodation is available in a converted dairy next door, where youngsters can sleep in bunk beds. This is a good base for watersports and hill-walking.

Loughcrew House

Oldcastle, Co. Meath, t (049) 854 1356, www.loughcrew.com (*expensive*)

The Napers run a school for gilding and painting restoration as well as this B&B in their grand house on an estate that's been in the family for centuries. Children are welcome, and families find the house and nearby Loughcrew refreshing and fascinating.

Hostels

Slane Farm Hostel

Harlinstown House, Slane, Co. Meath, t (041) 988 4985, www.slanefarmhostel.ie (*inexpensive*)

This independent hostel is in the middle of the Boyne Valley on a working farm with a faery fort. En suite family and dormitory rooms are available, plus a laundry room, bike hire and kitchen.

Self-catering

Kiltale Cottage

Kiltale, Dunsany, Co. Meath, t (046) 943 6679, www.irishholidayhomes.com (*moderate*)

This self-catering 16th-century cottage in rural surroundings sleeps 6. A playground, pony rides and a farm may be visited nearby.

Slane Farm Cottages

Near Slane Castle, Harlinstown, Slane, Co. Meath, t (041) 982 4390, www.slanefarmcottages.com (*inexpensive–moderate*)

Old horse stalls here have been skillfully renovated into individual wood-floored three-room cottage-apartments that hold an open-plan parlour with fully equipped modern kitchen, a bedroom with double and single beds and a bathroom with a short-burst shower. Within the complex, which also houses a hostel, is a laundry room you can use. Located between many Meath attractions beside a road, touring the Boyne Valley is easy from here. Information about sites may be obtained in the reception area or from the friendly staff. All around this place lies the past and when the full moon spreads its mystical white glow over everything, it's easy to feel that Angus Óg could be hovering in bird form in a nearby tree where bird wings are rustling.

Camping and caravanning

Gyles Caravan and Camping Park

Riverstown, Co. Louth, t (042) 937 6262 (*moderate*)

Set in the Cooley peninsula beneath the Slieve Foy mountains overlooking Dundalk Bay, facilities here include a pool room, leisure centre with gym and sauna, bar and children's playground.

Westmeath and Longford

Hotels

The Village Inn

Tyrellspass, Co. Westmeath, t (044) 23171 (*moderate*)

A cosy, period townhouse hotel offering excellent service and food. The building forms part of an elegant crescent around the village green.

Country houses

Mornington House

Mornington, Multyfarnham, near Mullingar, Co. Westmeath, t (044) 72191, www.mornington.ie (*moderate*)

Teenagers and parents seeking quiet will enjoy this lovely country house where two dogs act as the welcoming party and proprietors Anne and Warwick O'Hara will ensure your stay is restful. Their own vegetables and herbs flavour the delicious candlelit dinners served before a peat fire. The beautiful grounds are close to Lake Derravaragh, to which you can walk.

B&Bs and guesthouses

Shannon Side House

Termonbarry, near Cloondara, Co. Longford, t (043) 26052 (*inexpensive*)

A comfortable house on the edge of the Shannon. Its proprietor is an expert on fishing matters and has a boat that you can use.

Toberphelim House

Granard, Co. Longford, t (043) 86568 (*moderate*)

A pleasant old farmhouse owned by a friendly family, the Smyths, who are also family friendly.

Woodlands Farm

Streamstown, Mullingar, Co. Meath, t (044) 26414 (*inexpensive*)

Very typical of Irish farmhouses, Mrs Maxwell's welcoming place is crammed with holy pictures and offers delicious food.

Self-catering

Mullingar Equestrian Centre

Athlone Rd, Mullingar, Co. Westmeath, t (044) 48331/40569, www.mullingarequestrian.com (*moderate*)

A self-catering cottage sleeping eight, and four ensuite rooms, at a well-equipped riding centre.

Camping and caravanning

Lough Derravaragh Camping and Leisure Park

Multyfarnham, near Mullingar, Co. Westmeath, t (044) 71500 (*inexpensive*).

This site offers good facilities in a lovely location near the lough, excellent for walks, riding, sailing and other sports.

MUNSTER

County Cork

Cork City

Hotels

Metropole Gresham Hotel
McCurtain St, **t** (021) 450 8122, **www.gresham-metropolehotel.com** (*moderate*)

This hotel offers old-fashioned charm together with excellent facilities, including three swimming pools, two dining areas with views over the River Lee, and the Met Tavern.

Country houses

Farran House
Farran, Cork, **t** (021) 733 1215, **www.farranhouse.com** (*luxury*)

Families are welcome at this elegant country house set in 12 acres of mature beech woods just to the west of Cork City. The guest rooms have enormous bathrooms.

B&Bs and guesthouses

Garnish House
Western Rd, Cork, **t** (021) 427 5111, **www.garnish.ie** (*inexpensive–moderate*)

A surprising jewel of a guesthouse. In the morning you will find tables covered in crisp white linen and tastefully laid with fresh flowers and china, and be amazed by an extraordinary array of stewed and fresh fruits, home-made breads, cakes and yogurts, Irish cheeses and more. A very extensive menu is also available, which will make even the most fussy vegetarian feel they are in heaven. Children are made very welcome in the old Brehon manner.

Hostels

Cork International An Oige
1/2 Redclyffe, Western Rd, **t** 454 3289 (*inexpensive*)

Just across from the University of Cork, this central hostel has en suite family rooms, a kitchen and a laundry. It's a bit bare, but clean and private.

Sheila's
4 Belgrave Place, Wellington Rd, **t** (021) 450 5562 (*inexpensive*)

A conveniently central option north of the river, with family rooms.

Around County Cork

Hotels

Blarney Park Hotel
Blarney, **t** (021) 438 5281, **www.blarneypark.com** (*moderate*)

Not far from Cork city, this hotel has a large, child-friendly leisure centre, with toddler pools, a waterslide, a pool, saunas, a steam room, a gym and a play room, plus a therapy centre with alternative therapies, and babysitting/listening.

The Blue Haven
Pearse St, Kinsale, **t** (021) 477 2209 (*moderate*)

A strong candidate for the title of best hotel in Kinsale (3 star), this is cosy and comfortable with excellent food.

Casey's
Baltimore, **t** (028) 20197 (*moderate*)

The best type of small hotel: welcoming and comfortable, with excellent food served in its bar and restaurant.

Inchydoney Island Lodge and Spa
Inchydoney Beach, Clonakilty, West Cork, **t** (023) 33143, **www.inchydoneyisland.com** (*expensive–luxury*)

Families are welcome in this modern spa hotel and holiday apartment complex beside a magnificent, virtually untouched beach. Toiletries and 4-star accompaniments, including complimentary flip-flops and fluffy white housecoats, are provided in each en suite room, many of which face the ocean. Gourmet fare is served in a large restaurant from which you can survey the ocean beyond the heli-pad and car parks. The modern haute cuisine, including good vegetarian dishes, is great for both adults and children. Starters include figs with blue cheese, and among the fresh home-made breads is an unbelievably good walnut bread. Buffet-style breakfasts include fruit compôtes/salads, cheese and cold meats, and a cooked Irish buffet breakfast with Clonakilty black pudding. The beauty and therapy spa features clay and seaweed wraps. You can swim in a seawater pool where whirlpools and waterfalls massage away your aches and pains while you watch your children play in the kiddies' pool beside it. Outside you can walk on the sandy Blue Flag beach (check with hotel staff before you surf the waves, however, as the tides can be dangerous). Be sure to request a quiet room, as the nightly entertainments can go on into the wee hours.

Midleton Park Hotel and Spa

Midleton, t (021) 463 5100 (*moderate–expensive*)

This is quite a luxurious residence for the price, with a leisure and 'wellness' centre, and an indoor pool. The décor is beautiful, the atmosphere relaxed and the restaurant food superb. There are low rates for children sharing with parents.

O'Donovan's Hotel

44 Pearse St, Clonakilty, t (023) 33250 (*moderate*)

An old-fashioned hotel in the town centre, with a public bar and family rates.

Sea View House Hotel

Ballylickey, t (027) 50073 (*moderate*)

Cots, highchairs and babysitting are provided in this hotel offering old-fashioned Irish hospitality and good food. Two cottages are available to rent.

Westlodge Hotel

Bantry, t (027) 50360, www.westlodgehotel.ie (*moderate*)

A hotel with a scenic location just outside town, activities for children (June–Aug), a leisure centre with toddler and children's pools, a sauna, a Jacuzzi and a gym, and gardens, pitch'n'putt, tennis courts and a playground. Babysitting and kids' meals are available, as are some self-catering cottages.

Country houses

Assolas Country House

Kanturk, t (029) 50015, www.assolas.com (*luxury*)

Children are welcome at this superb 17th-century house among mature trees that run right down to the river. Monks lived at this site until the 16th century. Tennis, fishing and croquet are possible, and delicious food is served.

Ballymaloe House

Shanagarry, t (021) 465 2531, www.ballymaloe.com (*expensive*)

A special trip to Myrtle Allen's Georgian house paradise is well worth it, for the elegant rooms, friendly service and generous helpings of fabulous food, served in a room with a rustic French atmosphere. Chefs from all over Ireland come here to learn at the celebrated Ballymaloe School, which sparked the current revolution in Irish cuisine. The whole Allen family are involved in the enterprise, and have created organic gardens that curl around grey-stone farmhouses and a summerhouse covered in seashells. Children can have special early meals, and babysitting can be arranged. In summer they can swim in an outdoor pool (not supervised) or play in a sandpit and on a slide. A small golf course, a tennis court and a craft and kitchen shop are on-site, and fishing and riding can be organized.

Ballyvolane House

Castlelyons, near Fermoy, t (025) 36349, www.ballyvolanehouse.ie (*luxury*)

Run by a friendly family who are welcoming to children, this lovely old Georgian house is set in beautiful grounds, and locally produced vegetables are used in the cooking.

Bantry House

Bantry, t (027) 50047 (*luxury*)

Children are welcome in this converted wing of one of Ireland's most beautiful stately homes, with a plush library, snooker room and extensive gardens at guests' disposal.

Rock Cottage

Barnatonicane, near Schull, t (028) 35538

A renovated Georgian hunting lodge with bright bedrooms, wicker furniture and wooden floors, run by a German lady chef who spent happy holidays in Ireland as a child and invites families.

B&Bs and guesthouses

Avonmore House

South Abbey, Youghal, t (024) 92617 (*inexpensive*)

This elegant old house with beautiful rooms is a good bargain.

Ballymakeigh House

Killeagh, Youghal, t (024) 95184, www.ballymakeighhouse.com (*expensive*)

Margaret Browne, award-winning cook and owner of Browne's County Restaurant (*see* p.152), runs this guesthouse with aplomb, ensuring you feel at home. In the middle of her husband's dairy farm, its plant-filled conservatory is a fine spot for nouveau-Irish dinners and breakfasts sprinkled with herbs. You'll have a peaceful time here.

Castle Salem
Near Rosscarbery, **t** (023) 48381 (*inexpensive*)
A family room is available in this atmospheric B&B where Pennsylvania founder William Penn once slept. Donations are gratefully received to help preserve this impressive 15th-century castle now owned by the Daly family.

Grove House
Ahakistra, Durras, **t** (027) 67060 (*inexpensive*)
An old and pretty farmhouse on the Sheep's Head Peninsula, where you can sample delicious honey from the garden and free-range eggs.

Magannagan Farm
Derryconnery, Glengarriff, **t** (027) 63361 (*inexpensive*)
A small, good-value cottage where you can enjoy fine high teas.

Schull Central B&B
Schull, **t** (028) 28227 (*inexpensive*)
An efficiently run B&B handy for Schull harbour, with all en suite rooms.

Seacourt
Butlerstown, **t** (023) 40151 (*inexpensive*)
A beautiful historic house (1760) with views of the Seven Heads peninsula.

Self-catering

The Castle
Castletownshend, **t** (028) 36100 (*moderate*)
A choice of apartments in 18th-century buildings.

Courtmacsherry Coastal Cottages
Courtmacsherry, **t** (023) 46198 (*inexpensive–expensive*)
Eight luxury cottages enjoying the use of nearby hotel facilities.

Glenview House
Midleton, **t** (021) 463 1680, **www.glenviewmidleton.com** (*expensive*)
Two self-catering coach-house cottages beside a Georgian guesthouse, one with disabled facilities, both sleeping 2–6. Guide dogs are welcome.

Green Lodge
Trawnamadree, Ballylickey, Bantry, **t** (027) 66146 (*inexpensive*)
A single-storey terrace in an enclosed courtyard, with disabled access, next to an organic garden on 10 acres in a beautiful part of West Cork.

Hostels

Cape Clear Island An Oige
Cape Clear Island, **t** (028) 41968 (*inexpensive*)
This hostel offers basic family rooms in summer (from 1 June) in an isolated spot.

Shiplake Mountain Hostel
Dunmanway (3 miles/5km from Dunmanway Sq via Castle Rd), **t** (023) 45750, **www.shiplakemountainhostel.com** (*inexpensive–moderate*)
This restored traditional farmhouse on top of a mountainous hill has a communal kitchen and parlour, small dormitory rooms, caravan and garden. You're close to nature here, which leads to interesting conversations with people who prefer to visit places far from the usual tourist routes. Ask about the courtesy pick-up/drop-off service from the nearby old-fashioned village of Dunmanway.

County Kerry

Hotels

Brandon Court Hotel
Tralee, **t** (066) 712 9666, **www.brandonhotel.ie** (*expensive*)
A hotel offering babysitting/listening, price reductions for kids, children's meals, a swimming pool and other sports and leisure facilities. Cots and highchairs are also available.

Butler Arms Hotel
Waterville, **t** (066) 947 4144, **www.butlerarms.com** (*moderate–expensive*)
There are fantastic sea views from this intimate, family-run, pleasantly old-fashioned hotel. It's a lovely place to stay for salmon or trout fishing, and there's also a sandy beach and riding for kids, plus children's meals, babysitting, price reductions for families and gardens to run around in.

Castlerosse Hotel and Leisure Centre
Killarney, **t** (064) 31144, **www.castlerossehotelkillarney.com** (*moderate*)
Great lake and mountain views may be seen from Castlerosse's self-catering suites and main hotel, which caters well for disabled guests. Children's

meals, babysitting, price discounts for families, gardens, a swimming pool and tennis courts are all available, and riding and fishing can be enjoyed nearby. Golf packages are offered and an inviting leisure centre offering Swedish massage is available.

The Climbers' Inn

Glencar, t (066) 976 0101, www.climbersinn.com (*moderate*)

Get away from it all at this wild mountain location, 30mins yet a million miles from Killarney. There are cottagey bedrooms in the inn and a hostel behind. The on-site walking and climbing centre offers wilderness walking tours.

Dingle Skellig Hotel

Dingle, t (066) 915 0200, www.dingleskellig.com (*moderate–expensive*)

A family-friendly hotel with leisure facilities that include a children's pool with waterfall and bubble feature, Fungi Kids Club during weekends and school holidays, indoor and outdoor play areas and a playroom. There's also a crèche, interconnecting rooms, a babysitting service and separate kids' menus and meal times.

Glencar House Hotel

Glencar, t (066) 976 0102, www.glencarhouse.com (*moderate*)

A remote, comfortable, clean and efficient country house hotel in a stunning area of special conservation framed by mountains, with boats to hire on nearby lakes. Child-friendly features in this golf and fishing resort include price reductions, kids' meals, a games room, a tennis court and gardens, and the menu is largely organic.

Killarney Park Hotel

Kenmare Place, t (064) 35555, www.killarneyparkhotel.ie (*expensive*)

An oasis of modern luxury, with marble floors, antique furniture, huge suites, and a pool and health spa. Children's meals, price reductions, a babysitting service and a playroom are available.

The Park Hotel

Shelbourne St, Kenmare, t (064) 41200, www.parkkenmare.com (*luxury*)

For first-class service, visit this award-winning hotel with a new spa and every modern comfort in rooms furnished with fine antiques. Thoughtful extras are provided – children will exult over the nuts and home-made biscuits. The views are exemplary and you feel a deep sense of rest as you breathe in the soothing Kerry air. Finely judged, delicious meals are made with organic local produce. Babysitting/listening, price reductions for families, a games room, gardens and tennis facilities are at hand.

Quality Hotel and Leisure Centre

Killarney, t (064) 31555, www.qualityhotelkillarney.com (*luxury*)

Facilities here include a children's activity programme in school holidays and at weekends, crèche (up to age 3), supervised activities (ages 3 and up), family events, 24hr parents' kitchen, babysitting, playroom/outdoor playground and leisure centre.

Sheen Falls Lodge

Kenmare, t (064) 41600, www.sheenfallslodge.ie (*luxury*)

A beautifully located hotel popular with families for its leisure centre and child-pleasing activities, and its elegant rooms and lavish food. Parents can enjoy health treatments in the spa and fine dining overlooking the Sheen Waterfalls. For children there are gardens, an outdoor play area, a games room and special meals, price reductions and a babysitting service.

Country houses

Glendalough House

Caragh Lake, Killorglin, t (066) 976 9156 (*moderate*)

A lovingly furnished house with great views over the lake.

B&Bs and guesthouses

Aisling House

Castlegregory, t (066) 713 9134 (*inexpensive*)

A clean, comfortable choice, with good breakfasts.

Castlemorris House

Ballymullen, Tralee, t (066) 718 0060 (*expensive*)

Children are welcome in this large 18th-century house in extensive gardens, a short walk from Tralee city centre. It has a pleasant drawing room, spacious bedrooms, open fires and a friendly atmosphere.

Doyle's Townhouse

John St, Dingle, t (066) 915 1174, www.doylesofdingle.com (*moderate*)

One of the most enjoyable places to stay in the country with rooms full of individuality and sitting-room shelves groaning with books over which you can linger by a warm fire. The Seafood Bar and Restaurant next door (*see* p.152) are famous for their conviviality and food.

Fuchsia House
Muckross Rd, Killarney, **t** (064) 33743, **www.fuchsiahouse.com** (*moderate*)

Children are welcome in this peaceful, modern Victorian-style house.

Hawthorne House
Shelbourne St, Kenmare, **t** (064) 41035 (*inexpensive*)

Families are welcome at this comfortable B&B, with en suite bedrooms and delicious food.

Inveraray Farm Guesthouse
Beaufort, Killarney, **t** (064) 44224 (*inexpensive*)

A guesthouse offering a playground, playroom, pony rides for children, babysitting and home-baking. Tours can be arranged.

The Phoenix
Shanahill East, Boolteens, Castlemaine, **t** (066) 976 6284 (*moderate*)

This slightly hippyish B&B serves vegetarian and vegan foods in a little café run by its Swiss-trained cook/owner and her Kerry-born husband.

Suan na Mara
Camp, **t** (066) 713 9258 (*moderate*)

An award-winning Laura Ashley-style home with mountain views, a private walk to a sandy beach, an extensive breakfast menu, a pitch'n'putt course, a cot and a babysitting service.

Self-catering

The Cottage
Patrick O'Leary, Sneem, **t** (064) 45132 (*inexpensive*)

A two-bedroom cottage near the sea.

Stone House
Ventry, **t** (066) 915 9962 (*inexpensive–moderate*)

A traditional three-bedroom stone house. The owner also has other comfortable properties.

Hostels

There are An Oige Hostels with family rooms at Dunquin, Ballyferriter, Beaufort and Killarney, and on Valentia Island.

Ballintaggart House Hostel and Camping Site
Tralee Rd, Dingle Town, Co. Kerry, **t** (066) 915 1454, **www.dingleaccommodation.com** (*inexpensive*)

Plans are afoot to turn this converted 18th-century hunting lodge into a hotel, but it would be a real pity to lose the history of its enclosed stableyard, where the starving came during the 19th-century famine to partake of soup made in the large iron 'famine' pot that sits there empty now. (Today visitors use the communal kitchen beside it.) Family rooms are available, including private ones in the old stables, where you'll have your own shower, although it's one of those button-press ones once common in hostels, and the water isn't constant or necessarily pure.

Collis Sandes House
Oakpark, Tralee, **t** (066) 712 8658, **www.colsands.com** (*inexpensive*)

Family rooms, self-catering kitchens and a laundry in an imposing 19th-century country house in 15 acres of woodland on the edge of Tralee, with camping areas. It hosts traditional music sessions in the evenings.

Fáilte Hostel
Shelbourne St, Kenmare, **t** (064) 42333 (*inexpensive*)

A virtually spotless place run by a mother-and-daughter team, with en suite family rooms.

Camping and caravanning

Campail Teach An Aragail Oratory House Camping
Gallarus, Dingle, **t** (066) 915 5143 (*inexpensive*)

Killarney Flesk Caravan and Camping Park
Killarney, **t** (064) 31704 (*inexpensive–moderate*)

County Limerick

Hotels

Adare Manor Hotel
Adare, **t** (061) 396 566, **www.adaremanor.ie** (*luxury*)

The former house of the Earls of Dunraven, in a mix of Victorian, Gothic and Tudor fantasy architectural styles, has beautiful grounds, riding facilities, clay-pigeon shooting, an 18-hole golf course and an indoor swimming pool and fitness centre. Children's meals, family discounts and babysitting are available.

Castletroy Park

Dublin Rd, Limerick, t (061) 335 566, www.castletroy-park.ie (*expensive*)

This modern 4-star hotel offers fine food, a swimming pool with its own gardens, children's meals and family price reductions.

Dunraven Arms Hotel

Adare, t (061) 396 633, www.dunravenhotel.com (*expensive*)

An olde-worlde hotel, with appealing rooms, friendly staff, a large swimming pool and garden, children's meals, family price reductions and a babysitting service.

Country houses

Ash Hill Stud Farm

Kilmallock, Limerick, t (063) 98035 (*moderate*)

A bed and breakfast in a crumbling 18th-century mansion, where two terriers greet you as you're invited in for tea by the fire in a parlour with the atmosphere of a century ago. Horsebreeder-owner Simon Johnson's crested white cockateel may sit on your shoulder – be sure to offer it some crumbs from your biscuit as it's the polite thing to do and he will expect it. A high-ceilinged bedroom with windows opening onto vast quiet grounds holds a bed so soft you feel you're sinking into 100 years of history. Shades of Anglo-Irish splendour remain in the antique-filled dining room, outside the windows of which chickens cackle and peck. You must love animals and deep night silences to enjoy your stay here, but don't expect the gloss of a hotel.

B&Bs and guesthouses

Cussens Cottage

Ballygreennan, Bulgaden, Kilmallock, t (063) 98926 (*inexpensive*)

Nearly two acres of organic gardens supply the kitchen here, which provides vegetarian breakfasts and dinners, and vegan and macrobiotic meals by request. Children are welcome, and there is disabled access.

Self-catering

Springfield Castle

Drumcollogher, t (063) 83162 (*expensive*)

A fabulous historic home that is available for holiday lets.

Hostels

Barrington's Lodge and Hostel

Georges Quay, Limerick, t (061) 415 222 (*inexpensive*)

Children's meals, a playground, indoor playroom, babysitting, cots and highchairs are available here.

County Clare

Hotels

The Falls Hotel

Ennistymon, t (065) 707 1004, www.fallshotel.net (*moderate*)

With a reputation of 50 years' standing, this hotel sits above the river that runs through Ennistymon. Its faded charm is perked up by a lively bar, but quiet rooms for families are available, as are children's meals, family rates and babysitting. The grounds cover 50 acres of woodland and glen, with riding, fishing and river walks possible.

The Old Ground Hotel

O'Connell St, Ennis, t (065) 682 8127, www.flynnhotels.com (*moderate*)

Built in 1749, this pretty ivy-covered hotel in the middle of Ennis has 83 rooms furnished with antiques, plus a garden. Its pub has entertainment from cabaret to Irish music in summer. Babysitting, children's meals, family rates and highchairs in the restaurant are available.

Temple Gate Hotel

The Square, Ennis, t (065) 682 3300, www.templegatehotel.com (*moderate*)

Built on the site of a 19th-century convent in central Ennis, this excellent modern hotel retains a sense of its former inhabitants' prayerful peace. It has an award-winning restaurant and an enjoyable pub where you can have light meals or snacks. Family rooms, children's meals and babysitting are available, as are riding and fishing nearby.

Country houses

Berry Lodge

Annagh, Milltown Mowbay, t (065) 708 7022, www.berrylodge.com (*moderate*)

Good food and lodgings from a lady who teaches home economics to local pupils in her kitchen.

Fergus View

Kilnaboy, Corofin, t (065) 683 7606 (*moderate*)

Families are welcome here, and there's excellent food (give notice if you are on a special diet) and a garden sloping to a river. You can also rent a self-catering cottage next door.

Gregan's Castle

Near Ballyvaughan, t (065) 707 7005, www.gregans.ie (*expensive*)

This is not actually a castle but an old manor house, with comfortable rooms and delicious food. Set at the top of the Corkscrew Hills amid green gardens, it makes a fantastic contrast to the Burren's moonscape, with views over Galway Bay.

Lismacteigue

Ballyvaughan, t (065) 707 7040 (*inexpensive*)

Children are welcome in this 500-year-old thatched farmhouse in a ring fort, on a green road in the Burren, open in summer only.

Tinarana House

Killaloe, t (061) 376 966, www.tinaranahouse.com (*inexpensive–moderate*)

A Victorian mansion in 300 acres of woods and open countryside, with deer, pheasants and other wildlife. Bedrooms have magnificent views across a valley by Lough Derg. Organic cuisine and health treatments are offered.

B&Bs and guesthouses

Doolin Activity Lodge

Doolin, t (065) 707 4888, www.doolinlodge.com (*inexpensive–moderate*)

Restored stone buildings near Doolin Pier, with modern en suite guestrooms and self-catering apartments (available weekly or nightly), best for outdoor types who don't place too much importance on fine breakfasts and the like. The helpful staff can book (preferably with advance notice) many local sports activities for you, including caving, diving, walking, cycling and golf.

Self-catering

The NatureQuest Centre

Blackweir Bridge, Kilkee, t (065) 905 6789, www.naturequest.ie (*moderate*)

Serenity is assured as you gaze from the living room of one of these five superb, wooden-floored apartments onto Poulnasherry Bay. NatureQuest's owners can tell you about the natural history of Loop Head. Dolphin-watching, walks, riding, and birdwatching and photography workshops can be arranged. An indoor swimming pool and some exercise machines are also on site, and the owners often offer guests freshly baked bread and other amenities.

Tipperary and Waterford

Hotels

Cashel Palace Hotel

Main St, Cashel, Co. Tipperary, t (062) 62707, www.cashel-palace.ie (*luxury*)

An elegant 18th-century house just off the main street. Family rooms are not available, but there is a mews house with interconnecting rooms.

O'Shea's Hotel

Strand St, Tramore, Co. Waterford, t (051) 381 246, www.osheas-hotel.com (*moderate*)

This small family-run hotel is set close to the beach, and offers family rates, children's meals and babysitting.

Round Tower Hotel

College Rd, Ardmore, Co. Waterford, t (024) 94494 (*inexpensive*)

Simple accommodation in a former convent, with a restaurant offering children's meals. Family rates, a playroom and babysitting are available.

Waterford Castle Hotel

The Island, Ballinaskill, Waterford, t (051) 878 203, www.waterfordcastle.com (*luxury*)

A luxurious Anglo-Norman castle on its own 310-acre island 3 miles (5km) downstream from Waterford, with an indoor pool, golf course, tennis courts and beautiful grounds. Families get special rates, children's meals and babysitting.

Country houses

Ballycormac House

Aglish, Borrisokane, Co. Tipperary, t (067) 21129, e ballyc@indigo.ie (*moderate*)

A lovingly restored 300-year-old farmhouse, with exceptional breakfasts, dinners and activities for guests.

Bansha House

Bansha, Co. Tipperary, t (062) 54194, e banshahouse@eircom.net (*moderate*)

Children will love this early Georgian farmhouse covered in ivy, where a tiny terrier may greet them inquisitively upon arrival. After you settle in, it's likely you'll be given a hot drink and home-made cake or biscuits. Then you can look out at some of the 100 acres of farmland owned by hosts John and Mary Marnan. In the morning, after a fine Irish breakfast, Mary may encourage you to explore the walker's paradise beyond the house, or perhaps show you some of her horses. If you're not careful, you may find yourself renting their guest cottage and staying longer in this charming village.

Castle Country House

Milstreet, Cappagh, Co. Waterford, t (058) 68049, www.castlecountryhouse.com (*moderate*)

Recently upgraded, this homely country house has a lovely restored wing dating back to the 15th century. Tennis, trout fishing and horse-riding are all available.

Lismacue House

Bansha, Co. Tipperary, t (062) 54106 (*expensive*)

A beautiful lime-tree avenue leads to this gracious 17th-century house. The owners offer a warm welcome, delicious gourmet dinners and breakfasts and a sense of Anglo-Irish tradition – not to mention local advice, particularly about horses. This is horse country. Trekking parties often stay here and people come to the area looking for horses to buy.

B&Bs and guesthouses

Brown's Townhouse

29 South Parade, Waterford, t (051) 870 594, www.brownstownhouse.com (*moderate*)

This charming late-Victorian house, which is decorated in period style, was recently taken over by a new owner. It's very conveniently located for exploring Waterford.

Sion Hill House

Ferrybank, Waterford, t (051) 851 558 (*moderate*)

Families are welcome to come and stay in this early-19th-century house complete with beautiful views of Waterford and the River Suir. Its lovely gardens have been restored to their original condition and the house itself is full of antiques and memorabilia.

Self-catering

Anner Castle

Ballinamore, near Clonmel, Co. Tipperary, t (052) 33365, www.annercastle.com (*moderate*)

Accommodation in a romantic 19th-century folly in landscaped parkland.

Garrykennedy Cottage

Garrykennedy, Co. Tipperary, t (01) 633 5487, www.garrykennedycottage.com (*expensive*)

This lovely terraced cottage (*c*.1780) not far from Killaloe (35miles/56km from Shannon Airport), in a small village on Lough Derg, has a small garden, three bedrooms (two of them up a spiral staircase), and two bathrooms. As many of its original fittings as possible have been retained, and the cottage is a perfect spot for settling into a small community. It's between two pubs, one of which serves good food and often hosts music. It's also ideal for boat trips and morning walks by the lake with its swans.

Eco Booley

Clogheen, Co. Tipperary, t (052) 65191, www.ecobooley.com (*inexpensive*)

A pioneering eco-friendly cottage created as an experiment in eco-tourism by Bord Fáilte.

Killaghy Castle

Mullinahone, Co. Tipperary, t (052) 53112 (*inexpensive*)

An 18th-century manor farmhouse with a Norman castle attached, and horse-riding close by. The castle accommodates 18 people, self-catering.

Riverrun Cottages

Terryglass, Co. Tipperary, t (067) 22125, www.riverrun.ie (*moderate*)

Three and 4-star cottages in the middle of the country, near a small village with two pubs, a craft shop, post office, village store and church. There are outdoor activities on and around Lough Derg.

Hostels

Cashel Holiday Hostel

John St, Cashel, Co. Tipperary, t (062) 62330 (*inexpensive*)

A cheerful hostel in an old townhouse.

Rock House

Dundrum Rd, Cashel, Co. Tipperary, t (062) 61003 (*inexpensive*)

This restored 18th-century coach house has a hostel and self-catering accommodation.

CONNACHT

County Galway

Hotels

Ardilaun House Hotel

Taylors Hill, Galway City, t (091) 521 433, www.ardilaunhousehotel.ie (*luxury*)

This large mansion in wooded grounds, the childhood home of Lady Gregory, now boasts a leisure centre and an indoor swimming pool. Children under 15 sharing a room with their parents stay for less, and under-3s stay free.

Brennan's Yard Hotel

Lower Merchant's Rd, Galway City, t (091) 568 166, (*moderate*)

A pleasant town hotel with stripped pine décor and local pottery. Children aged 2–12 staying in a room with their parents pay half-price; kids under the age of 2 stay free.

Day's Hotel

Inishbofin Island, t (095) 45809 (*moderate*)

This family-run hotel on the pier on remote Inishbofin has recently been renovated and a spa has been added to it. The son of the house runs music nights to which children are welcome.

Ostan Inis Meáin

Inishmann, Aran Islands, t (099) 73020, www.galway.net/pages/inismeain/ (*moderate*)

The only hotel on the island, made famous by playwright JM Synge when he came here in the 1900s, has family rooms.

Renvyle House Hotel

Renvyle, Connemara, t (095) 43511, www.renvyle.com (*expensive*)

This hotel on the edge of the Atlantic is going green by recycling and instituting sustainable energy systems. It sits on the edge of a peninsula covered by Mesolithic and Neolithic settlements near Grace O'Malley's Renvyle Castle – the seat of the O'Flaherty clan, who ruled Connacht until Cromwell's arrival in the 17th century. Once the site of physician Oliver St John Gogarty's home, it was burnt down by rebels against Gogarty taking office in the Republic's post-partition government. Rebuilt, its ghosts remained; WB Yeats encountered them on his honeymoon there. In 1991 a flood ruined the building's ocean-facing side; new family suites – with modern Jacuzzi-style baths, separate showers and sitting rooms – now face the rocky shore. The older part of the hotel has first-floor rooms with balconies overlooking an outdoor swimming pool (used only on warm days) and a dark 19th-century-style library. The downstairs bar offers traditional Irish and popular acoustic music and a pianist accompanies generous dinners of imaginative, contemporary Irish cuisine served by black-suited waiting staff.

Zetland Country House Hotel

Cashel Bay, Connemara, t (095) 31111, www.zetland.com (*expensive*)

This converted hunting lodge in an isolated setting overlooking Cashel Bay offers award-winning cuisine, tennis, billiards and other activities and children are welcome.

Country houses

Cregg Castle

Corrandulla, near Galway City, t (091) 791 434, www.creggcastle.com (*moderate*)

Children are welcome to explore this estate-sized farm with its friendly dogs, cat, donkey, chickens, sheep and cattle. This old manor house has family rooms that are big and airy, with space for two or three youngsters. Board games are on hand to keep them entertained on wet evenings and the friendly proprietors, Pat and Ann Marie, often play Irish music, usually inspiring a few budding musicans to join them for a session.

Crocnaraw House

Moyard, near Clifden, t (095) 41068, e lucyfretwell@eircom.net (*moderate*)

This small, cosy Georgian country house has an otherworldly atmosphere – not surprising since Crocnaraw means 'hill of the faery fort'. Children are welcome. Delicious food is prepared from local organic produce.

Delphi Lodge

Leenane, t (095) 42222, www.delphilodge.ie (*expensive*)

The former Marquis of Sligo's sporting lodge, this 19th-century house is run along traditional lines, with tea and biscuits provided in your room on arrival. Fly-fishing can be arranged, and owner Peter Mantle makes every dinner conversation unique and meals are perfectly judged and delicious. Even Prince Charles wrote to thank him for his visit here. Children are offered early dinners separately from adults. Self-catering cottages are available.

Dolphin Beach Country House

Lower Sky Rd, Clifden, t (095) 21204, e dolphinbeach@iolfree.ie (*moderate*)

Children are welcome in this luxurious 19th-century farmhouse where the owners grow their own organic vegetables. You might be able to watch dolphins in the bay from your bedroom window if you're lucky, then pop over to a private cove for a swim. Book dinner in advance.

Lisdonagh House

Caherlistrane, t (093) 31163, www.lisdonagh.com (*moderate–luxury*)

Near the Hill of Knockma, where Finvarra, King of the Faeries, holds court, you'll find this relaxing faeryland. Dinners and breakfasts prepared from home-grown organic ingredients magically appear in your luxurious 18th-century room, Victorian gate lodge, French-style coach-house apartment or 'honeymoon' pavilion suite with pyramid roof and Venetian window. Families are welcome to explore the grounds and fish or row out to the *crannóg* on Lough Hackett, where St Patrick is said to have converted the King of Connacht to Christianity. Your hosts are friendly but unobtrusive, offering helpful advice when requested. A guests-only restaurant serves dinner at 8pm.

Man of Aran Cottage

Kilmurvy, Inishmore, Aran Islands, t (099) 61301, e manofaran@eircom.net (*moderate*)

Older children and teenagers are welcome here in high season, while families can rent the whole cottage – built for the movie *Man of Aran* by Robert Flaherty (*see* p.191) – from November to February. In the summer season, the delightful proprietors, Joe and Maura Wolfe, serve healthy breakfasts, teas and dinners. Joe is an enthusiastic organic gardener and Maura prepares tasty drinks and freshly cooked dishes using his herbs and vegetables. She can also tell you all about how people lived on Inishmore in her youth.

B&Bs and guesthouses

Ard Alainn

Inishmaan, Aran Islands, t (099) 997 3027 (*inexpensive*)

Near Synge's Chair, this recently built three-bedroom old-style Aran cottage has a lovely view of the ocean and play space for children.

Ben View House

Bridge St, Clifden, t (095) 21256 (*inexpensive*)

A truly traditional family-run B&B in the middle of Clifden, with TVs in ensuite rooms.

Camillaun

Eighterard, Oughterard, t (091) 552 678, www.camillaun.com (*moderate*)

After an excellent breakfast in this homely, modern, wooden-floored home, you can play tennis on hard courts or paddle down the River Owenriff, which runs alongside the garden. Environmentalist proprietor Greg Forde can arrange for a guide to take you to Lough Corrib in one of his boats, where you can fish or explore the ruins of two monasteries on Inchagoill Island, and the village of Oughterard is a short stroll away down a leafy lane. Good home cooking is offered for dinner.

Col-Mar House

Salahoona, Spiddal, t (091) 553 247 (*inexpensive*)

The owners of this house are very welcoming and offer especially good breakfasts in a lovely setting.

Hazel House Farmhouse

Mausrevagh, Headford, t (091) 791 204 (*inexpensive*)

You'll get a traditional Irish welcome at this modern bungalow from Mrs Cunningham, who provides tea and scones when you arrive. Matt, the man of the house, is happy to play the accordion, banjo and fiddle to guests.

Killary Lodge

Derrynasliggaun, Leenane, t (095) 42276, www.killary.com (*moderate*)

Family rooms are available in this bed and breakfast on the shores of Killary Harbour. With advance notice, the owners can cater for special diets and arrange guides for cycling, walking and other outdoor activities.

Norman Villa

86 Lower Salthill, Galway City, t (091) 521 131, www.normanvilla.com (*moderate*)

This city house has a country atmosphere, with elegance and lighthearted banter indoors and oak trees in the field behind. Children are welcome. Two family rooms are available.

Self-catering

Lucy O'Toole

Annaghvane, Bealadangan, t (091) 572 120 (*moderate*)

Two 200-year-old traditional reed-thatched cottages by the sea, with 3 bedrooms in each.

Renvyle Thatched Cottages

Renvyle, Tullycross, Connemara, t (095) 43464, www.irishcottageholidays.com (*moderate–expensive*)

Nine modernized traditional cottages.

Hostels

Clifden Town Hostel

Sean Joyce, Market St, Clifden, t (095) 21706, e seancth@eircom.net

Clean and central.

Inishbofin Island Hostel

Inishbofin, t (095) 45855, www.inishbofin-hostel.ie (*inexpensive*)

Once upon a time two fishermen saw an old woman driving a white cow across this island, which appeared magically out of nowhere. But the moment the strangers stepped upon it, she and the cow disappeared. Ever since, it has been called 'The Island of the White Cow'. Your friendly hosts at this self-catering hostel (open Mar–Sept) with family rooms and a conservatory-like breakfast room at the front of the house will tell you the best way to get to know 'Bofin is to walk. You need time to stand and stare, if you are to notice the wild-flowers and the way the light changes the colours of its treeless landscape or to see the rare corn-crake and hear its song, or the low howling of a ghost that is really a dog. A new airport is being built for the islanders, but until then a boat from Cleggan will deposit you here.

Camping and caravanning

Ballyloughane Caravan Park

Ballyloughane Beach, Renmore, t (091) 755 338/ 752 029 (late Apr–Sept) (*inexpensive*)

A two-star camping site.

Renvyle Beach Caravan Park

Renvyle, t (095) 43462 (July and Aug only) (*inexpensive*)

Another two-star camping facility.

County Mayo

Hotels

Ashford Castle

Cong, t (092) 46003, www.ashford.ie (*luxury*)

During World Wars I and II, the moneyed and the military ate and drank here to their hearts' content. The grounds were farmed and its Guinness brewing family landlords never ran out of drink. Today American-owned, its Irish staff make you feel as if you are accustomed to living in castles. You adjust surprisingly quickly with the help of strawberries and sherry in your room and traditional Irish musicians who serenade you on a boat ride on the glass-smooth Lough Corrib. Ride horses through leafy woodland, learn about falconry, have a massage or take a tour to Inchygaoill Island. Ask historian Michael Maye (*see* p. 172) to tell you about the Norman French de Burghos (later Brown) family, who built the first mansion here, and how the Guinnesses turned it into their own mini-kingdom. Dinner brings succulent entrées, crisp vegetables, artisan breads and creamy desserts under silver domes lifted with ballerina-like flourish. After putting the children to bed, visit the Dungeon Bar for storytelling and a sing-a-long. On your last morning, after a sumptuous faeryland buffet, you'll depart this Tír na n'Óg reluctantly, feeling as if you are leaving old friends.

Downhill House Hotel

Ballina, t (096) 21033 (*moderate*)

Family rooms, a leisure centre with an indoor toddler pool and a summer children's activity club.

Hotel Westport

Westport, t (098) 25122, www.hotelwestport.ie (*moderate–expensive*)

Families can enjoy delicious meals together in this modern, purpose-built hotel, then go down the backstairs way to comfortable leisure facilities that include a pool, sauna, steam room, Jacuzzi, separate children's pool and health treatment centre. In summer, supervised activity sessions and a children's dinner time (5.15–6) are offered by the Panda Club, while a call to Cubs Corner will ensure you a babysitter for under-3s. You can walk into central Westport from this quiet well-planned hotel with attentive staff.

The Olde Railway Hotel

North Mall, Westport, t (098) 25166, www.anu.ie/railwayhotel (*moderate*)

Artefacts and antiques fill every nook and cranny of this atmospheric 27-room hotel, many of whose rooms face the grey stone bridge in the middle of Westport. While waiting for your meal to be ready in the bistro, you can have a drink in the library-cum-sitting room, where children's books and games are available, and where a fire warms cold days. You can breakfast on incredibly flaky croissants, home-made brown bread and hot porridge smothered with Bailey's Irish Cream (for adults only) or honey, all served in the sunny rear conservatory, beyond which is an organic garden where herbs and produce are grown for the kitchen. Coffee and tea are provided on a complimentary basis throughout your stay.

Westport Woods Hotel

Quay Rd, Westport, t (098) 25811, t 1-850 304050 (IR Callsave), t 0800 282007 (NI and UK freephone), www.westportwoodshotel.com (*expensive–luxury*)

With its backdrop of woods in Westport town, this lively modern hotel is notable for its 'Kiddie Organisers' Club' for 3–16-year-olds, held at Easter and in summer. Youngsters take part in everything from crazy golf and watersports to treasure hunts and face-painting. Events such as Pyjama Breakfasts or Fancy Dress Dinners add to the fun. Family rooms (2+3), a children's play area and pool and babysitting are available all year. For adults, horse-riding and golf can be arranged, or you can relax in a Jacuzzi, swim in the indoor pool, use the new adults-only spa or the fitness studios and health and beauty treatment rooms (which include facilities for the disabled) or take part in a murder mystery weekend. Call **t** (087) 260 5672 for special breaks and offers.

Country houses

Newport House

Newport, t (098) 41222 (*moderate*)

Cots, highchairs, a babysitting service and early-evening meals are available for children in this superb Georgian house with old-fashioned service and the owner's home-smoked salmon. Antiques add to the elegance and beauty of the house, which overlooks a river.

B&Bs and guesthouses

Boheh Loughs

Liscarney, near Westport, t (098) 21797 (*inexpensive*)

This traditional cottage stands in 40 acres with two lakes at the foot of Croagh Patrick beside Togher Patrick walk, near St Patrick's Chair (*see* p.178). Children are welcome. The non-smoking ensuite rooms have herbal toiletries. Organic and vegan/macrobiotic breakfasts and dinners are served here just 5 miles (8km) from Westport, home to many musicians and craftspeople.

Rathoma House

Killala, t (096) 32035 (*inexpensive*)

A pleasant farmhouse in the country, with lots of activities, including horse-riding.

Self-catering

Enniscoe House

Castlehill, near Crossmolina, Ballina, t (096) 31112, www.enniscoe.com (*expensive*)

Families with teenagers might enjoy renting one of the cottages in the grounds of this Georgian house in parklands on the shores of Lough Conn more than a stay in the house itself.

The Harbour Mill

The Quay, t (098) 28555, www.theharbourmill.com (*luxury*)

These fully equipped self-catering apartments complete with wooden floors and new furnishings will make you feel as if you're in the first-class section of a very steady ship, particularly as the front doors face a nautically designed interior courtyard. The location of this complex beside the bay makes it a perfect spot for families who want to spend time exploring Westport town and the Clew Bay area and having fun at Westport House.

Kiltartan House

Botharnasup, Ballina, t (096) 73301 (*inexpensive–moderate*)

This is a modern house with one-, two- and three-bedroom self-catering apartments. Your supremely helpful host Jim Henry will be delighted to introduce you to his home county of Mayo, should you request a tour. If you or your children are curious about Irish folklore, he can tell anecdotes of his own and put you in touch with locals who can tell you even more. For anglers, Ballina is a great place, famous for its salmon fisheries; you can even fish in the middle of the town.

Camping and caravanning

Parkland Caravan and Camping Park

Westport Country House, t (098) 27766, www.westporthouse.ie (*moderate*)

County Sligo

Hotels

Castle Arms Hotel

Enniscrone, t (096) 36156, www.castlearmshotel.com (*moderate*)

Two brothers run this 2-star roadside hotel, set in a seaside town where everyone knows everyone else. You only need to ask, and they will send you to the fellow or lady down the road who'll be glad of a chat about this or that subject. From the hotel, you can walk to the seaweed bathhouse, Waterpoint leisure centre and 3 miles (5km) of sandy beach. In summer, there's entertainment nearby, as well as horse-riding and golf, pitch'n'putt for children, surfing, snooker, tennis courts and a playground. The restaurant offers good wholesome Irish cooking for breakfast, lunch and dinner.

Yeats Country Hotel and Leisure Club

Rosses Point, t (071) 917 7211, www.rossespoint.com/hotel (*moderate*)

Special family activities are arranged by this large family-run hotel with indoor swimming and kids' pools, a sauna, Jacuzzi, gym, tennis and basketball courts and indoor bowling. Supervised crèche and indoor play areas are available on bank holiday weekends and in July and August. Facilities include children's meals and family rates, a playroom and a babysitting service.

Country houses

Coopershill House

Riverstown, t (071) 916 5108, www.coopershill.com (*expensive*)

Children are welcomed at this, one of Ireland's finest Georgian mansions, by its friendly owners Brian and Wendy O'Hara, who maintain a clean, crisp feeling in their spacious rooms – some of which are interconnecting. They are filled with furniture and books and warmed by log fires in the cooler months, and the house is surrounded by woodland with roaming peacocks.

Markree Castle

Collooney, t (071) 916 7800, www.markreecastle.ie (*expensive*)

Bring your children here to give them a sense of what living in a real castle must have been like. Markree has a castellated façade looming up out of grounds where royalty once hunted and today visitors ride horses. Inside, three interconnecting reception rooms hold tall mirrors and plasterwork from 1845. The views over the countryside are magical, and the formal gardens lead down to the River Unsin.

Markree House

Coolooney, t (071) 916 7800, www.markreecastle.ie (*moderate*)

A family room is available in this house converted from the stables of Markree Castle. It has a garden, and riding and fishing nearby, and children's meals and family discounts are available.

Ross House

Ross, Riverstown, t (071) 916 5787 (*moderate*)

There are three family rooms in this farmhouse, where children are surrounded by farm activity and animals. Nearby are Carrowkeel passage tombs.

Temple House

Ballymote, t (071) 918 3329, www.templehouse.ie (*moderate*)

Since 1665 the Perceval family have looked after some of the most beautiful land in Ireland here. Within the house, the faded grandeur of old Ireland's Anglo-Irish aristocracy remains, with canopied beds, ancient curtains and family paintings. By the lake are the remains of a Knights Templar castle from 1200, and various other ruins are scattered around the grounds.

B&Bs and guesthouses

Ardtarmon House

Ballinfull, t (071) 916 3156, www.ardtarmon.com (*moderate*)

Families are welcome at this peaceful country house with its 19th-century ambience and a treehouse perched in a huge cedar in the grounds. Simple breakfasts are prepared by the friendly owners Charles Henry and his German wife Christa. The house, a mixture of Victorian styles, grew up around the original thatched cottage, which is now used by self-catering guests. The interiors are a little austere, but there is a lovely easy walk to the sea, and the quiet atmosphere is something to savour.

Hostels

Eden Hill Holiday Hostel

Pearse Rd, Sligo Town, **t** (071) 43204/44113 (*inexpensive*)

Family rooms and bicycle hire.

Camping and caravanning

Greenlands Caravan and Camping Park

Rosses Point, **t** (071) 77113/45618 (*inexpensive*)

A caravan and campsite set on sand dunes above two Blue Flag beaches.

Leitrim and Roscommon

Hotels

The Abbey Hotel

Galway Rd, Roscommon, **t** (090) 662 6240 (*expensive*)

An attractive Georgian building offering 20 en suite bedrooms. Children's meals may be ordered, and family rates and a babysitting service are available.

Royal Hotel

Bridge St, Boyle, Co. Roscommon, **t** (071) 966 2016, (*moderate*)

This inn in the town centre by the River Shannon has been in business for more than 250 years. It has a Chinese restaurant and a coffee shop on-site, and riding and fishing facilities nearby. Special rates are offered for those with children.

Country houses

Glebe House

Ballinamore Rd, Mohill, Co. Leitrim, **t** (071) 963 1086 (*moderate*)

Fishing and riding excursions can be arranged by the Maloney family at this old rectory (minimum stay two nights), and there is a pony that children may ride.

Glencarne Country House

Ardcarne, near Carrick-on-Shannon, Co. Leitrim, **t** (071) 966 7013 (*inexpensive*)

Children are welcome at this fine Georgian farmhouse near Lough Key Forest Park, with pleasant rooms, lovely old furniture and well-cooked meals.

Riversdale Farm Guesthouse

Ballinamore, Co. Leitrim, **t** (071) 964 4122 (*inexpensive–moderate*)

This Edwardian-era farmhouse has spacious rooms, an indoor swimming pool, a squash court and a sauna. Home-cooking is provided by the delightful hosts, who also offer trips on the Shannon–Erne waterway.

B&Bs and guesthouses

Gleeson's Townhouse

Market Sq, Roscommon, **t** (090) 662 6954 (*moderate*)

This is centrally located with well-appointed rooms and a restaurant. Babysitting is available.

Self-catering

Abbey House

Boyle, Co. Roscommon, **t** (071) 966 2385 (*inexpensive–moderate*)

Lovely old houses available to rent in the grounds of Boyle Abbey, with babysitting available.

Clonalis House

Castlerea, Co. Roscommon, **t** (094) 962 0014 (*expensive*)

A Victorian-Italianate house on a lovely wooded estate. Shooting and fishing can be arranged, as can dinner, with notice. Several four-bedroom mews houses can be rented.

Primrose Cottage

Killukin, Carrick-on-Shannon, Co. Leitrim, **t** (071) 962 1658 (*inexpensive*)

A two-bed cottage on an eco-friendly dairy farm.

Camping and caravanning

Lough Key Caravan Park

Rockingham, **t** (071) 966 2212 (*inexpensive*)

A site within Lough Key Forest Park, with a children's play area, a café and a shop.

ULSTER

County Antrim

Belfast

Hotels

Culloden Hotel and Spa

142 Bangor Rd, Craigavad, t (028) 9042 1066, www.hastingshotels.com (*luxury*)

This is one of Belfast's best hotels, on the shores of Belfast Lough. It's very plush, with lovely grounds, an indoor swimming pool, a fitness centre and luxurious old-style furnishings.

The Wellington Park Hotel

21 Malone Rd, t (028) 9038 1111, www.wellingtonparkhotel.com (*expensive*)

A modern and comfortable hotel, close to the Botanic Gardens, with secure car parking, children's meals, family rates and babysitting.

B&Bs and guesthouses

Many of these are in the quiet, leafy streets of the university district. They are often busy in summer, so it's best to book ahead.

Ash-Rowan Townhouse

12 Windsor Ave, t (028) 9066 1758 (*moderate*)

Children are welcome in this non-smoking, cosy, attractive family home near Queen's University, 10mins from Belfast centre. It was once the home of the designer of the *Titanic*. The ex-restaurateur owners cater for special diets.

Camera Guesthouse

44 Wellington Park, t (028) 9066 0026 (*moderate*)

A comfortably elegant Edwardian terraced house with a friendly proprietress, Caroline Drumm, who is happy to advise families on things to do with children in Belfast. Two family rooms are available, as are discounts for children, self-catering apartments and organic options for breakfast.

Ravenhill House

690 Ravenhill Rd, t (028) 9020 7444, www.ravenhillguesthouse.com (*moderate*)

This non-smoking Victorian home in the tree-lined university area is an ideal base to use for exploring Belfast. One family room contains two beds and sleeps up to three. Rooms are bright, spacious and furnished with locally made hardwood furniture. Breakfast features seasonal organic produce, home-made bread and preserves. Cots, cribs, highchairs, babysitting, laundry services and a free car park are available.

Around Co. Antrim

Hotels

Bushmills Inn

9 Danluce Rd, Bushmills, t (028) 2073 3000, www.bushmillsinn.com (*moderate–expensive*)

This attractive and charming inn offers turf fires, gaslights and intriguing rooms. Although not specifically geared to catering for families, it is comfortable, with good service, excellent food, including children's meals, family rates, gardens and a babysitting service.

Causeway Hotel

40 Causeway Rd, Giant's Causeway, Bushmills, t (028) 2073 1226/2073 1210, www.giants-causeway-hotel.com (*moderate–expensive*)

This delightful family-run hotel offers children's meals, family rates, babysitting and gardens for kids to run around in.

Galgorm Manor Hotel

136 Fenaghy Rd, Ballymena, t (028) 2588 1001, www.galgorm.com (*luxury*)

Children's meals, family rates and babysitting are provided at this spectacular 17th-century castle with lovely lawns, transformed into a plush hotel with river views. Riding and fishing are available nearby.

Radisson Roe Park Hotel and Golf Resort

Roe Park, Limavady, t (028) 7772 2222, www.radisson.com (*moderate–expensive*)

This hotel and its grounds date from the 18th century. Facilities include an indoor pool, whirlpool, sauna and health club with a steam room and fitness suite. Families enjoy price reductions and upgrades, and free breakfasts for four.

Country houses

The Moat Inn

12 Donegore Hill, Templepatrick, t (028) 9443 3659, www.themoatinn.com (*expensive*)

This former coaching inn (1740) is decorated with William Morris wallpaper and has a library filled with old books, antiques and a grand piano (owners Rachel and Robert Thompson are accomplished pianists). All the breakable objects strewn about mean this may not be such a good place for toddlers or active school-age kids, but family rooms are available, and the very comfortable country house has won awards for its candlelit dinners, luxurious bedrooms and fabulous breakfasts.

Whitepark House

150 Whitepark Rd, Whitepark Bay, Ballintoy, t (028) 2073 1482, www.whiteparkhouse.com (*inexpensive*)

This pretty 17th-century house on a hill overlooking the Atlantic, luxuriously furnished with mementoes from the owners' Asian travels, is better for families with teenagers than young children. It's a good stopping place for coastal walkers, and is not far from the Giant's Causeway by car. Its friendly, award-winning hosts make sure their guests are comfortable, and pamper them with one of the north's best full-Irish breakfasts, both for meat-eaters and vegetarians. Three bedrooms share a large bathroom.

B&Bs and guesthouses

Ahimsa

243 Whitepark Rd, near Ballintoy, Bushmills, t (028) 2073 1383 (*inexpensive*)

A traditional cottage with two rooms and an organic garden providing ingredients for vegetarian meals. Yoga and reflexology are available.

Maddybenny Farmhouse

20 Maddybenny Park, Loguestown Rd, Portrush, near Coleraine, t (028) 7082 3394, www.maddybenny.freeserve.co.uk (*inexpensive*)

The riding centre here is a great attraction for children, not to mention the animals and space out in the fresh air. It has an easygoing atmosphere and great breakfasts. The owners also have self-catering cottages you can rent.

The Manor House

The National Trust, Rathlin Island, t (028) 2076 3964, www.ntni.org.uk (*inexpensive*)

Five en suite rooms are available in this old manor house situated on the very special island of Rathlin (*see* p.210).

Self-catering

North Irish Lodge Holiday Cottages

Islandmagee, 161 Low Rd, Larne, t (028) 9338 2246, www.activityhols.ni.co.uk (*expensive*)

These multi-award-winning luxury Irish cottages, equipped for the disabled, are set in a Victorian farmyard in the centre of Islandmagee, 5mins from three sandy beaches. A unique hotel service package is offered, in which guests may choose traditional Irish dishes to be delivered to their 3- or 4-star cottage. A play area is here for under-12s, and guided walks, horse-riding, diving and sea fishing can be arranged.

O'Harabrook Old Dairy

Bann Rd, Ballymoney, t (028) 2766 6273 (*moderate–expensive*)

Three large secluded apartments in stone-built outhouses, each of which sleeps six people, are on this farm, which has a laundry and games room.

Hostels

Sheep Island View Hostel

42a Main St, Ballintoy, t (028) 2076 9391, www.sheepislandview.com (*inexpensive*)

In a handy position for exploring the Causeway coast, this hostel has five en suite family rooms, ocean views and bikes for rent.

Waterside House

Oxford Island, Lurgan, Craigavon, t (028) 3832 7573 (*inexpensive*)

This hostel situated in the conservation area beside Lough Neagh offers a wide range of water-sports and other activities.

Whitepark Bay International Youth Hostel

157 Whitepark Rd, Whitepark Bay, Ballintoy, t (028) 2073 1745 (*inexpensive*)

A hostel on Whitepark Bay near the Giant's Causeway and other Antrim attractions, with excellent facilities, 11 en suite family rooms and sea views.

County Down

Hotels

Burrendale Hotel and Country Club

51 Castlewellan Rd, Newcastle, **t** (028) 4372 2599, **www.burrendalehotel.com** (*expensive*)

Hydrotherapy baths are available in the modern rooms here, along with tea- and coffee-making facilities and television sets, and cots are available by prior request. The hotel's country club has the best golf centre in the area and a leisure centre with an indoor pool, Jacuzzi, sauna, steam baths and exercise equipment across from a beauty salon. Everything is clean, comfortable and quiet in this 1980s hotel, and children's meals, a playroom and family rates are available.

Clandeboye Lodge Hotel

10 Estate Rd, Clandeboye, Bangor, **t** (028) 9185 2500 (*expensive*)

A hotel with rooms for families and for non-smokers, situated in the Clandeboye Estate in extensive landscaped gardens. Golf can be arranged here.

Slieve Donard Hotel

Newcastle, **t** (028) 4372 1066 (*expensive*)

A hotel with new leisure facilities and special rates for children.

Country houses

Edenvale House

130 Portaferry Rd, Newtownards, **t** (028) 9181 4881, **www.edenvalehouse.com** (*moderate*)

Diane and Gordon Whyte are delighted to have children here, as they have five of their own grandsons and Diane even helps run a local toddlers' group. They keep cots, highchairs and toys in their perfect Georgian home, a climbing frame and swing near the big flower garden, and ponies, a dog and two cats who are used to children. They don't provide dinner but are happy to make snacks for children before parents go out to eat, and to arrange babysitting. Breakfast is a feast. The bedrooms and bathrooms have all the comforts you could possibly need. A stay here offers an inspiring introduction to Co. Down, as Mrs Whyte is most helpful with touring advice.

B&Bs and guesthouses

Drumgooland House and Equestrian Centre

29 Dunnanew Rd, Seaforde, near Downpatrick, **t** (028) 4481 1956 (*inexpensive*)

B&B is offered particularly to horse-riders, including families, in this fully modernized 100-year-old home. Disabled riders are welcome too.

Dufferin Coaching Inn

31 High St, Killyleagh, **t** (028) 4482 8229, **www.dufferincoachinginn.co.uk** (*moderate*)

This B&B does not have family rooms, but a discount is offered for those with children, depending on their age. In or near the small village of Killyleagh (close to Strangford Lough), sailing and horse-riding are available. The pub/restaurant next door is happy to serve families early in the evening.

Self-catering

Castle Espie Cottages

11 Ballyglighorn Rd, Comber, **t** (028) 918 73011 (*moderate*)

Two cottages on a working farm, with a play garden for children, sleep four to six people. Babysitting, cots and highchairs are available.

Corralea Activity Centre and Cottages

Belcoo, **t** (028) 6638 6668 (*moderate*)

Self-catering accommodation in cottages.

The Courtyard Motel

Lusty Beg Island, Kesh, **t** (028) 6863 3300, **www.lustybeg.co.uk** (*expensive–luxury*)

Self-catering chalets, including new Finnish log houses, are available, plus an indoor swimming pool, tennis, canoeing and other activities. A ferry takes you to and from the island.

Camping and caravanning

Murlough Cottage Farm Caravan Park

180 Dundrum Rd, Newcastle, **t** (028) 4372 3184/2906 (*inexpensive*)

A site open March–Oct for touring caravans only, situated next to Murlough Bay National Nature Reserve and beach. Children like the sand dunes. It's a short walk into town for the supermarket.

Tollymore Forest Park

176 Tullybrannigan Rd, Newcastle, **t** (028) 4372 2428 (*inexpensive*)

Camping facilities for families only, open all year.

County Armagh

Hotels

The Charlemont Arms Hotel

63 English St, Armagh City, t (028) 3752 2028 (*moderate*)

A family-run hotel with kids' meals and family rates.

B&Bs and guesthouses

Deans Hill

34 College Hill, Armagh, t (028) 3752 4923 (*inexpensive*)

This pretty 18th-century house with lovely gardens is close to the observatory. You have a choice of two en suite rooms, one with a four-poster, and also a self-contained, self-catering chalet with room for four.

De Averell Guesthouse

3 Seven Houses, English St, Armagh, t (028) 3751 1213 (*moderate*)

A Georgian townhouse with a good restaurant.

Hillview Lodge

33 Newtownhamilton Rd, Armagh, t (028) 3752 2000, www.hillviewlodge.com (*inexpensive*)

Beside a floodlit golf driving range just outside Armagh City, this purpose-built B&B is a bit like a small hotel. Run by friendly, helpful Alice and Dermot McBride, it has well-equipped rooms with modern amenities, including family rooms.

Hostels

Armagh City International Youth Hostel

39 Abbey St, Armagh, t (028) 3751 1800, www.hini.org.uk (*inexpensive*)

A purpose-built and well-sited if somewhat functional hostel with good security, offering ensuite two-, four- and six-bed rooms.

County Londonderry

Hotels

Beech Hill Country House Hotel

32 Ardmore Rd, Derry City, t (028) 7134 9279, www.beech-hill.com (*expensive*)

This hotel has lovely grounds and is renowned for its cuisine. Facilities include a sauna, steam room, Jacuzzi, fitness suite, tennis courts and a treatment programme including massage and Reiki. Children's meals, family rates and babysitting are offered.

B&Bs and guesthouses

Aberfoyle B&B

33 Aberfoyle Terrace, Strand Rd, Derry City, t (028) 7128 3333 (*inexpensive*)

A 19th-century mid-terrace house located just 5mins from Derry centre, 10mins from Donegal and 40mins from the Giant's Causeway. Late breakfasts are available.

Brown Trout Golf and Country Inn

209 Agivey Rd, Aghadowey, south of Coleraine, t (028) 7086 8209, www.browntroutinn.com (*expensive*)

Set in pretty grounds near a river, this place offers good food, including children's meals, family rates, gardens, a play area, gym, babysitting, and riding, golf and fishing tuition.

Drumcovitt House

704 Feeny Rd, Feeny, t (028) 7778 1224, www.drumcovitt.com (*moderate*)

Families and children are welcome at this lovely Georgian farmhouse set in scenic countryside. Three self-catering cottages are also available.

Elagh Hall

Buncrana Rd, Derry City, t (028) 7126 3116 (*inexpensive*)

An 18th-century farmhouse 2 miles (3.2km) from the city centre, overlooking the hills of Donegal.

Laurel Villa

60 Church St, Magherafelt, t (028) 7963 2238 (*moderate*)

Run by Blue Badge guide Eugene Kielt and his wife Geraldine, this house was the home of a Victorian doctor and is full of antiques. The present owners' influence is felt in the framed, illustrated poems on the walls. Eugene is an inspired student of Irish history and can tell you all sorts of intriguing snippets about his country. Families are welcome (the Kielts have two sons), and breakfasts are good. Guided tours of South Derry, based on the works of Seamus Heaney, are your host's speciality, but whatever your interests, he will locate the best places to take you.

The Merchant's House

16 Queen St, t (028) 7126 9691, www.thesaddlershouse.com (*inexpensive*)

This narrow house makes up for its lack of ensuite bathrooms with its pleasing Victorian and Georgian decorations. You can relax in a carefully furnished 19th-century parlour with family history photographs and linger over an old-fashioned Irish breakfast, with good home-baking. Your genial hosts also offer en suite rooms at The Saddler's House around the corner at 36 Great James St, but The Merchant's House holds more historical interest.

Streeve Hill

25 Dowland Rd, Drenagh, Limavady, t (028) 7776 6563 (*moderate*)

A lovely 18th-century house with delicious food, pleasant walks in parkland and a 'moon garden'.

Self-catering

Lough Beg Coach Houses

Ballyscullion Park, Bellaghy, t (028) 7938 6235 (*moderate–expensive*)

Six well-appointed cottages (each sleeps six) on a large estate bordering Lough Beg share a games room, horse-riding and lovely walks. Breakfasts and dinner may be ordered here.

Hostels

Downhill Hostel

12 Mussenden Rd, Castlerock, t (028) 7084 9077 (*inexpensive*)

A sociable hostel on a stretch of beach, with a kitchen, laundry, dorms and family rooms.

Dungiven Castle

Main St, Dungiven, t (028) 7774 2428, www.dungivencastle.com (*inexpensive*)

En suite and dorm rooms and a kitchen in a restored Gothic/Tudor-style castle in parkland, with walking, gliding, riding, cycling, fishing and birdwatching.

County Tyrone

Hotels

The Valley Hotel

60 Main St, Fivemiletown, t (028) 8952 1505 (*moderate*)

This 2-star hotel is comfortable and cheerful, offering 22 bedrooms and has some family rooms and a restaurant.

Country houses

Charlemont House

4 The Square, Moy, Dungannon, t (028) 8778 4755 (*inexpensive*)

This Georgian townhouse with period furnishings and lots of atmosphere has a lovely garden with a view of the Blackwater River at the back.

Grange Lodge

7 Grange Rd, Dungannon, t (028) 8778 4212 (*moderate*)

Children over 12 are welcome at this comfortable Georgian house by the Blackwater River, with outstanding breakfasts and non-smoking rooms

B&Bs and guesthouses

Braeside House

23 Drumconvis Rd, Coagh, Cookstown, t (028) 8673 7301 (*inexpensive*)

There's a family and a double room in this old house with a garden on a working farm, with fishing available on the Ballinderry River and Lough Neagh.

Self-catering

Blessingbourne Luxury Flats

Near Fivemiletown, t (028) 8952 1221 (*expensive*)

Three self-catering apartments in a Victorian mansion in wooded grounds, with comfortable rooms that sleep 6–8.

Gortin Accommodation Suite and Activity Centre

62 Main St, Gortin, t (028) 8164 8346, www.gortin.net (*moderate*)

An outdoors-oriented centre, with self-catering apartments sleeping 4 and 6 and a hostel for independent travellers, in a village from which you can explore the Sperrins on foot or by bike or canoe. Facilities include breakfast and TV.

Grange Court

21–27 Moyle Rd, Newtownstewart, t (028) 8166 1877, www.grangecourt.co.uk (*moderate*)

This 4-star self-catering apartment complex on the Mourne River is central for visiting the Sperrins. Facilities include a café, TV, laundry, garden, play area, barbecue, cots and highchairs.

County Fermanagh

Hotels

Killyhevlin Hotel

Dublin Rd, Enniskillen, t (028) 6632 3481, www.killyhevlin.com (*moderate*)

This modern hotel overlooking Lough Erne offers children's meals, family rates, a play area and babysitting. The bar is a noisy venue for weddings and fishermen's gatherings. Book a room with a lake view, which is lovely.

Country houses

Rosfad House

Killadeas, P.O. Ballinamallard, t (028) 6638 8505 (*inexpensive*)

Children are welcome at this Georgian/Victorian house not far from Enniskillen, where in summer they can swim in Lower Lough Erne with parental supervision. They can also play croquet or badminton in the beautiful gardens.

Tempo Manor

Tempo, t (028) 8954 1450, www.tempomanor.com (*expensive*)

This Victorian manor house stands in 300 acres of grounds and overlooks gardens and lakes. Guests are treated to home-cooked breakfasts and log fires. Three bedrooms with four-posters and a twin are available, and the informal atmosphere is child-friendly.

B&Bs and guesthouses

Arch House Tullyhona

Marble Arch Rd, Florence Court, t (028) 6634 8452, www.archhouse.com (*inexpensive*)

This old-fashioned farmhouse in its own grounds beside Upper Lough Erne offers family rooms, a play area, children's play house and baby-listening service. Award-winning home-cooking, including children's menus, and highchairs are available.

The Cedars

301 Kiladeas Rd, Castle Archdale, Irvinestown, t (028) 6862 1493, www.cedarsguesthouse.com (*moderate*)

This family-friendly guesthouse with antique furniture offers traditional fare made from fresh local produce for all meals, and a children's menu. It has good rates for families.

Drumrush Lodge

Boa Island Rd, Kesh, t (028) 6863 1578, www.drumrush.co.uk (*inexpensive*)

A family-run watersports centre with en suite rooms and all the mod cons. The restaurant serves home-cooking, and its camping and caravan park overlook a marina. Lake swimming and tennis are available.

Self-catering

Belle Isle Estate Cottages

Lisbellaw, t (028) 6638 7231, www.belleisle-estate.com (*moderate–luxury*)

This estate of traditional buildings converted into luxurious apartments and cottages with spacious, modern interiors is on an island at the northern end of Upper Lough Erne. Cookery courses and other activities may be arranged.

Corralea Holiday Cottages

Corralea, Belcoo, Fermanagh, t (028) 6638 6668 (*moderate*)

Five self-catering cottages at an outdoor activity centre on Lough MacNean. Full board is possible.

Crom Estate Cottages

Newtownbutler, t (028) 6773 8118 (*luxury*)

Cottages in 2000 acres of woodland and wetland.

Hostels

Castle Archdale Youth Hostel

Lisnarick, Irvinestown, t (028) 6862 8118 (*inexpensive*)

Family rooms available in a historic listed building.

Camping and caravanning

Lough Melvin Holiday Centre Caravan Park

Main St, Garrison, t (028) 6865 8142, www.fermanagh-online.com (*inexpensive*)

An outdoor activity centre on a lough, with dorms and bedrooms, a restaurant and disabled facilities.

Cavan and Monaghan

Hotels

Creighton Hotel

Fermanagh St, Clones, Co. Monaghan, t (047) 51055, (*moderate*)

A family-run, traditional hotel on Clones' main street, with a full menu, including children's meals.

Hillgrove Hotel
Old Armagh Rd, Monaghan, Co. Monaghan, **t** (047) 81288, **www.hillgrovehotel.com** (*moderate–expensive*)

Children's menus and babysitting services are available at this comfortable, welcoming hotel.

Country houses

Glynch House
Newbliss, Clones, Co. Monaghan, **t** (047) 54045, **www.glynchfarmhouse.com** *(moderate)*

Children are welcome at this Huguenot farmhouse built in 1772, with comfortable rooms.

Lisnamandra Farmhouse
Crossdoney, just west of Cavan town, Co. Cavan, **t** (049) 433 7196 (*inexpensive*)

Family rooms a 10mins drive from Lough Oughter at an award-winning traditional-style farmhouse with home-cooking.

B&Bs and guesthouses

Bavaria House
Garrymore, Ballinagh, Co. Cavan, **t** (049) 433 7452 (*inexpensive*)

Children are welcome in this house located close to local historic sites. Organic produce and vegan, macrobiotic and non-vegetarian food are available on request.

Fort Singleton
Emyvale, Co. Monaghan, **t** (047) 86054, **www.fortsingleton.com** (*moderate*)

Children love sleeping in this house's Victorian train carriage, Bedouin's tent, boat-shaped bunkbed or bishop's chamber rooms. Those seeking a country-house style can move upstairs to rooms filled with antiques.

MacNean House
Blacklion, Co. Cavan, **t** (071) 985 3022 (*inexpensive*)

This comfortably furnished bed and breakfast with 10 en suite rooms offers a babysitting service and children's meals and can arrange horse-riding, trekking and angling. It has a great reputation for its fine food and books tables well in advance.

Self-catering

Cabra Castle Hotel
Kingscourt, Co. Cavan, **t** (042) 966 7030, **www.cabracastle.com** (*luxury*)

Stay in this lavish 15th-century pile with landscaped gardens or one of its self-catering units. Children's meals, family rates, a babysitting service, riding, golfing and fishing are available.

Killykeen Forest Chalets
Killykeen Forest Park, Co. Cavan, **t** (049) 433 2541, **www.coillte.ie** (*moderate*)

Wooden chalets and cabins may be rented here within Killykeen Forest Park.

Tara House
Jampa Ling Tibetan Buddhist Centre, Bawnboy, Co. Cavan, **t** (049) 952 3448, **www.jampaling.org** (*inexpensive–expensive)*

Quiet families seeking a peaceful, meditative environment can rent part or all of this recently renovated wood-floored house, which can accommodate up to 20 people.

County Donegal

Hotels

Rathmullan House Hotel
Rathmullan, **t** (074) 915 8188, **www.rathmullanhouse.com** (*expensive–luxury*)

Children are welcome at this 18th-century country house situated on the edge of Lough Swilly, which offers children's meals, family rates and a babysitting service. The hotel has a very cosy bar with a turf fire, excellent gourmet meals, an indoor pool and sports courts. You can stroll from here along a sandy beach.

Country houses

Ardeen House
Ramelton, Co. Donegal, **t** (074) 915 1243, **e** ardeenbandb@eircom.net (*inexpensive–moderate*)

Anne Campbell's house facing the bay on the edge of Ramelton village is spotless, comfy and clutter free. In the morning you're treated to scrumptuous freshly baked scones, amazing brown bread made with ground sunflower seeds and nuts, and poached plum or fresh strawberry fruit salads that will have you reaching for second helpings (resist if you want one of her perfect traditional Irish breakfasts). Anne introduces her visitors to each other, with perhaps a mischievous comment thrown in to stimulate conversation. Staying in this place brings on a light heart, and it's also an excellent base from which to explore Donegal. Family rooms holding both a double and single bed are available.

Bruckless House

Bruckless, t (074) 973 7071, www.iol.ie/~bruc/bruckless.html (*expensive*)

A charming 18th-century house near Donegal Bay. Its owners Clive and Joan Evans will point you in the right direction, whether your interest is walking, prehistoric sites or just exploring. It's a good base for families who want to ride, as it's just down the road from Deane's Equestrian Centre. Visitors may stroll through surrounding woodland and cultivated gardens. The four-roomed Gate Lodge may be rented for self-catering.

Frewin House

Ramelton, t (074) 915 1246, www.accommodationdonegal.net (*moderate–expensive*)

This 17th-century rectory in its own grounds is owned by farmer Thomas Gibson, a goldmine of local folklore and history, and his wife, Regina, who prepares excellent breakfasts with fresh ingredients, including unsweetened fruit and home-made bread. The house is more suited to children over seven, but a self-catering cottage is also available for two adults and one child. For a sense of the peace once enjoyed in Irish homes, you should visit the benign ghost who haunts this place.

B&Bs and guesthouses

The Green Gate

Ardvally, Ardara, t (074) 954 1546 (*inexpensive*)

For families who want to experience what living in a Donegal stone cottage must have been like a century ago, this is the place. Welcomed by French proprietor Paul Chatenoud, guests relax and really talk to each other here, breathing in the scent of a turf fire in winter, or socializing over breakfast on a summer's morning. Chatenoud is determined to give back to the Irish the magic that they have given him and to convey it to the world, which, he says, visits him here so that he doesn't have to travel anywhere.

The Hall Green

Near Lifford, Co. Donegal, t (074) 914 1318 www.thehallgreen.co.uk (*inexpensive*)

That this farmhouse is a well-loved home becomes immediately apparent as you arrive to see its brightly painted façade and neat flowers in the front car park. Indoors, one steps back into a way of life almost forgotten in Ireland, with family heirlooms filling every space. The mixture of styles and colours is very pleasing in comparison to many slick hotels. Rooms are individually decorated and one family room has an en suite bathroom. The night here is so quiet that it's easy to fall into the deepest sleep. Mrs McKean ensures that her guests feel comfortable with each other, inspiring friendly conversation, and her very good baking and traditional breakfasts cut no corners. She also sells her own excellent home-made jams and knitting.

Self-catering

The Gate Lodge and Buncronan Cottage

Salthill House, Mountcharles, t (074) 973 5014 (*moderate*)

Either of these two places close to the lake near Mountcharles will help you to shed the cares of modern life. Children can explore the beach and woods, swim in the sea or explore the organic garden.

Hostels

Cliff View Holiday Hostel

Coast road (to Killybegs), Donegal Town, t (074) 972 1684 (*inexpensive*)

This purpose-built hostel 2mins from the town centre, with en suite rooms, offers full Irish breakfasts, children's meals and laundry and babysitting services.

Malin Head Hostel

Malin, Inishowen, t (074) 937 0309 (*inexpensive*)

A clean and comfortable but simple place to stay, complete with an organic garden and an orchard in which guests are free to wander.

Camping and caravanning

Lakeside Caravan and Camping

Belleek Rd, Ballyshannon, t (071) 985 2822, www.donegalbay.com (*inexpensive*)

Travel

GETTING THERE 280
By air 280
Flights 280
Arriving in Ireland 283
By bus 284
By sea 284
Border Formalities 286
GETTING AROUND 286
By air 286
By bus 286
By car 287
By train 288

GETTING THERE

All kinds of general information on travel to Ireland and on transport throughout the island can be obtained from **Tourism Ireland**, **t** UK 0800 039 7000, **t** US and Canada 1 800 223 6470, **www**.tourismireland.com.

This is now the sole international tourist information service for the whole 'island of Ireland', covering the Republic and Northern Ireland.

By air

Flights

Since the low-cost revolution in European air travel it's easier – and cheaper – than ever before to fly to Ireland from Britain and many parts of Europe, and there's also a choice of flights from different departure points in North America.

From Britain

Thanks to the low-cost airline boom, there are now direct flights to a number of airports in Ireland from most parts of Britain, and fares can be less than £20 one-way. The occasional problems of no-frills airlines are well known – long check-in times and delays – but the low-cost operators claim that punctuality has improved significantly since 2002. An essential part of the low-cost package is that no food or drink is included with the ticket, and should you then buy any of the refreshments available on board they are notably expensive (so take at least some snacks, water and/or other drinks with you, especially for kids).

These problems aside, something else to highlight is that low-cost airlines are not always as cheap as their advertising can suggest (note, too, that to get significant extra savings you must book online rather than by phone). Fares for each airline vary greatly on the same route, according to when you travel and how far in advance you book; the real rock-bottom deals are often for seats at inconvenient times (very early in the morning, early in the week), and on popular routes prices leap up at busy times, such as on Friday evening.

Also, one benefit of the no-frills revolution that often goes unnoticed is the concessions it has forced on the older mainstream carriers. Obliged to compete, they have responded with lower and lower fares – especially Aer Lingus, which now operates as a low-cost airline itself, with prices comparable to Ryanair's. Because of this changing price system, the rules to follow when booking flights are – **always check all the airlines operating on the route you want**, and bear in mind that the **new-model no-frills airlines may not always be the cheapest**, especially on very popular routes at peak times.

Good to know...
Airfares for Children

The terms under which children fly vary from airline to airline. A few offer discounts of around 20%–30% from a full adult fare for children aged 2–12, but on most airlines operating between Britain and Ireland (especially low-cost ones) any child occupying their own seat will simply be charged the full normal fare.

Children under 2 who do not have their own seat (i.e., who travel in an adult's lap) travel for free on several airlines, but others charge 10% of the adult fare, or a set fee.

On long-haul (i.e., transatlantic) flights, the discounts available vary not only between airlines but also between flights of the same airline, so check carefully when booking. On most airlines children under 2 travel for 10% of the full fare if they share the adult's seat, but this can be an uncomfortable option on long flights.

Airlines Operating between Britain and Ireland

Since the airline market has become so changeable nowadays, routes change frequently, and new airlines are also still starting up, so always check current routes and future plans on websites and in the travel press.

Aer Arann
t UK 0800 587 2324, **t** IR 061 704 428, **www**.aerarann.ie

Routes: to **Dublin** from Isle of Man; to **Cork** from Birmingham, Bristol, Edinburgh and Southampton; to **Galway** from Luton and Manchester; and to **Kerry** and **Waterford** from Luton.

Fares for children Discounts of around 33% are offered for children aged 2–12 on many flights; for children under 2 sharing a seat the charge is 10% of the normal fare. No car seats are allowed.

Good to know...
Flying with babies and toddlers

Sucking on a bottle or dummy (a soother) helps ease earache on take-off and landing; many chemists/pharmacists (especially at airports) stock 'earplanes', small plastic devices that fit in the ear and are quite effective if you or your child suffers from air pressure problems.

Insist that you take your buggy up to the door of the aircraft – it's more convenient and the buggy is less likely to get damaged. Inside, if you don't want to have your baby sitting on your lap all through the flight, it can be a good idea to book a separate seat and take a familiar car seat for the child to sit in comfortably. If you do, though, you will usually have to pay full fare for the seat, and if you want to do this, check carefully with your airline when booking: some airlines do not allow car seats inside the aircraft, or only allow specific types.

On long-haul (transatlantic) flights, most airlines offer facilities for small children – infant cots, child seats, on-board bottle-warming, baby-changing facilities, children's meals – on request, but they must be ordered in advance. Check what is available when booking, and be sure to make clear exactly what you need. Many airlines will also allow you to use your own child seats, cots and so on, but, again, check when booking to ensure that the type you have is one the airline allows on board.

Aer Lingus
t UK 0845 084 4444, **t** IR 0818 365 000, **www.**aerlingus.com
Routes: to **Dublin** from Birmingham, Edinburgh, Glasgow, Jersey, Heathrow and Manchester; and to **Cork** and **Shannon** from Heathrow.
Fares for children Discounts of around 15% of the adult fare for children aged 2–11 on some flights, depending on the class, but on most UK–Ireland flights they must pay full fare. For children under 2 sharing a seat with an adult, the fare is 10% of the normal fare.

Air Wales
t UK 0870 777 3131, **www.**airwales.co.uk
Routes: to **Dublin** and **Cork** from Cardiff, Plymouth and Swansea; and to **Belfast City** from Cardiff.
Fares for children No discounts for children aged 2–12; for children under 2 sharing a seat, the fare is £5/€8, for any flight. No car seats are allowed on board.

Bmibaby
t UK 0870 264 2229, **www.**bmibaby.com
Routes: to **Dublin** from East Midlands, to **Belfast International** from Cardiff, East Midlands and Teesside, and to **Cork** from Cardiff, East Midlands and Manchester.
Fares for children No discounts for 2–12s, but children under 2 sharing a seat travel for free.

British Airways
t UK 0870 850 9850, **www.**ba.com
Routes: to **Dublin** from Bristol, Gatwick, Manchester and the Isle of Man; to **Belfast City** from Edinburgh, Glasgow and Manchester; to **Cork** from Glasgow and Manchester; to **Knock** from Manchester; to **Derry** from Glasgow and Manchester; and to **Shannon** from Manchester.
Fares for children No discounts for children aged 2–12 on European flights. Children under 2 sharing a seat are charged 10% of the adult fare.

British Midland (bmi)
t UK 0870 607 0555, **www.**flybmi.com
Routes: to **Dublin**, **Belfast City** and **Cork**, from Heathrow.
Fares for children No discounts for 2–12s; children under 2 sharing a seat pay 10% of the full fare.

British Northwest Airlines (BNWA)
t UK 0800 083 7783, **www.**bnwa.co.uk
Routes: to **Belfast City Airport** from Blackpool and the Isle of Man.
Fares for children Only airport taxes are charged for under-3s; fares for children 3–14 are a little over half adult fares.

***Good to know...* Cheap flights online**

With so many flights running between Ireland and Britain, it's usually pretty easy to get tickets directly from the airlines, but in case you get stuck, the services below are handy ports-of-call for finding a wide range of bargain flight options.

www.cheapflights.com
www.cheaptickets.com
www.dialaflight.com
www.farebase.net
www.flightline.co.uk
www.lastminute.com
www.openjet.com
www.travelocity.com

easyJet
t UK 0871 750 0100, 0905 821 095 (£0.60/min); 0871 244 2366 (£0.10/min); 0905 560 7777 (£1/min; Sat and Sun 9–5 only), **www.easyjet.com**
Routes: to **Belfast International**, **Cork**, **Knock** and **Shannon** from Bristol, Edinburgh, Gatwick, Glasgow, Liverpool, Luton, Newcastle and Stansted.
Fares for children No discounts for children aged 2–14. Children under 2 sharing a seat travel for free.

Flybe
t UK 0871 700 123, **t** IR 1 890 925 532, **www.flybe.com**
Routes: to **Dublin** from Exeter, Jersey, Isle of Man and Southampton; to **Belfast City** from Birmingham, Bristol, Exeter, Gatwick, Isle of Man, Leeds-Bradford, London City, Newcastle and Southampton; and to **Cork** and **Shannon** from Birmingham.
Fares for children Variable discounts for children aged 2–12 on many flights; for children under 2 sharing a seat the fare is 10% of the adult fare.

Jet 2
t UK 0871 226 1737, **www.jet2.com.**
Routes: **Belfast International** from Leeds-Bradford.
Fares for children No discounts for 2–12s, but children under 2 sharing a seat travel for free.

MyTravel
t UK 0870 1564 564, **t** IR 0818 300 012, **www.mytravel.com.**
Routes: to **Dublin**, **Belfast International** and **Knock** from Birmingham.
Fares for children No discounts for children aged 2–12. For children under 2 sharing a seat there is a fare of £5/€8, for any flight.

Ryanair
t UK 0906 270 5650, **t** IR 1503 787 787
www.ryanair.com
Routes: to **Dublin** from Aberdeen, Birmingham, Blackpool, Bournemouth, Bristol, Cardiff, Edinburgh, Gatwick, Glasgow (Prestwick), Leeds-Bradford, Liverpool, Luton, Manchester, Newcastle, Stansted and Teesside; and to **Cork**, **Kerry**, **Knock**, **Derry** and **Shannon** from Stansted.
Fares for children No discounts for children 2–12. For children under 2 sharing a seat there is a fare of £7/€10, for any flight. No car seats are allowed.

From North America

Direct flights from North America to Ireland arrive in **Dublin** and **Shannon** airports – Aer Lingus offers the widest choice of departure airports around the US. Fares have been falling overall, and at many times of year you can get return fares of around $200 or less. There are also many charter flights, especially in summer, and many more flight options, often with good fare deals, are also available with a change in Britain or at another European airport. Flying indirect like this via Britain is the best way to get to Ireland from Canada.

Airlines with Direct Flights between the USA and Ireland

Aer Lingus
t US and Canada 1 800 IRISH AIR, **t** IR 0818 365 000, **t** (001) 888 474 7424, **www.aerlingus.com**
Flights to Dublin and Shannon from Baltimore, Boston, Chicago, Los Angeles and New York (JFK).

Delta Airlines
t US and Canada 1 800 241 4141, **t** IR 1 800 768 080, **www.delta-air.com**
Flights to Dublin and Shannon from Atlanta.

Continental Airlines
t US and Canada 1 800 231 0856, **t** IR 1 890 925 252, **www.flycontinental.com**
Flights from Newark to Shannon and Dublin.

US Airways
t US and Canada 1 800 428 4322, **t** IR 1 890 925 065, **www.usairways.com**
A direct service from Philadelphia to Shannon and Dublin, May–October only.

Good to know... Consolidators in North America

Tickets are often cheaper than usual if bought via consolidators, but beware that their tickets are usually non-refundable or carry stiff cancellation penalties, often as high as 50–75% of the ticket price. The following are US telephone numbers:

Air Brokers Travel, t 1 800 883 3273, **www.airbrokers.com**
TFI Tours International, t 1 800 745 8000
Travac Tours and Charters, t 1 800 872 8800, **www.travac.com**
Unitravel, t 1 800 325 2222, **www.**unitravel.com

Charter Operators in the USA and Canada

Air Transat Holidays, t 1 800 587 2672
Signature Vacations, t (US) 1 800 268 7522, **t** (Can) 1 800 268 7063
Sunquest Vacations, t 1 800 268 8899
World of Vacations, t 1 800 387 4860

Arriving in Ireland

Airports in the Republic of Ireland

The Republic's three main airports – Dublin, Cork and Shannon – are all run by the same national body, Aer Rianta. The other regional airports are run by local authorities.

As well as bus services from the different airports to the nearest cities and towns, there are bus services between the airports and from towns further away to Dublin and Shannon airports, run by national bus company **Bus Éireann**. For contact details for timetable and fare information, *see* p.286.

Cork Airport

t 021 431 3131, **www**.aer-rianta.ie
Getting there 3 miles (5km) south of Cork City on the Kinsale road (N27)

There are around 2 buses an hour, 7.50am–8.45pm Mon–Fri, between the airport and Cork city, with a less frequent service at weekends. The trip takes abou25 mins. A taxi into Cork city costs €11–15.

Donegal Airport

t (091) 755 569, **www**.donegalairport.ie
Getting there At Carrickfinn on the coast

Flights to Dublin.

Dublin Airport

Information **t** 01 814 1111, **www**.aer-rianta.ie
Getting there 6 miles (10km) north of Dublin near Swords, just west of the Dundalk road (M1).

The quickest and most convenient bus service between the airport and Dublin is the **Aircoach** (**t** 01 844 7118, **www**.aircoach.ie), which runs every 15mins every day in each direction during the day, and every 30mins about 12 midnight–4.30am, on a circular route from the airport, through the city centre and down to south Dublin, and then back again. There is a flat-fee fare of €7, one way, from any stop on the route, or €12 return. There are set stops on the route (which are not the same as city bus stops), which are well signposted.

Several city bus (**Dublin Bus, t** 01 872 0000, **www**.dublinbus.ie) routes also serve the airport. Routes **747** and **748** are the main **Airlink** buses between the airport and the city centre, stopping at the Central Bus Station (Busáras) and Connolly and Heuston rail stations; other routes run to different parts of Dublin. These buses are cheaper (€5) than the Aircoach (€7); Airlink routes run approximately 6.40am–11pm, Mon–Sat, and less frequently on Sundays.

A taxi from the airport into central Dublin usually costs around €25, depending very much on traffic.

Galway Airport

Carnmore, **t** 091 755 569, **www**.galwayairport.com
Getting there 4 miles (6km) east of Galway City.

As well as flights from Britain, this has Aer Arann flights to the Aran Islands. There is a very infrequent bus service, and the airline often provides a shuttle bus into town, but otherwise the main way to get into Galway is by taxi; the fare should be about €15.

Kerry Airport

Farranfore, Co. Kerry, **t** 066 976 4644/4350, **www**.kerryairport.ie
Getting there 9 miles (14km) north of Killarney on road to Tralee (N22)

Kerry has flights from Luton and Stansted in the UK. A shuttle bus runs regularly to Killarney, stopping in Farranfore village, where you can change onto buses for Dingle and the Ring of Kerry.

Knock International Airport

Knock, near Charlestown, Co. Mayo, **t** 1 850 672 222, **t** 094 67222/67232, **www**.west-irl-holidays.com
Getting there Next to the N17 Galway–Sligo road, 24 miles (38km) east of Castlebar

Only a shuttle bus operates intermittently to local villages, but taxis go to all towns in the region for €1.27 per mile (e.g., about €25 to Westport). All passengers departing from Knock (over 12) must pay a special extra local airport charge per ticket.

Shannon Airport

Shannon, Co. Clare, General information **t** 1 890 742 6666, Flight information **t** 061 712 400, **www**.aer-rianta.ie
Getting there 16 miles (26km) west of Limerick just off the Ennis road (N18)

Buses operate between the airport and Limerick city centre approximately 8am–midnight, daily. The journey time is about 40mins. Bus Éireann also runs direct buses from Shannon to many towns in Ireland; check the company website for details (*see* p.286). A taxi to Limerick will cost around €25–35.

Sligo Airport

Strandhill, **t** (071) 68280
Getting there 5 miles (8km) west of town

Flights from Dublin.

Waterford Regional Airport

Killowen, Co. Waterford, t 051 875 589, www.flywaterford.com
Getting there **8 miles (13km) south of Waterford town on local road to Clohernagh**

Taxis are the only means of transport between this small airport and Waterford town. The usual fare is around €15–20.

Airports in Northern Ireland

Belfast has 2 airports, 1 of them (Belfast International, once known as Aldergrove) much further from the city than the other. Make sure that you are very clear about which airport your airline is using.

Belfast City Airport

t 028 9093 9093, www.belfastcityairport.com
Getting there **4 miles (7km) from central Belfast, east of the city on the A2 Holywood–Bangor road**

Airport buses run every 40mins between the terminal and Europa Bus Terminal in Belfast, 6.25am–9.50pm daily. Shuttle buses also run to Sydenham Halt rail station, from where there are 2 trains each hour to Belfast, 6am–6pm Mon–Fri, and 1 hourly Sat and Sun; and Citybus 21 runs from near the airport terminal to the city (and is cheaper than the airport bus).

Belfast International Airport

Aldergrove, Co. Antrim, t 028 9448 4848, www.belfastairport.com
Getting there **18 miles (29km) northwest of Belfast and 6 miles (10km) to the west of the M2 motorway**

This is Northern Ireland's largest airport. An **Airbus** service runs every 30mins between the airport and Belfast city centre, 5.45am–11.30pm Mon–Sat, and every hour on Sundays. A taxi to Belfast costs around £25.

City of Derry Airport

Airport Rd, Eglinton, Co. Derry, t 028 7181 0784, www.cityofderryairport.com
Getting there **7 miles (11km) northeast of Londonderry on A2 Coleraine road.**

A variety of Ulsterbus services run from the airport to Londonderry/Derry City and Coleraine, and Bus Éireann buses run to several destinations in the Republic. The taxi fare to Derry City is approximately £12.

By bus

Travelling to Ireland by coach with children in tow can seem an endurance test, with the ferry journey and plenty of stops en route. The plus is that you can travel direct from many departure points in Britain to a huge range of small towns and villages in Ireland, without the need to transfer from an airport or ferry port. And, since air fares have fallen so much, bus fares are even cheaper.

The international bus network **Eurolines**, which includes National Express in Britain and Bus Eireann and Ulsterbus in Ireland, offers many routes between Britain and Ireland, and has a central booking service. In London, coaches leave from Victoria Coach Station; a bus to Dublin takes 11–12 hours (each way).

There are many more small companies that run buses to Ireland, often to provincial towns. A good way to find out about them is through ads in Irish newspapers such as the *Irish Post*.

Eurobus Express

t 0870 608 8806, www.eurobusexpress.net

Eurolines

In the UK: National Express, t 08705 808080, www.eurolines.co.uk; In the Irish Republic: Bus Éireann, t 01 836 6111, www.eurolines.ie

By sea

Ferries across the Irish Sea run from a variety of British ports to **Dublin**, **Dun Laoghaire** (just outside Dublin), **Rosslare** (near Wexford) and **Cork** in the Republic, and **Belfast**, **Larne** and the little port of **Ballycastle** in Northern Ireland. There are also direct ferry services to Dublin, Rosslare and Cork from Cherbourg and Roscoff in France.

The great attraction of crossing by ferry is, of course, if you want to travel around with your own car, and all the many things you can pack into it. As with airlines, it may be worth shopping around for different prices. Comparing prices is sometimes complicated. Fares on each route vary according to season and how long you intend to stay. Between Holyhead and Dublin a return ticket for a trip of more than five days for a car, two adults and two under-15s costs from around £250, low season, to about £340 in midsummer. Most companies still base their fares on a simple return fare for a car and one driver, to which must be added extra charges for each additional person and any extras, such as cabins (which families with kids will almost certainly want on longer overnight crossings). This can make working out fares annoyingly difficult. The 'extra person' charge is generally lower for under-14s or under-15s, and under-4s usually travel free. It tends to be the smaller companies – Norse Merchant, Swansea–Cork – that have more generous (or at least simpler) fare structures, with which up to four people with a car can cross, perhaps with cabin included, for around £300–£320 return. Virtually all the companies now offer cheaper rates if you book directly online, not through agents.

For foot passengers, fares are very low. From Dublin and Dun Laoghaire harbours there are frequent buses travelling to central Dublin, and from Rosslare there is a direct rail link to Wexford and Dublin and many Bus Éireann services to these or other towns. From Larne harbour there is a rail link to Belfast.

Sailing times vary a great deal between routes (*see* below). Ferries are comfortable and offer a range of family facilities, especially on the longer crossings – child-friendly restaurants, baby-changing rooms, play areas, video rooms. Take note, though, that the Irish Sea can often grow rough, especially in the winter months.

Ferry companies between Britain and Ireland

Irish Ferries

t Britain 08705 171717, **t** IR 1 890 31 31 31, **t** Northern Ireland 0800 018 2211, **www.irishferries.com**

Several standard 'Cruise Ferries' and faster 'Swift Ferries' run daily between Holyhead and Dublin and between Pembroke and Rosslare. Swift Ferries are slightly more expensive.

Isle of Man Steam Packet Company

t UK 01624 661 661, 08705 523 523, **www.steam-packet.com**

Liverpool–Dublin, Feb–Nov only, plus several routes to the Isle of Man. This company has absorbed SeaCat and the Argylle & Antrim Steam Packet Company.

Norse Merchant Ferries

t UK 0870 600 4321, **t** IR 01 819 2999, **www.norsemerchant.com**

Liverpool–Belfast, with at least 1 ferry daily each way, all year. This has some of the best fare offers.

P&O Irish Sea Ferries

t UK 0870 242 4777, **t** IR 1 800 409 049, **www.poirishsea.com**

Liverpool–Dublin, Mostyn (North Wales)–Dublin, Fleetwood–Larne, Cairnryan–Larne and Troon–Larne. On the Larne routes from April to October only there are both standard ferries and fast catamarans, for which fares are higher.

Stena Line

t UK 08705 707070 **t** IR 01 204 7777, **www7.stenaline.co.uk**

Sailings all year, Holyhead–Dublin, Holyhead–Dun Laoghaire, Fishguard–Rosslare, Stranraer–Belfast. Stena has some of the most modern Irish ferries, both conventional 'Superferries' and HSS Fastcraft giant catamarans, which offer the fastest crossings to the Republic. Fastcraft fares are predictably a bit higher.

Swansea–Cork Ferries

t UK 01792 456 116, **t** IR 021 427 1166, **www.swanseacorkferries.com**

Overnight ferries between Swansea and Cork. Fares are very competitive.

Good to know...

Average Crossing Times

Cairnryan–Larne 1hr 45mins
Campbeltown–Ballycastle 2hrs 45mins
Fishguard–Rosslare 1hr 40mins Fastcraft, 3hrs 30mins Superferry
Fleetwood–Larne 8hrs
Holyhead–Dublin 3hrs 15mins
Holyhead–Dun Laoghaire 1hr 39mins Fastcraft, 3hrs 15mins Superferry
Liverpool–Belfast 8hrs
Liverpool–Dublin 7hrs 30mins
Mostyn–Dublin 6hrs
Pembroke–Rosslare 3hrs 45mins
Stranraer–Belfast 1hr 45mins Fastcraft, 3hrs 15mins Superferry
Swansea–Cork 10hrs
Troon–Belfast 2hrs 30mins
Troon–Larne 2hrs

Ferry companies between France and Ireland

Brittany Ferries

t IR 021 427 7801, France 00 33 (825) 828 828, www.brittany-ferries.ie

Ferries once a week between Cork and Roscoff in Brittany, Apr–Sept only. Sailing time 11 hours.

Irish Ferries

t IR 1 890 31 31 31, 08705 171717, www.irishferries.com

Ferries once a week from Rosslare to Cherbourg and Roscoff in France. Sailing time around 12 hours.

Border formalities

UK citizens do not need a passport or visa to enter Ireland, but most airlines and ferry companies require you to show some form of identification with a photograph when boarding, usually either a passport or driver's licence. Check with your airline, ferry or tour operator what form of identification is required before travelling. Other EU nationals and citizens of other countries must have a valid passport or national identity card to enter the Republic or Northern Ireland.

No visas are required for travel to the Republic or the UK by citizens of the USA, Canada, Australia, New Zealand or South Africa. Citizens of other countries should check with their nearest Irish and/or British Consulate before travelling. There are not usually any customs checks between the Irish Republic and the UK, but there are still limits on the amount of goods that can be brought in by travellers arriving from non-EU countries.

VAT Refund Scheme

Residents of non-EU countries can reclaim the VAT or Value-Added Tax (currently 20.6% in the Republic, and 17.5% in Northern Ireland) paid on some goods when they leave Ireland. They must spend more than €180, or £150, in any one shop, which must be part of the Retail Export Scheme (it will have a sticker on the door). Show your passport to the shop staff and ask for a Tax-Free Shopping Form, which you present it to Customs when you finally leave the Irish Republic or the UK to go home, to reclaim the tax. You cannot reclaim VAT when travelling between Ireland and Britain or another EU country.

GETTING AROUND

By air

Given the size of Ireland, few travellers are in such a hurry that they want to take internal flights, but there's a wide range of domestic services, mainly operated by **Aer Arann** and **Aer Lingus** (*see* pp.280–1), and to airports such as Sligo and Donegal as well as those listed on pp.283–4. One local air route that can be both handy and memorable is the light-plane service run by Aer Arann from Galway to the **Aran Islands** (*see* p.164).

By bus

Bus Éireann, in the Republic, and Ulsterbus in Northern Ireland are the two main, interconnecting bus companies that, between them, cover the whole of Ireland. Translink controls all bus and rail services in Northern Ireland. In addition, many towns have their own local transport authorities (notably Dublin Bus, and Citybus in Belfast), and there are many small regional and county-based companies. There are few places in rural Ireland that cannot be reached by bus in some way – so long as you're able and ready to take your time. Country buses can be infrequent and very slow. Local tourist offices are the best guides to the full choice of bus services in each area.

Bus Éireann

The Travel Centre, Busáras (Central Bus Station), Store St, Dublin 1, t 01 836 6111, www.buseireann.ie

The Republic's national bus lines have routes to every part of the country from Dublin, and many others between regions. There are reduced fares for children under 16, and student discounts. Bus Éireann also offers several kinds of multi-journey tickets for discount travel, some allowing you to combine train and bus (*see* right, **Discount Tickets**).

Ulsterbus/Translink

Europa Bus Centre, Great Victoria St, Belfast, t 028 9066 6630, www.ulsterbus.co.uk

Ulsterbus runs all buses in Northern Ireland except those in Belfast city. As well as sharing some multi-journey tickets with Bus Eireann tickets, Ulsterbus has its own **Freedom of Northern Ireland** unlimited travel tickets (*see* right, **Discount Tickets**), which link up with rail companies.

Good to know...
Discount Tickets

There are reduced fares for children under 16 on all public transport in Ireland, north and south, and also significant discounts for students in possession of a student card. Fares in general are reasonable but change quite often, so check current rates when you travel. Ireland is also part of the Eurail Pass and Interail networks, which allow unlimited rail travel on European railways, including the Republic of Ireland but excluding the UK, and discount ferry crossings from France to Ireland. To obtain a Eurail Pass you must be resident of a non-European country and purchase it outside Europe. For details of these schemes, check **www**.raileurope.com.

Ireland's bus and train companies also offer a range of multi-journey, unlimited travel tickets directed at foreign visitors, some of which can be used across different networks. These include:

Emerald Card Unlimited travel on buses and trains in the Republic and Northern Ireland (all Iarnród Éireann, Bus Éireann, Northern Ireland Railways and Ulsterbus services). Valid for 8 or 15 days' (adult €375, under-16s €187.50) consecutive travel.

Freedom of Northern Ireland Unlimited travel on Northern Ireland bus or trains for 1 day (£12), 3 days (£30) or 7 days (£45), with reductions for under-16s.

Irish Explorer Unlimited travel on buses and trains in the Republic (Iarnród Éireann and Bus Éireann) for 8 of 15 days (adult €194, under-16s €97).

Irish Rambler Unlimited travel on all Bus Éireann buses in the Republic, for 3 days (adult €53, under-16s €32), 8 days (adult €116, under-16s €74) or 15 days (adult €168, under-16s €105).

Irish Rover Unlimited travel on all Bus Éireann buses in the Republic and Ulsterbus services in Northern Ireland. Can be bought for 3 days (adult €68, under-16s €38), 8 days (adult €145/ £105, under-16s €80/£58) or 15 days (adult €226, under-16s €124).

By car

Taking a car around Ireland is a great option when you're travelling with a family. It gives you the freedom to pace your journey to suit yourself, and it makes it easier to travel around once you get where you're going. Remember too that large parts of Ireland, particularly in the west, are only accessible by car – unless you spend ages waiting for buses. However, it's equally worth considering that travelling by train and bus might be more fun and less stressful if your children are old enough to be mobile themselves. We're not recommending it, but it's worth noting that the Irish travel writer Dervla Murphy rode all over India on a bike with her baby and then wrote a book about it, *Full Tilt*. That's not to mention Connacht's pirate queen Grace O'Malley who, just after childbirth, fought a battle on a ship, grumbling all the while about her male mariners losing heart.

If you take your own car from Britain to Ireland, it is advisable to have breakdown cover with the AA or RAC, your home insurance company or another specialist breakdown service. Be sure to take your car registration and insurance papers as well.

Car hire

Valid UK, US or Canadian driver's licences are all accepted for hiring a car in the Irish Republic, but you will normally have to show another form of ID as well (a passport). Hire-car companies in the Republic and Northern Ireland usually require that the hirer must have had a licence for at least 1 year, or in some cases may ask for an international driving licence issued in the home country.

The major international car-hire chains such as Avis, Hertz, Europcar and so on are all present in Northern Ireland and the Republic. Car hire tends to work out cheaper if you rent a car in advance before you arrive in Ireland, especially if coming from North America. However, it's still best to contact different companies and compare prices. It will usually be cheaper to hire in a city rather than at an airport. Most hire cars have manual gearshifts, and automatics will cost more to rent.

If you hire a car in Northern Ireland, make sure that its insurance will cover you if you take the car to the Republic, and vice versa. Collision damage waiver and other insurance coverage may also vary, so check the details before you sign up.

Seatbelts and child seats

It is mandatory for all car drivers and front seat passengers in Ireland to use seatbelts, and motorcyclists must wear crash helmets. In both the Republic and Northern Ireland, the law requires all children travelling in cars to use an appropriate child restraint or adult seat belt. These must be in

Good to know...
Speed limits
Speed limits in Northern Ireland are the same as in Britain:
30mph/50kph in towns unless otherwise signposted
60mph/95kph on most dual carriageways with no hard shoulder
70mph/112kph on motorways and highways without any other speed restriction.
Speed limits in the Republic of Ireland are:
30–40mph/50–65kph in built-up areas
63mph/100kph on most roads
70mph/112kph on motorways and dual carriageways

place on infant carriers, baby or child car seats or booster cushions. Children normally cannot be carried in the front seat of a car unless they are either in a child restraint or are using a seat belt, but please check current laws. If a child under 18 years of age is sitting in the front passenger seat of a car, make sure that the airbag on that side has been removed. It is the driver's responsibility to ensure that children under age 14 are using an appropriate child restraint or an adult seat belt. For information on car seat types, try **www**.childcarseats.org.uk.

If you are hiring a car, make sure that you order a child's seat in advance. Baby or child car seats can be hired from most car-hire companies for a weekly rate.

Some rules of the road

A vital note for visitors from North America and most of Europe: drive on the left and overtake on the right. Cars already on a roundabout (traffic circle), circulating clockwise, have right of way over those entering the roundabout – so look to your right carefully before going ahead. Distances on road signs can be confusing: in Northern Ireland, they're all in miles, but in the Republic they may be in miles (on older signs) or kilometres.

Never park in restricted areas or your car will be towed away. In the Republic and Northern Ireland, a single yellow line parallel to the kerb indicates restricted parking (with a sign usually nearby indicating the times when parking is banned), and double yellow lines indicate that you cannot park there at any time. Do not park in a clearway or bus lane between designated times; if it is towed away it may cost €100 to get it back. Always lock your car and do not leave tempting items exposed to view.

By train

Ireland's railways are centred on its main cities, Dublin and Belfast, and there are few local lines, except suburban networks around the 2 capitals. Trains, though, can be very useful and enjoyable for getting from cities to smaller towns. Also, as well as the multi-journey tickets most useful for people doing a lot of touring (*see* p.287 **Discount Tickets**), the rail networks offer very attractive **low fares** for anyone travelling with children, such as the 'Family Fares' on Iarnród Éireann (for 2 adults and up to 4 children) and the 'Kids Go Free' scheme on some Enterprise trains (no charge for up to 4 children travelling with 2 adults). It's always worth checking on current family train fares when planning a trip.

Enterprise Trains

t UK 028 9066 6630, t IR 01 703 4070, www.translink.co.uk, www.irishrail.ie

Run jointly by Irish Rail and Northern Ireland Railways, this special Dublin–Belfast express service has 8 trains daily in each direction Mon–Sat, and 5 Sun. It also stops in Drogheda, Dundalk, Newry and Portadown. A single ticket costs around €31/£22, and there are very good 'Kids Go Free' offers for adults travelling with children.

Iarnród Éireann (Irish Rail)

Travel Centre, 35 Lower Abbey St, Dublin D1, info t 1 850 366 222, (01) 703 1885, reservations t 01 703 4070, 01 836 6222, www.irishrail.ie

Irish Rail's lines run out Dublin's 2 main stations: from Dublin Heuston there are trains to the west and southwest (Ballina, Westport, Galway, Ennis, Limerick, Tralee, Cork, Kilkenny and Waterford, and stops en route), and from Dublin Connolly lines run along the east coast and to Northern Ireland (Wexford, Leitrim, Sligo, Belfast, Derry). There are 2 classes on most trains. For details of **DART** suburban trains in the Dublin area, also run by Iarnród Éireann, *see* p.47.

Northern Ireland Railways

Central Station, Belfast, t 028 9066 6630, www.translink.co.uk

NIR has trains from Belfast to Coleraine, Portrush and Derry, local lines around Belfast to Bangor, Larne harbour and Portadown, and runs the Belfast–Dublin line (via Newry) with Irish Rail. It's administered by the same Translink authority as **Ulsterbus** (*see* p.286), and many services connect.

Practical A–Z

Babysitters 290
Beaches 290
Climate and when to go 290
Clothing 290
Electricity 291
Embassies and consulates 291
Emergency numbers 291
Environmental matters 291
Food and eating out 291
Insurance 292
Lost property 293
Medical matters 293
Money and banks 294
Opening hours 295
Post and post offices 295
Public holidays 296
Safety 296
Shopping for children 296
Smoking 296
Special-interest and activity holidays 297
Special needs 298
Sports 298
Telephones 299
Time 299
Tipping 300
Toilets and Baby Facilities 300
Tourist information 300

10

Babysitters

Many hotels in Ireland will provide babysitters on request, usually for an extra charge, but check the details of the services available when you book. B&Bs and guesthouses can normally arrange babysitting so long as you inform them of what you need well enough in advance.

Beaches

Many Irish beaches have now been awarded Blue Flag status, under a Europe-wide quality-control scheme. If a beach carries the Blue Flag this means that local authorities (such as county councils) have committed themselves to maintaining certain standards during each summer season. In brief, Blue Flag status means that beaches are kept tidy and clean; that they have toilets, showers and other sanitary facilities that are well maintained; that camping, driving motor vehicles and dumping on the beach are prohibited; and that dogs, horses and other pets are not normally allowed in bathing areas. Lifeguards should be on duty throughout the summer season and there should be adequate lifesaving equipment. Look out for the Blue Flag (or just the Blue Flag symbol) on signs by any beach you think of using.

The local authorities are also committed to passing on any complaints they receive about the state of their beaches to the Foundation for Environmental Education in Europe.

Climate and when to go

Ireland's weather is notoriously changeable, and in a single day you can experience 'a fine mist' (as the Irish call it) under a cloud-heavy sky, then strong winds, and end up with bright sunshine. You can also suffer a whole month of rain and storms in midsummer, or be lucky enough to come across 2 weeks of warm, balmy sunshine in the months of autumn.

The weather in April, May and September is sometimes better than that from June to August, which can be especially variable. From late November to February you can usually expect dull cloudy weather that makes you want to sleep a lot and dream, with the occasional very cold snap. In March it's usually still a bit cool for spring clothes, but you will probably experience the odd beautiful day, as you will in October, when in addition the leaves are changing colour and the days turn brisk.

Good to know...

Average Daily Temperatures

Jan/Feb	3–7°C (37–44°F)
Mar/Apr	4–10°C (39–51°F)
May/June	8–16°C (46–61°F)
July/Aug	10–18°C (51–65°F)
Sept/Oct	8–15°C (46–59°F)
Nov/Dec	3–8°C (37–46°F)

The sunniest months are usually May and June (though September can be bright); average annual rainfall is 43 inches. Temperatures in Ireland have scarcely ever fallen below freezing (0°C, 32°F) in winter, or topped 32°C (90°F) in summer.

For more information, you can consult:

Met Éireann, t IR (01) 806 4200, **www**.weather.ie
The Irish Republic's national weather service.

Met Office, t UK 0870 900 0100, **www**.metoffice.co.uk
The official British government weather centre.

Clothing

It's best to be frank: the best thing to do is expect the worst and hope for the best, making sure you and your kids have clothing you can add or remove as required. At some point during any stay in Ireland, it will rain. It's especially important to bring some good, comfortable and rain-secure walking shoes, warm sweaters or fleeces, tights or socks, rainwear, a cap (you can buy lovely woollen ones in Ireland) and/or a scarf and gloves, even in summer. Wearing layers of clothes is the safest thing to do in Ireland, with plenty of items you can remove and carry easily, such as a cagoule or sweatshirt, with a T-shirt underneath in case it suddenly gets hot, just as unpredictably as when it decides to rain.

For a winter stay, of course, you will need a bigger supply of warmer clothes. However, you can always buy sweaters, scarves and other items that are perfect for the climate in Ireland if you find you haven't brought what you need. Plan for them in your budget for the trip, as you may be unable to resist the amazing Aran knits, even though you probably won't need the heavier versions in the summer. Lightweight, loose windbreakers with hoods and pockets are good to have at any time of year, and perfect for walks beside the seashore on a brisk sunny day. Good pockets are important for collecting seashells and rocks or carrying sandwiches, fruit and bottles of water.

Electricity

The standard electricity supply in the Republic is 220 volts AC and in Northern Ireland 240 volts AC. Both systems use the same 3-pin plugs. Visitors with equipment with either North American- or European-style 2-pin plugs will need plug adaptors to convert them to Ireland's 3-pin plugs, and anyone with North American 110-volt appliances will also need a current transformer.

Embassies and consulates

For Ireland and Northern Ireland/Britain:

Canada

Canadian Embassy 65–68 St Stephen's Green, Dublin 2, **t** (01) 478 1988
Canadian High Commission Canada House, Trafalgar Sq, London W1, **t** (020) 7258 6600

British Embassy in the Irish Republic

31–33 Merrion Rd, Dublin 4, **t** 01 269 5211

USA

US Embassy 42 Elgin Rd, Dublin 4, **t** (01) 668 8777
US Consulate 223 Stranmillis Rd, Belfast, BT9 5GR, **t** (028) 9038 6100
US Embassy 24 Grosvenor Sq, London W1, **t** (020) 7499 9000

Environmental matters

Children need to know that the land is the home of animals as well as humans, not to mention unseen beings. Irish country people used to throw their washing water outdoors, and every time they did so they'd cry out 'feet water', just in case a passing invisible person was about; they believed that if they didn't do that a faery might play a trick on them. So please don't pick wildflowers, light fires outdoors (especially in forests), disturb wildlife or leave behind food, pets' waste or rubbish you bring to picnic and tourist sites (there can be on-the-spot fines for doing all these things).

Horse-riding, walking, camping, swimming and so on may not be allowed everywhere, so check for regulations or ask local people about restrictions and permitted places. If you want to see a site marked as being on private land (even when it's an official heritage spot), people expect you to knock on the door of the nearest farmhouse and ask if permission is required to walk on it, especially since the Foot and Mouth disease outbreak.

Emergency Numbers Republic of Ireland

112 or **999**
Call one of these freephone numbers for **fire, police** or **ambulance** services. They must only be used in cases of genuine emergency.
Crime victims can also call **t** (01) 478 5295.
In case of a vehicle breakdown:
Automobile Association (AA), **t** 1800 667 788
RAC, t 1800 535 005

Northern Ireland

999
This is a freephone number for **fire, police** or **ambulance** services, and must only be used in genuine emergencies.
Crime victims can also call **t** (028) 9065 0222.
In case of a vehicle breakdown:
Automobile Association (AA), **t** 0800 887 766, info **t** 08705 722 722, **www**.theaa.com
RAC, t 0800 828 282

Some Irish environmental organizations are:
Irish Wildlife Trust, Sigmund Business Centre, 93A Lagan Rd, Dublin Industrial Estate, Glasnevin, D11, **t** (01) 860 2839
The Woodland Trust in Northern Ireland, 1 Dufferin Court, Dufferin Ave, Bangor, Co. Down, **t** (028) 9127 5787

Food and eating out

Many Irish restaurants offer children's portions from their main menus, others offer them special menus. It's a good idea to check with the restaurant beforehand, and also whether any special rules or limited hours apply to kids. Families with small children usually book an early meal at restaurants. Many have 'early-bird menus' (normally 5–7pm) for children. Restaurants and other establishments in Ireland with licences to sell alcohol must, by law, ensure no one under 18 is on their premises after 9.30pm if they continue to serve alcohol.

Restaurant price categories

Restaurants listed in this guide are categorized in the price bands shown here, based on the cost of a 3-course meal for an adult, without drinks.

Luxury	Cost no object
Expensive	More than €65/£42
Moderate	€32–65/£22–42
Inexpensive	Less than €32/£22

Pub rules

Ireland's pubs are a near-unmissable alternative to restaurants for refreshments, socializing and, increasingly, eating. Pubs in the country generally have more relaxed rules when it comes to admitting families than those in cities, as in Ireland the local village pub quite often doubles as a community centre. However, it is the law in the Republic that children are not allowed to remain in pubs past 9pm, although this may be extended for private functions where significant amounts of food are being eaten, or in hotel restaurants and so on. An area where food is being served is not considered a pub. Just ask and people will tell you whatever the policy is. In Northern Ireland, the laws are stricter (being those of Britain): children under the age of 18 are not allowed in pubs where no food is served.

Children may have soft drinks and snacks in pubs, but otherwise there's not much for them to do unless the establishment has a play area. If restaurant-style meals are not offered, you can often get a sandwich, tea or coffee, or possibly soup. Live music does not usually start in pubs until 9 or 10pm, especially during the summer. You're more likely to see musicians playing in pubs during the day at town festivals.

Good to know...

Country Markets

The markets listed here are among the best places to find and buy Irish farm produce, organic and traditional foods, direct from producers.

Co. Cork

Bantry Market. **Open** Fri am, plus a fair in the market square on the first Fri of each month.

Castletownbere, Beara Peninsula. **Open** first Thurs of each month.

Cork: Cornmarket, Cornmarket St. **Open** Sat.

Macroom Market. **Open** Tues am.

Skibbereen Market **Open** Fri 12 noon–2pm.

Dublin City

Cow's Lane Market, Meetinghouse Square, Temple Bar, Dublin 2. **Open** Sat 9–6. Organic fruit, fish, cheeses, breads, preserves.

Moore Street Market, behind O'Connell St, Dublin 2. **Open** Sat am, Dublin's oldest open-air market.

Co. Galway Galway City Saturday Market, outside St Nicholas Church. **Open** Sat am.

Co. Kerry Kenmare Farmers' Market, Casey's Car Park, Sneem Rd, Kenmare. **Open** Weds am.

Milltown Organic Farmers' Market. **Open** Sat.

Co. Kildare Friday Country Market, Town Hall, Naas. **Open** Fri 10.45–12 noon.

Co. Mayo Westport Thursday Market, Town Hall, Westport. **Open** Thurs 10–5.

Co. Wexford Country Market, The Bull Ring, Wexford. **Open** Fri from 9am.

Co. Wicklow Brook Lodge Inn Sunday Market, Macreddin Village, **t** 0402 36444. **Open** Sun am.

Roundwood Market, Roundwood. **Open** Sun.

Northern Ireland St George's Indoor Market, near Waterfront Hall, Belfast. **Open** Sat am.

Shopping for food

Traditional Irish foods such as salmon, barm brack (*see* p.103), soda bread, organic cheeses and medieval mead are available from many specialist local producers. For gluten-free, vegetarian or wholefood products, you can find health shops and delicatessens in most large towns.

Around Ireland there are fine weekly country markets where local growers sell their produce. For information, contact the **Irish Country Markets Association**, Swanbrook House, Morehampton Rd, Dublin 4, **t** (01) 668 0560. For places where organic growers sell their products, contact the **Organic Trust**, **t** (01) 853 0271, or the **Irish Organic Farmers & Growers Association**, **t** (0506) 32563. Selected local markets are listed on the left, but bear in mind that market times and locations tend to change; see **www**.bordbia.ie or **www**.irishfarmersmarkets.ie for up-to-the-minute information, or ask locally.

Insurance

It's essential to take out travel insurance before your trip. The policy should cover cancellation due to illness, delays, accidents, lost luggage, loss of passports or other belongings, theft, personal liability, legal expenses, emergency flights and medical cover. A wide range of travel insurance policies is available, so it's worth shopping around.

Most insurance companies offer free insurance to children under 2 as part of their parents' policy. When travelling, keep the insurance company's 24hr emergency number close to hand, and store it in the memory of your mobile/cellphone. Report stolen or lost items to the police, however trivial, so you can make a claim when you get back home.

In the UK

Association of British Insurers, t (020) 7600 3333
Insurance Ombudsman Bureau, t (020) 7964 1000
These government-appointed regulators of the insurance industry can help with complaints.
ABC Holiday Extras Travel Insurance, t 0800 171 000
Columbus Travel Insurance, t (020) 7375 0011
Endsleigh Insurance, t (020) 7436 4451
Medicover, t 0870 735 3600
World Cover Direct, t 0800 365 121

In North America

Access America, t US 1 800 284 8300, **t** Canada 1 800 654 1908
Travel Assistance International, t US and Canada 1 800 921 2828
MEDEX Assistance Corporation, t US 1 410 453 6300

Lost property

If you lose important documents such as a passport, contact your consulate or embassy. For insurance purposes, you must report the loss to the local police.

Medical matters

In a medical emergency, the best thing to do is to call an ambulance, by phoning **112** or **999** in the Irish Republic or **999** only in Northern Ireland (*see* p.291). Don't try to drive a sick child to hospital if you don't know a city; it could waste valuable time. If you are staying in self-catering accommodation, make sure you have either a landline or a working mobile phone. Be sure too to ask the house owners or keyholders about local doctors and taxis, which sometimes double up as ambulance services in very rural areas, and on what to do in the case of a medical emergency.

Medical insurance

British visitors to Northern Ireland receive treatment as they would in Britain. In the Republic, British visitors are covered under an agreement with the Irish Department of Health but need to show some form of identification or a European Health Insurance Card (EHIC; *see* below). Visitors from all other EU countries travelling to Ireland should obtain an EHIC card prior to departure.

The Irish National Health Plan does not cover US or Canadian visitors. Check the details of your private medical insurance policy before travelling to ensure that you have full health cover in Ireland.

First-aid kit

Be sure to have with you a basic first-aid kit for dealing with children's minor ailments. Always keep it out of reach of small children.

Antiseptic cream, spray and wipes
Calamine lotion and aloe vera gel (for soothing bites, burns and stings)
Calpol or equivalent for lowering high temperatures
Cotton wool, bandages and plasters (Band Aids) – both fabric and waterproof
Decongestant and children's aspirin
Earplanes (plastic devices that fit in the ear and help prevent air pressure problems on flights)
Scissors and tweezers (prohibited in cabins)
Strip or digital thermometer
High-factor sun protection cream
Chewable vitamins and/or drinks
Travel sickness preparations
Vaseline or similar nappy/diaper cream

For all visitors from non-EU countries to Ireland, private medical insurance is pretty much essential, especially if you are travelling with children. If you are from the US or Canada, your existing insurance plans may provide you with sufficient medical cover while abroad, so, again, check your policy details thoroughly before taking out additional travel insurance cover.

The EHIC

The European Health Insurance Card (EHIC), which replaced the **E111** form at the end of 2005, allows EU citizens to make free use of the health services in any other EU country. In the UK, application forms are available from post offices.

Many travellers, though, prefer to take out a private travel insurance policy with full medical cover in addition to this option.

Visiting a doctor

For non-emergencies, ask hotel staff or the owners of your accommodation to help you contact a doctor. The local police will always have the number of a local doctor on duty, and during office hours tourist offices should be able to help.

If a medical problem seems more serious or urgent, especially if you're in a town, make your way to the Casualty (Emergency) department of a local hospital. EU visitors may go into any hospital to find a doctor, so long as they have an EHIC card (*see* p.293); non-EU visitors should follow the instructions of their insurance carrier.

To get prescriptions for drugs renewed in Ireland, visit an Irish general practitioner (local doctor), explain your situation and get an Irish prescription, which you can then use in any local pharmacy. Hospital admissions, where necessary, are also usually arranged by a doctor. EHIC cards should be presented to the doctor or hospital, along with ID, if and when required. In emergencies, initial hospital services will be provided free of charge for all visitors, but you and/or your family should be able to present some form of identification.

If British or EU citizens think they are entitled to cash benefits while in the Republic, they should apply within three days of becoming ill to:
Department of Social Welfare EU Records, Floor 1, O'Connell Bridge House, Dublin 2.

Medication

If you or any of your children have a pre-existing medical problem, you will need a letter from your doctor describing the illness and any prescription medications being taken, including the generic name of the drugs, to obtain further supplies in Ireland. Bring your own pre-packed sterile needles and syringes as required.

Good to know...
Travelling with children – first-aid tips

Countering in-flight air pressure: breastfeed or give a bottle to your baby; give toddlers something to swallow or suck (i.e., have them drink juice with a straw); give older children something soft to chew or get them to yawn or blow their noses
Eye protection: UVA/UVB sunglasses
Minor cuts on skin (for external use, to avoid infections): iodine, diluted hydrogen peroxide, Bach's Rescue Remedy
Skin irritations, bites or rashes: aloe vera, calamine, calendula, neem or zinc creams or gels; diluted hydrogen peroxide
Sleeplessness and anxiety: herbal sleep remedies are available, but ordinary foods such as bananas, milk and lettuce are soporific also; sugar tends to stimulate children, so honey is a better option before bedtime than sweets or biscuits; milk helps to counteract sugar's speedy effects
Stomach aches: chamomile or peppermint tea
Sunburn: waterproof UVA/UVB sun cream with a factor of 15+ or more, and calamine lotion; infants should not be exposed to direct sunlight
Travel sickness: get some fresh air or nibble a dry cracker or biscuit; avoid big meals, greasy foods and lots of fluid before travelling, especially by sea.

Good to know...
Natural remedies for children

Aloe vera: skin injuries or irritations (check if a product should be used internally or externally)
Arnica cream: bruises
Calamine lotion: heat rash, skin irritations and sunburn
Calendula cream: skin rashes and abrasions
Calendula liquid: use on scalp to deter or get rid of nits (or vinegar and water as a hair rinse)
Lavender oil: use diluted on young skins (never get it near the eyes, and wash them out immediately with warm water if any oil gets into them) as an insect repellant, against burns and sunburn, and for a bedtime bath (for its soporific qualities)
Lemons: fresh juice repels insects
Neem cream: soothes skin irritations
Rosemary oil: mild stimulant, soothes headache when sniffed on cotton wool or a pad
Tea tree oil: deters bugs and nits, and is antiseptic

Money and banks

The Republic of Ireland is one of the European Union countries that uses the European single currency, the **euro**, the symbol for which is €. Each euro is divided, like the US dollar, into 100 cents. There are 8 euro coins, for 1, 2, 5, 10, 20 and 50 cents and 1 and 2 euros, and 7 notes, for 5, 10, 20, 50, 100, 200 and 500 euros. The notes are entirely the same throughout the EU, but euro coins have a common design on one side, with the amount, and a design specific to each country, on the other. However, all euro coins can be used equally in any of the eurozone countries.

In Northern Ireland, the currency is the British **pound** (£), each one of which divides into 100 pence (abbreviated as the letter p, so you have 10p, 20p and so on). There are 8 coins (1p, 2p, 5p, 10p, 20p, 50p, and £1 and £2), and 4 denominations of notes, for £5, £10, £20 and £50.

Many businesses in border areas, especially those in towns such as Dundalk on the Republic side and Newry in the North, accept both euros and pounds, and so do many places all across Northern Ireland. Otherwise, though, you'll need to change money if you go between the Republic and Northern Ireland.

Exchange rates vary; you can check current rates on Internet currency converters such as **www**.xe.com.

Money can be exchanged in banks and at private bureaux de change, or obtained direct from bank ATMs (cashpoints). All small towns have at least 1 bank; otherwise, though, exchange offices can be scarce in the south and west of Ireland, so make sure you have enough cash with you. Be careful when carrying money around with you. Ireland is safer than most European countries regarding pickpockets, but they may operate in the shopping areas of big towns and at tourist attractions.

Bank opening hours

Banks are generally open Mon–Fri 10–4.30, with some branches, often those in shopping centres, open until 5pm on Sat and Thurs. In Northern Ireland, banks are usually open Mon–Fri 9.30–4.30. All banks are closed on public holidays. Most banks have ATM (cash) machines, which accept most credit and debit cards

Credit cards

Many shops and restaurants in the Republic and Northern Ireland accept all the big-name credit and debit cards – Visa, Delta, MasterCard, American Express, Cirrus – but in country areas many places are cash-only. Nearly all Irish cash dispensers (ATMs) dispense money on foreign credit or bank cards linked to the international Cirrus or Maestro networks. There will be a handling fee for each withdrawal, which can vary between banks; your own bank will be able to advise you on different rates. Diners Club cards are less widely accepted.

In Northern Ireland, most ATMs accept Visa, Cirrus and MasterCard, but if in doubt check with your home bank before travelling. AmEx and Diners Club are not widely accepted in Northern Ireland.

Traveller's cheques

Traveller's cheques in US dollars, British pounds and euros are readily cashed at any bank, for a commission. Most banks also cash traveller's cheques in other major currencies, such as the Japanese yen. Hotels will usually cash traveller's cheques but charge a big transaction fee. The main airports all have banks with exchange windows.

Opening hours

In the Republic of Ireland opening hours vary according to the habits of the local population, although, as a rule, Sundays are still usually quiet on the commercial front – both the Republic and Northern Ireland still consider Sunday to be a day of rest. On the other hand, you will often find shops open in the evenings, especially in the Republic, until 10pm or even later, according to their location.

In general, though, most shops in the Republic and the North are open Monday to Saturday, 9am to 6pm. Some close for lunch, usually for an hour 12 noon–2, and in main towns many stores have a weekly late-opening day, usually Thursday, when they stay open until 8 or 9pm. In cities, large department stores and shopping centres also open on Sundays, from 12 noon to 5–6pm in the Republic and 1–5pm in Northern Ireland. Many country towns, in contrast, still have an 'early closing day' once a week (usually Wednesday or Thursday) when all shops are closed after 1–2pm.

Tourist attractions are generally open Mon–Sat, 9–10am until 5–6pm or dusk, or sometimes earlier. Museums often open on Sundays but close on Mondays; theatres are often closed on Mondays and Tuesdays as well as Sundays.

All tourist attractions are open in the June–Aug high season, but in May and September they may close earlier or not open at all on some days. Variations also occur due to public holidays; some places, for example, open for Easter then close again until summer. It's always a good idea to ring before you drive a long way to see a tourist site, as you will find that time is a little bit more malleable in Ireland than in some countries of the world.

Post and post offices

Post offices, north and south, are usually open Mon–Fri 9–5.30, and Sat 9–1 and 2.15–5. In main towns, there's always one prominently placed in the middle of town, but in villages they may be hidden away in shops or even pubs. There is usually 1 closing day or afternoon each week, but it varies from place to place. You can buy telephone top-up cards for mobile/cellphones in post offices, as well as stamps and stationery. Postal charges to the UK are the same as those within Ireland.

To mail a letter or postcard, in the Republic you should look for green letterboxes, while in Northern Ireland, as in Britain, they are red.

Public holidays

All shops, banks and visitor attractions close on St Patrick's Day, Christmas Day and usually Boxing Day. However, many open on other public holidays.

In the Republic of Ireland
New Year's Day 1 January
St Patrick's Day 17 March
Easter Monday March/April – date varies
May Bank Holiday 1st Monday in May
June Bank Holiday 1st Monday in June
August Bank Holiday 1st Monday in August
October Bank Holiday last Monday in October
Christmas Day 25 December
St Stephen's Day/Boxing Day 26 December

In Northern Ireland
New Year's Day 1 January
St Patrick's Day 17 March
March/April Good Friday is widely observed as a holiday, but is not official
Easter Monday March/April – date varies
Spring/May Bank Holiday first and last Mon in May
The Twelfth 12 July (Battle of the Boyne)
Summer/August Bank Holiday late August
Christmas Day 25 December
Boxing Day 26 December

Safety

Lost children

It's easy to get separated from children in busy airports, railway and bus stations and markets. Make sure toddlers know their full names and that, if they are lost, they should go into a shop and ask an assistant for help. Generally people in Ireland will be only too happy to assist. Teenagers also can easily stray. Make sure they know where to go to make a public announcement at a station or airport, and fix a place to meet if you are separated.

Road safety and awareness

Make sure your children are fully aware that the Irish drive on the left side of the road, and that they know where to look for oncoming traffic. The dangers are the same in Ireland as they are at home. In cities, be as vigilant and as cautious, if not more so, as you would normally be at home.

Teen issues

Mobile phone theft is a problem everywhere. Make sure your children are careful where they use their telephones, and are aware that it's not worth a fight if someone tries to steal them.

The drug scene in Ireland is similar to that of the rest of western Europe. Soft and hard drugs are available. It's illegal to be in possession of drugs and even a small amount of marijuana could land you in jail. In the UK, look for the leaflet *Drugs Abroad*. For more information, in the UK call the National Drugs Helpline, **t** 0800 776 600.

Shopping for children

Gifts of quality for children can be found all over Ireland. Apart from leprechaun figurines, souvenirs that might interest them are the St Bridget's Cross, Crolly dolls, toy soldiers and child-sized *bodhrán* drums or tin whistles, if not a real Irish harp made by an Irish instrument maker. Irish bookshops often have good stocks of mythology and fairytales, and towns tend to promote famous authors associated with them. As a special gift you could buy children's stories by Oscar Wilde or Jonathan Swift in Dublin, the Narnia tales of CS Lewis in a Belfast store or poems by WB Yeats at Thoor Ballylee. Music is in the blood in this part of the world, and as well as the most popular Irish acts such as Enya or Westlife you could consider Gael-Linn's excellent recordings of traditional artists singing in Irish, available in traditional music shops. Recordings of Irish storytellers are riveting also (*see* p.26).

Irish crafts, from pottery to bogwood sculptures, and Irish lace, linen, crochet, tweed and knitwear will interest old and young. For hardy woollen goods that are warm as well as beautifully coloured, visit shops such as Magee's in Donegal and Avoca in Wicklow, or skilled independent knitters who sell intricately hand-woven Aran sweaters in the Arans and Connemara. Among many other things, you will also see fine crystal in Galway, Tyrone and Waterford, Parian china in Belleek (Fermanagh), ceramics, blackthorn walking sticks, compressed peat ornaments, and jewellery produced by excellent craftspeople on this island.

Smoking

In an unprecedented move, smoking was banned from pubs and restaurants in the Republic of Ireland in March 2004. All public premises must comply by law.

Currently, Northern Ireland retains British laws about smoking, which is not yet completely banned in pubs and restaurants. If you require a smoking or non-smoking bedroom, check when you book that what you want is available.

Special-interest and activity holidays

For more on family holiday possibilities, *see* pp.246–8 and pp.298–9. More locally based agencies offering tours, walks and so on are listed in the province chapters of this book.

In Britain

Angler's World Holidays, 46 Knifesmithgate, Chesterfield, Derbyshire, S40 1RQ, **t** (01246) 221 717, **www.anglers-world.co.uk**

This firm can arrange for families to holiday in Ireland and try a spot of game fishing for salmon and sea-trout, and coarse fishing in Irish rivers and lakes.

Back-Roads Touring Company, 14a New Broadway, London W5 2XA, **t** (020) 8566 5312, **www.backroadstouring.co.uk**

Off-the-beaten-track tours of Dublin, Killarney, Galway, Sligo and Donegal.

HF Holidays, Imperial House, The Hyde, Edgware Rd, London, NW9 5AL, **t** (020) 8905 9558, **www.hfholidays.co.uk**

Dingle Way and West of Ireland guided walking holidays, or stays in Killarney National Park.

In Ireland

Adams & Butler, 71 Waterloo Rd, Dublin 4, **t** 01 660 7975, **www.tourismresources.ie**

Informative tours anywhere in Ireland, with tailor-made itineraries, cars with driver-guides and accommodation ranging from homely farmhouses to stately castles. Tours can take in gardens, genealogy, ghosts, gourmet cooking and sites of historical importance.

Ardress Craft Centre, Kesh, Co. Fermanagh, **t** (028) 6863 1267

Arts and crafts courses.

Association of Irish Riding Establishments (AIRE), 11 Moore Park, Newbridge, Co. Kildare, **t** (045) 431 584

Horse-riding and pony-trekking information.

British Horse Society, House of Sport, Upper Malone Rd, Belfast, **t** (028) 9038 1222

Horse-riding information for Northern Ireland.

Equestrian Holidays Ireland, 1 Sandyford Office Park, Foxrock, Dublin 18, **t** (01) 295 8928, **www.ehi.ie**

Horse-riding holidays.

Go Ireland, Killorglin, Co. Kerry, **t** (066) 976 2094, **www.goireland.com**

Guided or independent walking, golfing, cycling and cultural holidays, including tours of the Aran Islands and the Dingle Peninsula.

Irish Country Holidays, Old Church, Mill St, Borrisokane, Co. Tipperary, **t** (0672) 7790, **www.country-holidays.ie**

This company gives you the opportunity to live as part of a small, rural community in self-catering properties or B&B-style accommodation.

Irish Cycling Safaris, Belfield Bike Shop, University College, Belfield House, Dublin 4, **t** (01) 260 0749, **www.cyclingsafaris.com**

Leisurely 1wk cycling holidays, with bikes supplied and luggage transported for you, in many parts of Ireland, especially Cork, Kerry and Connemara.

Kerry Holidays, t UK 0800 039 0088, **www.kerryholidays.com**

Fly-drive, B&B or self-catering accommodation, city breaks and golf.

Vagabond Irish Adventure Tours, t (01) 660 7399, **www.vagabond-ireland.com**

Award-winning multi-activity trips in 4x4s.

In the US and Canada

Travel companies specializing in Ireland can be found through the Shamrock Club, **www**.shamrockclub.net

Backroads, 801 Cedar St, Berkeley, CA 94710-1800, **t** 510 527 1555, **www.backroads.com**

Multi-sport: golf, walking and biking, with packages in counties Kerry, Cork and Galway.

CIE Tours International Inc, 100 Hanover Ave, PO Box 501, Cedar Knolls, NJ 07927-0501, **t** 1 800 CIE-TOUR, **www.cietours.com**

Escorted coach, self-drive or independent holidays, including theme tours.

Classic Adventures, t 1 800 777 8090, **www.classicadventures.com**

Guided biking holidays in southwest Ireland.

Green Earth Travel, 7 Froude Circle, Cabin John, MD 20818, **t** 301 229 5666, **t** 1 888 246 8343, **www.vegtravel.com, www.irelandtrips.com**

A specialist firm catering to vegetarian and ecologically oriented families.

Irish Folklore Tours, Hemisphere Travel Service, Inc., 5 Washington St, Biddeford, ME 04005, **t** 1 800 848 4364, **www.irishfolkloretours.com**

Tours for families interested in exploring aspects of Irish culture, including music, mythology, archaeology and the landscape.

Special needs

Access facilities for wheelchair users and other disabled people are more common in Ireland than they used to be, but it is still a good idea to check beforehand any time you wish to visit a tourist attraction, hotel or guesthouse that facilities are available or that there are rooms at ground level. Where possible, information on access has been listed for attractions and accommodation in this guide. In general you will find the Irish helpful to anyone with special needs. There are often facilities to accommodate wheelchairs on boats and coaches, and many restaurants have suitably large toilets, so don't hesitate to ask.

Information for Northern Ireland is available from **Disability Action**, 2 Annadale Ave, Belfast, BT7 3JH, **t** (028) 9029 7880, **www**.disabilityaction.org. For the Republic, contact the **National Disability Authority**, **t** (01) 608 0400, **www**.nda.ie, or **The National Rehabilitation Board**, 25 Clyde Rd, Dublin 4, **t** (01) 668 4181.

Useful addresses

In the UK

National Children's Bureau (Council for Disabled Children), **t** (020) 7843 6000

Information on travel health and resources.

Holiday Care Service, 2nd Floor, Imperial Building, Victoria Rd, Horley, Surrey RH6 9HW, **t** (01293) 774 535

Information sheets for families with disabilities. All sites have been visited and assessed by Holiday Care representatives.

RADAR, Unit 12, City Forum, 250 City Rd, London EC1V 8AF, **t** (020) 7250 3222

Specialist advice on travelling with mobility problems, and a guide to facilities at airports, *Getting There*.

Royal National Institute for the Blind, 224 Great Portland St, London W1S 5TB, **t** (020) 7388 1266

Advice for blind people on travel matters.

In the US

American Foundation for the Blind, 15 West 16th St, New York, NY 10011, **t** 1 800 232 5463

Mobility International, PO Box 10767, Eugene, OR 97440, **t** (541) 343 1284

SATH (Society for the Advancement of Travel for the Handicapped), 347 Fifth Ave, Suite 610, New York 10016, **t** (212) 447 7284

Sports for the disabled

Irish Wheelchair Association, Aras Chuchulain, Blackheath Drive, Clontarf, Dublin 3, **t** (01) 833 8241

Share Centre, Smith's Strand, Lisnaskea, Co. Fermanagh, **t** (028) 6772 2122

Activity holidays for families with special needs.

Sports

Canoeing

White-water racing and slalom can be tried on the rivers Liffey, Barrow and Nore in the east of Ireland. For sea canoeing, try activity and leisure centres in counties Clare, Cork and Galway. The Barrow in Wicklow is probably the best river for canoeing, but canoeing centres can also be found on the Boyne, the Nore (Co. Kilkenny) and the Suir (Co. Waterford) and on the Lee, Blackwater and Shannon (best for lake canoeing). All along the western seaboard from Donegal to Cork are good sites for sea canoeing and canoe surfing.

Diving

Underwater swimming and diving are superb in the Gulf Stream surrounding Ireland. Noted diving centres can be found in Dublin, Waterford and Wexford; some other popular ones are on the Atlantic coast in counties Donegal, Mayo and Galway. Cork and Kerry also have wonderful conditions.

Fishing

Central Fisheries Board, **t** (01) 837 9206

The board will tell you to how to get a fishing licence for the area where you wish to fish, and has information on fishing in Ireland with kids.

Fermanagh Lakeland Visitors' Centre, Enniskillen, Co. Fermanagh, **t** (028) 6632 3110

Foyle Fisheries Commission, 8 Victoria Rd, Derry City, Co. Londonderry, **t** (028) 7134 2100

Game-rod licences in Northern Ireland.

Sailing

There are sailing schools all around Ireland's coasts; many are residential, and provide other outdoor sports as well. Tuition standards are high. In the southwest, in Co. Cork, excellent courses are given at Baltimore, Bere Island in Bantry Bay and Cobh. In the west there are fine facilities at Renvyle in Connemara and Clew Bay, Co. Mayo. More sheltered lakeland sailing schools are on Lough Derg, Co. Tipperary, and the Blessington lakes in Wicklow. Sailing holidays can be enjoyed north of Dublin in Malahide, and just to the south in Dun Laoghaire.

Surfing

Great surfing conditions can be found on Ireland's west and south coasts. Ireland's largest surf club is in Rossnowlagh, Co. Donegal. Not far away in Co. Sligo, there are renowned surf beaches at Easkey, Enniscrone and Strandhill. Farther south in cos. Clare (Doolin Point) and Kerry (Inch) there are more excellent places to surf. Small, medium and even high levels of surf can be found from southern Kerry through Cork and Waterford to Wexford. There are occasional rideable waves, particularly in winter, along the east coast. Make sure children surf with a qualified instructor.

Walking and mountaineering

For contact details for the Republic and Northern Ireland's youth hostel associations, *see* p.248.

The House of Sport, Upper Malone Rd, Belfast, **t** (028) 9038 1222

This provides details on climbing in the Mournes, handles grants and serves as an advice centre.

Irish Ways, Ballycanew, Gorey, Co. Wexford, **t** (055) 27479

Courses and holidays.

National Mountain and White Water Centre, Tiglin, Ashford, Co. Wicklow, **t** (0404) 40169, **www.tiglin.com**

Details of training courses in mountaineering.

Tullymore Mountain Centre, Bryansford, nr Newcastle, Co. Down, **t** (028) 4372 2158

Climbing in the Mourne Mountains.

Ulster Federation of Rambling Clubs, Queen's University, Lanyon North, Belfast, **t** (028 9027 3107)

Water-skiing

There are several well-equipped water-ski centres in the Republic that also offer training. Favourites are in Macroom, Farran Forest Park and on the River Lee (an official site for the disabled) – all in Co. Cork; Parknasilla on the Ring of Kerry; Ballymore Eustace and Blessington on the Blessington Lakes in Co. Wicklow; and Lough Muckno in Co. Monaghan.

Windsurfing

Conditions are delightful for windsurfing in Ireland. Along the west coast there are excellent locations at Cobh, Oysterhaven and Schull in Co. Cork, and Glenans Sailing Club for Clew Bay in Co. Mayo. On the east coast, Carlingford in Co. Lough, Malahide, the Grand Canal Dock in Dublin, and Rosslare in Co. Wexford are good places also. A good inland spot is Lough Allen in Co. Leitrim.

Telephones

Eircom was once the Republic's sole national phone company, but today other companies can provide public phones. Similarly in Northern Ireland, as in the rest of the UK, while British Telecom (**BT**) is still predominant, there are also pay phones of other companies around. However, non-Eircom payphones in the Republic are expensive.

Both Eircom and BT provide coin and card phones in their territories, some with (overpriced) e-mail devices. It's much better to use phonecards (of the right company) than coins, as they give substantial discounts. They can be bought in newsagents, train stations, post offices and many shops.

Mobiles/cellphones are popular in Ireland. Only digital mobiles will work in Ireland, but check charges and roaming agreements with your phone provider. US cellphones only work in Europe if they have a tri-band facility. In mountainous or distant places, a mobile may not work, but it's a good idea to keep one with you, especially when travelling by car.

To call Northern Ireland from the rest of the UK, the prefix for the whole province is **028**, but within Northern Ireland you need only dial the remaining 8-digit number, without 028. To call Northern Ireland from the Republic, simply replace the 028 area code with **048**. Calling the Republic from Northern Ireland counts as an international call (but at cheaper rates): dial the international access code (**00**), followed by the code for the Republic (**353**) and the number, **omitting** the initial zero.

To phone the Republic from mainland Britain or any other country, the process is the same (the international access code, **00** in the UK, then **353** and then the number, **omitting** the first 0). To call Northern Ireland from outside Ireland or Britain, dial the international access code, the UK code (**44**) and the number, **omitting** the 0 before the 28.

The way to make an international call **from** Ireland is the same north and south: **00** followed by the country code (UK, from the Republic, **44**; US and Canada **1**; Australia **61**; France **33**; New Zealand **64**), then the area code (minus the 0 in UK numbers) and the number.

Time

The saying 'When God made time, He made plenty of it' is no longer heard quite so often in Ireland, but there is still a sense of it, mainly in country towns and villages.

Ireland and the UK are in the same time zone. Therefore, they are 5hrs ahead of US Eastern Standard Time and 8hrs ahead of Pacific Standard Time. Each country moves to Summer Time (daylight saving) roughly at the same time, so these differences are maintained. By mid-December, it can be dark in Ireland by 4pm, but during summer it may stay light until 11pm.

Tipping

Some people claim that tipping is not expected in Ireland, as it hasn't always been the custom, but leaving something behind discreetly is appreciated. In hotels and restaurants, when a service charge is not included, 10–15% of the bill is appropriate. Taxi drivers are usually tipped 10% of the fare, and porters about €4–5. In pubs, tipping is unusual but at the customer's discretion.

Toilets and baby facilities

In just about every public place you go, there are toilets in Ireland. The better tourist attractions usually have excellent clean ones, often with baby-changing areas where mothers can also breastfeed if they need to. Attitudes towards breastfeeding in public are less liberal here than in many other countries, so you may prefer to do it somewhere private – ask at information or reception desks, and very often a space will be provided if possible.

Many museums, restaurants, hotels and tourist attractions now have wheelchair or disabled access toilets also. If you stay near tourist attractions, it is unlikely you will find yourself anywhere without easy access to clean public toilets. Even in remote places, there will probably be pubs and hotels not far away that will have places you can stop off at, but it is polite to buy something if you intend to use the toilets, or at least to ask permission.

Useful Websites

www.visitbritain.com	UK tourist info
www.tourismireland.com	Tourist info
www.heritageireland.ie	Irish heritage sites
www.irelandonthenet.ie	General info
www.shamrock.org	Info on Ireland
www.goireland.com	Info on food, etc.
www.nci.ie	Irish Yellow Pages
www.local.ie	Regional info
www.rollercoaster.ie	Parents' tips

Good to know...
Sightseeing discounts

The card schemes below can give big savings if you expect to visit a range of heritage sites.

OPW Heritage Card
The Office of Public Works, **t** (01) 647 6587, **www.**heritageireland.ie
Annual card prices Adult €20, over-65s €15, child (5–16) €7.50, family ticket (for 4) €50

Unlimited admission to around 70 fee-paying parks, buildings and monuments. It can be bought in advance or at any of the heritage sites.

National Trust Northern Ireland
t (028) 9751 0721, **www.**ntni.org.uk

The National Trust administers some 50 properties (historic houses, monuments, places of natural beauty) in Northern Ireland. At most sites, family tickets are available; annual membership charges are complicated, with several options, but all give unlimited admission to Trust sites. National Trust members from Britain can use their cards equally in Northern Ireland. Many family and children's events are held at Trust sites in school holidays.

Tourist information

There is a single information and international promotion service for the whole of Ireland, **Tourism Ireland**, combining the work of the Republic's Irish Tourist Board (still called Bord Fáilte) and the Northern Ireland Tourist Board. Each of them still runs information offices in its own territory.

Irish tourist offices, north and south, are plentiful and helpful; as well as providing all sorts of advice, leaflets, maps and information, they have local accommodation booking services. For their addresses, *see* under the individual destinations in this guide.

Tourism Ireland offices outside Ireland

Freephones UK **t** 0800 039 7000, US and Canada **t** 1 800 223 6470 **www.**tourismireland.com.

Main Office in Britain Tourism Ireland, Nations House, 103 Wigmore St, London W1U 1QS, **t** (020) 7518 0800

Canada 2 Bloor St West, Suite 1501, Toronto, Ontario M4W 3E2, **t** (416) 929 3403

USA 345 Park Ave, 17th Floor, New York, NY 10154, **t** (212) 418 0800

Index

Main page references are in **bold**.
Page references to maps are in *italics*.

Abbeyleix 112
Abbeyshrule 113
accommodation **246–78**
Achill Folk Life Centre 177
Achill island **180**, 192
Adams, Gerry 42
Adare 153
Adventure Viking Cruise 106
Aengus Óg 30, 100
Agricultural Museum 88
Aillebrack 170
Aillwee Cave 141–2
airlines 280–2, 286
airports 283–4
Altamont Gardens 80
An Cláchán Folk Village 236
An Creagán Visitor Centre 228
An Dún Transport Museum 108
Animal Magic 72
Annamore Leisure Park 79
Antrim **201–10**, 240–1, 271–2
aquariums *see* sealife centres
Aran Islands **164–5**, 191
Ardara 244
Ardgillan Castle 72
Ardmore **150**, 154
Ardress House 219
Argideen Valley
  Heritage Park 124
The Argory 219
Ark Open Farm 214
Arklow 109
Armagh **216–22**, 241–2, 274
Arranmore island 236
Arthurstown 90, 111
Ashtown Riding Stables 73
Athenry
  Arts Centre 168
  Castle 167
Athlone **106**, 114
Athy 112
Atlantaquaria 161–2
Aughnanure Castle 167
Aughrim Heritage Centre 168
Avoca 109
Avondale House 80

babies 290, 300
Ballina 150
Ballinamore 194
Ballinasloe 191
Ballinskelligs 152
Ballintubber Abbey 176
Ballon 109
Ballycastle 192
Ballyclare 240
Ballyconneely 170
Ballyconnell 243
Ballyhack Castle 87
Ballyhoura Mountain Park 139
Ballyhugh Art Centre 233
Ballykeenan House
  Pet Farm 79
Ballymagibbon Cairn 177
Ballynabola 111
Ballyvaughan 153
Balor 29, **30**, 183
Balscadden Beach 72
Baltimore 151
Banagher 112
Bandon 151
Bangor 241
banks 294–5
Banshee 30
Bantry 151
Bantry Bay 126
Bantry House 123–4
barm brack 103
Barrontop Funfarm 227
Barryscourt Castle 124
beaches 290
  see also under
    individual places
Beaghmore Stone Circles 227
Beal Boru 141
Bective Abbey 103
bed and breakfast 246
Belfast **202–6**, 240, 271
  airport 284
Belle Isle School of Cookery 232
Belleek Pottery Factory 230
Beltaine 30
Belturbet Railway Station 233
Belvedere House 107
Benaughlin 230
Benbulben 185
Benvarden Garden 209
Bere Island 126
Berkeley, Bishop 35, 42, 84
Berkeley Costume and
  Toy Museum 86
Birr **92**, 112
Black Pig's Dyke 42
Black Pool 52
Blacklion 243
Blarney Castle 122
Blasket Centre 132
Blasket Islands 128
Blennerville Windmill 131
Blessington Lakes 81
Boa island 230
bodhrán 169
Bog of Allen 95
border formalities 286
Boyle **189**, 194
Boyne, Battle of 35, 100
Brandon 152
Bray 76, 110
Brian Boru 42, 141
Brigid (goddess) 30
Brigid, Saint 93, 94
Bród Tullaroan
  Heritage Centre 88
Brookhall Historical Farm 208
Brown Bull of Cooley 187
Browneshill Dolmen 80
Bruree Heritage Centre 138–9
Bunratty **141**, 153
Burns, Robert 101
Burren 141–3, 153
Burtonport 244

buses and coaches 284, 286–7
Bushmills 240
Buttercup Farm 138
Byrne, Martin 26

Caher 174
Caherdaniel 152
Cahir Castle 148
Cairn Visitor Centre 237–8
Campile 111
camping 247
canoeing 298
Cape Clear Island 126
caravans 180, 247
Carlingford 113
Carlow 74–81, **109–10**, 251–2
Carne 111
Carnfunnock Country Park 209
Carnlough 240
Carraig Craft Centre 234
Carrick-on-Suir Heritage Centre 149
Carrickfergus Castle 206
Carrowmore Megalithic Cemetery 183
cars 287–8
Carson, Sir Edward 42
Cashel **147–8**, 154
Castle Coole 231–2
Castle Espie 212–13
Castle Ward 214
Castlebaldwin 193
Castlebar 192
Castlederg Castle 227
Castledermot 112
Castlegarron 193
Castletown 242
Castletown House 92
Castlewellan Forest Park 215
Catholics 35–6
Cauldron of Plenty 163
Causey Experience 98
Cavan **233–4**, 243, 276–7
Cave Hill Country Park 204
Céide Fields 178
Celtic Furrow 176
Celtic Park and Gardens 137–8
Celts 28–31
Ceoláras Coleman 185
Cessair 29
Charles Fort 124
Charles II 35
Charlestown 192–3
Children of Lir 177
china and pottery factories 163, 230
Christ Church Cathedral 148
Christianity 31–2
Claddagh Ring 161
Clare **140–5**, 153–4, 262–3
Clare island 174, 179, 180
Clarinbridge 191
Claypipe Centre 190
Cleggan 170
Clew Bay 174, 179, 180
Clifden 191
Cliffs of Moher 144–5
climate 290
Clonakilty 151
Clonalis House 189
Clonea Bay 150
Clonfert Cathedral 167
Clonmacnoise Monastic Site 93
Clonmel 154
clothing 290
Cloverhill 243
coaches and buses 284, 286–7
Cobh 122–3
Coleraine 242
Collins, Michael 38–9, 42, 124
Collon 113
Collooney 193
Columcille, Saint 42, 238
Comber 241
Conchobhar Mac Nessa 30
Cong 193
Congreve, William 35, 42, 84
Connacht *156–7*, **158–94**, 191–4, 265–70
Connemara National Park 170
Connolly, James 42
consulates 291
Cookstown 243
Coole Park 170
Cooley Hills 103
Coolwood Wildlife Sanctuary 128
Cork **120–6**, 151–2, 257–9
  airport 283
Cormac MacArt 30
Courthouse Visitors Centre 238
Courtown 90
Crag Cave 134–5
Craggaunowen 142–3
Cranfield Bay 215
credit cards 295
Croagh Patrick 178–9
Crolly 244
Cromwell, Oliver 34, 42
Croom Mills 138
croppy boys 88
Cruachan Ai Visitor Centre 187–8
Crunnchu 199
Cúchulainn 30, 50, 199, 219
Curracloe 90
Cushendall 240
customs formalities 286

The Daghda 30, 163
Dalkey **69**, 109
Dan O'Hara's Homestead Farm 168–9
Dartfield Horse World 167
Dathí's Stone 188
Davitt, Michael 37, 42, 176–7
De Valera, Eamon 38–9, 42
  museum 138–9
Deane's Open Farm 237
Déirdre of the Sorrows 30
Delamont Country Park 215
Derry City **222–3**, 242
  airport 284
Derryglad Folk Museum 188
Derrynane House 133

Desmond Castle 124
Devenish Island 231
Diarmait McMurrough 33
Diarmuid 30
Dingle Maze 132
Dingle Peninsula **131–3**, 135, 152
disabled travellers 298
discount schemes 287, 300
diving 298
Doagh Famine Museum 238
Dogs and Hares game 25
dolmens 80, 103, 142
Dolphin Tours 144, 145
Donabate 72
Donaghadee 241
Donegal **235–9**, 244, 277–8
  airport 283
Doneraile Wildlife Park 125
Donkey Sanctuary 123
Doolin 153
Down **211–16**, 241, 273
Downhill Estate 224
Downpatrick 212
Drimnagh Castle 58
Drogheda Heritage Centre 102
Dromahair 194
Drum Manor Forest Park 228
Drumcliffe 193
Drumshanbo 194
Drumskinney Stone Circle 232
Duanguaire Castle 166
Dublin *46–7*, **48–64**
  accommodation 249–50
  airport 283
  attractions 50–6
    outside the centre 58–61
  entertainment 57
  food and drink 62–4
  parks and gardens 57
  shopping 49
  tourist information 49
Dublin Butterfly House 72
Dublin County **68–73**, 109, 251
Duiske Abbey 87
Dun Aonghasa 164–5
Dún na Sí Centre 107
Dunbrody Abbey and Castle 86
Dunbrody Heritage Ship 86
Duncannon 90, 111
Duncannon Fort 88
Dundalk 113
Dundrum **215**, 241
Dunfanaghy 244
Dungannon 243
Dungloe 244
Dunluce 206–7
Dunmore Cave 89
Dunmore East **150**, 154
Dunsany Castle 101
Durrow **94**, 112
Durrus 151
Dwyer McAllister Cottage 77
Dwyer, Michael 77
Dysert O'Dea Castle 144

Earhart, Amelia 224
Easter Rising 38, 50–1
ecos Millennium Centre 210
electricity 291
Elizabeth I 33–4
Elphin windmill 190
embassies 291
emergencies 291, 293
Emo Court 94
English Civil War 34–5
Ennis **141**, 153
Enniscorthy 84–5
Enniskerry 110
Enniskillen **230**, 243
environmental issues 291
Eóghan Mór 42
Eóghanacht 42
Eustace 112
Exploris 213

faeries 118
Falls Road (Belfast) 205
False Bay 170
Famine 36–7, 238
Faughart Hill 104
Fenians 37
Fermanagh **229–32**, 243, 276
ferries 284–6
festivals
    see under individual places
The Fianna 30, 184
Finn McCool 30, 184, 207, 234
Fiónn MacCumhail 30
Fionnbharr 30
Fir Bolg 28, **29**, 30, 163, 175
First World War 38
first aid 293, 294
fishing 298
  see also sports and activities
Flight of the Earls 34, 238
Florence Court **232**, 243
Flying Boat Museum 139
Fomorians 28, **29**, 30, 183, 237
food and drink 291–2
  see also under
    individual places
Fore Abbey 106–7
The Forge 223
Fort Dunree 238
Fort Lucan Adventureland 73
Fota Wildlife Park 123
Foxford **179**, 193
Frenchpark 194
Friar Murphy Centre 84
Fry Model Railway
    (Malahide) 71
Fungi the Dolphin 132

Gallarus Oratory 132
Galway **159–71**, 191–2, 265–7
  airport 283
games 25
Garinish Island 125
geography 22
Giant's Causeway 207–8
Giant's Ring 209
Gilligan's World 183
Gladstone, William Ewart 42
glass
  Cavan Crystal 234

Irish Crystal Heritage Centre 162
Waterford Crystal 148
Glasson 114
Glebe House 236
Glen Inchaquin Waterfall Park 135
Glenariff Forest Park 208
Glencomcille 244
Glencullen 109
Glendalough **77–8**, 110
Glendeer Pet Farm 108
Glenroe Open Farm 79
Glens of Antrim 208
Glenveagh Castle 236
Glenveagh National Park 239
Glin Castle 139
Good Friday Agreement 41
Gortlin Glen Forest Park 228
Gosford Forest Park 220
Graiguenamanagh 111
Gráinne 30
Grant Ancestral Home 227
Granuaile *see* O'Malley, Grace (Granuaile)
Gray's Printing Press 226
Great Famine 36–7, 238
Greenan Farm Museums and Maze 79
Gregan's Wood 142
Gregory, Lady Augusta 42
Grey Abbey 214
Greystones 110
Grianán Ailigh 236–7
Grove Gardens 101

health 293–4
Hell's Kitchen Bar and Railway Museum 190
Helen's Bay 215
Hennigan's Heritage Centre 174
Henry II 33
Henry VIII 33
Hezlett House 208
Hill of Tara 100, 102
Hill of Tivereagh 208
Hill of Uisneach 106
Hillsbrough 241
history **28–42**
Holycross Rare Breeds Farm 149
Holywood 241
Home Rule 37
Hook Lighthouse 88
horse-drawn caravans 180, 247
horse-riding
see sports and activities
hostels 247
hotels **246–78**
Howth **69**, 70, 109
Hume, John 42
Hunt Museum 137
Hyde, Douglas 188, 190

Illnacullin 125
Imbolg 30
Inishbofin 192
Inisheer 165
Inishglora 174
Inishkea 174
Inishmann 165
Inishmore 164–5
Inishowen Maritime Museum 238
Inishturk 174
Inistioge 111
Inniscrone 185
insurance 292–3
Ionad an Bhlascaoid Mhóir 132
IRA 39, 40–1
Irish Agricultural Museum 88
Irish Crystal Heritage Centre 162
Irish Linen Centre 209
Irish National Heritage Park 85

Jacobites 35
James I 34
James II 34–5, 42
Jerpoint Abbey 87
Jewish Museum 59
John F. Kennedy Arboretum 89
Jonathan Swift Park 108
Joyce, James 59

Kavanagh, Patrick 234
Kells **102**, 113
Kenmare 152
Kennedy Homestead 89
Kerry **127–35**, 152–3, 259–61
airport 283
Kerry the Kingdom Museum 131
Kevin of Glendalough, Saint 78
Kia Ora Mini Farm 87
Kilbrittain 151
Kildare **91–6**, 112–13, 254–5
Kilfane Glen and Waterfall 89
Kilfenora 153
Kilkenny **82–90**, 110–12, 252–4
Kilkenny Cats 84
Killarney **128–31**, 152–3
Killeavy 242
Killenard 113
Killiney 72
Killiney Hill Park 69
Killorglin 153
Killruddery House and Gardens 76
Kilmacurragh Gardens 80
Kilmainham Gaol 59
Kilmessan 113
Kilmokea Gardens 89
Kilmore Quay 90
Kiltartan Gregory Museum 166, **169**
King House 188
King John's Castle 137
Kinlough 194
Kinsale 151
Kissane Sheep Farm 134
Knappogue Castle 144
Knock 174–5
airport 283

Knockabbey Castle 104
Knowth 99
Kylemore **167–8**, 192

lace museum 232
Lagan Lookout Centre 204
Lahinch **145**, 154
Lalor's Open Farm 79
Land League 37
Laois **91–6**, 112–13, 254–5
Laragh 110
Larchill Arcadian Garden 92
Leap Castle 94
Ledwidge Cottage Museum 102
Leenane Sheep and Wool Centre 169
Leighlinbridge 110
Leinster **66–114**, *67*, 251–6
Leisureland 162
Leitrim **186–90**, 194, 270
Lenihan, Eddie 26
leprechauns 30
Leslie Hill Open Farm 208
Letterfrack 192
Letterkenny 244
Lewis, CS 202–3
Lifford 244
Limerick **136–9**, 153, 261–2
Linen Centre 209
Lios na Croi 133
Lir, King 30, 177
Lisburn Museum 209
Liscannor 154
Lisdoonvarna **144**, 154
Lismore Castle 149
Lismore Heritage Centre 149
Lissadell House 184–5
Londonderry **221–4**, 242, 274–5
Longford **105–8**, 113–14, 256
lost property 293
Lough Derg 145
Lough Erne 230–1
Lough Gur Heritage Centre 138
Lough Key Forest Park 190
Lough Neagh Discovery Centre 220
Loughcrew 99
Loughgall **220**, 242
Louth **97–104**, 113, 255–6
Lugh 30, 183, 237
Lullymore Heritage Park 94

Macha, Queen 217
Macreddin Village 110
Maeve, Queen 30, 187
Magherafelt 242
Malachy, Saint 33
Malahide **70–1**, 72, 109
Marble Arch Caves 231
marble games 25
Marian Shrine 174
markets 292
Markethill 242
Markievicz, Constance de 42
Marlay Park 61
Marsh, Richard 26
Maudabawn Centre 234
Mayo **172–80**, 192–3, 267–9
Meagher, Lory 88
Meath **97–104**, 113, 255–6
medical emergencies 293–4
Miach 172
Midleton 151
Milesians 30, 118
Millbridge Farm 237
Millisle 215
Millmount Museum 102–3
Millstreet Country Park 123
Mitchelstown Cave 149
Monaghan **233–4**, 243, 276–7
Monasterboice Round Tower 103
money 200, 294–5
Moone 113
Morell Open Farm 95
Mount Stewart House 215
Mount Usher Gardens 78
Mountsandel Fort 206
Moycullen 192
Moytura, battles of 175, 183
Muckross House 129
Mulcahy Pottery 133
Mullaghmore 185, 193
Mullet Peninsula 180
Mullingar 114
Munster *116–17*, **118–54**, 151–4, 257–64
Murrisk Abbey 179
Museum of Country Life 175
music 26, 131, 133, 169, 185

National Botanic Gardens 61
National Garden Exhibition Centre 81
National Sealife Centre (Bray) 76
National Stud 95
National Wax Museum 51
Navan 113
Nemedians 28, **29**, 30
Nendrum Monastic Site 214
New Ross 111–12
Newbridge House 72–3
Newgrange 99
Newgrange Farm 101
Newmills Corn and Flax Mills 238
Newport 193
Niall of the Nine Hostages 30
Niamh of the Golden Hair 30
Nine Years' War 34
Nore Valley Park Open Farm 87
Normans 33
North Bull Island 72
North Down Heritage Centre 215
Northern Ireland 39–41
Nuadhu 175

O'Carolan's grave 189
Ocean and Country Centre 167
O'Connell, Daniel 36, 42, 133
O'Donnell, Red Hugh 34

Offaly **91–6**, 112–13, 254–5
Oísín 30, 130, 208
Old Leighlin Cathedral 80
Old Mellifont Abbey 102
Omagh 225
O'Malley, Grace (Granuaile) 70, **178**, 179
Omey Strand 170
O'Neill, Hugh 34, 42
opening hours 295
Orange Order 36, 40, 219
Organic Centre 190
Ormond Castle 149

Paisley, Ian 42
Palace Stables Heritage Centre 218
Parnell, Charles Stewart 37, 42
Parson's Green Pet Farm 149
Partholonians **29**, 30
Partry House 176
passports 286
Patrick, Saint 31, 42, 178–9, 212, 213, 214
Patterson's Spade Mill 209
Pearse, Pádraic 42, 60, 169–70
Penal Laws 35, 36
perfume-making 142
pewterware 94, 107
Phoenix Park 61
planetariums 124, 217–18, 238
Plantation settlers 34
Pooka 30
Portadown 242
Portaferry 241
Portlaoise 113
Portmarnock 72
Portnoo 244
Portrane 72
Portroe 150
Portrush 241
Portsalon 239
Portstewart 242
Portumna Forest Park 170
post offices 295–6
pottery *see* china and pottery factories
Poulnabrone Portal Dolmen 142
Powerscourt Estate 79
practical A–Z **290–300**
prehistory 28
Primrose Hill 73
Prince August Toy Soldier Factory 125
private home accommodation 247
Proleek Dolmen 103
Protestantism 35–6
public holidays 296
Púca 30

Queen Macha 217
Queen's University Centre 204–5
Queenstown Story 122–3
Quiet Man Heritage Centre 179

railways 288
  Cavan and Leitrim 189–90
  Clonmacnoise and West Offaly 96
  Giant's Causeway and Bushmills 207
  Narrow Gauge 96
  Peatlands Park 228
  Preservation Society 210
  Tralee and Blennerville 135
  Waterford and Suir Valley 150
  West Clare 145
  West Cork Model Railway Village 125
Ramelton 239, 244
Rathcroghan Mound 188
Rathdrum 110
Rathfarnham Castle 58–9
Rathlin island 210
Rathmore 188
Rathmullen 244
Rathnadarve 188
Rebellion of 1798 36, 42, 85, 88
Recess 192
Red Branch 30
The Reek 178–9
Reginald's Tower Museum 148
Relignaree 188
restaurants 291–2
  see also under individual places
Riches of Clare 141
ring games 25
Ring of Kerry **133–4**, 135
Roberts, Michael 26
Rock of Cashel 147–8
Rock of Dumasne 95
Roscommon **186–90**, 194, 270
Ross Castle 131
Rosscarbery 151
Rosslare Strand 90
Rossnowlagh Beach 239
Rothe House 84
Roundstone 192
Roundstone Music and Crafts 169
Roundwood 110
Rowallane Gardens 215
Royal Tara Visitor Centre 163

safety 296
St Canice's Cathedral 84
Salmon of Knowledge 142, 234
Saltee Islands 90
Samhain 30
Scanlon's Pet Farm 133
Scattery Island 144
Schull **124**, 152
Seaforde Butterfly House 213
sealife centres
  Atlantaquaria 161–2
  Dingle Oceanworld Aquarium 132
  Dolphin Tours 144, 145
  Exploris 213
  Fungi the Dolphin 132
  National Sealife Centre 76
  Ocean and Country Centre 167

Sea Safari 71
Seanchaí 134
self-catering 246
shamrock 214
Shankill Road (Belfast) 205
Shannon airport 283
Sherkin Island 126
shopping 292, 296
VAT refund scheme 286
Siamsa Tíre 131
Sídh 30, **143**
Siege of Derry 223
The Skelligs 128, **133–4**
Skerries Mills **73**, 109
skipping games 25, 201
Slane **101**, 113
Sligo **181–5**, 193–4, 269–70
airport 283
smoking 296
Soldier's Tig game 25
Spanish Point 154
Spear of Lugh 163
special-interest holidays 297
The Sperrins 228
Spiddal 192
sports and activities 298–9
Antrim 210
Armagh 220
Cork 126
Donegal 239
Down 216
Dublin County 73
Fermanagh 232
Galway 171
Kerry 135
Kildare, Laois and Offaly 95–6
Kilkenny and Wexford 90
Leitrim and Roscommon 190
Limerick 139
Londonderry 224
Mayo 179–80
Meath and Louth 104
Tipperary and Waterford 150
Tyrone 228
Westmeath and Longford 108
Wicklow and Carlow 81
Springhill House 223–4
Staigue Fort 134
Steam Museum 96
Stephenstown Pond 101
Stoker, Bram 55
Stone of Destiny 163
Stonehenge 107
Stormont 205
storytellers 26
Strandhill 185
Strangford 241
Strokestown Park House 189
Strongbow (Earl of Pembroke) 33, 42
Swift, Jonathan 35, 42, 84
Swiss Cottage 149
Sword of Nuadhu 163

Talbot Botanic Gardens 71
Tannaghmore Gardens and Animal Farm 219
Tara's Palace Doll's House 71
Tarbert Bridewell Courthouse 134
Tayto Castle 220
Teach an Phiarsaigh 169–70
telephones 299
emergency numbers 291
Northern Ireland numbers 200
Thomastown 112
Thoor Ballylee 166
Tiglin National Mountain Centre 81
time 299–300
Tintern Abbey 88
Tipperary **146–50**, 154, 263–4
tipping 300
Tír na n'Óg 30, 130
toilets 300
Tollymore Forest Park 216
Tone, Wolfe 36, 42, 85
Tory island **236**, 244
tourist information 300
trains *see* railways
Tralee 131
Tramore 150
Transport Museum (Killarney) 129
travel **280–8**
with children 24–6
disabled travellers 298
planning 23–4
when to go 290
Trim Castle 101–2
Trimble, David 42
Tuam 192
Tuatha Dé Danaan 30, 119, 125, 163, 175, 183
Tullow 110
Tully Castle 232
Turlough Park 175
Turoe Pet Farm 167
Tyllynally Castle 107
Tyrella Beach 215
Tyrellspass 114
Tyrone **225–8**, 242–3, 275

Ulster *196–7*, **198–244**
accommodation 271–8
curse of Ulster 199
food and drink 240–4
money 200
telephones 200
Ulster American Folk Park 226–7
Ulster Museum 205
Ulster Transport Museum 213–14
United Irishmen 36

Valentia Island 134
VAT refund scheme 286
Vikings 32–3, 54
Virginia 243
visas 286
walking 299
see also sports and activities
Waterford **146–50**, 154, 263–4
airport 284

Waterford Harbour 83
watersports 298–9
  see also sports and activities
Watertop Farm 209
Waterways Visitor Centre 60
websites 248
Wellbrook Beetling Mill 227–8
Westmeath **105–8**, 113–14, 256
Westport 193
Westport House Estate 176
Wexford **82–90**, 110–12, 252–4
Wexford Wildfowl Reserve 86
where to stay **246–78**
Whiddy Island 126
White Island 231
Whowhatwherewhywhen (Belfast) 205
Wicklow **74–81**, 109–10, 251–2
Wicklow Town 76
Wilde, Oscar 42, 56
William of Orange 35, 42
Wilson Ancestral Homestead 227
Winter, Dan 219–20
Witches of Wexford 87
Woodstock Gardens 89
Yeats, William Butler 42, 185
Yola Farmstead Filk Park 86
Youghal
  beaches 126
  food and drink 152
  Heritage Centre 124

zoos 58, 204

A Story to Tell

The Invasions of Ireland 29
Faery Origins 32
The Death of Cúchalainn 50
The Black Pool 52
The Vikings are Coming 54
The Ransom of Grace O'Malley 70
Michael Dwyer the Rebel 77
St Kevin of Glendalough 78
The Kilkenny Cats 84
The Witches of Wexford 87
St Brigid and Her Magic Cloak 93
The Burning of the Hill of Tara 100
The Hill of Uisneach 106
The Coming of the Sons of Míl 119
Them 125
Óisín and Tír na n'Óg 130
The Way to Sing a Song 143
The Claddagh Ring 161
The Tuatha Dé Danaan or People of the Goddess Dana 163
A Galway Folk Tale 166
Knockma: The Great Hill 169
The First Battle of Moytura 175
The Children of Lir 177
Connacht's Pirate Queen 178
The Second Battle of Moytura 183
Diarmuid and Grainne 184
Cruachan and the Brown Bull of Cooley 187
O'Carolan's Last Tune 189
The Curse of Ulster 199
Finn McCool and the Giant's Causeway 207
How St Patrick Came to Ireland 213
Queen Macha 217
Cúchulainn 219
Finn McCool and the Salmon of Knowledge 234
The Fomorians and the Arrival of Lugh 237

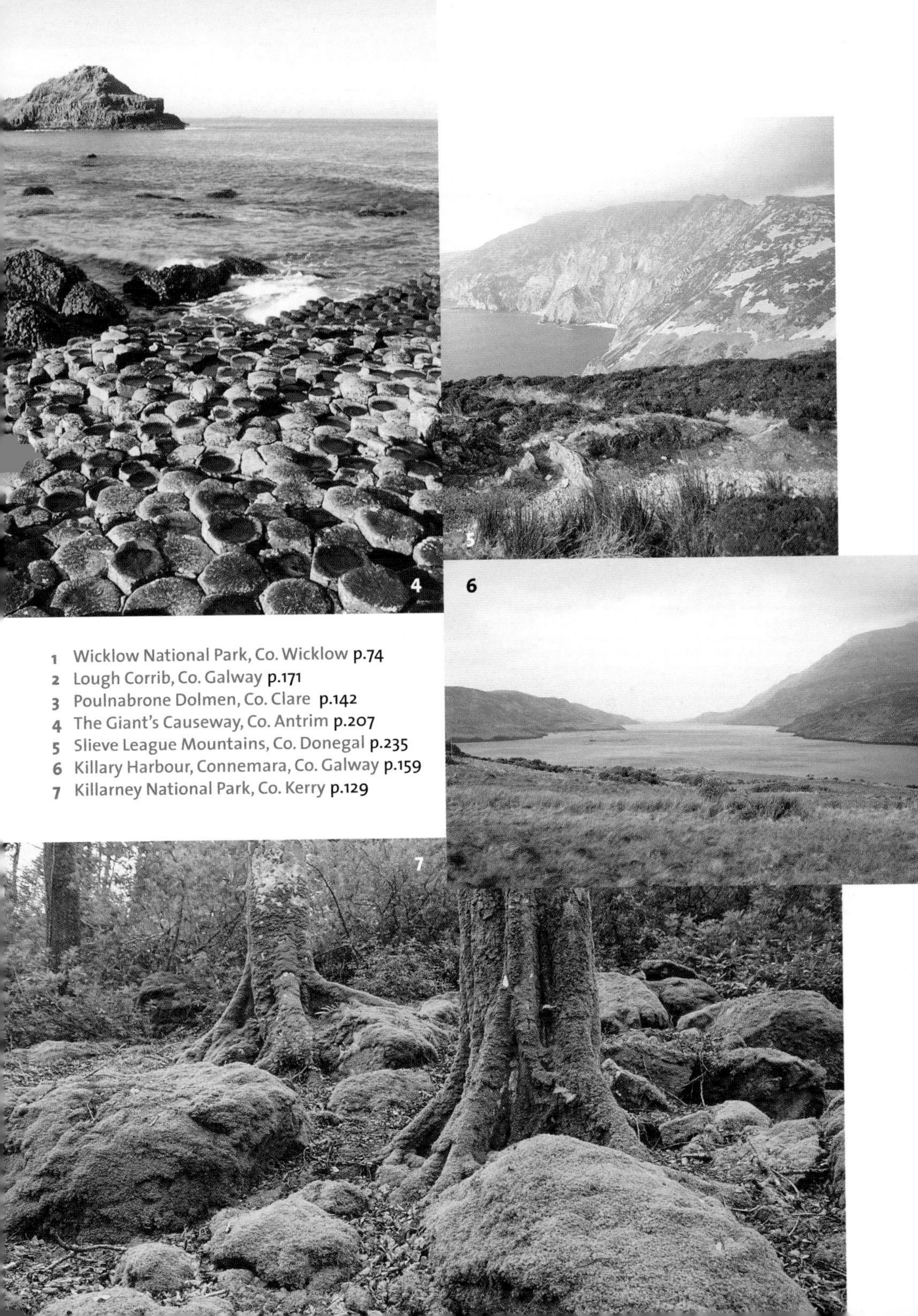

4

5

6

7

1 Wicklow National Park, Co. Wicklow p.74
2 Lough Corrib, Co. Galway p.171
3 Poulnabrone Dolmen, Co. Clare p.142
4 The Giant's Causeway, Co. Antrim p.207
5 Slieve League Mountains, Co. Donegal p.235
6 Killary Harbour, Connemara, Co. Galway p.159
7 Killarney National Park, Co. Kerry p.129

8 Powerscourt Waterfall, Enniskerry, Co. Wicklow p.79
9 Bog, Wicklow Mountains, Co. Wicklow p.74
10 Lauragh Bay, Co. Kerry p127
11 Cliffs of Moher, Co. Clare p.144
12 Glengash Pass, Southern Co. Donegal p.235

11

12

Trains, planes and automobiles

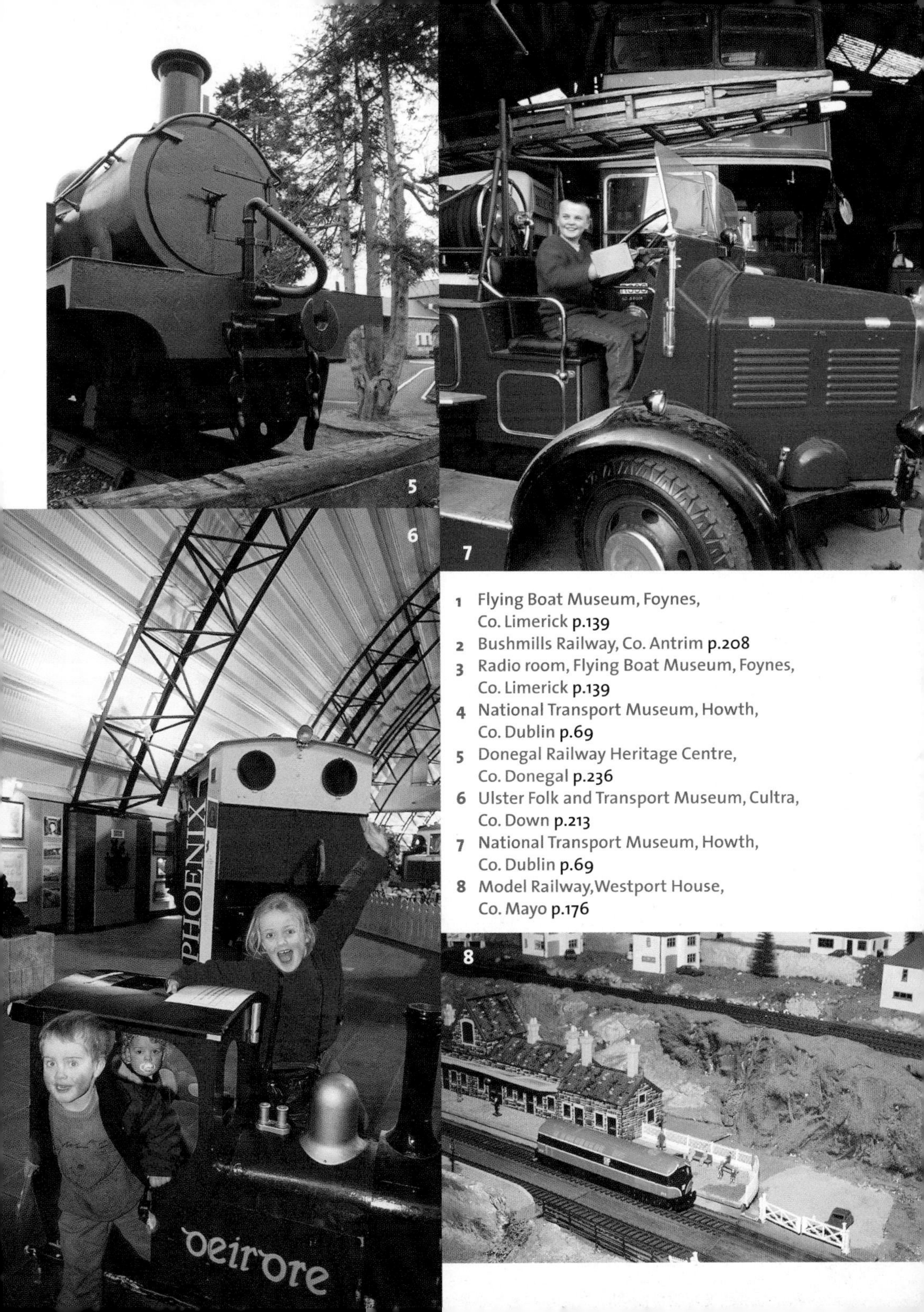

1 Flying Boat Museum, Foynes, Co. Limerick **p.139**
2 Bushmills Railway, Co. Antrim **p.208**
3 Radio room, Flying Boat Museum, Foynes, Co. Limerick **p.139**
4 National Transport Museum, Howth, Co. Dublin **p.69**
5 Donegal Railway Heritage Centre, Co. Donegal **p.236**
6 Ulster Folk and Transport Museum, Cultra, Co. Down **p.213**
7 National Transport Museum, Howth, Co. Dublin **p.69**
8 Model Railway, Westport House, Co. Mayo **p.176**

Eating Out

1 Juice, Dublin p.63
2 The English Market, Cork, Co. Cork p.122
3 Saturday market, Temple Bar, Dublin p.292
4 Bad Ass Café, Dublin p.62
5 Pastries, Dublin
6 Bewley's restaurant, Dublin p.62

Chapter Index Map